AF333627

*To Be or Not
to Be Human*

TO BE OR NOT TO BE HUMAN

The Traits of Human Nature

Ben Freedman

VANTAGE PRESS
New York / Washington / Atlanta
Los Angeles / Chicago

FIRST EDITION

Published by Vantage Press, Inc.
516 West 34th Street, New York, New York 10001

Manufactured in the United States of America
ISBN: 0-533-06964-5

Library of Congress Catalog Card No. 86-90012

To my esteemed wife,
Miriam,
and
to my longtime friend and mentor,
Dr. Jack Sparer

Contents

Acknowledgments   ix

 1. Introduction   1
 2. The Need for a Scientific Model   11
 3. The Nature of Human Nature   47
 4. Freudian Theory on the Nature of Man's Behavior   112
 5. The Phylogenetic Characteristics of the Family and the
    Bonding-Sharing-Exchange Trait in Human Nature   128
 6. The Bonding-Sharing Trait   147
 7. The Trait of Freedom to Choose   173
 8. The Unifying Orientation of Behavior Trait   198
 9. The Trait of Striving to Satisfy One's Appetites,
    Inclinations, and Talents   216
10. The Self-Image and Self-Esteem Trait   241
11. Prospection: Man's Time-binding Trait   256
12. The Trait of Challenge and Competence to Control   268
13. The Cumulative Creative Action Trait   284
14. The Relations of Emotions to Traits of Human Nature   307
15. Some Epidemiological Considerations about the Dynamics
    of Human Nature   318
16. Democracy without Limits: Chaos   347
17. Human Nature and Governmental Life-Style: Marxian
    Implications   385
18. The Essence and Essentiality of Capital   427
19. Human Engineering and Political Action   475

Index   511

Acknowledgments

The accumulation of the background data for this study began well over two decades ago. It consumed much time that normally is devoted to family affairs, for which my wife sustained an unusual sense of understanding and encouragement.

For an extended span of our professional collaboration as physicians, Jack Sparer shared with me his unique philosophy of life, his erudition, and his acute insight into the behavior of people.

My secretary, Pauline McAuliffe, managed the typing and filing of my voluminous data with consummate devotion.

During the actual composing of this manuscript, Dr. Munro Edmonson, professor of anthropology at Tulane University, gave me his generous and valued guidance. I also appreciate the counsel of Dr. Michael Smith, professor of social science at Tulane University.

To Be or Not to Be Human

1

Introduction

"For Freud as for Marx, it was a broad humanistic interest that led [them] to pioneer in the borderlands of science."[1] Such fascination with the physical and mental exploits of humankind—with the historical development of the variety of social systems, with the flood of cultural creations, with the infinity of intellectual pursuits, and with the bivalent origin of *Homo*'s ingenious behavior—such humanistic wondering and wandering by this author led to the crystallization of this study of the anatomy, dynamics, and quest into the epidemiology of human nature.

Human consciousness begins in infancy as an inchoate awareness and builds up with time as an interpenetrating complexity of preceptive functions that enable one to interact with and interpret experience within one's surroundings. The preceptive functions are largely implicit and operate automatically as natural cognizance.[2] Human nature begins with human consciousness—the medium in which the human conscience comes into existence. Whether all animal life or only the mammalian class has an inherent consciousness is not the concern of this dissertation. That human consciousness is a unique level of development in the genus *Homo* is a factual observation, considering the quality of humankind's mental powers. Whether this study be on the borderlands of science or *in* the medium of science itself is the question that provoked the author throughout the incubation period of this thesis.

It is the content of the consciousness of humans that determines their mode of existence, but it is their sociocultural conditions of existence that determine the content of their consciousness. And, to elaborate this principle further, it is the creation of cultural resources that determines human perception of social change, and it is the mental response to the basic social relations evolved in the process of securing survival that gives the sense of permanence to *Homo*'s humanness and to the nature of human nature. It is the exploration of the latter thesis that, perforce, elicits the quest into the question of man's eternal moral-ethical struggle as to whether the problem "to be or not to be human" is solvable and whether this is epidemiologically amenable to etiological understanding.

Capitalism and socialism are the two main social systems competing on the world fronts. When they are each defined in general terms expressing their essential nature, as in the dictionary, such definitions never describe for a particular country the degree of humanistic or exploitative practices abounding to the various sections of its population. Therefore, comparing one capitalist or socialist country with another such country just on the basis of definition tells little about how compatible either nation is with the traits of human nature of its population. A comparison of the social services and levels of income available to the general population in two capitalist countries, the United States and Brazil, and the resulting well-being (physical and mental) of their people is impossible to derive from the definition of capitalism. Capitalism under a dictatorship and capitalism under a democratic governmental structure are two entirely different social systems and have quite different impacts on the traits of human nature, even though the stereotype ideological heritage that capitalism is the dictatorship of the capitalist class still lingers on with tenacious justification. The significance of the capitalist class's dictatorship in today's power struggle is as different from its pre–World Wars meaning as the specific functions of the right hemisphere of the brain is from the left hemisphere.[3] Legend notes that ideologies have tendencies to freeze and to remain frozen like glaciers, thereby also freezing their methodologies. One of the important causes of this freezing process is the institutionalization of the ideas therein. Once ideational systems become institutionalized, the intellectual proponents become a governing dictatorship of those ideas. When the institutionalization takes place in academia, scholarship and scholastic literature become the bearers of these glaciers, as Linder[4] points out in this study titled *Anti-Samuelson*, concerning Nobelist Samuelson's economics teachings.

Not only has this process taken place in capitalist economic theory, where the economists of academia are incapable of solving the present-day economic problems of the Western capitalist nations, but also in socialist theory, whereby the socialist economists are as incapable of solving the socialist economic problems. The same impotence abounds in their efforts to solve with their sociological theories the growing epidemics of social problems of various forms of mental and emotional disorientations rearing their heads in all these countries.

The basic problem is that the intelligentsia of both worlds have failed in their appreciation that the *nature of human conduct* is the essence of human behavior in all social orders and therefore the *traits* of human nature are the foundation on which to build socio-economo-political theories. Without being cognizant of the historical significance of the *behavioral* implications of such terms as "bonding-sharing," "exchange," "challenge," "competition," "creativity," "value," "exchange-value," "surplus-value," and "capital," all of which have their basis in the traits of human nature, socio-economic-political theories are fruitless in solving human problems. Marx understood this in developing his theories in class struggle. Neither Marx's followers nor Adam Smith and his followers were aware of the psychosocial foundations in socio-economo-political dynamics. The significance of these terms in basic human behavior and how such behavior has made and continues to make man's history can be more accurately observed from comparative study of the history of humankind revealed by social and cultural anthropology. Enough of this has been brought to light to open new vistas of understanding the nature of human nature, thereby laying a valid basis for social theory.

In developing his economic theory, Adam Smith relied basically on very strong instinctual qualities of *Homo*'s behavior, which were inherited from his primate forebears: relentless, aggressive competition—competition and aggressiveness whose relentlessness no capitalist democracy has really tried to reasonably control in spite of the innumerable laws enacted that cram the legislative libraries, competition, which Marx described as "the great civilizing influence" because of its ability to create and accumulate capital, which produced "a stage of society compared with which all earlier stages appear to be merely *local progress*,"[5] competition, which during the history of capitalism, has alienated the workers, generated antagonistic economic classes, and violated, for one class or another, every trait of human nature, competition, which was eliminated in the economies of the Soviet Union and China at the same time creating major deficiencies in their abilities to produce much needed capital, competition, which, to date, no government has been able to manage for the comparably equal good of its entire people.

This competitive-aggressive instinct, when piloted by *human* brains, can violate all the traits of human nature that *Homo* evolved through the long years of his psychosocial development while trying to forge rational norms of behavior to be able to live in a human community mode of life. Since *Homo* cannot divest himself of this (or any other) inherited animal instinct, he must adopt a community methodology for controlling it, because his human traits of "challenge " and "striving" may become engulfed in destructive levels of the animal trait of aggressive competition. The destructiveness of behavior when the human completely surrenders to his animal instincts is such that Freud created his entire system of psychic dynamics on repairing the damage that *Homo*'s uncontrolled animal instincts can render to human conduct.

The physical sciences must begin with understanding the dynamics of the interactions, under all environmental conditions, between the elements and forces composing the physical world. The psychosociological sciences must begin with understanding the nature of the elements of human behavior and how they react in the media of various types of social orders.

The social scientists are more prone to study and be concerned about the impact of the social, economic, and political forces on the physical and physiological nature of people, almost to the exclusion of how these forces interact with the traits of human nature and what the responses of these traits are in forging the history of these societies. The present study attempts to explain the latter topic.

It appears that sociologists and social psychologists, with few exceptions, are not expressly guided in their studies by methodologies that are epistomologically in consonance with historically evolved principles and theories of human behavior. Thus we note that the main differences usually apparent between the physical and the psychosocial methodological accommodations are how to deal with the two unique human factors: (1) how to harmonize the teleological needs and motivations with the traits of human nature, and (2) how to objectify the subjective in order to validate as much as possible observations of cognitive-behavioral expressions. Thus done, these factors do not divert from adherence to the broad principles and philosophy of general scientific methodology. The second chapter of this study, "The Need for a Scientific Model," is addressed to this problem. The third chapter, "The Nature of Human Nature," develops the specific methodology for laying a scientific foundation for the sociological and social psychological sciences. It predicates the existence of a *specific behavioral pattern in all human societies* defined as the traits of human nature upon which sociological and sociopsychological studies must be based to be relevant to human society. This nature is composed of an enduring well-defined set of behavioral traits. Each trait has been found to be a unity of biphasic behavioral propensities, each phase being a contradiction of its counterphase. This contradictory nature, the human versus primate, evolved as a hominid's heritage from the subhuman primates. The study could as well be titled "The Nature of Human Nature," since it attempts to filter out of the historical drama of *Homo sapiens sapiens* those constant behavioral characteristics that have manifested themselves in every society from the most primitive times. The physiological characteristics manifested in the behavior of animal life, including primate life, such as sex and hunger are considered only as examples of the strength of humankind's psychosocial ability to pervert even the physiological processes, thus producing such behavioral disorientations as homosexuality, bulemia, anorexia nervosa and drug abuse. We are here concerned mainly with the *human* characteristics, those that distinguish *Homo* from his primate relatives. These are the psychosocial behavioral traits of humankind that are in a continual state of contention with the phylogenetic traits inherited from the primate forebears. The historical process accountable for the emergence of these characteristics or traits, their importance in the well-being of society, and the effect on these traits of the various social systems whose dynamics are not in harmony with the traits are researched in this study.

Is the methodology here used valid in accordance with the accepted scientific method? What kind of laboratory can accommodate a research project of such universality in sociological history, i.e., which concerns all of human society since the emergence of primates of the human genus and which is the foundation of sociological and social psychological dynamics?

Since what is human concerns all of what is scientifically classified as belonging to the genus *Homo,* it becomes necessary to examine the social anthropological history of *Homo* as far as that history is available. This approach is necessary lest we find that what was *human* for *Homo erectus* and *Homo sapiens neanderthalensis* is not human for *Homo sapiens sapiens.* To decide this, we need to know what *was* human in the past and what *is* human today. If each of these stages were essentially different as to the meaning of humanness, then the term "human" becomes a relativistic concept like "culture" and there is no difference in the durability between the cultural and the social categories, both concepts being relegated to the imprecision of relativism. But even from superficial observation, there seems to be a difference in the persistence of their particularity. In one lifetime, one easily sees and experiences the *cultural* world of material and mental phenomena to be changing drastically. Yet basic *social relations* appear to maintain a sense of permanency, since families continue to exist and children continue to be born to these families, and parents continue to have responsibility to raise these children, and families still have one or more breadwinners, and people continue to strive for the betterment of their lot. These social relations and interrelated efforts have existed since time immemorial.

Thus the laboratory of this kind of study must become the repository of the accumulated written records and artifacts depicting and giving descriptions of the ways people have lived. The research, then, becomes a search into the history of humankind, filtering out and classifying the data concerning the cognitive (if that be possible) and behavioral characteristics that were common as far as the records reveal for all these various epochs and that persist to the present. What help is the technique of uniformitarianism in uncovering this past behavioral record?

The biphasic nature of the human is phylogenetically unavoidable, as is the nature of evolution itself. The human and the primate characteristics are indivisibly interpenetrating. What is primate in the human can never be exactly the same as what is primate in the non-human primate. This is so because the mental capacity and dynamics of the human brain produce cognition and behavior that cannot be isolated effectively from the meta-primate cognition and behavioral characteristics produced by the same brain. Some of these characteristics, like exaggerated aggressive behavior, can be destructive or, at least, disturbing to human society if not harnessed. But much of the fascinating drama of human life and human history has resulted from an indissoluble combination of human and meta-primate behavior, which is both admirably credible and shamefully discredible to the human species, such as the American and French revolutions on the one hand and the holocausts of the Jews and the Armenians on the other hand.

Thus, this study has adopted the historical method, utilizing the experience and documented observations of those who have investigated and given much thought to the behavior of people and primates. The classification of such data creates a reservoir for scientific analysis and interpretation. Such an approach must, perforce, animate a philosophic perspective. This study, therefore, radiates the philosopher's panoramic sweep.

The world of knowledge is becoming minutely departmentalized. The specialist has become the accepted and esteemed purveyor of valid, precise, and decisive judgments. There are science specialists, however, whose intellectual curiosity drives them to savor the exhilaration of probing other fields of knowledge. Excursions of this nature eventually lead to philosophic meandering into new worlds of harmonious synthesis of previously unrelated phenomena. Knowledge, then, begins to crystallize into a cosmic outlook. Attaining such an outlook is the essence of becoming a philosopher—a status not perceived with favor by too many specialists, since the philosopher dabbles in their special fields without himself being such a specialist. Does this really invalidate the philosopher's judgment? The history of the development of knowledge answers this question emphatically in the negative.

Knowing the principles and major theories of a science without knowing the detailed current investigative minutiae does not hamper the philosopher's ability to synthesize the knowledge of various fields. The knowledge in social science, in its broad meaning, is not as precise as that of the physical sciences, nor have the findings of social anthropology been sufficiently integrated into the reservoir of social science knowledge; therefore, the need for developing new syntheses of all these data is obvious for more comprehensive understanding. The present study is such an attempt. The above premise is well stated by the eminent physicist Niels Bohr: "History of science teaches us again and again how the extension of our knowledge may lead to the recognition of relations between formerly unconnected groups of phenomena, the harmonious synthesis of which demands a renewed revision of the presuppositions for the unambiguous application of even our most elementary concepts."[6]

There are a number of pertinent points, cognizance of which beforehand will help orient the reader concerning the author's intent in elaborating this study, although these points are not the original stimuli that animated this effort. These points are as follows.

First, in 1955, Erich Fromm predicated five basic human *needs stemming from the conditions of human existence,* a subject that had attracted my attention for some time.[7] They were discussed and described by Fromm as though they were traits of human nature, although not distinguished in these terms. This was the period when the explosion of genetic science occurred. It was also in the midst of a surge in the augmentation of anthropological data and the contention between the cultural relativists and those who were beginning to see some *permanent* characteristics in the evolution of social life—the permanent characteristics that a few anthropologists classified as traits of human nature. In 1953, Kroeber's voluminous symposium of anthropological knowledge, *Anthropology Today,* was published. Fifty-three of the most eminent social scientists contributed to its composition. In these articles were some very pertinent discussions of the subject that so intrigued me in Fromm's book. Hallowell cited two references from David Bidney's works of 1947 and 1949, in which Bidney specifically postulated a "human nature" that "is logically and genetically prior to culture, since we must postulate human agents with psychobiological powers and impulses capable of initiating the cultural process as a means of adjusting to their environment."[8] Bidney in his article stated: "The constant factor in history was human nature, and it was conceived to be the task of the historian to demonstrate the universal principles of human nature as they manifest themselves in the course of historical experience."[9]

In perusing the anthropological literature, however, except for occasional reference to the concept of human nature, I have found that little has been done to study the subject with concentrated application. Robert Redfield explained this dearth: "[T]here is a return in our time of a conscious concern, as yet unprovided with dependable methods of work, with human nature. This term, replacing a misconceived 'psychic unity,' may be understood to refer to the characteristics of all human beings as acquired in whatever society."[10] Thus Redfield's hopeful observaton that anthropologists will return to the study of human nature has not been as industrious or prolific as the subject deserves. The present study is an outgrowth of the author's own estimation of the importance of this subject in understanding the fundamentals of the social sciences.

Second, this study brings attention to social theorists that history of social behavior rather than concentration on the manipulation of statistical data is the prime factor in developing social theory. This is not to depreciate the value of statistical methods as an instrument in research. But it is only an adjunct to the essential factor of people expressing their behavioral traits in response to stimuli from their ecosystem and thereby making human history. Basic social theory is not built on such meta-human events as economic depressions, prosperity, and monetary or fiscal events. These are resultants, not beginnings or initiators of socioeconomic events. All the fundamentals of social theory must begin with human needs, physical and psychosocial, and how these needs are satisfied.

Third, as this study demonstrates, social theory is cross-disciplinary, involving sociological sciences, including economics and politics, psychology and social psychology, social and cultural anthropology, biology, and such disciplines as pertain to health, education, and spiritual development and those related to the physical environment. Social systems, in order to be humanly adequate, must satisfy the psychosocial traits of human nature as well as the physical and the physiological. Since the two most vibrant social systems in the world today are in the Western and the Eastern worlds, a comparison of the relation of these systems, based on the theories of Karl Marx and Adam Smith, to the traits of human nature must be studied in as much detail as will clarify their differences and their similarities.

Fourth, one of the quandaries that has plagued the development of the social sciences has been the problem of how to deal objectively with the subjective. A tenable system of psychosocial dynamics can be built from research into the behavior and cognition of people. As already indicated, some anthropologists believe that a scientific basis for the study of human nature can be developed by anthropology's findings in the social evolution of human society. The behavior of people in relation to their cognitive processes has recently been favored with concentrated research.[11] By applying the technique of uniformitarianism, as done by the anthropologist Lee,[12] objectifying the subjective is further advanced. The interrelation of the senses and cognition to the brain processes and brain mapping has in recent years been studied by such investigators as Roger Sperry, who concluded that "the mental forces of the conscious mind are restored to the brain of objective science from which they had long been excluded on material-behaviorist principles."[13] The fact is that the subjective by various scientific mechanisms is being objectified. Such development will more and more demonstrate the essential nature of the traits of human nature in societal dynamics. Objectification of the subjective in the above sense must not be confused with the proposition of the crass materialists who assert that mental substance is a form of material substance.

Fifth, since this study deals with concepts of fundamental human needs arising from basic human relations, it is necessary to define the terms expressing these concepts. Such terms as "value," "exchange," and "exploitation" are at the basis of the human relations in political economy, but, in this inchoative world economy, have lost their rational meaning. Such discussion does not mean that a critique on political economy is here being attempted, any more than dealing extensively with the concepts of social, cultural, and alienation makes this a critique on sociology, psychology, or social anthropology.

Sixth, unless the reader apprehends from the beginning what the aims of this study are, both its clarity and persuasiveness will suffer. For example, the amount of references pertaining to sociobiology, psychology, anthropology, and political economy is considerable. This does not mean that the subject matter of this study is lacking if reference is not made to some of the great contributors to any of the above fields. This is not an exhaustive study of any of those fields. Such a presumption would be ridiculous. The references chosen were indeed from recognized authorities, but only for the purpose of validating my thesis on the traits of human nature.

Last, the breadth of the areas of the social sciences involved in this study and the presumption that the validity of the very foundations of those sciences depend upon recognition of the pervasiveness of the impact of the traits of human nature in all science pertaining to society give this subject a paradigmatic appearance.

NOTES

1. Daniel J. Boorstin, *Discoverers* (New York: Vintage Books, 1983), p. 622.

2. Charles T. Tart, "States of Consciousness and State-Specific Sciences," in Robert E. Ornstein (ed.), *The Nature of Human Consciousness* (San Francisco, California: W. H. Freeman and Co., 1974), pp. 43–44.

3. Ibid.

4. Marc Linder, *Anti-Samuelson,* (New York: Urizen Books, 1977).

5. Karl Marx, *The Grundrisse,* edited and translated by David McLellan (New York: Random House, Inc., 1971), p. 94.

6. Niels Bohr, "Analysis and Synthesis in Science," in Otto Neurath, Rudolf Carnap, and Charles Morris, *International Encyclopedia of Unified Science,* Vol. 1 (Chicago, Illinois: University of Chicago Press, 1955), p. 28.

7. Erich Fromm, *The Sane Society* (New York: Henry Holt and Company, Copyright © 1955, 1983), pp. 27–66.

8. A. Irving Hallowell, "Culture, Personality, and Society," in A. L. Kroeber, *Anthropology Today* (Chicago, Illinois: University of Chicago Press, 1953), pp. 597–620.

9. David Bidney, "The Concept of Value in Modern Anthropology," in A. L. Kroeber, *Anthropology Today* (Chicago, Illinois: University of Chicago Press, 1953), pp. 682–99.

10. Robert Redfield, "Relations of Anthropology to the Social Sciences and Humanities," in A. L. Kroeber, *Anthropology Today* (Chicago, Illinois: University of Chicago Press, 1953), pp. 728–38.

11. V. F. Guidano and G. Liotti, *Cognitive Processes and Emotional Disorders* (New York: The Guilford Press, 1983).

12. Richard B. Lee, *!Kung San: Men, Women and Work in a Foraging Society* (New York: Cambridge University Press, 1979), pp. 434–37.

13. "Some Efforts of Disconnecting the Cerebral Hemisphere," *Science,* Vol. 217, no. 4566 (September 24, 1982), pp. 1223–226.

2

The Need for a Scientific Model

THE SCIENTIFIC APPROACH TO KNOWLEDGE OF THE PSYCHOSOCIAL

What has made the physical world so amenable to scientific probing, analysis, and prognostic knowledge? One is prompted to opine, "Because the nature of its structure has been revealed, to a large extent, from its macroscopic whole to its microscopic parts, and the motion of a significant portion of its parts and its whole can be measured with some facility." This renders the behavior of the physical world subject to predictive comprehension. The reduction of knowledge of the physical world to its elemental structure and to the dynamics of its motion for precision measurement is fundamental in the development of precision knowledge about it. Science is strikingly "reductionist," although within certain hierarchical levels of complexity of matter and motion, "constructionism" complements reductionism[1,2,3] as a phase of methodology, i.e., in scientific method, analysis must, at certain points, accompany synthesis. In the actual cognitive processes, these are complementary interpenetrating phases. These basics are common knowledge to scientists in general.

Science is organized knowledge of the principles, laws, theories, and hypotheses of the structure and motion of matter in its various phenomenal manifestations. The natural sciences include the organized knowledge of the patterns of structure and motion of the first three levels of material organization, the physical, the chemical, and biological, each level respectively being more complex than the previous, but, at the same time, resting on the previous level's organized knowledge.

The third level of the material world, the biological, brings into existence a remarkably new quality to matter, that of life. Whereas physical and chemical levels of the structure and motion of matter are not self-propagating, the essence of life is self-propagation, and the essential quality of living matter is its capability of being excited and conditioned by and being able to respond to stimulation. It is this nature that is the basic concern of epidemiology, epizoology, and epiphytology. The rationale for an epidemiology of infectious and nonmental chronic diseases is the need for information on the dysfunction of physiological processes resulting from stimulation by external and internal physical agents and factors and by the human organisms' self-impelled activities, such as running, skating, swimming, football, and the like. The epidemiology of psychosomatic diseases is on the transitional plane between that of the physical and the mental. The need for an epidemiology of infectious diseases is to obtain knowledge for maintaining human health by the investigation of the dynamics of the various microorganisms in the environment, how they reach the bodies of human beings, and their effects on the various physiological processes of the various components of the human population in the various parts of the world. This is the basis for the elaboration of preventive techniques. The epidemiology of the noninfectious chronic diseases has a similar methodology, including the dynamics of the genetic process.

Life forms in the higher orders of animals have the ability to react not only automatically or instinctually to external stimulation, including situations, and to internal biological urges such as sex, hunger, taste, smell, touch and sleep, but also are subject to feeling the sensations of being stimulated and responding emotionally as the result of such sensory and perceptual stimulation. Among human primates, sensations are associated with a wider range of perceptions to which they respond and from which they can learn an infinitely richer complex of cognitive processes, all set in a matrix of the conscience that guides their biphasic behavioral process (human versus primate) toward the human direction. The behavior resulting from this level of living substance brings into being a new quality to matter in motion, that of cognition. Whereas the epidemiology of physical diseases studies effects of the various external physical and internal physiological factors on the various physiological processes of the members of a population, the epidemiology of behavioral disorientations must study the effects of the various *whats* of the ecosystem on the various *whats* of the behavior of the people in that ecosystem. What are these *whats?* If the whats of the ecosystem be *anything* in the ecosystem without definiteness, such as the microorganisms in the ecosystem in the study of infectious diseases, then we must conclude that the science of behavior today is equivalent to what the status of the science of communicable diseases was before the time of Pasteur. And if the *whats* in the behavior of the human population be *any kind* of human expression without definitiveness, such as the general term physiological processes in the study of physical diseases, then we must also conclude that, from this point of view, the status of the science of human behavior is not much more developed than that which was rendered by Charles H. Cooley in 1902, Alfred Korzybski in 1921, and George H. Mead in 1934 and as the anthropologists David Bidney in 1947 and Robert Redfield in 1953 reminded us.

What are these *whats?* The whats in the ecosystem are the socio-functional relations and all those factors that have an impact on the sociofunctional relations of people, i.e., those factors in the sociocultural complex of the society that tend to alter or vitiate the basic social interrelationships necessary to function as human society and that determine the nature of human nature. But human nature, like that of human physiology, is composed of various very specific processes, each process of which is called a trait of human nature. Like the physiological processes, these traits are interdependent and interpenetrating. They function as a whole in a state of dynamic equilibrium or dynamic disequilibrium. Behavioral disorientation may occur in those individuals whose thresholds to compensate are overcome, just as happens when physiological processes are faulted. The traits of human nature are not only interrelated, but are psychosocial responses to the basic human interrelations necessary between people as the result of the genus *Homo* struggling to create those societal characteristics that his endowed human potential made possible for forging into existence a human society.

The psychosocial sciences include psychology/psychiatry and the social sciences, such as social anthropology, sociology, economics, and political economy. These sciences are the knowledge of the principles, laws, theories, and hypotheses of the structure and behavior of human phenomena, including phenomena in the ecosystem composed directly and ubiquitously with the creations of human labor. To designate these as psychosocial is not the customary way of classifying them. Actually, it is not the accepted way. How can one call economics a psychosocial science? Not to call economics a predominantly psychosocial science and not to see it from that point of view is the main problem with its lack of predictability. This is as surely true for sociology, political science, and political economy.

Let us examine one facet of this problem to illustrate the deficiency. The most basic trait of human nature is that of bonding-sharing. The bonding aspect is phylogenetic in origin, and the sharing aspect is a hominid characteristic. But this trait, being ensconced in the behavioral complex of *Homo* and also being endowed with all the rest of the characteristics that make *Homo* human, particularly the processes of speech and cognition, initiated a unique transaction early in the evolution of human society whereby one human group *exchanged* vital products with another. This trait could just as well be called the bonding-sharing-exchange trait. The exchange transaction, now called *trade*, is purely a human characteristic, which has become the very basis for the whole system of local, national, and world economy. Engel's discussion of the history of the trade concept is revealing.[4] Adam Smith discussed exchange in a nonremarkable way. But Marx was the first economist who elaborated with intensity on the psychosocial implications of exchange, emphasizing its behavioral significance throughout the history of mankind[5] and making note of Ben Franklin's contribution.[6] This phenomenon is indeed psychosocial behavior. No matter how complex the exchange transactions become, they are basically the outcome of human interrelational and interactional behavior and cannot be evaluated with predictive (scientific) consequence without understanding human interrelational behavior and its teleological essence. The same holds for psychology/psychiatry, social anthropology, sociology, and political science.

Knowledge in the area of economics is fundamentally knowledge of the behavior of individuals *interrelated* and *interacting* in the process of purposeful production and exchange. To predict what will happen in the market, one must contend with innumerable variables, such as exist among the particles in a volume of gas. The predictability of the formulae of how the gas particles will react was formulated by Dalton, Avogadro, Boyle, and Charles. Their formulae gave accurate results, because the disparity of the variables in a gas—the molecules, electrons, and ions—are not so great, since their motions and sizes and weights rigidly adhere to natural law, i.e., their patterns of behavior cannot vary from automatic motion. The randomness of the components of a gas, therefore, results in definite statistical parameters. For exchange in the market, however, the human interrelations exerted to produce the commodities are *primarily* 'capital' employed human labor, mental and physical, regardless of the use of machinery or robots. The size and power of the component participants and those who control the money market that finances production are very disparate and incongruous, each with its own *teleological* drive, sometimes manifesting statistical equilibrium and, at other times, statistical disequilibrium, i.e., depressions, prosperity, inflation, foreign trade balance and imbalance, monopoly maneuvers. To predict when one state or another state will occur is almost like a guessing game, and if one guesses correctly, there are few measures that authorities will take presently. The amount of theoretical formulae for modern economics gets continually greater, but the predictive level of answers remains static, for the most part. Economics Nobelist Wassily Leontief had this to offer about this situation in a letter to *Science:* "Year after year economic theorists continue to produce scores of mathematical models and to explore in great detail their formal properties; and the econometricians fit algebraic functions of all possible shapes to essentially the same set of data without being able to advance, in any perceptible way, a systematic understanding of the structure and operations of a real economic system."[7] Such theories mask the teleological and psychosocial nature of exchange and also the teleological and psychosocial factors in the contradictory and antagonistic tensions behind production of the commodities entered into the market. The amount of unknowns, due to the unrestricted and unaccountable randomness of the participants, are so numerous that neither accurate science nor reliable predictability is possible. It is not the psychosocial and teleological nature of exchange that renders it nonamenable to scientific methodology, but the unaccountability of the participants in the process of modern exchange. Under present conditions, the randomness of the market forces will remain unmeasurably random, because it is effected by so many participants whose aims and purposes are allowed to remain secret in the false perception of the meaning of democracy. We know that the overall purpose of market participants is to make a profit. But, in the process of making a profit, some participants also aim at accumulating power to enhance their drive to make profit by the use of unscrupulous means. Much of this is hidden behind the interlocking directorships in the executive boards of large industries, banks, and insurance companies that supply the funds to producers. Making a profit ethically is getting to be unprofitable. It no longer means creative production for the market that contributes to the community well-being. Profits can also be made by such wasteful practices as not producing while receiving government subsidies for doing nothing, investing in money-losing enterprises that generate tax write-offs, colluding with others to produce less of a product vital for community survival, such as oil, and then increasing prices inordinately and investing tax-relief funds, earmarked by government for specific productive ventures, for the unproductive pursuits of devouring other industries to create tax write-offs and to enhance unfair economic power.

To eliminate unaccountability in behavior in modern production and exchange without weakening the incentive and challenge to participate in the production process is the crux of the crisis of modern economic practice. In order to accomplish this, it will require revolutionary techniques to set standards for market participation that will be equitable from a completely different point of view than the facade that exists today in favor of raw private politicoeconomic power. Ethical codes should be the basis of standards used to prevent powerful private forces from manipulating the market and should give a hopeful opportunity for less powerful but ethical private entrepreneurs to participate. Behavior in the market must be open, not chaotic, and therefore amenable to reasonable predictability, and the competition must be based on real quality of product or service.

New standards for market participation must be brought into existence to preserve the democratic form of society against perversions by the amoral and immoral economic and social depredations of the multinational industrial-financial forces, and to satisfy the needs of a healthful environment. Multinational *private* enterprising forces have, by their very nature, a similar code of ethics and morality as the oldtime privateers of the high seas. Society had to declare them null and void.

The fact is that *Homo,* at the very beginning of his emergence, recognized that he could not continue to exist as human unless he inhibited the primate animality of his behavior and in his social organization and replaced it with a *planned* social *order* to foster *human* relations. Out of necessity, therefore, he organized a human social order for the precise purpose of suppressing the social order of his primate forebears. This was done by developing norms of social interrelations that would enhance the human need to dominate man's inherent primate nature, thereby suppressing the violence of the patriarchal sex-dominant nature of primate community life.

Out of the needs to act humanly, therefore, which were initiated by the pressures of the newly emergent conditions for human living (see charts 1, 2, and 3 in the chapter on "the nature of human nature"), the molding of *Homo*'s traits of human nature began to take shape. Those traits did not come into being abruptly, as a chick breaks through its eggshell. Yet, comparing the hundreds of thousands of years ago since the genus *Australopithecus* emerged into the genus *Homo* to the time it took for the primate trait of "bonding" to change into the human trait of "bonding-sharing" (soon adding the practice of exchange) and for the primate trait of "troop dominance by a patriarch" to be replaced by a human code of social behavior in sex relations (including norms of sex and other conduct inhibitions), such extended changes in the evolution of interrelations could be considered revolutionary. Thus the traits of human nature that the *Homo* conditions of living made potentially inherent in the evolution of that genus became intermittently manifest in individuals and groups, hordes, clans, tribes, and communities of various stages of social evolution, depending upon the nature of the social organization and the sociofunctional interrelations established as its norms of conduct. The more popularly organized, the more the society nurtures the maturing of the traits of human nature, but always subject to certain controls and inhibitory norms lest the primitive urges regain dominance. During periods when society is organized on a less popular system, those favored with power and privilege tend to overexercise the expression of their traits toward extremism, i.e., toward the least inhibitory pressure—toward primate dominance.

That we do not have an organization of knowledge for the psychosocial sciences with comparable predictability as holds for the natural sciences is to be expected. One of the critical reasons why the present study was initiated was to find an answer to this problem. In a general way, the deficiency can be summarized as follows from the above exposition:

1. Social sciences lack a precise structural organization of the behavioral nature of the people whence all social action emanates. There is no precise perception of the specific traits of human nature.
2. Little significance is attributed to the crucial role that the teleological forces and the factions play commensurate to their actual performance in social movement and social development, such as discussed above in relation to "exchange" and "market." That people purposefully make their own history out of the conditions they have at hand is lost in the maelstrom of "impersonal" *social* forces and probability statistics that the socioeconomic scientists hynotize themselves into presenting as though they were natural laws.
3. There is a need for a well-developed methodology for dealing scientifically with the subjective factors that motivate people to act. Progress has begun in this area.

It would be foolhardy to pretend that the psychosocial sciences are vistas of deserts. Quite the contrary. We do have some psychosocial knowledge that could be called principles, some formulations that may be called laws, an abundance of rhetoric that has the flavor of theories, and philosophical propositions by the hundredweight that could be called hypotheses. The problem with all this is that there is no preponderant course of agreement among the scientists as we have in the natural sciences. This lack of consensus is scientifically a good sign, since consensus would be a catastrophic mistake under the limited validity of the present organization of psychosocial knowledge.

SCIENCE OF THE PSYCHOSOCIAL PHENOMENA

We know from the nature of the various hierarchical levels of scientific knowledge that we do not expect the pattern of the interrelationships of the basic entities in one science level to be repeated at another level. Thus the elementary particles of physics, the molecules and their parts, are different from the elementary particles of chemistry, the positive and negative ions. The same is true for the cells, chromosomes, and genes of biology and the enzymes, hormones, vitamins, antibodies, and essential amino acids of physiology.

Whereas natural science deals with a vast universe of more or less durably structured objects and their laws of motions, psychosocial science deals with *thinking* people who think about their thinking, behaving more or less freely, but restricted to this little planet and by the conditions they have at hand. The people in the process of behaving are the molecules in motion of the teeming mass called society. The nature of their movement (social behavior) has so far shown reluctance to yield to a reasonably precise predictability. The scientific discoveries of neurophysiology have not even begun to fathom the gap between what is electrochemical action and what is symbolic representation in the neopallium, if this "gap" can ever be reduced to scientific physical formulation. Concerning this gap, Francois Jacob reasoned: "Despite such generalizations [about how scientific discovery in the past has eliminated important gaps in our knowledge], however, large gaps remain [between] . . . each branch of science . . . some of which probably will not be bridged for a long time, *if ever*" (italics added).[8] Concerning the hierarchical levels and the gaps, Jacob describes this principle with undoubted clarity as follows:

> Science can be arranged in a certain order—physics, chemistry, biology, psychosociology—an order that corresponds to the hierarchy of complexity found in the objects of these sciences. Following the line from physics to sociology, one goes from the simpler to the complex of objects and also, for obvious reasons, from the older to the younger science, from the poorer to the richer empirical content, as well as from the harder to the softer system

of hypotheses and experimentation. . . . each system at a given level uses as ingredients some systems of the simpler level, but some only. The hierarchy in the complexity of objects is thus accompanied by a series of restrictions and limitations. At each level, new properties may appear which impose new constraints on the system.[9]

Anderson's discussion of the nature of the hierarchical structure of science[10] is in line with Jacob's point of view and also that of Engels.[11] The essence of this concept actually comes from Hegel's *Doctrine of Being,* the first volume of his *Science of Logic.*[12] This Hegelian principle was adopted by Marx and Engels and named the principle of transformation of quantity to quality.[13]

Anderson described this hierarchical arrangement as follows: "The elementary entities of science X obey the laws of science Y:

X	Y
Solid state or many-body physics	Elementary particle physics
Chemistry	Many-body physics
Molecular biology	Chemistry
Cell biology	Molecular biology
Psychology	Physiology
Social science	Psychology"

Anderson could have placed: "Physiology . . . Cell biology" in the hiatus between "Cell biology" and "Psychology." Thus the above principle, as applied to the organizational development of matter, states that physics, chemistry, cell biology, physiology, psychology, and sociology are each specific levels in the organization of matter and respectively as listed represent increasing complexity in organization. Each higher level of complexity is based on the laws of movement of the lower levels, but each higher level of complexity is unique in possessing laws of its own not possessed by the lower levels.

Odum expresses this basic principle from another perspective:

It is self-evident that science should not only be reductionist in the sense of seeking to understand phenomena by detailed study of smaller and smaller components, but also synthetic and holistic in the sense of seeking to understand larger components as functional wholes. A human being, for example, is not only a hierarchical system composed of organs, cells, enzyme systems, and genes as subsystems, but is also a component of supraindividual hierarchical systems such as populations, cultural systems, and ecosystems . . . An important consequence of hierarchical organization is that as components, or subsets, are combined to produce larger functional wholes, new properties emerge that were not present or not evident at the next level below.[14]

But to Wilson[15] and the sociobiologists and to many scientists who reason in terms of nineteenth-century mechanistic materialism, the meaning of the gap between symbolic representation and the material of the brain eludes them. They believe that the gap can be dissipated by molecular biology and neurophysiology, i.e., a symbol in the mind can be explained by specific molecular configuration in neurophysiological dynamics. Stent, in a very scholarly presentation of this gap problem, discusses the history of the problem as it relates to various philosophic systems and concludes that the brain-mind interrelational structure cannot be explained by relating the molecular dynamics of brain function to the corresponding structure of mental abstraction, and he asserts that: "We thus encounter the barrier to an ultimate scientific understanding of man which Descartes had recognized more than three centuries ago. . . . Descartes had realized that physiological studies really leave the central problem of visual perception untouched. For the percept is obviously a function of the *soul,* or in modern psychological parlance, of the *self,* whose nature Descartes thought to be inaccessible to scientific analysis. No matter how deeply we probe into the visual pathway, in the end we need to posit an "inner man" who transforms the visual image in a percept."[16]

The hyperbolic dualism of Descartes that crystallized from his hyperbolic skepticism in describing the relation of mind to body is, as Straus described it in his Phenomenological Psychology, an invention that had "devastating consequences . . . in the conceptual formation and development of psychology, physiology, medicine and psychiatry."[17] Cohen, in describing Straus's criticism of Descartes, states with quotations from Straus:

> With Descartes the universe is divided ontologically between two types of entities: the *res cogitans* which is mental, and the *res extensa* which is physical. The two are said to be mutually exclusive substances. . . . In order to show the novelty of the Cartesian "discovery" of consciousness, Straus emphasizes that the Cartesian *res cogitans–res extensa* dichotomy goes far beyond

the old-fashioned Christian soul-body dichotomy. In the Christian tradition it is only in death that the soul departs the body, "but so long as a man was alive body and soul . . . belonged together . . . the soul was part of the world . . . intramundane."[18] This is not the case with Descartes's *res cogitans*. Cartesian consciousness is not part of the physical world which is governed by the mechanical laws of physics. The Cartesian "thinking thing" is "extramundane."

This concept is also alien to the Aristotelian and entire Greek world of conceiving the essence of consciousness.

Stent, indeed, makes a "scientific" case against the idea that man can be understood scientifically by equating Descartes' isolated and independent *soul* with the *self* of man. But then, at the same time, he negates this proof by rejecting the scientific understanding of self. He does this by misunderstanding the meaning of those gaps in knowledge that exist between the various levels in the hierarchy of the branches of science. *The gaps exist because the developmental principle relating to the uniqueness of the motion of matter manifested at each hierarchical level of the structure of matter has its own unique laws of motion. The gaps are not breaks in the continuity of knowledge, but steps in the manifestation of the different levels of organization and dynamics of substance.* Therefore, the nature of symbolism cannot be explained by the dynamics of molecular biology and neurophysiology any more, for example, than the physical laws of gravitation can explain the chemical laws of oxidation and reduction. Not being able to define "self" in the scientific terms of the dynamics of molecular biology and neurophysiology, as Stent correctly claims, he proceeds to opine incorrectly that self cannot be understood. However, self, as the behavioral nature of the average person, can be understood by examining the unique dynamic relations between the traits of human nature and the culture which that nature created and in which that nature operates, as we shall see.

The unenthusiastic future for social science perceived by Stent is not unusual, considering the amount of peripherally directed studies based on philosophically uninspired trivia congesting the literature in this field in recent years by sociological, psychological, and social and cultural anthropological branches of science. Nevertheless, some of the citations presented by Stent have some significance insofar as this study of human nature is concerned. The fact that Franz Boaz sought to establish a common sameness to be present among all cultures is a very pertinent observation in spite of the cultural relativism he inspired by overemphasizing the myriad differences manifested between these cultures. Although the deeper structure of sameness, cited by Stent, is considered by him to be innate, it will be shown subsequently in this study that the traits of human nature that correspond to this deeper structure of sameness have not been proven to be innate, even though they have an innate and an ecological base, i.e., the psychosocial is ultimately biopsychosocial.[19] His observation, nevertheless, that "any theoretical framework for understanding man must be based on the deep structures whose discovery ought to be the *real goal* of the human sciences" is indeed pertinent. The traits of human nature appear to fill this counsel, as will be demonstrated.

Pertinent to Stent's thesis about the "deep structures" is Bidney's asseveration concerning the priority of human nature in relation to culture, i.e., that culture is created by human nature: "The general thesis I have sought to establish . . . is that *human culture in general may be understood as the dynamic process and product of the self-cultivation of human nature as well as of the natural environment, and involves the development of selected potentialities of nature for the attainment of individual and social ends of living.* I am especially concerned to make it clear that *culture is essentially a correlative, polar concept and is unintelligible apart from its reference to nature.* . . . If there were no determinate human nature and natural environment for man to cultivate and transform there would be no cultural process or product."[20]

Although certain aspects of biology, particularly relating to the microcosm of the living cell's structure and function and the biochemistry of physiology and pathology of an organism are adoptable to the scientific methodology of physics and chemistry, the knowledge of the *behavior* of the animal itself and the process of its evolution must rely mostly on *field observations* in the natural ecology of the animal. Ernst Mayr, the most eminent modern biologist of evolution, changed the course of evolutionary biology by his ability to interpret the meaning of his field observations and those of other biologists by deriving therefrom the theory of geographic speciation. *This is a valid methodology for scientific investigation of animal evolution. It is also valid when applied to the social world of* Homo *using the world as the laboratory, and using its history, social and anthropological, and the myriad observations of trained and otherwise critical observers, including philosophers, as a data bank. It is the method used in this study for filtering out the essential traits of human behavior. The extensive use of full quotations is for the purpose of being accurate with the data and assuring their pertinency. By this method of the naturalist, the constants (the traits of human nature) abounding in the great cultural variability of human behavior were derived.*

The development of an organized system of knowledge based on the psychosocial responses of people, which are generated in the process of them interacting with the basic conditions of human living, is the subject this study is attempting to probe. Because of the difficulty in subjecting the "subjective" responses of *Homo* to the objective rigors of scientific methodological investigation, the relation between the cognitive processes and human behavior has not been objectively (scientifically) established, as noted by Stent. The result has been that Freud's theories have been rejected by many scientists on this basis, the behaviorist school gained popularity by disregarding cognition, and the mechanical materialist school of thought has gained favor by divining that future scientific developments will overcome the gaps between the levels of the basic branches of science by materializing cognition. The dialectic materialist school of Marx has had no scientifically logical problem in this area. It postulates that the only absolute in the world is matter in motion and that the cognitive processes are properties of the brain expressed as ideational reflections of the material world in the dynamics of brain function. Mind and material operating as a process are therefore a unity of opposites with material as the primary factor.

For Marx, ideas organized as theories, laws, and principles have scientific validity if these concepts are collated correctly to the dynamics of material existence and if they are confirmed in relation to repeated similar historical circumstances and social interrelations. As an apparent confirmation of this thesis, Roger Sperry, in experiments on the brain, has demonstrated ·that the cognitive process could be subjected to scientific methodology, for which work he received the Nobel Prize in 1981. In this Nobel lecture, he concluded, "one of the more important indirect results of the split-brain work is a revised concept of the nature of consciousness and its fundamental relation to brain processing. The key development is a switch from prior noncausal, parallelist view to a new causal, or 'interactionist' interpretation that ascribes to inner experience an integral causal control role in brain function and behavior. In effect, and without resorting to dualism, the mental forces of the conscious mind are restored to the brain of objective science from which they had long been excluded on materialist-behaviorist principles. The spreading acceptance of the revised causal view and the reasoning involved carry important implications for science and for scientific views of man and nature. Cognitive introspective psychology and related cognitive science can no longer be ignored experimentally or written off as a 'science of epiphenomena' or as something that must in principle reduce eventually to neurophysiology. The events of inner experience, as emergent properties of brain processes, become themselves explanatory causal constructs in their own right, interacting at their own level with their own laws and dynamics. The whole world of inner experience (the world of the humanities), long rejected by twentieth-century scientific materialism, thus becomes recognized and included within the domain of science."[21] Thus the subjective has come into its own scientifically by its objective expression.

To attribute the same laws of movement (behavior) to human individuals and to human society as to the rest of biological taxa, as the sociobiologists are apt to do, and to reduce the explanation of all behavior of humans (as individuals or as society) to molecular biology and neurophysiology was such a gross misinterpretation of science for Sahlins that he wrote a polemic on the subject, being so outdone by this tendency of the sociobiologists.[22]

THE BIPHASIC NATURE OF HOMO: HUMAN VERSUS PRIMATE

It is true that animals show behavior characteristics that are also inherent behavior manifestations in *Homo,* such as sexual, environmental resourcefulness, spatial, and territorial *competition;* territoriality, parent-offspring conflict, parental discipline, sex dominance, nonpredatory *aggression, courtship, altruism, kinship,* and *parental care* behavioral traits and *aggression-submission* relations, and playing for fun. These have been thoroughly discussed by Wilson in his *Sociobiology.* MacKinnon, in his many years of observing the behavior of apes in natural habitats, cited a number of behaviors in these animals that are also found in adult man as *negative* types of conduct so far as man is concerned, such as *sex excesses, child abuse, rape, competition accompanied by trickery and guile, violent aggression and fighting, terrorizing to gain an immediate objective, blindly following the leader, lack of conscience in conduct,* and *maliciousness.*[23]

In the process of development of *human* behavior, one aspect of the deeper structure of behavior can be observed as the child develops, i.e., as the process of socialization teaches the thinking child in his cognitively maturing mental processes the necessary *inhibitions* that help to *humanize* him, he is deflected from manifesting the antihuman heritage of his *primate* behavior. Each phase has an individual pattern of expression. The young child does not react like an adult. Adolescents may not become completely socialized to adult conduct until they actually become adults in years. The comparison may not be too far-fetched, but to a striking degree, childhood behavior resembles primate behavior in various aspects of conduct and even seems to resemble chimpanzee behavior in some features. Reference is made to such behavioral features as *aggressiveness, distractability, uncontrolled conduct, lack of inhibitions,*[24,25,26] *egocentrism and solipsism,*[26,27] *learning by play,*[26,28,29] *imitation,*[26,27] *assimilation,*[26,28] *repetition,*[28,29] and *object manipulation.*[29]

A number of these behavioral features are for the human or the negative side of desirability. There are also certain features of primate behavior that were further developed by *Homo* to become valuable behavioral assets to his humanness. Farb in his "Humankind" study, pages 26 and 27, observes certain behavioral features of primates that distinguish them from other animals and are important in understanding certain aspects of human behaviors. Those are, the ability for:

1. social learning;
2. tool making;
3. cooperation in hunting;
4. organizing the social group;
5. securing protection for companions known since infancy;
6. maintaining kinship ties with mother and siblings who can be counted upon for protection;
7. maintaining safety of the group by the continued presence of adult males; and
8. maintaining pleasurable social interactions of a predictable way of life.

As indicated above, higher primates, particularly the apes, have behavioral *anlage* of some of the basic human behavioral characteristics. This observation is not made in the same context that some sociobiologists, such as Wilson, and some ethologists, such as Lorenz, hold in discussing this subject. The term "anlage," as used here, really means its dictionary meaning—the first recognizable commencement of a developing part—and nothing more. The nature of man's behavior has a *human quality* (human nature) that is beyond comparison to that of the other primates. If an ape shows affection or disaffection to another ape, how can this be compared to that complexity of love and sharing and commitment of conscience or of hate and feeling of guilt expressed by the human, except in terms of such ape expression being an anlage? The bonding force without the sharing is the most developed of these traits in the higher primates. In *Homo*, however, this trait is very intricately involved with other *human* traits such as relate to challenge, to self-image–self-esteem, to norms of conduct, and to sense of competence, all of which may appear to have anlage in higher primates, but barely so. The time-binding trait is completely absent in any organism except *Homo* and so is the psychosocial element of conscience.

People living in certain sociocultural conditions react with certain predictability, but for psychosocial and cultural reasons. This is obvious when one considers that otherwise demogogues, politicians, advertising agents, and family and friends could not maintain successful interrelations among those of interest to them. But what is the behavioral anatomy of *Homo sapiens sapiens?*

Knowing the structure of a substance and the nature of its motion as a whole and of its elemental parts means knowing the processes by which such a dynamic system *operates* and *changes*. The operation is its *repetitive* process. The changing is its *developmental* process. All things manifest themselves in this manner. For example, the cells of an organism have a set of processes that cause them to perpetuate themselves by dividing and producing daughter cells which for the most part are replicas of themselves. This is the repetitive process of the cell. The repetitive nature of natural events could very well have been the stimulus for the origin of arithmetic counting.[30] It could also have been the influence on living cells and organisms to evolve circadian systems.[31] The cell is basically composed of two components parts: the nuclear material which carries on reproduction, and the extranuclear material, including the cytoplasm and the cell membrane, which carries on many vital functions, among which are food assimilation, respiration, excretion, and growth. The dynamic interaction between the functional processes of these two structural elements is the essence of the life process. Assimilation, excretion, respiration, growth, and division are directed by the genes. This is the repetitive process. The dynamics of meiosis and mitosis and the effects of the extranuclear environment on this vital activity are the developmental process—the process of evolution. These are the life processes on which biomedical scientific knowledge is built—knowledge that emphasizes the physiological nature of the individual. But what are the fundamental dynamics of the psychosocial processes that generate the durable, definitive characteristics of the cognitive-behavioral nature, the traits of human nature of people, manifested most distinctly in social groups and more or less manifested in individuals?

The movement in every process is a unique phenomenon in that the movement results from interaction between two particular tension-actuating forces. These forces can be described as contrarieties, as Aristotle[32] named them. Hegel called them opposites.[33] Marx and Engels called them contradictions. The above description of the vital processes of the cell as an integrated tension between the nuclear and extranuclear forces is a good example. Thus every process is biphasic, each phase being a counterforce to the other, such as negative and positive electric charges, acidic and basic reactions, anabolism and catabolism, human and primate (or subhuman) behavior in *Homo,* and so on, *ad infinitum.* But these opposites are not necessarily antagonistic; they are complementary and interdependent within the limits of extremities. We will see how important this principle is in delving into the psychosocial nature, the human nature, of man—his cognitive-behavioral processes churning in the social medium of the basic human condition.

In summary, it is clear that the genus *Homo* evolved as a primate with primate instincts and continues *ad infinitum* to reproduce that vigorous heritage. In order to become human, *Homo* had to develop a process of humanization that is designated as socialization. In this process, hominid children are taught to control their primate instincts. This is done by their learning *inhibition* by means of the *educability* attribute of their brain potential, which particularly distinguishes them from the pongids. They are also taught the basic behavior that hominid society had to elaborate during the tens of thousands of years of its emergence from the primeval horde that gave it the capability to live as a human society under its newly evolved conditions of living. This basic behavior was composed of the traits of human nature. The conditioning of its children to behave as humans did not prevent the primate instincts from continuing to plague the people by their unremitting struggle to dominate the human traits of behavior. This unremitting nature of the force of the primate instincts animated Freud to study the sociocultural history of humankind for clues to man's behavior. It led him to elaborate his elegant theories on the behavioral processes of the human race in its contention—its crucial struggles—to contain the disorienting influences on *human* behavior by the primate instincts. Freud's theories deal primarily with the disorienting influence of the primate instincts on the human behavior of individual cases by the push of the instincts for dominance. As a system that is amenable to developing primary prevention in community mental health programs, Freudian theory is ineffective. It deals only cursorily with some of the traits of human nature, whereas a system based on the traits of human nature is capable of being used for such community programs.

THE SCIENCE OF THE SUBJECTIVE

When one contemplates science, concepts such as molecules, atoms, matter, physics, chemistry, biology, and behavior flash across one's mind. But when one directs the same awareness of science toward such concepts as feeling, love, pain, happiness, joy, anger, and the like, the distinctiveness that accompanies the contemplation of the science of material substances vanishes. The subjective reveals itself as quite a different substance than the material substance of the objective brain, and yet this different substance is really a qualitatively new expression of the inherently unique molecular motion of the same brain matter that sees and feels and contemplates.

Although we are not dealing here directly with the *extrinsic* manifestation of molecular motion, such as is encountered in neurophysiology, we are dealing with an *intrinsic* expression of this energy revealed as mental representations. Let us examine the relation of this process to that of the material world. The basic process of the world is that of the biphasic relation between matter and its motion. This process is universal in nature, since all existence is expressed as a relation between *quantity* of matter and energy and *quality* of form and function.

The biphase is always between *interpenetrating* and *interdependent* but *not* interchangeable forces. This is true for the subjective and the objective aspects of living organisms that have the capacity to feel and ideate. The subjective in the human is more than to feel and to ideate. It is permeated by the state of self-consciousness, self-awareness, and self-estimation. Roger Sperry, in discussing "the higher, reflective, self-conscious kind of inner awareness that is special to the human mind," which he researched in his ten years of brilliant work on split-brain patients, claims that "self-awareness in particular is reported . . . to be a predominantly human attribute and is rated by developmental as well as by evolutionary standards to be a highly advanced phase of conscious awareness."[34] As the result of Sperry's and related research, no *duality* of independent mental and brain forces is any longer valid as philosophers such as Plato, Aristotle, Aquinas, and Descartes saw the relation between mind and matter to be. The subjective and objective are now proven to be scientifically interpenetrating and interdependent forces of a single biphasic process. Brain dynamics are reflected in mental dynamics. The subjective has become scientifically "objective," i.e., has become subject to the methodology of scientific study. In the subjective, we are dealing with a process whereby physical, chemical, and biological energies are transformed into mental energy, manifested subjectively as psychic substance—a quality of energy found *only* in living organisms—a quality of life whereby the extrinsic becomes and is reflected in the intrinsic. The scientist of the material world may look upon such a description of the mental world as nonscientific, since we have not "explained" the dynamics by which the extrinsic (matter) becomes and is reflected in the intrinsic (mind). By the same logic, we could ask such a scientist to explain the dynamics of the chemical process of oxidation and reduction by the laws of physics, for is that not the same as asking for the explanation of the dynamics of the extrinsic becoming and being reflected in the intrinsic by the laws of biology, i.e., neurophysiology and molecular biology?

The science of the subjective must be sought in the *behavior* of living organisms, behavior, which in *Homo* is accompanied by interrelated, interdependent cognitive processes. The dictionary of the intrinsic symbolism and cognitive processes is written in the reflected language of extrinsic behavior as Sperry was able to correlate certain specific cognitive processes with specific locations in the brain. In animals where the genetic and instinctual predominate, the qualities of behavioral manifestations are much easier to classify and to organize into paradigms of scientific coherence. In man, his physical attributes (including his genetic nature and expanded neopallium) give him the widest range of behavioral action (associated with expansive cognitive processes), constrained only by the conditions in which he finds himself in his particular ecosystem. Thus the problem of classifying and organizing his behavioral manifestations into a coherent scientific paradigm has, to a large extent, stymied social scientists, although the attempts have been infinite. The task, of course, is much more difficult of solution than using the methodology ethologists and the sociobiologists have presented. It is much easier to delineate genetic and instinctual behavior, i.e., *animal behavior,* than behavior originating in the tremendous reservoir of psychosocial stimuli of the mind, i.e., *human behavior* and the cognitive and emotional activity accompanying it. Of this almost infinite variety of behavioral responses in the spheres of numerous cultures and subcultures, what are, if any, the patterns of sameness—the generic traits of human behavior common to all cultures? Ay, there's the rub.

Luckily, the literature is rich with philosophic and scientific observations on the matter of universal traits of human behavior, from the Bible to the present-day social scientists' writings. However, few social scientists have grasped the panoramic concept of filtering out the generic patterns of human behavior lurking in the massive complexity of behavioral expressions and organizing them into a paradigmatic pattern of man's behavioral nature. These generic patterns compose the behavioral complex common to all human societies, denoting the nature of social man—the nature of his human nature.

THE SCIENCE OF SOCIETY

Now let us consider further the nature of the basic process of human society, i.e., the process of population development. This is the process that must be understood if we are going to delve into the well-being of society. Without social well-being, a society will develop a deteriorating trend till it disappears. What is the nature of the process of population development? This process is actually a *double* biphasic process, not, as for animals whose survival process is a single biphasic process, e.g.,

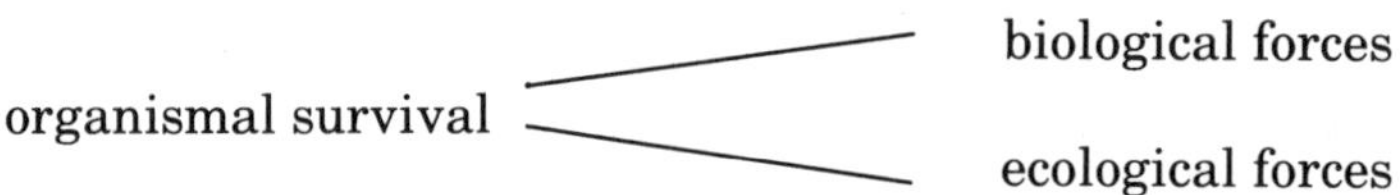

Animal life survives or perishes, depending on the outcome of the process of tension between the biological and the ecological forces of the particular species. For the human population, its survival and development are due to the resultant of the following double integrated, interpenetrating biphasic processes, with the organismal survival process in the background:

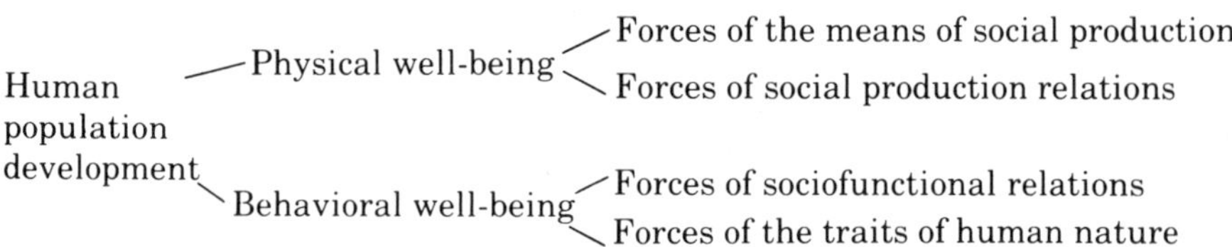

The reason that animal survival is the result of a single process while the human population development is not only dependent on the latter process but is also subject to a human interpenetrating biphasic process is because of the capacity of human society to make its own

history not out of the whole cloth, but out of conditions found at hand, whereas animal survival has no active self-initiating cognitive aspect to contend with as the human has in his activities of creating and changing the ecosystem.

At this point, there is a need to distinguish the meaning of "sociofunctional relations" in contrast to "social relations." The latter encompasses, in general, all interrelations pertaining to people in the organized community process. The sociofunctional relations are those social relations that are pertinent influentially in the process of organized community life to the *functioning* of that society, i.e., to the making of human history out of the existing ecosystem. For example, the social relations between twin siblings in a society cannot be pertinent to the overall functioning of that society even under very unusual circumstances, if ever, while the social relations between generations in any society is very pertinent to comprehensive functioning of that society.

Lee, in his discussion of the economic organization of the !Kung peoples asserts that "Marx made the important point that the distinct social and political forms and ideology of each society within a mode of production were closely related to the ways people organized their work and to the ways the ownership of the means of production was allocated."[35] This is equivalent to saying that the physical and, *to some extent only,* the behavioral well-being of a population are closely related to the forces of the means of production as the latter relate to the forces of production relations. The nature of the economic organization includes the level of technology and determines the amount of the productive yield that the workers receive for maintenance of their physical well-being. Only to a limited degree but an important degree, does the economic organization effect the mental well-being, but *basic* in effecting the mental-behavioral well-being is the relation of the pattern of sociofunctional relations (of which production relations are a part) to the traits of human nature.

We have glanced hurriedly at some important basic concepts relating to scientific methodology, because they pertain to the development of this thesis of dealing with the subjective aspect of human nature in an objective scientific method. Many perceptive writers have discussed various aspects of human nature, but none in present times has developed a model of its specific traits and how they react to the social forces around them in the process of societal development. Only such a model of specific traits of human nature as a complex of enduring entities of human behavior could be dealt with objectively in fathoming the behavioral dynamics of society.

Human nature is not a fuzzy agglomeration of the behavioral manifestations of people. It is an integration of specific modes of behavior manifested in humankind more or less since the genus *Homo* embarked on its humanization process and emerged as a culture producing force in nature. These specific traits of behavior have fused into a relatively enduring pattern as human nature. Yet in this pattern of behavior each trait is a distinct, discernible entity, the result of a cognitive process steeped in the social medium of surviving as a society of human beings. Emotions infuse their force in these traits, but are themselves not an essential component of the traits of human nature.

MATERIAL AND MENTAL WELL-BEING

The foregoing process of population development is not new to political economy. It is very similar to Marx's formulation of the determinants "of the social, political, and spiritual process of life," in which he predicated that the two forces in the process of social development are the means of production and the forces of production relations.[36] This formulation is a powerful theory. This process is basic to the *material* well-being of society. It also affects the mental health of society, being a component of the sociofunctional relations. But here our thesis diverts. It agrees that increasing the ability to produce also increases the physical well-being of a society, but it does *not* agree that the higher level of material well-being of a society *ipso facto* endows it with a higher level of mental well-being. This is where adherents to the modern interpretation of the socialist philosophy make a basic error in expecting that changing the relations in ownership of the means of social production will *automatically* also be accompanied by the disappearance of the social factors leading to mental stress and disorientation. The mental well-being of society is *not* significantly determined by, although it is affected by, the level of forces of production and the pattern of the forces of production relations. But it is directly determined by the forces of sociofunctional relations, which include production relations, as these are or are not in harmony with the traits of human nature. As already stated, but bears repetition, the sociofunctional relations describe how people function in their whole sociocultural setting and to what extent these relations are in concordance with the traits of human nature. This is well illustrated by the fact that the forces of the means of production and the forces of production relations in the United States and in the Soviet Union are quite different and much more developed in the United States than the

Soviet Union. But the problem of alcoholism, a mental health (behavioral) problem resulting from the disharmony between the sociofunctional relations and the traits of human nature, is as epidemic in one country as in the other, because in both countries disharmony exists between the sociofunctional relations and the traits of human nature. This would be an excellent area for epidemiological study.

The ability of a country to produce material things is certainly essential to the physical well-being of that society and the physical well-being reflects in a positive way on the mental health, but it does *not* determine the whole well-being of the cognitive-behavioral, emotional, spiritual, and social aspects in the process of living. This was known even in biblical times and was expressed as "Man doth not live by bread alone" (Deuteronomy). The fact that the most important means of production are government controlled or owned does not guarantee that the distribution of wealth will be equitable, nor is there the slightest indication that governments place the mental well-being of their people as a top priority. Government control of ownership does not mean people's power. A government may be controlled by a personal dictatorship of which a number exist, such as the regime in Libya, which nation claims the name: People's Socialist Libyan Arab Republic, and whose secretary-general of the General People's Congress, Col. Muammar el-Qaddafi, operates the country's affairs as the dictator. There are other such "people's socialist" countries in the Third World that are neither the people's nor socialist. There are governments that are controlled by military juntas and call themselves people's republics and are neither the people's nor republics, such as Chile. There are governments that are controlled by an only recognized political party but are really controlled by a small group of such party, as in the Republic of Iraq where the party is "socialist." In this case, the country is neither a republic nor socialist, but a dictatorship of almost a single person, the "president." There are socialist countries that are republics controlled by their communist parties, such as the Union of Soviet Socialist Republics and the Socialist Republic of Romania. While there are some of these in which liberalization is being practiced, as in the Socialist Federal Republic of Yugoslavia and the Hungarian People's Republic, these are single-party dictatorships that own and control the major means of production or tolerate modified private initiative in agriculture and small business. From a physical (material) point of view, the overwhelming majority of their people are better off than they were under their prior monarchies. From the point of view of the people's behavioral-mental well-being, there is no available reliable evidence of such progress.

For the well-being of the population of a country, besides its productive ability to serve the physical needs, to exist *the country also requires an ecosystem that harmonizes with the traits of human nature.* As far as human ingenuity is concerned in the area of social organization that fosters compatible human relations, democracy has been its best invention. John Dewey has eloquently defined this social form in *The Shaping of the American Tradition:*

> The foundation of democracy is faith in the capacities of *human nature* [italics added]; faith in human *intelligence* and then power of pooled and cooperative experience. It is not belief that these things are complete but that if given a show they will grow and be able to generate progressively the knowledge and wisdom needed to guide collective action. . . .
>
> Democracy is much broader than a special political form, a method of conducting government, of making laws and carrying on governmental administration by means of popular suffrage and elected officers. It is that, of course, but it is something broader and deeper than that. The political and governmental phase of democracy is a means, the best means so far found, for realizing ends that lie in the wide domain of human relationships and the development of human personality. It is . . . a way of life, social and individual. The key-note of democracy as a way of life may be expressed . . . as the necessity for the participation of every mature human being in formation of the values that regulate the living of men together, which is necessary from the standpoint of both the general social welfare and the full development of human beings as individuals. . . . no man or limited set of men is wise enough or good enough to rule others without their consent; the positive meaning of this statement is that all those who are affected by social institutions must have a share in producing and managing them.
>
> The very fact of natural and psychological inequality is all the more reason for establishment of law of equality of opportunity, since otherwise the former becomes a means of oppression of the less gifted.
>
> Unless freedom of individual action has intelligence and informed conviction back of it, its manifestation is almost sure to result in confusion and disorder.[37]

DEMOCRACY AND DICTATORSHIP DEFINED

Democracy is a system of humanistic social interrelations fitting the traits of human nature, which are formalized into a pattern of civil and personal rights ordained by laws, customs, mores, and institutions to govern the social interrelational behavior of those affected. Every system of government is a teleological instrument. The patterns of relations, except such basic biosocial relations as between mother and child, are purposefully established with their rights and duties and inhibitions defined. Therefore, teleological phenomena are always articles of faith or faith-involved, since purpose is never set forth for translation into action without the hope and faith for fulfillment. Democracy, one of these systems of social relations by which man is governed, is identified by:

1. Faith in the capacity of human nature and the dominance of the human aspect over the primate aspect.
2. Faith in the power of human intelligence to generate progressively the knowledge and wisdom to choose freely what is needed for collective action when human experience is pooled, shared, and used cooperatively. This requires:

    a. A system of popular suffrage for choosing representatives of government who govern with the consent of the people.
    b. A system for assuring equal rights to each person to express his judgement and to participate as a mature human being in the formulation of values that regulate the living of people together.
    c. A system assuring everyone the right of expression and such other rights as the freedom of the press, the freedom of assembly, and the freedom of communication—freedom with popularly agreed upon limits lest chaos supervene.

3. Faith in developing a conscience of individual and social responsibility in the individual as reflected in his appreciation of his self-image in the context of his community participation. This requires:

    a. A system assuring the equality of opportunity to develop one's capacity.

b. A system for assuring freedom of the mind in order to produce a freed intelligence necessary to warrant freedom of individual action for self-development within the bounds expressed as: Freedom is not the right to *do* as one pleases without considering the freedom of others.

c. A system for assuring that those wielding political power are responsible to the voters.

4. Faith that the freedom to act and choose will initiate the creative power in the individual and the group to strive to satisfy the appetites, inclinations, and talents vested in them. This requires a system for assuring the means for attaining the general social well-being and full development of the people and the strivings of the individuals.

5. Faith that humankind's ability to evaluate and to judge will fittingly guide people's actions for realizing their future hopes and needs as human beings. This requires a system for realizing the present and future needs in human relations and development of the human side of personality.

6. Faith that, given the freedom and the means for developing their competence for role performance, individuals will be stimulated to accept the challenge to achieve. This requires a system for assuring the individual's share in producing, shaping, and managing those institutions in which and by which people are challenged to succeed.

7. Faith that the predictive expectancy hoped for in the social conscience will be maintained in a salubrious state by having the freedom to satisfy the human need for commitment and engagement in a unifying code of behavioral orientation. This requires:

a. The system of governmental regulations to be based on a code of social inhibitions voluntarily arrived at but with the profoundest of perspection and perspicacity by mutual consultation and voluntary agreement and not on arbitrary coercion and with equality of treatment of each individual by the law and its administration.

b. A social philosophy, democratically developed and agreed upon, for guiding and unifying the orientation of the mores and institutions that mold attitudes, dispositions, abilities, and personalities in the direction of the balanced needs of the traits of human nature.

Democracy as an ideal pattern of interrelational behavior should be engraved in the customs, mores, and institutions of community life—in the governmental regulations as well as in the nongovernmental codes of conduct. Since human nature is a biphasic phenomenon, the struggle between the human conduct and the primate urges are *always* present. Therefore, democratic behavior as an ideal is continually being compromised by latent primate tendencies. That is why laws and codes of morality and ethics are unconditionally necessary as human instrumentalities and coercion for some people will be unavoidable.

Dictatorship is a system of coercive social interrelations for most of the community that are discordant with the traits of human nature and are formalized into a pattern of restrictive civil and personal rights ordained by a system of laws and decrees to govern the social interrelational behavior of those affected.

Dictatorship, by application of coercion to society, violates each trait of human nature whose essences are appreciation of self-image, freedom to choose, challenge to accomplish and act with competence, creativity, striving to satisfy inclinations and talents, adhering to a rational and humanistic philosophy for living, time-binding action implying hope, and bonding-sharing commitment in interrelations. The violation of these traits is effected by the following practices:

1. Rule by one, or a few, or a minority that operates by the principle that the *right* to rule is based on heredity, family position, wealth, physical or military strength, or the like, but not by mutual agreement.
2. The right to control others by corralling their productive work to satisfy political rather than social, economic, and psychosocial benefits.
3. Leadership imposed from above by various systems of force.
4. Control arbitrarily applied by an ubiquitous espionage system.
5. Reducing the psychosocial response of challenge to a spirit of collective passivity, conformity, and submission to unconditionally imposed discipline.
6. Shifting of self-responsibility to the shoulders of the leader or party, thus surrendering the right for self-chosen self-development.
7. The use of terror to maintain order and submission to conformance through fear.

8. Inducing mental, social, and spiritual demoralization to the subjects.

9. Substitution of a restricted social philosophy for the humanism of democracy and, at the same time, modifying traditions, loyalties, and relationships.

10. Abnegation of freedom of speech, press, and assembly and other human rights.

11. Building an all-pervading bureaucracy, against the subjects' will, that increases the growth of corruption and apprehension, and reduces efficiency in productive activities. A centralized bureaucracy breeds rigidity.

DEMOCRACY VERSUS DICTATORSHIP

In a democracy, universal education is an essential facet. But in a dictatorship, this may or may not be part of its system. In the Eastern European and Chinese socialist republics, education is a primary social form and is certainly basic in helping to expand their industrial bases. But *education has an essential quality that abhors dictatorship*. This is due to the fact that human beings have specific traits of human nature that are incompatible with the social relations created by dictatorship. In an economically underdeveloped country where a socialist party seizes power and in time raises the material conditions of the overwhelming majority and introduces universal education, the change for this majority is to the good so far as their basic material conditions are concerned. For that generation of persons, the dictatorship raises the level of living both materially and intellectually by the educational process. The traits of hope, challenge, creativity, self-image–self-esteem, striving to satisfy one's appetites, inclinations, and talents, and philosophy for living are fired up. Even a glimmer of freedom to choose emerges to a hopeful level. But, in a dictatorship, those individuals in power strive to stay in power. Things do not change enough in socio-functional relations for the people so far as the satisfaction of their human traits are concerned. A new generation is born and grows up without having experienced the welcome change that occurred when the socialist party first seized power. The new generation of youth begins to feel only the cramping of their nature as human beings, because their *education widens their wisdom as to possible ways of living*. Whereas the morale of the population was elevated after the seizure of power changed their living conditions for the better, the new generations do not have that experience so that morale in the younger people regresses more and more unless democratization creeps forward. The threshold of tolerance for the discordance of the ecosystem in relation to their traits of human nature grows thinner. Then the trouble begins. In the Soviet Union, alcoholism was decreasing up to about 1950.[38] By this time, two generations had come into existence and a war for survival had rallied the morale of the people. With this increased morale, alcoholism decreased. Since the 1950 period, however, with another generation coming into being, which did not experience the morale elevating circumstances, use of alcoholic beverages (using 1940 as the base)[39] increased 283 percent in 1965, 439 percent in 1970, 501 percent in 1972, and 531 percent in 1973. Today alcoholism is epidemic in the Soviet Union. It can be expected that if the Soviet government does not begin inaugurating a more democratic atmosphere in the conduct of its operations, morale will continue to sag, due to the perception of the several younger generations that their nature as human beings is being stifled. This will occur regardless of how the material conditions of life get better. The same increase will continue in the United States, but for opposite reasons, i.e., because of the sociofunctional chaos resulting from democracy being stretched too far, freedom from inhibition, and glorification of excessive permissiveness, which allows moral and ethical corruption and crime to filter into every nook and cranny of American life. This continues to disrupt the economy, pervert the elected and bureaucratic government officials, break up families, disorient children and youth, increase violence, *ad infinitum*.

TO SUMMARIZE

Individuals make up population. Population organizes community life. The way these people act in relation to each other and to their ecosystem is the study of sociology, social psychology, and social anthropology. But behavior is a complex phenomenon. What are the particulates that compose human behavior? The sociobiologists and the ethologists have isolated these particulates for animals' behavior. For human behavior, this complex is called human nature, its particulates being the traits of human nature. But human behavior is distinguished from animal behavior by its teleological orientation and intrinsically or subjectively being motivated by cognition, emotion, and biological urges. For the human to act with purpose, except in extremes, *faith* and *hope* (time-binding behavior) in the outcome is assumed. How can faith and hope, so teleologically and intrinsically involved with cognitive and emotional processes, be subjected to scientific methodology? Basically, that which is scientific is expected to give predictive information. Can faith in a system of social interrelations be put to sophisticated probing and come out with predictive information? As previously cited, Roger Sperry is highly persuaded that this is feasible as the result of all the recent split-brain research, which points to the premise that "the whole world of inner experience . . . thus becomes recognized and included within the domain of science."[40]

When dealing with the subjective in animal life, there is no way for an animal to convey its subjective ideational representations as a correlate to its behavior. Therefore, we study animal psychology in accordance to their overt behavior, as Pavlov demonstrated. The behaviorist school of psychology, not knowing how to "objectify" the subjective for purposes of the human, applied the methodology of research in animal psychology to the human, thereby reducing human psychology to nonpsychology since the mind, the psyche, was being eliminated from the "ology." What was really being eliminated was the cognitive processes. But can the subjective be subjected to scientific objective methodology? Since an idea cannot be reduced to electromolecular representations in neurophysiology and molecular biology, can there be correlation between cognition and brain activity expressed as behavior? The very fact that sensations such as hearing and actions such as speaking can be *localized* as brain activity is an indication that it is possible to study and observe objectively ideation and cognition. This is done by examining group reaction manifested physically, verbally, and mentally (including emotional and spiritual) to particular circumstances, by noting the various types of descriptive observations made in the works dubbed "the humanities" and by extracting commonalities from these observations that imply the existence of enduring features manifested in the nature of human nature. The main reason why this study quotes verbatim the human behavior observations of so many sources generally accepted as reliable is precisely because, for the present, this is the obvious method of objectifying the cognitive processes associated with specific types of behavior common to all societies.

The *only* reason why *Homo* has been able to develop an organized society is because, very early in his primordial stage, he was ingenious enough to create a system of norms of conduct to dominate and even to replace as much as possible the primate instincts, which receded to the background in the process of evolution. Primate instincts made it possible for individuals to live in organized bands by endowing the behavior of each individual in the group with predictive behavior. Chaotic behavior is abhorred by living organisms whose survival depends on group organization and interrelationships. It is well documented among ethologists' observations that when animals are subjected to chaotic stimuli that create disruption and conflict in instinctive responses, it is possible to provoke in them behavior responses similar to what is known in man as psychoneurosis. Man has not lost the need for expecting his associates to respond in predictive patterns of behavior. It was unconditionally necessary, therefore, for *Homo,* in order to maintain his societal needs, to replace the relatively uniform automatic responses of *primate* instinctual behavior with reliably steady normative responses induced by adapting to a system of self-created norms compatible with the needs of *human* social existence. Incompatible with these needs is any system of norms that allows extreme degrees of permissiveness. Such circumstances tend to confuse and to depreciate social behavioral norms that steady social relations and social tranquility. Such tendency is toward social chaos.

The almost limitless permissiveness developing in the United States as a result of the misapplication of the tenets of civil and human rights and the subsequent abuse in practically all areas of social life tears at the fabric of American democracy; to wit: in such areas as violence and the coddling of lawbreakers; drug abuse, including alcoholism and children's use of it; sexuality; fraudulent advertising and other illicit methods of making a buck; tolerance of unethical and lawbreaking conduct of elected officials. The norms of social life are being successfully attacked as antidemocratic violations against personal freedom. The remarkable role and function that the Bill of Rights has played in the development of democracy in our country are being testily questioned as restriction on the personal freedom unless interpreted to protect extreme permissiveness in personal behavior. What is going on is not altogether negative for the future of American democracy. The present trend toward extreme permissiveness is very likely to indicate a period of testing the limits to which we should allow our freedom to develop for their optimum application to the present and future of the American social order set in a medium of high-technology and dense population concentrations. In the meantime, however, *disorientation* of behavior in patterns similar to those expected under dictatorship are appearing in our social medium, resulting from *discord* of the ecosystem with various traits of human nature, but a discord caused by different factors. It must also be noted that the increase in crime in the United States is supported by discordance of our ecosystem with the traits. This discordance is also present under the Soviet dictatorship, except that the latter controls criminal manifestations through vigorous coercion.

In order for democracy to learn to maintain the dominance of the human aspect of the traits over that of the primate and therefore to control by social consent such behavioral disorientations as crime, alcoholism and abuse of other drugs, child abuse, and behaving habitually on the periphery of law and social norms, we need to embark on the following types of epidemiological research:

1. Since the various traits are more or less prominent in the various people of a community, there is a need to study the proportional distributions of the degrees of strength each trait exhibits in the personalities of the population. For example, in considering the trait of creativity: What percentage of people have a strong propensity to creativeness, i.e., a high threshold against demoralization of this trait in presence of discordance in the ecosystem? What percentage have a moderate propensity, and what percentage have a low propensity or are easily demoralized against creative activity? The term "creativity" will have to be defined precisely. For the general population, the definition should include as wide a range of usual activity that people perform as feasible without faulting the meaning of the term.
2. What are precisely the social *interrelationship* factors in the ecosystem that affect favorably or unfavorably specific traits, and how strongly does each factor have its effect on each trait in relation to the effects on each trait by the other factors?
3. What are the most important specific sociofunctional relations in a democracy like the United States and in a dictatorship like the Soviet Union, and how strongly does each such sociofunctional relation affect favorably or unfavorably each trait of human nature?
4. To what extent do the economic production relations in the capitalist economy in the United States have a harmonious or discordant effect on each trait? The same question can be posed concerning the socalist economy in the Soviet Union.

That production relations are important in creating harmonious or discordant conditions in the ecosystem in relation to the traits of human nature is exemplified by Dr. Joseph Goldberger's adventure in seeking the etiology and prevention of pellagra. For hundreds of years, this disease was an enigma to the medical profession and the world. Early in Goldberger's epidemiological study, he observed the striking fact that the attendants in the institutions caring for pellagra cases never contracted the disease, which he found concentrated among the poor people. This led him to conduct dietary experiments among children in some orphanages in Georgia. The results convinced him that the disease was a nutritional deficiency. Then, in retrospect, he observed that the commencement of the very steep increase in cases of pellagra occurred in 1909, the second year of the 1907 worldwide economic depression that created havoc among the poor rural people of the South.

In this situation, there still prevailed some of the pristine form of the raw production relations inherent in capitalism. Monopoly had not yet become the effective deterrent to economic progress and freedom of trade. In industry and commerce, most people made their living working for a wage or salary. In the rural South, a great number of the workers were tenant farmers who scarcely eked out a subsistent living even in good times. In large sections of the South, the farm product was still cotton, raised largely by tenant farmers. When an economic depression struck the country, unemployment rose steeply in industry and commerce and the price of cotton dropped to a devastating level for the farmer in the Cotton Belt, who was beholden to the owner of the land and to his general store, where the demoralized tenant farmers were coerced by circumstances to buy the products for their subsistence. Usually they remained in debt to the general store unremittingly. Social services for easing the material conditions of these poor as we know today were still in limbo. However, public education was available for all who took advantage of it, and the labor movement was beginning to infect the morale of the workers. The civil rights granted by the Bill of Rights could be taken advantage of effectively by a Horatio Alger here and there, and John Dewey's ideal of the virtues of democracy was beginning to animate and invigorate the first and second generations of the immigrants who had come flooding into the United States during the latter half of the nineteenth century and the early years of the twentieth century. These were mostly the denizens of the rapidly growing urban jungles. Under the above conditions, there was an ample measure of demoralization. but because of the democratic potential, the country was well populated with vibrant, fighting, struggling, and determined people. In spite of the rapid, intermittently recurring periods of prosperity and depression, the technological advances in methods of production made this country bloom with profusion. Even the restrictions on the full expression of the traits of human nature imposed on large sections of the population due to the shaping of the sociofunctional interrelations by the nature of the economy and social institutions could not dampen the tremendous force of capital formation and accumulation. Why such progress in spite of the restrictions on the traits? Precisely because the freedom in the economic field, although extreme, impinged forcefully on the other areas of social life (which could not happen under dictatorship) to inspire and motivate a large enough section of the population with democratic zeal to pursue its myriad creative inclinations and talents. The epidemiology of pellagra brought to light that malnutrition was the direct cause of pellagra, but that the ultimate cause was the disjointed pattern of the sociofunctional relations of a demoralized section of population whose traits of human nature were being vitiated by an ecosystem that allowed the traits of freedom-to-choose among the economically powerful to dislocate the nation's potentially democratic heritage.

A similar disjointed pattern of sociofunctional relations was imposed on the Soviet Union's peasantry by Stalin when, in the mid-thirties, he forced the brutal measures of collectivization in agriculture. The result was millions of deaths from starvation. But unlike in the United States, the Soviet Union's agricultural production never recovered its real potential.

Other studies in the vitiation of the traits of human nature should be made to show how the dislocation of the sociofunctional relations created conditions in the ecosystem to cause such disasters as:

    a. the Love Canal hazard in New York State;
    b. the Bhopal catastrophe in India;
    c. the Seveso disaster in Italy; and
    d. the Times Beach mishap in Missouri.

Sociological principles must be based on ultimate causes, but not to the neglect of direct or sufficient causes. Knowing how to control direct causes directly does not give assurance that a particular direct cause will not be a continual threat. This continual threat is removed by removing the ultimate causes. Ultimate causes emanate from the relation between the traits of human nature and the organization and functioning of the ecosystem. Much of such information comes from the studies of social anthropology, social psychology, and political economy.

We need, therefore, to widen the science of social dynamics for developing and maintaining rational cognitive pattern based on the needs of the specific traits of human nature and untrammeled as much as possible from the urges of the primate nature.[41] Such patterns of cognition and behavior induce a *predictive* course of social dynamics that gives man a rational approach to making his history by helping with planned foresight to create the conditions out of which that history is made. Only then can we understand the details of why human nature abhors dictatorship of any type, why education generates the forces against such dictatorship, why an exaggerated expression of the traits of "freedom to choose" and self-image–self-esteem" lead to a negation of democracy, and why we must study the dynamics of the types of social institutions that will be in concordance with the traits of human nature and then develop the methodology for implementing such social forces.

Let it not be forgotten that *Homo,* from the very beginning of his career, organized human society specifically for the purpose of being able to support the dominance of the human phase over the primate phase of his nature by establishing a pattern of social interrelations to be in harmony with the traits of being human. *For human beings who have the capacity to plan and to devise methods for implementing such plans, the dominance of their primate phase of behavior would be much more destructive to human society than the aggressive furor and violence of purely primate behavior itself.*

NOTES

1. P. W. Anderson, "More Is Different," *Science,* vol. 177 (June 4, 1972), pp. 393–96.

2. H. Soodak and A. Iberall, "Homokinetics: A Physical Science for Complex Systems," *Science,* vol. 201, (August 18, 1978), pp. 579–82.

3. F. Engels, *Dialectics of Nature* (International Publishers, 1940), pp. 319–24.

4. K. Marx, *The Economic and Philosophic Manuscripts of 1844* (International Publishers, 1964), pp. 202–203.

5. Karl Marx, *Capital* (Chicago, Illinois: Charles H. Kerr and Co. 1926), p. 208 *et passim.* Karl Marx, Grundrisse, vol. 3, (New York: Vintage Books, 1973), p. 88 *et passim.*

6. Marx, *loco supra citato,* p. 59, Vol. 1, footnote. Benjamin Franklin, *The Works of Franklin,* vol. 2, (Jared Sparks, Charles Tappan, Publishers, 1844), p. 267.

7. Wassily Leontief, "Academic Economics," *Science,* vol. 217 (July 9, 1982), p. 107.

8. Francois Jacob, "Evolution and Tinkering," *Science,* vol. 196, no. 4295 (June 10, 1977), pp. 1161–66.

9. Ibid., pp. 1161–66.

10. P. W. Anderson, "More Is Different," *Science,* vol. 177, no. 4047 (August 4, 1972), pp. 393–96.

11. George Engel, "The Need for a New Medical Model: A Challenge for Biomedicine," *Science,* vol. 196, no. 4286 (April 8, 1977), pp. 129–36.

12. G. W. F. Hegel, *Science of Logic* (London: Allen and Unwin Ltd., 1929), section 3, chapter 1, "The Specific Quantity," pp. 351–366.

13. Friederich Engels, *Dialectic of Nature* (International Publishers, 1940), pp. 26–34.

14. Eugene P. Odum, "The Emergence of Ecology as a New Integration Discipline," *Science,* vol. 195, no. 4284 (March 25, 1977), pp. 1289–93.

15. E. O. Wilson, *Sociobiology* (Cambridge, Massachusetts: Harvard University Press, 1975), pp. 574–75.

16. Gunther S. Stent, "Limits of the Scientific Understanding of Man," *Science,* vol. 187 (March 21, 1975), pp. 1052–57.

17. Avner Cohen, "Consciousness and Depersonalization: Viewing the History of Philosophy from a Strausian Perspective," *Journal of Medicine and Philosophy,* vol. 9, no. 1 (February 1984).

18. Ibid.

19. Ibid.

20. David Bidney, "Human Nature and the Cultural Process," *American Anthropologist,* vol. 49, no. 3 (July-September 1947), pp. 375–99.

21. Roger Sperry, "Some Effects of Disconnecting the Cerebral Hemisphere," *Science,* vol. 217, no. 4566 (September 24, 1982), pp. 1223–26.

22. Marshall Sahlins, *The Use and Abuse of Biology* (Ann Arbor, Michigan: University of Michigan Press, 1977).

23. John MacKinnon, *The Ape Within Us* (New York: Holt, Rinehart and Winston, 1978).

24. J. Bowlby, *Maternal Care and Mental Health* (Albany, New York: World Health Organization, 1952), p. 39.

25. E. O. Wilson, *On Human Nature* (New Haven, Connecticut: Harvard University Press, 1978), pp. 20–32.

26. J. Bowlby, *Attachment and Loss* (New York: Basic Books, Inc. 1969), vol. 1: pp. 99–102, 153–56, 214–15, 352–54, vol 2: pp. 384–87.

27. Jean Piaget, *The Essential Piaget,* edited by H. E. Gruber and J. J. Vonèche (New York: Basic Books, Inc.. 1977), pp. 198–214.

28. Piaget, *loco supra citato,* pp. 70–72, 216, 844.

29. Wilson, *loco supra citato,* pp. 166–67, 175.

30. Alexander Marshack, "The Art and Symbols of Ice Age Man," *Human Nature* (September 1978), pp. 32–41.

31. Gay Gaer Luce, *Body Time* (New York: Pantheon Books, 1971).

32. Aristotle, *Metaphysics,* vol. 8: *Works of Aristotle, Translated into English* (New York: Oxford University Press, 1940), pp. 986a–986b, Book A5.

33. George W. F. Hegel, *Science of Logic* vol. 1 (London: George Allen and Unwin Ltd., 1929), p. 95.

34. Sperry, *loco supra citato.*

35. Richard B. Lee, *!Kung San: Men Women and Work in a Foraging Society* (New York: Cambridge University Press, 1979), p. 437.

36. Karl Marx, *A Contribution to the Critique of Political Economy* (Chicago, Illinois: Charles H. Kerr and Co. 1904), p. 11.

37. Louis M. Hacker, ed., *The Shaping of the American Tradition,* (New York: Columbia University Press, 1947), Vol. 2: *Democracy,* John Dewey, p. 1161–62.

38. Joseph Wortis, *Soviet Psychiatry* (Baltimore, Maryland: Williams and Wilkins Co., 1950), p. 173.

39. Segal, B. M., "Drinking Patterns and Alcoholism in Soviet and American Societies," in S. A. Corson, ed., *Psychiatry and Psychology in the USSR* (New York: Plenum Press, 1976), p. 184.

40. Sperry, *loco supra citato.*

41. R. and I. Z. Greigerl, eds., *Cognition and Emotional Disturbance* (New York: Human Sciences Press, 1982), pp. 12–13.

3

The Nature of Human Nature

ASKING THE QUESTION ABOUT HUMAN NATURE

The maxim "know thyself" was already an epigram in Greece when Socrates began his teaching, but as far as our records reveal, no one before him had so relentlessly pursued the exploration of the realm of self with the objective of discovering the nature of human nature. The intellectual approach to the subject of cognition in Socrates' day was not cluttered with professional jargon, so it was not difficult from the very beginning to approach this subject with the obvious observation that human behavior was inherently biphasic—a characteristic of natural movement common to Greek thought. Since the time of Socrates, philosophers and theologians have worked over the subject of human nature endlessly, either from the point of view of moral conduct or that of general behavior of people. Not until about a century ago, with the emergence of the modern scientific approach to the psychosocial disciplines, was there an attempt to treat the subject of human nature as a complex natural (as distinguished from supernatural) phenomenon of elemental traits. This is stated philosophically with deference to earlier sages such as Rousseau, Hobbes, Helvetius, Hume, James Madison, and Adam Smith. The psychosocial behavioral scientists of particular note for their contributions in developing systematized paradigms were Charles H. Cooley (1902), A. Korzybski (1921), and George Mead (1920s) and later Ashley Montagu (1951), Erich Fromm (1955), and Amitai Etzioni (1968). These will be discussed in detail. There were also two modern philosophic works that need to be especially considered—one by the philosopher-educator John Dewey (1922), and the other by the historian of ideas, Arthur O. Lovejoy (1961). None of these authors specifically defined the term "human nature." They took for granted that their understanding of its meaning was, in general, similar to that of everyone else.

Dewey's work[1] does discourse in great detail about various aspects of behavior, such as habits, morality, impulses, instincts, desires, and freedom. He made many profound observations that are important in considering the nature of human nature, but the observations are not tied together as a paradigm of the biopsychosocial science of human nature, particularly the psychosocial-behavioral aspect. He made a point of the biphasic nature of behavior of self: "There is no one ready-made self behind activities. There are complex, unstable, *opposing* attitudes, habits, impulses which gradually come to terms with one another [italics added]."[2] This is not a very pithy observation, since the real anthropological explanations of the opposing attitudes are not expounded, nor is the profundity of the part played by the force of *inhibition* particularly stressed. Neither Dewey nor Lovejoy, being philosophers, mention Schopenhauer's discussion of the subject of human nature. The latter certainly added nothing of importance to the subject. However, he repeats over and over again the moralists' diphasic view of human nature, which is valid indeed: "These two diametrically opposite qualities [envy and sympathy] exist in every man. . . .[3] Every human perfection is allied to a defect into which it threatens to pass; but it is also true that every defect is allied to a perfection."[4]

Another example of naming a study with an imposing title involving human nature and discoursing all around the subject without defining the term is Eisenburg's article "The *Human* Nature of Human Nature."[5] Of course, as a psychiatrist, he makes some relevant remarks about the subject, distilling from the stream of perception that language and the struggle for human betterment are traits of human nature. These are certainly fundamental factors in the emergence of the traits of human nature, but are themselves not distinguishable traits of human nature. Language is *one* of the very basic ways by which symbolization is expressed and by which traits of human nature are facilitated to manifest themselves, and the struggle for human betterment is a cognitive development on a higher level of the basic impulse to survive—an impulse that fosters the traits of human nature.

Dewey's explanation of the origin of conscience as it applies to behavior is very well done, and his explication of the meaning of freedom is excellent.[6] The modern degeneration of moral norms is analyzed with perspective: "When social life is so disturbed that custom and tradition fail to supply their wonted control, men resort to Nature as a norm. They apply to Nature all the eulogistic predicates previously associated with divine law; or natural law is conceived of as the only true divine law. . . . In our time, this notion has been perpetuated in connection with a laissez-faire social philosophy and the theory of evolution. Human intelligence is thought to mark an artificial interference if it does more than register fixed natural laws as rules of human action. The process of natural evolution is conceived as the exact model of human endeavor."[7] Thus, since morals are *manmade,* they interfere with the natural impulses generated by natural law. The natural impulse takes priority over manmade rules to limit "natural" expression. Inhibition thereby takes a backseat in human relationships. Such destructive rationalization becomes more and more common.

Lovejoy, a contemporary of Cooley, Korzybski, Mead, and Dewey, was known best as the historian of ideas. In reference to the maxim that the knowledge man needs most is of himself, he opines that "to no generation of men can it [the injunction to know thyself] have come with more force than to our own. For self-searching is most commonly the offspring of self-distrust and misgivings. . . . And never before, it is probable, has the reflective portion of mankind suffered a more acute attack of self-distrust or experienced more sudden and disquieting misgivings about its species."[8] He quotes from religious and moralist sources to provoke the search to answer the problem:

> The Christian ethic has been taught for almost two thousand years; the present spectacle of Christendom is, or should be, a profoundly thought-provoking commentary on that fact. The presentation of excellent ideals, in short, has not been lacking; the question is, why they have so little efficacy in shaping the actual life of man. And if we are to find an answer to that question, we shall need a better knowledge of the inner constitution, of the nature, interaction, effects, and relative potency of human motives or springs of action. . . . Such a knowledge . . . might best be called the theory of *Human nature;* it is *not* yet, I think, sufficiently systematically and penetratingly pursued [italics added].[9]

The question asked by Lovejoy and the knowledge needed to answer it are what this dissertation is all about. Both Dewey and Lovejoy carry on detailed analyses in the many phases of human conduct, but never develop what Lovejoy called a systematically developed theory of human nature.

The nature of the human being had its origin in the struggle of the genus *Homo* to survive and to better its conditions of living, given its special anatomical developments of the cerebral cortex, the voicebox, the thumb-fingers arrangement of the hand, bipedality, and its physiological potentials relating to sexuality and the nature of the reproductive process requiring intensified parenting.[10] These factors (see Chart 1) gave new quality to *Homo* to initiate stimuli and to receive and respond to external stimuli of the ecosystem* in which man had to organize his interrelationships, particularly the male-female pair bonding already germinally developed, and to sharpen his discerning abilities to make judgments, evaluations, and choices of directions to take in order to make existence tolerable. This new capacity, which differentiated *Homo* as a new genus emerging from the genus *Australopithecus,* gave him the critical advantages of a highly regenerated memory to store and to interrelate images, facilitating a new ability unique in biological history for symbolization, developing language and art, communication, creation of ideas (fantasizing and planning), and an incredibly increased cognitive potential for educability. This composite of characteristics is the basis of *Homo*'s biosocial nature, which, in the maelstrom of the ecosystem, in turn, elicits a psychosocial behaviorial response called human nature. Thus *human nature* is defined as *the composite of specific behavioral traits* (see chart 2) *characteristic of the species* Homo sapiens. *These traits are the psychosocial responses generated in the process of the human biosocial nature interacting with the basic conditions of human living in the struggle for survival and the drive for betterment of those conditions of living.*

CHART 1
Original Nature of Hominid Conditions of Living that Induced the Generation of the Traits of Human Nature

1. Bipedality
    a. Freed the dexterous hands for making tools and other manipulation
    b. Enhanced reproductive fitness
    c. Increased ability to carry loads, such as food and infants
    d. increased the ability to hunt with weapons
    e. increased creativity of material culture that was accumulated for the next generation
2. Laryngopharyngeal sound-producing organ for speech articulation
    a. Enhanced language communication in the socialization process
    b. Stimulated and improved the cognitive processes
    c. Made the accretion of culture possible

*This term is taken to mean the entire social and natural environment.

3. Expansion of the neopallium (neocortex)
    a. Increased educability and the perspective to see the need for development of competence
    b. Increased the capacity for storage of ideas
    c. Increased the complexity of the cognitive powers
    d. Increased the planning and creative powers
    e. Increased anticipation and prospection, the ability to compare and to make judgments and, therefore, to hope and make choices
    f. Increased hominid's resistance to environmentally induced mortality, which enhanced his capability to expand into novel and varied habitats
    g. The massive increase in brain capacity in the Pleistocene intensified the development of the material and mental culture
4. Epigamic and parasexual characteristics
    a. Female
        (1) Prominent and permanently enlarged mammae
        (2) Other shapely characteristics of the anatomy
        (3) Continuous sexual receptivity pointing to one's self as a noteworthy individual
    b. Male
        (1) Facial hair
        (2) Distinctive somatotype
        (3) Conspicuous penis
    c. Since copulation showed little or no synchronization with ovulation, copulatory vigilance in both sexes would be required to ensure fertilization. This was favorable for the stability of the monogamous mating structure.
    d. The above characteristics compose a mechanism for establishing and displaying individual sexual uniqueness, which played a major role in pair bonds, emphasizing the awareness of the self.
5. Survivorship
    a. The altricial infant and foraging mother
        (1) To reduce infant mortality
            (a) Mother had to become less mobile by the reduction of male competition for local resources
            (b) Had to establish a home base and a limited, circumscribed, foraging area—the core area in which she maximized her familiarity

(c) Had to depend on male to supplement the diet with calories and protein
(d) Had to intensify the amount and quality of child care
(e) Had to decrease exposure of offspring to predators and to accidents

(2) Biological factors related to the increasing need for investment in the survival of the fewer offspring
(a) Increasing length of the gestation period
(b) Increasing length and intimate nature of breast-feeding
(c) Increasing need for more calories and protein for mothers and children
(d) Increasing length of childhood dependency and learning period, including emotional patterns of response to essential cultural norms
(e) The need to enhance the iteroparous reproductive strategy by reducing the space between births
(f) The increasing delay in sexual maturation (puberty) favoring a longer play and socialization period
(g) The above factors cause fewer offspring and therefore the need for reducing infant mortality.
(h) The increasing longevity and population size

b. The male consort
(1) Established a sexual bond to the mother of his offspring in order to enhance his status to the changing of the mother's status and to avoid the competitive circumstances arising from his offspring
(2) Planned hunting excursions for protein food increased the status of the male as food provider.
(3) Participated in the parenting process and thereby decreased competition with offspring
(4) Enhanced the security of his monogamous pair bonding unit
(5) Established relations with other nuclear families. The above factors strengthened bonding-sharing and generated new qualities in relations.

6. Bonding-sharing relations in the nuclear families
a. Increased protection of the group, reduced fear, anxiety and anger, and satisfied the feelings of attachment and dependency
b. Increased the food supply by sharing
c. Increased variety of food and other products by exchange

d. Necessitated the formulation of rules for behavior and development of the sense of self and the conscience
   (1) To control the disruptive effect in the group of sexual violence
   (2) To organize the conduct of exchange
   (3) To socialize and educate children into the ways of the community
   (4) To recognize the conduct of establishing a family grouping and eventually a nuclear family
   (5) To establish rules of relations with older generations and the infirm
   (6) To establish relations between the families of the pair composing the union in the new nuclear family
   (7) To establish the rules for disposing of the dead
   (8) To formulate how the community as a unit will be administered

The remarkable quality about these traits is their continued persistence throughout human history. From their primitive behavioral structure, they have developed to a set of behavioral characteristics unique to the human species. They persist today in the world communities, because the very essence of the conditions of living that brought them into being persists, although intensely conditioned by a myriad of the varied cultures extant. Chart 2 is an outline of the factors of *Homo*'s conditions of living in primitive times that persist in present-day society.

CHART 2
**Factors of the Primitive Hominid Conditions of Living
that Persist in Present Society**

1. Bipedality
2. Speech–language has expanded greatly in content and usage.
3. The massive neopallium registers an infinitely greater variety of data and usages.
4. The epigamic and parasexual characteristics are being exploited for creating cults of hedonism.
5. Survivorship has become easier for most people on earth, but is still primitive for many and dilapidated for large sections of urban dwellers.

6. Bonding-sharing relations of the nuclear family are still strong but showing weakness in the younger generations
7. Biological factors related to increasing investment in the survival of offspring continue in relative sameness, although affected by new cultural factors.

CHART 3
The Traits of Human Nature

1. *The Bonding-Sharing-Exchange Trait:* This is the basic trait of social relations. It has an extensive phylogenetic history through the animal kingdom, except, for the sharing-exchange phase, which emerged with the emergence of *Homo.* The whole system of hominid conditions of living necessitated bonding, sharing and exchange behavior just to survive as hominids as distinct from subhuman primates. More specificially, the great expansion of the potential of cognition, of language and mental symbolization, of the stimulation of epigamic and para-sexual characteristics to sensitize and consolidate the male-female-offspring interrelations, to establish a home base, a nuclear family, an extended family or clan and tribe, and the bonding-sharing-exchange practices of human social interrelations. A new trait of human nature was thus born. This trait provides the love and trust relations in the family and beyond the extrafamilial relations. Sharing means more than mother-child relations, although phylogenetically it began there. The sharing process, when taken a step further, becomes the exchange process between unrelated individuals and groups and finally the barter and community exchange process in the world market.

2. *The Freedom-to-Choose Trait:* The physical and mental endowments of *Homo,* such as the cognitive powers to discriminate and to realize what is desirable and the dexterity of the hands to manipulate liberated him from the thralls of instinctive response to the exigencies of life. His responses to the exigencies inherent in the nature of the hominid conditions of living were characterized by a quickened spontaneity to cogitate and a richness of perception of the surrounding world as presented to him by the expanding panorama of life. This all generated a conscious freedom to choose from a variety of judgments made by him as to how, when, and where to satisfy his newly perceived growing needs. In present-day life, it refers to the freedom we cherish in making choices. It refers to the restraints on freedom to choose as punishment for violations of social norms. It refers to the difference in the freedom to make choices in a democracy and under a dictatorship, in a state of

54

poverty and in the lap of wealth, and in the position of responsibility.
3. *Homo*'s cognitive powers sparked his awareness of the realization
that his existence in human guise was threatened by the violence
inherent in his primate sociosexual behavior—this violence being further enhanced by his epigamic and parasexual characteristics. Thus,
out of the necessity for nascent *Homo* to orient himself to the human
potential in his state of existence, he had to accommodate his conduct
teleologically to a *social structure of planned interrelationships*. These
relationships refer to the need for an ordered, peaceful, and mutually
agreeable social ecology and for the need to create norms of behavior
to accomplish this. They refer to the ability to rear children in a medium of controlled conduct according to rules of family interrelations
concerning sexuality, satisfying hunger and rest and recreation. They
refer to the need for education and how to act among people beyond
the family harbor. They refer to the ethics in professional activity, in
business and sports and in social life. They refer to the making of laws
and regulations for conducting government, in prosecuting violators
of the sociolegal norms, of operating prisons, the courts, the religious
affairs.
4. *The Trait of Striving to Satisfy One's Appetites, Inclinations, and
Talents:* Endowed with a productive central nervous system, self-conscious hominids were showered with newly perceived stimuli, both
desirable and undesirable, pressing on their conditions of living. Desire
is generically a trait of animal life. The higher in the scale of evolution,
the more prominent is this trait, manifested in violent aggressiveness,
predation, and the energy exerted in sating appetites. Some types of
animals, like squirrels, bees, and ants, have developed specialized
urges to gather and store food. Such urges in *Homo* are conscious,
cognitively modulated drives called human desires. *Homo*'s desires are
continually provoking him to strive to appease them, be they sexual
urges, physical security needs, mental probes of prospections to fulfill
inclinations or develop talents, securing egocentric hungers and the
like. It even appears that, in some instances, striving is so inchoate as
to resemble pure, uncogitated instinct, such as the sex drive. Out of
the uncontrolled combinations of human and primate traits, all types
of undesirable strivings may emerge, such as are productive of greed,
treachery, or other unconscionable behavior. Historically, *Homo* became an active participant in his surrounding ecology and became
impelled to action in efforts to ameliorate his precarious circumstances,
and to strive with whatever means were at hand to satisfy his newly
perceived needs, be they biological appetites, psychosocial inclinations

imprinted by social practice, or talents that, if satisfied, would magnify his abilities to act advantageously.

5. *Self-Image–Self-Esteem Trait:* The cognitive processes, greatly enhanced by the expansion of the neopallium, initiated the development of the primate self from essential "itness" of the animal primate to the budding consciousness of the human self. The human self's discriminatory ability transduced the self-consciousness into self-image. The increasing domestication of parenting and reproductive behavior, inspired largely by the altricial infant, magnified the appreciation of the self to the self and to its position in relation to other selves so that self-esteem became an integrated element of self-image and bore a new quality to the self—the conscience. Today, child rearing emphasizes the blooming of this trait. "Doing one's thing" has almost become a cult. It is a precarious exaggeration of the the self-image–self-esteem trait. Doing one's thing with a minimum or without guidance and restraint is the tragedy of many young lives. Parenting should be more than tending to the physical needs of children. Accentuating this trait with disregard of reaching its limits leads to an egocentrism that is destructive of orderly interrelations and disorienting when facing the adult world of reality. The mass media is an accomplice in this disorientation process.

6. *The Prospection Trait:* It became inevitable that the pristine appreciation of the uniqueness of the self should arouse desires for self-preservation beyond the instinctual level and that the great enrichment of the cognitive processes by the domestication of mating and the rearing of offspring should stir desires to perpetuate the values in these interrelations and to plan to do so. Animals instinctively accommodate to diurnal and seasonal changes in time. To *Homo,* time was and is a conscious element of awareness of things that were and things to come. As culture accumulated, time consciously became historical and prospective. More and more, the clock, the watch, and the schedule became the tyrants of our behavior. Getting the children to school, getting to work on time, catching the train or plane or bus, and arranging the schedule not to miss the favorite TV program—these became the dictators of our lives.

7. *The Challenge and Competence Trait:* The expansion of the neopallium and the stimulation to secure family and group life increased *Homo*'s ingenuity, developed his dexterity, and prepared his abilities to accept challenges to resist environmentally induced predicaments such as, for example, infant mortality. His enhanced capabilities expanded his activities into a variety of new places and new problems, always preparing himself through experience to act with increasing

competence to achieve through building his self-image–self-esteem. The need to accept challenges and be aware of the competence required to be successful and to try to attain that competence is basic to man's existence. Competition is a *natural* process among plants and animals. In man, competition is a social relations phenomenon resulting from more than one person or group of persons responding to a challenge for attaining the same desirable objective. Uncontrolled competition is like war, without the destructive weapons, but it can become physiologically and psychosocially destructive and, when involving nations, can become military war. The *human* aspect of challenge is to respond rationally and competently rather than by emotionally motivated impulse. Competition is *Homo*'s inherited primate behavioral trait and must be controlled in *human* society to prevent its dehumanizing effects. It *cannot* be eliminated, but it can be controlled and utilized for the benefit of human society.

8. *The Cumulative Creative Action Trait:* The *human* needs that confronted primitive, self-conscious, and conscionable *Homo* as the result of his conditions of living, i.e., providing sustenance, shelter, and clothing and planning for environmental and social security of family and social group, activated him to embark on purposeful tasks to preserve and to improve his conditions of living. Man, however, in the process of humanizing himself, never lived by bread alone. His cognitive powers to elaborate on the self, on the family and clan, on the nature and needs of social interrelationships, on his ability to make rational choices, and on planning the future required, as Marx called it, disposable time or nonworking time.[11] The facts are, as Lee described them,[12] that primitive man did not always need to occupy himself with the tasks for securing life. There was time available for recreation and boredom. Since man abhors boredom, a substantial number pursued physical or mental or both types of tasks that augmented the nature of their physical environment, their mental activities and store of knowledge, and their social life. They thus initiated the creation of culture. In modern society, this trait manifests itself in going to school to learn how to practice health care, build bridges and buildings, decorate homes, paint pictures, write and create literary works, play musical instruments, participate in sports, perform onstage, raise children, organize entertainment and political action groups, and run a successful business or organize and maintain a home. Thus culture keeps accumulating and changing.

These traits of human nature express themselves as intertwined modes of behavior. Each one, however, is as ultimate and persistent as man's basic biosocial conditions of living and his responding psychosocial behavior. Since man's nature also harbors *primate* nature, these traits also tend to express themselves interpenetratingly with the traits of *human* nature, but as contradictory modes of behavior, except in such modes of action as sports under controlled circumstances. Thus the nature of man's behavior is bivalently composed of human and primate natures, each thrusting itself for the dominant role in man's behavior. Combined actuation of various traits in various degrees of prominence express themselves in various compounded behavior forms. For example, the prominent behavioral manifestation in man, *greed,* is the negation of the positive aspect of some traits of *human* nature. It is a compounded primate-human behavioral expression. It is the predominance of the primate traits of egocentrism and lack of conscience and control in conduct, thus exaggerating and perverting the human traits of satisfying the appetites and inclinations, self-image–self-esteem, freedom to choose, and prospection. In this case, the primate trait of egocentrism dominates the human trait of bonding-sharing, and the primate trait of uncontrolled expression of impulses dominates the human trait of unifying orientation of conduct. The bivalency of *Homo*'s behavior is a continuous struggle for the dominance of the traits of *human* nature over the primate nature in the behavioral expression of man. Considering the fertility of man's mind, all types of nonhuman behavior may become dominant in the course of social intercourse. Man's reversion to primate behavioral dominance can be much more destructive than pure animal behavior.

The embryologists Bailey and Miller, in correlating the embryological development of human and lower animal pallia (cerebral corteces) and higher mammalian neopallia give credence to the following description of the genus *Homo:*

In addition to the increasing projection of stimuli from all parts of the body upon the neopallium and the consequent increase in centripetal fibre terminations and in centrifugal neurone bodies lying in its [neopallium's] walls, a . . . factor in the development of the neopallium is the enormous increase of its association neurones. It is the latter features which especially distinguish the human from other mammalian brains. The biological significance of these changes [as compared to the other mammalian brains] lies in the fact that there is thus produced a mechanism not only for the association of all kinds of stimuli, but also for very complex coordinations between these stimuli. In this way an extensive symbolization and formulation of individual experience (memory, language, etc.) can take place. The formulated experience of one generation can be immediately transmitted (by education in the broad sense of the term) to the plastic late-developing neopallia of the next generation. In this way, a social experience may be rapidly built up without the direct intervention of the slow process of heredity and natural selection and each generation profits by the accumulated experience of the past generations to a much greater extent.[13]

A RECAPITULATION OF BASIC PSYCHOSOCIAL DEVELOPMENT

Besides the changes in the brain, there were other structural and functional changes that further facilitated the development of the ideational and cognitive potentials of the brain in humanizing the genus *Homo* and that other primates do *not* possess. These are:

a. The changes in the laryngopharyngeal area associating the function of the voice box with the symbolizing function of the brain, resulting in spoken language communication and the imagination for the arts and crafts.
b. The bipedal stance, which liberated the hands to develop the dexterity needed for performing and creating in the development of culture and speed in the chase for game and allowed liberation of hands for weapon and other manipulations.
c. The position of the thumb in opposition to the other four fingers, giving the hand the dexterity to manipulate in the most skillful way.
d. Male and female display of elaborate dimorphic epigamic features, which hastened the adhesive nature of monogamous pair bonding into an effective nuclear family for child rearing; female suppression of estrus.

With the remarkable capacity of man to increasingly and cumulatively manipulate and change his ecosystem, certain types of behavior were absolutely necessary in his social relations if he were to survive and be in a position to develop and transmit an increasing body of culture. For example: How could mankind manipulate the environment to suit its purpose without being *creative?* How could humankind attain a certain goal that it deemed *desirable* if it had not the ability to *choose* between courses of action? How could society have developed without a very basic sense of *sharing* and *cooperation* upon which *love* and *brotherhood* are nourished? How could society have continued to develop without some stability in social relations and a sense of *rootedness,* a home base in the group? How could humankind keep carrying on through all its troubles without *hope?* How could society have achieved so many wonderful cultural results without an inner sense of *striving to accomplish?* How could humankind have developed a sense of order in community life without a *frame of orientation,* an ethics and normal code in conducting itself? Could man have accomplished what he did without an inner urge to *challenge* the obstacles confronting him, to confront *risk?* How could man have ventured at all if he had no appreciation of himself—his *self-image* and his *self-esteem?*

Social organizational systems depend on the creativeness of individuals, resulting from attitudes to contribute one's activities with or without being aware of contributing to the cultural accumulation of the society. How can an individual, conscious of himself, want to live without an orientation as to the desirability of living? Could society continue to exist over an extended period of time without such orientation of most of its members? Is it possible to conceive of an individual, conscious of what he is doing, being creative without feeling a challenge to accomplish what he chose to accomplish? If man's creativeness and creations augment him as an individual, how could he feel so augmented, i.e., appreciate the work he does, unless it be self-fulfilling? The essential traits of man's behavior cited above, which compose his human nature, did not suddenly come into being. It took actually some millions of years for the germination of the cognitive process and the behavioral anlage to evolve in order to launch *Homo* on its remarkable course of development.

The speculation of the father of social anthropology, Lewis H. Morgan, in the 1880s that: "With one principle of intelligence and one physical form, in virtue of a common origin, the results of human experience have been substantially the same in all times and areas in the same ethical status. The principle of intelligence, although conditioned in its powers within narrow limits of variation, seeks ideal standards invariably the same."[14] These judgments about the "narrow limits of variation" of psychosocial behavior (principle of intelligence) "meets us in the savage, in the barbarian, and in civilized man."[15] Williams, a century later, remarked: "The evidence I have considered in the earlier chapters would suggest that a historical construction of the psychosocial evaluation of the hominid lines is no longer a matter of pure speculation. Much of the new knowledge we now possess, particularly from ethology and physical anthropology, has developed rather than refuted the main hypotheses in the work of the pioneer anthropologist Lewis H. Morgan."[16]

Let us trace this course as perceived by the present-day anthropologist C. Owen Lovejoy. The history of the origin of the traits of human nature is the history of the origin of *Homo*. In the last several decades, Lovejoy states: "The study of human origins has proved remarkably successful. Crucial fossils and primate behavioral data are now available from which to reconstruct man's evolution during the last 15 million years." It is self-evident that survival of offspring is the most elemental factor in the perpetuation of a species. But such survival for hominoids whose offspring had an infancy period of at least five years and a subadult period of six or seven years required an effective mechanism of child rearing and availability of a food supply. Thus Lovejoy asserts:

> Survivorship of offspring must have been critical to Miocene [at least 15 million years ago] hominoids. . . . Miocene ecological conditions required a generalist feeding strategy. Conditions were prime for the establishment of male parental investment and a monogamous mating structure. . . . Strong social bonds, high levels of intelligence, intense parenting, and long periods of learning [for children] are among factors used by higher primates to depress environmentally induced mortality [accidents, predation, infectious conditions]. It is of some interest that such factors also require greater longevity (for brain development, learning, acquisition of social and parental skills) and that they constitute reciprocal links leading to greater longevity. . . . It is probable that significant preadaptations were present in early hominids that served as a behavioral base from which the "breakthrough" adaptations of later hominids could progressively develop. We are therefore in search of a novel behavioral pattern in Miocene hominoids that could evolve from typical primate survival strategies.[17]

The primate characteristic of requiring mother-infant mobility in order for the mother to both care for the increasingly altricial infant and to forage for herself was an important circumstance for cause of infant mortality. This situation is described by Lovejoy:

> Lowered mobility of females would reduce accident rate [of children] . . . maximize familiarity with the core area, reduce exposure to predators, and allow intensification of parenting behavior,

thus elevating survivorship. . . . A sex ratio [close to male-female parity in pair bonding] would obtain if the mating pattern were monogamous pair bonding. In this case males would avoid competition with bonded mates and biological offspring. . . . In short, monogamous pair bonding would favor feeding divergence by assuring males of biological paternity and by reducing feeding competition with their own offspring and mates. . . . If the model [presented above] is correct, the conventional concept that material culture is pivotal to the differentiation and origin of the primary characters of the Hominidae is probably incorrect. Rather, both advanced material culture and the Pleistocene [beginning about 3 million years ago] acceleration in brain development are sequelae to an already established hominid character system, which included intensified parenting and social relationships, monogamous pair bonding, specialized sexual-reproductive behavior, and bipedality.

Lovejoy concludes his study with the following statement about the ancient nature of the nuclear family: "It implies that the nuclear family and human sexual behavior may have their ultimate origin long before the dawn of the Pleistocene."

Thus the bonding and sharing trait of human nature began to develop its human qualities in the early epochs of hominid history. This was supported by special qualities in sexual behavior and features of anatomy.

Human females are continually sexually receptive and have essentially no externally recognizable estrous cycle; male approach may be considered equally stable. . . . Copulation would increase pair bonding adhesion. . . . The selective emergence of a monogamous mating structure and male provisioning [of food and protection] would require that males not be disadvantaged in obtaining consorts. [Anatomically] man displays a greater elaboration of epigamic characters than any other primate. . . . If pair bonding was fundamental and crucial to early hominid reproductive strategy, the anatomical characters that could reinforce pair bonds would also be under strong positive selection. . . . In man, marked epigamic dimorphism is achieved by elaboration of parasexual characters in both males and females.

These are: "the body and facial hair, distinctive somatotype, the conspicuous penis of human males, and the prominent and permanently enlarged mammae of the females."

Lee, in his masterful review of the !Kung San people, in which he skillfully showed how their socioeconomic organization and culture reflect on the early organization and development of *Homo,* brought to light a wealth of critical evidence. He pointed out that "Marx never postulated hunting and gathering (foraging) as a distinct mode of production. It was always included together with other pre-class societies based on fishing, horticulture, and pastoralism in a category labeled 'primitive communism'. . . . Foraging was not only the original mode of production, but it was a way of life that characterized the first 80 to 95 percent of the total history of the human species."[18] He quotes from Marx a passage that expresses the essence of Marx's historical materialism, i.e., that "the mode of production of material life determines the general character of the social, political, and spiritual processes of life. It is not the consciousness of men that determines their existence, but, on the contrary, their social existence that determines their consciousness."[19] To clinch this point, Lee states: *"Sharing* [italics added] is an example of such a cultural practice. Sharing deeply pervades the behavior and values of !Kung foragers within the family and between families, and it is extended to the boundaries of the social universe. . . . Sahlins . . . found the principle of generalized reciprocity to be a universal among hunting and gathering peoples."[20] What Lee asserts about Marx's appraisal of primitive man's mode of production is essentially valid, although Lovejoy's thesis that during *Homo's* transitional period some biosocial factors were as important as the mode of production is also important. Concerning this matter, Williams quotes from Levi-Strauss's *Structural Anthropology* (Penguin, 1968), [p. 340]: "According to their [Marx and Engels'] view, in the pre-capitalist societies kinship ties played a ·more important role than class relations. I do not believe I am being unfaithful to their teachings by trying, seventy years after Lewis H. Morgan, whom they admired so greatly, to resume Morgan's endeavor—that is, to work out a new typology of kinship systems in the light of knowledge acquired in the field since then, by myself and others. . . . Lewis Morgan's genius at one and the same time founded social anthropology and kinship studies and brought to the fore the basic reasons for attaching such importance to the latter: permanency, systematic character, continuity of changes."[21]

Exchange as a human activity was made possible as a further development of the sharing aspect of man's basic trait of human nature, sharing and bonding. Concerning the importance of exchange as a human behavior trait, Levi-Strauss, in reassessing one of his previous works *(Les structures élémentaires de la parenté),* in which he analyzed kinship structure in primitive societies, quotes himself from that study: "I should have made more distinction between *exchange as it is ex-*

pressed spontaneously and forcefully [italic added] in the *praxis* of groups and the conscious and deliberate rules by which these same groups—or their philosophers—spend their time in codifying and controlling it. If there is anything to be learnt from the ethnographic enquiries of the last twenty years, it is that this latter aspect is much more important than has generally been realized by observers. . . "[22]

Marx considered *exchange* as a distinctly human form of behavior attributed as well to the barter system existing between primitive human groups as between individuals or groups in later history. The following gives Marx's analysis of the subject:

> All commodities are non-use-values for their owners, and use-values for their non-owners. . . . The articles A and B . . . are not as yet commodities, but become so only by the act of barter. The first step made by an object of utility towards acquiring exchange-value is when it forms a non-use-value for its owner, and that happens when it forms a superfluous portion of some article required for his immediate wants. Objects in themselves are external to man, and consequently alienable by him. In order that this alienation may be reciprocal, it is only necessary for man, by a tacit understanding, to treat each other as private owners of those alienable objects and, by implication, as independent individuals. . . . But such a state of reciprocal independence has no existence in a primitive society based on property in common. . . . The exchange of commodities, therefore, first begins on the boundaries of such communities, at their points of contact with other simular communities, or with members of the latter.[23]

For Marx, therefore, exchange is nonexistent or a potential existent within a social group in which property is owned in common. The gap between *Homo*'s bonding-sharing trait and the act of exchange is not difficult to bridge, considering his neocortical gift of cognition and rationality. Exchange, therefore, appears as an act intimately associated with the nature of man's behavior. This was cogently understood by Marx, whose appreciation of the nature of human nature was indeed auspicious:

> *Exchange,* both of human activity within production itself and of *human products* against one another, is equivalent to *species-activity* and species-spirit, the real, conscious and true mode of existence of which is *social* activity and *social* enjoyment. Since *human* nature is the *true community* of men, by manifesting their

nature men *create,* produce, the *human community,* the social entity, which is no abstract universal power opposed to a single individual, but is the essential nature of each individual, his own activity, his own life, his own spirit, his own wealth. Hence this *true community* does not come into being through reflection, it appears owing to the *need* and *egoism* of individuals, i.e., it is produced directly by their life activity itself.[24]

Lee found two methodologies applicable and fruitful in assessing historical phenomena by the retrospective technique. The two methods are uniformitarianism and the historical materialism of Marx. Uniformitarianism is a methodology borrowed from geology, which predicates that certain basic processes that operated in the past continue to operate into the present. Thus Lee formulates the following four processes as the uniformitarian basis in *Homo*'s evolution: "Four fundamental variables provide our starting point: energy, space, resources, and vital statistics. Foragers have to expend energy in work in order to absorb energy in consumption. They have to move around their range in order to find the resources necessary to life. Their caloric intake has to provide for their own needs; for the needs of nonproductive young, sick, and old; and for the extra demands of reproducing the next generation. And they have to live in social groups as do all territorial primates, for their health, safety, and social needs."[25]

Lee claims that there is no evidence that foragers (at least, *Homo sapiens* primitives) lived in precarious and hardship-laden ways. It appears that they usually had an ample food supply and were able to make this available in a twelve-to-twenty-one–hour workweek per person, which increased to forty to forty four hours per week during periods of tool making and maintenance and housework: "The key point is the central position of *work.* . . . If food supply decreases, humans do not respond by dying like fruit flies; they respond by working harder. . . . Like many other hunter-gatherers, the !Kung sought both kinds of social existence—the intensity and excitement of a larger grouping and its attendant risks, and the domestic tranquility and leisure of smaller groupings. . . . This dynamic of movement in space—of coalescing [into larger groupings] and splitting [into smaller groupings], of rearranging groups, and of cycles of social intensity and tranquility—probably characterized the life of humankind for thousands of years before the cycle of movement was permanently altered by sedimentarization accompanying the invention of agriculture."[26]

Lee in line with Marx's appreciation of "exchange," asked the question:

> What is the basic difference in economic organization between humans and their nearest relatives? The answer is summed up in the word *exchange*. Whereas each nonhuman primate organism (in common with most of the vertebrates) is a self-sufficient subsistence unit, no human eats or works alone. Much of a human individual's energy expenditure goes into feeding others, and much of what an individual consumes is food produced by others . . . Each individual [chimpanzee] is a self-sufficient unit. . . . This is truly a hand-to-mouth existence. . . . But, unlike the beast, the consumption of food ["produced" by man] is delayed. . . . For by *exchange* humanity breaks down individual animal self-sufficiency. . . . Exchange of food is basic to all human societies, even the most nomadic, yet is absent from the societies of nonhuman primates. The consequences of this pattern of food use for early society were revolutionary. First, the expectation of exchange of foodstuffs led protohumans to develop the *home base* [italics added], an improved site where members of a group could rendezvous on successive days and pool resources. Second, exchange allowed the development of varied subsistence activities. . . . Third, differentiation of tasks allowed a most important step in human affairs—risk taking—whereby an individual could attempt a difficult subsistence task such as hunting, which has a potentially great return but a rather small chance of success. . . . Finally, exchange and home base permitted a breaking of the lockstep of primate subsistence. . . . The universality of this cluster of economic features in humans makes it likely that its origin is early and probably bound up with the very origin of human society itself.[27]

Lee brings to light a new feature in tool development by early man. We are accustomed to believe that such durable objects as stone and bone devices were critical tools, whereas Lee logically predicates that nondurable carrying devices such as pouches and baskets made of hide, bark, or crude net were the first critical tools of humankind: "The invention of the carrying device made possible a human way of life, but with the increased efficiency of labor came the twin problems that have plagued humans ever since: the problem of surplus and the problem of leisure."[28]

Thus what Sahlins in 1960 in his study, *The Origin of Society,* developed as "an exercise in inference," Lee in 1979 and Lovejoy in 1981 were able "to reconstruct" from "crucial fossils and primate behavior data" in *The !Kung San* and *The Origin of Man*. It was these anatomic features of the hominids and the basic behavior patterns of sociofunctional interrelations necessary for survival and improving the lot of humankind that forged, over ages, the traits of human nature.

VALUES, NEEDS, AND DESIRES

The term "values" should be defined, since it is a basic concept of psychosocial reference and since each trait of human nature is a value and a need desirable for fulfillment. Herrick has done as scholarly a study of these terms as is available. His approach is from the evolutionary development of human behavior. In the consideration of value and needs, he states that in order to be scientific: "We start with the proposition that it is biologically good to be alive."[29] This is not philosophically controversial, transcendental, or supernational. It is a fact without which no fact could be conceived or scientifically pondered over. "It is biologically good to enlarge and diversify the organism's capacity for productive behavior and to enhance the satisfaction won.... With this connotation of the word [good], what is good and what is evil is a factual question to be answered by appeal to actual experience.... Goodness as science views it is nothing inherent in things, persons, or acts as such. What is good is a judgment which cannot be made apart from the questions good for what? and good for whom?... There is general agreement that what is good is valuable. Since life is intrinsically valuable to the organism that has it, whatever is good for the organism is a value."[30]

Values are indeed judgments. As Herrick quoted the sociologist Bouglé:

Judgments of value—whether of esthetic, religious, or moral order—express, not the relations of things among themselves, but the relations of things to human tendencies.... True values are the things men set their hearts upon.... These extracts [from Bouglé] put emphasis where it belongs, upon the *relation* between desires and needs and the things that give satisfaction. This is a biological criterion which is applicable throughout the whole range of animal life, for all animals have need and most of their behavior is concerned with satisfaction of those needs.... The desires of men and the needs of all other creatures arise as expressions of their own inner natures. . . . This sets the most significant criteria of value within the organism, and our search for the biological antecedents of the desires of men must be directed to the intrinsic properties of the organism as such, its needs and satisfactions, not primarily to the things that satisfy the needs. This postulate is basic for a biological analysis of values as motivators of behavior.[31]

Herrick continues: "Because the basis of all value is life itself, what the biologist properly calls 'survival value' is primeval and inescapable. It can never be outgrown, however much may be added to it. From this primordial value all others have been individuated in a hierarchy of values that culminate in man's most refined intellectual, esthetic, and moral satisfaction."[32]

Although Herrick does not specifically define "human nature" and does not differentiate specific traits, he does declare, as many writers on the subject do, that human nature is changeable. He declares it changeable because he does not differentiate human nature from the differences in behavior of individuals and from the differences of behavior in each culture. However, his explorations of the meanings of values, needs, and desires are a real contribution, but require some discussion lest the origins of all animal needs and all human needs be conceived as identical and lest the object of human desire in some instincts, such as a child in relation to the mother, not be considered as having some causal relation to the *inner* need of the mother for the child. There is no question that hunger, thirst, sex, and such biological needs originate from within, though some stimulation may come from outside. But man has more than biological needs. Unlike animals, man is an active participant in his ecosystem and creates human needs.

Let us take an example in group value and need. Early hominids found that sex violence interfered with and even prevented the formation of firm group social relations. They also found that certain inhibitions in the relations between those in the monogamous pairing bond structure and between the parents and offspring had to be formulated and made obligatory for the development of social life. The mental need to do the latter originated from the mental processes of those involved. But was the mental awareness of the problem the only source of the origin of the need? This is not a hunger pain generated by an inner biological process alerting the body of the need for food. This is an external circumstance alerting the mental processes that the conditions of living need to be modified to secure the stability of human group existence. The threat to survival is external. The realization of the threat is internal. The *need* to act is a consensus judgment made after surveying the situation—a psychosocial group phenomenon. The *desire* to act is a further group consensus judgment to satisfy the need for social stability. The need for firm group social relations is a social *value* of the group—a judgment made by group consensus.

There are indeed social and personal values. The traits of human nature are humankind's very basic behavioral values. They are psychosocial behavioral responses to the conditions of human living by the society and, in *various degrees of intensity,* by each individual. The need to act as human is a value. To want to act as a human is a desire. In the human being, there are two levels of needs, biological needs, such as hunger, which are automatically initiated by physiological prompting, and psychosocial needs, which are produced by the conditions of living and formulated by the consensus of cognitive processes as value judgments for the group.

THE TRAITS OF HUMAN NATURE AS HUMANIZING FORCES

It should become obvious that although each trait of human nature is an essential and specific entity in the panorama of activities fundamental for social development, yet not one trait stands alone without the others, lest some damage to the human behavior of individuals becomes evident. When the damage does take place, the biphasic nature of these behavioral traits becomes more obvious. Each is a process, and every process is biphasic, i.e., in this case composed of a human force and a nonhuman or subhuman force. The designation of the primate force of the traits of human nature as unhuman and negative should not be perceived in a pejorative context. We are here dealing with elements of phylogenetic behavior—behavior that developed through millions of years and served as survival responses that got us to the *Homo* stage of development. In this stage was attained the development of certain physical characteristics that placed us in a position to become human. These physical attributes gave us certain behavioral potentialities that primates did not possess. The primate traits are vigorous behavioral forms of action that can reinforce the human traits when *controlled* properly by *inhibitions,* but can disrupt and destroy *human* relations when allowed free rein.

Human nature, being biphasic, is composed of a contradiction: that nature that is human and that nature that is primate and therefore nonhuman. Is it not a contradiction to use the term "human nature" when one aspect of it is human and the other aspect is primate? But the nonhuman is not purely nonhuman, since it derives from the body of the genus *Homo*. Therefore it is subhuman or metahuman. Being a contradiction makes the term no less the description of reality. The purely human aspect of human nature is the complex of psychosocial behavioral traits that are *only* attributes of *Homo sapiens* and therefore by themselves are not a concrete reality, since *Homo* is also a primate. The aspect of human nature derived from the psychobiological nature of the primate (animal urges, instincts, drives) modified by the psychobiological aspects of *Homo* (human brain potential) are themselves not a concrete reality, since this complex is a deflection from the human. Only as a mutually interactive set of behavioral attributes with the human aspect predominating over the primate are they a concrete reality of human behavior. As humans, we had to inhibit certain primate urges that were contradictory to the behavior we needed to adopt in order to develop our human potentials. Not all of our primate urges, however, are in opposition to our human needs, except when expressed with extreme response. For example, defense against predators is a phylogenetic reaction. But as human beings, we do not take the law into our own hands to punish predators, because we are human and compassionate. Yet we do restrain predators with human justice, sometimes even with extreme lenience. Progress in societal development has been possible because *Homo* has been strong-willed enough to cause the positive or human phases of human nature to predominate. Each trait gets its name from the positive phase of the process because this is the human phase. Primitive *Homo* was faced with his primate behavioral heritage, which has persisted and will continue so indefinitely, and this in the presence of his new *Homo* potential orientation. His new *Homo* potential gave him the ability to rationalize, to evaluate, and therefore to see the two sides of the problem. The cognitive force gave his behavior a new direction. He thus developed the *need* to be *free to choose* the direction to act, which he saw as being favorable to him and his family group. The need to be free to choose over the tens of thousands of years became a trait of human nature. *Homo* also realized early in his evolution that the violence inherent in primate male sexuality was a deterrent in the development of the potential in human social relations. Therefore, by his ability to rationalize, evaluate, and freely choose, he developed a *system of norms* of behavior that proscribed primate violence in sexual relations and promoted norms for maintaining stability in the family group. Thus came into being the the revolution in *Homo* sexual behavior that generated the human behavioral capacity for inhibiting impulses of antisocial consequences. *Inhibitions,* therefore, are essential behavioral characterics in human relations, since the primate impulse of a trait is not destroyed, but only inhibited and modified.

The very nature of *Homo* sexuality and the reproductive process drew the opposite sexes together, and the protection of the young until they could fend for themselves was another factor directing *Homo* toward cooperation, mutual aid, and protective tendencies. Whether the long period of helplessness of the *Homo* child developed during the latter hominoid period or in early *Homo* existence or whether it came about more rapidly in the generation of the new genus *Homo* is not known. Cooperation and mutual aid evoked a growing acuteness of *Homo's* sensibilities, which eventually blossomed into emotionally charged behavioral relations called love. This has become a powerful aspect of the bonding trait of human nature. It is difficult to imagine that individuals who have a need for freedom to choose and to inhibit impulses should not be aware of themselves and able to make judgments as to their image in relation to their group. Thus, in the emergence of *Homo* as a human being, the concentration on the individual to behave in a human way toward others eventually converted man's need to appreciate his *self-image* into a trait of human nature. One would expect that the love of life, of children, and of relatives would produce a *hope* in a reasoning individual with a mind capable of fantasizing and looking into the future that the conditions of existence for which he is *striving* will be realized so that his progeny and other kin will be in better circumstances after he is gone. This wish for fulfillment in the future of plans and goals, this *hope*, this *time-binding* nature, has become a powerful trait of human nature. An ecosystem that does not generate hope in its social relations is subject to much social disorientation. It goes without saying that people with hope, with appreciation of their self-images and, with a philosophy of the social value of love would be urged by reason to participate in the betterment of life's conditions and would be challenged by their various social roles to magnify their self-esteem by striving to perform with competence. This type of striving has resulted in the remarkable creations of man's cultural world, and the *need to create* has become another unique trait of human nature.

Humanization has been a long and remarkable process, proceeding respectively from *Australopithecus afarensis* to *Homo erectus* to *Homo sapiens neanderthalensis* to *Homo sapiens* (Cro-magnon man).[33, 34] The primate behavioral impulses have not been bred out of man, although they have been modified. They have, however, in the humanization process, been submerged or inhibited to a greater or lesser degree, depending upon the situation. Therefore, the cognitive process in humanization has always been a tensional struggle for the human being when motivated, consciously or unconsciously, to act—whether to respond in the direction impelled by the primate impulses or to behave according to *human* needs. This is not to depreciate the positive social impulses of primates and early hominids. Man is destined forever by his evolutionary history to struggle between positive and negative choices—between good and evil and right and wrong—because the human aspect of one of his traits (the trait of behavior being guided by moral-ethical norms) endows him with a strong sense of *conscience*.

Without cultivating systems of inhibitions, chaos would prevail and social life on the human level would become untenable. Such inhibitions were translated into systems of social relationships that have been transmitted from generation to generation by culture as codes of moral and ethical behavior. Thus culture became the dominant evolutionary force for *Homo sapiens,* replacing in dominance the forces of biology. This does not mean that there is no biological aspect in the psychosocial-behavioral expression of human nature, for without the neurological, hormonal, anatomical, physiological, and biochemical background factors, there could not be a manifestation of human nature. These background factors are the biological, including genetic, factors that give the potential to mankind to develop human nature. Human nature is itself the psychosocial behavior consequent to humanization of sociofunctional relations inherent in the reproductive process, child rearing, and the survival strategies necessary for protection, subsistence, and the striving toward easing the conditions of living, including the diversions practiced as leisure time accumulates.

As indicated above, each of the traits is a process of opposite movements. Dubos describes this biphasic nature of man: "The vicissitudes of life come in large part from conflicting tendencies inherent in human nature. Taking to the open road gives many satisfactions but we never forget our origin and for this reason we want to return to camp. On the other hand, sedentary life is not completely satisfying either, because we never perfectly adapted to our social environment, and furthermore we yearn for adventure. We thus oscillate between two ideals of being and becoming. These hesitations are responsible for much human uneasiness. They are creative, nevertheless, because they engage human beings in a process of self-searching and external exploration which helps them to escape from biological bondage and to humanize the earth."[35] Fromm expresses these inherent tendencies in man's nature as: "Man cannot live statistically because his inner contradictions drive him to seek for an equilibrium, for a new harmony instead of the post-animal harmony with nature."[36] He describes his formulation of the traits of human nature as biphasic forces such as "Relatedness vs. Narcissism," "Creativeness vs. Destructiveness," "Brotherhood vs. Incest," "Individuality vs. Herd Conformity." and "Reason vs. Irrationality."[37]

Montagu speculates as an anthropologist upon the meaning of the facts cited above:

> *Homo sapiens* is a pleistocene form. That is to say, he may be about one million years old as a distinct species. The really important part of this history lies in the period in which those significant evolutionary changes occurred which eventually led to the appearance of man, and this period is the pliocene—a period which lasted for some 12 million years. During the pliocene, the African homeland of the higher primates was affected by a series of climatic changes which may be summarized as reducing the forested land and turning much of it into open savanna or treeless plains covered with low vegetation. Such environmental changes made adaptive demands upon apelike creatures who, as herbivores, had been accustomed to live upon the abundant yield of the forest. These demands were constituted by the necessity of adapting oneself to an environment in which the vegetation was sparse, and in which, therefore, one would have to turn to a new and supplementary food supply, that is to animals. The hunting of animals required a totally different series of adjustments to the environment than that which was sufficient in the forest. On the savannas one needs speed in order to succeed in the chase . . . and at the same time have one's hands free for the use of implements. Above all, one requires intelligence, the ability to scan, forecast, and make rapid adjustments to rapidly changing conditions.[38]

Primitive *Homo* was so equipped.

Speculating further concerning the facts we know about primitive man, we may ask, how did he feel when he first perceived that he had cognitive powers to plan the manipulation of nature that the rest of animal life around him did not possess, i.e., to generate fire, to make tools, and to use these effectively, to plan for tomorrow, to be aware that he, the person, was self-activated? How did he react to such feelings and to such realizations? It is, of course, impossible to retrace precisely the steps of man's evolution and to regain objective testimony about how primitive man felt, thought, and reacted to his new situation. We must remember that the new situation did not present itself to a particular generation of primitive man, but took thousands of generations to be realized. Is it possible that in studying the in utero and early childhood mental, emotional, and social behavior, we may be able to some extent to reconstruct primitive man's reactions to his "new situation"? This approach, plus conjecture based on reasonable and, to some extent, apparently objective observations of anthropologists, psychologists, and psychiatrists, was taken by Fromm: "From all we know about the evolution of the human race, the birth of man is to be understood in the same sense as the birth of the individual. When man had transcended a certain threshold of minimum instinctive adaptation, he ceased to be an animal; but he was as helpless and unequipped for human existence as the individual infant is at birth."[39] The problem with Fromm's description is whether the psychoanalytic adaptation of the recapitulation theory of Haeckel in assuming that "he [man] was as helpless and unequipped for human existence as the individual infant at birth" is valid considering that the infant at birth is suddenly, in minutes, virtually catapulted from a completely dependent symbiotic existence to a nonsymbiotic existence, while primitive man took tens of thousands of years to transcend the threshold of minimum instinctive adaptation. It is possible that the study of such primitive people as the Tasaday[40] may throw light on the problem. They certainly confirm the validity of most of the above identification of the basic traits of human nature, such as love, the ability to choose between courses of action, of self-image self-esteem, conduct by a specific normative orientation to life, and stability in social relations and rootedness in the group. Life was a challenge to them, but in their circumstances, the challenge appears to be to maintain the status quo, since the Tasaday were, as Marshall Sahlins called them, the "original affluent society." More study needs to be made of the mental, emotional, and social characteristics of this society.

Fromm further asserts that: "The most powerful forces motivating man's behavior stem from the condition of his existence, the 'human situation.' "[41] But he also asserts that "Man's life is determined by the inescapable alternative between regression and progression, between return to animal existence and arrival at human existence."[42] On the basis of these observations, he speculates that "Man is torn away from the primary union with nature, which characterizes animal existence. Having, at the same time, reason and imagination, he is aware of his loneliness and separateness; of his powerlessness and ignorance; of the accidentalness of his birth and of his death. He could not face this state of being for a second if he could not find new ties with his fellow man which replace the old ones, regulated by instincts. Even if all his phys-

iological needs were satisfied, he would experience his state of aloneness and individuation as a prison from which he had to break out in
order to retain his sanity."

In examining and evaluating Lee's comprehensive study of the
!Kung San, one must conclude that these primitive people's behavior
is in accordance with the traits of human nature, although each trait
is conditioned by the particular characteristics of the prevailing culture. Fromm's assertion that "man's behavior stems from the condition
of his existence, the human situation" is indeed a prevalent anthropological thesis. That *Homo*'s cognitive potential extends back to the
Pleistocene and possibly into the late Miocene is also an accepted anthropological thesis. That the very basic "condition of man's existence"
has not changed in any critical way for *Homo* since he become human
has been pointed out by the work of various anthropologists. The research of Earl W. Count,[43] done under the prodding and observation
of Prof. A. L. Kroeber, is fundamental and detailed and confirms
Fromm's above cited observation.

PRIMATE BEHAVIOR

What do we specifically mean by man's primate behavioral nature?
Do we mean that man has the capacity to behave like an ape? First
of all, let us enumerate the behavioral characteristics of an ape that
resemble those of man. Peter Farb observes that:

> Although various mammals exhibit kinds of behavior similar to
> those of primates, only the primates display the full constellation
> of these behaviors [new ways of responding to the environment].
> Four major behavioral characteristics in particular distinguish
> the primates—social learning, tool-making, cooperation in hunt-
> ing, and social organization—and each has had important impli-
> cations for the later development of the human way of life. Most
> mammals learn from experience. They modify their behavior in
> response to events they have both participated in themselves and
> observed in others of their species. The anthropoids are notable
> for having carried this kind of social learning far beyond that
> found in other mammals. From earliest infancy, primates spend
> considerable amounts of time simply observing behavior: first
> that of their mother, later that of siblings, peers, and other mem-
> bers of the group. Eventually, the maturing monkey or ape enters
> fully into the group.

In contrast to other animals living in groups, Farb says: "Primates . . . have exploited group living in a way that confers numerous adaptive advantages. The list of such advantages is long, but those of particular importance in understanding human behavior are: the security of companions known since infancy; kinship ties with the mother and with siblings who can be counted upon for protection; the safety afforded by continued presence of adult males; and the pleasurable social interactions of a predictable way of life."

Although a "humanlike" bond may be displayed in a very few monkey or ape species, the primate sexuality is of a definite different quality than that of the human. Farb observes:

> The female primate is sexually receptive ("in heat" or, technically, "in estrus") for a few days before and after the egg passes from the ovary to the uterus. During this time she may copulate with as many as twenty adult males, thus ensuring fertilization—but making it virtually impossible to determine which male is the father. Adult males can obviously show no interest in offspring whose paternity is unknown. Although the human female has retained the menstrual cycle of other primates, she has suppressed estrus and presents no visible signs of ovulation (which in some primate females consists of a swelling of the brightly colored skin in the area of the vagina). Instead, the level of human sexual activity remains constant during the year—*a behavioral and biological change* [italics added] that has undoubtedly strengthened the bond between human males and females, as well as given human sexuality a prominence and intensity unmatched in any other member of the animal kingdom. Once a monkey or ape female has conceived, on the other hand, she will not come into estrus again until her infant has been weaned.[44]

The closest condition to "estrus" in the human female is the pathological behavioral condition known as nymphomania. If all human females had this condition as a normal attribute, human society, if such could exist in such circumstance, would be completely different from what it is.

What needs to be understood is that even though primitive people like those in Malaysia (before being touched by civilization) called the apes of Borneo and Sumatra "orangutan," meaning, in the Malaysian tongue, "wild man," these apes behaved in a manner, though similar to these primitive people, *entirely inferior in quality than the latter.*

Other characteristics of primate behavior that are mostly on the negative side of *Homo*'s social well-being are aggressive competition, dominance, predation, selfishness, distractibility, irrationality, and uncontrolled conduct.

Let us, therefore, not make the same mistake that the primitive Malaysians made in equating ape's behavior with that of man. Farb affirms this in less emphatic language, even though the emphasis should never be forgotten: "Nonhuman primates in the wild during recent decades have revealed an unsuspected potential for acquiring information and for developing innovative forms of behavior. These accomplishments, though, are unimpressive when compared with those of humans, and even of some mammals. Only when primates are brought into the laboratory in contact with human trainers does their potential for solving problems, cooperation in tasks, and symboling become clear. . . . No one has yet completely explained why these flexible skills, the very hallmark of the hominids, emerge in laboratory primates but not in primates living in the wilds."[45] That no one has yet completely explained this phenomenon is due to the failure of having formulated into specific traits of *human* nature certain basic behavioral characteristics *not present* even embryonically in *primate* nature, such as: the inner generated impulse to act by accumulated experiential initiative, the challenge to be effective by developing one's competence, and the time-binding capacity to project one's comprehension into the future. The complex "time-binding" capacity of the human has no parallel in primates, although the "tool preparation" that chimpanzees perform in preparing to search for termites is declared by Farb as a clear display of "foresight."[46] When compared to mankind's time-binding capacity, it dwarfs into practically nothing. It is like Iago comparing his name, his reputation, to his money purse: " 'tis something, nothing."

The important similarities between ape behavior and that of man are well described by Farb. The enthusiasm of the biologists, the sociobiologists, and the ethologists about these similarities is understandable. Whether the primitive peoples of Malaysia were astounded by the looks and behavior of the Sumatran apes to the point of calling them wild men or were not astounded and merely called them wild men as they would probably have called any other newly discovered primitive people of a different tongue and other cultural differences we cannot know. To the scientist, new discoveries are exciting. The discovery that chimpanzees can be conditioned to perform certain humanlike behavior in the "laboratory" has stimulated some enthusiasts to try to teach them to talk. Psychologist G. C. Gallup claims with great ado that he can prove that chimpanzees display "self-aware-ness."[47] The claims have been fantastic. However, on close examination of these studies, psychologist Terrace, after five years of hoping to prove the validity of such a claim came to the conclusion: "I am now dubious. . . . The apes appear to be able to learn words, but they cannot produce new and original sentences—the benchmark of language use."[48] Terrace *et al.* declare also that: "Psychologists, psycholinguists, and linguists are in general agreement that using a human language indicates knowledge of a grammar. . . . However, objective analyses of our data, as well as of those obtained by other studies, yielded no evidence of an ape's ability to use a grammar."[49] Considering further the evidence gathered concerning the criteria for recognizing when a child uses sentences having objective meaning (governed by a gram-mar), as pioneered with such scientific and philosophic detail by Piaget and later by others, and when a child first distinguishes himself from his surroundings (self-awareness as distinguished from childhood so-lipsism), then the experiments attributing these behavior traits to chimpanzees have *far* from proven that these animals have such ca-pabilities. Terrace further asserts: "Most of those who work with non-human primates vehemently disagree with this conclusion, but many others feel that, at best, the pioneers in this research have overstated their subjects' abilities. . . . No matter how many word relationships chimpanzees learn, no matter how many original usages they produce, none of them matches the linguistic dexterity and spontaneity of the average three-year-old human child."[50, 51] How many "cultures" could a population of three-year-old children create, let alone a population of apes? Such is the reasoning that must be followed in comparing the *nature* of *similar* types of behavior between humans and nonhumans. The quality becomes so different that, for example, human sexuality, as already indicated,[52] and parenting[53] are aeons apart. The similari-ties, therefore, are so superficial, arbitrary, and remote due to the rudimentary nature of one as compared to the highly developed and remarkably creative nature of the other. This comparison is reflected in the structure-function gaps that exist between the higher and lower organisms resulting from the tens of millions of years of evolution of the phylum Chordata, through its various orders and classes and even-tually furcating into the simian and hominid branches. This process, reflecting further the aeons through which the reproductive and sur-vival patterns of praxis predisposed these organisms into close relations with their own kind, should not surprise one that circumstances have generated certain group similarities in behavior, such as cooperation and kindred relations, nor should one be surprised that the various similarities between various groups of organisms should also be quite different in nature as the level of evolution becomes higher, particularly for that of mankind.

MENTAL UNIQUENESS OF HOMO

Being aware of one's self and one's surroundings is the nature of higher orders of animal life. What is unique to *Homo sapiens sapiens* in relation to this awareness is the extent, i.e., the quantity and quality, of this awareness and the influence this attribute has had in differentiating man from the rest of animal life. *Man's awareness about himself in relation to the world around him* we designate *as his consciousness*. It is an aspect of his actual life process. Consciousness cannot be anything else than one's awareness of relationships to one's ecosystem. The existence of man is manifested in the functioning of his life process. Life is, therefore, primary, and ultimately in its very essence is not contingent on the existence of consciousness, but consciousness is dependent on the life process. Both interact intimately in the ecological crucible.

Consciousness is the matrix in which *conscience* generates by accumulating cognitively appreciated experience. Man's conscience is the complex of ideological reflexes and echoes of his developing consciousness molded into a system of norms for guiding behavior—behavior that brings out the variations of individual human beings and also the basic similarities of their behavioral patterns in the process of being human.

Man's consciousness and conscience are fundamental potentials of the cognitive processes of the brain. These attributes of his brain make him unique among living organisms, giving him the ability to reason by a process of analyzing and synthesizing symbols, to generate mental images of the future and plan ahead, to store concepts in a memory pool, to learn by instruction—to be *educable*—to learn by imitation, and to communicate by language. These capacities of the brain, plus the bipedal stance, freeing the hands for manipulatory coordination when stimulated by the ecological pressures to take action to survive, are constrained in the choice of such actions we take by the unique dynamics of the human reproductive cycle, which is a very basic determinant of human interrelationships and social organization.[54] In this crucible, a pattern of traits of basic human behavior has been generating through the hundreds of thousands of years of development of *Homo*. These generic traits, in ensemble, constitute a pattern of cognitive behavioral interrelations depicting the nature of being human. This nature is the fundamental essence from which man's unique behavior stems and on which culture builds and accumulates. This point of view was anticipated by Redfield in his discussions of the relations of anthropology to the social sciences: ". . . There is a return in our time of a conscious concern, as yet unprovided with dependable methods of work, with human nature. This term, replacing a misconceived 'psychic unity' may be understood to refer to the characteristics of all human beings as acquired in whatever society. The conception of universal human qualities has reappeared, among other places, in the recognition recently given by such men as Firth and Kluckhohn to the existence of moral values universal in all cultures *because necessary conditions for these values are present in all societies*" [italics added].[55]

Even earlier, the anthropologist Wallis anticipated that the potentialities of the human brain in relation to basic human needs determine the nature of man: "The constituents of human nature are in the (human) race, which in all its branches evinces a biological unity and similar psychic processes. Human reactions to the natural environments are analogous, and forecast the stages through which all tribes appear to pass, insofar as they do pass."[56]

SPECIFICITY OF THE TRAITS: DEFINITION
OF HUMAN NATURE

We need not belabor with scientific proof that each individual human is a unique variable within the species and that the species itself has a behavioral pattern composed of basic traits by which the species is recognized. There is, however, a problem in agreeing on the specific pattern of behavior traits that composes the holistic nature of the human species and of the specific character of each trait by which we recognize the behavioral uniqueness of the human species.

Montagu claims that, based on anthropological and paleontological findings, there are three fundamental characteristics of human nature, i.e., man's unique educability, his competitiveness in terms of cooperation, and his need for love.[57] Frank does not specifically define human nature, but devotes a whole book to elaborating its meaning as being "capable of almost any conduct, for good or otherwise."[58] In his dissertation, he opines that, basically, the nature of man is flexible, adaptable, potentially intelligent, and endowed with a unique imagination and pair of skillful hands. Human beings are personalities, he relates "who are *in* nature, *in* culture, and *in* society and, at the same time, nature, culture, and social order are in them."[59] With the same eloquence as Frank, Dubos discourses all around the term "human nature," but does not define it, although he does contribute to the subject.[60] In Lorenz's fascinating comparative studies in behavior, he does not technically use the term "human nature," to describe the basic behavior pattern of man. One of the terms he uses is "structure of human social behavior." This, he depicts as the "unique, phylogenetically unprecedented (in the animal world) phenomenon of rational responsibility" that "incorporates a whole series of functions which are generally regarded as rational (responsible) ethical phenomena" and that should be classified "together with the innate social behavior patterns of higher animals exhibiting *only* [emphasis added] functional analogies to ethical processes."[61]

Wilson defines the task of comparative sociobiology to be the tracing of human qualities as closely as possible back through time. Such an exercise, he states:

> . . . will help to identify the behavior and rules by which individual human beings increase their Darwinian fitness through the manipulation of society. In a phrase, we are searching for the *human biogram* [italics added]. One of the key questions, never far from the thinking of anthropologists and biologists who pursue real theory, is to what extent the biogram represents an adaptation to modern cultural life and to what extent it is a phylogenetic vestige. Our civilizations were jerrybuilt around the biogram. How have they been influenced by it? Conversely, how much flexibility is there in the biogram, and in which parameter particularly? Experience with other animals indicates that when organs are hypertrophied, phylogeny is hard to reconstruct. This is the crux of the problem of the evolutionary analysis of human behavior.[62]

Thus, the term "human biogram," which Wilson does not use later in his works *On Human Nature* and *Genes, Mind, and Culture,* gives a connotation which involves the sense of human nature although its meaning is much broader. Wilson's term, "sociogram," refers to phenotypic behavior traits for a society of animals as contrasted to "biogram," which is, at least, phylogenetic in nature. As in his later book, human biogram is different from human nature in that it not only has a phylogenetic nature and should eventually be able to be traced through man's phylogeny, but should also eventually be explainable by means of neurobiology, i.e., he reduces everything to molecular biology and neurophysiology.

Harris is so intent, and rightly so, on refuting Wilson's and the sociobiologists' genetic theory of human nature and in pushing his theory of cultural materialism that he ends up with a concept of human nature based on cultural dynamics to the complete neglect of the psychosocial dynamics in the evolution of the traits of human nature.[63] He, however, does agree that there is a human nature: "Nothing I have said about the gene-free status of most cultural variations is opposed to the view that there is a human nature shared by all human beings.[64]

Harris, like Wilson, equates the "human biogram" with human nature, except that Harris would constrict the list of psychobiological drives composing this term, while the sociobiologists would enlarge the list.[65] The problem with Harris's definition of human nature is that he relates its origin to psychobiological determinants, while the traits *are* psychosocial responses to the basic conditions of man's existence. He justifies his list of psychological constants as follows: "My justification for this list is that its generality is guaranteed by the existence of similar biopsychological predispositions among most members of the primate order. You may wish to postulate that human beings also naturally seek to create music and art, to dichotomize, to rationalize, to believe in God, to be aggressive, to laugh, to play, to be bored, to be free, and so forth. By succumbing to the temptation to open this list to all nominations, you will rapidly succeed in reducing every recurrent cultural trait to the status of a biological given."[66]

Among Harris' minimal list of traits and those listed beyond the minimal list, some do suggest various psychosocial traits of human behavior, such as "to be free" and some are purely psychobiological, such as sex, but his exposition of specific traits of human nature with definity and clarity are lacking.

Maslow wrote a complete and very perceptive book on human nature, and yet not once in over 400 pages did he define the term, always taking for granted that the reader knew the definition.[67] To paraphrase Mark Twain: Everybody talks about human nature but no one takes the trouble to define it. It appears that most people who talk about it seem to be referring to a different notion. Maslow described what human "basic needs" are, stating that such needs had an "instinctoid" nature and also a cultural factor:

"What we have found during the last ten years or so is that, primarily, the sources of creativeness of the kind that we're really inter-

82

ested in, i.e., the generation of really new ideas, are in the depths of human nature."[68]

Those portions of ourselves that we reject and repress (out of fear or shame) do not go out of existence . . . but rather go underground. Whatever effects these underground portions of our human nature may thereafter have upon our communications tend . . . to be unnoticed by ourselves. . . . To me this phenomenon means that expression is not alone a cultural thing; it is also a biological phenomenon. We must talk about the instinctoid elements of human nature, those intrinsic aspects of human nature which culture cannot kill but only repress, and which continue to affect our expression . . . in spite of all that culture can do. Culture is only a necessary cause of human nature, not a sufficient cause. But so also is our biology only a necessary cause and not a sufficient cause of human nature.[69]

By definition, self-actualizing people (more matured, more fully human) are gratified in all their basic needs (of belongingness, affection, respect, and self-esteem). This is to say that they have a feeling of belongingness and rootedness, they are satisfied in their love needs, have friends and feel loved and love worthy, they have status and place in life and respect from other people, and they have a reasonable feeling of worth and self-respect.[70]

Maslow makes very perceptive observations, but does not place these observations in an organizational pattern of human nature. He refers to the "instinctoid elements of human nature, those intrinsic aspects of human nature which culture cannot *kill* but only *repress,* and which *continue to affect* our expression . . . in spite of all that culture can do" (italics added). He fails to realize that the "instinctoid" elements are really the "negative" aspects (the primate behavioral impulses) of the processes by which the traits of human nature are expressed. Then he cites the "basic needs" that, when gratified, make the "self-actuating people." These needs, he declares, are belongingness, affection, self-respect, self-esteem, being respected by others, rootedness, and creativeness. These needs are indeed aspects of various traits of human nature. When he opines that "culture is only a necessary cause of human nature, not a sufficient cause," he would be correct if he asserted instead that the sufficient cause is the psycho-social-behavioral reaction of *Homo sapiens* to the social interrelationships intrinsic to the human condition assumed in response to the struggle to survive and to mitigate the conditions imposed by the ecosystem, that culture has no causal effect here, and that culture only colors the expression of these psychosocial-behavioral responses (human nature) as they are manifested in each culture.

Matson, like Maslow, devotes a whole book to the idea of what man is, and no place in his discussion does he come to grips with a definition of human nature.[71] He writes: "More than any other single spokesman, it was Abraham Maslow who, in a succession of highly original and provocative writings, laid bare the morbid preoccupation of psychology with pessimistic negative and limited conceptions of human nature. . . . An important corollary of the humanistic commitment to normality is the affirmation of sociality as an intrinsic, almost a defining, characteristic of man's nature."[72]

The anthropologist J. E. Pfeiffer finds human nature quite a variable factor, not amenable, from a practical standpoint, to definitive exposition: "People played new roles in their new societies. It is an old opinion that human nature cannot be changed, whatever that means. But human behavior certainly can be."[73] Pfeiffer is apparently not differentiating the secondary behavior of people resulting from current types of cultural change from the basic cognitive pattern and behavior of *Homo sapiens sapiens* due to the nature of his sex drive, of his reproductive cycle, of his quest for subsistence, and of his will to protect himself and his kin and to seek to ease his human condition. Since Pfeiffer does not distinguish between human nature and other behavioral manifestations of people, he refutes the opinion that human nature does not change. The fact is that there are good reasons for the "opinion" that human nature is a very stable psychosocial-behavioral complex. It does *not* appear to change because the traits are the result of humankind's response to the above *durable* factors, which forge the nature of the human condition in the ecosystem, as illustrated in charts 1 and 3.

The psychiatrist Levine discusses the need to change human nature, which to him is at least partially determined by culture and is therefore changeable, but he does not define what he wishes to change, since he takes for granted that we all know what he means by *his* term "human nature." He opines that one point in the needed attempt to add to the technique of changing our destructive ethics "is that such changes in man and his ethics would contradict the fact or the dogma that human nature can not be changed. Human nature can be changed, at least in certain ways. Human nature is in good part an expression of the culture, and changes in culture can change human behavior."[74] In such generalities most writers about human nature express themselves.

Levine's discussion of human nature is as prosaic as that of Pfeiffer in not distinguishing between the stability of the intrinsic psychosocial nature of human nature and its extrinsic cultural variability. The more recent (1978) contribution to this subject by Gordon is well presented, but does not add any new pioneering concepts that really enlarge our basic understanding of the essential dynamics of human nature.[75] He must be given credit for grasping the importance of this subject as a sociologist.

Barash, a zoologist and psychologist, sees human nature as a set of behavioral inclinations having significant grounding in biology.[76] This generalized expression about human nature is the usual socio-biologist's version of the subject.

Montagu's treatment of the term is a real contribution to the subject. But just as significant are the contributions of Charles H. Cooley, Alfred Korzybski, George H. Mead, Erich Fromm, and Amitai Etzioni. These social scientists have perceived human nature as a unity of specific basic traits of human behavior.

Although the psychosocial aspect of human behavior is its essential human quality, the emotional aspect of behavior attributes the physiological changes apprehended as feeling, as affective-cognitive experiences that reinforce the expression of the positive or negative aspects of the traits of human nature. What is emotional in man is the mammalian heritage *humanized* by the positive phase of the traits of human nature, i.e., the raw emotions are colored and harnessed and directed by the humanly generated cognitive forces. Both the traits of human nature and the emotional qualities in their expression are intimately involved with cognition and with each other and, thereby, with consciousness. Human thinking, as a conscious process, generates the behavioral responses to the human condition, but the same conscious mental process will call forth an accompanying emotional response that colors the feelings associated with the behavioral response to the human condition. *Cognition, therefore, is the generator of the psycho-social-behavioral as well as the psychophysical emotional responses.* Human behavioral science is, fundamentally, a psychosocial-psychophysical discipline. In order for this discipline to grow into a structurally productive science such as physics, chemistry, and physiology, a more functional anatomy will need to be developed, particularly in the psychosocial domain. This means that human nature will have to be reduced to its elemental traits, to its molecules. Then we will need to study and understand the laws of motion of these molecules, i.e., the dynamics of the traits of human nature. This is what this monograph is attempting to initiate.

WILSON'S NEW THEORY ALMOST BYPASSES HUMAN NATURE

The newly elaborated behavior theory of Lumsden and Wilson unmindful of the existence of human nature is described by them as "the formal conceptualization and analysis of [the interaction between genes and culture factors that] may be called gene-culture coevolution theory or, more concisely, gene-culture theory."[77] The only reason to consider this theory is because it almost disregards human nature as a behavioral entity, although it presents an elaborate complexity of detail concerning human behavior that allows only fortuitously for the inclusion of a human nature. The theory does, however, try to mitigate the extreme genetic position taken as to the nature of human nature in Wilson's book *On Human Nature,*[78] but not successfully.

Wilson and Lumsden criticize Marx for his "tendency to conceive of human nature as relatively unstructured and largely or wholly the product of external socioeconomic forces."[79] However, they themselves describe human nature in such broad and indefinite terms as to make it practically worthless as a concept, to wit: "Idiosyncrasies in concept formation and valuation obviously distinguish one human being from another. But the epigenetic rules are sufficiently tight to produce a broad overlap in the mental activity and behavior of all individuals and hence a convergence powerful enough to be labeled human nature."[80] Compare "broad overlap" with Redfield's clear term "universal human qualities" for human nature. For further reference, Wilson refers the reader to his work *On Human Nature,* written in 1978. This is an apt reference, for among the attributes he assigns to human nature, such as it being "the full set of innate behavioral predispositions that characterize the human species,"[81] he says it is also "a hodgepodge of special genetic adaptations to an environment largely vanished, the world of the Ice Age hunter-gatherers."[82] Human nature, therefore, is an obsolescent biological phenomenon and not a subject that can be handled by social science with expertise. Then, displaying his own Marxian dialectical expertise, he suggests "that biology, and especially neurobiology and sociobiology, will serve as the antidiscipline of the social science [i.e., will succeed social science by reordering its subject matter, which, of course, is the complex network of human relations and forms of organization enabling people to live together]. I will now go further and suggest that the scientific materialism embodied in biology will, through reexamination of the mind and the foundations of social behavior, serve as a kind of antidiscipline to the humanities." Thus Wilson's scientific materialism of biology will eventually supplant humankind's subjectivity, its mind, its emotions, and its senses of feeling with molecular biology. Human nature will be replaced by molecules of matter instead of molecules of behavior. Is it possible that the following observation on human nature by Dobzhansky will one day be reduced to molecular formulae?: "Self awareness and foresight brought . . . the awesome gifts of freedom and responsibility. Man feels free to execute some of his plans and to leave others in abeyance. He feels the joy of being the master, rather than a slave, of the world and of himself. But the joy is tempered by a feeling of responsibility. Man knows that he is accountable for his acts: he has acquired the knowledge of good and evil. This is a dreadfully heavy load to carry. No other animal has to withstand anything like it. There is a tragic discord in the soul of man. Among the flaws of human nature, this one is far more serious than the pain of childbirth."[83]

It is important that Wilson's point of view on human nature be given special attention since he is the inventor of and most productive writer on the subject of sociobiology. His latest production, in a sense, reduces the importance of the behavioral complex of human nature by the invention of the concept of epigenetic rules, which is the solution of his previous difficulty with sociobiology when "attempting to treat the transition from genes to culture."[84] Except for the latter attempt to redeem his losses in the estimation of scientists by the obvious unacceptable concept of human nature given in his book on that subject, the latest book is useless in revealing any aspect of the nature of human nature. However, Wilson's eminence in the area of biosocial science requires that we consider some of the philosophic predilections and elements of theory structure engendered in his latest book, *Genes, Mind, and Culture.*

The basic problem with the Wilson and Lumsden theory in relation to the nature of human behavior, therefore also to human nature, is that it relates the foundation of the theory to artifacts, the culturgens and epigenetic rules, instead of to the factual data that have accumulated concerning man's origin and behavior since Darwin posited the theory of evolution. However, in the context of these genetically biased artifacts, they do assert the importance of cognition in the shaping of human behavior, which Wilson neglected in his previous works, to wit: "Almost all of human behavior is based on knowledge structures that are learned to some degree."[85] Wilson and Lumsden skirt the possibility that traits of human nature could compose the entity human nature, but conjure up "genetic assemblages" to explain the phenomena of the psycho*social* responses of *Homo* to the basic human conditions that are factual data in the history of humankind. Continuing: "But human nature may be simpler and more transparent than we thought. If epigenetic rules are made the 'molecular units' of learned behavior, the analysis of human behavior can be streamlined. Relatively elementary epigenetic rules generate greater diversity at the cultural level, while remaining obedient to complex genetic assemblages that prescribe relative simplicity in the sensory and neuronal responses. Under appropriate conditions simple rules can be employed to generate an arbitrary amount of detail in either direction." The yes–no–maybe-so explanation as to what may eventuate when millions of genes react with billions of culture-events leads where?—To epigenetic rules? This cannot be denied as a theoretical mechanism of explanation of the origin and dynamics of human behavior, but how does it explain the history of *Homo* and the eventuation of the traits of human nature?

What a complicated problem to solve if we were to reduce the *bonding-sharing trait* of human nature to culturgens and epigenetic rules, i.e., reduce the biophysical-social state of *Homo*'s fundamental conditions of existence as outlined in charts 1 and 3 to the culturgens and epigenetic rules that elicited the psychosocial behavior called human nature!

Another problem with the Wilson-Lumsden theory is that the essence of the theory is built on genes and culture, with no reference to the *social* basis for human existence. Hiller's comprehensive analysis of social relations as the foundation of the structure of human society states: "Because . . . sociology is concerned with human relations, principles of sociology necessarily deal with the content, forms, organization, and enforcement of the relations among the members of a society. To the extent that social relations become stabilized, they constitute what is variously called structures, institutions, groups, social order, and organization. The content of norm-regulated social relations is found in the reciprocities, rights, privileges, and obligations referring to prestige, respect, justice, power, transfer of utilities, and the like."[86] "The social is not something that is opposite of individuals. Rather it is the life they have in common. . . . In other words, that is social which pertains to relations between persons or groups of persons. . . . The genuinely social implies interdependent, coordinated living; and this consists of conduct and mutual life which embody not only norms of social relations but also other fields of culture content."[87]

It should be clear that although the social and cultural are tied intimately together, the social are the fundamentals upon which a culture is built. Human culture was built on the social relations that were absolutely necessitated for early *Homo* to develop its *human* potentialities—social relations that were generated by *Homo*'s cognitive powers, i.e., by psychosocially impelled behavior, the essential elements of which became the traits of human nature. How can such artifacts as culturgens and epigenetic rules lead to credible theory for the origin of human nature while subsuming, contrary to reality, the social under cultural without mentioning the social and without a complicated series of derivatives and syntheses with a decided bias toward the genetic? As Wilson-Lumsden assert: "We expect the complete patterns of causation, from genes to behavior, to be commonly multivalent and reticulate [meaning here: relating or constituting evolutionary change dependent on genetic recombination involving diverse interbreeding populations]."[88] "The central tenet," they assert, "of human sociobiology is that social behaviors are shaped by natural selection . . . Sociobiological theory to the present time has consisted largely . . . of the principles of population genetics and ecology."[89] Not only is this point of view too rigidly a simulation of the formulation of the dynamics of the inanimate, but also of the nonhuman type cerebration of animal life. Most anthropologists and some eminent biologists do not hold such point of view, and this certainly applies to few social scientists and psychologists who have diligently studied this area of cognition as relates to human behavior.

Wilson always justifies his theory as emanating from the principles of evolution. His sociobiological theory, as applied to animal life, certainly adheres credibly to evolutionary theory. But his human sociobiology, which does not recognize the *uniqueness* of man and disregards and even negates with his culturgens the subjective, the cognitive, and the affective, is rejected vigorously by some anthropologists and is in opposition to the view of the most eminent of present-day evolutionists, Ernst Mayr. Mayr declares concerning the uniqueness of man: "Man is a product of evolution. . . . Man is a species of animal, as is self-evident as soon as one applies the concept of evolution to man. . . . But no more tragic mistake could be made than to consider man 'merely as animal'. Man is unique; he differs from all other animals in many properties, such as speech, tradition, culture, and an enormously extended period of growth and parental care."[90]

Wilson and Lumsden have made their presentation as physical and biological scientists, and that is fine for physics, chemistry, and biology. This is evident (1) in their nondiscriminant and interchangeable use of mind and brain; (2) in subsuming of the meaning of "social" under the concept "cultural," thus abasing the dominant importance of human interrelations in the gene-culture theory, since human nature came into existence before the rapid accretion of culture began; (3) in expectation that mental pictures or ideas of "meaning" studied in cognitive psychology will one day be resolved into molecular biology, i.e., the subjective being resolved into the objective as the material substance, water, is resolved into the material substances $2H + 0$; (4) in that neurophysiological dynamics of the brain in cognitive psychology plus the biological dynamics of population can explain the intricate emotional and ideational human behavioral trait of bonding-sharing, a psychosocial-behavioral phenomenon.

They state that: "Bonding results from the virtually automatic positive linking of mothers and infants during their initial contacts." The canalization of this trait "results in part from the peculiar constraints that lead to algebraic rules of risk estimation and other forms of decision making."[91] The important facet of the bonding trait in the human being is not that it has a biogenetic basis and a phylogenetic history, but that it is inseparably linked to the practice of sharing and exchange. This is scientifically an indisputable essentiality in the nature of man. The important concern is social anthropology's finding that it is a common trait in all cultures and that, in its commonality, it differs so greatly from primate and other mammalian bonding that we must describe this exceptional quality as *human* in nature. But *Homo* cannot divest himself of his primate nature. He can only inhibit it when necessary. The bonding-sharing-exchange trait in *Homo* is therefore intrinsically biphasic, manifesting the capacity to express itself both in its rich human form and in its poor primate form. In its human form, its richness emanates from the *psycho*social-behavioral response of man to the sociofunctional relations basic to his human condition. In its primate form, it is a *modified* expression of its primatial essence precisely because it emanates from *Homo* and when given expression in preference to the human aspect, it is due, for various reasons, to less favorable socialization exposure to untoward vicissitudes, whereby his inhibition against responding in his primate mode becomes relaxed. Although all this has an ultimate basis in molecular and population biology and in genetics and neurophysiology, yet the symbolization that represents the intrinsic psychosocial stimuli giving rise to the bonding-sharing-exchange trait in the human can never be resolved in terms of molecular biology, population biology, genetics, or neurophysiology. The principles and laws of mental level dynamics do not exist in the level below, the biological dynamics, even though there be interpenetrating inseparability of the two levels of substance at the interface. Good examples of this interpenetrating inseparability of dynamics between two levels of material substance, the higher level of complexity having laws not found in the lower level of complexity of organization, are physics and chemistry. Nuclear physics is science at the interface between physics and chemistry, yet the oxidation-reduction and the acidity-alkalinity processes remain laws of chemistry and do not pertain to physics even at the interface between the two. In the same sense, neurophysiological and population biological processes that appertain to human behavior will never portray the subjective dynamics of the psychosocial essence of the traits of human nature that express themselves in human behavior. The social anthropologists, the sociologists, and the social psychologists will not find the answers to their scientific problems in the fields of neurophysiology and population biology, regardless of how detailed and particularized the analysis of structure and function may be, although being a votary of these sciences certainly gives general perspective to their tasks.

The specific traits of human nature will be described in detail as this thesis develops. But it should be clear from the foregoing that human nature is not some generalized, nondescript, nonspecific concept, as so many social scientists and would-be social scientists depict human nature to be.

MEAD'S CONTRIBUTION

It appears to me that the most pertinent observations on the nature of human nature made by a social scientist in the more pioneering days of this study were made by Mead in the 1934 compilation of his thinking. What he has to say is so basic to this subject that I will quote at length:

> Among these fundamental socio-physiological impulses or needs (and consequent attitudes) which are basic to social behavior and social organization in all species of living organisms, the one which is most important in the case of human social behavior, and which most decisively expresses itself in the whole general form of human social organization (both primitive and civilized), is the sex or reproductive impulses; though hardly less important is the parental impulse or attitude, which is of course closely connected or associated with the sex impulse, and the impulse or attitude of neighborliness, which is a kind of generalization of

the parental impulse or attitude and upon which all co-operative social behavior is more or less dependent. Thus the family is the fundamental unit of reproduction and of maintenance of the species: it is the unit of human social organization in terms of which these vital biological activities or functions áre performed or carried on. And all such larger units or forms of human social organization as the clan or the state are ultimately based upon, and (whether directly or indirectly) are developments from or extensions of, the family. Clan or tribal organization is a direct generalization of family organization; and state or national organization is a direct generalization of clan or tribal organization—hence ultimately, though indirectly, of family organization also. In short, all organized human society—even in its most complex and highly developed forms—is in a sense merely an extention and ramification of those simple and basic socio-physiological relations among its individual members (relations between the sexes resulting from their physiological differentiation, and relations between parents and children) upon which it is founded, and from which it originates. These socio-physiological impulses (reproductive, parental neighborliness, cooperative impulses) on which all social organizations are based constitute, moreover, one of the two poles in the general process of social differentiation and evolution, by expressing themselves in all the complexities of social relations and interactions, social responses and activities. *They are the essential physiological materials from which human nature is socially formed* [italics added]; so that *human nature is something social through and through, and always presupposes the truly social individual.* Indeed, any psychological or philosophical treatment of human nature involves the assumption that the human individual belongs to an organized social community, and derives his human nature from his social interactions and relations with that community as a whole and with the individual members of it. The other pole of the general process of social differentiation and evolution is constituted by the responses of the individuals to the identical responses of others, that is, to class or social responses, or to responses of the whole organized social groups of other individuals with reference to given sets of social stimuli, these class or social responses being the sources and bases and stuff of social institutions. Thus, we may call the former pole of the general process of social differentiation and evolution the individual or physiological pole, and the latter pole of this process the institutional pole.[92]

Mead, as already cited, not only correctly deciphered the basic bio-social origin of the psychosocial-behavioral traits of human nature,[93] but also differentiated this nature of humankind from the sociocultural contingent of behavior (Herkovits's source of cultural relativism) whose origin is mainly *cultural*. It is fitting to let Mead summarize his thesis on human nature:

> Human society as we know it could not exist without minds and selves, since all its most characteristic features presuppose the possession of minds and selves by its individual members; but its individual members would not possess minds and selves if these had not arisen within or emerged out of the human social process in its stages of development—those stages at which it was merely a resultant of, and wholly dependent upon, the physiological differentiation and demands of the individual organisms implicated in it. There must have been such lower stages of the human social process, not only for physiological reasons, but also (if our social theory of the origin and nature of minds and selves is correct) because minds and selves, consciousness and intelligence, could not otherwise have emerged. . . . The behavior of all living organisms has a basically social aspect: the fundamental biological or physiological impulses and needs which lie at the basis of all such behavior—especially those of hunger and sex, those connected with nutrition and reproduction—are impulses and needs which, in the broadest sense, are social in character or have social implications, since they involve or require social situations and relations for their satisfaction by any given individual organism; and they thus constitute the foundation of all types or forms of social behavior, however simple or complex, crude or highly organized, rudimentary or well developed. . . . All living organisms are bound up in a general social environment or situation, in a complex of social interrelations and interactions upon which their continued existence depends.[94]

The important contribution of Mead is his detailed analysis of the biosocial mechanism that gives rise to the basic psychosocial-behavioral traits of *human nature*. He did not elaborate with detailed analysis the scientific structure of the individual traits as processes operating in tensional biphasic movement, although he did evaluate and amply dissected and delineated with valuable discussion the biosocial origin of human nature and the psychosocial-behavioral responses to the basic biosocio-environmental relations. He affirmed with clarity and vigor how the traits of human nature are formed in the crucible of responding to the bio-physiological factors such as the sex impulse and the reproductive process, hunger and nutrition, the parental impulse or attitude, and the neighborliness impulse upon which cooperative behavior depends. He also analyzed the psychosocial interrelations of mind, self, and society as few had the perception to do.

Mead recognized but did not emphasize the biphasic nature of human responses to various aspects of social relations, e.g., he pointed out that content of self (the basic, unsocialized, prehuman (primate) nature of self) is essentially selfish while the structure of self (the socialized, humanized self) is essentially social.[95]

As a colleague of Cooley and Dewey, Mead lived at a time when social psychology was in the process of becoming a science and the field was not cluttered with pseudoscientific jargon and philosophic frippery that obstructs the scientists' view of the essential dynamics of the nature of human nature. Sociology has suffered from lack of concern by sociologists of the part played by the traits of human nature. Let us now examine the contributions to this science by Cooley.

COOLEY'S CONTRIBUTIONS

Charles Horton Cooley wrote his thesis on human nature and the social order at the turn of the twentieth century. It was published in 1902. His contribution to understanding the nature of man, which is basic to the development of both sociological and psychological theory and principles, has not been recognized until recently by most psychologists and sociologists. Extensive psychological works such as R. E. Ornstein's *Nature of Human Consciousness,* and B. Bernard and G. A. Steiner's *Human Behavior* and *Psychological Issues,* edited by G. S. Klein, do not mention the existence of Cooley's work. However, the social psychologist M. Brewster Smith gives a good deal of attention to Cooley and his basic contributions: "Sociologist-social psychologists, beginning with G. H. Mead (1934) and C. H. Cooley (1902) had created an important body of theory concerning the processes of 'symbolic interaction' through which the biological raw materials of human potentiality are transmuted into *human nature* [italics added] to provide the psychological basis for organized society. But they were slow to refine and test these ideas in empirical research."[96] "One of the most hopeful features in the current situation . . . is the emergence from diverse quarters of incipient consensus on a model that rejects the sterile dichotomy of isolated individual versus disembodied group. The model is by no means new; Cooley (1902) and Mead (1934) had the essential insights early in the century. But the tradition springing from Mead and Cooley tended to remain the private property of sociologists, in whose hands it retained a speculative flavor. What is new today is that the insights are being rediscovered on all sides, and—more important—they are being employed, refined, and tested as never before in empirical and experimental research."[97] The sociologist, Gordon in 1978 also recognized the importance of the contributions of these two social scientists.[98]

Although Cooley does not come to grips with a precise definition of human nature, he described with elegant insight a number of specific traits of behavior that he attributed to a composite core of traits qualified as human nature. In relation to a trait of human nature called the bonding-sharing force, Cooley philosophized under the heading of "Sympathy or Communion as an Aspect of Society": "In common thought and speech, sympathy and love are closely connected; and, in fact, as most frequently used, they mean somewhat the same thing, the sympathy ordinarily understood being an affectionate sympathy, and the love of a sympathetic affection. . . . However, the excitant of love, in all its aspects, is a felt possibility of communication, a dawning of sympathetic renewal. We grow by influence, and where we feel the presence of an influence that is enlarging or uplifting, we begin to love. Love is the normal and usual accompaniment of the healthy expansion of *human nature* [italics added] by communion, and in turn is the stimulant to more communion."[99]

Under the rubric of "love," Montagu, from an anthropological point of view and with elaborate citations and discussion, designates this characteristic as a trait of human nature.[100] Fromm, likewise, predicates love as a trait of human nature, but in the biphasic concept of Relatedness vs. Narcissism.[101] Actually this trait is attributed to human nature by many scientists, such as Dubos,[102] Erikson,[103] Loevinger,[104] May,[105] Lewis *et al.*,[106] and some of the sociobiologists who trace this trait back to animal behavior, such as Barash,[107] Lorenz,[108] and Alcock.[109]

Cooley considers "sociability" to be a trait of human nature: "Alone one is like fireworks without a match; he cannot set himself off, but is a victim of *ennui*, the prisoner of some tiresome train of thoughts that holds his mind simply by the absence of a competitor."[110] "The impulse to communicate is not so much a result of thought as it is an inseparable part of it. They are like root and branch, two phases of a common growth, so that the death of one presently involves that of the

95

other."[111] "Sociability in this simple form is an innocent unself-conscious joy, primary and unmoral, like all simple emotions."[112] Cooley quotes Montaigne on sociability. He describes Montaigne as one who understood human nature as well, perhaps, as anyone who ever lived and then cites the following: "There is no pleasure to me without communication; there is not so much as a sprightly thought comes into my mind that it does not grieve me to have produced it alone, and that I have no one to tell it to."[113] Fromm cites the same concept of sociability under his biphasic trait, Relatedness vs. Narcissism, which he describes as follows: "Man is torn away from the primary union with nature, which characterizes animal existence. Having at the same time reason and imagination, he is aware of his aloneness and separateness; of his powerlessness and ignorance; of the accidentalness of his birth and of his death. . . . Even if all his physiological needs were satisfied, he would experience his state of aloneness and individuation as a prison from which he had to break out in order to retain his sanity. . . . The necessity to unite with other beings, to be related to them, is an imperative need in the fulfillment of which man's sanity depends."[114]

Sociability that implies social relationship and the impulse to communicate is expressed by Montagu as follows: "The fundamentally social nature of all living things has its origin in the reproductive relationship between genitor and offspring . . . and that the social relationships existing between organisms up to and including man represent the largely unconscious development of the interdependent relationship between mother and child as experienced in the reproductive state."[115] Sociability as a fundamental trait of man's nature and the process of socialization that implies the existence of this trait are propounded by many social scientists among whom are Opler,[116] Young,[117] Thomas and Chess,[118] Jensen,[119] and Matson.[120] The sociobiologists generally, including Edward O. Wilson, consider socialization a basic biological characteristic in animal behavior, even attributing human socialization to an evolutionary biological process.

Self-awareness is a trait in Cooley's ensemble of traits of human nature: "The emotion or feeling of self may be regarded as an instinct, doubtless evolved in connection with its important function in stimulating and unifying the special activities of individuals. It is thus very profoundly rooted in the history of the human race and apparently indispensable to any plan of life at all similar to ours."[121] Fromm also considers this one of the traits of human nature under the title "Sense of Identity—Individuality vs. Herd Conformity": "As with the need for relatedness, rootedness, and transcendence, this need for a sense of identity is so vital and imperative that man could not remain sane if he did not find some way of satisfying it."[122]

Cooley believes that hostility and conflict are traits of human nature: "Conflict is a necessity of the active soul, and if a social order could be created from which it were absent, that order would perish as uncongenial to human nature."[123] Montagu would thoroughly disagree with this. However, if we define a trait of human nature as having a biphasic essence, a socially positive and a socially negative or a human and a primate aspect such as Fromm posits for his traits, to wit, Relatedness vs. Narcissism, creativeness vs. destructiveness, et cetera, then Cooley has an important point. Cooley actually sensed this biphasic nature of the traits of human nature when he stated: "It would not be very difficult to take the seven deadly sins—Pride, Envy, Anger, Sloth, Covetousness, Gluttony, and Lust—and show that each may be regarded as undisciplined manifestation of a normal or functional tendency."[124]

Under the title "The Social Aspect of Conscience," Cooley discussed a trait of human nature that Fromm chose to call "The Need for a Frame of Orientation and Devotion—Reason vs. Irrationality."[125] Cooley described this trait as follows: "The mind is the theatre of conflict for an infinite number of impulses, variously originating, among which it is ever striving to produce some sort of unification or harmony. . . . It is mostly an unconscious or subconscious manipulation of the material presented, an unremitting comparison and rearrangement of them which ever tends to organize them into some sort of a whole."[126] "It (sense of duty) is like obedience to some external authority; any clear way, though it leads to death, is mentally preferable to the tangle of uncertainty."[127]

The drive for freedom is also a trait of *human nature* in Cooley's system: "The social order should not exaggerate one or a few aspects of human nature at the expense of others, but extend its invitation to all our higher tendencies. Thus the excessive preoccupation of the nineteenth century with material production and physical science may be regarded as a partial enslavement of the spiritual and aesthetic sides of humanity, from which we are now struggling to escape."[128] Dobzhansky affirms this conception of freedom: "But this new evolution, which involves culture, occurs according to its own laws, which are not deducible from, although also not contrary to, biological laws. The ability of man to choose freely between ideas and acts is one of the fundamental characteristics of human evolution. Perhaps freedom is even the most important of all the specifically human attributes."[129]

Cooley also considered emulation a trait of human nature and he related the motives to conform as a manifestation of emulation. Emulation is intimately concerned with imitation, and Dawkins gives this element of behavior a very basic place in the development of culture.[130]

ETZIONI'S CONTRIBUTIONS

Etzioni uses the term "human nature" sparingly, but his term "basic needs," actually, from the context of its use, means "traits of human nature." In discussing the problem of the fulfillment of the basic needs of human beings in their social settings, he invokes Marx's basic thesis on this matter: Alienation. He defines alienation in the partial context of Marx's meaning, i.e., being estranged from authentic participation in one's social existence. In Etzioni's words:

> Alienation . . . is not only a feeling of resentment and disaffection but also an expression of the objective conditions which subject a person to forces beyond his understanding and control. . . . Even if a person is only vaguely aware of his own deprivation, dependency, and manipulation, he is still alienated so long as he is unable to participate authentically in the process that shapes his social being. Alienation, thus, has *structural* [sociopolitical] bases and *psychic* consequences [italics added]. As these two aspects of alienation are often confused, we refer to the society as *alienating* and to its members as being alienated [i.e., society appropriates something, usually essential from its members]. It should be noted, however, that the roots of alienation are not in interpersonal relations and intrapsychic processes but in the societal and political structure.[131]

To further understand Etzioni's thinking: "When alienation exists, it encompasses most, if not all, social relations. . . . Alienation is encompassing in still another sense: It affects both the excluded groups and those who exclude them. The excluded are affected because the society is particularly unresponsive to their need. The excluding groups are affected because the process of exclusion creates a distorted social world which they cannot elude. Highly alienating structures . . . rely relatively heavily on coercion; this brutalizes the wielder of force as well as those who are whipped."[132] Etzioni also discusses another term closely related to alienation, i.e., "inauthenticity": "A relationship, institution, or society is inauthentic if it provides the appearance of responsiveness [to basic human needs] while the underlying condition is alienating."[133]

The politicoeconomic *followers* of Marx maintain that once the interrelationships of the forces of the means of production and those of production relations are altered in favor of the alienated workers, there is no longer any need for research in social science and the modalities of the social structure in relation to the human being. Utopia is then on its way to being achieved for the development of the human being, and this development will now take place naturally and unhindered and will follow like night follows day. But this is not so, and Etzioni sensed this very well. He realized that although human beings are extremely adaptable to their ecosystems, their basic human needs or traits of human nature have limitations to such adaptability. When the ecosystem is not in harmony with the traits of human nature, it will "cost" the people in their well-being: "What we seek to illustrate are the opportunities to test *empirically* the key proposition that the *flexibility of basic human needs is limited in that they can be more readily and fully satisfied in some societal structures than in others. Thus, some societal structures, as a whole, are less responsive and more alienating than others, and there are significant limits to the manipulability of the members.*"[134]

Contrary to the interpretation of Marx by the political adherents who believe that solving the class struggle will automatically purify the social relations imperative for a good life, Marx's description of the nature of alienation presupposes the existence of a patterned nature of man's behavior that has a stability that can be in discordance with the social system when the latter's structure interferes with the expression of man's human nature. True enough, making food, shelter, clothing, and education available to all the people is an excellent and basic foundation for rendering some relief to the psychosocial nature of its anxiety in the materialistic struggle. But then the rest of the structure of social relations must also be fitted to the organizational pattern of the traits of human nature. Etzioni suggests six basic needs or traits of human nature, indicating that there may be more. He states:

Human needs seem to include the need for *affection,* also referred to as the need for solidarity, cohesion, or love, and the need for *recognition* variously referred to as the need for self-esteem, achievement, or approval. . . . A third need is for *context,* variously referred to as the need for orientation, consistency, synthesis, meaning, or wholeness. . . . The person seems to have a need for some degree of "harmonization" among these various inputs and demands. . . . Fourth, there is the need for *repeated gratification;* . . . whatever the source of gratification, large lapses of time between instances of it are frustrating. . . . Two "second order" needs arise out of these basic ones; one concerns the longitudinal and the other the lateral organization of gratification. The first is the need for a degree of stability in the pattern of the distribution of rewards—of their expectability independent of the level and frequency of gratification. If there is not sufficient stability, the level of anxiety is expected to rise. . . . The other "second order" need is the need for *variance in a social structure.* . . . There is the need for a variety of social roles and norms to provide outlets for the varied personalities.[135]

Etzioni further states, and the author of this study agrees:

that the more a social structure allows for the satisfaction of the basic needs of its members, the less the structure will be alienating. The participation of the members in a societal structure comes to assure the responsiveness of that structure to the basic needs. *Ultimately, there is no way for a societal structure to discover the members' needs and adapt to them without the participation of the members in shaping and reshaping* the *structure.* Thus, participation, besides serving psychological needs, is a major societal instrument. But complete satisfaction is not possible; the gratification of some needs reduces the ability to gratify others. . . . The realm of social life entails . . . some frustrations. . . . *Most alienation is the result of a specific societal and cultural pattern and can be reduced by changing that pattern.*[136]

Etzioni further considers the "costs"—the depreciation—concerning the well-being of the individual or society by the discordance of the ecosystem in relation to the traits of human nature:

The empirical verification of the validity of the concept of basic human needs ought to concentrate on comparisons of the socialization and social control "costs" of various roles, societal sectors, and total structure, and on the visible indications of underlying frustrations. (We refer to psychic costs as "personal" and to all others, especially socialization and social control as "social." The fact that a man can be socialized and/or controlled to carry out almost any role is not a sufficient indicator of the extent of his flexibility, so long as the social and personal costs of the effects are not taken into account. We suggest (a) that the socialization and social control costs as well as the levels of frustration of any two roles differ, and (b) that they are higher when roles are less natural, i.e., allow for less satisfaction of the basic human needs.[137]

Etzioni is certainly on the right track, although his traits of human nature are too few but certainly valid. His assertion that the untoward effects of the discordance in the relation between the ecosystem and the traits of human nature could be used for measuring criteria for the level of discordance between the two. For example, the degree of alienation might be measured by the levels of such factors as frustration and anxiety neurosis, family disintegration, divorce, psychosomatic disease, alcoholism and drug abuse, suicide, illegitimacy, households composed of unmarried couples, battered children, rapes, homosexuality, venereal diseases, juvenile delinquency, mass demonstration, crime, and police force increase. *Sociological and psychological research could be directed toward determining what societal structures best accord with the traits of human nature.*

Etzioni is among the present-day social scientists who have succeeded in building a system that defines human nature, isolates the specific traits of human nature, attributes to human nature a sense of stability, describes the relation of the traits to the ecosystem, and suggests a method of measuring the benign or malign effects of societal structures and organization on the traits of human nature.

SUMMARY

The most basic problem plaguing sociological theory development is the illusive factor of human behavior—the essence of what gives validity to sociology, psychology, and social anthropology, i.e., social science in general. Since Marx's time, social structure has become the subject of objective study. True enough, the underlying elements of social study must, perforce, be based on philosophic values, such as the term "value," in economic theory, or the terms "freedom," "self-esteem," and "love" in psychosocial theory. Although, in essence, such value terms are not measurable, as matter is, nevertheless, they can be *evaluated* in weighted degrees of significance in relation to the human being, i.e., in the appraisal of humaneness. And humaneness is the mark of acceptability of social life itself. Human nature is the essence of such a concept, for it provides the measure of what is humane.

Human experience has demonstrated that the structure of social life and its dynamics influence the physical well-being of people of that society. The social scientists have described in detail the forces and the material components involved in the operation of various types of social systems, i.e., the elemental forces and factors and their interrelations that determine the paradigms of each type of social order.

Human experience has also demonstrated that the structure and dynamics of each type of social system influence the behavior of the people of that society. Some social scientists, such as Herskovits (an anthropologist), have asserted that human behavior is totally plastic, i.e., that culture, which describes the behavior of people, is altogether *relative. Cultural relativism* abhors behavioral structure. As Harris put it: "[C]ultural relativism, at its best, would represent a state of moral and ethical confusion characterized by contradictory, weak, unconscious, or disguised value judgments."[138] However, to the contrary, the same underlying, durable pattern of behavioral structure *does* exist in every known society. It exists in the composition of human nature by the fact that it is composed of very specific traits of behavior, the essences of which are found in the behavior of all societies, primitive and modern. This is the nonrelative aspect of behavior. The relative aspect is the fact that the culture of each society gives its particular color to the manifestation of these traits. The following diagram (chart 4) illustrates the course of development of the forces responsible for the patterns of human behavior, from primitive times to the present.

Just as social science has been able to dissect the structural elements of society and to synthesize the dynamics of these elements into workable theories of social structure, so now, with dissection of human nature into its specific traits and correlating the dynamics of these traits with the stream of social movement in particular types of social structure, it becomes possible to elaborate workable theories of behavior structure. Paradigmatic theory therefore becomes possible concerning the psychosocial behavior of people exposed to the stresses of the various types of social structure.

This analysis of the structure of human behavior as a complement to social structure gives social science a complete set of dynamic elements, material and psychosocial for developing a comprehensive science of sociology, social psychology, and social pathology. The basic questions that such theory *must* be able to answer if it be accepted as valid are: How does the social structure effect the psychosocial structure (the traits of human nature), and what kind of social structure is necessary so that it will be in harmony with the traits of human nature? How does the discord between these two cause psychosocial (i.e., cognitive and emotional) disorientation or pathology, and what kind and how much psychosocial disorientation is necessary for the development of mental (i.e., cognitive and emotional) disturbance? A formidable task for sociological research!

However, research is rapidly veering in this direction. But, at the sociodynamic level, the fruits of research are not of the quality as in

CHART 4
Diagram of the Course of Development from Primitive to Modern Times of the Forces Responsible for Patterns of Human Behavior

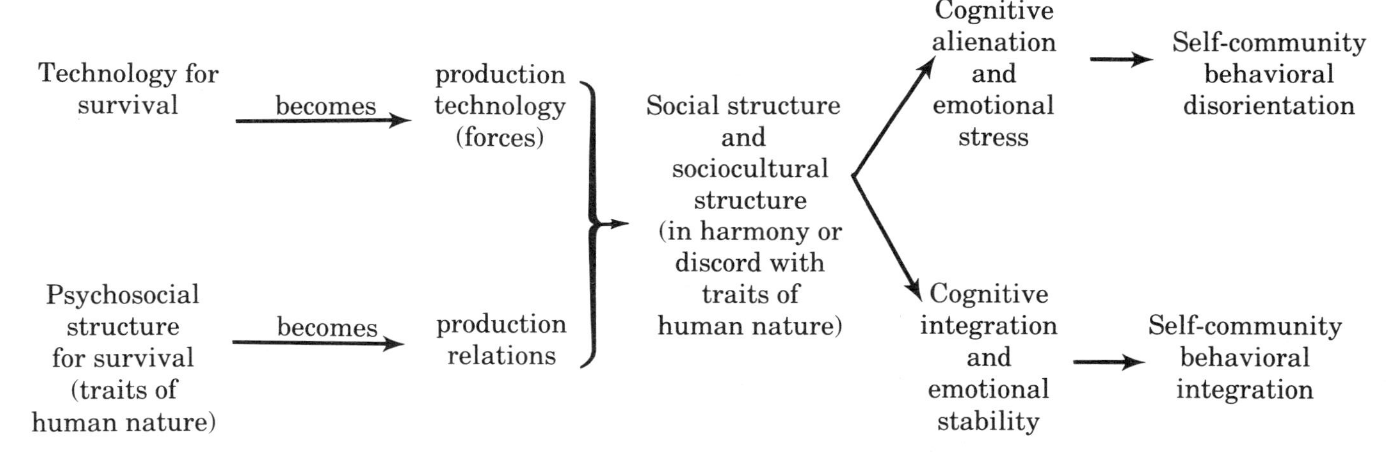

the biodynamic field. In relation to biodynamics, Dr. Hamburg, president-elect of the American Association for the Advancement of Science, opined that effective inquiry is taking place

> at every level of biological organization, from molecules and cells to organisms and population. . . . These recent discoveries grew out of investigations into the brain's control of the endocrine system and the hypothalamic hormones (peptides) that mediate control. It was discovered that such peptides [constituent parts of proteins] not only are present in the hypothalamus and pituitary but are widely synthesized and distributed throughout the brain; that they have neurotransmitter or neuromodulatory functions; that they are involved in the regulation of homeostatic systems in many ways; and that they mediate such crucial behavioral systems as those involved in pain and pleasure, learning and memory, and stress and coping. . . . Curiosity about stress-related disorders has led to fundamental progress on neuropeptides and other neuroregulators. . . . The Centers for Disease Control have estimated that about half the mortality from the ten leading causes of death in the United States is strongly linked to long-term patterns of behavior (life-style). Such known behavioral risk factors as cigarette smoking, excessive consumption of alcohol beverages, use of illicit drugs, certain dietary habits, insufficient exercise, reckless driving, noncompliance with medication regimens, and maladaptive responses to stress are involved in the pathogenesis of cardiovascular diseases and cancer as well as accidental disabilities and other disorders. . . . Eventually, advances in disease prevention and health promotion may result from fundamental research on the effects of brain peptides on behavioral systems.[139]

This quotation is an excellently stated concise exposition of the scientific basis that could lead to the eventual bringing to light how the social system under which a population lives can affect the traits of human nature when that social order *is* or *is not* in harmony with those traits.

The behavioral risk factors cited above, if examined in depth, are problems of behavior brought about by maladaptive responses to stress or by behavior diversions initiating stressful activities or both, all of which modify the quantity and quality of the various peptides in and associated with the nervous and hormonal systems and resulting in the modification of the physiology of the body organs and the mental and emotional processes.[140] Therefore, not only is it necessary to study the way the processes of the body are affected by the conditions of living; it is also necessary to study the detailed dynamics of the social structure under which people live in order to uncover what qualities the social structure must have in order to be most harmonious to the traits of human nature. Thus, as Cooley pointed out so aptly in his 1902 contribution, the dynamics of behavior must be understood in relation to the dynamics of the particular social order to be able to rationally devise measures for preventing behavioral dysfunction of the people and its society.

The microcosm of the dysfunction is the physiology of peptides, proteins, and deoxyribonucleic acid (DNA). The macrocosm is in the behavior of people in response to their conditions of living. Because of the general unrest over the world after the Second World War and the increasing activities of left-wing nations and political groups, the U.S. Congress became interested in this macrocosm. Thereby the Senate Committee on Foreign Relations organized a series of discussions on the subject of the nature of revolution, beginning February 19, 1968. The chairman of the committee opened the session with the following statement: "The Committee on Foreign Relations this morning is beginning a series of public hearings on the nature of revolution and the significance of revolutions abroad for American foreign policy. The broad purpose of these discussions is, first, to develop information about the tendency of revolutions, regardless of their ideological origin, to pass through certain relatively distinct stages, and second, to try to identify the implications of the process in the context of current and future formulation of foreign policy by the United States."[141] It appears that the U.S. government's interest in the cause of sociopolitical violence is for outward considerations, not for the impact of the sociopolitico-economic forces of its own social order on the psychosocial nature of the American people. Its internal interest is almost zero except as, for the most part, it superficially affects the outcome of elections. Its outlook on the sociopolitical behavior of foreign peoples is biased and superficial, and therefore, the foreign policy is biased in relation to governments under which social unrest exists. The United States relies on the FBI to monitor the disposition of its own people, and this is only from the point of view of adherence to the law. The business interests of our country concern themselves with the behavior of the American people only as it effects their consumer attitudes and activities. Luckily, of course, a democracy allows for a greater amount of resiliency in the expression of the traits of human nature than does a dictatorship or an autocracy.

There are few, if any, governments that have openly demonstrated a manifest acumen in monitoring the in-depth psychosocial disposition of its people in relation to the long-term behavior of the government to the conditions of societal dynamics. Government interest in this area must one day become one of its basic functions for long-term survival.

Relation of Macrocosmic to Microcosmic Factors

When speaking of the traits of human nature, we refer to the psychosocial behavior of the human population or groups of human population. The concept "people" implies that each individual in the group or the whole is an organism unto itself and that each such organism has its own set of chromosomes and genes and its own exposure to its ecology. This renders each individual a unique personality with a specific character, each having its own share of each trait of human nature—some being more and some less endowed with each trait. Whatever that endowment may be, it is part of the statistical mean of the group's or population's capacity to express the essence of each trait. The concordance or discordance of the particular ecosystem in its relation to the traits of human nature determines the psychosocial behavior of that group or population to its conditions of living. The expression of group behavior, although it is the resultant of the combined behavior of each individual, is quite different from each individual's behavior. Thus, in pinpointing the behavior of an individual, we must take into consideration the individual's particular biological and social heritages and the evolutionary result of the continuous impact between the individual's biological and social heritages in the process of the individual's development. Consequently, in studying the anatomy, dynamics, and epidemiology of the traits of human nature in relation to, let us say, alcoholism in an individual, we must take into consideration a set of microcosmic factors that are distinct from but mutually related to the macrocosmic factors when studying the origin and evolution of alcoholism in a population.

Just as it is essential to study the concordance or discordance between the traits of human nature and the ecosystem in order to understand the resultant behavior of a population to its ecosystem, so, as Chess and Thomas predicate, it is necessary to study the "goodness of fit" or the "poorness of fit"[142] between an individual's temperament, abilities, motivations, and goals and the *impact* on that individual of his intrafamilial characteristics and extrafamilial factors. Chess and

Thomas state it well: "When the organism's capacities, motivations and style of behaving and the demands and expectations of the environment are in accord, the *goodness of fit* [emphasis added] results. Such consonance between organism and environment potentiates optimal positive development. Should there be dissonance between the capacities and characteristics of the organism on the one hand and the environmental opportunities and demands on the other hand, there is *poorness of fit* [emphasis added], which leads to maladaptive functioning and distorted development. Goodness of fit and consonance, poorness of fit and dissonance are never abstractions. They have meaning only in terms of the values and demands of a given socioeconomic group or culture."[143] If one were to examine the specific factors Chess and Thomas attribute to the intrafamilial characteristics and the extrafamilial factors, one would find that each characteristic and each factor would fit into one or more of the traits of human nature. Individual behavior is a psychosocial and biosocial response of the individual to the microcosmic complexity of the interactionist framework in which the individual develops.[144] For the most part, Freudian theory is also anchored in individual behavior.

Chess and Thomas distinguish among the intrafamilial characteristics *parenting attitudes, child care practices,* and *sib influences,* which are aspects of most traits of human nature, particularly of the "bonding-sharing" trait and the "self-image–self-esteem" trait. Also distinguished are *ethical standards* and *sociocultural values,* which are inherent in the "unifying orientation of behavior" trait, and *aspirations,* which are aspects of the "time-binding" trait, "striving to satisfy one's appetites, inclinations, and talents" trait, the "challenge and competence" trait, and the "cumulative creative action" trait, and finally the *personality attributes* characteristics, which are the combined resultant of the conditioning of the individual's temperament categories,[145] abilities, motivations, and goals.

The extrafamilial factors, as distinguished by Chess and Thomas, include *peer group standards* and *community value systems* that are aspects, particularly, of the "unifying orientation of behavior" trait; *school expectations and demands,* which are aspects of the "time-binding" trait, the *"striving* to satisfy one's appetites, inclinations, and talents" trait, the "self-image–self-esteem" trait, the "challenge and competence" trait, and the "cumulative creative action" trait; and the *opportunities* factor, which is concerned with the "bonding-sharing" trait and practically all the other traits and the nature of the social order.

NOTES

1. John Dewey, *Human Nature and Conduct* (New York: Modern Library, 1957).

2. Ibid., p. 130.

3. A. Schopenhauer, *On Human Nature* (Aberdeen, Scotland: University of Aberdeen Press, 1957), p. 7.

4. Ibid., p. 14.

5. Leon Eisenburg, "The *Human* Nature of Human Nature," *Science,* vol. 176, no. 4031 (April 14, 1972), pp. 123–28.

6. John Dewey, *Human Nature and Conduct* (New York: Modern Library, 1922), pp. 276–86.

7. Ibid., pp. 272–73.

8. Arthur O. Lovejoy, *Reflections on Human Nature* (Baltimore, Maryland: Johns Hopkins Press, 1961), p. 1.

9. Ibid., pp. 9–10.

10. C. Owen Lovejoy, "The Origin Of Man," *Science,* vol. 211, no. 4480 (January 23, 1981), pp. 341–50.

11. Karl Marx, *The Grundrisse,* edited by David McLellan (New York: Harper Torchbooks, 1971), p. 144.

12. Richard B. Lee, *!Kung San: Men, Women and Children in a Foraging Society* (New York: Cambridge University Press, 1979), p. 492.

13. F. R. Bailey and A. M. Miller, *Textbook of Embryology* (William Wood Co., 1929), pp. 439–41.

14. Lewis H. Morgan, *Ancient Society* (Chicago, Illinois: Charles H. Kerr and Co.), p. 562.

15. Ibid., p. 562.

16. Leonard Williams, *Challenge to Survival* (New York: New York University Press, 1977), p. 124.

17. C. Owen Lovejoy, "The Origin of Man," *Science,* vol. 211, no. 4480 (January 23, 1981), pp. 341–50.

18. Richard B. Lee, *!Kung San: Men, Women and Children in a Foraging Society* (New York: Cambridge University Press, 1979), p. 437.

19. Ibid., p. 436.

20. Ibid., p. 437.

21. Leonard Williams, *Challenge to Survival* (New York: New York University Press, 1977), p. 124.

22. Claude Levi-Strauss, *The Savage Mind* (Chicago, Illinois: University of Chicago Press, 1966, pp. 251–52.

23. Karl Marx, *Capital,* volume 1: *Capitalistic Production* (Chicago, Illinois: Charles H. Kerr and Co., 1906), pp. 97 and 99–100.

24. Karl Marx and Friederich Engels, *Collected Works,* volume 3: *1843–1844* (International Publishers, 1975), pp. 216–17.

25. Ibid., p. 435

26. Ibid., pp. 444, 446, and 447.

27. Ibid., pp. 490–91.

28. Ibid., pp. 491–92.

29. C. Judson Herrick, *The Evolution of Human Nature* (Austin, Texas: University of Texas Press, 1956), p. 147.

30. Ibid.

31. Ibid., p. 142

32. Ibid., pp. 146–47.

33. Jacquetta Hawkes, *The Atlas of Early Man* (New York: St. Martin Press, 1976), pp. 16–23.

34. Ernst Mayr, *Populations, Species and Evolution* (Cambridge, Mass.: Harvard University Press, 1970), 390–409.

35. Rene Dubos, *Beast or Angel* (New York: Scribners, 1974), pp. 137–38.

36. Erich Fromm, *The Sane Society* (New York: Henry Holt, 1955), p. 28.

37. Ibid., pp. 27–66.

38. M. F. Ashley Montagu, *Anthropolgy and Human Nature* (Boston, Massachusetts: Porter Sargent Publ., 1957), pp. 15–16.

39. Fromm, *loco supra citato,* p. 26.

40. John Nance, *The Gentle Tasaday* (New York: Harcourt, Brace, Jovanovich, 1975), pp. 134–39.

41. Fromm, *loco supra citato,* p. 28.

42. Ibid., pp. 27–28.

43. Earl W. Count, "The Biological Basis of Human Sociality," *American Anthropologist,* vol. 60 (1958), pp. 1049–85.

44. Peter Farb, *Humankind* (New York: Houghton Mifflin Co., 1978), pp. 26–33.

45. Ibid., pp. 36–37.

46. Ibid., p. 27.

47. G. C. Gallup, "Self-Awareness: Humans Are Not Alone," *Science News,* vol. 111 (May 28, 1977), p. 340.

48. H. S. Terrace, "How Nim Chimsky Changed My Mind," *Psychology Today,* vol. 13, no. 6 (November 1979), pp. 63–76.

49. H. S. Terrace, L. A. Petitto, R. J. Sanders, and T. G. Bever, "Can An Ape Create a Sentence?" *Science,* vol. 206. no. 4421 (November 23, 1979), pp. 891–902.

50. *Loco supra citato,* ref. 26

51. Jean Piaget, *The Essential Piaget,* edited by H. E. Gruber and J. J. Vonèche (New York: Basic Books, Inc., 1977), part 5: "The Mind of the Baby: From Action to Thought," p. 197–294.

52. Farb, *loco supra citato.*

53. Alice S. Rossi, "A Biosocial Perspective on Parenting," *Daedalus* (Spring 1977), pp. 1–31. Reprinted by permission of *Daedalus,* Journal of the Academy of Arts and Science Spring 1977, Boston.

54. L. A. White, *The Evolution of Culture* (New York: McGraw-Hill Book Co., 1959), p. 67.

55. Robert Redfield, "Relations of Anthropology to Social Science and to the Humanities," *Anthropology Today* (1953), p. 730.

56. Wilson D. Wallis, *Culture and Progress* (New York: McGraw-Hill Book Co., 1930), p. 152.

57. M. F. Ashley Montagu, *Anthropology and Human Nature* (Boston, Massachusetts: Porter, Sargent Publishers, 1957), pp. 10–14.

58. Lawrence K. Frank, *Nature and Human Nature* (New Brunswick, New Jersey: Rutgers University Press, 1951), p. 174.

59. Ibid., p. 165.

60. Rene Dubos, *Beast or Angel* (New York: Charles Scribner and Sons, 1974).

61. Konrad Lorenz, *Studies in Animal and Human Behavior,* vol. 2 (Cambridge, Mass: Connecticut: Harvard University Press, 1971), p. 148.

62. E. O. Wilson, *Sociobiology* (Cambridge, Mass: Harvard University Press, 1975), p. 548.

63. Marvin Harris, *Cultural Materialism* (New York: Vintage Books, 1980).

64. Ibid., 127

65. Ibid., p. 127

66. Ibid., p. 63.

67. A. H. Maslow, *The Farther Reaches of Human Nature* (New York: Viking Press, 1973).

68. Ibid., p. 82.

69. Ibid., p. 158.

70. Ibid., p. 299.

71. Floyd W. Matson, *The Idea of Man* (New York: Delacorte Press, 1976).

72. Ibid., p. 206–207.

73. J. E. Pfeiffer, *The Emergence of Society* New York: McGraw-Hill Book Co., 1977), p. 34.

74. Maurice Levine, *Psychiatry and Ethics* (New York: George Braziller, Inc., 1972), pp. 211–12.

75. Milton M. Gordon, *Human Nature, Class, and Ethnicity* (New York: Oxford University Press, 1978), pp. 30–64.

76. David P. Barash, *Sociobiology in Behavior* (New York: Elsevier North-Holland, Inc., 1977), p. 286.

77. C. J. Lumsden and E. O. Wilson, *Genes, Mind, and Culture* (New Haven, Connecticut: Harvard University Press, 1981), p. 11.

78. E. O. Wilson, *On Human Nature* (New Haven, Connecticut: Harvard University Press, 1978).

79. *Loco supra citato,* p. 355.

80. Lumsden and Wilson, ibid., p. 253.

81. E. O. Wilson, *On Human Nature* (Cambridge, Massachusetts: Harvard University Press, 1978), pp. 217–18.

82. Ibid., p. 196.

83. Theodosius Dobzhansky, *Mankind Evolving* (New Haven, Connecticut: Yale University Press, 1962), p. 338.

84. Lumsden and Wilson, *loco supra citato,* p. 255.

85. Lumsden and Wilson, *loco supra citato,* p. 345.

86. E. T. Hiller, *Social Relations and Structures* (New York: Harper and Brothers, 1947), p. xi.

87. Ibid., pp. 81–82.

88. Lumsden and Wilson, *loco supra citato,* p. 100.

89. Ibid., p. 99

90. Ernst Mayr, *Population, Species, and Evolution* (Cambridge, Massachusetts: Harvard University Press, Belknap Press, 1970), p. 375

91. Lumsden and Wilson, *loco supra citato,* p. 253.

92. George H Mead, *Mind, Self, and Society,* edited by C. W. Morris (Chicago, Illinois: University of Chicago Press, 1934), pp. 228–30.

93. Ibid., p. 229.

94. Ibid., p. 230.

95. Ibid., p. 230.

96. M. B. Smith, *Social Psychology and Human Values* (Aldine Publishers, 1969), p. 2.

97. Ibid., pp. 58–59.

98. Milton M. Gordon, *Human Nature, Class, and Ethnicity* (New York: Oxford University Press, 1978).

99. Charles Horton Cooley, *Human Nature and the Social Order* (New York: Charles Scribner and Sons, 1902), 125–26.

100. M. F. Ashley Montagu, *Anthropology and Human Nature* (Boston, Massachusetts: Porter Sargent, 1957), p. 12.

101. Erich Fromm, *The Sane Society* (New York: Henry Holt, 1955), pp. 30–31.

102. Rene Dubos, *Beast or Angel* (New York: Charles Scribner and Sons, 1974), pp. 46–47.

103. Erik H. Erikson, *Insight and Responsibility* (New York: W. W. Norton, 1964), pp. 142–43.

104. Jane Loevinger, *Ego Development* (San Francisco, California: Jossy-Bass Publishers, 1976), pp. 72–3.

105. Rollo May, *The Courage to Create* (New York: W. W. Norton, and Co., 1975), pp. 17–18.

106. J. M. Lewis et al., *No Single Thread* (New York: Bruner/Mazel, Inc. 1975), pp. 206–207.

107. David P. Barash, *Sociobiology and Behavior* (New York: Elsevier, 1977), p. 310.

108. Konrad Lorenz, *Studies in Animal and Human Behavior,* vol. 2, (Cambridge, Massachusetts: Harvard University Press, 1971), p. 186.

109. John Alcock, *Animal Behavior* (Sunderland, Massachusetts: Sinauer Associates, Inc., 1975), p. 479.

110. Cooley, *supra cite,* p. 48.

111. Ibid., p. 56.

112. Ibid., p. 51.

113. Ibid., p. 56.

114. Fromm, *supra cite,* p. 30.

115. Montagu, *supra cite,* p. 34.

116. Marvin K. Opler, *Culture and Social Psychiatry* (Atherton Press, 1967), p. 7.

117. J. Z. Young, *An Introduction to the Study of Man* (New York: Oxford University Press, 1974), p. 495.

118. Alexander Thomas and Stella Chess, *Development and Evolution of Behavior* (San Francisco, California: W. H. Freeman and Co., 1970), pp. 537–38.

119. A. R. Jenson, *Socialization and Learning,* Vernon L. Allen, ed., *Psychological Factors in Poverty* (Markham Publishing Co., 1970), p. 67.

120. F. W. Matson, *The Idea of Man* (New York: Delacorte Press, 1976), pp. 207–208.

121. Cooley, *supra cite,* p. 139.

122. Fromm, *supra cite,* pp. 60–63.

123. Cooley, *supra cite,* p. 269.

124. Ibid., p. 381.

125. Fromm, *supra cite,* pp. 63–66.

126. Cooley, *supra cite,* p. 326.

127. Ibid., p. 338–39.

128. Ibid., p. 402.

129. Theodosius Dobzhansky, *The Biological Basis of Human Freedom* (New York: Columbia University Press, 1956), p. 134.

130. Richard Dawkins, *The Selfish Gene* (New York: Oxford University Press, 1976), p. 206.

131. Amitai Etzioni, *The Active Society* (London: Collier, MacMillan Ltd, 1968), p. 618. Reprinted with permission of The Free Press, a Division of Macmillan, Inc., from THE ACTIVE SOCIETY by Amitai Etzioni. Copyright © 1968 by The Free Press.

132. Ibid., p. 618–19.

133. Ibid., p. 619.

134. Ibid., p. 624.

135. Ibid., pp. 624–25.

136. Ibid., pp. 625–26.

137. Ibid., pp. 626–27.

138. Marvin Harris, *The Rise of Anthropological Theory* (New York: Thomas Y. Crowell Company, 1968), p. 163.

139. David A. Hamburg, "Frontiers of Research in Neurobiology," *Science,* vol. 222, no. 4627 (December 2, 1983), p. 969.

140. Dorothy T. Krieger, "Brain Peptides: What, Where, and Why?," *Science,* vol. 222, no. 4627 (December 2, 1983), pp. 975–85.

141. *The Nature of Revolution,* hearings before the Committee on Foreign Relations, U.S. Senate, February 19, 21, and 26 and March 7, 1968, Washington, D.C.: U.S. Government Printing Office, 1968).

142. Stella Chess and Alexander Thomas, *Origin and Evolution of Behavior Disorders,* (New York: Bruner/Mazel Publishers, 1984).

143. Ibid, p. 21.

144. Ibid, p. 183.

145. Ibid., pp. 42–43.

4

Freudian Theory on the Nature of Man's Behavior

FREUD, THE PIONEER IN SCIENTIFIC THEORY OF THE SUBJECTIVE

The Freudian contribution to the understanding of human behavior is on a different level than all the other contributions to this subject. Therefore a separate chapter is necessary to elaborate in this area. I have demurred long enough from embarking on this critique of Freud's psychological theories as they relate to the nature of human nature. This hesitancy was in deference of the high esteem that animates my viewing of his epochal contributions to psychology and the behavioral processes. To have opened up the vistas of scientific inquiry into the dynamics of ideas and cognition was in itself a monumental contribution to social science. And then to have elaborated a structure of human behavior in the context of the pattern of biological and neurological processes, to have demonstrated the significance of childhood in behavioral development, to have objectified the idea of sexuality, to have discovered the importance of the unconscious, to have demystified the art of dream interpretation, to have elaborated a logical theory of neurosis, to have initiated a trend to deal scientifically with the subjective, and to have enlisted what knowledge of anthropology that was available in his day to give evolutionary perspective to the nature of human behavior was an eminent triumph in rendering scientific method to psychology.

THE AUTHOR'S INVOLVEMENT

However, my engagement in the analysis of the nature of human nature was sparked not by Freudian postulations, but by dissatisfaction with political economic theory as I found it in my researches as a dilettante in the philosophy of social theory during my medical school days. During those Great Depression days when my mind became boggled with Havelock Ellis, Karl Marx, Friederich Engels, John Dewey, G. Bernard Shaw, Geothe, Franz Boas, Jacque Loeb, Bertrand Russell, George Santayana, Romain Rolland and a host of others, everything was in a state of flux, and economic hardship for a large section of the ordinary folk did not encourage satisfaction with the way things were. The field of public health, which seemed to me to engulf philosophically the knowledge of the humanities and the sciences, was the field of choice for one whose mind revolted against containment in one constricted field. Medicine appeared to me as the proper way to begin such a career. My original dissertation in this area was on the sociological basis of health and longevity. The structure of its basis was of population development based on economic class division, nutrition, and all the lack of benefits resulting from economic and social deprivation. The application of these principles gradually revealed their *limitations* in explaining the dynamics of the cognitive processes involved in alienation, particularly as defined by Hegel and Marx, and in effecting the psychosocial responses of human behavior.

It was Erich Fromm's *Sane Society* that, in the midfifties, triggered my concepts in the direction of specific structure of human nature. Fromm convincingly demonstrated to me by logical analysis that: "The most powerful force motivating man's behavior [rather than the libido] stem from the conditions of his existence, the 'human situation'. Man cannot live statically because his inner contradictions drive him to seek for an equilibrium, for a new [human] harmony instead of the lost animal harmony with nature."[1] Freud attributed man's inner contradictions to the nature of the libido. Although this is valid up to a point, there are other powerful forces involved. Freud expressed this countervalence with a less appropriate set of contradictions. "After long doubts and vacillations we have decided to assume the existence of only two basic instincts, Eros [libido] and the destructive instinct."[2] *Homo*'s particular conditions of existence emerged when he found himself to be an active contender with the forces of nature, i.e., when he began to become *human*. This probably began sometime in the period of his *Homo erectus* existence or maybe even during his status as *Homo habilis*. As Freud correctly indicated, the lessons of social anthropology must be learned in order to perceive the structural nature of human nature. As Fromm posited, the nature of man is biphasic. This implies that *Homo* as a *human* species has the human behavioral traits and as a member of the order Primates has also inherited the primate traits.

It became *necessary* for man, finding himself in a new, bewildering ecological circumstance, to seek to assuage this confusion. This required him to conceive those new circumstances in an intelligently unified frame of reference, to perceive the structure of man's behavior as subject to self-control—behavior that arises from his *human* potential as distinguished from that which arises from his primate instinctual heritage. We today differentiate that behavior originating in the physiological processes from that resulting from psychosocial processes, and we dissect each phase of this duality of man's behavior into its specific human traits, on the one hand, and its specific nonhuman primate traits, on the other hand. In the process of doing this, we find that modern knowledge in ethology, sociobiology, and anthropology has led to the entertainment of new interpretative patterns of man's nature that are not in consonance with some of Freud's basic theory.

LIMITATIONS OF FREUDIAN SOCIOLOGICAL THEORY

Freud's theories give cognitive processes and ideas an important place in the psychology and behavior of people, but, for the most part, not as initiating factors in the development of psychopathology and behavioral disorientation. The causal agents of the latter he attributed to the instincts and accompanying emotions, with particular emphasis on the sexual instinct, the libido, which he opportunely defined in much broader terms than common usage gives it.

Freudian theory is directed toward the mental and emotional disorientation of the individual. Psychoanalysis is individual-pathology oriented for the most part. Although Freud built elaborate interpretative patterns of historical events based on speculative assumptions, he applied the methodology for individual cases while attributing a phylogenetically inherited folk conscience to groups of people, then, as with neurosis, treating the group as an individual. Example: "[T]here probably exists in the mental life of the individual not only what he has experienced himself, but also what he brought with him at birth, fragments of phylogenetic origin, an archaic heritage. . . . [T]here is the universality of speech symbolism [that] . . . we cannot trace the way in which they [the children] learned it. . . . It is original knowledge which the adult later on forgets. . . . This then would be a case of inheriting a thought-disposition as elsewhere one inherits an instinctual disposition. . . ."[3]

Freud explained religion on the basis that it originated "in the Oedipus complex, the relation to the father. . . . If on the one hand religion brings with it obsessional limitations which can only be compared to an individual obsessional neurosis, it comprises on the other hand a system of wish-illusions, incompatible with reality."[4] According to the thesis of the present study, religion originated out of the need to seek peace of mind—the need to experience a sense of commitment and responsibility to and engagement in a unifying frame of behavioral orientation—a teleological intent of acting together so that order, predictive expectancy, direction, and purpose be felt in the process of social interrelations to satisfy the social conscience, the sense of not being alone in one's beliefs and in having others as supportive of one's position. In sophisticated phraseology, it means the need for having a philosophy of life to live by and one shared by others in one's social interrelations. This philosophy of life based, for the most part, on the ten commandments has, to a large extent, been embodied in the laws of nations and the ethics and morality of social and professional organizations worldwide. This need for a unifying outlook for behavioral orientation is a trait of human nature. In cases where a person satisfies this need to the extreme with religious rigidity and develops an obsessional neurosis, the problem rebounds to the individual, whereas when a person satisfies this trait as a community need, the problem becomes social. Although religion has been satisfying this trait of human nature since time immemorial, other socially but nonreligious unifying institutions could serve as well. Thereby an individual with a highly developed, socially intelligent outlook on life could satisfy his individual need for a unifying orientation in approaching life. Although Freud, like Marx, denigrated religion, he admitted that "the true believer is in a high degree protected against the danger of certain neurotic afflictions; by accepting the universal neurosis he is spared the task of forming a personal neurosis."[5]

In discussing primitive society as speculated by Darwin, Freud stated: "I attempted to show that the fortunes of this horde have left indestructible traces upon the history of human descent, and especially, that the development of totemism, which comprises in itself the beginnings of religion, morality, and social organization, is connected with the killing of the chief [of the horde by] violence and the transformation of the paternal horde into a community of brothers."[6] He also attributed exogamy to the taboo of incest: "With this [the killing of the father and the reconciliation of the brothers] the taboo of incest and the law of exogamy came into being."[7] This psychoanalytic interpretation places the cart before the horse. Beginning with the dean of American anthropology, Franz Boas, a significant portion of anthropologists strongly disagreed with Freud's interpretation of the meaning of totemism. However, some eminent anthropologists such as Ruth Benedict, Gésa Roheim, and Margaret Mead applied psychoanalytic method to their theses for describing the national character of peoples from their cultural history.[8] Harris, in his comprehensive survey of the history of theories of culture, asserted that "Psychoanalysis . . . had little to offer cultural anthropology by way of scientific methodology. In this respect the meeting of the two disciplines tended to reinforce the inherent tendencies toward uncontrolled, speculative, and histrionic generalization which each in its own sphere had cultivated as part of its professional license."[9] Religion is a human phenomenon. To be human means to behave in accordance with the psychosocial norms that distinguish the *Homo* primate from the non-*Homo* primate. Freud attributed totemism to all primitive human societies, thereby attributing to this primitive practice characteristics beyond its due. Kroeber's extensive study of totemism around the time that Freud wrote *Totem and Taboo* leads to the conclusion that there is no evidence that totemism was universal among primitive people. "[B]oth in eastern and western hemispheres the most primitive and backward tribes are, with fair regularity, sibless* and non-totemic."[10] "Wherever social exogamy appears among larger group of nations, social totemism also crops out, and vice versa. . . Exogamy and totemism, then, are theoretically separate factors. Yet . . . it is remarkable that in probably seven or eight tenths of all cases they coincide."[11] "Sibs are social facts, totems a naming device with magico-religious implications."[12] From these observations by Kroeber, it is evident that totemism did not antedate primitive social organization and therefore was not the "beginning of religion, morality, and social organization." In Harris's review of the origin of the incest taboo, he amply discussed the history of exogamy and totemism.[13] In assessing the theories of the most eminent contributors to this subject, Freud's contribution of the primordial significance of totemism as the primal force in the origin of religion, morality, and social organization and exogamy as resulting from incest taboo is not supported with any weight of evidence.

Freud identified the dynamics of individual psychology with that of mass psychology by the process of *analogy*. Thus he related the genesis of obsessional neurosis as an ethnological disturbance of the Jewish people, being due to the special dynamics in the origin of the Jewish religion, which, he stated, were practically identical to the dynamics of the etiology of individual neurosis: "It [the history of the Jewish religion] is very complete [in its genesis of obsessional neurosis

---

*A sib is a group, such as a clan, whose individuals are blood-related.

in the Jewish personality], approximating to identity [with the genesis of individual neurosis]. . . . This *analogy* [emphasis added] is met with in psychopathology, in the genesis of human neurosis, that is to say, in a discipline belonging to individual psychology, whereas religious phenomena must of course be regarded as a part of mass psychology. We shall see that this analogy is not so startling as it appears at first sight; indeed it is rather in the nature of an axiom."[14] Further he stated: "If we accept the continued existence of such *memory traces* [emphasis added] in our archaic inheritance, then we have bridged the gap between individual and mass psychology and can treat peoples as we do the individual neurotic."[15]

It is logical to assume and evidence exists to affirm the interdependence of individual and mass psychologies. This must follow from the fact that both deal with all human behavior. Just as changes in the cumulation or diminution in quantity of substance results in qualitative changes in the substance, so mass psychology must have basic differences from individual psychology. Freud was well aware of this:

> It might be said that the intense emotional ties which we observe in groups are quite sufficient to explain one of their characteristics—the lack of independence and initiative in their members, the similarity in the reactions of all of them, their reduction, so to speak, to the level of group individuals. But if we look at it as a whole, *a group shows us more than this.* [italics added] Some of its features—the weakness of intellectual ability, the lack of emotional restraint, the incapacity for moderation and delay, the inclination to exceed every limit in the expression of emotion and to work it off completely in the form of action—these and similar features, which we find so impressively described in LeBon, show an unmistakable picture of a regression of mental activity to an earlier stage such as we are not surprised to find among savages or children. A regression of this sort is in particular an essential characteristic of common groups, as we have heard, in organized and artificial groups it can to a large extent be checked.[16]

Freud quoted LeBon* in discussing the transformation of individuals into a group: " . . .the fact that they [individuals] have been transformed into a group puts them in possession of a sort of *collective mind* [italics added] which makes them feel, think, and act in a manner quite

---

*Freud praised LeBon's work as "deservedly famous work *Psychologie des foules* (1895)," from which he quoted amply.

different from that in which each individual of them would feel, think, and act were he in a state of isolation. "[17]

The "collective mind" of LeBon is certainly not the same as Freud's "memory traces in our archaic inheritance." The former is *not* an assumption but a reality. The latter is a speculative assumption for which no experimental grounds exist. Thus Freud's identification of the dynamics of individual psychology with mass psychology by a process of *analogy* in comparing the psychopathological processes of mass obsessional neurosis with individual neurosis stretches scientific theory rather tautly.

Freud also attributed the origin of both religion and totemism to the Oedipus complex. Thus the Oedipus complex and totemism both become the foundation from which religion stems. Now, if totemism is itself a feature and not *the* feature of primitive social organization, how could it have antedated social organization in order to be its origin? Then again, was a reasonable relationship between father-mother-siblings well enough understood in the primal stage of human society of hundreds of thousands of years ago when the *Homo* horde was beginning to develop human social relations to attribute the Oedipus complex to it? It is far more reasonable to attribute human social organization, as Sahlins did, to the need for *Homo* to overcome the nonhuman violence associated with primate sexuality in order to establish the cooperative norms for human social relations required for the existence and maintenance of a human societal way of life. This, Sahlins considered the first great revolution of human society.[18] Concerning this sexuality battle, Sahlins recognized the profundity of Freud's observations in this area: "In Sigmund Freud's famous *allegory* [italics added[, the conflict between the self-seeking, sexually inclined id and the socially conscious super-ego re-enact the development of culture that occurred in the remote past."[19] It was, therefore, the sexually aggressive non-human primate violence and the necessity for developing inhibitions or at least effecting some control of this instinctual aggressiveness in order to satisfy the *human* need to establish human societal interrelationships that resulted in the coming into being of human social organization, morality and ethical norms, and religion.

LIMITATIONS OF FREUDIAN INSTINCT THEORY

A significant limitation of Freudian theory is its restriction, for the most part, to the effects of the excitation of the instincts and emotions on the mental apparatus to the exclusion, to a large extent, of the effects of the psychosocial processes such as the traits of human nature on mental behavior as posited in this study. Nowhere does Freud define "human nature," although he uses the term occasionally. For example in discussing the response of human beings whose "virtue is not rewarded here on earth," he stated that "the recognition of this fact among socialists has been obscured and made useless for practical purposes by a fresh idealistic misconception of human nature."[20] This observation Freud made in criticism of the doctrine that "the communists believe that they have found the path to deliverance from our evils. According to them, man is wholly good and is well-disposed to his neighbor; but the institution of private property has corrupted his nature. If private property were abolished . . . ill-will and hostility would disappear among men."[21] In refuting this doctrine, Freud asserted: "Aggressiveness was not created by property. It reigned almost without limit in primitive times, when property was still very scanty. . . . It is clearly not easy for men to give up the satisfaction of this inclination to aggression."[22] Freud's correctness in exposing the futile idealism of the above cited doctrine that the elimination of private property will solve the disadvantages of man's primate nature inherent in his instincts is affirmed by this present thesis of the biphasic nature of man's behavior. However erudite and wise Freud's thesis on this aspect of human nature is, his pessimism about man's ability to nurture the human traits of his nature restricts the comprehensiveness of his methodology, particularly in the area of primary prevention of behavioral disorientations in community life—a basic aspect of public health.

Practically all of the psychosocial traits of human nature depicted in the present study as composing the *human* aspects of man's nature are alluded to and even amply discussed by Freud in his various writings. But they are practically always noted as effects rather than basic qualities or as accessory behavioral factors to more fundamental instinctual behavioral processes rather than the *human* nature of *Homo*. They are *not* of essence—not initiators in his estimation. They are *responses* to fundamentals. For example, the need for a unifying orientation, a moral-ethical code, is not a *basic human* trait according to him, but a means to restrict instinctual gratification.[23] Freud only occasionally distinguished the human from the animal, but usually the instinctual are treated as human essence. The fact is that the instinctual traits are primary to the psychosocial traits *only* phylogenetically. But once the primate *Homo* emerged on the scene, the instinctual and psychosocial traits became fundamental interpenetrating, contradictory forces on the same level in man's nature. And since man *needed*, perforce, to become *human*, the drive to achieve human trait predominance over nonhuman primate instincts became the most basic concern of human social life, as demonstrated in the ubiquitous laws, rules, and regulations and moral and ethical norms prevalent in all phases of life. Although a physician, Freud was basically a biologist. He dealt with the instincts so effectively because they are rooted in the physiological nature of man. Thus the instincts became the foundation of his appraisal of human behavior. The traits of human nature as here presented are purely psychosocial phenomena. They are ideational, not physiological. They have no counterpart physiologically except the energy of cognition and the emotional and other physiological energy required to act out the traits. Freud understood this but did very little about it, because he felt discouraged "at the feeble mentality of man"[24] when he is confronted by the impulsive strength of his instincts. Yet Freud counseled that "we have no other means of controlling our instincts than our intelligence. And how can we expect people who are dominated by thought prohibitions to attain the psychological ideal, the primacy of the intelligence?"[25] Freud had no confidence that *human* intelligence and intellect could favorably contend with the *primate* instincts. The present study contests this view offering Freud's *same* contentious history of mankind as evidence to the contrary. This evidence maintains that the traits of human nature reflect the psychosocial response of *Homo sapiens* to the human conditions of living in order to support and develop a human way of existence. Human history is evidence of this. Concentrating on the instincts emphasizes only the nonhuman primate behavior of *Homo* while at the same time, deemphasizing the nature of the human traits of behavior. This was recognized several decades ago and was described as follows by Ralph Linton: "Unfortunately, the earlier psychoanalysts carried on their investigations entirely within the frame of European culture and largely within that of a single class in European society. Lacking comparative materials, they took many environmental factors for granted and built up an elaborate theory of universal human instincts. The various attempts which were made by Freud and others to apply this instinctual approach to the explanation of cultural phenomena and even to reconstruction of cultural history struck the average anthropologst as fantastic and led him to minimize the very real contributions which psychoanalytic techniques might make to the solution of many of his own problems."[26] Kardiner *et al.*, who were adherents to psychoanalysis, state further: "The only psychology that can approach these [all psychological] problems with any hope of success is psychoanalysis. To render this psychology useful some modification in operational concepts must be made; but the clinical observations which Freud originally described have not been amended."[27]

120

The problem with using the Freudian theory sociologically for primary prevention against behavioral disorientation is that it deals predominantly with only half of the behavioral content of *Homo*—the *primate instinctual* traits as distinguished from the *human psychosocial* traits.

A program of primary prevention in behavioral disorientation based on the Freudian instinct-dominance approach has actually been in the process of development since time immemorial, although its proponents were unaware of the Freudian theory. It is based on the externally applied forces for inducing *inhibitions* in people that have been crystallized into the legal structure of the governments of the world, in the police and military organizations so prevalent in the political jurisdictions of the world, in the morality taught by the religions operating worldwide, and in the "don'ts" so abundant in the socialization processes practiced by family rearing of children and public educational systems. This method has been successful enough to have gotten the world to its present civilized state from its old stone age existence. No more brilliant effort to illustrate the battle between *Homo*'s nonhuman primate instincts and his human intelligence-intellect has been produced than *The Federalist Papers*. No country in the world has accommodated its governmental apparatus to consciously concentrate its efforts on the *human* aspects of humankind's behavior. Countries utilize mostly the "don'ts" instead of embarking on research methodologies of community and personal interrelationships for emphasizing the positive. We need to know, for a starter, the most effective methods for socializing children to become adults who have been conditioned to utilize the intelligence-intellect potential to effectively predominate over their instincts in the course of daily living. Much research pointed to this problem will be required and must be initiated. The Western world, particularly the United States, is lapsing into an irrational rendering of democracy that verges on a chaotic tendency toward unrestricted permissiveness as the solution to our behavioral problems. This method is further tilting the balance toward the predominance of the instinctual nature of man.

It would be negligent to leave the impression that nothing is being done in this area. But much that is being done is based on the misleading premise that unrestricted permissiveness allows for the best development of native talents—thus the cliché "doing one's thing." The permissiveness is being synergized by the increasing social sensitivity toward humaneness, producing the maudlin protestations for the dole system of welfare instead of a job system for those who need to work. Another area where social guidance for good is deflected to the opposite is the religious teachings of brotherhood where the religious leadership involves itself in destructive political partisanship, in the community educational processes where bigotry and bias are *supposed* to be negated, and the economic, recreational, and mass media areas of making a living where unrestricted competitive operations corrupt these very sensitive social instruments of popular usage and produce socially undesirable behavioral effects on community life. Then many of the above instruments are allowed to function on instinctual methods of operation.

Freud's final classification of the instincts of man was a system composed of those instincts that build up and preserve the homeostasis of the person designated as Eros and those that break down that equilibrium designated as Thanatos. This duality of forces is referred to by Freud as the life and death contradiction.[28,29] The instincts as outlined in Fletcher's study, *Instinct in Man*,[30] are much more elaborate than Freud's but no more comprehensive than what Freud intended in his duality of instinctual forces. Freud, however, gave special emphasis to the instinct of sexuality, which was extended widely to include a vast number of protective impulses. We must recognize that some of the most important instincts of the human being are of the emotional type. Certainly the ones Freud emphasized are emotion-laden, and that is probably one of the reasons that he found them so difficut to deal with by a methodology that would appeal to the intelligence of people. The more recent development in psychotherapeutic theory, however, which is mainly based on the *cognitive* processes rather than instinctual in solving emotional disorders, indicates the credibility of enlisting the dynamics of intelligence-intellect to solve problems. This is so because cognition, emotion, and behavior are separate and independent entities, because people are chronic thinkers and thinking evokes emotions, because they think about their thinking, because they think rationally and can therefore make themselves disturbed, and therefore it becomes possible to redirect disturbed thinkers into rational ways of thinking.[31] On this basis, an understanding of the dynamics of the traits of human nature in relation to the human ecology becomes a must for the development of societal structure and operations.

Freud's pessimism about the future of mankind is expressed in the opening sentence of his book *Civilization and Its Discontents:* "The impression forces itself upon one that men measure by false standards, that everyone seeks power, success, riches for himself and admires others who attain them, while undervaluing the truly precious things in life."[32] And, to support his pessimism further, he states that this work "faithfully corresponds to my intention to represent the sense of guilt as the most important problem in the evolution of culture, and to convey that the price of progress in civilization is paid in forfeiting happiness through the heightening of the sense of guilt."[33] Then he quotes from the desperate, despondent Hamlet's soliloquy: "Thus conscience does make cowards of us all. . . . " Since the above work was first published in 1930, during the period of the threatening rise to power of Hitler, one can scarcely expect this threat not to have constricted the panoramic sweep of world history even in the mind of a genius like Freud.

FREUDIAN INSTINCT THEORY VERSUS HUMAN INTELLIGENCE-INTELLECT THEORY

Although the instincts are the foundation of Freud's dealings with human behavior, he nevertheless touches on the psychosocial traits of behavior here and there in a way that attributes such behavior to the biophysiological foundation of the instincts. This is indeed inadequate. The truth of the matter is that all human behavior, instinctual and noninstinctual, has an ultimate biophysiological background. However, the psychsocial traits are purely mental in their immediate manifestation. For example, the bonding-sharing trait of human nature has a phylogenetic background so far as the bonding aspect is concerned and even so far as the sharing aspect is somehow related to the feeding relation between mother and offspring. Phylogenetically, this trait probably has its origin, as Freud claimed, in the libido, holding to his inclusive biosocial definition. But when developed as a psychosocial entity of *human* behavior, it is more than biosocial—for instance, when applied to political economy. Freud's expression of this trait is: "The same thing [formation of ties] occurs in man's social relations as has become familiar to Psychoanalytic research in the course of the development of the individual libido. The libido props itself upon the satisfaction of the great vital needs and chooses as its first object the people who have a share in that process. And in the development of mankind, love alone acts as the civilizing factor in the sense that it brings a change from egoism to altruism."[34] The fact is that the bonding-sharing trait, perforce, had to be a characteristic of *Homo's* nature in the process of humanization for him to contend in a *human* way with the basic conditions under which he *had* to act and continue to act in order to maintain and better his existence.

The trait of striving to satisfy appetites, inclinations, and talents that Leighton developed so well is expressed by Freud as follows: "The repressed instinct never ceases to strive for complete satisfaction. . . .

No substitutive or reactive formations and no sublimations will suffice to remove the repressed instinct's persisting tension; and it is the difference in the amount between the gratificatory pleasure which is demanded and that which is actually achieved that provides the driving factor which will permit of no halting at any established position. . . . "[35] Where the teleological psychosocial aspect of striving differs from Freud's is that his trait is no more or less than the nonteleological drives of other animals. In discussing this matter, he stated: "The present development of human beings requires, as it seems to me, no different explanation from that of animals. What appears in a minority of human individuals as an untiring impulsion toward further perfection can easily be understood as a result of the instinctual repression upon which is based all that is most precious in human civilization."[36] Here Freud does not discriminate between the striving trait and that of creativity, which cannot be other than teleological.

In relation to the trait that responds to the human need for orderly, peaceful, and productive relations and that has already been discussed as the unifying orientation trait, Freud attributed its origin to man's need to overcome the "constitutional tendency in men to aggressions against one another." This is in line with anthropological knowledge that aggression is a primate instinct that is a biological heritage in *Homo*. But for Freud something like the unifying orientation trait was attributed to the superego. This functional division of the psyche is the conscious-unconscious cybernetician of human behavior. It may have intelligence and it may not. Can the heir of the Oedipus complex have much intelligence, much less intellect? The term "cybernetician" is therefore too generous a rubric for function resulting from frustration and resorting to primitive methods of defense. Freud described this situation as follows:

The cultural super-ego has elaborated its ideal and erected its standards. Those of its demands which deal with the relations of human beings to one another are comprised under the name of ethics. The greatest value has at all times been set upon systems of ethics, as if men had expected them in particular to achieve something especially important. And ethics does in fact deal predominantly with the point which is easily seen to be the sorest of all in any scheme of civilization. Ethics must be regarded therefore as a therapeutic effort: as an endeavor to achieve something through the standards imposed by the super-ego which had not been attained by the work of civilization in any other way. We already know . . . that the question is how to dislodge the greatest obstacle to civilization, the constitutional tendency in men to aggression against one another. . . . [37]

Freud had no confidence that this trait can be successful because the superego "troubles little about the happiness of the ego, and it fails to take into account sufficiently the difficulties in the way of obeying it—the strength of instinctual craving in the id and the hardships of the external environment. . . . Even in so-called normal people the power of controlling the id cannot be increased beyond certain limits."[38] This estimation of the origin of the ethics as due to the need to control the primate behavior characteristic of aggression is certainly correct, but the pessimism of its effectiveness due to the eternal dominance of instincts over the traits of human nature and the cognitive processes finds no evidence in the history of mankind. The tremendous creations of human culture are evidence of its predominance over man's destructiveness resulting from aggression. The battle, of course, is eternal.

SUMMARY

The Freudian system of human behavior has its roots mainly in the primate instincts as modified by the human brain potential, which are lodged in the id and are continually seeking immediate gratification. Accordingly, the theory states that human society has been developing as the result of the struggle of the superego to control the id-ensconced instincts that continue unendingly to disrupt the well-being of the individual and society. The present study, contrary to the Freudian theory, concentrates not on the nonhuman primate behavioral characteristics of man, but on the *human* traits of man's nature based on the intelligence-intellectual potential of the human brain rather than on the instinctual nature of mankind. This human nature emerged long after the instincts that are a heritage from *Homo*'s primate ancestors. The human nature originated from the ability of *Homo*'s brain potential to respond humanly to the survival exigencies presented by the nature of the human conditions and the need for man to better his lot. Even though Freud had little confidence that the intelligence and intellect of man could tip the scale over the instincts in the development of society, the evidence is clear that these brain potentials have been responsible for creating the imposing culture that fascinates even the genius of mankind. In fact, in the great volume of writings Freud produced, he showed moods of optimism. He admitted that giving vent to the gratification of the instincts could be controlled by "instinctual renunciation." Instinctual renunciation, he further asserted, is possible if a father authority be imposed[39] to wield the power of punishment, such as family or government. In the extreme, dictatorship may serve as such father authority. This *negative* method is the only way to control the instinctual nature if the cognitive power of the brain be faintly employed. In psychoanalysis, the subject is guided to recall from the unconscious the cause of his or her trauma hoping that by becoming conscious of what caused the trauma then he can dissipate it. The present study brings to light the specific psychosocial traits of human nature that lend themselves to management by the cognitive processes and to the health ecology dynamics involved in social interrelationships. Thus the traits of human nature when in harmony with the dynamics of the social interrelations created by the nature of the social ecology tend to prevent behavioral disorientations. Thereby a *positive* approach to the prevention of behavioral disorientation becomes possible.

It is in the behavioral area of "striving" that Freud's psychological theory based on instincts adjoins the psychosocial theory of human nature of this present study. It is also at this point where cognitive processes are brought into play to control the expression of the instincts and, at the same time, to apply the human considerations as to how far appetites should be satisfied. It is here also where the striving in the pursuit of one's inclinations is in harmony with being human and pursues the development of one's talents to be of human value to the individual and to society.

NOTES

1. Erich Fromm, *The Sane Society* (New York: Henry Holt, Inc., 1955), p. 28.

2. Sigmund Freud, *Dictionary of Psychoanalysis* (New York: Philosophical Library, 1950), p. 100.

3. S. Freud, *Moses and Monotheism* (New York: Alfred A. Knopf, 1939), pp. 154–56.

4. S. Freud, *The Future of an Illusion* (New York: Liveright Publishing Corporation, 1949), p. 76.

5. Ibid., p. 77.

6. S. Freud, *Group Psychology and the Analysis of the Ego* (Honolulu, Hawaii: Hogarth Press, 1948), p. 90.

7. Sigmund Freud, *Moses and Monotheism* (New York: Alfred A. Knopf, 1939), p. 129.

8. Marvin Harris, *The Rise of Anthropological Theory* (New York: Thomas Y. Crowell Co., 1968), pp. 426–448.

9. Ibid., p. 488.

10. A. L. Kroeber, *Anthropology* (New York: Harcourt, Brace and Co., 1923), p. 233.

11. Ibid., p. 237.

12. Ibid., p. 236.

13. Marvin Harris, *The Rise of Anthropological Theory* (New York: Thomas Y. Crowell Co., 1968), pp. 196–199, 346, 425, 478.

14. Sigmund Freud, *Moses and Monotheism* (New York: Alfred A. Knopf, 1938), pp. 113–114.

15. Ibid., p. 158.

16. Sigmund Freud, *Group Psychology and the Analysis of the Ego* (Honolulu, Hawaii: Hogarth Press, 1948), pp. 81–82.

17. Ibid. p. 7.

18. Marshall D. Sahlins,"The Origin of Society," *Scientific American,* vol. 203, no. 3, (September 1960), pp. 88–96.

19. Ibid.

20. S. Freud, *Civilization and Its Discontents* (Honolulu, Hawaii: Hogarth Press, 1946) pp. 140–142.

21. Sigmund Freud, *Civilization and Its Discontents* (New York: W. W. Norton, 1961), pp. 59–60.

22. Ibid., pp. 60–61.

23. Sigmund Freud, *Moses and Monotheism* (New York: Alfred A. Knopf, 1939), p. 187.

24. S. Freud, *loco supra citato,* pp. 82–83.

25. Ibid., p. 83.

26. Abram Kardiner and Associates, *The Psychological Frontiers of Society* (New York: Columbia University Press, 1945), pp. vi–vii.

27. Ibid., p. 22.

28. S. Freud, *Beyond the Pleasure Principle* (New York: Liveright Publishing Corp., 1950), p. 84.

29. S. Freud, *The Ego and the Id* (Honolulu, Hawaii: Hogarth Press, 1942), pp. 54–67.

30. R. Fletcher, *Instinct in Man* (New York: International Universities Press, 1957) pp. 309–315.

31. Russell and Ingrid Z. Grieger, *Cognition and Emotional Disturbance* (Human Sciences Press, Inc., 1982) pp. 12–14.

32. Freud, *loco supra citato,* p. 7.

33. Ibid., p. 123.

34. Sigmund Freud, *Group Psychology and the Analysis of the Ego* (Honolulu, Hawaii: Hogarth Press, 1948) p. 57.

35. S. Freud, *Beyond the Pleasure Principle* (New York: Liveright Publishing Co., 1950), p. 56.

36. Ibid., p. 56.

37. S. Freud, *Civilization and Its Discontents* (Honolulu, Hawaii: Hogarth Press, 1946), p. 138.

38. Ibid., p. 139.

39. Sigmund Freud, *Moses and Monotheism* (New York: Alfred A. Knopf, 1939), p. 189.

5

The Phylogenetic Characteristics of the Family and the Bonding-Sharing-Exchange Trait in Human Nature

COMMUNITY ORGANIZATION

Community organization of any species of animal life depends on how the species reproduces and the ability of its members to survive long enough to reproduce. *Aggregation* is the community organization of unicellular animals in which organization is almost absent, although the slime mold amoeba *Dictyostelium* displays the most advanced colonial behavior of single-celled organisms.[1] There is practically no group protection exerted to foster the survival of the individuals long enough for them to reproduce. However, to compensate for this lack, the reproduction period is very short and the method of reproduction is very simple—asexual binary fission and budding. As simple as this is, the biochemistry and the DNA mitotic division are already established as the basic complexity of every living system. What basic interrelations exist between the individual members of a group of amoebae in a drop of water? Apparently practically none, although, as Wilson points out, what is apparent is not necessarily factual, for there is a definite intercommunication system operating in the aggregation process of the slime mold amoebae.[2] Therefore the biogram, i.e., the way of life of amoebae, is of the greatest simplicity to the eye, although one amoeba may relate to another by emitting AMP (a biochemical intracelluluar messenger in all organisms) pulses at fractions of a minute intervals—a stimulus-response mechanism that organizes the relationships in the aggregation.

Microscopic unicellular animals that reproduce sexually by conjugation and fission, such as the paramecium, are less group-oriented than the slime amoeba, but also have a pheromone intercommunication system to effect conjugation in the reproduction process.

Multicellular animals demonstrate group action for group self-protection in a much more manifest manner than unicellular organisms. The protective maneuvers of the higher organisms are more protracted, complex, and effective and thereby compensate for the shorter reproduction intervals of the unicellular animals. In fact, so uncomplicated and rapid is the fission method of reproduction that it can be said that the unicellular organisms never die. For certain types of metazoa, "a potential bonus of living in groups is the enhancement of repellent powers. If a predator were more likely to be turned away by the defense systems presented by two individuals side by side than by that of a single individual, then (all other things being equal) aggregation will be favored in evolution.[3] This principle is indeed valid through the animal kingdom. For the large, powerful animals, the aggregate may get as small as a parent and its offspring. Although there could be no animal world without there first being a plant world, nevertheless, the animal world is prevalently composed of prey and predator—one animal being the food of another animal. One of the basic mechanisms for survival in the natural world is the *aggregation* of conspecific organisms that, in the evolutionary scale, develop increasingly intercommunicating cooperative relations of higher and higher levels of organization designated as a *society*. Axelrod and Hamilton in much more detail explore the evolution of the dynamics of the process of cooperation by probability statistics and establish the "conditions under which cooperation based on reciprocity can evolve."[4] There is still some contention whether the words *social* and *society* should be used in reference to animal life. The very essence of this natural process is manifested as the unavoidable propinquity and association between organisms resulting from the inevitable interrelations created by their pristine behavioral activities in reproducing and struggling to survive. In the human, this interrelationship is manifested by self-realization in relation to the group and the need for struggling to better the human condition. Such circumstances activate the origin of the traits of human nature of which the "bonding" trait, modified by the distinctive feature of "sharing" that is associated with "exchange", is the cornerstone. To what extent such behavior is genetic or learned remains a moot question, although both are involved except for the purely human "exchange" aspect. Certainly, for the human being, who has a highly developed neopallium, a versatile pair of hands and arms, bipedal locomotion, fertile imagination with its symbol-bearing capacity, a unique speech apparatus, a prodigious memory, an intellectual capacity of foresight and planning and the ability to use these in the responsibility for survival of the altricial children, dexterity of manipulation and the freedom to do so by the upright stance, there is plenty of reason to believe that the bonding-sharing trait is as much a matter of responding intelligently to a pattern of ecosystem circumstances as to expect that such behavior is elicited from genetic responses. One must expect, however, that given the above behavior potential over tens of thousands of years, genetics must have played its part in the development of man's pattern of behavior. Lancaster gives a good example of this in discussing bipedalism, which began in our ancestors 5 to 15 million years ago, long before man developed a large brain and had a language and before he learned to manipulate the environment to suit his own needs. This "two-legged gait slowly changed prehuman life. It freed both hands, enabling our forebears to develop complex tools; it led them into dangerous places, forcing them to use their wits to survive and resulting in an enlarged brain; it remodeled the pelvis so that future generations were born exceedingly immature, leading to a highly dependent relationship between mother and child. . . . The adaptive value of bipedalism lay in the social behavior that it facilitated; sharing and carrying things in order to share and exchange them. Collaboration has always characterized our species and bipedalism expanded the area of human collaboration."[5] It is clear that bipedalism is both genetic and phenotypic and gives a tremendous potential for augmenting the bonding-sharing-exchange trait.

PHYLOGENETIC MEANING OF "SOCIAL"

Let us not make the mistake of attributing a sameness beween the social relations of human beings and the "social" relations or interrelations inherent in aggregation or the community relations of other animals, even though the propinquity and associations between all organisms are a necessary result of the natural process of reproduction and struggle to survive. The quality of the interrelationships between human beings is utterly and completely different from the interrelationships between the individuals of any other species.[6] One wonders whether the term "social" should be used to describe even the interrelations that pervade a troop of animals in so high a stage of evolution as the pongids. This question is valid, recognizing the fact that in such animal behavior the automatic reflective nature of response is so predominant while the sharing quality is so insignificant or absent except between mother and offspring, thus rendering this "social" element in the behavior of nonhuman primates so rudimentary in comparison that the use of the term is, indeed, questionable. This should not be taken to mean that much of human reactive behavior is not automatic, i.e., habitual, and, in the context of Freudian theory, instinctual. Much of habitual behavior is conditioned by many previous responses to similar circumstances or factors in which a certain amount of deliberation and conscious choice took place. Yet Wilson certainly has a point in declaring: "The terms *society* and *social* need to be defined broadly in order to prevent the exclusion of many interesting phenomena. Such exclusion would cause confusion in all further *comparative* discussions. . . . The definition of a society as a cooperating group of conspecific organisms is about the same as that used by writers as early as Alverdes (1927), Alles (1931), and Darling (1938). There has, nevertheless, been some ambiguity about . . . the level of organization at which we cease to refer to a group as a society and start labeling it as an aggregation or nonsocial population."[7] Then he defines *aggregation* as "a group of individuals of the same species, comprised of more than just a mated pair or family gathered in the same place but not internally organized in cooperative behavior."[8]

THE UNIQUENESS OF MAN?

Wilson places greater emphasis on relatedness, similarity, and sameness of the behavior between "social" animals and man that do not appear to be warranted on the basis of present knowledge. He attributes this interrelation to genetic factors, and there may well be genetic factors involved. If evolution is a valid principle, there must be some type of a genetic continuum in the stream of evolving organisms, and indeed there is a genetic continuum in the basic pattern of cellular organization and the process of mitosis and meiosis in reproduction and growth, and there is an environmental continuum that involves the organisms in a struggle to survive. To some extent, there are similarities in the molecules of deoxyribonucleic acid (DNA) that compose the genes of living organisms. There is a similarity in tissue response, at least among the mammalian organisms, which gives us valid scientific data in studying physiology, pathology, and response to bacterial, toxic, and drug challenges.[9] There is also a similarity between human and nonhuman primates and even lower mammalia in such behavior as bonding, kinship, selfishness, and aggression. Even the smartest population of chimpanzees could not develop a number reckoning system up to five in a million years, or invent an alphabet with only three letters or, uncoached, draw a circle or a square as respresenting an idea or compose a five-word poem like "A rose is a rose." These potentialities are millions and millions of years away from the potentialities of the chimpanzee, yet Wilson writes: "The status of the chimpanzee deserves especially close attention. Our growing knowledge of these most intelligent apes has come to erode to a large extent the venerable dogma of the uniqueness of man."[10]

The fact is that the uniqueness of man is not in his general and purely physical constitution, which distinguishes him as a living organism. Embryologically, man may be considered a recapitulation, in a very condensed way, of his phylogeny. There is nothing unique about his anatomy and physiology except for a larger brain, hands with opposing thumbs, bipedalism, and a special speech apparatus, but what that brain can direct those hands, vocal apparatus, and bipedalism to do!—there is the rub. The uniqueness of the human being is the ability to symbolize freely and amply, to classify symbols in an orderly manner, and to utilize this order with facility by converting and using materials for changing the ecology in accordance with plans elaborated to satisfy human needs and fancies. If this be not a fantastic uniqueness, what else could it be?

Lee, in summarizing his study of primitive man, elucidates on the "sharing" characteristic of man, a simple trait that no other primate has been able to adopt: "When we discuss sharing and other central features of !Kung foraging, we are not simply looking at a cultural practice unique to them, but rather at an expression of a universal theme in the foraging mode of production." Lee further distinguishes human from chimpanzee behavior by referring to the area of economic organization. The basic difference, he avers, "is summed up in the word *exchange*. Whereas each nonhuman primate organism . . . is a self-sufficient subsistence unit, no human eats or works alone." The chimpanzee lives "a truly hand-to-mouth existence."[11] Exchange, of course, basically involves an act of sharing. Lee does assert that a *protoexchange* form of behavior in relation to food sharing does exist as a primogenial manifestation among chimpanzees and some baboons, as cited from Goodall.[12]

One of the most detailedly documented studies of exchange, based on evaluation of archeological findings from the fourth millenium B.C., was in Greater Mesopotamia at Farakhabad in southwest Iran. It was done by Henry T. Wright and a team of archaeologists. They described an already developed form of exchange where statehood and competition were evident: "During Middle and late Uruk, when established states were growing and competing with each other, various efforts were made to re-organize . . . production and participation in exchange."[13] Comparing Lee's discussion of the exchange process among the !Kung to that of Wright's seems to indicate that the present-day !Kung are no farther developed in this basic human activity than were the people of the Uruk culture.

If man retains some semblance of animal nature, that is not to be regarded with amazement. After all, he is a primate. But he also developed far beyond by a qualitative jump. The fact is that the first great revolution in the history of the humanization of humankind was *Homo*'s decision to *inhibit* certain of his primate sexual impulses that were destructive to his newly developing human potentialities being revealed by the bonding-sharing* trait.[14] If man's animal biogram has a "social" semblance, how could it be otherwise? The animal biogram of primates is a biosocial phenomenon. As can be expected, the animal nature of the human is biosocial also. But the human has both an animal nature and a human nature completely intermingled, and, for the most part, even the animal nature is psychosocially directed. The human nature is an expression of man's uniqueness, and that uniqueness is a psychosocial phenomenon. The ability to organize society in order to create a culture is a psychosocial force to the core. True enough, the psychosocial cannot be separated from the biosocial. But Wilson confuses these two levels of behavior, or, at least deaccentuates the profound distinction between them. As an example, describing the abilities of the chimpanzee, Wilson summarizes: "This account of the life of the chimpanzee is meant to establish what I regard as a fundamental point about the human condition; that by conventional evolutionary measures and the principal criteria of psychology we are not alone, we have a little-brother species. The points of similarity between human and chimpanzee social behavior, when joined with the compelling anatomical traces of relatively recent divergence, form a body of evidence too strong to be dismissed as coincidence."[15] There is scarcely any place today for educated people to get involved in an argument as to the validity of evolution. But to overemphasize the psychological achievements of the chimpanzee, which leads to the impression of the similarity between the traits of human nature and the traits of pongid nature, is misleading, to say the very least.

Wilson has written so much in his *Sociobiology* that some contra-

---

*The use of the term "bonding-sharing" should be understood to mean "bonding-sharing-exchange."

dictory points of view are expressed. The deaccentuation of the uniqueness of man is contradicted in the following statement by him: "We
(man) have leaped forward in mental evolution in a way that continues
to defy self-analysis. The mental hypertrophy has distorted even the
most basic primate social qualities into nearly unrecognizable forms.
Individual species of Old World monkeys and apes have notably plastic
social organizations; man has extended the trend into a protean ethnicity."[16] This partially confirms my thesis expressed above. But this
does not exculpate Wilson's overall and general exaggeration of the
subhuman primate traits in comparing them favorably with human
behavior traits.

Wilson's deaccentuation of the uniquness of human capability of
symbolization is in line with his reduction of the whole process to
integrative neurophysiology and sensory physiology.[17] The reduction
of symbolization (psychic phenomena) to biological principle is the essence of Wilson's scientific methodology, which he calls scientific materialism.[18] Unfortunately, his scientific materialism is of the same
vintage as nineteenth-century crass materialism. Human nature,
which is a psychosocial behavioral expression of the cognitive processes, he reduces to "an essentially biological phenomenon." Of course,
this is a biological phenomenon, but with the extension into the mental.
What he implies in his descriptions of that phenomenon appears as a
facade to eliminate the "mental" by describing it in terms of mechanisms explained by neuro and sensory physiology and cellular transducers at the molecular level. Certainly, the latter explains the
material aspects of brain biology, but not that of mental symbols which
are transduced from the material, even though he refers to transducers.
In a later work on human nature, he continues his "scientific materialism" with: "The conventional treatment of 'social biology' and 'social issues of biology' in our colleges and universities present some
formidable intellectual challenges, but they are not addressed to the
core of social theory. This core is the deep structure of human nature,
an essentially biological phenomenon that is also the primary focus of
the humanities."[19] Although we must agree that social theory has its
core in human nature, Wilson's mechanistic, materialistic reductionism is contrary to the dynamic materialism of modern science, which
propounds that matter in motion is primary to the existence of mind,
but that mind as the reflection of the material world has laws of movement of its own. Psychosocial phenomena are not biological phenomena, but are a higher level of the manifestation of matter in motion
than is the biological, although biology is basic to this process, just as
chemistry is the expression of a lower level of complexity of such matter

in motion than is biology. Each level has laws of motion of its own. The concepts composing the principles and laws of mathematics whose mental symbolization is subjective in nature cannot be reduced to the objective dynamics of neurobiology.

HUMAN NATURE'S GENETIC FOUNDATION

Some traits of human nature resemble some of the traits manifested in the animal biogram. The "bonding" trait without the sharing quality appears to be the most obvious. The sharing between mother and young among mammals is instinctive and distinctly different from the social sharing among humans. The bonding trait in the human is also completely different from that manifested in the animal biogram, even though both had their source in the propinquity and association of organisms in the process of reproduction, growth, and struggle to survive. Only contingently do they look the same, although basically having similar roots. Wilson, in his later book, *Human Nature,* asserts that human nature is genetically primed, just as he did in previous works declare the human biogram to be so based. Here are precisely his ideas on this matter:

> Chimpanzees are close enough to ourselves in the details of their social life and mental properties to rank as nearly human in certain domains where it was once considered inappropriate to make comparisons at all. These *facts* [italics added] are in accord with the hypothesis that human social behavior rests on a genetic foundation—that human behavior is, to be more precise, organized by some genes that are shared with closely related species and others that are unique to the human species.... The heart of the genetic hypothesis is the proposition, derived in a straight line from neo-Darwinian evolutionary theory, that the traits of human nature were adaptive during the time that the human species evolved and that genes consequently spread through the population that predisposed their carriers to develop those traits.[20]

The gist of Wilson's description of Darwinian theory is indisputable from a physical anthropological approach. His reference, however, does not apply to any element of adaptation that may still influence the nature of the traits of human nature, nor does he enumerate what the traits are except to say that they are similar to the traits that compose the behavioral complex of the higher animal biogram. He specifically defines human nature to be: "In the broader sense, the full set of innate behavioral predispositions that characterize the human species and in the narrower sense, those predispositions that affect social behavior."[21] One cannot find anywhere in his writings an enumeration of "the full set of innate behavioral predispositions" that he asserts characterize the human species. They are, according to his theory, biological and innate. Somehow, one is stymied in seeking in his depictions what part man's "mental hypertrophy" has played in the evolution of man. One would have to be as rigidly oriented as Wilson in the heredity-environment perspective to believe that heredity was not important in the nature of human nature. But its importance lies in the *physical* nature of the brain, in the ability to symbolize and evaluate, in the process of reproduction, and in other physical traits that made it possible for humankind to express behavior teleologically, which ability, at least partially, is not hereditary. The poverty of such discussion must be due to Wilson's closeness to behaviorism, where mind is a superfluous element of behavior.

THE BASIS FOR THE BONDING-SHARING-EXCHANGE TRAIT

The most pristine of the traits of human nature is the "bonding-sharing-exchange" trait, which impelled man toward human socialization and served as the anlage for the system of human economics by initiating the process of *exchange*. This trait, therefore, can and has been studied from its phylogenetic origins. A very basic characteristic of the phylum of Vertebra is the ability of an individual organism to stimulate another proximal organism and be stimulated in return. This mutual stimulation is the prime cohesive stuff from which sociality develops.[22] What are the specific factors involved that predispose to the socializing interrelation for the class Mammalia? Such factors must have their origin in some pattern of association between organisms. The closer the association, the firmer the interrelation. The longer the association, the more durable. The more involvement between the associated organisms, the stronger the attachment. The five factors that generate association are:

1. The act of fertilization—copulation—male and female sexual relations.
2. The period of gestation—female and childbearing process.
3. The act of birth (delivery)—intimate ordeal between female and offspring, with conscience operating on the human mother's part.

4. Supplying nourishment to the offspring of which suckling is the most intimate method, resulting in the most durable intimacy beween female and offspring and an extended period of socialization of the child in the human.
5. The age-peer interstimulation.

Over the millions of years that this whole process has been operating, kinship and altruism accumulated a certain amount of genetic nature. How much is a question. Certainly, throughout the history of living material, the quality of self-preservation must also have accumulated as a genetic force; otherwise life would have disappeared a long time ago. Such bivalence is the nature of the bonding-sharing trait. It is endowed with all the richness of active and reactive behavior, which can manifest itself in many ways, such as love and hate, trust and suspicion, self-indulgence and altruism, forgiveness and revenge, generosity and envy, gratitude and ingratitude, cooperation and antagonism, friendliness and hostility, sympathy and antipathy, empathy and callousness, sharing and exchange, etcetera.

Count points out: "The cardinal fact about vertebra biogram is that it is a drama with two alternating phases: a non-reproductive and a mating phase. The former lasts longer in the lowest vertebrates, but as we ascend the phylogenetic scale and the reproductive efforts become greater and more complex, the two phases change in relative length."[23] In the human, the reproductive phase is almost continuous for many years of an individual's life. With the emergence of the order Primate, the oestrous cycle began losing its rigid behavioral responses. "The adult primates [males particularly] never have a period when their psychoneural mechanisms are without the tonic stimulus of the sex hormones. . . . Together with the high capacity of the primate brain [and the infinitely higher capacity for *Homo*] for making associations that can produce endlessly complex motivations for action, this makes for a versatile psyche."[24] Thus sociality (bonding-sharing) in the human is a biosociopsychic phenomenon intiated by the associations (interrelations) compelled by the neurohormonal[25] sex drive,[26] which is a continuous mechanism and which results in the five factors cited above that generate associations between individuals, particularly strong and emotion-laden in the human.

Count further describes another basic developmental phenomenon that determines vertebrate behavior and is critically operative in the human: "The vertebrates possess innate neuropsychic mechanisms which must be appropriately stimulated at the *right point* [italics added] in maturation if they are to become properly activated; otherwise the animal's maturation is permanently stunted and its personality [animality] is deformed."[27] Piaget[28] and Bowlby[29] have amply demonstrated the importance of this mechanism in the human child.

Count further describes how the age-peer group is such a powerful influence in behavior development: "Among those mammals which produce only one offspring at a birth, interreaction with the parent precedes interreaction with age-peers. Nonetheless, any human parent who has twins or triplets is fully aware of the socializing powers of interreaction with one's age-peers, and every human parent knows what he has to contend with as soon as the single youngster begins to interreact with age-peers outside the family. The juvenile age-group occurs as a subsociety throughout the vertebrate gamut, from the fish level up."[30] Let it not be interpreted that the human potential in the socializing process, and thereby the development of the bonding-sharing trait, is the same as that of fishes or monkeys. Yet the interstimulation between individual vertebrates resulting from the propinquity and association inherent in the biological process of reproduction and survival is present in fish as well as in humans. But in humans the cognitive processes are stimulated and developed by such biological interactions, thereby creating the psychosocial armamentarium for *Homo*'s development.

MALE AND FEMALE AND OFFSPRING

The sex phenomenon in living organisms is an archetype present in all levels of development of animal life. Sex in the human being is *not* a trait of human nature, although this inherent biological force has a powerful influence on human nature. Because of similarity in the basic interrelations that are elicited by the propinquity and associations necessitated in the reproduction process, it is not surprising that some of these basic interrelations may provoke interreactions among organisms that have basic similarities. Count describes such similarity of interreactions as follows:

From all this [the dynamics of parentalism] we derive the following about the vetebrate mating phase: the males initiate and conduct the reproductive cycle, as far as the cycle involves behavior and is not merely physiological (e.g., gestation). Wherever the male selects a nesting site, courts the female, and keeps out intruders, the female is accepting a situation which the male created for her. The mating phase very commonly finds intra-sex competition—males competing for the females, females competing for the males. This reinforces the tendency to social hierarchialism, but both observations of natural events and laboratory experiments show that the two phenomena are not identical . . . the hierarchialism can be exercised even during the non-reproductive phase of the biogram. The hierarchialism is intrasexual, so that a hierarchy exists for each sex. More often than not, the male hierarchy tends to dominate the female hierarchy.[31]

The above quotation will evoke a cry of "male chauvinism"[32] from the extremists of the women's lib movement. The above is quoted to show how the biological nature of animal life elicits certain patterns of behavior throughout the groups of organisms whose biograms are initiated by similar biological processes. In the field of biology, the male has certain strengths, which generally give him a dominance in certain behavior patterns. When these biological strengths were inherited by the hominids, male dominance continued to be manifest and became a social heritage down to modern times. Biologically and physiologically, these strengths still obtain, as explained by Alice Rossi,[33] but such strengths never were present in greater predominance in the mental-intellectual spheres of life, except that the idea of male biophysical dominance was also traditionally transferred (without justification in reality) to the tasks requiring mental-intellectual powers. The quality of the neopallium was never inherited as a sex-dominant characteristic. In this area there was and is equal male-female distribution of genetic heritage. Nevertheless, some of the leadership in the feminist movement appear to be preaching a type of physical unisex that is hurting the validity of the need for *psychosocial equality.*

There is indeed a special relation and bond between parent and young, particularly between mother and offspring, described so well by Rossi[34] and discussed phylogenetically by Count: "When a parent tends young, the young react to the parent, and we have a true sociopsychological ingredient in the total reproductive situation."[35] "If a parent remains with the incubating young until they emerge, whether by hatching, simple extrusion, or parturition, a new set of parental actions ensues immediately without exception; these actions elicit from the young an innately-determined behavior which attaches them to the source of the elicitation. This occurs in every class from fishes to mammals and birds. Here is a psychological parent-offspring mutualism that justifies the appellation 'familialism'."[36] Thus comes into existence the bonding characteristic in animals that develops into the bonding-sharing trait of human nature.

The child-mother bond, just like the young-parental bond of animals, must change, since the child or the young animal must grow up. Count observed that: "It is not fully appreciated by some students of animal society (and this certainly is true of many a human parent) that to emancipate the young from parental bond is a part of the parental behavior pattern quite as genuinely as parental care is, and that in many species it requires positive and definite acts."[37] However, except for man, "once the parent has dismissed the offspring, they no longer have the parent-offspring relation."[38] This is another important difference between human and animal bonding.

The unisex pattern of behavior in some of the young extremists has extended to the males equal participation in caring for infants and children. The male certainly has a social function in such family affairs, but for human society to go unisexual in child rearing is as fruitless a quest as hoping to change the mother's physiology to that of the father's and vice versa. Rossi discusses this subject with detailed clarity in her essay:

> Many cultural determinists now claim that the only difference between men and women is that women bear young and lactate [let alone menstruate]. This use of "only" implies that pregnancy, childbirth, and nursing are insignificant activities, especially because few women breast-feed nowadays and because women are having fewer children than they once did. But the reproductive and endocrine systems that underlie childbearing and lactation function throughout the woman's life cycle. To deny their importance to female psychology or to the organization of the family devalues the woman's role in the survival of the species, ignores the findings of science, and reveals the profound degree to which many women accept masculine technocratic thinking, which places exceedingly heavy stress on rational control over nature and on purely technical solutions to human problems.[39]

Count observes that " . . . for the mammals generally the definition of family becomes that of mother and offpsring. There is a uniquely intimate and complex gestation within a very specialized uterus, and a corresponding endocrine drama."[40] "The mammalian female, the human not excepted, has a more elaborate sexual cycle and a double orientation: toward a male as a sex partner, and toward a brood as its parental fosterer."[41] "It does not seem far-fetched to see in this dual pattern the prerequisite for the human scheme of familialism. . . . "[42]

THE FAMILY: THE PHYLOGENETIC BASIS

The real nidus of the family in the class Mammalia is the mother and her offspring. However, for the primates, apes and monkeys, the rudiments of male permanance in the family circle began to develop, as Count observed: "Male familialism in apes and monkeys is fractional, even when present, but males are ramparts for the entire herd against intruders."[43] "Where males show interest in the offspring of their partners, the matter requires a less obvious explanation."[44]

The human family appears to have a phylogenetic, but particularly a Mammalian class basis—a basis having its origin in the dynamics of the reproductive-survival processes. Although the biophysiological nature of these processes is similar in the various orders and genuses of the Mammalian class, there are indeed differences in the behavior of these groups, the greatest differences being in the genus *Homo*. The differences are fundamentally anatomical, the physiological and behavioral characteristics issuing therefrom, the most important of which are the greatly enlarged neopallium and its *conscience* and the infinite flow of symbols generated therein and actions responding thereto. Most probably, the original groups of *Homo* had a social structure in which family relations served as the primary cohesive force to unify the family unit, even though its structure was extended as in the gens and clan. The latter were completely and qualitatively different from the subhuman primate horde, even though both may have had their origin in the essential characteristics of animal nature expressed in cooperative association and in affinitive relations called kinship. Sahlins, in reflecting on anthropology's contributions to sociology, states: "Comparison of sociology with the findings of anthropological research immediately suggests a startling conclusion; the way people act, and probably have acted, is *not* the expression of *inherent* human nature. There is a quantum difference, at points a complete opposition, between even the most rudimentary human society and the most advanced subhuman primate one. The discontinuity implies that the emergence of human society required some suppression, rather than a direct expression, of man's primate nature. Human social life is *culturally,* not *biologically* [italics added] determined."[45] The victory of culture in replacing the *primate* bonding trait with the *human* bonding-sharing trait was one of the great social revolutions. This trait became the phylogenetic keystone in the structure of human nature. Sahlin's meaning of the term "culture" in the above statement may include that of the term "social." If so, some comment need be made here. The victory of culture over biologically determined primate nature is a basic scientific observation. That culture is a powerful force in shaping human behavior is just as basic an observation. However, the very essence of human behavior is a set of psychosocial traits of human nature determined by the *social,* not the cultural, dynamics necessary for *Homo* to adapt to the human condition in which he found himself. He was and is a *cognitive* animal with the physical characteristics that made it possible to symbolize into language the imagery of the brain and to modify his environment with the versatility of his hands. Thus *Homo* began to create his culture, but under the pressure of *social* forces.

Sahlins, with deep insight, observes that human nature is not hereditary, i.e., "is not the expression of *inherent* human nature," and that humankind, because of its *inherent* primate nature, had to suppress some of that nature in order to support the emergence of human society. Thus human nature became *biphasic,* with a human and a primate aspect. It was the social relations resulting from *Homo's* response to his conditions of living that evoked his human practices, his human nature, through which culture began to be created and thereafter accumulated. Once the social relations initiated the basic structure of the nature of human behavior, the cultural aspects gave color, warmth, variety, and richness to the evolving traits of this human nature.

From the knowledge presently available, it appears that one of the earliest significant cultural practices of human society, an offshoot of the bonding-sharing trait, was the practice of *exchange.* Eventually this sociocultural practice became the foundation of all the subsequent social systems invented by man. Adam Smith, in his classic analysis of capitalism, treated exchange as operated by the self-interest nature of man and devoid of its original humane social interaction:

> But man has almost constant occasion for the help of his brethren, and it is in vain for him to expect it from their benevolence only. He will be more likely to prevail if he can interest their self-love in his favor, and show them that it is for their own advantage to do for him what he requires of them. Whoever offers to another a bargain of any kind proposed to do this. Give me that which I want, and I shall have this which you want, is the meaning of every such offer; and it is in this manner that we obtain from one another the far greater part of those good offices which we stand in need of. It is not from benevolence of the butcher, the brewer, or the baker that we expect our dinner, but from regard to their

own interest. We address ourselves not to their humanity but to their advantages. . . . and thus the certainty of being able to *exchange* [italics added] all that surplus part of the produce of his own labour, which is over and above his own consumption, for such parts of the produce of other men's labour as he may have occasion for encourages every man to apply himself to a particular occupation, and to cultivate and bring to perfection whatever talent or genius he may possess for that particular species of business.[46]

Karl Marx's classic analysis of capitalism treated exchange as a most basic factor in social relations in economics, relating its essence to the labor of workers who were the real creators of capital.[47]

Another of the very early significant cultural practices of human society was the development of a code of conduct relating to sex relations. Sahlins described how sex naturally played a powerful role in animal and human societies. "The powerful social magnet of sex was the major impetus to subhuman primate sociability."[48] But, as he also declared: "Sex is not an unmitigated social blessing for primates. Competition over partners, for example, can lead to vicious, even fatal, strife. It was this side of primate sexuality that forced early culture to curb and repress it. The emerging human primate, in a life-and-death economic struggle with nature, could not afford the luxury of a social struggle. Cooperation, not competition, was essential."[49] Thus emerged a code of conduct based on *inhibition* of the brutish nature of primate behavior relating to sex in order to be able to establish and function as a human community to replace the primate troop. The human community had to be based on behavioral traits that promoted social interrelations, allowing the development of a human philosophy of living together—a moral-ethical code, a basic trait of human nature: the trait of "unifying orientation of behavior." One of the earliest rules to control sex violence was that against incest, which effectively enlisted the service of cooperation kin relations, as Sahlins expressed it.

In discussing sexuality in primates, Williams concluded that: "Copulation between mother and son is rarely seen, from which it seems possible that the incest taboo originated earlier than in human cultures."[50]

How did man become familialized? This question has not been precisely and with complete satisfaction determined. Sahlins stated with assurance that "No one . . . can be absolutely certain who his father is in a genetic sense, but in all human societies fatherhood is a fundamental social status. Almost all societies adhere implicitly or explicitly to the dictum of the Napoleonic Code in this respect: the father of the child is the husband of the mother. Many hunters and gatherers carry kinship to an extreme that is curious to us. By a device technically known as classificatory kinship they ignore genealogical differences between collateral and lineal kin at certain points, lumping them terminologically and in social behavior. Thus my father's brother may be 'father to me, and I act accordingly'."[51]

Count states: "Multiple status is a human social characteristic. A human does not cease to be a son or a daughter on becoming a husband or wife. . . . Of all the new statuses that are involved in the human kind of society, none is as decisive as the familialization of the male. The sex which has but one orientation toward reproduction—the erotic toward a heterosexual partner—is brought to polarize many of his interests and skills upon the familial circle."[52] This did not happen because of female weakness, particularly during pregnancy and parturition, since women have demonstrated that they can take care of themselves very well. It did not happen because man wished to possess his offspring, since his familialization took place before man was aware of biologic paternity. The fact is that to become familialized as the father, man had to accept this obligation. But to accept this obligation, he had to have already assented to a moral code. Did man develop a moral code before becoming familialized, or did sheer prolonged sexual associations develop such a companionship, which, being reinforced by the kinship urge of the primate nature, at the same time generated gradually a family code of morals? Was the self-image–self-esteem trait already beginning to influence the bond-sharing relation between man and woman? Count states:

In proportion as the male becomes familialized and so develops a stake in the circle that he comes to share with a female and her offspring, he brings to bear upon his domestic world the skills which he develops and elaborates outside that world [e.g., as a hunter]. His mate has her own skills and inventions which she often can exercise simultaneously in the interest of her double orientation—that toward her mate and that toward her offspring. Extrafamilial and intrafamilial activities are thus brought into mutual support; there is a cultural integration of the two vertebrate biogrammatic phases, the reproductive and the nonreproductive. But most cultural inventions take shape outside the familial polarity and it is out here that culture develops most elaborately. This reverses the relative complexity of the two bio-grammatic phases; for, as we have had occasion to notice, it is in the reproductive phase that the nonhuman vertebrates display the more complex social behavior.[53]

It should be clear how the bonding-sharing trait developed out of the phylogenetic dynamics of hominid evolution. It must also be clearly appreciated that the quality of the bonding-sharing trait as manifested in man's psychosocial behavior is an entirely different and higher level of behavior than that of the bonding trait among the rest of the primates, not to slight the Mammalia.

NOTES

1. Edward O. Wilson, *Sociology: The Abridged Edition* (Cambridge, Massachusetts: Harvard University Press, Belknap Press, 1980) pp. 388–92.

2. Ibid.

3. Ibid., p. 43.

4. R. Axelrod and W. H. Hamilton, "The Evolution of Cooperation," *Science*, vol. 211, no. 4489, pp. 1390–96 (March 27, 1981).

5. Jane E. Lancaster, "Carrying and Sharing in Human Evolution," *Human Nature* (February 1978), pp. 82–89.

6. G. B. Kolata, "Human Evolution: Life-Styles and Lineages of Early Hominids," *Science*, vol. 187 (March 14, 1975), pp. 940–42.

7. Wilson, *loco supra citato*, pp. 7–8.

8. Ibid., p. 8.

9. Ernst Mayr, *Population, Species, and Evolution* (Cambridge, Massachusetts: Harvard University Press, 1970). Mayr deals potently with this problem on pp. 373–74.

10. E. O. Wilson, *On Human Nature* (Cambridge, Massachusetts: Harvard University Press, 1978), p. 25.

11. Richard B. Lee, *!Kung San: Men, Women and Children in a Foraging Society* (New York: Cambridge University Press, 1979), pp. 437, 490.

12. Ibid., p. 489.

13. *An Early Town on the Deh Luran Plain* (Ann Arbor, Michigan: University of Michigan, 1981), p. 278.

14. Peter Farb, *Humankind* (New York: Houghton Mifflin Co., 1978), p. 83.

15. Wilson, *On Human Nature*, p. 31

16. Wilson, *Sociobiology, cite supra*, p. 548.

17. Ibid., p. 6.

18. Wilson, *Human Nature, loco supra citato*, p. 10.

19. Ibid., p. 10.

20. Ibid., p. 32.

21. Ibid., pp. 217–18.

22. Earl W. Count, "The Biological Basis of Human Sociality," *American Anthropologist*, vol. 60 (1958), pp. 1049–85.

23. Ibid., p. 1052.

24. Ibid., p. 1064.

25. A. Rossi, "The Biosocial Side of Parenthood," *Human Nature* (June 1978), pp. 72–79.

26. M. D. Sahlins, "The Origin of Society." *Scientific American,* vol. 203 (September 1960), pp. 76–87.

27. Count, *loco supra citato,* p. 1053.

28. Jean Piaget, *The Essential Piaget,* edited by H. Gruber and J. Voneche (New York: Basic Books, 1977), pp. 180–83.

29. J. Bowlby, *Maternal Care and Mental Health* (Albany, New York: World Health Organization, 1952), pp. 59–63.

30. Count, *loco supra citato,* p. 1053.

31. Ibid., p. 1054.

32. David Abraham, "Tamarins in the Amazon," *Science,* vol. 85, pp. 58–63.

33. Alice S. Rossi, "The Biosocial Side of Parenthood," *Human Nature* (June 1978), pp. 72–79.

34. Ibid.

35. Count, *cite supra,* p. 1054.

36. Ibid., 1057.

37. Ibid., 1060.

38. Ibid., p. 1078.

39. Rossi, *cite supra,* pp. 72–79.

40. Count, *cite supra,* p. 1060.

41. Ibid., p. 1063.

42. Ibid., p. 1064.

43. Ibid., p. 1064.

44. Ibid., p. 1066.

45. Sahlins, *cite supra.*

46. Adam Smith, *The Wealth of Nations* (New York: The Modern Library, 1937), pp. 14–15.

47. Karl Marx, *Capital,* vol. 1 (Charles H. Kerr and Co., 1906), pp. 43—45.

48. Sahlins, *cite supra.*

49. Ibid.

50. Leonard Williams, *Challenge to Survival* (New York: New York University Press, 1977), p. 129.

51. Ibid.

52. Count, *cite supra,* pp. 1075–76.

53. Ibid., p. 1078.

6

*The Bonding-Sharing Trait**

IT'S HUMAN NATURE

The need for rootedness in a social group based on mutual commitment that engenders a significant bonding and sharing and exchange force of fruitful social interrelations is the essence of being human.

There is need for rootedness, i.e., having a home base in a social group, even if that group eventually becomes all of mankind or as small as the family. The sensibilities of the human have transcended primate behavior by establishing a home base, to wit, Lee's observation of primitive man: "Among primates, the young, the old, the sick and the disabled, and nursing mothers, all must keep up with the group or die. The human home base allowed rest and recovery without requiring the weak members to forfeit their lives or even a day's food. . . . The existence of a home base [is] not only a sleeping [and care] site but also a locality where individuals meet to *exchange* [italics added] goods. . . . "[1] The home base therefore creates a pattern of social relations and humanized sensibilities that bears the warmth and security of social well-being as reflected in cooperation, mutual aid, sympathy, compassion, love, care, and trust, but also serves as the economic base for exchange of material products and psychosocial forms. Exchange, therefore, is a more discrete form of sharing. This is what Edwin Markham meant in the lines:

> There is a destiny that makes us brothers;
> None goes his way alone;
> All that we send into the lives of others
> Comes back into our own.

---

* The word *Exchange* is understood in title, but not used because it is historically subsequent to bonding-sharing.

Markham expresses the human aspect of bonding most appropriately by succinctly differentiating human bonding from nonhuman bonding. The first two lines of the stanza are the nonhuman primate descriptions of bonding, although the word *brothers* may be correctly applied to both the nonhuman and human. The last two lines are the human aspect—the giving and receiving, the sharing and exchange, as Lee puts it in analyzing the foraging economy of the !Kung San: "What is the basic difference in economic organization between humans and their nearest relative? The answer is summed up in the word *exchange*."[2] This has been the basis of all systems of human economy since the first foraging state. Lee recognizes a *protoexchange* behavior in chimpanzees and some baboons, but "although this does not amount to *exchange* in the human sense, it does appear to be a rudimentary form of something that could be called *protoexchange*."[3]

These *bonding* and *sharing* forces between individuals and groups can also be directed toward social destructiveness generated by various forms of individual and group antagonism and hostility.[4] Such practices are based on reversion to primate impulses modified by the devious abilities of human intelligence, which could be more destructive than the blind rage of the primate urge and could lead to exaggerated self and group aggrandizement, restriction of the sharing practices, intemperate self and group indulgence, retaliation, and predatory aspects of self-preservation. It appears to be an irreconcilable contradiction to attribute the bonding force to practically all forms of animal life and then call behavior disruptive of bonding in human society when humans adopt the dominance trait of subhuman primate behavior. But what is good for the primate is not necessarily good for *Homo*.

Traits of human nature, being psychosocial in origin, are molded into specific patterns by cognition. Cognitive processes that made it possible for *Homo* to support "human" behavior *can be used* to keep social interrelations accommodated to the needs of human nature. When the ecosystem is in violation of the traits of human nature, reaction of the cognitive processes may maintain a rational course or may veer to an irrational path, causing disruption in social behavior. The Griegers confirm this evaluation: "People have both innate and acquired tendencies to think rationally (thereby aiding their basic values and goals) and to think irrationally (thereby interfering with their basic values and goals.) Irrational thoughts by definition are absolution and antiempirical, and they logically lead to what we commonly call disturbed emotional states—anxiety, anger, depression, guilt, and severe frustration. These irrational cognitions correlate with almost all forms of emotional disturbance, and disturbed populations employ significantly more irrational thinking than do nondisturbed populations."[5]

Although the bonding force in animals manifests itself ontogenetically and phylogenetically as a biological trait, genetically programmed,[6] and is distinctly different in the various phyla and their genera, the class Mammalia has a special physiological mechanism that enhances the bonding relations: breast-feeding of the offspring. Among the primates, another factor enhances the bonding relations: the length of the infantile phase.[7] But among the primates, the genus *Homo* has other features that augment the genetically programmed biological patterns with learned characteristic such as sharing and exchange, so far beyond the level of the other primate patterns of behavior as to render *Homo*'s bonding force qualitatively different from the rest. Not only is the infantile period of *Homo*'s offspring longer and more helpless, but the symbolization capacity (the cognitive power) of the greatly enlarged neopalliun, the remarkable larynx and the language articulation, the bipedal stance and thumb-hand opposition that make manipulation and ambulation fantastic arts, are features that make *Homo*'s bonding force a humanly generated *psychosocial* trait.

A fundamental responsibility of human society is to organize its group effort toward the human expression of group and individual *action* and to develop *inhibition* to prevent the tendency of reversion to primate impulse expression except under controlled circumstances, such as boxing matches and football games, and even these have their human attributes, the skill involved, the forethought and planning, and the prevention of relentless finality.

Rootedness in a social group engendering bonding and sharing and exchanging behavior for

human

Cooperation, mutual aid, trust, love, care, sympathy, commitment to welfare of others (sharing), and just practices of exchange of material and mental products

primate

Self-aggrandizement, hostility, retaliation, intemperance, self-indulgence, and even destructiveness

ATTACHMENT: ROOTEDNESS

Man has a need to be securely rooted in a home base with social relationships of love, trust, and goodwill with the world of people about him. Man, in the dim past, developed this need supported by his physical and mental attributes to unite with his world of people in order to overcome his bewildering aloneness consequent to his emergence from his primary union with nature, i.e., his emergence as an intelligent, self-conscious, self-directed *Homo*.

Bowlby has tried to explain the process of early social (human) bonding by the principles of modern biology and psychology.[8] He believes that infants have genetically determined (instinctive) predispositions to seek the proximity of the adult figure who protects and cares for them, and that parents are predisposed to respond. Bowlby considers attachment behavior the quintessential relationship in the development of personality. Since the bonding-sharing force is the primary trait of human nature and has an evolutionary history of primordial essence, the argument as to how much of this trait in the human is genetic is irrelevant. Certainly, a significant portion of the human aspect of bonding has a *psychosocial* basis. The bonding-sharing trait, which has its origin in the mother-offspring relations and subsequently with the father-family relations, has its roots therefore in the sexuality-survival dyad.[9] Both are, at their roots, biological forces. Sexuality is therefore not a trait of human nature, but a biological force, like hunger. Yet, like hunger, it is humanized (socioculturized) into love, marriage, morals, and child training on the one hand and culinary art, restaurants, agriculture, and food processing on the other hand. Certainly such biological, forces have their profound influence on coloring the traits of human nature with cultural artistry.

In anthropology, A. L. Kroeber is credited with developing the concept of "persistent cultural patterns" that are observed in the comparative study of culture. In discussing this subject, Spicer stated: "The essential features of any identity system is an individual's belief in his personal affilation with certain symbols, or more accurately, with what certain symbols stand for. There are collective identity systems as well as individual ones."[10] This basic behavioral characteristic of individuals and groups is an expression of the bonding-sharing trait of human nature.

This urge to be rooted in a meaningful relationship is primary in sustaining life. It is the fundamental psychosocial force in the sociocultural development of humankind. Union with other human beings manifests itself as love of *his* mate, of *his* progeny, of *his* forebears, of *his* family, and of *his* world. The child, on growing into adulthood, compensates for his loss of parental security by developing special forms of social relations that serve as powerful instruments for mutual aid such as his own family, new in-law relations, community organizations and alliances with other communities. An example of a reversion to primate impulse is the practice of incest, which early hominids and even pongids to some extent proscribed to prevent the disruptive violence associated with sex competition in the family or close kinship group and to promote economic and social relations by forming outside alliances. The incest taboo itself implies that the human family *cannot* be the social outcome of uncontrolled erotic urges, particularly since these urges are not limited by estrous cycles. Incest taboo could have originated before the emergence of *Homo*.[11] Because of the biphasic nature of the behavioral process and the presence of certain phases of the ecosystem in relation to the traits of human nature, incest in greater or lesser prevalance has persisted. Today there is even a movement toward legitimizing incest.[12,13] How the lifting of this inhibition will effect the integrity of the family and the nature of human nature is nowhere discussed by these "progressive" social scientists. Such a release of inhibition is quite in line with the chaotic sexual behavior being advocated in arrogant and cynical disregard of "inadequate manmade" behavioral codes.

The traits of human nature express themselves as behavioral processes. Each trait functions as a process of opposing forces. This biphasic contention of contradictory forces of behavior becomes manifest in the course of responding to the vicissitudes of life. The nature of the impact on man's interrelationships by the particular ecosystem or social system determines which of the opposing forces of the particular trait is encouraged to be inhibited and which is supported to express itself.

THE FAMILY: HISTORY

The history of the human family is the story of the origin of society. As the eminent anthropologist Sahlins put it:

The nearest contemporary approximation to the original cultural conditions [of man] are societies of hunters and gatherers, preagricultural peoples exacting a meager livelihood from wild food resources. This cultural order dominated the Old Stone Age (one million to 10,000 or 15,000 years ago). . . . The emergence of human society required some suppression, rather than a direct expression, of man's primate nature. *The decisive battle between early culture and human nature must have been waged on the field of primate sexuality* [italics added]. . . Sex is not an unmitigated blessing for primates. Competition over partners, for example, can lead to vicious, even fatal, strife. It was this side of primate sexuality that forced early culture to curb and repress it. The emerging human primate, in a life-and-death economic struggle with nature, could not afford the luxury of a social struggle. Co-operation, not competition, was essential. Culture thus brought primate sexuality under control. More than that, sex was made subject to regulations, such as the incest taboo. . . . Thus the incest taboo is a guardian of harmony and solidarity within the family. . . . At the same time, the injunction on sexual relations and marriage among close relatives necessarily forces different families into alliance and thus extends kinship and mutual aid. . . . "Kinship" here means a cultural form, not a biological fact. . . . The progressive emancipation of sex from hormonal control in the primate order . . . seems to be paralleled by a progressive development from promiscuous mating to the formation of exclusive, permanent heterosexual partnerships. . . . Marriage and the family are institutions too important in primitive life to be built on the fragile, shifting foundations of "love." The family is the decisive economic institution of society. It is to the hunter-gatherer what the manor was to feudal Europe, or the corporate factory system is to capitalism: it is the productive organization. The primary division of labor in band economy is that between men and women. . . . In selective adaptation to the perils of the Stone Age, human society overcame or subordinated such *primate propensities as selfishness, indiscriminate sexuality, dominance,* and *brute competition* [italics added]. It substituted kinship and cooperation for conflict, placed solidarity over sex, morality over might. In its earliest day it accomplished the greatest reform in history, the overthrow of *human primate nature,* and thereby secured the evolutionary future of the species [italics added].[14]

HUMAN NATURE VERSUS PRIMATE NATURE

The above most pithy statement by Sahlins condenses in a short essay the essence of a million years of development of that primate species that eventuated in the emergence of *Homo erectus.* Sahlins, in line with the thesis of this study, also affirms the psychosocial basis of human nature. He also differentiates the drives (traits) of human nature from the social structures of human culture between which, he asserts, there enters a "critical indeterminacy."[15] He further posits the thesis of the bivalent nature of human nature, i.e., the opposing tendencies between human primate nature and human nature. Sahlins's critical observations that "the decisive battle between early culture and human nature must have been waged on the field of primate sexuality" is being fought again in our day on a *higher level* of sociocultural development. Early Stone Age culture had to inhibit such primate propensities as selfishness, indiscrimate sexuality, male dominance, and brute sex competition and had to substitute kinship, altruism, and cooperation over conflict, solidarity over sex, and morality over might. The early primate propensities have never disappeared from *Homo sapiens'* behavioral nature. They have only been submerged or inhibited or restrained by social and legal norms from expression. But they are gaining permissiveness to be expressed again in rebellion not only against past institutionalized patterns of prudery, but also against the institutional memory of a million years of human experience. The swing is now to the opposite extreme: although if not altogether back to the sex violence and sex dominance of the primate type, it looks, from the mass media reporting, that sex violence is rapidly increasing. Are we beginning to pay our debt by the vicarious derangement of our bio- and socio-sexuality? Are we going to continue employing our human endowments of rationality, educability, and manipulative dexterity in pursuing the following perversions?: (1) A subhumanized sex violence in the form of killing, maiming, child abduction and abuse, and rape; (2) a highly sophisticated eroticism in the form of pornography; (3) a rejection of the normal bivalence of the sexual process in the perversive form of homosexuality and unisex socialization; (4) the perversion of the legitimate aspiration of attaining equal justice for womanhood to the covetous aspiration of mimicking the activities that are biophysiologically expedient for the male and downgrading the development to the highest degree the potentialities that are advantageously female attributes; and (5) a return to sexual indiscriminateness.

BRINGING THE FAMILY UP TO DATE: MOTHER AND CHILD

Today the inordinate abandon in expressing the trait of "freedom to choose" is playing havoc with the concordance of our culture in relation to the other traits of human nature. In the early Stone Age culture, the need for the development of a stable family required the establishment of sex norms to secure such stability. The family, clan, or gens became the social unit that made possible the humanization and the socialization of humankind. The present return to uninhibited freedom of sex expression is, in a crucial sense, a return to the primate propensities supported by the premise of civilized sophisticated rejection of jealousy (if such rejection were indeed possible). The result as already stated, is an increase in sex violence, and in child abuse and abandonment and increase in behavioral disorientation of the youth, with increase in homicide and suicide among the youth. To what extent will such a course eventually erode the most basic trait of human nature, the bonding-sharing force? And what effect will this have on the future course of the development of mankind? What social glue will be substituted for the family—the commune?, the child care institution? Sahlins's masterful summarization of the scientific information available on the origin of society in 1960 is a reminder of a similar scholarly effort by Friederich Engels, whose study in a similar vein in 1884 in *The Origin of the Family* was likewise of classical quality. The temper of Engels's synthesis of historical data, in spite of some of its outdated detail, renders it valuable, in broad principle, for present-day explanatory examination in relation to this study:

According to the materialistic conception, the decisive element of history is pre-eminently the production and reproduction of life and its material requirements. This implies, on the one hand, the production of the means of existence (food, clothing, shelter, and the necessary tools): on the other hand, the generation of children, the propagation of species. The social institutions, under which the people of a certain historical period and of a certain country are living, are dependent on these two forms of production: partly on the development of labor, partly on that of the family. The less labor is developed, and the less abundant the quantity of its production and, therefore, the wealth of society, the more society is seen to be under the domination of sexual ties. However, under this formation based on sexual ties, the productivity of labor is developed more and more. At the same time, private property and exchange, distinctions of wealth, exploitation of the labor power of others, and by this agency, the foundation of class antagonisms, are formed. These new elements of society strive in the course of time to adapt the old state of society to the new conditions, until the impossibility of harmonizing these two at last leads to a com-

154

plete revolution. The old form of society founded on sexual relations is abolished in the clash with the recently developed social
classes.[16]

Continuing further:

> We have, then, three main forms of the family, corresponding in
> general to the three main stages of human development. For
> savagery group marriage, for barbarism the pairing family, for
> civilization monogamy supplemented by adultery and prostituion.
> Between the pairing family and monogamy, in the higher stage
> of barbarism, the rule of men over female slaves and polygamy
> is inserted. . . . Since monogamy was caused by economic condi-
> tions, will it disappear when these causes are abolished? One
> might reply, not without reason: not only will it not disappear,
> but it will rather be perfectly realized. . . . With the transfor-
> mation of the means of production into collective property the
> monogamous family ceases to be the economic unit of society. The
> private household changes to a social industry. The care and ed-
> ucation of children becomes a public matter. Society cares equally
> well for all children, legal or illegal. . . . Here a new element
> becomes active, an element which at best existed only in the germ
> at the time when monogamy developed: individual sex love. . . .
> Our sex love is essentially different from the simple sexual crav-
> ing, the Eros, of the ancients. In the first place, it presupposes
> mutual love. In this respect woman is the equal of man. . . . In
> the second place our sex love has such a degree of intensity and
> duration that in the eyes of both parties lack of possession and
> separation appear as a great, if not the greatest calamity.[17]

Regardless of whether Engels' anthropological data lack the newer
knowledge of today and his interpretation follows with a critical eye
the exploitation of classes, these quotations, given at length from the
studies of two eminent scholars, summarize very concisely the high
points in the origin and the history of the family, which has been the
essential social unit supporting the humanization of mankind. It gave
roots to and secured the social relations among humankind. It served
as the womb for generating the human intimacy in the bonding-sharing
force between group members and between groups of people. It has
been the stabilizing force of society.

The very fact is that the biological nature of the relation of human
offspring to parents makes a long dependence an absolute necessity for

human survival and that the psychological and social nature of this dependence solidifies the bonding-sharing force in family and fosters the practice of exchange between clans, tribes, and nations for the improvement of the human condition. All this elicits certain very stable psychosocial patterns of human behavior. Engels's dictum that "the care and education of children becomes a public matter" refers to the legitimatization of community support complementing family care.

The integrity of the family depends upon the strength of the bonding-sharing trait. This integrity has been more and more fractured in recent years. It is not difficult to find sociocultural factors that could be attributed as causes of this fracturing, but we do not often cite obstetric management as *one* of these causes. Rossi contributes the following:

There is hardly an instance in human life in industrial societies that has shown so great a degree of technological interference with a natural process than American obstetric management of pregnancy and birth. In the past fifty years, spontaneous birth in a familiar setting has been replaced by medically managed deliveries, and breast feeding has been largely replaced by bottle feeding.

Until very recently, obstetric practice received very little criticism in the United States, despite the fact that many aspects of obstetric management have warranted it—to name just some of them: heavy reliance on anesthetics which produces drugged babies prone to respiratory distress and apathetic response at birth, the use of instruments which risk brain damage and newborn trauma, obstetric insistence on horizontal delivery tables which prolong second stage labor because the body is not working with but against gravity, foot stirrups which stretch the perineal tissue so that physicians feel justified in performing routine episiotomies that would otherwise be unnecessary in most cases, premature cutting of the umbilical cord which robs the newborn of up to a quart of its blood supply and prolongs the third stage of labor because the placenta remains engorged, and perhaps most important from a psychological perspective, the use of general anesthesia which cheats the mother of consciousness at the moment of birth, at precisely the point when hormonal levels and the euphoria of accomplishment could contribute to a positive experience for the woman and a deep attachment between mother and child. . . . Klaus and his associates have found that the earlier the contact of a mother with her newborn and the longer that contact, the greater the mother-child attachment at the end of the first month. . . . By neglecting the biosocial dimension of human life, American society may set the stage for unprecedented stress in the lives of young mothers and an impoverisment of the quality of their relationship with their children.[18]

Fromm is always eloquent in describing man's relations to nature and to society: "When the infant is born he leaves the security of the womb, the situation in which he was still part of nature—where he lived through his mother's body. At the moment of birth he is still symbiotically attached to the mother, and even after birth he remains so longer than most other animals. The more complete the separation is, the greater the need to replace the original biological roots by new affective roots."[19] "He can dispense with the *natural* roots only insofar as he finds new *human* roots, and only after he has found them, can he feel at home again in this world."[20] The new roots he finds by his own efforts in seeking and developing close relationships with the people about him. A new sense of security is attained.

CONSCIENCE

Loevinger, in discussing the origin of conscience, without which psychosocial bonding-sharing is impossible, attributes five elements to this phenomenon, all dependent on the basic psychosocial relationship between the child and the parents: "Distinguishable elements of conscience originate in difference stages of ego development. Seen from the viewpoint of man as animal, conscience is a sickness, as Nietzsche and Ricoeur have noted; yet it is also a sublime achievement and the beginning of all culture, as Freud noted. The sources of conscience lie in both conscious and unconscious mental life. Conscience is grounded on narcissism and on interpersonal relations. Conscience has its origin in love and in aggression. Conscience in its nature reproduces and memorializes the inequality of station of parent and child; yet in its fullest and rarest reach conscience transcends all inequalities of station."[21]

Loevinger further summarizes: "We have noted five more or less independent sources that contribute to the evolution of a mature conscience. These sources are, in their developmental order, (1) the formation of a sense of self, (2) turning of aggression against the self, (3) the need for mastery, (4) adoption of parental precepts and standards, and (5) mutual love and respect. Each source has its origin in one of the stages of ego development."[22] Loevinger elaborates on the element of love. "The origin of this fifth contributor to conscience lies in love, or, if you will, the *human bond* [italics added]. In explaining altruism, love and conscience are alternatives. Sacrificing one's own interests so as to further the interests of one's own children or spouse is a less decisive evidence for conscience than doing so for some person more remote. At the same time, it is hard to believe that a person would develop much of any conscience without love for other people. The child's love for his parents and it is involved somewhat less directly in other aspects of the . . . formation of conscience."[23] Such explanation of the bonding force is about an aeon away from the sociobiologists' description of bonding in animals.

Mead expounds on the origin of sympathy, an aspect of the bonding-sharing force:

> The attitude that we characterize as that of sympathy in the adult springs from this same capacity to take the role of the other person with whom one is socially implicated. . . . Sympathy always implies that one stimulates himself to his assistance and consideration of others by taking in some degree the attitude of the person whom one is assisting. The common term for this is "putting yourself in his place." It is presumably *an exclusively human type of conduct* [italics added] marked by this involution of stimulating one's self to an action by responding as the other responds. As we shall see, this control of one's conduct, through responding as the other responds, is not confined to kindly conduct. We tend to reserve the term "sympathy," however, for those kindly acts and attitudes which are essential bonding-cords in the life of any human group. . . . There can be no doubt that the fundamental attitude of giving assistance in varied ways to others gets striking exercise in relation to children. Helplessness in any form reduces us to children and arouses the parental response in the other members of the community to which we belong.[24]

RELATEDNESS

When one considers how dependent a child must be for years to survive and develop, how dependent parents become on one another in creating the ecosystem for child and self survival against the physical and biological phenomena of nature, how families cluster together for creating social protective and productive means for survival, and what a bewildering loneliness must have pervaded the human spirit at the dawn of man's emergence from his primary union with nature, and what an extended period of perplexity that must have been for him, then it is not difficult to realize that survival and protection are activities that are and have been common to all races and cultures of *Homo* and the need for a relationship of trust, love, sympathy, and mutual aid among people is basic to maintain the survival and protective system. The urge for relatedness in the human may, in its profound, pristine origin, spring from the nature of propinquity of relationships in the reproductive process of all animal life, but the psychosocial qualities of this relationship are purely human and are distinctly different from the "altruism," "kinship," and "cooperation" described by the sociobiologists in animal behavior. Thus the urge for relatedness became part of human nature and expressed itself as a higher union than *Homo*'s former union with nature, i.e., a union with other human beings manifested as a pervading mutuality for living together, which in the progress of human relations from primitive times blossomed into love relations—love of his mate, his progeny, his forebears, his family, and his world. He became rooted and bonded in his social relations. He felt secure in "belonging socially," which served him as a powerful instrument of "mutual aid" in such groupings as the clan, the tribe, the family, or other protective associations.

Modern man firms up his feeling of security by rooting himself in such social bonds as will generate mutual aid not only by establishing a home and an organized community of neighborly homes, but a community of such communities, a state, a nation, and strives even to establish a friendly world of nations.

CHILD REARING: THE FORGOTTEN RESPONSIBILITY

Alice Rossi has contributed brilliantly in elucidating the dynamics of the bonding-sharing trait:

A remarkable shift has occurred during the past decade in society's opinion of the family, from a general endorsement of it as a worthwhile and stable institution to a general censure of it as oppressive and bankrupt one whose demise is both imminent and welcome. What was defined a decade ago as "deviant" is today labeled "variant" in order to suggest that there is a healthy, experimental quality to current social explorations into the future "beyond monogamy," or "beyond the nuclear family!" . . . More recently, the emphasis in family analysis has been on sex, with a heavy reliance on an egalitarian ideology that denies any innate sex differences and assumes that a "unisex" socialization will produce men and women that are free of the traditional culturally induced sex difference. This egalitarian ethos urges several programmatic changes in family organization: a reduction of maternal investment in children to permit greater psychic investment in work outside the family, an increased investment by men in their fathering roles, and the supplementation of parental care by institutional care. Frequently associated with this emphasis on equal commitment to work and family for both men and women is a corollary emphasis on the autonomy and the "rights" of the child. . . . It is the position of this paper that the older sociological view of the family distorted, and that the new one neglects, the central biological fact that the core function of any family system is human continuity through reproduction and child rearing. More specifically, the paper will argue that the particular version of egalitarianism underlying current sociological research on, and advocacy of, "variant" marriage and family forms is inadequate and misleading because it neglects some fundamental human characteristics rooted in our biological heritage.[25]

Continuing with Rossi's thesis:

During this very long period of human history [millions of years of mammalian primate heritage] adaptation and selection processes contributed to sexual dimorphism and a sexual division of labor. That division of labor did not mean that women were restricted to child-bearing and rearing and men to productive labor for food and group defenses. . . . What it did mean was that reproductive success went to those females capable of two conjoint activities: the bearing and rearing of their young and the hunting of small game and gathering of food within a restricted geographic range compatible of infant and child care. . . . Biologically, males have only one innate orientation, a sexual one that draws them to women, while women have two such orientations, a sexual one toward men and a reproductive one toward the young. . . . No known society replaces the mother as the primary infant-tender except in cases of small and special categories of women. . . . Mother-infant interaction carries a cluster of characteristics that suggest the presence of unlearned responses. . . . The reproductive and endocrine systems that underlie childbearing and lactation are functioning systems within the female throughout her life cycle, and to deny their significance to female psychology or to the organization of family systems is to devalue a central fact in human-species survival for which the human female plays the most critical role, to reveal the profound degree to which many women accept masculine technocratic thinking, and to bypass the significant findings of science pertaining to reproductive and endocrine functioning. . . . The new family sociology seems to be modeled on what has been a male pattern of relating to children in which men turn their fathering on and off to suit themselves or their appointments for business or sexual pleasure. . . . The report [of Rothchild and Wolf on children of counterculture parents] provides an overall portrait of children almost uniformly neglected, deprived, and tormented; many are uneducated, disorganized, and disturbed; a pervasive boredom and lack of joy and serious problem of mal- or under-nourishment were prevalent. . . . By neglecting the biosocial dimension of human life, American society may set the stage for unprecedented stress in the lives of young mothers and an impoverishment of the quality of their relationship with their children. . . . The application of a biosocial perspective to current explorations of marriage and parenthood puts serious questions to the *cultural determinism* to which the social sciences have long adhered [italics added]. . . . In my judgement, by far the wiser course to such a future is to plan and build from the most fundamental root of society in human parenting, and not from the shaky superstructure created by men in that fraction of time in which industrial societies have existed.[26]

MONOGAMY OR PRIMATE SEXUALITY?

Rossi skillfully and with all presently available scientific background reveals the naivete, the unscholarly interjection of claims and conclusions, and the ignorance of the history of humankind with which the social scientists of the counterculture use their bankrupt ideology of *cultural determinism* to prove how oppressive the family is to their lingering, childish self-indulgence in sex, in free-wheeling, in irresponsibility, and in pursuing their "thing." A good example is the Smiths' *Beyond Monogamy*.[27] In dealing with such a biosocial phenomenon as the family and the psychosocial traits of human nature involved in its structure and function, cultural factors may support or deter the attaining and maintaining individual and social well-being.

However, where it is taken as *the* determinant of the social process, it becomes impossible to understand what induces discord between human nature and the ecosystem, since it denies the existence of human nature and biosocial forces. The Smiths' scholastic finesse is revealed in their misjudgment of Marx's philosophic rendering of the origin of monogamy to support their free-wheeling sex commentary.[28] Engels, Marx's collaborator, would have demolished their misapplied comparison of the origin of commodities in capitalistic production with the origin of monogamy as a capitalistic invention. A hundred years before the Smiths made their observations, Engels predicted, based on the best anthropological information available that the highest stage of monogamy (which, he states, originated with the emergence of civilization, not capitalism) would be attained in the future under communism.[29] Engels's main sources of information in study of the history of the family were Lewis H. Morgan, E. A. Westermarck, Charles Darwin, J. F. McLennan, and J. J. Bachofen. Such popular writers on the subject at the present time as Masters and Johnson state emphatically concerning the counterculture "philosophers" that "this kind of conjecturing, which totally repudiates the established principles of sexual commitment, owes less to disciplined observation of what most people require in order to live sexually effective lives than it owes to wishful fantasies about how they ought to live."[30] The present-day popular versions of egalitarianism that preach no obligation, no responsibility, untrammeled freedom of action, the right of everyone "to do one's thing" are philosophies of complete social chaos, and this is beginning to show up in our social lives today.

The dislocation of the bonding-sharing process in families or among other close relations may spark mental disorder as observed by Abrams:

> Stressful life events have consistently been found to be related to psychological problems. . . . It is current social stressors which seem to have an even stronger association with depressive symptoms [than similar past events]. Research indicates that marital stressors appear to have the highest and most significant relationship with depression. Parental stressors (for mothers) and job stressors (for married men) have a statistically significant correlation with depression (Ilfeld, 1977). Making a comparison with past sources of stress, Ilfeld states, "My view is that current social stressors that are patterned into our everyday roles as marital partners, breadwinners, and parents are equally as important in affecting mental status.[31]

In such circumstances of family involvement, the bonding-sharing trait is, for the most part, the dominant trait affected. The cognitive factor determines how one interprets life's circumstances, i.e., whether there be harmony or discord in the relation of the ecosystem to the traits of human nature and therefore is basic to the development of mental disorder.

DiGiuseppe further elaborates in this vein: "From clinical observations, Spirak (1975) hypothesized that disturbed populations appear to lack specific thinking proceses that would enable them to adequately solve social problems, the result being anxiety or inappropriate behavioral excesses. . . . Beck (1976) and Ellis (1962, 1972) view the role of cognition in maladaptive behavior similarly. They stress the existence of maladaptive thoughts which bring about disturbed emotional states such as anxiety, depression, or anger. Maladaptive thoughts are illogical and/or exaggerated ideas which falsely represent reality."[32] Adaptation, of course, does not mean giving in to disruptive social conditions that violate the traits of human nature by merely adapting to them passively. To devise methodology for social change is also adaptation, but in an active, participatory way.

Thus it is of fundamental importance to understand what in the social environment induces certain patterns of irrational cognition in people resulting in maladaptive behavior. What is the process that elicits emotional disturbance in some and motivation for changing the circumstances in others when the ecosystem is in disharmony with the traits of human nature?

LOVE BONDS AND THE FAMILY

Love, the most powerful element of the bonding-sharing force, is recognized by Montagu and by many other cultural anthropologists, ethologists, and other social scientists as an all-pervading trait of human behavior. Let some of the eminent anthropologists and other social scientists speak for themselves on this matter. Montagu strongly advises that: "The evidence, such as it is, all points in the same direction, namely, that love is the most important of all developers of the potentialities of human beings, and that love is the most adaptively valuable trait of the species."[33] This, in a general way, affirms Friederich Engels's predictive interpretation in 1884 of the future development of monogamy from an economic basis to a love relationship.

Montagu defines *love* as: "behavior calculated to confer survival benefits in a creatively enlarged manner upon the other. For the dependent infant it consists in the satisfaction of its basic needs as well as such perceptual needs as touch, vision, hearing, and the vestibular, oral, and gastrointestinal experiences, to name the more obvious ones. Even more important than these is the communication of the feeling of deep involvement in the welfare of the other, that the infant can depend upon you for the support, sustenance, and stimulation it requires for that feeling of security so essential to healthy development."[34]

In discussing the ability of the Winnebago Indians to formulate ethical codes, Radin quotes the following two precepts of the Winnebago code of behavior: Precept 1: "If you hear of a person travelling through your country and you want to see him, prepare your table and send for him. In this manner you will do good and it is always good to do good." Precept 2: "What does life consist of but love? All the members of the clan have given me counsel and all the women and children have pleaded in my behalf with the spirits. What love was that! And of what does life consist but of love?"[35]

Some sociobiologists [36,37,38,39] stress the importance of altruism as a basic impulse in the history of the development of mankind. Regardless of whether they attribute a genetic basis for this human trait, phylogenetically as well as ontogenetically, the important consideration is that even the sociobiologists regard as fundamental to the nature of man the manifestation of "love" as defined by Montagu. Dubos discusses the existence of altruism and affection as human traits as far back as Neanderthal times, based on archaeological findings in the Shanidar cave of Iraq and in Stone Age tombs.[40] Soleci, the author of *Shanidar*, states: "From archaeological findings elsewhere we already know that Neanderthal man seems to have had a spiritual concept, since he evidently practiced funerary rites over his dead. But the occurrence of flowers with Neanderthal burials raises the question, where else in prehistory is there any parallel? Searching through the literature on Stone Age cultures yields nothing. . . . With the finding of flowers in association with Neanderthals, we are brought suddenly to the realization that the universality of mankind and the love of beauty go beyond the boundary of our own species. No longer can we deny the early men the full range of human feelings and experience."[41] Dubos affirms further: "Whether or not the words altruism and love had equivalents in the language of the Stone Age, the social attitudes which they denote existed."[42]

Love binds all the traits of human nature together in an interpentrating unity. This is so well stated by Erikson:

> Love is the greatest of human virtues, and in fact, the dominant virtue of the universe. . . . It must be an important evolutionary fact that man, over and above sexuality, develops a selectivity of love: I think it is the *mutuality of mates and partners in a shared identity,* for the mutual verification through an experience of finding oneself, as one loses oneself, in another. . . . Identity proves itself strongest where it can take chances with itself. For this reason, love in its truest sense presupposes both identity and fidelity. . . . Intimate love thus is the guardian of that elusive and yet all-pervasive power in *psychosocial* evolution: the power of *cultural and personal style,* which gives and demands conviction in the shared pattern of living, guarantees individual identity in joint intimacy, and binds into a "way of living" the affiliations of procreation and of production. . . . *Love,* then, *is mutuality of devotion forever subduing the antagonism inherent in divided function.*[43]

The force of bonding-sharing is the cement that holds together as a unit the other traits of human nature. If this force be not hindered from operating because of an unfavorable ecosystem, any obstructive circumstances restraining the adequate expression of the other traits of human nature are mitigated in their discordant effect by the bonding-sharing force. The importance of this force cannot be exaggerated, therefore, as the most fundamental essence of human society's origin, maintenance, durability, and development. The bonding-sharing force is the generating center of the other aspects of this force, i.e., love, mutual aid, cooperation, sympathy, care, trust, empathy, commitment to the welfare of others, altruism, and family attachment. Even the basic political-economic motor of social development, exchange, has its essence in this force. It has molded the family from its organization based on the division of labor of the sexes to its organization based on the economics of the slave and feudal periods to its present transitional nature based on sex love. It welded families into clans, gens, tribes, city-states, and nation-states and has been trying to weld the nation-states into a United Nations organization. Through all these hundreds of thousands of years of development, the family has been the keystone of the societal structure, i.e., just as essential to human society as the means of production.

THE FAMILY FALTERS

The modern Western family has gone through a number of changes, which have increasingly weakened the children's identification with it, have rendered them psychologically alone, have given them a freedom from coercion with minimal constraints, and have deprived them of close ones in whom to invest strong emotions. As Kagan put it: "We take as an axiom that the self resists depersonalization. As modern environments make a sense of potency and individual effectiveness more difficult to attain, freedom from all affective involvements becomes more and more intolerable. Involvement with a family is the only viable mechanism available to satisfy that hunger. The forces that initially weakened the family—urbanization and industrialization—have produced conditions a century later that are now likely to strengthen it."[44] This is a good illustration of the law that "changes in quantity beyond a certain threshold will produce a change in quality." Kagan obviously understands the deep-rooted nature of certain aspects of human behavior, especially the bonding-sharing force that resists the sense of loneliness that tends to depersonalize the individual. The need for rootedness in a group assures the feeling of individual effectiveness and competence, and the need for constraints to individual autonomy and freedom to choose further assure affective involvement and commitment to others. These deep-rooted needs are expressions of traits of human nature. An ecosystem that is discordant to these traits generates behavioral disorientations in those affected.

The basic philosophy of the Smiths expressed in the following citation shows how immature sentiments and lack of scholarly delving into the history of humankind can breed distorted reasoning particularly when based on discredited cultural determinism as valid theory for human behavior:

> Liberation from sexual possessiveness and all that it feeds and thrives on in the self and the environment must be gotten rid of in order to achieve the state of open, free, permissive marriage. We have not been divested of sexual possessiveness because of the damnable consequence of a process of repressive primary sexual socialization which, in fostering the cultural ideology of monogamy and perpetuating the procreative sex ethic as the indispensable dual standards of sexual relationships and sexual expression eventuates in feelings of sex jealousy and renders many persons emotionally lame and even physiologically impo-

tent in the adult years. Their sexuality is stifled, truncated, and subject to a myriad minor handicaps and self-negating blind spots.[45]

Monogamy on Trial?

The Smiths have not learned that sexual possessiveness and monogamy are not necessarily capitalist expressions of its private property system, anymore than they are expressions of the Soviet Union social system. Primate behavior had a strain of possessiveness, but, of course, in a different context, and it was not based on private property or monogamy as one could expect. Primitive people as we know them from ancient written history and present-day remnants were monogamous and polygamous. They were not capitalistic, yet they were sexually possessive. Primitive people as we know them from present-day primitive societies have a sense of sexual possessiveness as expressed in the marriage contract and expressions of jealousy [46,47]. Although these marriages were both group or monogamous, they were not rigidly so, since the real sense of solidarity was in the clan. Sexual possessiveness was present among the slaves and serfs of ancient and feudal societies, although they were themselves private property and owned practically no property themselves, nor did they live under capitalism, nor were they dedicated and engaged in free monogamous practice.

As far as we know, jealousy has been a human response since time immemorial and has nothing to do with being culturally determined. It seems to be largely an emotional response associated with the cognitive process engendering the trait of self-image–self-esteem, whereby thoughts of oneself being depreciated are involved.[48] Culture merely gives it various and specific colors of expression. *Jealousy* is defined as a disposition, attitude, or feeling of intolerance of rivalry or unfaithfulness, of being disposed to suspect rivalry or unfaithfulness, of being apprehensive of loss of another's exclusive devotion, of hostility toward a rival or one believed to enjoy an advantage, of being vigilant in guarding a possession, or of being depreciated by various circumstances.

Such a reaction is a complex of a number of basic psychosocial traits of the human being. Like some human reactions to personally concerned situations, it may become exaggerated by intense cognitive discursiveness eliciting emotional responses to the point of behavioral disorientation. The psychosocial traits involved besides the self-image–self-esteem trait could be the bonding-sharing trait, the trait of devotion to a philosophy of life, the trait of freedom to choose, the trait of role performance, and the trait of self-competence. Since each trait of human nature is biphasic, in jealousy there is a tendency for the negative phases of the traits to express themselves. But since the negative phases are also part of human nature, jealousy can never be completely eliminated from human reaction. But not all jealousy is an expression of negativity. For example, when a person produces a work of art, it becomes the expression of that person's life—it is a part of his or her life. When the work of art is depreciated or defaced or destroyed, a part of the artist's life has been diminished. The same is true when a person gives a part of his or her life in a love bond to another person. If the bond appears to be in jeopardy, the response will be strong or moderate, inhibited or demonstrable, violent or controlled, depending as much on the biological makeup of the person as on training. Othello's nature (of precapitalist vintage) was one of strong loyalty, simple and straightforward in carriage, sober in justice. Shakespeare, a profound student of human behavior, created the character, and Verdi's librettist, Arrigo Boito, wrote character studies to aid the singers in the principal roles. After Iago provoked Othello, Boito wrote: "Othello utters a cry and Iago suddenly says, 'Beware, my lord, of jealousy.' *Jealousy!* The word is uttered. Iago has first pierced Othello's heart, then rubbed salt in the wound. The torture of the Moor is begun. The man is transformed [primate reactions are taking over]. He was judicious, now he raves; he was strong, now he is a criminal; he was sane and joyful, now he moans and falls and faints like a body poisoned or stricken with epilepsy. And Iago's words truly are poison injected into the Moor's blood. . . . Othello undergoes, step by step, the most horrible tortures of the human heart—doubt, fury, lethal depression."[49]

It is clear what flimsy logic the antimonogamy adherents use in proving that "liberation from sexual possessiveness" that is equated to the capitalistic monogamy ethos will be the next great revolution in human behavior. A revolution against the traits of human nature!

EGALITARIANISM

The misinterpretation of egalitarianism among present-day activists needs clarification. Douglas Rae, in his most exhaustive discussion of the egalitarian state, concludes that even the most powerful state cannot attain equality of opportunity "for the same reason that it cannot square a circle."[50] Rossi has clarified the issue well: "One of the characteristics an active egalitarian movement has in common with social science thinking is an extreme emphasis on cultural determinism. The activists ... base their political efforts on the belief that adults have the ability to change their values and goals. ... Activists who are also social scientists are under a double social pressure to argue from a strong cultural determinist perspective. The result is a tendency in much contemporary thinking to *confuse equality* with *identity* and *diversity* with *inequality*. But where age and sex are concerned, diversity is a biological fact, while equality is a political, ethical, and social precept" (italics added).[51] Early in the long hunter-gatherer period of hominid history, plant food and small animals were foraged by females to feed the children. Male hunters shared their larger animal meats with their own maternal relatives. Thus, far from being dependent on the males for food for survival, females were themselves crucial to the survival of the group.[52,53] The female certainly had social equality and maintained her female diversity and did not attempt to pretend to behave identically as males in accordance with their modern counterparts in the feminist and unisex movements. Later the sexual division of labor and the males' specialization in hunting added a new element to this system. Males *and* females for the first time in primate evolution shared responsibility for feeding the children. This mutual economic interest led eventually to emotional attachment that linked specific males to specific females. Gradually, dependence on meat led to male dominance.[54,55]

Today there is no reason why the female should not have political, ethical, and social (including economic) equality without societal dislocations resulting mainly from the psychosocial trauma to children growing up in a disorganized family atmosphere. In such a situation, besides the bonding-sharing force being counterposed, practically all the other traits of human nature would be violated. Of course, an exceptional mother here and there might be emotionally prepared and ingenious enough to prevent grievous results.

SUMMARY

The most predominant trait of human nature is the bonding-sharing trait, which is the begetter of altruism, mutual aid, love, cooperation, sympathy, empathy, family attachment, compassion, care, and trust—all this with the help of a conscience which is born from this interrelation. This is the trait that humanizes the potentials of the other traits. It muffles egocentrism with altruism. It directs creativity toward social uses. It steers striving toward goals of compatibility with social good. It modulates the freedom to choose toward social behavior. It colors the mind's projection into the future with hope. It activates those challenges that involve the eventual social good. The bonding force, although phylogenetically present in practically all animal life, is ontogenetically specific in each genus and even species. However, in the genus *Homo* it became so specific and unique with its sharing and exchange aspects that its humanizing effect on the other traits of human nature made possible *Homo*'s domination of the earth by progressively harnessing nature to its use. The bonding-sharing force, therefore, is basically the humanizing trait—humanizing force against what? It could be only the antithesis of the humanizing force—the antihumanizing force. What is antihumanizing? It is that state of behavior that the humanizing force replaced as dominant in *Homo,* i.e., primate behavior. But since *Homo* is no longer a non-*Homo*, his primate behavior can be expressed *only as modified* primate behavior—primate behavior as modified by the potentialities of the *Homo* brain's cognitive powers, i.e., modified by a free will, a conscience, and a symbolization process expressed in language and art and the ability to evaluate and to create and plan and hope for the future. Let it not be inferred from the above that primate behavior is malevolent and reprehensible. Not so. For the nonhuman primate, primate behavior is suitable and necessary. But the human cannot behave as a nonhuman primate, only as a human primate. Thus *Homo* has buried in his being the impulses to behave as a primate, but modified by the potentials of the *Homo* brain which can transmute that primate potential for eliciting devious antihuman and antisocial expressions. For example, in the care of ape children, parental and nonparental adults will protect the juvenile, but among aggressive subordinate males are those impulses to strike against the dominant male and thereby possibly incurring the violence of the dominant male. To protect itself, the subordinate male may snatch up an infant and interpose it as protection (agonistic buffering).[56] A human being with a more creative mind for maneuvering may, in a state of behavioral disorientation develop a pattern of child abuse that may spill over to spouse abuse and, in cases of social disorientation, devise ritual infanticide. Thus, by a reversion to primate behavior, the more mentally versatile human primate whose faulted socialization netted him little native intraspecific inhibitions against violence and killing as some primates do will conjure up greater destructive methods of antisocial behavior than the nonhuman primates are capable of. What makes the disoriented human's behavior more vicious to a human is the fact that the human has a conscience, whereas in the nonhuman primate the action is, for the most part, automatic response. Is it any wonder that, during more ancient times and even in the recent past, *Homo* conjured up evil spirits, Satans, devils, and gods of evil as "possessing" those with disapproved behavior, which was a way of alluding unwittingly to primate behavior.

One of the most urgent tasks of the human race is keeping the human aspect of the bonding-sharing trait dominant in human behavior.

NOTES

1. Richard B. Lee, *!Kung San: Men, Women and Work in a Foraging Society* (New York: Cambridge University Press, 1979), p. 491.

2. Ibid., p. 490.

3. Ibid., p. 489.

4. Erich Fromm, *The Anatomy of Human Destructiveness* (New York: Holt, Rinehart, and Winston, 1973), pp. 216–17.

5. Russell and Ingrid Z. Grieger, ed., *Cognition and Emotional Disturbance* (New York: Human Sciences Press, 1982), 13–14.

6. Edward O. Wilson, *Sociobiology* (Cambridge, Mass.: Harvard University Press, 1975), p. 336.

7. Ibid., p. 348.

8. John Bowlby, *Attachment,* vol. 1 (New York: Basic Books, Inc., 1969), pp. 177–234.

9. "Patterns of Attachment: A Book Review by Michael E. Lamb, *A Psychological Study of the Strange Situation,* Mary D. Ainsworth, M. C. Blehar, E. Waters, and S. Wall, Erlbaum, Hillsdale, 1978," *Science,* vol. 204 (May 18, 1979), pp. 730–31.

10. E. H. Spicer, *Science,* "Persistent Cultural Systems," vol. 174, no. 4011 (November 19, 1971), pp. 795–800.

11. Leonard Williams, *Challenge to Survival* (New York: New York University Press, 1977), p. 129.

12. Benjamin DeMott, *Psychology Today,* "The Pro-Incest Lobby," vol. 13, no. 10 (March 1980), pp. 11–18.

13. Yehudi Cohen, *Human Nature,* "The Disappearance of the Incest Taboo," (July 1976), pp. 72–78.

14. M. D. Sahlins, *Scientific American,* "The Origin of Society," vol. 203 (September 1960), pp. 76–87.

15. Marshall Sahlins, *The Use and Abuse of Biology* (Ann Arbor, Michigan: University of Michigan Press, 1976), p. 11.

16. Friederich Engels, *The Origin of the Family* (Minneapolis, Minnesota: Charles H. Kerr and Co., 1902), pp. 9–10.

17. Ibid., pp. 90, 91, 92, 93.

18. Alice S. Rossi, "A Biosocial Perspective on Parenting," *Daedalus* (Spring 1977), pp. 1–31.

19. Erich Fromm, *The Anatomy of Human Destructiveness* (New York: Henry Holt, 1973), pp. 232–233. From *The Anatomy of Human Destructiveness* by Erich Fromm. Copyright © 1973 by Erich Fromm. Reprinted by permission of Henry Holt and Company.

21. Jane Loevinger, *Ego Development* (San Francisco, California: Jossy-Bass Publishers, 1976), p. 411.

22. Ibid., p. 408–409.

23. Ibid., p. 407.

24. George H. Mead, *Mind, Self, and Society* (Chicago, Illinois: University of Chicago Press, 1934), p. 366.

25. Alice S. Rossi, "A Biosocial Perspective on Parenting," *Daedalus* (Spring 1977), pp. 1–31.

26. Alice S. Rossi, "The Biosocial Side of Parenthood," *Human Nature* (June 1978), pp. 72–79.

27. J. R. Smith and L. G. Smith, *Beyond Monogamy* (Baltimore, Maryland: Johns Hopkins University Press, 1974).

28. Ibid., p. 33.

29. Friederich Engels, *The Origin of the Family* (Minneapolis, Minnesota: Charles H. Kerr and Co., 1902), pp. 90–93.

30. W. H. Masters and Virginia E. Johnson, *The Pleasure Bond* (New York: Bantam Books, 1975), p. 192.

31. Eliot Abrams, "Cognition and Major Mental Disorders," in *Cognition and Emotional Disturbance,* Russell and Ingrid Z. Grieger, ed. (New York: Human Sciences Press, 1982), pp. 135–36.

32. Raymond DiGiuseppi, "Problems of Children and Their Parents," in *Cognition and Emotional Disturbance* by Russell and Ingrid Z. Grieger, ed. (New York: Human Sciences Press, 1982), p. 217–220.

33. M. F. Ashley Montagu, *Anthropology and Human Nature* (Boston, Massachusetts: Porter Sargent Publisher, 1957), p. 13.

34. M. F. Ashley Montagu, *The Nature of Human Aggression* (New York: Oxford University Press, 1976) p. 224.

35. P. Radin, *Primitive Man as Philosopher* (Pasedena, California: D. Appleton and Co., 1927), p. 70. From PRIMITIVE MAN AS PHILOSOPHER by Paul Radin. Copyright 1927 by D. Appleton & Co., renewed 1955 by Paul Radin. A Hawthorn book. Reprinted by permission of E.P. Dutton, a division of New American Library.

36. E. O. Wilson, *Sociobiology* (Cambridge, Massachusetts: Harvard University Press, 1975), p. 120.

37. D. P. Barash, *Sociobiology and Behavior* (New York: Elsevier, 1977), pp. 70–103.

38. J. Alcock, *Animal Behavior* (Sunderland, Massachusetts: Sinauer Assoc., Inc., 1975), pp. 485–492.

39. J. L. Brown, *The Evolution of Behavior* (New York: W. W. Norton and Co., 1975), pp. 196–213.

40. Rene Dubos, *Beast or Angel?* (New York: Scribner and Sons, 1974), p. 46.

41. R. S. Soleci, *Shanidar: The First Flower People* (New York: A. A. Knopf, 1971), p. 250.

42. Dubos, *loco supra citato*, p. 47.

43. E. M. Erikson, *Insight and Responsibility* (New York: W. W. Norton and Co., 1964), pp. 127, 128, 129.

44. Jerome Kagan, "The Child in the Family," *Daedalus* (Spring 1977), pp. 33–56.

45. J. R. and L. G. Smith, eds., *Beyond Monogamy* (Baltimore, Maryland: Johns Hopkins University Press, 1974), pp. 2–3.

46. P. Radin, *The World of Primitive Man* (New York: E. P. Dutton and Co., 1971).

47. Alexander Goldenweiser, "Sex and Primitive Society," *Sex in Civilization,* V. F. Salverton and D. Schmalhausen, eds. (Macauley Co. 1929).

48. Virginia Adams, "Jealous Love," *Psychology Today,* pp. 38–47, 102–105.

49. Arrigo Boito, "Dramatis Personae," *Opera News,* vol. 44, no. 13 (February 9, 1980), p. 18.

50. Alice S. Rossi, "A Biosocial Perspective on Parenting," *Daedalus* (Spring 1977), pp. 1–31.

51. Douglas Rae, "The Egalitarian State," *Daedalus* (Fall 1979), pp. 37–54.

52. Gina Bari Kolata, "Human Evolution: Life-Style and Lineage of Early Hominids," *Science,* vol. 187 (March 14, 1975), pp. 940–42.

53. Gina Bari Kolata, "!Kung Hunter-Gatherers: Feminisim, Diet, and Birth Control," *Science,* vol. 185 (September 13, 1974), pp. 932-34.

54. Jane B. Lancaster, "Carrying and Sharing in Human Evolution," *Human Nature* (February 1978), pp. 82–85.

55. Ernestine Friedl, "Society and Sex Roles," *Human Nature* (April 1978), pp. 68–75.

56. David P. Barash, *Sociobiology and Behavior* (New York: Elsevier, 1977), p. 199.

7

The Trait of Freedom to Choose

DESIRE: THE MAINSPRING TO ACTION

The need to feel free to evaluate situations and to freely choose to satisfy what one judges to be necessary and desirous for oneself, but within the context of the recognized needs of others based on the community's moral and ethical conscience, is basic to the behavior that is supportive of being human.

Desire is the mainspring of human motivation. Man desires that, material and immaterial, which he creates or which has been created as components of his culture, or created by nature as part of his environment, and which he judges and finds to satisfy his sensibilities and his physiological needs, and, at the same time, he aspires to have the freedom to choose or not to choose from among various alternatives in satisfying his desires.

There is an element of primeval behavior in the trait of freedom-to-choose. When the process of cognition created a glimmer in the developing mind of the earliest hominid that an urge or need could be satisfied by consciously self-directing one's behavior and manipulating one's surroundings in such a way as to control the outcome, a sense of power must have passed a surging thrill through his mind and spirit. The power to control is like an indigenous impulse differentiated from an instinct in that it is associated with the behavior of consciously cognizing, self-directing primates. In the study of the development of speech in children, Kuczai makes the following observation in answer to the question: Why do children play with language?: "Children obviously enjoy play, and even the casual observer might be led to conclude that, to the child, play is its own reward. However, what is it about play that the child finds intrinsically satisfying? The intrinsic reward for play appears to be the control that the child possesses in play situations. While playing, the child is in control of the situation, creating processes and results more and more at will."[1]

It appears to be this primogenial sense of satisfaction in having the power to control that almost generates a sense of psychological addiction in the need of freedom to choose. It was a wonderful power to primitive man in being able to guide his behavior in the midst of the ever-changing conditions in which he found himself. It gave him the ability to become an active force in nature. However, this power to choose when exercised to the extreme in one direction to feed the ego is one of great corrupting influences in human behavior as well as one of the characteristics of genius. The freedom to choose in controlling what is extrinsic without exercising the freedom to choose in controlling what is intrinsic is a basic problem in human behavior.

To state that man needs to feel free to evaluate situations and to freely choose to satisfy his desires sounds idyllic and idealistic. But the truth of the matter is that the act of being *responsible* for making a choice, after the "period of primate innocence" of childhood, is a struggle. Depending on the circumstances, this struggle may be minimum for the less complicated circumstances or major and even life-threatening in the more complex circumstances. This is what one's counselor would empathetically call living. The nature of the traits of human nature makes living a struggle, since every trait is a contention between contradictory impulses—one urging to behave *humanly,* the other urging action in the cast of primate nature. Therefore, freedom to choose is a struggle if it be done with the social responsibility of a humanized *Homo sapiens sapiens,* since the latter has for tens of thousands of years harnessed his *freedom to choose* with responsibility for supporting the needs of his societal life. The greatest freedom to choose is manifested by having knowledge of the essential dynamics of one's social world and of the traits of one's human nature. Freedom to choose is not a cultural phenomenon, although what one chooses may be cultural. It is a psychosocial aspect of being human in one's relations with human beings, since choosing without discretion for human relations can destroy oneself and others. When the choice is at *no time* a contention, mental pathology exists.

The automatic responses of nonhuman primates may *resemble* rationally directed action and may even have the enlage of such an action, while many habitual responses of the human may resemble the automatic, the instinctual, actions of the nonhuman primate. There is, of course, a gray area of behavior where the automatic instinctual responses of the nonhuman *appear* equivalent to the split-second habitual response of the human, and yet, from the consideration of *Homo's* socioanthropological history as compared to the biosociological history of nonhuman primates, these two areas of behavioral responses are, seemingly, an aeon apart. Freedom to choose, i.e., the free-will potential to act, is the cognitive essence of *Homo's* behavior, that characteristic of it which gives it the element of purpose in the human drive. What is *human* about the split-second responses of the socialized person is that the habits learned in the socialization process, except such reflexes as withdrawal from fire, are psychosocio-cultural reactions based on societal experiences that at their inception were freedom-of-choice decisions based on considerations of what was compatible with social stability. But social man also operates family life, community life, and national interrelations on deliberately considered aims and plans of his own choosing, but framed within the boundaries of maintaining a dynamic social equilibrium. What "social" community of non-human primates operates in such a context of psychosocial and spiritual orientation that creates an Iroquois Confederation, a League of Nations, and a United Nations as well as a Congressional Library, a British Museum, a Smithsonian Institute, a Manhattan Project, the public and private school systems that train people to create the machinery for industrial revolutions, the architectural monuments of ancient Greece and Rome, and the modern metropolises and communications with the celestial bodies?

Sense of judging values and freedom to choose or not to choose between alternatives

Human — Choosing to act according to the precepts of the community behavioral norms, thus demonstrating to oneself the ability to inhibit antisocial impulses

Primate — Choosing to act according to one's uninhibited desires and impulses

The need to satisfy a physiological necessity is inherent in all animal life. If this were not so, life would terminate. As we examine this phenomenon on a comparative basis, we are led to judge, from all appearances, that the higher in the scale of evolution that we examine this phenomenon, the more this need resembles a conscious purposeful desire. But only in the human being are conscious purposeful desires, or, more correctly, self-conscious desires, both physiological and psychological, tremendous forces in motivating people to act teleologically and with imaginative forethought. The cognitive processes of the neopallium make possible the unique imagination, intelligent behavior, and intellectual performances of the human. The latter processes make him aware of his desires and are involved in creating them and urge him to satisfy them, usually within the bounds of the community conscience. The nature of the ego is such that it needs to be free to choose how and when to satisfy or to inhibit the satisfaction of the impulse of desire. This is a basic trait of human nature, which is either accommodated or violated by the ecosystem, i.e., by the personal interrelations inherent in the dynamics of society's structure and organization.

The basic nature of desire is described by Schneirla's protégés as follows:

> The emergence of a wish marks the phylogenetic as well as the ontogenetic beginning of psychic structure. The transition is from "somatic needs," a physiological concept, to the psychological concept of instinctual drives as mental representations of stimuli arising within the soma. In Schneirla's terminology the emergence of a wish marks the transition from "approach" to "seeking," from a biosocial to a psychosocial pattern. . . . The wish must extend not only to the recathexis* of the memory of satisfaction . . . but to the recathexis of more and more details of the situation of satisfaction. . . . The need to recreate any situation of satisfaction, or at least to recathect its memory trace, is regulated by the pleasure principle.[2]

Loevinger defines the pleasure principle by stating: "People act to maximize pleasure and minimize pain."[3] It is clear that desire is the basis also of the trait to strive to satisfy appetites, inclinations, and talents and ultimately to energize the other traits.

In order for people to be able to actuate their choice in satisfying their impulses of desires, they must be free to do so—not absolutely free to proceed positively, but also to choose *not* to proceed, for always to proceed headlong would lead eventually to chaos, and very few are free under chaotic conditions. To be free to choose on a reasonable, humane, and social-norm–guided basis is where their choices would be within the bounds of what is considered the social and individual

---

*Reinvestment with psychic energy.

good. Therefore, the human need to be free to choose is not a quality that stands alone beyond society, but one that is monitored by the social conscience. To be absolutely free beyond the social realm would be meaningless to a human being. The greatest freedom to choose that one could have is in a democratic society, primitive or modern—to be able to choose or to choose not to choose according to one's desires as guided by that democratic social ethos.

MARX ON ALIENATION

Much has been written on the subject of human freedom, ranging from its complete denial to its absolute affirmation, and philosophically, from the strictest materialistic behaviorism to extreme teleological idealism of solipsistic nature. Hegel, the philosophical idealist, was the first modern philosopher who gave this subject a dynamic form, showing its dialectic nature and giving it a form that showed its essential nature to be a basis for sociological study. This was done by describing the relation of freedom to choose to estrangement and alienation in his extensive, detailed, relentless, almost mind-boggling presentation of the subject in his *Phenomenology of Mind*.[4] At this point, an explanatory diversion needs to be pursued in order to stress a very practical consideration—the comparison of "freedom to choose" in a capitalistic democracy and in a Soviet socialist type of dictatorship. This is a practical consideration because of the entire world concern with the Helsinki Agreement's section on human rights, which basically involves this question. To understand the pros and cons of this problem, there is need to elaborate on Marx's contribution to the subject of alienation. Karl Marx, the Hegelian turned materialist, saw the importance of this philosophic relationship and developed this subject in a truly significant manner in relation to the everyday mundane world.

Marx adapted the usage of the term "alienation" in describing the dynamic relations of how "capital" is generated and the relations of labor to capital and the worker to the product he produced, which relations were for Marx the essence of capitalism. He defined "alienation" in the following terms: "The *alienation* of the worker in his product means only that his labor becomes an object, an *external* existence, but that it exists *outside him,* independently, as something alien to him, and that it becomes a power on its own [as capital] confronting him. It means that the life which he has conferred on the object confronts him as something hostile and alien."[5] To Marx, alienation also meant the appropriation of "the worker in his product" by capitalists. Torrance's scholarly study clarifies and expands Marx's contribution on the subject and defines the above terms as follows: Alienation is "the renunciation or relinquishment of possession, or of a claim to something, or of a liberty or power to do some action—usually, but not necessarily, in favor of some other person or persons specified or unspecified. . . . It denotes simply a type of social action or social practice: an action which has the effect of altering a social relationship previously existing between a person and others affected by the claims or powers relinquished. . . . If it is to be a scholarly or scientific concept at all, therefore, it is at least potentially a sociological concept."[6]

Although, in the English language, estrangement is another aspect of the meaning of *alienation,* Torrance separates this meaning from that of alienation, in order, as he sees it, to conform to Hegels and Marx's separate and distinct usage of *"Entausserung"* (alienation) and *"Entfremdung"* (estrangement).[7] Torrance then defines *estrangement* as denoting "a process, or condition, by which people become or are strangers or enemies to one another. Usually, but perhaps not necessarily, its use implies a contrast with a previous state of solidarity. Certainly, for this sense of mutual estrangement, 'solidarity' denotes the opposite condition."[8] This term does not refer to objective action, but to subjective feeling, i.e., it refers to "how people feel about one another and describes the affective tone of texture of a relationship, or the direction in which its emotional content is changing."[9] To some extent, this distinction of terms resembles Etzioni's distinction between alienation and inauthenticity.[10] However, sometimes Marx seems to use these terms interchangeably.

Marx began his philosophizing with the economic fact that ubiquitously presented itself to him that the wage-laborer was in a precarious predicament. Life, for the wage-laborer, Marx observed, began in the process of making a living. He had lost his *freedom to choose* (a trait of human nature that Marx called "species-being") how to use his labor, how to control the product of his creativity, how to utilize his spare time if he had any, how to pursue the challenge of developing his talents, how to take care of his family in accordance with a plan for the future, and so forth to the other frustrations of accommodating his social circumstances to the traits of being human. It was very clear to Marx that "an immediate consequence of the fact that man [the wage-laborer] is estranged from the product of his labour, from his life activity, from his species-being is the *estrangement of man from man.* . . . In fact, the proposition that man's species nature is estranged from him means that one man is estranged from the other, as each of them is from man's essential nature."[11] Thus Marx sensed that in the capitalist mode of production, man's very species nature or human nature is violated. From this *value* judgment, he built a devastating analysis of the whole fabric of the capitalist social structure. According to this analysis the capitalist system was not built by means of the emotion-laden concepts inherent in the term "estrangement," but Marx's awareness that the very essence of man's nature was being violated by a conscienceless system that drove him to his analysis of the alienating nature of the system.[12] His economic theory was actually built on the cognitive value concept of alienation, on which his whole analysis of commodity value and exchange, exchange-value, and surplus-value is based.

Freedom as a general and complete abstraction is meaningless. Freedom, to have social meaning, must refer to man's freedom to choose. When the terms "alienation" and "estrangement" are applied to specific social relations, their meanings would be empty unless freedom to choose were basic to the actions and feelings of the people involved. Freedom to choose also implies freedom *not* to choose. In real life, the freedom to choose or not to choose is conditioned by moral and ethical norms, coercion, emotional tones, power relations, and a complex of desires. These psychosocial phenomena that react with the traits of human nature must be considered in judging exchange actions between people upon which Marx built his whole analysis of the capitalist system. *The structure of society cannot be humanly dealt with without consideration of the psychosocial response of the people who must live under it.* This is exactly what Marx did, considering the state of knowledge of his time.

MARX AND THE SCIENCE OF SOCIOLOGY

Marx laid the foundation for the building of a sociological science by attacking the problem of the freedom to choose and the freedom not to choose. His studies in alienation, which are consequent to the vicissitudes affecting freedom of choice in the process of capitalist commodity production and exchange, have led to a massive development in the socioeconomic area, particularly in economics, political economy, and political action. But his studies in alienation, which should have led to the development in the psychosocial area by the claimants of Marxism, has not been so fruitful. Whereas the opposite of alienation is appropriation and the opposite of estrangement is solidarity, Marx's followers have not developed to any important degree these instruments of sociological theory as they relate to the traits of human nature. One would expect this area to have been developed in the Soviet Union. But sociology as a science was practically forbidden during Stalin's regime, and the new sociology that began there around 1956 is still in its infancy, let alone the adventures into the psychosocial studies of the nature of man with which we are here concerned.

In bringing the importance of alienation *out* of Hegelian metaphysics to the attention of socio-economo-political scientists, Marx opened psychosocial science of behavior on human beings to scholarly and public scrutiny and practical politics. Unfortunately, the sociologists, psychologists, and anthropologists did not respond to the challenge of investigating the traits of human nature with the energy that they expended on other side issues such as cultural relativism.

FROMM ON ALIENATION

Fromm described in detail how the alienated-estranged persons in the Western world lose their freedom to choose or are so confounded and immobilized about their positions in society that they lost their abilities to determine whether to choose or not to choose. But he also counsels that there are a number of positive factors still alive in our Western ecosystems such as the humanist tradition:

> The alienated person . . . cannot be healthy. Since he experiences himself as a thing, an investment, to be manipulated by himself and by others, he is lacking in a sense of self. This lack of self creates deep anxiety. . . . The alienated person feels inferior whenever he suspects himself of not being in line. Since his sense of worth is based on approval as the reward for conformity, he feels naturally threatened in his sense of self and in his self-esteem by any feeling, thought or action which could be suspected of being a deviation. Yet, inasmuch as he *is* human and not an automaton, he cannot help deviating, hence he must feel afraid of disapproval all the time. As a result, he has to try all the harder to conform, to be approved of, to be successful. Not the voice of his conscience gives him strength and security, but the feeling of not having lost the close touch with the herd. Another result of alienation is the prevalence of a feeling of guilt. . . . We find that people feel guilty about hundreds of things; . . . it is almost as if they had to find something to feel guilty about. . . . Not to be like the rest, not to be totally adjusted, makes one feel guilty

toward the commands of the great It. . . . He senses that his life is the one chance he is given, and that if he loses this chance he has lost everything. He lives in a world with more comfort and ease than his ancestors ever knew—yet he senses that, chasing after more comfort, his life runs through his fingers like sand. He cannot help feeling guilty for the waste, for the lost chance. . . . Consumption of fun serves to repress the awareness of his unhappiness. He tries to save time, and yet he is eager to kill the time he has saved. Having no faith, being deaf to the voice of conscience, and having a manipulating intelligence but little reason, he is bewildered, disquieted and willing to appoint to the position of a leader anyone who offers him a total solution. . . . The person who is in touch only with his inner world and who is incapable of perceiving the outer world in its objective-action context is insane. The person who can experience the outer world photographically, but is out of touch with his inner world, with himself, is the alienated person. Schizophrenia and alienation are complementary. In both forms of sickness one pole of human experience is lacking. If both poles are present, we can speak of the productive person, whose very productiveness results from the polarity between an inner and an outer form of perception.[13]

Such a person has adjusted his cognitive powers to choose freely, but with reasonableness in expressing this trait of human nature.

Fromm points out that:

Among all the threats to man's vital interests, the threat to his freedom is of extraordinary importance, individually and socially. In contrast to the widely held opinion that this *desire* [italics added] for freedom is a product of culture and more specifically of learning-conditioning, there is ample evidence to suggest that the desire for freedom is a biologically based reaction of the human organism. One phenomenon that supports this view is that throughout history nations and classes have fought their oppressors. . . . Another reason for assuming there is an inherent impulse in man to fight for freedom lies in the fact that freedom is the condition for the full growth of a person, for his mental health and his well-being; its absence cripples man and is unhealthy. Freedom does not imply lack of constraint, since any growth occurs only within a structure, and any structure requires constraint.[14]

Other fine scholars of this subject recognize the profundity that freedom plays in man's behavior, but do not emphasize enough that freedom alone is a complete abstraction unless it be related to concrete reality, i.e., freedom to choose between particular alternatives. Man's freedom is predicated on action or inhibition in responding to his desires and impulses, i.e., to have the freedom to choose or not to choose how to respond to his desires and impulses, which may be directed toward material, mental, or spiritual matters and are usually guided by ethical, moral, or other social norms—the social conscience.

Fromm may be a bit overemphatic in attributing the need for freedom to a biological urge. True enough, there is a biological basis to freedom, such as is exhibited when an animal is placed on a leash and it struggles to free itself. So every human action has a biological basis, but that basis is also complemented by the nature of the neopallium, which gives to man the cognitive power to think, to imagine, to correlate experience, to synthesize and analyze symbols, to judge, to evaluate, to be aware of his identity and his desires, et cetera. To have all of these potentials and not to struggle to use them is unthinkable, since having them implies the freedom to do so for the purpose of humanizing *Homo's* social life against the constant threat of reversion to primatelike existence.

HUMAN FREEDOM TO CHOOSE IMPLIES INHIBITIONS

Freedom to choose is not only a trait of civilized man's nature, but also of primitive man. Radin, who studied the psychosocial aspects of primitive man with diligence, asserted that freedom to choose to express oneself according to one's nature is a very basic prerogative of primitive man: "I think everyone competent to judge will admit that in primitive communities free scope is allowed for every conceivable outlet. No moral judgment is passed on any aspect of human personality as such. Human nature is what it is and each act, emotion, belief, unexpressed or expressed, must be allowed to make or mar a man. It is each man's inalienable right. . . . "[15] Radin also elaborates on the system of ethics and morality that inhibit freedom of choice within the bounds of social justice to others. Lee, in his most detailed study of the !Kung San people, developed a technology by combining *uniformitarianism* and Marxian dialectics to filter out these basic behavioral characteristics of people of present primitive societies that most likely were also the behavior patterns of peoples of past primitive societies who lived under foraging economies. Freedom to act or to choose not to act is described by Lee, to wit: "On the political level these characteristics of foraging life lead to a strong emphasis on egalitarian social relations. Egalitarianism is not simply the absence of a headman and other authority figures, but a positive insistence on the essential equality of all people and a refusal to bow to the authority of others. . . . Leaders do exist, but their influence is subtle and indirect."[16] Within this freedom, a code of conduct prevails. Lee quotes from Lorna Marshall's *The !Kung of Nyae Nyae* concerning !Kung behavior: "Their desires to avoid both hostility and rejection leads them to *conform* [italics added] in high degree to *unspoken social laws* [italics added]. I think that most !Kung cannot bear the sense of rejection that even mild disapproval makes them feel. If they do deviate, they usually yield readily to expressed group opinion and reform. They also conform strictly to certain specific useful customs which are like instruments for avoiding discord."[17]

The ability to choose or not to choose can be destructive to those whose ecosystem has conditioned them to vacillate interminably when making a choice, thus leading to behavioral disorientation. Abrahms describes this in what he calls individuals with borderline personality organization: "Those who vacillate in their relationship tend to believe that they must make the correct choice, and that the consequence of the wrong decision would be *catastrophic*." This inability to commit oneself, Abrahms believes, is "one reason for feelings of depression."[18]

Dubos is very clear on this basic trait of being human: "Human nature is good only to the extent that it represses part of itself so as not to do harm to another person. Such an early belief in the need to repress the evil in human nature is a startling expression of the philosophy that being human implies choices. The uniqueness of humankind comes indeed from its potential ability to escape from the tyranny of its biological heritage. Instead of being slaves to these genes and hormones, as animals are, human beings have the kind of freedom which comes from possessing free will and moral judgment. We can repress if we will the bad aspects of our animality. Human beings can choose not only between good and evil, but also between other opposite traits of their nature."[19] The animality to which Dubos refers is man's primate nature.

The two eminent biologists Dobzhansky and Simpson affirm this conception of freedom. Dobzhansky wrote: "The relative autonomy of cultural from biological evolution lies in a different plane. Biological evolution has produced the genetic basis which made the new, specifically human, phase of the evolutionary process possible. But this new evolution, which involves culture, occurs according to its own laws, which are not deducible from, although also not contrary to, biological laws. The ability of man to choose freely between ideas and acts is one of the fundamental characteristics of human evolution. Perhaps freedom is even the most important of all the specifically human attributes. . . . Man has freedom to defy necessity, at least, in his imagination. Ethics emanate from freedom and are unthinkable without freedom."[20]

Simpson expounds on the freedom of man to choose between the desirable and undesirable evolution: "Both organic and social evolution are now to some degree, even though a limited degree, within our own control. We alone, among all organisms, are aware of our own sociobiological evolution, can judge what seems to us desirable or undesirable in that evolution, and can deliberately work for the desirable."[21] The same assertion is made by Dubos: "The human species has exhibited for at least 100,000 years certain traits which are uniquely and pleasantly human and which are more interesting than those that account for its beastiality. . . . The human species has the power to choose among the conflicting traits which constitute its complex nature. . . . "[22]

Dubos describes how man's ability to choose interferes with biological determination in human affairs: "In ordinary biological systems, the progression from a low to a more complex level of unity occurs through a series of unconscious evolutionary phenomena, whereas in human life it involves conscious decisions taken to reach goals which appear desirable even if they are in conflict with biological necessities. The operations of free will constantly disturb the deterministic course of human affairs."[23] Dubos is impressed by the pristine beginnings of man's ability to make choices: "The knowledge of good and evil . . . implies an objective attitude toward the external world, both non-human and human. Furthermore, the sense of objectivity and therefore of separation from the rest of the world probably became sharper with the progressive increase in power to manipulate and transform the environment. Humankind's awareness of being different from the rest of creation must date from the time at least 100,000 years ago, when Neanderthalian people were already capable of profoundly altering their environment. . . . "[24]

Fromm quotes Dobzhansky's eloquent statement about man's freedom to choose from the final pages of his book *Mankind Evolving*: "Self-awareness and foresight brought, however, the awesome gifts of freedom and responsibility. Man feels free to execute some of his plans and to leave others in abeyance. He feels the joy of being the master, rather than the slave, of the world and of himself. But the joy is tempered by a feeling of responsibility. Man knows that he is accountable for his acts: he has acquired the knowledge of good and evil. This is a dreadfully heavy load to carry. No other animal has to withstand anything like it. There is tragic discord in the soul of man. Among the flaws in human nature, this is far more serious than the pain of childbirth."[25]

Fromm, realizing how powerful man's primate response to desire is, warns that "man is guided by his intellect to make right choices. But we know also how weak and unreliable this instrument is. It is easily influenced by man's desires and passions and surrenders to their influences."[26]

Fromm, like Marx, recognized *desire* as the mainspring of human action and recognized process (the process of man's nature) as the movement of interpenetrating contradictory forces, and further recognized that man makes his choices between these contradictions. In the following citation, Fromm discusses desire, choice, freedom, and contradiction and, at the same time, gives his definition of human nature:

These considerations suggest a hypothesis as to how to define the essence or nature of man. I propose that man's nature cannot be defined in terms of a specific quality, such as love, hate, reason, good or evil, but only in terms of fundamental *contradictions* that characterize human existence and have their root in the biological dichotomy between missing instincts and self-awareness. Man's existential conflict produces certain psychic needs common to all men. He is forced to overcome the horror of separateness, of powerlessness, and of lostness, and find new forms of relating himself to the world to enable him to feel at home. I have called these psychic needs existential because they are rooted in the very conditions of human existence. They are shared by all men, and their fulfillment is as necessary for man's remaining sane as the fulfillment of organic drives is necessary for his remaining alive. But each of the needs can be satisfied in different ways, which vary according to the differences of his social condition. These different ways of satisfying the existential needs manifest themselves in passions, such as love, tenderness, striving for justice, independence, truth, hate, sadism, masochism, destructiveness, narcissism. I call them character-rooted passions—or simply human passions—because they are integrated in man's character. While the concept of character will be discussed at length further on, it will suffice here to say that character is the relatively permanent system of all non-instinctual strivings through which man relates himself to the human and natural world.[27]

And further, in relation to the concept of desire, Fromm states: "Since our whole economic system rests on generating desires that the commodities can profitably satisfy, it is hardly to be expected that a critical analysis of the instability of desires would be popular."[28]

Freedom to choose for man when it concerns choices affecting others involves having a set of values (norms) to be guided by in the process of choosing, otherwise freedom to choose would be, in a sense, similar to that of an animal's impulse to act. Without a set of values, there would be little freedom involved in choosing. Too much freedom becomes equivalent to no freedom, and the animal with no freedom acts as if it had complete freedom. Considering this contradiction, Montagu disagreed with Lorenz that morals stem from animal ethology: "To be as deeply interested in morals and evil as Lorenz is, is of course commendable. What is questionable is whether animal ethology, at least at this stage of its development, has anything to contribute toward the understanding of either morals or evil in humans, which . . . are essentially cultural and metaphysical problems. Even though their effects may be biological it only serves to confuse the issue to approach them as biological problems."[29] Montagu rather attributes the "selective advantages" of animals to intelligence: "An animal narrowly confined within the walls of his instinctual equipment will not do as well under such challenging circumstances [i.e., changing conditions] as one which is free to use its intelligence for the making of decisions, and so the selective advantages would tend to favor those animals who exhibited fewer instinctive and more intelligently adaptive responses."[30]

Pfeiffer describes this aspect of man's nature as it first developed in primitive man: "The increasing complexity of life on the African savanna favored an increasingly complex nervous system, a larger memory and a greater capacity for weighing and choosing among an increasing number of alternative actions."[31] Thus, the vicissitudes of primitive life stimulated the evolutionary development of man's nervous system so that he could contend as an active force in manipulating his environment in order to be able to choose what was good or bad and right or wrong in fostering his survival.

Cooley, who was a profound observer of human nature, stated that: " . . . there is, of course, no such thing as the absence of restraint, in the sense of social limitation; man has no existence apart from a social order, and can develop his personality only through the social order, and in the same degree that it is developed. A freedom consisting in the removal of limiting conditions is inconceivable."[32] " . . . Any practical idea of freedom must connect it with some standard of right, in which, like opposing claims in a clearing-house, the divergent tendencies of each person, and of different persons, are disciplined and reconciled."[33] "The mind is the theatre of conflict for an infinite number of impulses, variously originating, among which it is ever striving to produce some sort of unification or harmony."[34] "It is the nature of the mind to form standards of better or worse in all matters toward which its selective activity is directed."[35]

I continue to quote from Cooley for his pithy observations of man's cognitive processes and behavior in relation to his freedom to choose and the values and norms qualifying his choice: "It would not be very difficult to take the seven deadly sins—Pride, Envy, Anger, Sloth, Covetousness, Gluttony, and Lust—and show that each may be regarded as the undisciplined manifestation of a normal or functional tendency."[36] "So far as discipline is concerned, freedom means not its absence but the use of higher and more rational forms as contrasted with those that are lower or lesser rational. . . . It is freedom to be disciplined in as rational a manner as you are fit for."[37] "The social order is antithetical to freedom only in so far as it is a bad one. Freedom can exist only in and through a social order, and must be increased by all the healthy growth of the latter."[38] "Now this increase of moral strain is not in all cases exactly proportional to the ability to bear it well, and when it is not well borne the effect upon characters is more or less destructive, so that something in the way of degeneracy results. . . . This is very plainly to be seen at the present time, which is one, on the whole, of rapid increase of freedom."[39] Also, in this vein, Maslow discusses present-day ethics and confusion in some detail.[40]

This ability to choose freely has greater implications than the routine course of daily choosing between one or another of mundane alternatives. If behavior becomes disoriented as a result of the interrelationships in the ecosystem being in discord with the traits of human nature, man has the remarkable potentiality to choose the type of ecosystem, including the social order, that will be in concordance with his traits of human nature. But to prepare the circumstances to get this done is the real problem. Thus Matson, in his own way, develops the theme of freedom to choose, fully cognizant of his disagreement with the ethologists Lorenz, Ardrey, and Morris: "Those characteristics which are unique to man, as moral aspiration, are seen to be fundamentally at odds with the biological characteristics that he shares with the animals."[41] "If in this view [that man makes his history] the central theme of human history is conflict, the central theme of human behavior is *freedom*. Man as the subject of history is a responsible mortal agent, free within the boundaries of biology and culture to shape the story of liberty, as Croce maintained a generation ago and Hegel proclaimed a century before." Matson further asseverated that lest scholarship of the historian become threatened with a moral vacuum, the historian must become a moral critic and the "new moral history would take seriously the values men lived by and died for in the course of history. . . ."[42] Matson further asserts: "Man has always possessed the capacity of saying No to his destiny, even as it closed in on him. He might dare to defy his fate; he could not think of daring to *change* it. Now, in a miraculous way confirmed by science as well as psychology, man has come into possession of the capacity to say Yes: to affirm his existence and to choose his destiny. Today, for the first time in history, to paraphrase Lewis Mumford, we must ask ourselves in all urgency and candor: What sort of society and what kind of man do we wish to have and to become? That which was once an academic question has suddenly become an existential choice."[43]

Cooley's keen observations into the type of influence the dynamics of the social order has on the cognitive processes and the behavior of its people has been studied far and wide in more recent times. Some of these studies have been done with deep perspective into the universality of the problem. A much larger number with sociopolitical interests in changing the economic forces of the social order have more or less limited their outlook to the effect of limited income and poverty on cognition and behavior. The most important limitation of most studies has been the absence or cloudiness in delineating with clarity the specific psychobehavioral factors that are being affected by the social order, including the traits of human nature. An illustration of this is Matson, whose many insights are excellent but who finally is transported to the flimsy realm of relativism and indeterminacy when considering the nature of human nature: ". . . the new psychology begins and ends in an act of faith. Its starting point is a conception of human nature—an idea of man—not as a fully determinate and predictable 'given' but as an open system of shifting parameters, live options, and definite possibilities of becoming. . . ."[44] This indeterminacy is spelled out in the preface of his book *The Idea of Man*: "The definition of man—or, more exactly, the *identity* of man—is an open question, a live issue, up for grabs. It has never been settled or agreed upon; possibly it never can be."[45]

Erikson's expressive eloquence on the cognitive and behavioral nature of the human is engaging to read and seems to have an orderly unit of perception, as the following citation illustrates, yet always eludes expressing an awareness of the basic structure of human nature: "Some of these prerogatives [which man can not be without] are a sense of *wholeness,* a sense of *centrality* in time and space, and a sense of *freedom of choice.* Man cannot tolerate to have these questioned beyond a certain point, either as an individual among his fellow men, or as a member of a group among other groups."[46]

POVERTY AND HUMAN NATURE

Poverty not only produces physiological deficiency diseases from lack in quantity or quality of food, but also various types of mental illnesses. All of the traits of human nature are disturbed. Excepting these mental illnesses caused by lack of adequate nutrition, poverty per se does *not directly cause* behavioral disorientation. But indirectly, by disturbing the traits of human nature, behavioral disorientations are provoked. One of the basic behavioral disorientations that poverty provokes in the economically deprived people is the restriction placed on their freedom to choose to act or not to act in response to their desires, many of which are stimulated by the products available in the culture of their social order. Strong desires, when inhibited under a faulty socialization process, can provoke neuroses, psychoses, or behavioral disorientation such as delinquency and criminality in those whose thresholds for withstanding trauma are low. Sarbin identifies the violation of the poor's traits of human nature in his study of poverty: "Until more direct evidence is reported, the conclusion appears warranted that participants in the subculture of poverty are unwilling or unable to defer to, or to plan for, the future. Such temporal behavior is predictable from membership in social organizations that limit *choice* [italics added] behavior, such as culture of poverty."[47] Thus not only freedom of choice but also the time-binding trait is disoriented: "A basic postulate in the model [social organization characterized by negatively valued identities] is that human beings constantly strive to locate themselves in their environment. In order to make efficient choices from among behavior alternatives, a person must locate himself with regard to the world of occurrences. This world may be differentiated into a number of ecologies, among them the social ecology, or role system. Constantly faced with the necessity of locating himself [the unifying orientation of behavior trait], a person's misplacement of self in the role system may lead to embarrassing, perilous, or even fatal consequences."[48]

Poverty is a socioeconomic status *relation* of *inequality* in a society having various economic class levels and is manifested, socially and psychologically, as deprivation "of something that is needed, desired, or generally recognized as having value. . . . Starvation, death from exposure, and loss of life due to some other total lack of resources are the only absolute forms of poverty. Even here we are dealing with only one end of a scale that extends toward a quite indefinite opposite extreme. . . . The idea of poverty is above all a comparative concept that refers to a relative quality. . . . As a quality, however, the condition of being poor does have a central significance: the essence of poverty is inequality. In slightly different words, the basic meaning of poverty is relative deprivation. The poor are deprived in comparison with the comfortable, the affluent, and the opulent."[49] This quotation shows how the anthropologist Valentine sees poverty in the panoramic view of his vocation. Valentine berates those social scientists who attribute to the poor a "culture of poverty" and who attribute special cultures or subcultures to almost any social category, such as "culture of violence" and "culture of drugs." "These formulations," he further asseverates, "support the long-established rationalization of blaming poverty on the poor. Nothing could be further from the meaning, the spirit, or the ideological implications of the original concept of culture. . . . A series of papers delivered at the 1966 meeting of the American Anthropological Association shows how the 'culture of poverty' notion and associated ideas distort the reality of life among the poor, prejudice our understanding of that life, and encourage policies which perpetuate the disadvantages associated with poverty."[50]

The thesis of this study is that social and cultural factors are intimately interrelated with the traits of human nature. These factors may be in harmony, in partial harmony, or in discord with these traits. The notion of a "culture of poverty" negates the existence of a specific, universal human nature by disregarding the impact of poverty on the psychosocial elements or traits composing the nature of humankind. Valentine affirms by implication this paradigm of social behavior: "Much of the behavior alleged to be specifically characteristic of the lower class, and therefore often invoked as evidence of cultural distinctiveness, has been explained on other grounds. For example, the correlation between poverty and crime has been interpreted as the outcome of a social structure combining unequal opportunity for different strata with the same goals for all. This interpretation not only omits any reference to a 'culture of poverty' but explicitly rests upon the finding that significant cultural values are shared by different social strata."[51] The sharing of these values really is the equivalence of possession of the traits of human nature by all strata, as it should be according to the thesis of this study.

A social scientist working in a relatively poor but very populous country like India, such as Prof. Udai Pareek, certainly has the opportunity to observe the effect of poverty everywhere he turns, both in its primitive and modern version. Not being aware of the organized, universal nature of the trait structure of human nature, he propounds a general theory of social behavior and its relation to poverty that takes into consideration some of the traits of human nature in limited structural dynamics to explain his "paradigm of Culture of Poverty": "The paradigm is represented as (SS) (M,V) (B)" where SS is the social system, M,V are motivation and values, and B is the resultant behavior."[52] As Pareek stated: "According to this paradigm a social system produces relevant motivational patterns in the members of the society."[53] The inaccuracy of this system is that motivation (M) and values (V) are factors of various traits of human nature that are not produced by the social system, although the specific culture will color the expression of an already existent trait. As already demonstrated, the basic nature of the traits of human nature is the psychosocial behavioral responses to *Homo's* need to survive, to accommodate to, and to develop as a species in the basic conditions of living, the latter being more fundamental than the social order. Relating poverty to his paradigm, Pareek continues:

> In the light of the above paradigm of behavior, poverty can be viewed psychologically both as a structure and as a product (resulting behavior) of a system. . . . The conditions of poverty produce a specific pattern of motivation and, through relevant processes of socialization, the expectancy that can be called the frame of powerlessness. The specific motivational patterns and the expectancy of powerlessness produce behavior seen among the culturally deprived people (the culture of poverty). . . . The important concept in this paradigm is that poverty is essentially a structural problem producing specific motivational patterns which are also important and deserve attention during consideration of the strategy of dealing with poverty. . . . According to the paradigm . . . poverty as a structural component produces a threefold motivational pattern characterized by low need for achievement, low need for extension, and a high need for dependency.[54]

This quotation is extensive, but explains the position taken by a large section of social scientists concerning their understanding of the dynamics of poverty.

The problem with Pareek's paradigm is that his model denotes poverty as structure of society that creates the culture of poverty, whereas it is the *result* of the social structure limiting opportunity, thereby creating poverty, but expecting the goals of achievement to be the same as for those having unlimited opportunity. Under these circumstances, the discordant impact of the flawed social structure and the cultural values involved on each of the traits of human nature creates both pathology and resistance to the disruptive impacts on the traits, of which Pareek's "motivation," "expectancy," and "reinforcing mechanisms" are aspects of specific traits of human nature. The "pathological" impact results in the feeling of "powerlessness," while the "resistance" impels to acts of violence and disorder. What is not mentioned in the paradigm is that the disruptive impact also strains such other traits as "freedom to choose," "self-image–self-esteem," "need for ordered orientation," "challenge and competence," and "creativity." What must also be considered is what such discordant impact will do in upsetting the dominance of the human aspect over the primate aspect in the biphasic nature of each trait and to what extent inhibitions and rationality are weakened so that the primate aspects of behavior become dominant over the human aspects. Much research needs to be done concerning these matters. For example, what were the flaws in the social structure and cultural dynamics of the German nation that propelled its psychosocial constitution to lose so precipitously the dominance of the human phases of its traits of human nature to their primate phases in the creation of the Hitler regime? It is remarkable how the forces to maintain humanness can be overcome so easily under certain circumstances. In the United States, the McCarthy period demonstrated how the psychosocial propensities of a significant sector of its people can revert so quickly to support the unhuman behavior of Senator McCarthy. The history of the world is replete with such events, which demonstrate how the human nature trait of freedom to choose can be so easily deviated to render behavior *un*human, which almost always becomes *in*human. Many such events may never become chronicled, as was illustrated by the uncovering recently of such an event that occurred sixty years ago in the Florida village of Rosewood, but was lost to recorded history until now. In this massacre of black folks, forty people were killed and their homes were destroyed by fire. The incident was reported on the "60 Minutes" television show.

LINKAGE OF TRAITS

Freedom to choose opens up a myriad of avenues to take or not to take for each person in the process of living as a human being, and the choices that he makes determine his ethics, although the choices his society made in the past (his social heritage) influences his cognitive processes in making choices. May asserts that "man or woman becomes fully human only by his or her choices and his or her commitment to them,"[55] and Levine states that "a good part of a man's ethics consists of the way in which he copes with his temptations."[56] He further states: "In human life, an individual who behaves in a way which simultaneously endangers his or her own survival but increases the chance of the survival of others or of the groups is regarded as one of the highest forms of ethical behavior."[57]

The traits of human nature are inseparable. The trait concerned with ethics is patently associated with the trait of freedom of choice. Thus Levine relates ethics "first, to those patterns, of individual human beings or of groups, which are restrictive or limiting or inhibiting toward destructive impulses or behavior . . . second, to those patterns, in individuals or in groups, which foster the growth of constructive and creative impulses and behavior in individuals or groups." Then, "perhaps a general definition must emphasize the process of a deliberate and conscious choice of one alternative over another."[58] Further, recognizing the multifaceted nature of ethics, Levine stated:

> The starting point can be that individual ethics consist of those principles and those inner drives or patterns which press the individual toward satisfactions or developments which can occur without significant damage to other human beings (and which at times may foster the interest of others) and which do not jeopardize other basic needs or satisfactions of the individual himself. Similarly, the ethics of a group would press it toward group satisfactions or developments which can occur without significant damage to individual members of the group, or to subgroups, and which at times may actually foster the interests of individuals or subgroups. Further, the ethics of the group must include the avoidance of damage to other independent groups, as well as the avoidance of damage to a larger group of which the first group is a part, in the course of its own satisfaction.[59]

THE PSYCHOSOCIAL BASIS OF TRAITS

So basic is the dialectic nature of man's human nature, i.e., the biphasic composition of each trait of human nature, each phase being a contradiction of its other, that man had to create social institutions to deal with his behavior in making choices such as systems of ethics, legal systems, religious systems, and psychiatric medicine. Levine/asserts with a sense of asssuredness that "the resolution of his internal conflicts may be man's most important task. In part, it is the central issue of ethics."[60] In making the correct choice, "an individual has a high degree of responsibility for his own life, for his own behavior, for having and using an intelligent self-interest and attention to the interests of others, to the extent that he can mobilize his Ego forces, his Ego strengths, to carry through on that responsibility."[61]

In discussing the freedom to choose, Simpson relates that trait as mutually interdependent with ethics and the time-binding trait, thus: " . . . the concept of ethics is meaningless unless the following conditions exist: (a) There are alternative modes of action; (b) Man is capable of judging the alternatives in ethical terms; and (c) he is free to choose what he judges to be ethically good. Beyond that, it bears repeating that the evolutionary functioning of ethics depends on man's capacity, unique at least in degree, of predicting the results of his actions. A system of naturalistic ethics, then, demands acceptance of individual responsibilities for those results, and this in fact is the basis for the origin and function of the moral sense."[62] "Man has risen, not fallen. He can choose to develop his capacities as the highest animal and to try to rise still farther, or he can choose otherwise. The choice is his responsibility, and his alone. . . . Evolution has no purpose; man must supply this for himself."[63]

SAFEGUARDING FREEDOM TO CHOOSE

The attitude of unrestricted laissez faire in behavior has created today a lassitude toward permissiveness that does border on chaos. This near chaos in freedom to choose cognitively irrational or ill-considered courses of action has supported family disintegration, the supercilious adventurism toward marriage and divorce, the growing incest lobby, the antimonogamy movement, the formal recognition of the virtues of homosexuality, and the pornographic, prurient, and dollar-making, mind-boggling contrivances of the entertainment intrusions into the mass communications media. Unless the fundamental significance of moral and ethical norms is understood in relation to the sustenance of human society, the societal fabric is bound to become more and more weakened. The tearing down of the moral-ethical values of a society in a haphazard manner by irresponsible, self-seeking individuals or groups, manipulating mechanisms that disorient the cognitive processes of children and youth while the society itself has not developed an approved direction for new norms is the symptom of a cognitively unprepared society. There is a very basic need for a democratic people not to allow the "freedom to choose" for individuals to be translated into chaotic conduct leading to an uncontrolled minority creating a new societal ethic and to the negation of that very freedom for the majority. Chaos is the antithesis of freedom to choose. The community *must,* teleologically and with cognitively prepared conviction, decide the nature of the moral and ethical norms by which it wishes to direct its evolution, and every individual child should be subject to such a socialization process. These norms must be in concordance with the traits of human nature and democratically hammered out. Absolute freedom to choose leads to chaotic behavior of individuals in their scramble to satisfy their individual appetites and inclinations when unguided by convincingly accepted societal norms. The deadly scramble will otherwise negate the freedom of all but the few who are cunning enough to juggle themselves into positions of power and with dictatorial craftiness exert their will over the rest. Freedom to choose must therefore be a relative freedom—a freedom that satisfies the self in the framework of the needs of community order. This is the nature of the greatest freedom and can only be achieved under well-structured democratic institutions of living.

Changes in the social conscience concerning the freedom-to-choose trait should be a deliberate social consensus process, not the random perversions that privately manipulated mass communications media perpetrates.

NOTES

1. Stan A. Kuczai, *Crib Speech and Language Play* (New York: Springer-Verlage, 1983), p. 13.

2. M. Schur and L. B. Rivito, "The Concept of Development and Evolution in Psychoanalysis" in Aronson, et al. eds., *Development and Evolution in Psychoanalysis* (San Franciso, California: W. H. Freeman and Co., 1970), p. 613.

3. Jane Loevinger, *Ego Development* (San Francisco, California: Jossey-Bass Publishers, 1976), p. 6.

4. G. W. F. Hegel, *The Phenomenology of Mind* (Atlantic Highlands, New Jersey: Humanities Press, 1977).

5. Karl Marx, *The Economic and Philosophic Manuscripts of 1844* (International Publishers, 1964), p. 108.

6. John Torrance, *Estrangement, Alienation, and Exploitation* (New York: Columbia University Press, 1977).

7. Ibid., pp. xi–xii.

8. Ibid., p. xiii.

9. Ibid., p. xiii.

10. A. Etzioni, *The Active Society* (London: Collier-Macmillan Ltd., 1968), pp. 618–26.

11. K. Marx, *The Economic and Philosophical Manuscripts of 1844* (International Publishers, 1977), p. 114.

12. Ibid., p. 45.

13. Erich Fromm, *The Sane Society* (New York: Rinehart and Co., 1955), pp. 204–208.

14. Erich Fromm, *The Anatomy of Human Destructiveness* (New York: Holt, Rinehart and Winston, 1973), pp. 198–99.

15. Paul Radin, *Primitive Man as Philosopher* (Pasadena, California: D. Appleton and Co., 1927), pp. 32, 58, 77–78.

16. Richard B. Lee, *!Kung San: Men, Women and Work in a Foraging Society* (New York: Cambridge University Press, 1979), p. 457.

17. Ibid., p. 370.

18. Eliot Abrahms, "Cognition and Major Mental Disorders," in Russell and I. Z. Grieger, eds., *Cognition and Emotional Disturbance* (New York: Human Sciences Press, Inc.), pp. 143–44.

19. Rene Dubos, *Beast or Angel* (New York: Charles Scribner and Sons, 1974), p. 47.

20. Th. Dobzhansky, *The Biological Basis of Human Freedom* (New York: Columbia University Press, 1956), p. 134.

21. G. H. Simpson, *Biology and Man* (New York: Harcourt, Brace, World, 1969), p. 146.

22. Dubos, *loco supra citato,* p. 45.

23. Ibid., p. 182.

24. Ibid., p. 54.

25. Fromm, *loco supra citato,* pp. 229–30.

26. Ibid., p. 224.

27. Ibid., p. 226.

28. Ibid., p. 261.

29. Ashley Montagu, *The Nature of Human Aggression* (New York: Oxford University Press, 1976), p. 286.

30. Ashley Montagu, *Anthropology and Human Nature* (Boston, Massachusetts: Porter Sargent, 1957), p. 16.

31. J. Pfeiffer, *The Emergence of Society* (New York: McGraw Hill, Co., 1977), p. 50.

32. C. H. Cooley *Human Nature and the Social Order* (New Brunswick, New Jersey: Transaction Books, 1983), pp. 392–93.

33. Ibid., p. 396.

34. Ibid., p. 326.

35. Ibid., p. 372.

36. Ibid., p. 381.

37. Ibid., pp. 396–97.

38. Ibid., p. 397.

39. Ibid., p. 403.

40. A. H. Maslow, *The Farther Reaches of Human Nature* (New York: Viking Press, 1971), pp. 155–95.

41. Floyd W. Matson, *The Idea of Man* (New York: Delacorte Press, 1976), p. 60.

42. Ibid., p. 178.

43. Ibid p. 109.

44. Ibid., pp. 109–10.

45. Ibid., p. xiii.

46. Erik H. Erikson, *Insight and Responsibility* (New York: W. W. Norton, 1964), p. 148.

47. T. R. Sarbin, "The Culture of Poverty, Social Identity, and Cognitive Outcomes," in V. L. Allen, ed., *Psychological Factors in Poverty* (Markham Publishing Co.), p. 33.

48. Ibid., p. 36.

49. Charles A. Valentine, *Culture and Poverty* (Chicago, Illinois: University of Chicago Press, 1968), pp. 12–13.

50. Ibid., pp. 15, 17.

51. Ibid., p. 16.

52. Udai Pareek, "Poverty and Motivation: Figure and Ground," in V. L. Allen, ed, *Psychological Factors in Poverty* (Markham Publishing Co.), pp. 300–17.

53. Ibid., p. 302.

54. Ibid., p. 303–304.

55. Rollo May, *The Courage to Create* (New York: W. W. Norton and Co., 1975), p. 14.

56. Maurice Levine, *Psychiatry and Ethics* (New York: George Braziller, 1972), p. 23.

57. Ibid., p. 65.

58. Ibid., p. 46, 68.

59. Ibid., p. 47.

60. Ibid., p. 139–40.

61. Ibid., p. 188.

62. Simpson, *Biology and Man,* p. 146.

63. Ibid., p. 148.

8

The Unifying Orientation of Behavior Trait

THE SENSE OF COMMITMENT

Basic to the peace of mind is the need to experience a sense of commitment and responsibility to and engagement in a unifying frame of behavioral orientation—a teleological intent of acting together—so that order, predictive expectancy, direction, and purpose be felt in the process of social interrelations to satisfy the social *conscience,* the sense of not being alone in one's beliefs and in having others as supportive of one's position.

Humankind needs to be oriented in its way of life to a socially familiar and generally acceptable cognitive and behavioral pattern and to a conscience, which, in turn, it needs to pass on to kith and kin, and which gives people a sense of order, predictive expectancy, direction, and purpose in their efforts to survive with an inner strength to live. The human needs to adhere to and to teach a philosophy of life that makes living meaningful and worthwhile. Fromm calls this trait: The Need for a Frame of Orientation and Devotion.[1] This stems from the fact that man has a mind and an imagination that comprehends a complex world that must not be chaotic in relation to him, lest his life be placed in jeopardy and his reason be confounded, for the human mind abhors confusion in relation to the world about him. He needs, as far as possible, an "objective" understanding and an animated faith and hope about the world around him. This psychosocial orientation he needs in order to maintain mental and emotional stability and sanity—although, on a different level of behavior, even an animal may develop a condition resembling neurosis when all of its impulses are thwarted over a period of time.

Among the early historical vestiges known to us that demonstrates man's abhorrence of chaos is his fertile imagination in creating cosmological and mythological epics during the dawn of *human* emer-

198

Sense of commitment to a unifying frame of behavioral orientation

human → Adherence to a code of purposeful behavior conducive to orderly and human social interrelations and guided individually by a social conscience, which needs to be passed on to others

primate → Behaving without heed of a code of conduct of social approval in relation to others and with little or no conscience as guide to living

gence, portraying his struggle between the need for societal "Order" and the relentless flux of the natural forces, the seeming "Chaos." This conceptualization metamorphosed eventually into theological creeds and codes of behavior. One such example is described in the scholarly investigation by Batto of the term *"yam sûp"* (pronounced "yahm soof"), a biblical term ordinarily taken to mean the Red Sea, first mentioned in the Bible in the "Song of the Sea," Exodus 15, which relates to the Jews crossing the Red Sea in their exodus from Egypt. Batto stated:

> The Song of the Sea is . . . recognized to be older than even the earliest textual strands [the four classifications of the temporal origin of biblical text]. The Song of the Sea follows the basic pattern of ancient mythological cycles such as Enuma Elish, the Mesopotamian epic about the god Marduk, and the Ugaritic cycle concerning the god Baal. In these mythological texts the creator god overcomes his watery foe of chaos, bringing order out of this chaos and creating a people in the process. The creator god then retires to his mountain sanctuary where as king he rules his newly ordered cosmos. As has often been observed, the Biblical description in Exodus 15 is heavily dependent on this mythological language. . . . The *yam sûp* was the sea at the end of the earth, a sea which in the ancient mind was fraught with connotations of the primeval chaos. These mythical associations explain the presence of *yam sûp* in the Song of the Sea. Traditional mythical language is used to express the belief that the emergence of Israel as a people during the exodus was due to a creative act by Yahweh equal to that of the original creation of the cosmos itself. The Egyptians, the evil force which threatens the existence of

this new creation, are appropriately cast into the sea to perish. A more powerful symbol for nonexistence can scarcely be found than submergence into the sea of End/Annihilation. . . . Biblical writers were less interested in reporting historical data than in symbolizing for their contemporaries the salvational significance of their traditions. The significance of those original symbols, so meaningful when first written, has been lost in our modern scientific and technological world. Nevertheless, if we are to understand the exodus as the ancient Israelites did, we must also learn to understand the meaning of their symbols.[2]

If the "Song of the Sea" was written more than 3,000 years ago, and the Babylonian author of the Hammurabic legal code lived about 4,000 years ago, and the Sumerians of Ur lived 5,000 years ago and longer, and the mythological struggles of "Order" against "Chaos" and the story of creation of the world and of man were inherent in all of their historical tradition, and considering that social tradition changed very slowly during the even earlier millenia than during the above citations, then it is not stretching historical perception to presume that human yearning for social order, i.e., unifying orientation to orderly existence, was a trait of human nature very deep in *Homo's* primeval past.

This trait, like all traits of human nature, has a human or rationally oriented order aspect and a primate or orderless biologically driven aspect. This is not to attribute lack of order to animal behavior, since biogenetic or instinctive behavior has a structured form of order, but lacks the creative rationalized behavior of the human. However, the order of animal behavior appears and to primitive man also appeared orderless or even chaotic if applied to the *human* needs for human behavior.

When man's behavior is committed to a frame of orientation whose norms are blindly self-centered, unpledged, and hostile to the world about, unifying only around the self, then the resulting behavior can be said to be dominated by the primate impulses struggling for release in the breast of man. This is man's eternal struggle—to act human or *un*human.

PRIMITIVE MAN AS PHILOSOPHER

This trait is as valid for primitive man as for civilized man, since without it, living could not be tolerated, considering the intellectual and psychological potentials of man's mind to evaluate his state of existence.

Sahlins contends that the first human social revolution was that pertaining to controlling conflict originating from sexual passions as inherited from the primate stage of existence. This was a primary problem in primitive society, and in order for thinking *Homo* to be able to live in groups or bands or large families, it was necessary to have rules for controlling conflict. This was done through group approval or disapproval of conduct of individual members—an orientation that became an instrument of behavior control. This instrument was able to become a control device as the result of the emergence into the consciousness of each person the recognition of one's *individual ego* and the development of that remarkable human attribute, the *conscience*—that primogenial process of cognition and self-evaluation that initiated another human trait, that of self-image–self-esteem. Since conflict was feared[3] because it created group dislocation and even dissolution, and since the members of the group controlled this primate behavior by directing their ridicule and rejection to the principals in the fight, this norm of controlling behavior could be considered among the very incipient rules on which grew and developed the moral and ethical codes for preserving the integrity of *human* existence. This is expressed by Radin: "The fear of ridicule is thus a great positive factor in the lives of primitive peoples. It is the preserver of the established order of things and more potent and tyrannous than the most restrictive and coercive of positive injunctions possibly could be."[4]

Primitive man created many instruments, in the process of his development, to help him maintain and enlarge the scope of his human state of existence, particularly to keep him oriented away from reverting to uncontrolled primate behavior. These intruments are the moral-ethical codes, the legal systems, the socioeconomic structural relations, and the external spiritual controls in magic and religion. The fact that these instruments have been manipulated by power-hungry forces in human history for self-aggrandizement does not detract from their primary role in societal development. Radin stated that religion and magic to primitive man are simple aids for attainment of goals, which in itself means having a purpose for continuing the struggle to live as human beings:

> Thus viewed, the facts of primitive life take on a new psychological orientation. The attainment of a goal, the clear realization of a specific objective, becomes the main factor. Everything else is either completely slurred or regarded as secondary. . . . Primitive man may not in our sense of the term provide for the morrow but he attempts something perhaps far more important—he bends all his energies, inward and outward, toward ensuring the success

of his objective on the morrow. With this determination steadily before him he completely identifies himself with the goal to be obtained. He prepares for it, previsions it, preenacts it, and pre-attains it. . . . But he is not interested merely in the fact that the world exists and that it has a definite effect upon him; he is impelled by his whole nature, by the innate orientation of his mind, to try to discover the reason why there is an effect, what is the nature of the relation between the ego and the world, and what part exactly the perceiving self plays therein. Like all philosophers, he is interested in the subject as such, the object as such, and the relations between them."[5]

The historian Yerushalmi, in formulating the essence of the spiritual-mental revolution that stirred the Israelite tribes with the emergence of their monotheistic religion, in a sense, describes an episode in the eternally repetitious struggle that *Homo* was destined to contend with when he originally perceived that he had to devise a human system of behavioral norms to be able to dominate his primate responses in the process of living in a human society. Yerushalmi philosophized: "The pagan conflict of the gods with the forces of chaos, or with one another, was replaced by a drama of a different and more poignant order: the paradoxical struggle between the divine will of an omnipotent Creator and the free will of his creature, man, in the course of history; a tense dialectic of obedience and rebellion."[6] The conflict of the pagan gods with the forces of chaos or among themselves describes the earlier supernatural perceptions of *Homo's* struggles with his primate proclivities as externally motivated behavior. The conflict between the divine will of the omnipotent Creator and the free will of the product of his creation, rebellious man, was a later, more personally oriented episode in the struggle of the human traits to dominate the primate urges.

Voltaire, a keen observer of human behavior, understood the significance of the human struggle to be human and the need of religion, there not being any other spiritual guide available to give guidance and strength to *Homo's* effort to maintain a sense of order in his existence when he remarked, "If there were no God, it would be necessary to invent him." The main weakness of Marx's observation of human behavior is in his prepossessing misapprehension of the place religion served in the development of the human nature of *Homo*. Marx saw clearly the historical tragedy of how clerical and secular demagogues and just outright narrow-minded fanatics used religion as a weapon to manipulate the emotions of the masses for their own ends. What he did not see, probably due to the childhood trauma he experienced with his father's shamefaced religious conversion to curry favorable acceptance by the Christian world about him, was whý, in the first place, religion occupied so persistently the spiritual life of humankind throughout history—the great need *Homo* had for the norms of orderly behavior that the moral and ethical principles of religion provided. The raison d'être for religion is based on *human* need. The raison d'être cannot be abolished without depraving the essence of being human. Only a form of spiritual humanitarianism could replace it.

A sense of the religious can be equated to a sense of direction in life—a sense of hope and trust. At the beginning, just a glimmer of such direction existed. Hope and trust came from an imagination and intellect that tried to fathom the "whys" in the experience (educability) of living. Thus Hawkes stated: "These first essays at representation (art) can be dated to 25,000 B.C. or even earlier. With the Gravettians, accomplishment, particularly in sculpture, became much greater. . . . These little carvings were made over most of the Gravettian range from Italy and the Pyrenees to the Don. . . . Essentially, unlike the animal portraits, they (the female figurines) came from an inner vision of fertility and motherhood. In this sense, they can be said to be the first evolved religious symbols; it might not be wrong to call them idols."[7]

How far back this trait of human nature reaches is not known, yet Solecki stated: "His own biological evolution is something man really does not have conscious control over. But his culture, his social and religious life, is something else. It is among the Neanderthals [25,000 to 75,000 years ago] that we have the first stirrings of social and religious sense and feeling."[8] Was it here that man first began to get the glimmer of a *direction* in life? He probably had it many thousands of years before he displayed it in durable artifacts. Radin's study of primitive man led him to believe that he already had a direction in life that played a dominant role deep in the past. Besides his ruthless realism and objectivity, which was one side of his relations to life, "happiness, love and affection, humility and modesty, kindness and forbearance, play a dominant role in their civilizations. *To attain them is*, in fact, *the goal of every* individual's life."[9] A *worthy direction,* indeed!

Dubos put it this way: "All civilizations have formulated ideals of behavior based on attributes which appear uniquely human. In each case, this ideal is the expression of forces originating, not from geography and race, but from a philosophical attitude; not from the animality in *Homo sapiens* but from his humanity."[10] Montagu asserted that

> .. it is possible to lay down certain broad generalizations to which all societies are found to conform. In the first place it is obvious that moral ideas have a regulative effect; they function as abstract or ideal but nevertheless very real controls of the behavior of human beings in relation to each other and to the world of institutions, objects, things, and creatures in which they find themselves. In the second place, at the basis of all moral ideas is the people's conception of the "Good." In whatever variety of ways it may be codified, the conception of the "Good" which all peoples have arrived at may be phrased in the following way: "Good" is that, and that is "Good" which confers survival benefits upon the group.[11]

He also wrote: "The good life was what Korzybski was passionately interested in, and so he said 'Ethics is too fundamentally important a factor in civilization to depend upon a theological or legal excuse; ethics must conform to the *natural law* of human nature.' "[12]

THE SOCIAL SELF: SOCIAL IDENTITY

The social self is the result of the integration of the individual into his social world. In this integration, the conscience luxuriates. Any impairment to this integration scars the conscience and blemishes the nature of the human. The need to understand the social self is, therefore, primary to understanding how the unifying orientation of behavior operates as a trait of human nature. The ethical-moral conscience that is the essence of the unifying process of orienting behavior is a bulwark of the human spirit. The social self is really the result of the process of the individual striving to identify himself in his social surroundings, i.e., to find his social identity.

To Loevinger, ethics is equivalent to socialization in child development: "Although ego development has been dealt with in the field of ethics as *moral development,* the term usually used in child psychology for the most closely related topic is *socialization.*"[13] The latter author further states in discussing ethics and morals as a phase of the dialectic of personal growth:

> James Mark Baldwin (1861–1934), one of psychology's great theorists, exemplifies the evolutionary point of view in his books

on mental development and on social and ethical development, published before the turn of the century. Baldwin (1897) made central to his theory of ego development the "dialectic of personal growth". . . . The young child's behavior exhibits a polarity; he imitates those more powerful and practices on those less powerful. . . . One cannot say that either the egoistic self or the altruistic one is more real; the real self is the bipolar self, the *social self* [italics added], in all its complexity. . . . Children differ in the relative strength of their needs for social confirmation and for a sense of aging, the former leading to adaptability, the latter to originality. Social judgment and private judgment are virtually equated in Baldwin. . . . The ethical sense remains throughout life largely social. Social approval induces self-approval, social disapproval induces self-disapproval. . . . This reaction is not simply a reflection of public judgment. Rather, the judgment of another is necessary to call forth the full ethical sense because of the similarity of ego and alter."[14]

In this vein of thought, Loevinger states further: "The origins of the self in social relations is a topic associated with Cooley, who used the term 'looking-glass' in *Human Nature and the Social Order* (1902). There is, Cooley said, no sense of *myself* without a correlative sense of you."[15] The basic analysis of self as a social phenomenon was well understood by such pioneers as Marx, Engels, Baldwin, Mead, and Cooley before the turn of the century, but has become befogged in present psychology and sociology by the hyperplasia of the self, as though it were isolated, distinguished, and serenely perched on Mount Olympus. The Constitution of the United States is too often interpreted in this way, so that the litigation process is becoming long and, too often, the criminal is protected and the social need to prevent further victimization of the community is disregarded. Thus, as Kagan concludes: "But in the modern Western world, the individual not the family is slowly becoming the basic unit [in society]. The high divorce rate, the large number of single-parent families, and the public's willingness to work toward a more egalitarian society through interventions that *abrogate the family's power* [italics added] make the person the central entity in the eyes of the law, the school, and the self."[16]

Human nature is not self nature. There could be no human nature without human beings organized in some social sense in order to survive the reproductive and child rearing processes and in order to express the behavioral tendencies latent in the brain as it relates to social existence.

FRAME OF ORIENTATION AND SANITY

Fromm also placed the need for a frame of orientation and devotion in man as a fundamental part of man's human nature: "Man finds himself surrounded by many puzzling phenomena and, having reason, he has to make sense of them, has to put them in some context which he can understand and which permits him to deal with them in his thoughts. The further his reason develops, the more adequate becomes his system of orientation, that is, the more it approximates reality. But even if man's frame of orientation is utterly illusory, it satisfies his need for some picture which is meaningful to him. . . . Unless man has such a subjectively satisfactory frame of orientation, he cannot live sanely."[17]

The sense of commitment to a psychosocially unifying frame of orientation has been as fundamental to primitive man as it is for modern. Animism and totemism are such systems of orientation. They gave meaning to life in primitive times, just as Buddhism and monotheism are systems of religious belief in more recent times that have given meaning and hope to the masses of poor and ignorant people exposed to the rigors of life. But religion has at times been used as an exploitive instrument of state power. Even the affluent and nobility needed some such spiritual system, because they too were members of the human race whose human nature was of the psychosocial substance as those whom they ruled, exploited, and oppressed, even using religion as their instrument of control. The fact that the power-hungry and the demogogues have used religion as a political instrument for some thousands of years to sunder the harmony between the traits of human nature and the ecosystems molded by them is no reason why we should not recognize the benign role played by religions in serving as systems of orientation for most of the billions of people during the past five millenia. The evidence is that such systems, not necessarily religions, but probably magical behavior codes, existed for Cro-Magnon and even for Neanderthal man and probably in some form even before the latter in the formative millenia of human nature. In those dimmer epochs of the past, there must have been some glimmer of hope expressed as a spiritual system that pervaded the evolution of the traits of human nature.

Loevinger summarized Alfred Adler's researches into ego development and purpose in life:

Throughout [his writings] he stressed the unity and coherence (Einheit) of personality. The drives, including the sex drive, are subordinated to a person's *goal* or *purpose* [italics added] in life, his *guiding fiction*. The philosophical concept of the fiction was developed by Vaihinger (1911). Fictions are not fantasies but predictive schemes necessary to orient *oneself in the world* [italics added], they are subjective, created by the person, and unconscious in some sense. Adler's *guiding fiction* combined this idea of fiction with that of goal or purpose and adapted it to the field of development. According to Adler, by the time the child is four or five he has selected or constructed some purpose, only partly conscious, that guides the remainder of his life."[18]

Purpose and goal or their absence are basic elements in creating morale or demoralization. In the *Report on a Preparatory Conference on the Social Sciences and Morale,* the definition of *morale* is given as follows: "Morale is that potential (motivation and affective state) to persist in an activity toward a goal which might be motivated by the appearance of an obstacle."[19]

Goal-striving was advanced as another dimension besides performance of the role expectation in the latter study. The following hypotheses on morale were formulated:

1. Morale (goal striving) increases with increasing identification in a group.
2. Morale (goal striving) in groups with high identification is less affected by obstacles than in groups with low identification.
3. Morale is the potential identification occurring in a group in the face of an obstacle.[20]

According to the definitions of *morale,* goal striving is not necessarily striving for positive social goals; it may also involve criminal or other negative types of goal striving. Thus one's guiding principles or philosophy of life may be socially positive or negative or absent (demoralized).

At the present stage of the American consumer-oriented economy, two predominant factors are unbridling human behavior from its socially molded inhibitions, which the hucksters of consumerism are exploiting to the detriment of society. These hucksters are aware that human behavior is endowed with a duality of contradictory forces. They direct their sales pitch at loosening the inhibitory moorings that maintain the homeostasis of *social* life. Sell at any cost except when profit is jeopardized! The appeal is to the negative side of human nature. The two disorienting factors supporting runaway consumerism are: (1) The disturbance of the homeostasis of the trait of self-image–self-esteem by the inordinate exaggeration of the narcissistic self beyond the limits of social stability, and (2) The exaggeration of the trait of freedom to choose to the point of unrestricted permissiveness of individual action. Together, these forces are driving into disarray the trait straining for a unified social orientation of behavior. There are among those who are involved in selling commodities for individual consumption or use some who have enough capital to advertise in the mass media. The nature of modern advertisement is to appeal to the most self-centered, self-aggrandizing characteristics of the individual. Overindulgence in the self is always the aim, since that means more sales and more profit. To achieve this aim, the pitch of the advertisement is directed solely to stimulate the feelings and emotions—feelings and emotions associated with the physiological processes such as relate to the gustatory, the visual, the tactile, the auditory, the olfactory, and the sexual. Then judgment and reason take a holiday. As an example, consider the recent changes in the cinema. This was well summed up by George Will in a commentary on the movie *Scarface:*

> To say that the movie is morally constructive because it shows the squalor of drug addiction and because the bad guys get massacred, misses a large point, which is: Realism is no all-purpose defense in art. . . . The principal worry is not that repeated exposure to depictions of cruelty will make persons act cruelly. Rather, it is that it will produce persons who can respond only to depictions of excess. A generation raised on what are known as "slash films" ("Prom Night," "Halloween," "Friday the 13th," etc.) may become unable to enjoy subtlety, nuance or delicacy. That is, they may be rendered immune to art. . . . The ratings board deserves praise for taking gratuitous violence as seriously as degrading sex. But how will it rate things when the "slash film" generation becomes parents? While the ratings board tries to conform to community standards, the movies are driving those standards steadily down.[21]

As permissiveness increases, the movies get more extreme, the youngsters get more immune to extremities, and self-gratification demands more extremes. Thus drug abuse becomes a way of life. School discipline gets more difficult. Criminality spawns more fruitfully. Dietary gluttons and cases of anorexia nervosa keep sprouting. Herpes viral venereal disease and AIDS run rampant among the youth. The airways blast more cacophony. Indictments are declared more frequently against political and white-collar operators. The unifying force in human society that has been orienting the social world toward tolerable conditions of existence since *Homo's* emergence is being tested toward the limit. The system of basic inhibitions that had been molded out of thousands of years of societal experience is being dissipated by randomness verging on chaos, resulting from the extremities of permissiveness and self-indulgence. We have not yet learned to live in a culture of affluence.

Schmalleger, a professor of criminal justice, appreciates society's ability to create ways of life: "Crime is a *way of life* for some and the result of unfortunate circumstances and personal pathology for others. . . . Most convicts are professional criminals. They have been socialized into lives of crime just as the rest of us have been socialized into lives of conformity."[22] Only when there is no purpose, no goal striving, is there demoralization—dispensing with life or creating a way of negative existence. Criminality is not a culture; it is a pathology where *conscience* is absent or disorientation becomes firmly established. It is *only* disorientation when the strength of inhibition is overcome temporarily.

May gives philosophy of life an elemental significance for humankind: *"You can live without a father who accepts you, but you cannot live without a world that makes some sense to you. . . .* Persons in therapy, like all of us, are trying to make sense out of nonsense, trying to put the world into some perspective, trying to form out of the chaos they are suffering some order and harmony."[23]

This need for "order and harmony" is the basis for the development of codes of morality or norms of behavior, which have been detected in every culture ever observed and which were basic to the development of society in order to control the social disruptive tendencies of primate behavior that *Homo* inherited from *Australopithecus* as Radin observed "This [the attainment of happiness and prosperity] . . . probably all primitive peoples would contend, the ethical-religious ideal is more likely to do because it emphasizes the cardinal fact of life, the sense of proportion . . . that dominates all primitive life in spite of the superficial impression to the contrary."[24]

Radin concluded: "They [the Winnebago] insist upon a definite inward purification, a reverent and humble spirit, persistent effort, strength of character, the saving grace of a sense of life's realities, and finally, a knowledge of oneself."[25]

CULTURE, RELATIVISM, AND HUMAN NATURE

Levine attributes human nature mostly to culture and therefore opens the door to relativism, i.e., to the ability more easily to change human nature by changing cultural conditions: "Human nature can be changed, at least, in certain ways. Human nature is in good part an expression of the culture, and changes in a culture can change human behavior."[26] He is identifying the culturally superimposed veneer on the traits with the basic nature of the traits themselves. These traits came into being and persisted as the result of the psychosocial behavioral patterns in social relations that man had to assume in the struggle for survival and development. These social relations are so basic to man's existence that they persist to this day in the maelstrom of the ever changing cultural patterns. Levine's problem is that he has not filtered out of man's behavior those elements that are purely human—behavior patterns that animals do *not* possess or may appear to have only in so primogenial a form as to be almost formless. He therefore assumes that the behavior that is so valuable to man must be biological, just as animal social behavior is. He expands his concept as follows:

> The existence of . . . organized social behavior in animals other than man, whether it is called ethical or not, seems profoundly important. Such behavior indicates that the social patterns in man, which are so valuable, are not to be regarded as psychosocial or cultural epiphenomena, superimposed on man's biologic heritage. Rather, the extensive and varied social behavior of the other animals indicates that man's socially oriented patterns may be a part of man's biologic heritage, as well as a part of his cultural heritage, the behavior he learns after he is born. If this be true, the strong forces of violence, of destructiveness, of war, and of other forms of man's inhumanity to man, which perhaps are biologic, cultural, and individual in origin, may be matched within man by the further development of strong counterforces of socially oriented patterns which also are biologic, cultural, and individual in origin.[27]

Levine, in an attempt to give biologic heritage, cultural heritage, and individual heritage their due consideration in evaluating human behavior, becomes so unspecific, uncritical, equivocal, and general about such behavior traits as violence and aggression that his statement really sheds no light on the subject. It is a bland statement to say, "If it be true that man's violent and aggressive nature be biologic and cultural, it is also true that the counterforces to these traits are also biologic and cultural in origin." Such profundities, although generally true, lead nowhere. This is like propounding that human reproduction is the result of male and female participation. What can result is a monstrosity, but there are also counterforces of male and female origin which prevent such perversion.

In relation to changing human nature, Levine warns that doing this by manipulating the chromosomes or by electric stimulation of the brain is a dangerous trend, but "my proposal is a different one. It is that human nature should be changed by using techniques which will foster the further development of individual freedom and its values, and to foster also the ethical combinations of the values of the individual and of the culture."[28] In making such statements, Levine does not seem to understand what human nature is. Why does he want to change human nature in the first place? What is wrong with human nature? The fact is that human nature is the best response of *Homo sapiens* to the needs to survive and to develop. It is the ecosystem which is out of concordance with the traits of human nature and actually favors the dominance of the primate traits that are causing humankind's problems, such as violence, aggression, and wars. Certainly we want to "foster the development of individual freedom and its values," but not to the extremes of abolishing inhibitions against primate urges that are inherent in *Homo's* behavioral responses. Levine recognizes this[29] just as he recognizes the interrelation of opposites (the biphasic nature) in every process.[30] But because he fails to recognize the evolutionary origin of human nature (giving too much credence to the assumptions of sociobiologists), the psychosocial rather than cultural basis, and the specific fundamental traits that compose it, his excellent observations about human behavior always have about them a sense of wanting. And yet his definition of *ethics* shows an unusual insight into human behavior: "Ethics has a defensive function of controlling or directing or balancing some of the potentially destructive impulses in life, or of preventing a healthy part of life (such as a workable conscience) from becoming a dangerous distortion of itself (such as a rigid, corruptible conscience)."[31] His book, which is devoted to a comprehensive discussion of ethics, gives testimony to the essential nature of this trait in human behavior.

MORALS AND ETHICS: A UNIFIED PHILOSOPHY OF LIFE

Jahoda discusses this trait of human nature as the unifying philosophy of life, in which she elaborates on the concept of self-actualization as understood by Goldstein (1940), Fromm (1941), Erikson (1950), Maslow (1954), Barron (1955), Mayman (1955), and Allport (1955), all of whom one way or another related this concept to "philosophy of life."[32] Allport, Jahoda asserts, "speaks about a unifying philosophy of life as . . . reconciling two otherwise conflicting tendencies. *Self-extensive*—i.e., losing oneself in the things of the world—and self *objectification*—i.e., looking at one's self with detachment. . . . Allport discusses several types of unifying philosophies. The first is *religion,* the search for a value underlying all things . . . [and] also the esthetic philosophy, where the quest for beauty is the prime value."[33] Jahoda continued: "Apparently, the unifying philosophy of life results in the individual's feeling there is purpose and meaning to his life. On a time dimension, the unity theme is presented by Allport as the intentions of the present which commits the individual to strive for specific aspects of the future."[34] Jahoda stresses the fact that all the scientists whom she cites consider these concepts as basic forces in life.

Steven Muller, president of Johns Hopkins University and Hospital, gave a perceptive review of the present-day problem concerning moral discipline:

> The impact of technology increases human population. The economies of technology cluster populations together in large aggregations. Large interdependent populations require a high degree of abstract order to serve all their members; but at the same time they create individual conditions of anonymity which tend to corrupt order. The more impersonal rules are, the less compelling they seem to the individual. The more anonymous one feels, the more one is tempted to break rules, because the risk of discovery and its consequences appear reduced. The genius of religion is to personalize the abstract rules of human order and meaning so that they become self-induced more than socially enforced. . . . When concentration of the mind on the maintenance of collective order is broken, the effort to maintain the rules primarily by punishing offenders will either disintegrate or require intensely repressive policies. . . . Nothing less than education in social ethics . . . has historically been seen as the role of the family and the church rather than the school. . . . It now seems necessary for a lay public institution to teach morality. The nuclear family, itself

largely the product of technological civilization, is unlikely to discharge the obligation and the so-called peer group culture teaches self-indulgence rather than discipline.[35]

Muller asks, then, why so much individual and collective anxiety exists. His answer: "In large part, the anxiety may result from increased awareness of the fragility of our human abstractions of order and meaning." This fragility, as emphasized above, has its origin in the cynical frame of mind that has prevailed among a large section of the population in view of more and more publicly exposed violations of our ethical and moral norms by the supposedly trusted personalities of our community life and the tolerance exhibited thereto by the latter and our own elders. The *man-made* guidelines for behavior have become as significant a guide for youth as the elders accede to their observance. Thus Muller cautions: "The greatest hazard to man is other men. Many of our most significant abstractions are designed to establish a human order within whose confines human beings behave predictably and non-violently—if you will, justly—toward one another. The achievement of such human order requires immense discipline, because men must follow abstract rules rather than their appetites and animal inclinations."

What needs to be understood thoroughly, lest we continue to look with callow eyes at the ultimate significance of morality and ethics, is that not everything that is man-made is necessarily ignoble and of common vintage, deserving a lack of veneration. Moral and ethical norms are man-made, like fashion. But unlike fashion, which is a cultural phenomenon and subject to change, like the whims of daydreamers, are the persistent *social* guides of conscience during the whole lifetime of each person. Moral and ethical norms change slowly, sometimes so slowly that, like most of the biblical commandments, they become ingrained in the legal structures of nations and persist for centuries. Why? Because they are the psychosocial creations of man, who could never have become human in behavior without these community preservation norms, which have become guides of behavior affecting every trait of human nature. The present frivolous attitude toward morality and ethics has been generated by a bored outlook on human affairs where anything man-made is as venerated as a pornographic moving picture film. The attitude of unrestricted laissez-faire in behavior has created a lassitude toward permissiveness that borders on orderlessness. This semblance of chaos in behavior permissiveness has supported family disintegration, the supercilious divorce adventurism, the growing incest lobby, the antimonogamy movement, the formal recognition of the virtues of homosexuality, and the pornographic and prurient intrusions into the mass communications media. Unless the fundamental significance of moral and ethical norms is understood in relation to the sustenance of human society, the societal fabric is bound to become more and more weakened. There is a very basic need for a democratic people not to allow freedom of choice of the *individual* to be translated into orderlessness and the negation of that very freedom.

André Cournand, although philosophizing about the need of a new ethics for scientists, actually elaborates the need for a new ethics that fits the whole society. His discussion is not a consideration of the norms of individual personal interrelationships, but the broader outlook of the need for specific social imperatives to dispel the chaos into which we are drifting:

> In a word, what we are witnessing are phenomena that I prefer to characterize as reflecting blind emergence, pictured as an evolutionary process having strict analogies with processes of biological evolution. From the interactions of individual interests of men, nations, and new technological capabilities emerges, not a finely tuned system in which the needs of all are met more effectively, but rather a wildly oscillating disequilibrium in which the disparities between those who have and those who have not are broadening while technology remains unchecked. . . . We need to find a means of establishing control over the processes of emergence so as to favor man's survival. A central requirement, it seems to me, is a new and potent ethic, one that might help to shape the development of nations, regions, and ethnic groups in desirable ways—that is, in the direction of greater humanization.

After discussing the contributions of Jacques Monod and Pierre Massé to this subject, Cournand stated: "In seeking solutions to these problems, Massé suggests that we remember that *there has been and can be no enduring society without a common system of imperatives*" [italics added].[36]

NOTES

1. Erich Fromm, *The Sane Society* (New York: Rinehart and Co., 1955), p. 63.
2. Bernard F. Batto, "Red Sea or Reed Sea: How the Mistake was Made and What Yam Sûp Really Means," *Biblical Archaeology Review,* vol. 10, no. 4 (July/August 1984), pp. 56–63.

3. Richard B. Lee, *!Kung San: Men, Women and Children in a Foraging Society* (New York: Cambridge University Press, 1979), pp. 370, 396–97.

4. Paul Radin, *Primitive Man as Philosopher* (Pasadena, California: D. Appleton and Co., 1927), p. 51.

5. Ibid., p. 23.

6. Josef Hayim Yerushalmi, *Zakhor* (Seattle, Washington: University of Washington Press, 1982), p. 8.

7. Jacquetta Hawkes, *The Atlas of Early Man* (New York: St. Martin's Press, 1976), p. 22.

8. Ralph S. Solecki, *Shanidar: The Flower People* (New York: Alfred A. Knopf, 1947), p. 269.

9. Paul Radin, *The World of Primitive Man* (New York: E. P. Dutton and Co., 1971), p. 340.

10. Rene Dubos, *Beast or Angel?* (New York: Scribner, 1974), pp. 152–53.

11. Ashley Montagu, *Anthropology and Human Nature* (Boston, Massachusetts: Porter Sargent, 1957), p. 56.

12. Ibid., p. 44; also in Alfred Korzybski, *Manhood of Humanity* (New York: E. P. Dutton and Co., 1921), p. 193.

13. Jane Loevinger, *Ego Development* (San Francisco, California: Jossey-Bass Publishers, 1976), p. 3–4.

14. Ibid., pp. 270–72.

15. Ibid., p. 274.

16. Jerome Kagan, *The Nature of the Child* (New York: Basic Books, 1984), p. 243.

17. Erich Fromm, *The Sane Society* (New York: Fawcett, 1977), pp. 63–4, 65.

18. Jane Loevinger, *Ego Development* (San Francisco, California: Jossey- Bass Publishers, 1976), p. 9.

19. Iago Galston, ed., *Panic and Morals* (New York: International University Press, 1958), pp. 268–70.

20. Ibid.

21. George Will, "Rating the Movies," *The Times Picayune,* December 15, 1983.

22. Frank Schmalleger, "World of the Career Criminal," *Human Nature* (March 1979), pp. 50–56.

23. Rollo May, *The Courage to Create* (New York: W. W. Norton and Co., 1975), pp. 127–28.

24. Paul Radin, *The Primitive Man as Philosopher* (Pasadena, California: D. Appleton and Co., 1927), p. 90–91.

25. Ibid., p. 82.

26. Maurice Levine, *Psychiatry and Ethics* (New York: George Braziller, 1972), p. 212.

27. Ibid., p. 68–68.

28. Ibid., p. 212.

29. Ibid., p. 117.

30. Ibid., p. 116–120.

31. Ibid., pp. 30, 46–48, 66–68.

32. Maria Jahoda, *Current Concepts of Positive Mental Health* (New York: Basic Books, 1958), pp. 33–40.

33. Ibid., p. 39.

34. Ibid., p. 39–40.

35. Steven Muller, "I Do Not Believe in the Good Old Days," *Johns Hopkins Magazine* (January 1978), pp. 20–24.

36. André Cournand, "The Code of the Scientist and Its Relationship to Ethics," *Science,* vol. 198 (November 18, 1977), p. 699–705.

9

The Trait of Striving to Satisfy One's Appetites, Inclinations, and Talents

LEIGHTONS'S PRINCIPLE

Desire is a human phenomenon, although there is a tendency to define the automatic instinctual responses of the higher animals as desires when they elicit an urge to seek food or water or sexual satisfaction. There is no clinching evidence that animals respond to wants in accordance with Webster's definition of *desire*: "To long or hope for; to express a wish for." For animals, the urge is psychobiological; for man, it is psychosocial with biological roots. For man, except for infants and small children, the difference in the nature of desire is his brain, which elaborates the desires or tempers instincts with his cognitive processes, thus giving desires specific direction, which plans for manipulating the course to take to satisfy the desires, which engenders a conscience for giving social considerations in fulfilling of desires, and which makes evaluations as to the immediate and long term effects in proceding to fulfill the desires.

The human has desires stemming from physiological appetites, such as the Freudian instincts, desires initiated by the psychosocial effects of being socialized in a particular culture and a particular home setting where conditioning inclines desires in certain directions, and desires for talent pursuits for which one's constitutional makeup is fitted.

The need to keep striving in the direction that satisfies the appetites is explained by Freud as due to man's repressed instincts striving endlessly for complete satisfaction.[1] However, striving to satisfy these appetites, inclinations, and talents together are a trait of human nature. Although Freud's striving is basically instinctual, it does, perforce, also deal with the psychosocial cognitive level of behavior since repressions can produce psychoneurosis, a condition associated with cognition.* Seldom do animals overindulge in their physiological appetites—for example, their appetite for food. They eat to satisfy their hunger and then stop. Seldom are wild animals obese. For humans, the problem is quite different. Not only do they eat when hungry, but they have developed their gustatory faculties by cognitive processes to the most discriminatory degree. There are wine and whiskey experts and chefs who are masters of meat dishes, seafood delicacies, vegetable ambrosias, and special combinations. Many amateurs become famous for their culinary skills. Restaurants are frequented for their exotic foods. The spice trade can claim some responsibility for navigational enterprises leading to the discovery of trade routes and new lands. This illustrates the difference in quality of the animal response to eating when hungry and the human response to appetite for food, for the human consumes food when hungry and when not hungry. He makes an art of the ways of satisfying his mind and senses, such as cooking, photography, music, and painting.

Man has instinctual desires because he is an animal, i.e., because he feels the wants for something like sex, food, water, or rest. Man has psychosocial-cultural desires also because he is human, i.e., he has a particular type of functioning brain that makes possible his traits of human nature—the *hopes* to be *free* within the *norms* of societal existence to be able to *choose* to train himself to *create* and to *share* in what is created. This is what makes *Homo* the animal act as *Homo* the human. Man's behavior can only be understood in the context of this *bivalency*. Striving, therefore, is bivalent. Striving in the behavior milieu of the traits of human nature is the essence of being human. But in the struggle to be human, the primate traits, particularly those of egocentrism and aggression, may become dominant. Dominant egocentrism becomes exaggerated self-image–self-esteem trait, and aggression could exaggerate the challenge trait into violent, relentless competition or other types of destructiveness. The struggle is consciously or unconsciously expressed. What may result from such animal trait dominance is cupidity, despotism, selfishness, narcissism, uncontrolled aggressiveness, conscienceless behavior, or other of man's nonhuman behavior. Considering the fertility of man's mind, all types of nonhuman behavior may become dominant and destructive to society.

Leighton's basic theory of individual human behavior is based on the trait of striving. His two fundamental, underlying propositions

---

*It is in the behavioral area of "striving" that Freud's psychological theory based on the instincts adjoins the psychosocial theory of human nature of this present study.

about behavior are that "a given personality exists more or less continuously throughout life in the act of striving; and interference with that striving has consequences which in turn often lead to psychiatric disorders."[2] Concerning the relation of cognition to striving or goal seeking as a cause of behavioral disorientation and mental disturbance—in this case, psychoneurosis—Ellis makes the following observations:

> The relationship of psychoneurosis and anxiety problems to cognition in general and to what, in particular, people say to themselves as they experience difficult or "traumatic" experiences has been seen vaguely at least for many centuries. Buddha recognized that people make themselves miserable by concentrating too much on the fulfillment of their desires, including their goals and values; and he advocated that they become nonanxious or nonfrustrated by surrendering these values and making themselves desireless (achieving Nirvana) or at least less desirous. Epictetus and Marcus Aurelius, a student of Epictetus, even more clearly saw that people's unrealistic cognitions made them anxious or miserable and that these could distinctly be changed so that they then made themselves serene or happy. Other philosophers, such as Spinoza and Russell, have also clearly seen that what we call "emotions" and "emotional disturbance" are largely created by cognitions and that changing our beliefs and philosophies significantly modifies our disturbances.
>
> In the realm of psychology and psychotherapy, several outstanding thinkers have arrived at similar conclusions, often without any real knowledge of their philosophic predecessors. . . . I shall review some of the main hypotheses and findings about cognition and emotional disturbance, and I shall particularly concentrate on several major forms of anxiety and how human thinking significantly helps to create feelings of overconcern, phobias, worthlessness, and various other forms of "nervousness."[3]

The United States Public Health Service endorses this approach to understanding human behavior. In its publication, *Mental Health Considerations in Public Health*, it stated: "A suitable model of personality is that set forth by Leighton in which the individual is seen as a striving creature who must satisfy his physical, psychological, and group membership needs if he is to attain mental wellness. Clearly, these needs can be satisfied only if his society affords pathways that make their realization appropriate and consonant with the need-satisfactions of numbers of other related persons."[4] As indicated below, these are psychic needs that can only be satisfied in social settings involving basic social relations.

Leighton enumerates the essential striving sentiments as follows:

1. Physical security
2. Sexual interrelational satisfaction
3. The expression of hostility
4. The expression of love
5. The securing of love
6. The securing of recognition
7. The expression of spontaneity
8. Orientation in terms of one's place in society and the places of others
9. The securing and maintaining of membership in a definite human group
10. A sense of belonging to a moral order and being right in what one does, being in and of a system of values.[5]

These "essential striving sentiments" all relate one way or another to the traits of human nature, although not to all the traits specifically. The trait manifesting the need to strive to satisfy appetites, inclinations, and talents is a powerful drive in the human being's nature.

STRIVING IN PRIMITIVE SOCIETY

Striving is apparently as old as *Homo*'s effort to transcend his primate pattern of behavior. This is observed by Radin in his studies of primitive man: "If now we turn to the most insistent desire of primitive man—long life, success, and happiness—this sense of an objective world distinct from supernatural causation obtrudes itself even more strongly. Deities do not control the success or lack of success of the normal events and happenings of life. It is only at crises that their aid is solicited."[6] Radin continues:

> Social reality is to him [the individual] something unique and definitely distinct from the individual and no more emanates from him than does the external world. It is coexistent with the individual, both constraining and in its turn being constrained by him. As soon as we realize this, and that much of the religious and magical background is secondary, at times even being an inert accretion that but represents the external dress of a *will-to-action* [italics added], then the true interaction of the group and the individual becomes apparent at once. . . . It [this background] gives him what he most desires in life, prestige and a heightened sense of existence. . . . Individualism . . . everywhere runs riot. Whether it be in the South Seas, in aboriginal Asia, Australia, Africa, and the two Americas, the atmosphere that pervades each community is always the same—a ceaseless pitting of man against man, endless bickering, jealousies, envies, hatreds, a delight in the discomfiture of others. This, of course, is the negative side. . . . There is a positive side, too, expressed in romantic and devoted friendship, in love, reverential family affection, in kindness, generosity, and pity, in the highest of all virtues, respect for individuality.[7]

Striving is a psychosocial phenomenon, a cognitive process relating the self to the society. To compare it to the primate struggle among males for sexual dominance in a troop or any similar struggle such as may eventuate in preventing territorial incursion is to fail to understand the mental and emotional forces involved as outlined in the above citation from Leighton. The impetus to strive, except for the instinctual urges, more or less seems to depend on the social order. If we figure that, as Wenke puts it: "by about 400,000 years ago our *Homo erectus* ancestors had become skilled hunters and gatherers, exploiting environments from the temperate zones of Pleistocene Europe and North

China to the tropics of Africa and Java"[8] and that *Homo erectus* came on the scene about 1½ million years ago, gradually developing its foraging abilities, and that the foraging economy lasted up to about 10,000–9,000 B.C., then the foraging economy or what has been called "primitive communism" had occupied well over 90 percent of *Homo*'s time on this earth. If we consider further the fact that *Homo* appears to have come into existence about 3 million years ago, then the Neolithic and civilization periods have occupied a mere "instant" in *Homo*'s history. The question that must be answered is: *How could this socioeconomic system have lasted so long with so meager a development of technology considering the physical development of* Homo, *especially his brain?* The brain is the fastest-growing organ in the history of evolution. It certainly must have had something to do with this problem, but probably was not the deciding influence. Let us explore the brain aspect first. The ape, who cannot develop a cultural society, has an average brain size of less than 600 cubic centimeters. There apparently were some *Paranthropus* before *Homo habilis*, but the latter species, which existed some time before and after 2 million years ago, had a brain volume of around 680 cc. *Homo erectus*, a species that evolved about 2 million years ago and developed into *Homo sapiens* about 300,000 to 200,000 years ago, made much more progress in brain size, being endowed with a brain capacity that gradually increased in size from 750 cc. to at least 1200 cc. Definitely classified stone tools began to be found with fossils at the beginning of the *Homo habilis* period.

Wenke stated: "The archaeological record of a million years ago and earlier is fragmentary, but from the evidence we do have it appears that these early primates painted no pictures, carved no figurines, and made unbelievably simple and 'ugly tools,' and thus we might suspect that they also lacked the symbolic capacities required for complex language. . . . The amount of brain tissue required for complex speech patterns is uncertain. . . . Doubtless considerable 'rewriting' of the human brain occurred over the last 2 million years."[9]

By about 900,000 years ago [Wenke observed], our hominid ancestors had spread out along the margins of the temperate latitudes and had begun to invade Pleistocene Europe and northern Asia. The intrepid individuals who made the first forays into temperate climates were probably either a transitional form between *Australopithecus* and *Homo erectus* or full fledged *Homo erectus*. These hominids (and all hominids, including ourselves) were tropical animals who could not possibly have survived Pleistocene European winters without clothing, fire, and tools. . . . Between about 1 million and 350,000 years ago, from the first occupation of northern areas until most of Europe and northern Asia were inhabited by humans, the versatility and efficiency of tools increased, and people became larger, bigger-brained, and more "modern" in facial structure. The hominid associated with these changes is *Homo erectus*.[10]

Homo sapiens neanderthalensis and *Homo swanscombe* appeared on the evolutionary scene about 300,000 years ago, with a brain capacity of about 1300 cc., and disappeared about 35,000 years ago, when *Homo sapiens sapiens* appeared with an average brain capacity of 1400 cc.

FOOD SHARING, HOME BASE, AND EXCHANGE IN THE FORAGING ECONOMY

Considering that the brain size of *Homo* was apparently within the range of modern man for about 1 million years, why did it take over 900,000 years before *Homo* discovered agricultural and stock raising technology? If the cause of this great delay in technological development cannot be explained biologically, then maybe it can be explained socio-psycho-culturally. Therefore let us explore the latter avenue. How long *food sharing* was practiced before *exchange* was introduced is indeterminate. *Sharing* and *home-base*, which are essential for the initiation of exchange practices between social groupings, appear to have already been present 2 million years ago. It is also possible that the rigors of having migrated to the colder northern climates could very well have intensified the hunting and sharing practices and the need for exchange between groupings.[11] But yet, with the intensification of the "striving" trait, the foraging *mode of production* still persisted as the way of making a living.

Concerning the origin of the foraging economy of our ancestors, Wenke states:

Our earliest culture-bearing ancestors probably appeared on the African savannah about 5 million years ago or earlier. . . . The selective advantages of hunting and human-like social organization may have been emphasized by climate changes that increased the amount of open savannahlike environments in Africa. . . . Early *Homo* or *Australopithecus* probably lived in social groupings of about twenty-five individuals, and the "home-base" . . . at Olduvai suggests some territoriality and perhaps group stability. . . . Hunting and other factors then probably contributed to the loss of estrus and the various other physical developments during our first several million years as a genus, as did the defensive and mobility requirements of life in open country. By about 2 million years ago our ancestors' tool-using repertoire had become quite complex: eleven different tools have been identified at one site in Olduvai Gorge, including choppers, chisels, and engravers. Some division of labor probably existed, with females specializing in infant care and collecting activities, and males in defensive, hunting, and scavenging activities. *Food sharing* [italics added] would have been a likely concomitant of these specializations, but its extent at this time is difficult to estimate.[12]

If striving to satisfy appetites, inclinations, and native abilities, a trait of human nature, what was the reason why this trait's expression in the first several million years of the hominid's existence was concentrated on the foraging mode of making a living? A million years ago, except for the techniques of utilizing fire, the manufacture of spears and arrows and some stone and bone tools for cutting, stabbing, piercing, and chopping, making carrying devices and clothing, and providing shelter, life was unadorned with amenities requiring more technically developed skill. We must then ask ourselves, what stimulates the expression of the striving potential? Certainly it is desire—desire of what one's senses are aware and what one believes will be satisfactory or beneficial. The more things there are in one's environment of which one is aware and believes will satisfy or be beneficial to one's needs, the more one will desire. In the foraging ecology, besides a few artifacts, almost everything else was natural. The challenge-competence trait was still archetypal and not creating new things to be desired. *The appetites were pretty well satisfied. One's inclinations for a fairly secure mode of existence was satisfied.* The women's talents were continually taxed in raising children, gathering food, and keeping home base livable. The men's talents were well employed in perfecting their hunting skills and protecting the social group. Everyone's striving was, therefore, directed toward maintenance of the status quo, with some slow movement forward in attaining a more and more secure way of living by developing hunting tools. *From all indications, there was no motivation for enriching the culture or changing the social order.*

There is a need at this point to distinguish the spheres in which the trait of challenge-competence differs from that of the trait of striving to satisfy appetites, inclinations, and native abilities. In examining the extended duration of the foraging life-style of primitive *Homo*, the manifestation of these two traits seem to merge so that the creativity aspect of the challenge-competence trait appears almost absent, even though the techniques for hunting and gathering were being improved slowly. Thus only in the very long term examination of man's development does the challenge-competence trait begin to be differentiated from the striving trait.

As stated before, all traits interpenetrate one into the other as an integrated whole human nature so that each trait has a common area of interaction with other traits. But the two cited above appear to have more commonality than other traits have to one another. Our ability to understand the dynamics of the commonality of these two traits is made possible by the accumulated anthropological and archaeological artifacts that reveal their historical interrelations. The harmony between the ecosystem and the emerging traits of human nature during those primordial times was satisfactory to the point where creativity was not stimulated to move noticably forward enough to supercede the foraging system of making a living. During the 2 million or so years of the foraging period, the challenge-competence trait began only very slowly to be differentiated from the striving trait. The real stimulus for differentiation to gather speed came in the late Paleolithic period, about 35,000 years ago, when the advanced hunters took advantage of the glaciations created by the last Ice Age and spread to all the continents from Africa across the newly exposed land masses. This was the dawn of the rapid cultural advance by the first modern *Homo sapiens sapiens*, the Cro-magnon man: "These advanced hunting people began to create works of art of high imaginative quality, executed in an amazingly wide range of techniques. Their fine sculpture, modeling, painting and engraving put us in touch with them on fully human terms. We can see them as already our brothers, with the same creative urge [italics added], the same gift for image making, they are already feeling their way toward religious symbolism."[13] This was the prelude of the creativity which emerged in the Neolithic period, accompanied by revolutionary advances in agriculture and animal domestication.

The most important difference between the two traits is that of creativity. The challenge-competence trait is behavior that drives toward self or group development, at the same time, driving toward creative activity. A challenge is a presentation to the self or the group of a goal to be attained with the development of competence for that attainment. Such activity is the essence of creativity. The striving trait is conduct propelling individuals or groups only to satisfy appetites, inclinations, or native abilities. The striving is not primarily related to self- or group-development sentiments. Creativity is not an essential attitude of such striving as understood in this author's thesis. *Striving* mainly refers to that general seething movement of people scurrying about trying to satify their quest for things and tolerable social inter-relations. Both traits may at points engender jealousy and competition.

RETROSPECTIVE METHODOLOGY FOR DESCRIBING ANCIENT SOCIETY

Lee has described the behavior of people in the prehistoric foraging societies by a scientific retrospective methodology that is highly cred-ible. The essence of his description is: "Modern foragers *are* different from each other and from ancient foragers. We will make no progress in this area [of knowledge] by simply applying specific ethnographic data to specific archaeological sites. But it seems equally implausible that the behavior of ancient foragers would fall outside the range of behavior of the modern ones.... [I]f we can discern the *principles underlying foraging behavior* in all its variability, we can apply these principles to more dynamic models of foraging societies past and pres-ent."[14] Lee's methodology is a synthesis of *uniformitarianism* and Marx-ian dialectics in political economy:

> We start with the assumption that some of the same processes we see at work in contemporary foragers were also at work in prehistoric foragers. What are these processes? ... [W]e can be quite sure that they ate, slept, moved around their range, repro-duced and died, and that they lived in groups of some sort. Thus four fundamental variables provide our starting point: energy, space, resources, and vital statistics. Foragers have to expend energy in work in order to absorb energy in consumption. They have to move around their range in order to find the resources necessary to life. Their caloric intake has to provide for their own needs; for the needs of nonproductive young, sick, and old; and for the extra demands of reproducing the next generation. And they have to live in social groups as do all terrestrial primates, for their health, safety, and social needs.[15]

Lee asks: What conclusions can justifiably be drawn from this study of !Kung ecology and how can these be applied to the past history of humanity? One conclusion is that among the !Kung, food supply is sufficient to their needs, and they achieve this state of affairs with only the simplest of tools. This finding challenges the widespread popular and scientific notion that the way of life of hunter-gatherers is precarious and full of hardship and that the life of man in the 'state of nature' was 'nasty, brutish, and short.' "[16] He adds: "The traditional !Kung are *not experimenters* [italics added] introducing exotic cultigens into new environments. Theirs is a conservative adaptation based on locally occuring food plants that have become genetically adapted over many generations to the full range of conditions the environment has to offer. . . . Perhaps the most telling evidence of the security of life as hunter-gatherers is its *extraordinary persistence* [italics added]. Foraging people have been operating in the Dobe area for thousands of years without evidence for major discontinuities. Personnel have changed, but the way of life has remained the same. During this long period there has been little evidence for technological change."[17] He concludes: "The limited direct evidence for the !Kung suggests that they meet their needs with only 12 to 21 hours of subsistence work per person per week. . . . Studies of other hunter-gatherers . . . show a similarly low level of work effort—a level that has led one observer to suggest that the foragers probably enjoy more leisure time than does any other level of society. . . . [T]he overall picture tends to strengthen the argument for the relative ease of subsistence and for the security of foraging life."[18]

Lee attributes the basic economic characteristics of present day foraging society to all ancient foraging societies:

> Exchange of food is basic to all human societies, even the most nomadic, yet is absent from societies of nonhuman primates. The consequences of their pattern of food use for early human society were revolutionary. First, the expectation of exchange of foodstuffs led protohumans to develop the home-base, an improved site where members of a group could rendezvous on successive days and pool resources. Second, exchange allowed the development of varied subsistence activities; individuals could forage in different parts of the range and concentrate on different foods. . . . Third, differentiation of tasks allowed a most important step in human affairs—*risk taking*—whereby an individual could attempt a difficult subsistence task such as hunting. . . . Finally, exchange and the home-base permitted a breaking of the lockstep of primate subsistence, not everyone had to forage every day in order to survive. . . . The human home-base allowed rest and recovery without requiring the weak members to forfeit their lives or even a day's food. . . . The invention of the carrying device

made possible a human way of life, but with the increased efficiency of labor came the twin problems that have plagued humans ever since: the problem of surplus and the problem of leisure.[19]

Striving to satisfy one's appetites, inclination, and talents is a psychosocial phenomenon. Therefore let us not confuse the concept of striving with the urge to eat when hungry or the blind sexual urge for satisfaction. These are physiological urges impelling any animal to action. There is, however, a psychosocial *human* aspect to these physiological urges. The human has created an array of rules for sexual behavior, such as inhibitions against certain modes of action, fantasies of romance between sex partners, and different types of expectations mandated for the two sexes. The same is true for satisfying one's hunger: chefs, cookbooks, restaurants, fruit- and vegetable-growers, agriculture agencies, et cetera. Both sexes strive to fulfill their physiological urges with psychosocial motivations, which are certainly *not* identical for each sex. Therefore striving to satisfy appetites, inclinations, and talents for any group of humans has both identical and different aims. These strivings are further modified by the constitutional makeups of people and by qualities of the cultural forces prevailing in the area, since culture adds its specific qualities to psychosocial behavior. The intensity of striving to satisfy the basic intrinsic and extrinsic needs depends on the difficulty people have to satisfy them. The greater the difficulty, the greater the striving. According to the retrospective methodology of Lee, as described above, the circumstances of ancient foraging people in their ecosystem is such as to be conducive to "relative ease of subsistence and security." This appears as a logical conclusion to draw from the data presented. That technological development takes plenty of time when starting from scratch is to be expected. But that the foraging mode of production *absolutely* had to take millions of years of incubation before agriculture and stock raising could have been achieved is not necessarily an accepted conclusion. The most logical explanation is that *it must have been the relative ease of maintaining a satisfactory subsistence and security that dampened the intensity of the striving trait and kept the creativity trait harnessed.* This also kept those people on the conservative side of behavior—on the side of maintaining the status quo. Since there was no provoking violation against the traits of human nature, "primitive communism" attained a state of living whereby the needs as felt and conceived by the people at that time appear to have been adequately met. Under such conditions, the strong push for "research and development," if these words can be used to describe the creativity and striving impetus of primitive people, is curbed.

STRIVING AND COMPETITION

The human response to satisfying an appetite can become quite a reaction whose chain of events can become world-encircling. No less true for the appetites of individuals, groups, and nations than for their propensities and talents. Striving is a two-edged sword. Striving to satisfy appetites, inclinations, and native abilities can, by proper socialization, lead in the direction of social and individual good, but may also be diverted by primate impulses in antisocial and even violent and destructive directions. As can be expected, the trait concerned with appetite and inclinations can provoke competition and competition can develop to extremities, such as in the drug war that is now going on. Some types of extreme competition can be good, such as when atheletes compete in the Olympics. Some forms of striving can lead to challenges and competence development, such as when students strive for excellence in competing for scholarships and for just recognition. From most points of view, the results of the process are socially good, mainly because they give vent to the strivings of those who have developed propensities of their physical prowess in sports or mental mettle in intellectual matches, and could transform into the creativity trait, putting to creative work native talents. At the same time, society's senses are stimulated by such encounters. However, when inclinations and talents are directed toward the acquisition of wealth and power, competition of an extreme nature can develop, which could be detrimental societally. There is, of course, good and evil in competition. Economic competition is the mainspring of the creation, development, and accumulation of capital, and that is good, historically, for any nation. It may, in the meantime, cause disparities in subsistence and living conditions, but almost never do starvation, disease, and death settle upon a democratic community to the same extent as when a lively process of capital development is lacking, as in a dictatorship.

Economic Competition

When economic competition develops concentrations of economic power in monopolies and cartels and political competition develops concentration of police and military power, the latter are always applied *over* the people instead of *for* the people, except usually for a short period after a democratic revolution against tyranny. There is always a risk when such concentration of police and military power occurs. This is so because, as world history has demonstrated over and over again, uncontrolled power in the hands of one or a group *always* corrupts because it disorients the trait of self-image–self-esteem by magnifying the ego out of all normal proportion. The common expression is that such corruption is inevitable because "of the nature of the beast" (the primate). Although, in a colorful way, this expression contains validity, it would be more correct to describe this corruption as occurring on account of the biphasic nature of man's behavior—his human nature. Those who wield power, i.e., exercise their feeling of having *control*, develop an extreme sense of self-inflation. Although this is not supposed to happen under socialism, the history of the Soviet Union under Joseph Stalin is a good example. Such events demonstrate how reversion to the primate sense of individual-centered tendencies and conscienceless aggression can occur, given the circumstances. An example of group reversion to primate behavior is: When the American oil companies became multinational and realized that the sheikhs and dictators of oil-producing countries were getting wise enough to nationalize their countries' natural resources, the oil companies saw an opportunity to milk the world—an opportunity that they alone, without the help and cooperation of the oil cartel (OPEC), were not in a position to accomplish. They became partners in world piracy. As John Blair, a recognized expert on the oil industry, put it: "Partly for the same and partly for different reasons, the [OPEC] countries and the [oil] companies had the same interests".[20] The main interests were money and power.

The outlandish prices per barrel of oil were as much the fault of the oil companies as of OPEC.[21] When the time was opportune during the 1973–74 period the price per barrel was increased, and thereafter it was increased a number of times more. The profits of these companies soared beyond any level in their history. They made sure that the exploration for oil in the United States came gradually almost to a limp. In a period of less than a decade, the price per barrel of oil increased about 1200 percent. The world economy became dislocated. The poorer the country, the more its economy suffered. Inflation became rampant. Unemployment rose precipitously. Even in the richest country, the United States, large sections of the poorer people and those retired on fixed incomes began to suffer. If large sections of the population could be so affected in a rich country, just imagine what was the lot of the people in the poorer countries—all due to monopoly power, the power to control for antisocial reasons.

What has been remarkable about this whole episode is that the "capitalist" countries in which "free enterprise" has long been losing ground and whose people have been seeing flaunted before their eyes the demise of free enterprises's principal law—"supply and demand"—did nothing against the perpetration of this world economic catastrophe. Not one of these countries raised an eyebrow in astonishment at what was happening, in spite of the fact that together they could have destroyed this extortion racket in short order. In fact, the craven attitudes of these countries made it appear as if they were collaborating (which indeed they were) with this brazen stroke of immoral behavior as if it were normal business practice which, in a sense, it was, but risen to a height never before achieved. It would be difficult to find a better illustration of the social destructiveness resulting from extreme competition leading to the negation of competition and the assumption of extreme power and corruption by private monoploy. This is the ultimate of conscienceless behavior, the conscience being one of the basic characteristics distinguishing man from brute.

Why hasn't the United States government done anything about this arrogant throttling of competition in such a *vital* commodity in the *life* of modern society?

RATIONAL INTERPRETATION OF STRIVING

The desire to strive in expressing such inclinations as instrument playing, music composition, and literary authorship can lead to the awakening of the creativity trait of individuals to discipline themselves for periods of endurance and exertion of efforts in practicing or working where the sense of competing could even become adverse to physical or mental health. But this type of competition is not looked upon as bad or ill-considered, especially since it may produce a Beethoven, a Heifitz, an Einstein, or a Shakespeare and do the society good. It does not lead to monoploy or concentration of economic, police, or military power.

The striving trait of human nature, like other traits, interpenetrates other traits. The trait concerning the need to feel free to evaluate situations and freely choose one's course of striving can be carried to extremes. When youngsters are taught, as many have been, that they must be free "to do their thing," this has led to innumerable tragedies through misinterpreting the rational meaning of doing one's thing. A rational interpretation, if our knowledge about the socialization process is correct, would certainly include living and learning to live in a steady social setting, learning to discipline oneself to the necessary inhibitions that make a person acceptable as a social human being, and being made aware that doing one's thing should be based not on a "raw" appetite, a frivolous inclination, or an untested talent. People may not be born completely without conditioning, but such conditioning is scarce indeed. Infants certainly do have some appetites and may have inchoate inclinations and potential talents, but a good socially ordered socialization process will develop equilibrium to the appetites and social adeptness to inclinations and talents, tested and tried as maturing natural endowments. Appetites, inclinations, and native abilities should not be left up to immature children or those with dislocated socialization environments to decide as their choice in the process of doing their thing. Too often, parents unconcerned about directing the enthusiasm of their children to be free in striving to satisfy their urgent desires to do their thing have allowed them to follow such extremes, with disastrous results for the children. Sometimes, caring parents cannot control their children, who have become victims of their age-group surrogates. But misdirected age-group surrogates are a community responsibility.

Another extreme that is dislocating social life is related to the striving trait and the trait of self-image–self-esteem. The misuse of the mass media, particularly television, has helped to push these traits into extreme limits of expression. Inconsequential terror groups are built up by undeserved publicity given them in comparison to their initial impact on society. Individual disoriented people who have developed inordinate desires for enlarging their self-image may commit acts hazardous to others, such as hijacking planes to get notoriety, which they are sure to get an ample supply of. Criminals may become courageous enough to perform spectacular feats of criminality to satisfy their craving for enlarging their self-image in the newsprint and on TV, for surely their feats will be "magnified"in the mass media. There are so many variations of this theme that one need only look for demonstrations in the newspapers and daily TV news to find infinite varieties.

COMMITMENT

Commitment to a way of life is an essential for high morale. A country that inspires patriotism will also generate citizen's morale. Morale is a positive factor in participation of the people. But the philosophy to which commitment is directed may be socially good or evil. Hitler was able to get the overwhelming majority of the Germans committed to a bigoted way of patriotic life. The goal of that way of life was the genocide of a people. An example of a particular person who was patriotically motivated to extremes was that of Nicholas Chauvin, who idolized Napoleon I for his military victories to the point that the word *chauvinism* has come to mean blind enthusiasm to any cause. This type of extremity in satisfying the commitment to a philosophy of life trait of human nature is itself discordant with other traits of human nature, such as rootedness in significant social interrelationships of mutuality that generate love, trust, and cooperation. If the commitment, however, is to a philosophy of life that supports interrelationships that harmonize with all the traits of human nature, a love of country becomes a virtue worth striving for.

EXPLOITATION AND CAPITAL

In a highly developed capitalist democracy, two basic concepts must be dealt with. From the point of view of humanism, the critical term in the Marxian definition of capital is "exploitation," and from an economic point of view, the critical advantage of *capital* is its *phenomenal growth potential*. Let us consider these terms as they relate to the striving trait.

What is the difference in the exploitation factor between that of a highly developed capitalist democracy like the United States and a socialist country like the Soviet Union? This needs to be examined in broad perspective in order to understand the dynamics of capital in both systems.

It is necessary to understand that it is possible that the Soviet Union may not call its capital capital, lest it admit exploitation in its system, or maybe it does use the term but in a hidden language. However, English translations of Soviet economic literature pertaining to Soviet investment planning do use the term "capital."[22]

It must also be understood that from a Marxian point of view, real socialism is not attainable until the productive forces have reached a certain high level. The Soviet Union has not yet reached that level. The United States is much closer to that level of production, but has a distance to go, considering the funds needed for waste on armaments. Where does the Soviet Union get the capital to develop its production? Does it or does it not come from surplus value, a product of exploitation? Is it possible that it comes from any other source?

THE TREND IN THE UNITED STATES

Does a capitalist democracy that has reached the level of production at which real socialism could be practiced necessarily have to change its system to socialism in order for the entire population to be able to live at a human and humane level of existence? The answer to this question depends upon what that capitalist country does with the *surplus value* it produces and with the revenue it collects.

In the United States, some dramatic trends have been taking place in the socioeconomic arena since the end of World War II. Actually, these changes have been taking root since the Great Depression and the passage of the Social Security Act. From the end of the depression until 1977, the Gross National Product increased about twenty times—from around $100 billion to around $2,000 billion. The federal government expenditure increased well over forty times—from about $9 billion to about $400 billion. The health and social services expenditures increased almost 1,000 times—from $250 million to $205 billion. The percentage of corporate profits paid in taxes in 1940 was about 28 percent. (See table 2.) This increased to an average of 45 percent in 1950 and thereafter. In 1940, the amount of revenue collected by the federal government was twice the amount of profits after taxes made by U.S. corporations. In that year, government revenues collected were $14.1 billions and the amount of profit after taxes of corporations was $7.2 billion. In 1950, revenues were $51.1 billion, as compared to corporate profits after taxes of $24.8 billions. Thereafter, the differences between these got continually greater, so that by 1975, the revenues collected by all levels of government were $519.3 billion, as compared to corporate profits after taxes of $71.4 billion, the government collecting over seven times the corporate profits after taxes.

What does all this mean? It means *first* of all that the government of the United States has rapidly expanded its philosophy of humanism. This is shown by the fact that the percentage of federal expenditure of the worth of the GNP for operations and for all services increased from 2.8 percent in 1929 to 21.0 percent in 1977—an eight times increase—yet the increase in the percent of the federal expenditures on health and social services increased from a small fraction of one percent in 1929 to 52 percent in 1977, at lest several hundred times greater. (See table 3.) During the same period, the population less than doubled. This shows that the capitalist democratic system allowed the *striving* (competition) *for profits and power* to make phenomenal strides in a short period of time by increasing its capital formation and growth, while at the same time greatly concentrating political and economic power in the central government. *The central government was able to do this by the nature of its revenue collection system.* Before receiving authority to collect income taxes in 1912, it was collecting 17 to 18 percent of all revenues. Since then, its revenue collections kept increasing so that it now collects one half to two-thirds of all revenues, while the reverse was the fate for local government revenue collections. (See table 4.)

Second, statistical data shows that, although the median family income had only tripled between 1947 and 1967, the percentage of families in the higher income brackets had increased and those in the lower income brackets had decreased dramatically, (See table 1)) and the substantial increase in health and social services has decidedly neutralized some of the deleterious effects on those remaining in the lower income levels. But despite this favorable trend, and in the midst of such wealth, the extreme freedom for persons and groups to pursue the wild scramble for satisfying their appetites for wealth and power still leaves a substantial proportion of the population in economic trouble.

Third, all this means that if this trend keeps up its momentum, no socialist country would be able to equal the physical well-being of most of the people in the United States. The question remains: Would the United States then be able to move in the direction of harmonizing its ecosystem to the needs of *all* the people in relation to all the traits of human nature without changing its capitalist democratic system, but by introducing relevant controls, particular on monopolies and ethics in competition, which could affect corporate operations and even organization?

Fourth, what the statistical data do not indicate is the critical contradiction that has shown its ugly head in the last few years, a contradiction never before manifested in the American economy and that indicates that the economy has reached a stage where some very basic decisions must be reached concerning it. For it cannot go on this way too long without losses in its democratic nature. This complex, which has been dubbed stagflation (recession or depression with inflation), has completely baffled the traditionally trained economists as to the causes or the methods of control. At the same time, fixed monopolies and spurious monopolies have become so strong that they can control the price of commodities even when the world market is glutted with them, while the solutions applied lay like incubi on the backs of the needy. Examples are oil, meat, sugar, coffee, automobiles, steel, and so forth.

The statistical data indicate that the profits after taxes, the surplus value, from 1940 to 1975 increased ten times while the median family income increased only three times. Even with all the social and health services, this gap in the well-being of significant proportions of the people still calls for stricter controls on the competitive ruthlessness of monopolies that keep increasing the precarious state of the economy. Control does not mean increasing the number of regulations while at the same time increasing the number of loopholes to negate compliance, as is usually the case. Regulations must be simple and direct and forthwith implemented. There are already ample laws and regulations to do what is needed if modified for present conditions, and if the implementation were based on the obvious intent of the laws and regulations instead of the underhand devious intent of those in government who are in sympathy with or outright controlled by special interests. This brings us back to the wisdom of our founding fathers, particularly the wisdom of James Madison. In No. 10 of the Federalist Papers, Madison deals with the most vexing problem in democratic government: the resolution of antagonisms created by the division of people into competing factions—economics being the most potent of factors.

Thus he asserted: "But the most common and durable source of factions has been the various and unequal distribution of property. . . . The regulation of these various and interfering interests forms the principal task of *modern* [italics added] legislation and involves the spirit of party and faction in the necessary and ordinary operations of the government."[23] Madison clearly understood the biphasic nature of human nature and that from this biphasic nature issues the excesses of man's strivings, to wit: "As long as reason of man continues fallible, and he is at liberty to exercise it, different opinions will be formed. As long as the connection subsists between his reason and his *self-love* [italics added], his opinions and his passions will have a reciprocal influence on each other; and the former will be objects to which the latter will attach themselves."[24] In the less complicated world of James Madison, it was easier to see the operation of socioeconomic and psychosocial forces. Those forces still operate in our complicated world, but are blurred from vision in the maelstrom of other complicating factors. The fact is that human beings still are motivated by similar desires, which broadly might be equated to appetites, inclinations, and native abilities, which our forefathers strove to satisfy. Depending on the circumstances, those strivings can be pursued with socially directed morale and hopes with benefit to the whole society or with antisocially directed morale and hope with benefit to individuals or groups in the society.

TABLE 1
Money Income of Families,
Percentage Distribution by Income Level,
1950–1977 (in constant 1977 dollars)

	under 3000	3000 to 4999	5000 to 5999	6000 to 6999	7000 to 9999	10000 to 11999	12000 to 14999	15000 to 19999	20000 to 24999	25000 and over	Median family income
1950	14.3	10.3	7.3	7.1	23.8	19.7	10.5	4.8	1.3	0.8	8,356
1960	3.6	8.5	4.1	4.7	15.0	14.8	13.2	17.2	6.4	7.4	11,500
1970	4.6	5.7	3.2	3.5	11.0	7.9	13.2	22.8	10.5	18.2	15,399
1975	3.9	6.0	3.6	3.6	11.5	7.7	12.1	18.4	13.8	19.4	15,447
1977	3.6	5.7	3.5	3.7	10.9	7.2	11.3	17.8	13.9	22.4	16,009

From: *Statistical Abstracts of the United States*

TABLE 2
Corporate Profits before and after Taxes,
Percentage of Profits Paid in Taxes,
United States, 1940–1975 (in millions)

	1940	1950	1955	1960	1965	1970	1975
Profits before taxes	10,000	42,634	48,607	49,712	77,787	72,100	117,100
Profits after taxes	7,200	24,864	26,991	26,680	46,461	44,200	71,400
% profits paid in taxes	28%	43%	44%	46%	40%	39%	39%

Average = 42%

From: *Statistical Abstracts of the United States*

TABLE 3
Gross National Product, Federal Expenditures, Health and Social Services Expenditures, Federal Expenditures as Percent of GNP, Health and Social Services Expenditures as Percent of Federal Expenditures
(in billions)

	1929	1933	1938	1945	1955	1965	1975	1977
GNP	103.9	55.8	85.0	212.3	399.2	688.1	1,498.9	1,887.2
Federal expenditures	8.9	4.3	8.7	98.3	67.3	118.4	356.9	394.2
Health and social services expenditures				0.25	1.0	11.5	168.0	205.3
Federal expenditures GNP	2.8%	8.0%	10.2%	46.3%	17.0%	17.2%	24.0%	21.0%
Health and social services expenditures Federal expenditures				0.25%	10.4%	10.0%	44.2%	52.0%

From: *Statistical Abstracts of the United States*

TABLE 4
Revenue Collections, Percentage Distribution among Federal, States, and Local Governments
(in millions)

	Federal	%	States	%	Local	%	Total	%
1912	320	14.8	370	17.1	1,470	68.1	2,160	100
1915	625	27.1	368	15.9	1,318	57.0	2,311	100
1930	3,468	32.7	2,108	19.9	5,018	47.4	10,594	100
1940	5,566	39.4	4,187	29.7	4,365	30.9	14,118	100
1950	35,186	68.9	7,930	15.5	7,984	15.6	51,100	100
1960	77,003	68.1	18,036	15,9	18,081	15.9	113,120	100
1970	146,082	61.6	47,962	20.6	38,883	17.9	232,877	100
1975	302,300	58.2	119,200	22.8	97,800	19.0	519,300	100
1977	383,524	49.0	204,475	26.0	196,321	25.0	784,320	100

From: *Statistical Abstracts of the United States*

NOTES

1. Sigmund Freud, *Beyond the Pleasure Principle* (New York: Liveright Publishers, 1950), p. 56.

2. Alex. H. Leighton, *My Name Is Legion*, vol. 1 (New York: Basic Books, 1959),p.136.

3. Albert Ellis, "Psychoneurosis and Anxiety Problems," in R. and I. Z. Grieger, eds., *Cognition and Emotional Disturbance* (New York: Institute for Rational Living), pp. 17–18.

4. *Mental Health Considerations of Public Health*, United States Public Health Service Bulletin, No. 1898 (May 1969), p. 54.

5. Leighton, *loco supra citato*, p. 148.

6. Paul Radin, *Primitive Man as Philosopher* (Pasadena, California: Appleton and Co., 1927), pp. 30–31.

7. Ibid., pp. 37–38.

8. Robert J. Wenke, *Patterns of Prehistory* (New York: Oxford University Press, 1980), p. 163.

9. Ibid., p. 136–37.

10. Ibid., pp. 138–139.

11. Ibid., p. 141.

12. Ibid., pp. 134–135.

13. Jacquetta Hawkes, *The Atlas of Early Man* (New York: St. Martin's Press, 1976), p.13.

14. Richard B. Lee, *The !Kung San* (Cambridge, England: Cambridge University Press, 1979), pp. 433–434.

15. Ibid. pp. 434–435.

16. Ibid., p. 438.

17. Ibid.

18. Ibid., p. 440.

19. Ibid., pp. 490, 491, 492.

20. John M. Blair, *The Control of Oil* (New York: Pantheon Books, 1976), p. 280.

21. Ibid., p. 281.

22. Harry Schwartz, *The Soviet Economy Since Stalin* (New York: J. B. Lippincott Co., 1965), p. 233.

23. Alexander Hamilton *et al.*, *The Federalist Papers*, edited by Clinton Rossiter (New York: New American Library, 1961), p. 79.

24. Ibid., p. 78.

10

The Self-Image–Self-Esteem Trait

SELF: A SOCIAL PHENOMENON

The need to *appreciate* one's *self-image* in the continuing process of self-development as reflected in the judgment of those in whose social interrelations one participates is basic in man's nature as a human being.

Man's awareness of his relation to the world around him generates in him a *conscience* regarding his behavior and the need for support from his social surroundings. Such *consciousness* of self and *conscience* of one's conduct generate further a sense of self-uniqueness and assessment of self-worthiness, in comparison to others, which begets the need to appreciate one's self-image in the continuing process of self-development as manifested by the reactions experienced from one's social interrelations. Shakespeare, the great student of human nature, never defined the term, but was the master in revealing its dynamic responses to the myriad circumstances of man's adventures through life. He dramatizes this trait in Iago's clever insinuations of Desdemona's infidelity while protesting his own fidelity to Othello:

> Good name in man and woman, dear my lord,
> Is the immediate jewel of their souls;
> Who steals my purse, steals trash; 'tis something, nothing;
> 'Twas mine, 'tis his, and has been slave to thousands;
> But he that filches from me my good name
> Robs me of that which not enriches him,
> And makes me poor indeed.
>
> —*Othello*, Act III, Scene 3

The recognition of the self as a unique entity is indeed a behavioral characteristic of *Homo*. The uniqueness of the self appears to be demonstrated by the early care with which even *Homo sapiens neander-thalensis*, 100,000 to 35,000 years ago, buried his dead. Wenke asserts:

> Neanderthals were probably very like recent hunters and gath-erers in habit and abilities. . . . Whatever their fluency [in speech and language] the many Neanderthal burials indicate that they invested life and death with considerable rituals. Excavations at La Chapelle-aux-Saints reveal a corpse laid out in a shallow trench with a bison leg placed on his chest, and the trench filled with bones, tools, and other debris—perhaps representing offer-ings of animal flesh and implements. . . . At Shanidar Cave in Iraq, a Neanderthal dated to about 60,000 years ago had been buried toward the back of the cave, and the soil around the burial contained massive quantities of flower pollen, mainly grape hy-acinth, bachelor buttons, and hollyhock. Ralph Solecki, the ex-cavator, and the paleontologist, Arlette Leroi-Gourhan, concluded that the skeleton had been buried with garlands of flowers. Some scholars, however, remain unconvinced of this interpretation.[1]

Lee developed a retrospective methodology for judging the behav-ior of ancient foragers by the *principles* of behavior of present-day primitive foraging societies and applying these principles to the ancient foragers. Concerning the self-image–self-esteem behavior of primitive foragers, he cites a passage from Lorna Marshall's "The Harmless People" and whom he describes as a careful ethnographer: "I think that most !Kung cannot bear the sense of rejection that even mild disapproval makes them feel. If they do deviate, they usually yield readily to expressed group opinion and reform their ways."[2] Radin found the same sense of self pervading primitive people in his extensive research into their ideological processes: "In one sense the fear of rid-icule is merely the obverse side of prestige hunting, and prestige hunt-ing is at bottom but a defensive mechanism against ridicule. . . . The fear of ridicule is thus a great factor in the lives of primitive people."[3] This psychosocial trait of self-identification was, in primitive society, so structured by the prevailing culture as to take the place of a modern police force.

Jahoda looked far and wide in the literature for criteria of positive mental health and found the works she examined more or less lacking. What she did find, however, was: "A recurring theme in many efforts to give meaning to the concept of mental health is the emphasis on certain qualitites of a person's self. . . . Self-acceptance implies that a person has learned to live with himself, accepting both the limitations and possibilities he may find in himself. Self-confidence, self-esteem, and self-respect have a more positive slant. . . . "[4] "Closely related to such balanced self-acceptance is another aspect of the self-concept which is frequently discussed in mental health literature: the sense of identity."[5]

In examining the term "self-actualization," which "probably originated with Goldstein (1940)" who "spoke about the process . . . as occurring in every organism and not only in the healthy one: 'There is only one motive by which human activity is set going: the tendency to actualize oneself'. The idea is echoed in Sullivan's dictum, 'the basic direction of the organism is forward', and it also dominates the thinking of authors such as Carl Rogers, Fromm, Maslow, and Gordon Allport. Sometimes the term is used as implying a general principle of life, holding for every organism; at other times it is applied specifically to mentally healthy functioning." Then Jahoda cautions that the various meanings of self-actualization may also include the meaning "that not only the development of civilization but also self-destruction and crime . . . are among the unique potentialities of the human species."[6] Jahoda's warning is concerned with the negation of the positive aspect of this trait—a negation whereby the primate impulses predominate, resulting in an inflated self-centeredness supported by antisocial acts.

Self-identity, self-conscience, self-worthiness, self-esteem, self-realization, self–social orientation

Human

Sense of self

Primate

Self-centrism, self-indulgence, self-seeking leading even to antisocial acts and self-destruction, self-actualization without conscience or social responsibility

Mead explains self most aptly: "In our statement of the development of intelligence we have already suggested that the language process is essential for the development of the self. The self has a character which is different from that of the physiological organism proper. The self is something which has a development; it is not initially there at birth, but arises in the process of social experience and activity, that is, develops in the given individual as a result of his relations to the process as a whole and to other individuals within the process."[7]

"A person is a personality because he belongs to a community, because he takes over the institutions of that community into his own conduct. He takes its language as a medium by which he gets his personality, and then through a process of taking the different roles that all the others furnish he comes to get the attitude of the members of the community. Such, in a certain sense, is the structure of a man's personality. . . . The structure, then, on which the self is built is this response which is common to all, for one has to be a member of a community to be a self. . . . It is a structure of attitudes, then, which goes to make up a self, as distinct from a group of habits."[8] The self, therefore, is a psychosocial phenomenon resulting from the social process, although an individual entity.

Historically, Fromm opines that man's need for a sense of self-identity supported by self-esteem and self-realization developed from his becoming aware, in the deep past, that he had lost his original unity with nature. No longer being a sufficient component of nature, he had to develop a new form of sufficiency, i.e., an adequate degree of self-sufficiency supported by self-esteem and self-realization of his individuality, lest he become a crippled, an inferior derelict in the maelstrom of the natural forces.[9]

Self-identity came early in *Homo sapiens'* existence, as Hawkes put it: "So far as we know, this was the first time that such rites (burial ceremony) had been practiced (by Neanderthals), and it can hardly be doubted that they manifest a belief in some kind of after-life, perhaps springing from a heightened sense of individuality."[10]

"As with the need for relatedness, rootedness, and transcendence, the need for a sense of self-identity–self-uniqueness is so vital and imperative that man could not remain sane if he did not find some way of satisfying it."[11] Fromm's psychological analysis of this trait of human nature is well matched with Dubos's sociological insight of this trait: "There exists in human nature . . . [a] drive toward biological and intellectual individualization. This drive is probably essential to the development of civilization."[12] Dubos, believing in the unrestricted plasticity of the nature of human beings' reasons in terms of the facility of human adaptation to the ecosystem and not in terms of specific needs of the ecosystem being in or out of concordance with the traits of human nature. This inclination toward Watsonian plasticity of behavior is the usual deficiency in the reasoning of a large portion of the social scientists. Thus Dubos writes that Montaigne wrote concerning the shaping of our character that it "can be 'our great and glorious masterpiece'. But this can be achieved only by living in a manner suited to the special conditions of our existence. Ideally, human beings should therefore strive for an intimate adaptation between their own unique organic and psychological endowment and the circumstances of their individual lives, which are necessarily unprecendented. Since such adaptive interplay differs from one person to another and according to the situation, diversity is an inevitable consequence of life and especially of civilized life."[13] Of course, the adaptation process is basic for humankind, but so is the process of shaping the ecosystem to be in concordance with the nature of man, since he does have a human nature composed of specific traits which when violated produce pathological or at least perverted behavior, as Fromm points out so well.

That this trait of human nature, when violated, may produce mental disorientations, as Fromm contended, or even mental disturbance is strongly supported by Ellis. In discussing how cognition plays an extremely important role in the creation and sustaining of neurosis in general and anxiety in particular, Ellis describes the various types of anxieties about which *ego anxiety* is the most dramatic:

> Ego anxiety is perhaps the most dramatic form of nervousness and one of the most pernicious because it involves people rating themselves, their essence, and feeling almost totally worthless or inadequate if they do not perform some task(s) well enough, or if they are not sufficiently approved or loved by others. When they have anxiety, they have emotional tension (or, better, hypertension) that results when they feel (1) that their self or personal worth is threatened; (2) that they *should* or *must* perform well and/or be approved by others; and (3) that it is *awful* or *catastrophic* when they don't perform well and/or are not approved by others as they supposedly *should* or *must* be. Ego anxiety is frequently called performance anxiety, since it is experienced when people feel that they have not performed some task or project well enough and are pretty rotten individuals for having failed to do better on it.[14]

This also illustrates the linkage of traits, as in this case, the challenge-competence trait with the self-image—self-esteem trait.

The mass media, particularly the lifelike visual presentations by television, can have so stimulated susceptibles in the population to magnify their self-image by doing something spectacular (which can be *translated* into news-worthiness, be those acts socially or individually beneficial or destructive), that large sections of the population seek publicity by acts that in some cases are criminally directed and other cases emotionally disoriented. Thus the self-image–self-esteem trait can and has been perverted by seeking publicity to solve this trait's problems. Instruments like television but also the other mass media, which could be marvelous means for influencing the ecosystem into concordance with the traits of human nature are actually being used to elicit discord by falsely conditioning the susceptibles to use the media for magnifying their self-image by spectacular acts that the media seeks. This is not a new way of swelling the self-image–self-esteem trait. Only the means of publicity are new and more potent. Politicians have used publicity since ancient times. Shakespeare knew this well and described it eloquently in Antony's oration at the funeral of Caesar, in which Antony berates Brutus for accusing Caesar of having *acted* to ambitiously with evil intentions: "I come to bury Caesar, not to praise him. The evil that men do lives after them; the good is oft interred with their bones" (Act III, Scene 2). Somehow the evil, the spectacular, acts make greater impression on the people since they violate basic social inhibitions and give the primate urges vent.

What is so plastic in human behavior is the rich ethological matrix of the personality and character of people, in which the specific traits of human nature are embedded like rods of reinforcement. That these traits have a certain plasticity in adapting to changing sociocultural conditions is indeed true. *But beyond certain thresholds, strains on the traits of human nature result in disoriented responses, although the ethological matrix has a great deal more residual malleability..*

The "I" as a unique individual member of the human race may become disoriented by dissociating itself from the wholeness of the human race. This may occur by overemphasizing the identification of the "I" with a particular nation, religion, class, race, or occupation. Such excessive self-identification to a special group to the exclusion of all others tends to be destructive by excessive conformity, which negates the self-assertion and the individuality and, at the same time, distorts the interrelationships among humankind. Such perversions eventually lead to destructive behavior such as tunnel-vision, bigotry, hatred, war, genocide, suicide, criminality, behavioral disorientations, and even mental disturbances in many other forms. This discussion of the effects of extremism is not meant to denigrate the human richness of the world because of the great variety of cultures and subcultures that abound and to which almost everyone has an attachment. These need to be encouraged to flourish and develop, but as part of the human race.

Dubos clearly identifies this trait as an essential human entity: "While the tendency to form complex ecosystems is universal and is manifested also in the creation of human societies, there exists in human nature . . . an opposite drive toward biological and intellectual individualization."[15] "Most human beings desire to participate in the adventures and spectacles of collective life, but they also want to make a unique creation of their own."[16] "It is probable that the sense of uniqueness and of self-awareness did not fully emerge until late in the evolution of the human species. Even the most independent among modern people still feel the need to belong to a social group."[17] "Humanness may owe its existence to the conditions that first caused self-awareness and the sense of uniqueness to emerge in primitive tribes."[18] "The development of individuality thus begins by an objectivation of the external world, and it evolves into the realization by each individual person that he constitutes a unique specimen of the human species."[19]

Clinard makes the pithy point that one of the most vital aspects of eliminating the slum dwellers from their slum way of life "is a change in identity or self-image of the residents of the slums. In most instances, such a change represents a new sense of personal worth."[20]

Loevinger places self-awareness at the very basis of personality: "There are two central aspects of a human personality that seem to resist a structural treatment, namely, self-awareness and the experience of freedom, both implicit in our conception of ego development."[21] She discusses at length Jahoda's contribution to the subject of self-identity as basic to positive mental health and the contributions of Maslow, Erikson, McDougall, and White to the subject.[22]

Lewis *et al.* in an excellent presentation of the psychosocial dynamics of family health[23] quote Westley and Epstein concerning self-identity: "Autonomy seems to be essential to the development of a satisfactory ego identity, for one must be permitted to consider oneself a separate person, and to experience oneself as such, to find an identity."[24]

JEALOUSY

At this point, it is relevant to consider the emotional response called jealousy, particularly because of the confusion being introduced into its meaning by the advocates of consensual adultery. The details of this problem will be discussed elsewhere. However, it needs to be stated here that most students of the subject consider jealousy to be an emotional response to a denigration of one's self-image, self-esteem, self-identity, and self-worthiness. It is admitted that the most poignant problem in utopian colony experiments and swinger-type associations is jealousy. The advocates of consensual adultery believe that they can overcome this problem if they attack it in the right way. Human nature, of course, can be bent here and there. But to change the human nature of the people in general, it will be necessary to change very basic social relations that have been generated by the fundaments of the human condition from which human nature issues. The advocates of consensual adultery do not seen to realize that jealousy is a response to a violation of at least one of the traits of human nature—the trait of self-appreciation. A more recent study of the subject by Virginia Adams is worth reading.[25]

THE CIVILIZED IDENTITY SOCIETY

Glasser, in a very interesting study, has come to the conclusion that present-day society is undergoing a rapid transition into "The Civilized Identity Society." This, he asserts, is the fourth phase of an approximately 4 million year interval "since man has been considered a more or less distinguishable entity." He calls

> The earliest human society the *primitive survival society*. It lasted three and a half million years. During that long period, man's primary goal in life was survival. . . . He was able to survive because he cooperated intelligently with other members of the species. . . . About 500,000 years ago . . . man evolved . . . the *primitive identity society*. . . . Able to take survival at least partially for granted, primitive identity man developed other priorities. He finally found time to have a little fun—to love and be loved, to become involved, or, for those who could not, to learn the pain of loneliness. He formulated complex kinship systems, ornate rituals, ceremonies, dances and religious beliefs . . . High on the list of pleasure activities was sex.
>
> Then entered mankind's phase three . . . the *civilized survival society*. Survival again became a paramount priority, but civilized men did not revert to the cooperative instincts of their forefathers. Once the idea of conquest became common, survival of the aggressive became the ruling theme of existence. . . . The American

frontier men were survival-oriented, and all but eliminated the Indian in the acquisition of power and land. The civilized survival society was a goal-oriented society. To survive in it, men relinquished their individuality and became subservient to the group. Work became necessary. . . . In the past twenty or so years, a new society has begun to emerge . . . the *civilized identity society* . . . it is motivated by a respect for individual integrity. . . . Led by the young, the half-billion people of the Western World have begun a tumultuous revolution toward a new, role-dominated society in which people concern themselves more and more with their identities and how they might express them. Of course, people still strive for goals, but increasingly these are vocational or avocational goals that their pursuers believe will reinforce the independent human role. The goals may or may not lead to economic security, but they do give people verification of themselves as humans. . . . In the new identity society few people renounce the opportunity to struggle for an independent role. In this struggle, however, many people fail; they are unable to find such a role. They do gain an identity but the identity is that of a failure. . . . Many retreat into unreality through the use of alcohol or drugs; or they find escape in psychosomatic ailments. . . . Others find independence in growing beards, participating in peace marches or in voter-registration drives. . . . Today, about twenty years into the new civilized identity society, most families in the Western World are culturally divided. . . . The young . . . believe role takes precedence over goal. They do so because *they have had security within their families* [italics added]. They believe an independent role is natural; they do not hear admonitions that security and freedom are temporary because they are provided by the family and by the society. . . . Work for them is not necessarily sacred. If one chooses not to work, he should have that right. . . . The new identity society is a regeneration of intelligent cooperation and involvment, reverting back hundreds of thousands of years of humanity.[26]

This analysis reminds me of Marx's animating observation that historic events repeat themselves, but as caricatures of the original. I am reminded of this observation because, as serious a situation as the present "civilized identity society" may be, it is still a caricature of the "primitive identity society." The main reason for this is that the present one is a distortion of the meaning of the original. The importance of the original identity society was:

1. It liberated the primitive survival society enough from the hazards of survival against the rigors of the natural ecosystem to allow human intelligence to develop intellectual pursuits whereby a symbolization system to synergize psychosocial behavior was molded into harmony with the vicissitudes of the human condition and initiated an accumulating culture, eventuating into domestication of animals and agriculture.
2. It sharpened the vision about the uniqueness of the individual so that the present traits of human nature began to crystallize rapidly into the complex of basic behavior that we designate as the nature of human nature.
3. Out of the self-consciousness, the self-esteem, self-realization, and self-actualization generated the humane conscience, which made possible the development of self-discipline, the importance of inhibitions and the freedom to choose, but circumscribed by *social* necessity and moral and ethical norms of behavior—a philosophy of life.
4. Cooperation and mutual aid blossomed into psychosocial stimuli of the emotional life, manifesting the various facets of love and family solidarity.
5. Stimulated by the mental capacity of foresight and insight (the time-binding trait of human nature) and by that mainspring of human motivation, desire, man's creativity, his work ethos gained acceleration.

Failure of Modern Identity Society

Now let us compare the above with the present "civilized identity society":

1. The first and most important fact is that the new identity society is heading toward a personal and social state of chaos resulting from the unrestricted permissiveness being bred by the philosophy that each individual has unrestricted freedom to choose his or her role in society—that is, freedom to do one's thing regardless of other person's or society's thing.
2. The first great revolution that initiated the predominance of human behavior over primate behavior by self-control in relation to sexuality, and thereby assuring cooperative social

action and family stability, is being negated by the new-identity society. The inhuman effect on the child population of family disintegration that is presently taking place is well documented in the Spring 1977 issue of *Daedalus*, which is devoted to the theme of family. The first two articles, by Alice S. Rossi and Jerome Kagan respectively, are particularly pertinent.

3. One of the basic aspects of human nature is the satisfaction of being competent in the role one chooses in identifying oneself in one's relation to one's social world. But when the whole force of people's energy is devoted to role acting, much being unproductive, to the minimization of the rest of the needs of human nature, and usually without a goal or goals, an imbalance in the psychosocial life of the community is bound to show up. This is particularly true when role acting demands *complete* freedom to choose and to act independently without any socially necessary inhibitions.

4. In the process of each person "doing his thing," independently and untrammeled, many fail to seek competence for their chosen role, and fail to test their native talents for that role and therefore many fail in their chosen role acting: "They do gain an identity, but the identity is that of failure."[27]

5. What has been blamed on a generation gap, implying pejoratively the conservative standpattism of the parents' and grandparents' generations is really a cultural gap. The fragmentation of the family has reached critical levels: "Whether children succeed or fail in their search for roles they can be proud of, the denials, the attacks, the rejections they encounter in the process are bound to separate offspring from parents. Today, about twenty years into the new civilized identity society, most families in the Western World are culturally divided."[28]

6. The reason why the children believe that role acting takes precedence over goal is "because they have had *security* and *freedom* within their families. They believe an independent role is *natural*; they do not hear admonitions that the security and the freedom are *temporary* because they are *provided by the family and not by society*."[29] It is at this point that we should engage the advice of Dennis Gabor concerning human nature: "Man is wonderful in adversity, weak in comfort, affluence and security. Man does not appreciate what he gets without effort."[30] This is the real problem with modern children. They

have not been educated to be proud of their heritage, of which they appreciate almost nothing. The education must be such that they get a *visceral* appreciation of their heritage rather than a purely cerebral understanding.[31]

7. The work ethos has been an aspect of human nature since it was formed as a means of survival. It is every bit as important today. The need for survival even with our greatly developed technology has not been eased since at least half of the people in the world are still in a hazardous state of not only nutrition, but also existence. Work, for the adherents to the role-acting ethos, is not necessarily an indispensable requirement for survival, since the family always supplies for their needs: "If one chooses not to work, he should have that right."[32] Yet in their confused and contradictory philosophism they "believe that not only each person but also the government has an obligation to work to improve the quality of life for all."[33] The good is all mixed up with the bad, for lack of perspective.

Carl T. Rowan in an editorial, "What Are We Doing to Our Youngsters?" quotes a mass of distressing data from the Department of Health, Education, and Welfare:

More than a million of them are running away from home each year, some to become prostitutes, others to live as nomads, to be abused, even murdered. . . . Millions . . . are killing themselves slowly with alcohol and drugs. . . . Suicide is now the second leading cause of death of Americans aged 15 to 24. . . . Violence is having a devastating effect upon our schools. . . . In our schools last year (1976) there were 8,000 rapes, 11,000 armed robberies, 256,000 burglaries, and 190,000 major assaults. . . . One of every nine . . . will have been hauled into juvenile court by age 18. . . . Our prisons hold a record population and our reform schools bulge at the walls. . . . One child in six now lives in a single-parent family. Of every eight women giving birth now, one is not married (compared with one of 20 in 1960). . . . More than half of American married women with children aged six to 17 are now in the labor force (double the 1948 rate), and a third of married women with children under three are in the work force. . . . Where mothers head households, about three-quarters of those with children six to seventeen and 56% of those with children under three are in the work force. . . . We are not giving them the love, discipline, guidance, food, health care, education and other support that American youngsters got before our families began to fall apart."[34]

The *Washington Report on Medicine and Health* states: "The American Psychiatric Association reports an *'alarming increase'* in the *number of severely mentally ill young adults* seeking emergency psychiatric care. The patients, part of the postwar baby boom, see themselves as social casualties, and are described as rootless, unemployed, and habitual drug or alcohol users. The pandemic comes at a time when many mental hospitals are closing, and community mental health systems are not prepared to handle more patients."[35]

What a record for the civilized identity society! Overemphasis on self-identity by independent role acting has to the same degree *de-emphasized* the identification with family. Kagan concludes that:

> Since there are no other institutions . . . to replace the family, he [the child] has no choice but to regard his beliefs and products as the primary locus of the sense of self. . . . He is psychologically alone. He has no other group or entity to rely on—a position that seems to have the advantage of freedom from coercion and minimal constraints on autonomy of action, but which exacts the prices of loneliness and the unavailability of any person or group in which to invest strong emotions. It is for this reason that marriage and the creation of a new family are likely to experience a recrudescence in the West. We take as an axiom that *the self resists depersonalization* [italics added]. As modern environment makes a sense of potency and individual effectiveness more difficult to attain, freedom from all affective involvements becomes more and more intolerable. Involvement with a family is the only viable mechanism available to satisfy that hunger. The forces that initially weakened the family—urbanization and industrialization—have produced conditions a century later that are now likely to strengthen it."[36]

Psychological literature universally acclaims the profoundness of self-image–self-esteem as one of the basic determinants of the behavior of people. It is presented here as one of the traits of human nature, arising from the necessary needs of life to behave as a unique individual. The psychosocial atmosphere of ecosystems may not be in harmony with a trait or traits of human nature, just as the psychosocial relationships developed under the processes of urbanization and industrialization became so discordant to the traits of self-image and self-esteem (and other traits). The result generated an over-response in the people's pursuit for adjusting to this imbalance. The consequence has been disastrous, but conditions can be created to reestablish the harmony. This reestablishment will not come about in an unplanned manner as the topsy-turvy development of our urbanization-industrialization ecosystem grew up. It will have to be planned and researched with great sociopolitical commitment and acumen.

NOTES

1. Robert J. Wenke, *Patterns in Prehistory* (New York: Oxford University Press, 1980), pp. 184–185.

2. Richard B. Lee, *!Kung San: Men, Women and Children in a Foraging Society* (New York: Cambridge University Press, 1979), p. 370.

3. Paul Radin, *Primitive Man as Philosopher* (Pasadena, California: D. Appleton and Co., 1927), p. 50–51.

4. Maria Jahoda, *Current Concepts of Positive Mental Health* (New York: Basic Books 1958), p. 24.

5. Ibid., p. 28.

6. Ibid., p. 31.

7. George H. Mead, *Mind, Self, and Society* (Chicago, Illinois: University of Chicago Press, 1934), p. 135.

8. Ibid., pp. 162–163.

9. E. Fromm, *The Sane Society* (New York: Fawcett, 1955), pp. 60–63.

10. J. Hawkes, *The Atlas of Early Man* (New York: St. Martin's Press, 1981), p. 19.

11. Fromm, *op. cit*, p. 61.

12. Rene Dubos, *Beast or Angel* (New York: Scribner, 1974), p. 185.

13. Ibid.

14. Albert Ellis, "Psychoneurosis and Anxiety Problems," R. and I. Z. Grieger, eds., *Cognition and Emotional Disturbance* (New York: Human Sciences Press, Inc., 1982), pp. 18–19.

15. Dubos, *op. cit*, p. 185.

16. Ibid., p. 100.

17. Ibid., p. 51.

18. Ibid., p. 53.

19. Ibid., p. 54.

20. Marshall B. Clinard, Chapter 17: "The Role of Motivation and Self-Image in Social Change in Slum Areas," in V. L. Allen, ed., *Psychological Factors in Poverty* (Markham Publishing Co., 1970).

21. Jane Loevinger, *Ego Development* (San Francisco, California: Jossey-Bass Publishers, 1976), p. 30.

22. Ibid., pp. 148–149.

23. J. M. Lewis, W. R. Beavers, J. T. Gossett, and V. A. Phillips, *No Single Thread* (New York: Brunner/Mazel Publishers, 1976), pp. 56–57.

24. W. A. Westley and N. B. Epstein, *The Silent Majority* (San Francisco, California: Jossey-Bass, Inc., 1969).

25. Virginia Adams, "Getting at the Heart of Jealous Love," *Psychology Today*, vol. 13, no. 12 (May 1980), pp. 38–47, 102–106.

26. W. Glasser, "The Civilized Identity Society," *Saturday Review* (June 19, 1972), pp. 26–31.

27. Glasser, *loco supra citato.*
28. Ibid.
29. Ibid.
30. Dennis Gabor, *The Mature Society* (New York: Praeger Publishers, 1972), p. 47.
31. Ibid., p. 172
32. Glasser, *loco supra citato.*
33. Ibid.
34. *Times Picayune*, New Orleans, Louisiana, December 8, 1977.
35. Jerome F. Brazda, ed., *Washington Report on Medicine and Health*, (July 27, 1981), vol. 35, no. 29.
36. Jerome Kagan, "The Child in the Family," *Daedalus* (Spring 1977), pp. 33–54.

11

Prospection: Man's Time-binding Trait

DEFINITION

Man has a need to nurture an integrated view, which explains the reasons for his coming into being, why he has the urge to survive, and the *prospect* that survival could be worthwhile. This is the essence of his time-binding nature, and it requires that he translate his past experience and present pursuits into a prospection of desires and hopes toward which he can direct his efforts for realization.

This trait is so basic to the nature of man's behavior that the disposition of the human brain to think, to evaluate, and to understand one's place in the ecosystem supported by the traits of human nature that relate to bonding-sharing, self-image, orientation, making choices, challenge, and creativity would have no psychosocial harbor lest he were endowed with this time-binding nature—this prospection of what could eventuate in the well-being of interrelations among his kith and kin from the circumstances in which he operates. *Where do I stand and where am I going?* he must ask himself.

Korzybski, who first distinctly developed the concept of time binding and attributed to it the characteristic of a natural law of human nature, asserted in the preface to his book, *Manhood of Humanity*: "It is obvious that to be able to speak about the great affairs of Man, his spiritual, moral, physical, economic, social or political status, it must first be ascertained what Man is—what is his real nature and what are the basic laws of his nature. If we succeed in finding the laws of human nature, all the rest will be a comparatively easy task."[1] Korzybski stated: "What is Man?—will be answered by saying that man is a being naturally endowed with time-binding capacity—that a human being is a time-binder—that men, women and children constitute the time-binding class of life."[2] Now let us examine in detail how Korzybski defines this term:

> The plants have a very definite and well known function—the transformation of solar energy into organic chemical energy. They are a class of life which appropriate one kind of energy, convert it into another kind and store it up; in that sense they are a kind of storage battery for the solar energy; and so I define The Plant as the Chemistry-Building class of life.
>
> The animals use the highly dynamic products of the chemistry-building class—the plants—as food, and those products—the result of plant-transformation—undergo in animals a further transformation into yet higher forms; and the animals are correspondingly a more dynamic class of life; their energy is kinetic; they have a remarkable freedom and power which the plants do not possess—I mean the freedom and faculty to move about in *space*; and so I define Animals as the Space-Binding class of life.

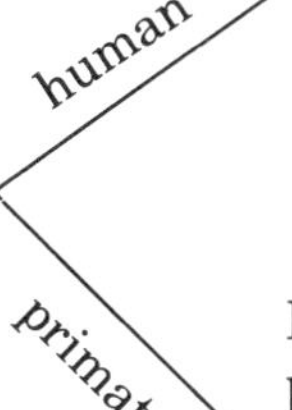

Prospection of one's lot: man's time-binding nature to project his attention to coming events

Hope, to have aspiring expectations, to accommodate to what is tolerable, planning with a social philosophy

Day-to-day living without prospect, accommodation to appetite response without thought of living beyond now, hopelessness from frustration, prospect of unsocial or antisocial activities

MAN AS TIME-BINDER

"And now what shall we say of *human* beings? What is to be our definition of Man? Like the animals, human beings do indeed possess the space-binding capacity but, over and above, human beings possess a most remarkable capacity which is entirely peculiar to them—I mean the capacity to summarize, digest and appropriate the labors and experiences of the past; I mean the capacity to use the fruits of past labors and experiences as intellectual or spiritual capital for developments in the present; I mean the capacity to employ as instruments of increasing power the accumulated achievements of the all-previous lives of the past generations spent in trial and error, trial and success; I mean the capacity of human beings to conduct their lives in the ever increasing light of inherited wisdom; I mean the capacity in virtue of which man is at once the heritor of the by-gone ages and the trustee of posterity. And because humanity is just this magificent natural agency by which the past lives in the present and the present for the future, I define Humanity, in the universal tongue of mathematics and mechanics, to be the Time-Binding Class of life."[3]

The time-binding trait of human nature, as Korzybski so graphically described, not only points to humankind's propensity of associating all events in the stream of time with the future, but also with the past—with the history of *Homo's* natural and cultural roots that shaped the attitudes and perceptions of the present. For the human, this is utterly inevitable. This trait also helps to influence the nature of the response of the other traits, particularly, in our present world, the trait that tends to unify behavior orientation and helps to shape our conscience and the trait of self-image–self-esteem, both of which influence the critical trait of freedom to choose. Certainly, the problems of the Middle East, Latin America, and East-West relations are deeply involved in the crosscurrents fashioned by the complex of these human propensities to behave. And since these traits are dualities of contradictions, which need inhibitions to direct their paths toward human and away from primate objectives, the problem of justice in human society as it contends with the traits of human nature becomes even more critical. Thus justice, like history, is as uniquely human, as are the traits that give them being. Time binding is as essential to being human as the cognitive process is to behaving humanly.

The early–seventeenth-century English poet John Donne expressed the same philosophic concept that Korzybski elaborated into a law of human nature. Porter quoted the Donne citation in the opening sentence of his work, *The History of Time*, as follows: " 'Creatures of an inferior nature are possest with the *present!*' declared the poet, John Donne: '*Man* is a *future Creature!*' Donne had in mind the Christian belief in Man's heavenly destiny, but he had seized on a basic distinction between Man and practically all other animals: Man has ingrained senses of memory and anticipation. He orders his life within a grid of past, present and future. This time sense dates back to primeval cultures. Neanderthal man (about 50,000 B.C.) was already burying his dead (no other animal does that), which probably means that he thought the departed had some continued existence."[4]

Fraser, in his discussion of the genesis and evolution of time, gives a physical scientist's interpretation of how the concept of simultaneities of need in primates and *Homo*'s expectations of the future and memories of the past fit into this evolution.[5]

It needs to be pointed out that thinking, memory, reasoning, and the ability of the brain to accumulate knowledge are not traits of human nature. They are psychological manifestations of biological processes. They are faculties of the brain that make *Homo sapiens*, as a species, possible. But the way man uses these abilities to behave like human beings—such as, to hope that certain things will happen, to devise ways of doing things, to decide to conduct oneself by certain rules—these patterns of behavior become traits of human nature. Since *Homo* is a primate genus, having evolved from a previous genus in the order of primates, the traits of the previous genus are retained but modified by the traits of the genus *Homo*. This renders the expression of every trait of human nature as a biphasic process. When the time-binding trait, expressed as hope, becomes frustrated by social circumstances, the human aspect of the trait is overcome by the primate aspect of living only in the present. This launches *human* living into disarray, with consequent manifestations of demoralization, crime, delinquency, suicide, or other expressions of disorders and antisocial behavior.

Thus time binding is, like the other traits of human nature, essentially a cognitive process. Like all cognitive processes, affective factors are always involved. Like all cognitive processes, they may become disoriented, resulting in neurotic and psychoneurotic behavior. This is well illustrated in Abrahms's discussion of the treatment of primary and secondary depression: "This [discussion] suggests that cognition plays a major part in the outcome of affective disorders, including both primary and secondary depression. Many people apparently define a nonremitting disease as catastrophic; in disproportionate numbers some even become hopeless. That cognitive state—hopelessness—has been found to be the best single indicator of an individual's suicidal intent."[6]

Knaus, in discussing procrastination, a time-binding process, asserted: "Most of us will periodically and purposely delay doing something *relevant* that we perceive as unpleasant and uncomfortable and rationalize this delay by promising ourselves to begin later. . . . But when acts of procrastination become recognizable patterns and are highly resistive to change, the pattern is indicative of mild to severe forms of psychological disturbance. . . . Self-doubt downing reflects a self-destructive, procrastination-generating process. . . . And this negative introspective process is characteristic of Raiport's *time-bound* [italics added] personality type. . . . Time-bound persons will procrastinate as a result of a process of thinking excessively."[7] It is clear that these negative states do not arrest the biopsychic process of brain cognitive action. The negative phase of a trait cannot separate itself from the time-binding cognitive process that makes *Homo* human.

Memory is the essential faculty of time binding. The motivation of memory with reasoning—the evaluation process—is the essential psychic maneuver that makes the ego comfortable and even vibrant with hope and expectancy or depresses it with frustration, hopelessness, and even dissolution. What may happen to the individual ego may also occur to the collective ego of a people, a nation, or any group. But hope may also be directed into vicarious ways by applying it in inhuman and unhuman projects.

Korzybski quotes the historian James H. Robinson to describe the relation of memory to history: " 'Man's abject dependence on the past gives rise to the continuity of history. Our convictions, opinions, prejudices, intellectual tastes, our knowledge, our methods of learning and of applying information we owe, with slight exceptions, to the past—often to the remote past. History is an expansion of memory, and like memory it alone can explain the present and in this lies its most unmistakable value.' "[8]

Montagu gives exceptional praise to Korzybski's "brilliant conception" of the time-binding capacity.[9]

History is social time binding, social memory. Epic poetry and the unwritten aphorisms, proverbs, and legends transmitted from generation to generation by primitive man are time-binding. The biblical prophets were more than spellbinders. They were time binders. Projection of the cognitive process into perception of the future immediately relates the past and the present to the future. Normal human beings are not neutral or indifferent creatures. Circumstances either are or are not to their liking. Those that are in harmony with their liking they desire to be prolonged, to be continued and stabilized, or to be available at their beckoning. Their desire for that future status is really a *hope*—an expectation of fulfillment, a morale elevator.

This time-binding trait is as human to primitive man as to modern man; otherwise it would not be a trait of human nature. This is best illustrated by the pithy observations of Radin concerning the mental processes in primitive man's behavior: "To primitive man they [religion and magic] are . . . simply aids, stimuli for the attainment of a goal. Thus viewed the facts of primitive life take on a new psychological orientation. The attainment of a goal, the clear realization of a specific objective, becomes the main factor. Primitive man may not in our sense of the term provide for the morrow but he attempts something perhaps far more important—he bends all his energies, inward and outward, toward ensuring the success of his objective on the morrow. *He prepares for it, previsions it, preenacts it, pre-attains it*"[10] (italics added). Could anyone today in the civilized world of the West be more time binding?

Lee's technique for retrospective interpretation of ancient foragers' behavior led him to the following reconstruction of events of time-binding behavior involved in the process of tool making: "When hominids began systematically to fashion stone tools during the Lower Pleistocene in Africa, they faced a set of special problems. First was the separation in space between the source of the raw materials and the areas where the tools could be put to use. Further, neither of these areas was necessarily the ideal spot at which to fashion the tools. A second problem was time. The collecting of the raw materials and the manufacturing of tools took time, and the makers at least temporarily had to leave off foraging in order to pursue these tasks. Although the tools might ultimately be of use in getting food, the task of making them removed the maker from the food quest."[11]

Dubos, the philosopher-scientist, in a similar vein described man's mastery over nature:

The possibility of choosing is an essential factor of the the human condition, but it is inoperative without a vision of the future. The ability to imagine the future, to "invent it," in Dennis Gabor's felicitous phrase, is a prerogative of human beings. Through anticipation they can modify the course of natural events. . . . In practically all human activities, the anticipation of the future thus precedes interventions into nature. Social structures likewise reflect the hopes of planners. The Declaration of Independence states certain social principles which were not self-evident, despite the affirmation of its signers, and certainly are not universally accepted but which correspond to the social patterns that the American colonists had in mind for the ways of life they were creating in the New World.[12]

"Hope springs eternal in the human breast" is a universally recognized sentiment—commonplace, yet true—but meaningfully expressed by the very quotable Alexander Pope in his *Essay on Man*. When the future looks bleak, hope is negated, eliciting frustration, futility, demoralization, and even antisocial behavior. This is well stated by Milton in *Paradise Lost* (Book IV): "So farewell hope, and with hope farewell fear. Farewell remorse: all good to me is lost. Evil, be thou my good."

The profundity of the time-binding trait of human nature is not difficult to demonstrate. Its contradictory manifestations in human behavior when guided by hope or its negation, frustration, fills the voluminous records in psychiatrists' files, in mental institutions, in prisons, and in historical libraries on social revolution the world over. As Korzybski expounded:

> It is the unique capacity of man for binding time, uniting past, present, and future in a *single growing reality* charged at once with the surviving creations of the dead, with the productive labor of the living, with the rights and hopes of the yet unborn; we know . . . and we can teach, that what is good in *present* civilization—all that is precious in it, sacred and holy—is the fruit of the time-binding toil struggling blindly through the ages against the perpetual barrier of human ignorance of human nature; we know at length, we can teach, and the world will understand, that in proportion as we rid our ethics and social philosophy of monstrous misrepresentations of human nature, the time-binding energies of humanity will advance civilization in accordance with their natural law, the forward-leaping function of time.[13]

HUMAN ENGINEERING

In discussing the reasons why the social sciences have lagged behind, Korzybski gives a long list of such reasons: "They have lagged behind, partly because they have been often dominated by the lusts of cunning politicians' instead of being led by the wisdom of enlightened statesmen; they have lagged behind, partly because they have been predominantly concerned to protect 'vested interests,' upon which they have in the main depended for support; the *fundamental* cause, however, of their lagging behind is found in the astounding fact that, despite their being by their very nature most *immediately* concerned with the affairs of mankind, they have not discovered what Man really is. . . . "[14]

The present-day discussion about human or social engineering is really not as new as it might seem to many. Korzybski devoted a good deal of argumentation to the subject: "There is no doubt that engineering of human society is a difficult and complicated problem of tremendous ethical responsibility, for it involves the welfare of mankind throughout an unending succession of generations. The science of Human Engineering can not be built upon false conceptions of human nature."[15] The subtitle of Korzybski's book is "The Science and Art of Human Engineering."

HOPE AND SOCIAL WELL-BEING

Erikson, in describing the time-binding nature of the evolution of the ego and the cycle of generations, declared hope to be the first and most basic virtue in the development of the human being. What could be more time binding than the future expectations involved in hoping: "In an epigenetic development of the kind here envisaged, each item [basic virtue] has its time of ascendence and crisis [turning point], yet each persists throughout life. Hope is the first and most basic, and yet it is also the most lasting; it is the most stable and yet acquires new qualities, depending on the general stage reached."[16]

Kosa described what happens when hope and perspective are negated by the influence of poverty: "[T]he lower-class lives in a world of anxiety about the immediate provisions for his basic needs of food, clothing, and shelter and learns to seek *immediate gratification* [italics added] in all his actions. Accordingly, he is likely to drop out of school and rationalize his behavior by referring to discrimination on the part of his teachers. While discrimination and mistreatment must not be entirely discounted, his behavior is just as much motivated by the fact that in his unstable environment he is unable to assess his actions and their contingent rewards; consequently, he regards the ulterior gratifications that higher education can give as too uncertain to renounce . . . his immediate gratification."[17]

Maslow finds that much of the "bad behavior of affluent, privileged, and basic-need–gratified high school and college students is due to frustration of the 'idealism' so often found in young people." His "hypothesis is that this behavior can be a fusion of continued search for something to believe in, combined with anger at being disappointed. . . . This frustrated idealism and occasional hopelessness is partially due to the influence and ubiquity of stupidly limited theories of motivation all over the world."[18]

Stotland, in his comprehensive study of hope, begins his book with: "The importance of hope for man has long been known to layman and professional. It is widely accepted that with hope, man acts, moves, achieves. Without hope, he is often dull, listless, moribund. Faced with a situation that threatens a loss of hope, he may desperately try to cling to it, to restore it, to protect it. Yet despite a common awareness of the role hopelessness plays in determining behavior, rarely has it been introduced into the mainstream of psychology and psychiatry. Psychologists are generally averse to the use of so subjective a term as *hope*. . . ."[19]

Stotland defines *hope* as "an expectation about goal attainment."[20] He treats the term as an equivalence of "confidence in a future event." It takes perspective to have such confidence: "Accordingly, hopefulness is treated here mainly, but not exclusively, as a construct used to tie together antecedent and consequent events." Concerning the Black American, Stotland wrote:

The highly anxious people may be so because they do poorly on tests. Furthermore, poor past performance of these highly anxious people leads them to expect to do more poorly in future tests, and part of the reason they do poorly is that they expect to do so. Their poor performance then enhances the anxiety, and the vicious circle continues. . . . The occasional violence that has characterized the movement [social change] is, of course, motivated by many purposes, such as that of communicating effectively with white Americans. Nevertheless, some of the aggression is no doubt a result of a high state of anxiety resulting from frustration of progress toward goals that are both very important and impossible to give up except at great psychological, social, and moral cost.[21]

Quoting Lewin from his book *Field Theory in Social Science* (1951), Stotland wrote: " 'Even more than suffering, persistency depends on the time perspective of the individual. As long as there is hope that the difficulty may be overcome for that price in effort or pain which the individual is ready to pay, he goes on trying. . . . Persisting depends on two factors: the value of the goal and the outlook for the future.' "[22]

Smith, in discussing the "competent self" trait of human nature, ties together other traits concerned in the same events but concludes that without "hope," which is the basic element of human perspective, nothing much is relevant in the resulting fatalism and passivity:

With self-respect go at least moderately favorable levels of general self-evaluation—self-esteem or self-acceptance—but favorable self-evaluation in the general terms according to which it has predominantly been studied would seem less important than the sense of efficacy or potency. . . . Distinctive attitudes toward the world are linked with these attitudes toward the self as the opposite side of the same coin. Coordinate with the feeling of efficacy is an attitude of hope—the world is a sort of place in which, given appropriate efforts, I can expect good outcome. Hope provides the ground against which planning, forbearance, and effort are rational. . . . While as Erikson has asserted, some degree of basic trust is essential to personal adequacy, I would think that given that essential minimum, hope is the more critical attitude. In the lack of hope, attitudes of fatalism and passivity that make a bad world tolerable at the cost of giving up the possibility of constructive action are natural adaptations that have been rediscovered perennially by individuals and cultures the world over.[23]

Korzybski clearly relates the mechanism how "man makes the past live in the present, and the present in the future,"[24] but this was before the modern explosion of anthropological information. We now know that *Homo sapiens* must have begun keeping symbolic records and making images about 40,000 years ago, as Marshack points out. Equally important is the fact that "efforts by still earlier forms of man toward the making of images are beginning to be tentatively considered. It is now clear, for instance, that long before modern man appeared in Europe, Neanderthal man was making and using symbols and images. . . . What Cro-magnon man apparently achieved was a more complex symbolic culture and social organization than Neanderthal man. . . . It was almost as though someone, 25,000 years before the development of writing and arithmetic, was keeping a record of some process or series of events and was structuring it in a manner that he could 'read'. . . . We may have found one of the intellectual and cultural threads that leads eventually to true writing and to history."[25]

When one casually observes the titles of books in a bookstore window, the thought that the germs of language communication and the symbols of writing began so many tens of thousands of years ago practically never comes to mind. Such remarkable symbol phenomena are taken for granted—not only taken for granted, but not even appreciated by large sections of the population. This is certainly not a criticism of the people, but of the leadership, which has been given the sacred responsibility of conducting community affairs to the best interests of the people. When one considers how, by trial and error, customs and traditions and morals and ethics developed over this extensive spread of years, should it not incite a spark of caution that changes in societal behavior should warrant the deliberate attention of those responsible for guidance in commumity life? What a world this past accumulation of our symbolic heritage has created! But in the routine of daily living, those sections of the population that have fared well in their fleeting span of years in the endless parade of generations look forward with hope that their desires for the future will be realized. There are, however, large sections of the population that have not fared well. Some of these have gotten a glimpse of the history of social struggle and have thereby been exhorted by an inner stimulation to contend for the vision of the future that had so excited them. Some, unfortunately, have not been fired with this inner warmth and have become depressed, with anxiety and frustration, passivity and inactivity, while some of these have become so angered that only violence and recklessness possesses them.

Prospection of one's lot in this world is such a basic trait of human nature that social stability is plainly impossible unless the ecosystem is in tolerable harmony with the positive aspect of this trait.

Erikson is eloquent, indeed, about hope as a basic need in the nature of the human:

> I will, therefore, speak of *Hope*, *Will*, and *Competence* as the rudiments of virtue developed in childhood; of *Fidelity* as the adolescent virtue; and *Love*, *Care*, and *Wisdom* as the central virtues of adulthood. In all their seeming discontinuity, these qualities depend on each other. Will cannot be trained until hope is secure, nor can love become reciprocal until fidelity has proven reliable. Also, each virtue and its place in the schedule of all virtues is vitally interrelated to other segments of human development. . . . Hope is verified by a combination of experiences in the individual's "prehistoric" era, the time before speech and verbal memory. . . . Hope, once established as a basic quality of experience, remains independent of the verifiability of "hope," for it is in the nature of man's maturation that concrete hopes will, at a time when a hoped-for event or state comes to pass, prove to have been superceded by a more advanced set of hopes. . . . *Hope is the enduring belief in the attainability of fervent wishes, in spite of the dark urges and rages which mask the beginning of existence.*[26]

Korzybski's expression could very well summarize the potency of this trait—the motivating, initiating nature of the time-binding power: "We know that time-binding capacity—the capacity for accumulating racial experience, enlarging it, and transmitting it for future expansion—is the peculiar power, the characteristic energy, the definitive nature, the defining mark of man."[27]

NOTES

1. Alfred Korzybski, *Manhood of Humanity* (New York: E. P. Dutton and Co., 1921), p. x.

2. Ibid., p. 4

3. Ibid., pp. 58–60.

4. Roy Porter, *The Book of Time* (Westbridge Books, 1980), p. 5.

5. J. T. Fraser, *The Genesis and Evolution of Time: A Critique of Interpretation in Physics* (Amherst, Massachusetts: University of Massachusetts Press, 1982), pp. 163–169.

6. Eliot Abrahms, "Cognition and Major Mental Disorders" in R. and I. Z. Grieger, *Cognition and Emotional Disturbance* (New York: Institute for Rational Living, 1982), p. 140.

7. William Knaus, *The Parameters of Procrastination*, ibid., pp. 174, 181, 194.

8. Ibid., p.31

9. Ashley Montagu, *Anthropology and Human Nature* (Boston, Massachusetts: Porter Sargent, 1957), pp. 13, 43–55.

10. Paul Radin, *Primitive Man as Philosopher* (Pasadena, California: D. Appleton and Co., 1927), p. 23.

11. Richard B. Lee, *!Kung San: Men, Women and Children in a Foraging Society* (New York: Cambridge University Press, 1979), p. 492.

12. Rene Dubos, *Beast or Angel?* (New York: Charles Scribner and Son, 1974), pp. 194–195.

13. Korzybski, *loco supra citato*, pp. 192–193.

14. Ibid., p. 22.

15. Ibid., p. 69.

16. E. H. Erikson, *Insight and Responsibility* (New York: Norton, 1965), p. 140.

17. John Kosa, "The Nature of Poverty," in John Kosa and I. K. Zola, eds., *Poverty and Health* (Cambridge, Massachusetts: Harvard University Press), p. 26.

18. A. H. Maslow, *The Farther Reaches of Human Nature* (New York: Penguin, 1976), pp. 320–321.

19. Ezra Stotland, *The Psychology of Hope* (San Francisco, California: Jossey-Bass, Inc., 1969), p. 1.

20. Ibid., p. 2.

21. Ibid., p. 46.

22. Ibid., p. 16.

23. M. Brewster Smith, *Social Psychology and Human Values* (Aldine Publishing Co., 1969), p. 219.

24. Korzybski, *loco supra citato*, p. 186.

25. Alexander Marshack, "The Art and Symbols of Ice Age Man," *Human Nature* (September 1978), pp. 32–41.

26. Erikson, *op. cit.*, pp. 115–118.

27. Korzybski, *loco supra citato*, pp. 174–175.

12

The Trait of Challenge and Competence to Control

CHALLENGE TO ACTION

The need to find one's social role–performance place in the community by accepting the challenges to become effectively competent in performing and controlling the outcome of such roles is the venture factor stimulating human achievement.

The response to challenge may initiate a moderate competitive reaction or, if uncontrolled, may eventuate in antisocial and even self-destructive, primatelike competition. The response to challenge is what changed the foraging existence of human society from its natural setting to its present rapidly accumulating technological world of endless amassing of amenities for living. It spearheaded the development of culture in general and in, particular, the myriad rich and fascinating cultures strewn over the earth. It filled the libraries and museums with the treasures of intellectual inspirations and artistic masterpieces. It crowded the cities with structural marvels and contending people. It speckled the countryside with vegetation and stock that would have dumfounded the foraging folk. It created a species of being that initiated a drive to achieve competence eventuating in establishing of schools of education leading to the control of the natural forces for the good of humankind.

The socialization process must stress that the urge of challenge must be primarily directed at one's self to achieve rather than against the potentialities of others. However, the self-image–self-esteem trait should not be unduly restrained, lest it be traumatized.

Man must act in order to survive. And act he does, with an objective in mind and facilitated by the dexterity of his hands, by the marvels of his vocalized symbolization, and by the freedom of movement unleashed by his bipedalism. Living is itself a process of perpetual challenge to self-initiated and external stimuli incident to the conditions

of living mandating one to achieve the competence necessary to control
the circumstances initiating the challenges. Challenge, then, is the
psychosocial response to the basic need of implementing one's selected
role performance in the process of accommodating the self to social
vicissitudes.

Challenge and role-performance with effective competence directed toward controlling one's circumstances

Challenge toward self and social benefit, balanced competitiveness

Challenge toward self-aggrandizement, uncontrolled and antisocial aggressive competition to the detriment of others

How much of challenge, as expressed in human behavior, has roots
in the primate impulse to act in order to satisfy a physiological appetite,
as expressed in simians by the impulse to dominate and in the immature and yet unsocialized child as the impulse to mastery?[1] It is
certainly interwoven with the trait of striving as propounded by Leighton.[2] The human response to challenge is striving, but not just appetite
satisfying or fancy-born chasing. It is challenge to achieve a new level
of creative activity. An animal's response to a physiological need or an
external stimulus is not a psychosocial response; it is biological. It is
conceivable that nonhuman primates and other animals on the higher
level of evolution have potentiality to respond in a very rudimentary
manner, which could be interpreted as a glimmer of the psychosocial
element. But a human psychosocial response has a basic essence, which
Korzybski described as time binding, that requires judgment and perspective into the future. This has never been observed with certainty
in nonhuman primates. When initiated to action, an animal will fight
to the death as prey or predator or instinctively retreat. This cannot
be interpreted as a psychosocial response to a situation, but one of

instinct to survive. The term "challenge," implying a calling oneself to account about a provocative situation and to dare oneself to action in order to achieve a foreseeable goal in relation to that situation, could not possibly apply to an instinctual response to a situation. The meaning of *challenge* as used here is not the actual pursuit toward the goal, since the pursuit is part of the striving trait, but the judgment made on how and whether to pursue to the resolution of the provocative situation and consideration of the competence to do so. It is the preparation to respond to a risk, based on the nature of the socialization of the individual and the particular social interrelations involved in the response. An instinct is usually considered an evolutionary process of spontaneous and unlearned response to internal or external stimuli.[3] Judgment is not involved here, although the instinct may be modified by conditioning from past experience.

Challenge is a trait of human nature because it is an inevitable psychosocial response to the human condition. Endowed with sensibilities, self-awareness, self-image, and the ability to reason and to evaluate situations and impelled to strive and to create, how could such an individual be insensitive to challenge, which may better one's condition and image, considering one's time-binding trait of projecting one's aim at the future.

Lee described an element of challenge as it came into being in the very early history of human development.[4] The very act of gathering food in the wilderness was a challenge to early *Homo*—a challenge that taxed the human band to exert a full day's work every day. In so acting, *Homo* learned to practice sharing and exchange as the most effective way of living under a foraging mode of production. This made time available for some of the males to *take the risk* of hunting game that had a potentially greater return, but a rather small chance of success. The more competent the hunters became, the more success with returns and the more leisure time for invention and development of competence. We need to take a lesson from this history of the evolution of human society, which particularly involved the challenge and competence trait of human nature. *Homo* came into being several million years ago, 80 to 95% of which was spent fixed in the foraging mode of production. What was the reason that during such a tremendous span of time, this highly intelligent species appeared satisfied to remain hunters and gatherers? Lee contends that the way of life of hunter-gatherers was *not* precarious and full of hardship and that the life of man in the "state of nature" was *not* nasty and brutish, at least for a very long period of that state of existence. Lee also makes the observation "that traditional !Kung are *not* [italics added] experimenters. . . . Perhaps the most telling evidence of the security of life as hunter-gatherers is its extraordinary persistence. Foraging people have been operating in the Dobe area [Africa] for thousands of years without evidence for major discontinuities. . . . During this long period there has been little evidence for technological change."[5] The *relatively easy way of life* in this period of "primitive communism" must have been the reason for the conservative attitude toward risk taking and experimentation, toward accepting a challenge beyond the needs of the status quo. This is a lesson that political economists must become acutely aware of—certainly the political economist of the left must understand the adverse effects of dictatorship on the traits of human nature, in particular, challenge and competence to control.

In the process of acting, man strives to act competently, i.e., to peform his self-chosen role and his goal seeking effectively. He is challenged to act this way because of the societal response to his behavior—responses that reflect on his self-image–self-esteem, his place socially, his feelings of success and of self-fulfilment. This challenge, which impels him to perform his role competently in achieving his goal, is a trait of human nature because it is a response to the fundamental human condition described elsewhere in this study. When the ecosystem is not in concordance with this trait, as revealed in the various studies discussed by Argyle, the result is "lowered self-esteem, discouragement, futility, feeling of failure and inferiority in contrast to a sense of personal growth and self-fulfilment resulting from more varied, responsible, *challenging* [italics added] undertakings that afford opportunity to develop and use one's ideas and skills."[6] An ecosystem that molds its socialization energies into fostering cognitive fantasies evoking "performance anxieties" must be guarded against, yet effective performance, competence, must not be discouraged. Ellis, in discussing anxiety problems, states: "[Anxiety problems] arise because people do not merely wish, want, or prefer to perform important tasks adequately; they insist that they *must*, that they *have to* do so. They have what Karen Horney called 'tyranny of the shoulds.' "[7]

The factors that pervert the behavioral trait of human nature involving (a) challenge to action, (b) conducting oneself with competence, and (c) striving for effective role performance, are:

1. absence, suppression, or diversion of challenge and responsibility, unemployment, unemployability;
2. no opportunity to use one's creative abilities in highly mechanized mass production involving repetitiveness, monotonous

work and higher skilled persons being forced to work at lower skilled positions; and

3. Low-grade, nonskilled, or other factors that do not promote one's image-building process in role performance.

Psychosomatic ailments are not only caused by psychic stress from the discord between the ecosystem and the traits of human nature, but also from the physiological stress caused by the tensions inherent in the work of executives, physicians, and the like and by overzealousness and compulsiveness to work.

The challenge intrinsic in man's impulse to perform resulting from cognitive processes dealing with self-worth as performer and the psychosocial response generated by the influence of his ecosystem may not only create conditions salutary to man's existence, but also those destructive of his social well-being. When security becomes too rigidly established, avoidance of the risk inherent in challenge may inactivate man and fetter him to a minimum productive state of security—a state of affairs reminiscent of an extreme manifestation of Schneirla's biphasic theory of *approach and withdrawal,*[8,9] i.e., elimination of challenge freezes the organism in the withdrawal phase to the point of permanent avoidance—inactivation. Inactivation leads eventually to deterioration and degeneration. The utility of man's creations must always be applied with circumspection. This caveat has become increasingly important as the population has increased and man's creation and manipulation of the environment have multiplied.

The challenge to act—to do, to perform a task—is the initial phase of work, although all work is not as spontaneous as man'a dynamic impulse to continue to act. The impulse to continue to act may be aimless when not initiated by challenge. But work is the initial phase of creativity. Work, by its creations, tends to make man's self-identity more unique and magnifies his individuality. Thus man's orientation to a world philosophy that is in consonance with his human nature stimulates his self-development, which, in turn, enriches his social sphere and improves his creativity and further challenges him to greater effort, ad infinitum. Therefore, man has developed a need to be challenged in order that his human faculties be excited to effective function. His use of his faculties develops their ability to function, as Dennis Gabor succinctly pointed out concerning man's heroic efforts in adversity, and his weakness in affluence and security and particularly that he does not appreciate what he gets without effort.[10] Gabor's observations strike a cord of a recognizable social phenomenon, the socialization process of each new generation, which could be controlled by a mechanism whereby each generation of human beings must be taught in its childhood and adolescent years to *relive* the struggles and sorrows and achievements of mankind's long past history, in order that, in George Santayana's words: "Those who cannot remember the past are condemned to repeat it." In a way, this is also the *psychosocial* analogue of Haeckel's biological theorem that the ontogeny is a recapitulation of the phylogeny.

C. P. Snow was asked to discuss the level of creativity in Britain in relation to its status as a world power. His response was to the effect that people must feel the spark of challenge in their country's atmosphere in order to produce great things: "On the whole, great literatures have usually come when countries are attaining their peak of power, not when they are actually at their peak of power. . . . People are probably at their best in times like our Elizabethan era, when England was struggling to be important, or like the Russian nineteenth century or your [American] nineteenth century. There is a certain vitality, a certain striving, a certain feeling that the best is not yet over."[11] Man is always being challenged, but the level of competence with which he performs his role to a large extent is influenced by the degree that the atmosphere in which he finds himself is charged with stimulation. This is an aspect of Gabor's thesis of effort and appreciation. There is indeed another aspect to this problem: We have yet to find an adequate method of raising children in an affluent society.

The biphasic nature of the traits of human nature is a most cogent contention in man's behavior. This is why children must be raised with discipline and adults must be guided by a moral-ethical code. Otherwise, chaos supervenes in behavior. This state of the contradictory nature of man's behavior is described concisely by Levine: "We can say that man is the only animal known with certainty to have major conflicts of high importance between his own internal forces. . . . Man's potential for conflict between the forces within himself may be one of the most important facts about man. And the resolution of such internal conflicts may be man's most important task, and still further, the resolution of man's internal conflicts may, in a way . . . help to resolve man's conflicts with other men."[12]

The biphasic nature of the traits of human nature and the essential place in man's behavior of challenge, competence, and workmanship are well stated by Erikson: "For true hope leads inexorably into conflicts between rapidly developing self-will and the will or others from which the rudiments of will must emerge. As the infant's senses and his muscles grasp at opportunities for more active experience, he faces the double demand for self-control and for the acceptance of control from others. *To will* does not mean to be willful, but rather to gain gradually the power of increased judgment and decision in the application of drive. Man must learn to will what can be, to renounce as not worth willing what cannot be, and to believe he willed what is inevitable."[13] Ericson also states: "Will, therefore, is the unbroken determination to exercise free choices as well as self-restraint, in spite of the unavoidable experience of shame and doubt in infancy."[14] He asks: "What shall we call the next virtue? Competence comes closest to what I have in mind. . . . A sense of competence . . . characterizes what eventually becomes *workmanship*. . . . Man *must* learn to work as his intelligence and his capacities are ready to be 'put to work' so that his ego's power may not atrophy."[15]

COMPETITION AND COOPERATION

Challenge cannot exist in a psychosocial vacuum. It exists in a human being who is endowed with a mental aura of conflict resulting from the contention of his human characteristics with those of his phylogenetic primate characteristics. The conflict is perpetual. Competition is a phylogenetic characteristic. It is part of the biosocial nature of *Homo* that influences the psychosocial behavior, forming the foundation of human nature. As indicated in other chapters, the biosocial behavior of *Homo* inherited from his primate nature does not express itself in the relatively fixed manner that it does for each species of the animal kingdom. The *Homo* nature of man modified these biosocial characteristics so they express themselves in "an infinitely fluid and malleable manner. Thus competition may intrude itself into man's challenging nature in an infinite number of ways, sometimes with favorable social consequence and at other times with unfavorable or even catastrophic results and sometimes with favorable and unfavorable consequence." As Ruben declares it: "Competition is an inescapable fact of life."[16]

Ruben's monograph on competition is detailed and comprehensive and is a good contribution to the subject, in spite of his lack of clarity on the relation of competition to human nature. He states that competition is an aspect of human nature: "Darwin's observations on the survival of the fittest in nature apply to humans as well, and for this reason it's perhaps unavoidable that a certain level of basic competitiveness be thought of as part of what we call 'human nature.' "[17] Here Ruben equates human nature to the biological principle of the "survival of the fittest" because this principle also applies to human beings. Yet

Ruben, as a psychiatrist, has the human sense about him in comparing *Homo* with the rest of animal life that the sociobiologists do not quite attain.

> The difficulty, [Ruben states] with comparing animal with human competition arises when the goals we compete for become more complicated than the goals of our fellow animals. It's one thing to admit that four people stranded on a desert island with limited food and water will naturally become rivals with one another; it's another to explain why, in our modern societies, people so often vie intensely with each other for such intangible goals as status and community approval. . . . One of the things that distinguishes us from the other animals, then, is the variety and complexity of goals. Human competitiveness serves many functions that animal competitiveness does not. Most importantly, it serves certain psychological functions that are simply superfluous elsewhere in the animal kingdom, since animals' psyches are apparently less flexible and less in need of pampering than our own.[18]

Ruben is a bit enamored with the sociobiologists' interpretations that "attempt to apply Darwinian principles to that all-too-human animal *Homo contendens*."[19] In discussing his theoretical approach to the problem, he asserts: "Many different theories for the motivations of human behavior can be applied to our competitive interactions, but when attempting to understand the pervasiveness of competition in our lives, I have found two theories most useful: the first is that human competitive behavior is an aspect of 'human nature,' that it is inherited and is therefore innate and relatively fixed; and the second is that such behavior is a result of specific training and education and is therefore infinitely fluid and malleable. The distinction between these two schools of thought may be seen as a distinction between a focus on *nature* and a focus on *nurture*: a focus on our genes versus a focus on our environment."[20] Ruben seems to be hedging in declaring his belief, nonspecifically, in the whole heredity-environment complex. One could not go too far astray in such a generalized statement. Since competition, according to him, is *an aspect* of human nature (which it is, but it is only an aspect and not a trait of human nature), it is both "innate and relatively fixed" and also "infinitely fluid and malleable." This does not explain in specific descriptive terms the relation of competition to human nature.

The term "challenge," as already discussed, means provocation to action by an external or a psychic stimulus eliciting a cognitive urge to achieve or overcome. Margaret Mead, in her excellent study of primitive society, defines *competition* as: "the act of seeking or endeavoring to gain what another is separately endeavoring to gain at the same time."[21] *Cooperation*, she defines as: "the act of working together to one end."[22] Mead found cooperation and competition in all the primitive societies she studied. The basic urge to confront situations and to solve them by overcoming and controlling them with the use of all native faculties and facilities, i.e., man's ability to meet and resolve a challenge, makes him different from his mammalian forebears. Some challenges he meets in a competitive medium and others in a social framework of cooperation. The problem resolves itself into the question, how much and at what point does competition result in social destructive competition, and how much and at what point will cooperation reduce individual initiative to a low grade lassitude and even to demoralization?

Mead, in studying the social organizations and cultures of thirteen primitive peoples, found that each fitted into a classification system based on its major emphasis, such as cooperation, competition, or individualism. The survey included contributions from the fields of child psychology, qualitative and quantitative adult psychology, psychoanalysis, sociology, and anthropology. It was found that "no society is exclusively competitive or exclusively cooperative. The very existence of highly competitive groups implies cooperation within the groups."[23]

Mead continues:

> The most significant specific conclusions which can be drawn from the sample and used for further research [are]:
>
> Strong ego development can occur in individualistic, competitive, or cooperative societies.
>
> Whether a group has a minimum or a plentiful subsistence level is not directly relevant to the question of how cooperative or competitive in emphasis a culture will be.
>
> The social conception of success and the structural framework into which individual success is fitted are more determinative than the state of technology or the plentifulness of food.
>
> There is a correspondence between: a major emphasis upon competition, a social structure which depends upon the initiative of the individual, a valuation of property for individual ends, a single scale of success, and a strong development of the ego.
>
> There is a correspondence between: a major emphasis upon cooperation, a social structure which does not depend upon in-

dividual initiative or the exercise of power over persons, a faith in an ordered universe, weak emphasis upon rising in status, and a high degree of security for the individual.[24]

Montagu succinctly states: "Man's evolution has not been competitive in terms of aggression. It has been competitive in terms of cooperation."[25]

As previously stated, the more individualistic the society, the more value is placed on property for individual ends, the more strongly the ego is developed, the more a single scale of success is appreciated and the more challenge is directed toward competitive rather than cooperative pursuits.[26] The cooperative pursuits are never completely inactivated, since society, per se, could not continue to exist without it. However, deflection of the human force of challenge and uncontrolled competition can lead to social perversions, which can destroy human life when the competition is directed toward unlimited freedom by individual or group competitors engaged in commodity exchange of such basic human needs as food, energy, shelter, land, and certain vital instruments of production. Throughout written history, such inordinate perversion of the trait of human nature that generates challenge has led to slavery, serfdom, and the worst conditions of capitalism, such as sweatshops, slums, starvation, and mortal strife. Competition, therefore, requires that it be controlled and channeled socially, but not stifled. Its adversary nature must be prevented from becoming destructive.

COMPETENCE

Dubos is expansive on the subject of challenge and competence and wonders why man deliberately accepts the challenge of exploring and testing dangerous situations even at the risk of pain or worse: "There is no obvious explanation for the fact that human beings deliberately place themselves in situations which require strenuous efforts and cause suffering. Similarly, there is no obvious answer to the question that Leonardo da Vinci asked himself in his notebook: 'Leonardo, perché tanto peni.'*"[27] When Dubos opines that "there is no obvious explanation" why man acts so, this merely represents the author's style

* Oh, Leonardo, why do you toil so much?

in presenting a situation since he answers this inquiry over and over again,[28] but does not specifically attribute such human behavior as a manifestation of a trait of human nature that it really is. Another aspect of this behavior, as described by Fromm, is man's motivation by challenge and his rejoicing at feeling the competence of his performance, to wit: ". . . the motivation of the primitive hunter was not pleasure in killing, but the learning and optimal performance of various skills, i.e., the development of man himself."[29] And further:

> Among the motivations of the primitive professional and the modern passionate hunter, at least two kinds must be distinguished. The first have their roots in the depth of human experience. In the act of hunting, a man becomes, however briefly, a part of nature again. . . . Of at least equal importance . . . is an entirely different motivation, that of enjoyment in the skill. It is amazing how many modern authors neglect this element of skill in hunting and focus their attention on the act of killing. . . . This point has been discussed in detail by William S. Laughlin, who also starts out with the thesis that "hunting is the master behavior pattern of the human species". . . . The efficiency of hunting is to be understood not on the basis of the advancement of its technical basis [i.e., the tools involved], but by the increasing skill of the hunter.[30]

The importance of hunting to the development of man's human characteristics is discussed with extraordinary perception by Mayr, who also happens to be of the opinion that unless something revolutionary occurs in man's currently developing ecosystem, it appears to threaten man with the loss of those most typical of human mental attributes and psychosocial characteristics:

> Early man's reliance on hunting, particularly the killing of big mammals, had several important consequences:
> The need for the invention and manufacture of improved weapons and tools was increased. . . .
> Cooperation among several males was required to achieve success in the hunting of large game. Eventually, this resulted in a considerable division of labor and responsibility. . . .
> The hunting of big game often required lengthy hunting expeditions involving strenuous traveling. The consequent prolonged absences of the men necessitated the establishment of base camps where nursing mothers, pregnant females, and children could be left under care of guards.

There can be little doubt that the rewards of successful hunting set up a strong selection pressure for an improved brain—for increased planning abilities, refined communication technique.[31]

Not only, Mayr claims, do the civilized modes of living encourage the vital human characteristics that were developed during the hunting phase to lapse into decelerating mediocrity, but the biological nature has been adding dysgenic effects in man's development: "As astounding as the precipitous increase in brain size is the fact that it came to a sudden halt some 100 thousand to 200 thousand years ago. There has been no increase in brain size since the time of Neanderthal. And there is no evidence whatsoever indicating internal improvement of the brain without enlargement of the cranial capacity, though we cannot decisively refute such a possibility. . . . Of all the possible answers that can be given to this question, the one that seems most convincing is that the breeding structure of *Homo sapiens* changed."[32]

Mayr continues: "The rapid increase in brain size between *Australopithicus* and *Homo sapiens* proves how drastic a change of phenotype is possible without any loss of fitness. . . . There is thus no genetic reason why the increase in brain size could not be continued if there were a selection premium on such a process. . . . These and other considerations support the conclusion that increase of brain size stopped not because it ran into a roadblock of direct counterselection, but rather because it was no longer rewarded by a reproductive premium."[33]

Fromm's historical approach, like Mayr's, in describing human nature is basic to understanding it. Fromm's description of why man must acquire a nature of competence in order to survive is excellent: "Man's awareness of himself as being in a strange and overpowering world and his consequent sense of impotence could easily overwhelm him. . . . To compensate for this he must acquire a sense of being able to do something, to move somebody, to 'make a dent,' or to use the most adequate English word, to be 'effective'. . . . To effect is the equivalent of: to bring to pass, to accomplish, to realize, to carry out, to fulfill; an effective person is one who has the capacity to do, to effect, to accomplish something. . . . The principle can be formulated thus: I am, because I effect."[34]

Competence could lead to very ample production so that the material aspects of living could become quite secure. A feeling of security is a phase of this fulfilment. But when security becomes too rigidly established so that those who "get" have not been required to have contributed to "what they get," the risk in the "getting" nullifies the trait that engenders "challenge" and thereby inactivates man's ability to produce as an essence of satisfaction of this basic need. The utility

279

of man's creations must always be applied with circumspection. Work, by its creations, tends also to make man's self-identity more unique and tends to magnify his individualistic nature. Thus man's orientation to a world philosophy (regardless of whether his world is small or large), which is in consonance with his human nature, stimulates his self-development, which, in turn, improves his creativity and further challenges him to greater effort, ad infinitum. Thus, man has developed a need to be challenged in order that his human faculties be excited to effective function. His use of his faculties develops their ability to function.

SUMMARY

Challenge has the tendency to engender competition. In present-day society, with the high development of the uniqueness of the individual by his education and his life-style, as he is living in hierarchical social structures practically the world over, it is evident that a great part of the challenges presented to people are imbued with strong elements of competition. This is as true in the socialist countries as it is in the feudal dictatorships of the Middle East and North Africa and the dislocated tribal societies of the African continent. However, the more individualistic the society, the more value is placed on property for individual ends, the more strongly the ego is developed, the more a single scale of success is appreciated, and the more is challenge directed toward competitive rather than toward cooperative pursuits.[35] The cooperative pursuits are never completely inactivated, since society could not continue to exist without them. Competition requires that this phylogenetic primate impulse be controlled and channeled socially.

Montagu's discussion of man's aggressive behavior from the view of the anthropologist puts a damper on the usual concept people have of the genetic essentiality of man's competitive spirit: "By competition, which is usually employed as a synonym for the struggle for existence, is generally meant the process of striving against others to achieve the same goal. . . . In the emphasis on 'struggle' it has been too often overlooked that cooperation also constitutes a form of competition, that those individuals or groups who are the most cooperative are likely to enjoy the greatest survival benefits."[36] He continues: "Men and societies have made themselves according to the image they have had of themselves, and they have changed in accordance with the changing image they have developed."[37] Montagu concludes: "There is no warfare

280

in nature. If there is a law of nature, it is the balance between cooperation and conflict leading to stable cooperative societies."[38]

In Pfieffer's description of the emergence of society, he noted that: "Whatever the future, man is moving into it faster and faster, swept up in a revolution which started ten thousand years ago when all the world was a wilderness. . . . Ten thousand years ago man's life-style, his original traditions and his ethics began to crumble."[39] The change from the hunter-gatherer to the farmer–livestock-raiser required a more sedentary existence and the development of a more concentrated community life. Crowding separated people as they had never been separated before. The equality of people that existed in the hunter-gatherer world was gone. "Proximity created a source of tension, a gulf separating people who had once been closer. Conflict reached newer levels of intensity among groups which had to stay put, having committed themselves to property and mass living."[40] This history of man's condition of existence indicates how essential it was in those dawning days to adhere to a code of morals and ethics in the face of competition, of the need for mutual aid for security of each village, of the need for working and creating to maintain what existed, and the need to act more effectively as man's cognitive faculties grasped and evaluated emerging vicissitudes of his world. The traits of human nature, although maintaining their basic sameness, began taking on new cultural coloration as the tempo of cultural change accelerated, which made man appear as a new species of *Homo* to come into existence.

Concerning the most prominent features of primitive man's response to his world, Montagu [41] quotes Radin [42] as follows: "If one were asked to state briefly and succinctly what are the outstanding positive features of aboriginal civilizations, I, for one, would have no hesitation in answering that there are three: the respect for the individual, irrespective of age or sex; the amazing degree of social and political integration achieved by them; and the existence there of a concept of personal security which transcends all governmental forms and all tribal and group interests and conflicts."

The force of effective competence manifested in man's nature is one of the factors that makes it possible for man to make his own history, which, of course, means to be master of his future, i.e., to be able to direct and control his course toward a goal chartered by him. Maslow puts this idea as follows: "Yes, man is in a way his own project and he does make himself. But also there are limits upon what he can make himself into. The 'project' is predetermined biologically for all men; it is to become a man."[43] "The project to become a man" is also what Marx meant in his statement: "Thus, the objectification [of human energy] of the human essence, both in its theoretical and practical aspects, is required to make man's *sense human*, as well as to create the *human sense* corresponding to the entire wealth of human and natural substance."[44]

Maslow's statement, to be rounded out, should include the fact that man is not only restricted biologically in his efforts toward making himself, which also means making his history, but also restricted by the material conditions under which he is living. It is very true that he can keep changing his material conditions, but material conditions will always be there. Matson describes man's potentialities in these words: "No longer is man the offspring of nature, the creature of natural selection. Science has provided him with technology to become his own maker."[45] In the process of man making himself, Matson correctly puts the problem of "making himself" into a "what?" The answer is: *making himself into a person who develops his human nature in an environment that does not frustrate it. But in order to do so, specific knowledge of those traits must be known so that man can create an environment that is in harmony with those traits.* Thus Matson declared: "The central thesis of this book [*The Idea of Man*] as documented in the previous chapters, is that underlying the competition of ideas in the market-places of science, politics, and culture is a deeper and deadlier conflict of ideas about man himself—his essential nature, his salient features, and his alternative futures."[46]

NOTES

1. Jane Loevinger, *Ego Development* (San Francisco, California: Jossey-Bass Publishers, 1976), pp. 404–06.

2. Alexander H. Leighton, *My Name is Legion*, vol. 1 (New York: Basic Books, 1959), p. 136.

3. Ronald Fletcher, *Instinct in Man* (New York: International Universities Press, 1957).

4. Richard B. Lee, *!Kung San: Men, Women and Children in a Foraging Society* (New York: Cambridge University Press, 1979), p. 438.

5. Ibid.

6. Michael Argyle, *The Social Psychology of Work* (New York: Taplinger Publishing Co., 1972), pp. 223–50.

7. Albert Ellis, "Psychoneurosis and Anxiety Problems," in R. and I. Z. Grieger, eds., *Cognition and Emotional Disturbance* (New York: Human Sciences Press, Inc., 1982), p. 22.

8. L. R. Aronson *et al.*, "Development and Evolution of Behavior," in Max Schur and Lucille B. Ritvo, eds., *The Concept of Development and Evolution* (San Francisco, California: W. H. Freeman and Co., 1970), pp. 8–10, 601.

9. E. Fromm, *The Anatomy of Human Destructiveness* (New York: Holt, Rinehart, and Winston, 1973), pp. 96–7.

10. Dennis Gabor, *The Mature Society* (New York: Praeger Publishers, 1972), p. 47.

11. J. R. Moskin, "A Conversation with C. P. Snow," *Saturday Review* (April 6, 1974), p. 20. © 1974 *Saturday Review* magazine. Reprinted by permission.

12. Maurice Levine, *Psychiatry and Ethics* (New York: George Braziller, 1972), p. 90.

13. E. Erikson, *Insight and Responsibility* (New York: W. W. Norton and Co., 1964), p. 118.

14. Ibid., p. 119.

15. Ibid., pp. 122–23.

16. Harvey L. Ruben, *Competing* (New York: Lippinott and Crowell, Publishers, 1980), p. IX.

17. Ibid., p. 194.

18. Ibid.

19. Ibid., p. 24.

20. Ibid., p. 17.

21. M. Mead, *Cooperation and Competition Among Primitive People* (New York: McGraw-Hill Book Co.), p. 8.

22. Ibid.

23. Ibid., p. 460.

24. Ibid., p. 511.

25. Ashley Montagu, *Anthropology and Human Nature* (Boston, Massachusetts: Porter Sargent, 1957), p. 12.

26. Mead, *op. cit.*, pp. 458–511.

27. René Dubos, *Beast or Angel* (New York: Charles Scribner and Sons, 1974), pp. 205–206. "Oh, Leonardo, why do you toil so much?"

28. Ibid., pp. 190–207, "On the Pleasure of Being Human."

29. Erich Fromm, *The Anatomy of Human Destructiveness,* p. 134.

30. Ibid., pp. 132–33.

31. Ernst Mayr, *Population, Species, and Evolution* (Cambridge, Massachusetts: Harvard University Press, 1970), p. 385.

32. Ibid., p. 386.

33. Ibid., p. 407.

34. Fromm, *op. cit.*, p. 235.

35. Mead, *op. cit.* pp. 458–511.

36. Ashley Montagu, *The Nature of Human Aggression* (New York: Oxford University Press, 1976), p. 42.

37. Ibid., p. 295.

38. Ibid., p. 303.

39. John E. Pfieffer, *The Emergence of Society* (New York: McGraw Hill, 1977), pp. 19, 54.

40. Ibid., p. 22.

41. Montague, *The Nature of Human Aggression,* p. 313.

42. Paul Radin, *The World of Primitive Man,* p. 11.

43. A. H. Maslow, *The Farther Reaches of Human Nature* (New York: Viking Press, 1971), pp. 349–50.

44. K. Marx, *The Economic and Philosophical Manuscripts of 1844* (International Publishers), p. 141.

45. F. W. Matson, *The Idea of Man* (New York: Delacorte Press, 1976), pp. 84–5.

46. Ibid., p. 154.

13

The Cumulative Creative Action Trait

CREATIVITY: A TRAIT OF HUMAN NATURE

Man's need for creative action is supported and stimulated by his capacity for accumulating and using his experiential knowledge and technology, thus adding, ad infinitum, from generation to generation to mankind's cultural treasure.

Our power to initiate production grows exponentially as we continue to accumulate our ever increasing achievements generation after generation. Culture is the objectivization of man's trait of creativity, his creative labor. Man is endowed with an *inner* spark that stimulates him to creative activity, as well as his capacity to respond creatively to outer stimulation. It is a distinctive mark of humankind—this power to initiate, to originate productive action, to accumulate this experience, to enlarge it, and to transmit it for future use and expansion. This capturing of the past for present use and enlarging it for the future is man's definitive mark—the mark of his time-binding capacity[1] to create.

Man, emerging as a human being, had to *transcend* the uncertainty surrounding him in his natural state as a *passive creature* buffetted about in the turbulence of the natural forces. This came about as a consequence of his time-binding capacity to act upon and to react to nature's vicissitudes. Also, having the native ability to *reason* and to *imagine*, mankind, as social units or as individuals in social settings, thereby became an *active creative* force in molding and developing his *social relations*. Creativity can only become manifest by work, mental and physical. Work is purposeful activity in transforming the energetic capacity to create into reality that serves to maintain human existence. Perversion of this thesis is illustrated by the creation of things and ideas for the purpose of destroying, such as with intercontinental missles.

Creative potential gener-
ated by living the human
existence

Human — Actualizing the creative force, self-development in the context of social need

Primate — Inertia of the creative potential, distractibility, subsistent living, habituated to play, moved toward destructiveness

Man needs to appreciate the way he functions, the work he does. The type of work he engages in should be self-fulfilling. Since man's creations augment him as an individual human being and since these creations represent to him the crystallization of *his* efforts—of his own life, i.e., the very fulfillment of his existence—man appreciates that which he attains or creates with his own efforts and appreciates considerably less that which accrues to him without such effort. Man does not appreciate the past, lest he make an effort to study and absorb it, i.e., to *live* through the history of mankind's struggles and successes. Yet every creation he achieves is based on accumulation of man's past experience, even though he may not appreciate this time-binding fact.

It is not unusual for the scions of "successful" parents or the plunderers of the public to squander the inherited or ill-gotten fortunes that they had no hand in creating, since the only effort exerted on their part is the perverted activity in dissipating the creations of others.

Man's creativeness is manifested in what he does, in the effort he expends. What he does is manifested in many types of behavior, a good part of which is the production of products basic to subsistence and material amenities, but also expressed as play, the elaboration of art and literature, the development of scientific knowledge, et cetera. These efforts may generically be considered an expression of work. What is work? Webster includes many different definitions of *work*, probably for the purpose of satisfying the variety of ways that people understand it. Common to all such definitions is the allusion to some kind of effort. Let us be more precise. Neff has explored this subject in depth. To him, work "is not merely to 'do something'; it is to do something 'for a purpose'. . . . It is probably fair to say that most widespread connotations of the term 'work' is that it is designed to get something for the person who performs it. If we ask what is the 'something' that work is designed to get, then common speech also tells us that work is the means by which man makes his living. . . . There appears to be a very close association between work as a human activity and the complex structure of procedures man has elaborated to procure his means of subsistence."[2] Neff asks whether "all animals work, or is work a peculiar *human activity*?" Neff answers this question with the observation: ". . . man has managed to erect upon these [fundamental animal] biological needs such an immense structure of social and cultural phenomena that the basic biological substratum [of his work] sinks under the weight [of the social and cultural phenonena] and almost vanishes."[3] Neff defines work as a purely human activity, asserting that it differs from animal activity in that man planfully alters the environment by his work: "Work . . . is an instrumental activity carried out by human beings, the object of which is to preserve and maintain life which is directed at a planful alteration of certain features of man's environment."[4] The term "planful alteration" includes mental exertion as a form of work.

No work at all may be a potent factor in causing depression and anxiety. This is an indication of how basic work is to the human. The positive human aspect of creativity is creation that is good for the self as well as the community. The negative aspect of creativity is when the human activity is guided by the primate impulses that negate the human impulses, i.e., when there is a state of human inertia or aggressive destructiveness. This fundamentalism of work to the human is defined by Neff:

Work is neither a blessing nor a curse, but simply one of the major conditions of man's existence. Through work, a naked half-ape, equipped with neither fang nor claw, has been able to establish his sway over stronger and better-armed animals, virtually extinguishing the latter in the process. Through work, we have domesticated useful animals, tamed the land, learned to control many of the indifferent and inimical forces of nature. Through work also, we have developed the most efficient means of subjugating and killing our fellowmen, which is the darker side of the process. The *entire aggregate of human culture, for better and for worse, is a product of work: without work, it is difficult to say how we would have become human at all* [italics added]. Like many other human characteristics, the ability to work has dual aspects. We can use it to destroy ourselves as a live species, or we can use it to improve our lot on earth . . . but the more we know *why* we work, what we are working *for*, what are the *consequences* of our labor, the more we will be in a position to control our destinies.[5]

Neff then discusses *why* man works: "One important set of unconscious motives for working is related to our needs for self-esteem. Other important motives may reflect our needs to identify ourselves, to assign ourselves certain recognized roles in society. Still others may be related simply to the need for activity, to avoid boredom. For some, work may gratify certain needs for creativity."[6] All these reasons refer to needs or traits of human nature. Man is and needs to be an active agent in nature.

Work, the basis for creativity, was probably never researched as assiduously as was done by Marx. He stated that: "Work is a positive, creative activity."[7] In relation to capital, which is the objectification of work or labor, he asserted "that the worker constantly creates a double fund . . . in the form of capital. One part of this fund constantly fulfils the conditions of his own existence [as wages] and the other part fulfils the conditions for the existence of capital [surplus labor or surplus value] . . . as objectified, appropriated *alien labour*."[8] Capital is a phenomenon of industrial production. It exists when the accumulation of surplus labor or surplus value occurs in the process of *exchanging* work for wages (money) and commodities (objectified labor) for money (objectified exchange value). Work, for Marx, is the essence of human existence. If that essence be misappropriated, then the subject (the worker) of the essence is subjected to alienation. The dynamics of alienation in all its material and psychosocial aspects of deprivation and appropriation is the foundation upon which a Marxian sociological science could be built. This theory is not all negative so far as the worker is concerned, since capitalist production is the most rapid method for creation and accumulation of capital (as Marx pointed out), whose benefits, in a democracy, can amply redound to the workers, as demonstrated in the United States.

CREATIVITY IN ANCIENT HOMO: HOMO ERECTUS

How far back in *Homo*'s evolution was this genus creative? Did the drive to be creative have an equal push forward from the time of ancient man—let us say 250,000 years ago, in the middle Pleistocene? The drive was there but not of equal acceleration from earlier to later times. This was the period as Jacquetta Hawkes described it "that saw the development of the culture known as Acheulean in which tool making reached a far higher standard, the hand axe with its carefully formed point and cutting edge being the characteristic among a number of more or less standardized implements."[9] These were the creations of *Homo erectus*, and they were quite an advancement over the stone tools created by *Homo habilis*, the first stone-tool makers, who created their objects hundreds of thousands of years before. The advanced skill of *Homo erectus* took place in East Africa, as illustrated by the findings at Olduvia Gorge. The Acheulean culture spread first "throughout north Africa and then north-westward through Europe where it reached as far as south-eastern England, and north-eastward into Palestine and on to Mesopotamia and southern India. . . . What is remarkable about the Acheulean hand-axe makers . . . is the immensity of the area they came to occupy. . . . The fact remains that the hand axe itself, *which was for such an immense stretch of time man's highest achievement in tool making* [italics added], was made and developed into more and more elegant and efficient shapes, over almost the entire African continent and from southern India across the whole of southern Asia and Europe to southern England."[10]

Hawkes's marveling that "for such an immense stretch of time man's highest achievement in tool making" was indeed the axe is justified. The Acheulean period dated from about 150,000 to 250,000 years ago. *Homo erectus* had a brain capacity of from 750 cc to 1200 cc. The Acheulean period was the last 100,000 years of *Homo erectus*'s existence. This period, in its later stages, also was frequented by the Swanscombe and Steinheim species of *Homo*, which may be classified as early forms of *Homo sapiens* just below the Neanderthals. Is 100,000 years an amazingly long time for a hominid with the brain size averaging 25 percent smaller than Neanderthal man's to be able to advance technologically no more than to making fairly high standard hand axes? Or should we expect no more rapid rate of creativity? How important is brain size? Wenke states that: "In 1957 a conference on Neanderthal problems produced evidence that Neanderthal brain size on the average was *larger* than that of most human groups, and it was demonstrated that there were no grounds for concluding that their brains were structurally inferior or that they did not walk fully erect."[11] It is, nevertheless, logical and credible that such a brain size difference as that between *Homo erectus* and *Homo sapiens neanderthalensis* makes a difference in mentation and thereby creative ability. But, how much?

Let us consider the Neanderthal period and its creativity—a period of well over 65,000 years of stone tool industry, 30,000 of which were classified as the Mousterian culture. This culture was rich with stone artifacts. More than 19,000 implements were discovered at one site alone—the cave in the Combe Grenal Valley. These people had developed great skill as hunters. They are presumed to have been able to symbolize and conduct ritual in relation to burial.

THE NEANDERTHALS

Hawkes gives the following commentary on the Neanderthals:

> By the time the last glaciation was building up about 70,000–100,000 years ago human evolution had produced some races already acceptable as *Homo sapiens*, but others under the bitter, harsh conditions prevailing gave rise to the true Neanderthal man. . . . These Neanderthals . . . had large brains and are in fact the earliest known human beings to have thoughts that led them to bury their dead in graves provided with food and implements. . . . The contemporary history of *Homo sapiens* remains bafflingly obscure. What is certain is that from about 35,000 years ago Neanderthal man as a recognizable breed disappeared, while man of our own species, fully evolved *Homo sapiens*, appeared in many parts of south-west Asia, north Africa and Europe, using skillfully made special tools and weapons.[12]

Here we observe that during a period of about 65,000 years, a species whose brain size had been declared by professionals to have been larger than *Homo sapiens sapiens*, could do no more than increase its skill in making stone tools, augment its ability to utilize fire, clothes, and shelter as protection against the rigorous climate during the first half of the last glaciation, and sharpen its skill in hunting. Was this the extent of creative progress to expect over such a long period of time?

These folks certainly did meet the challenge of survival in the glacial environment. Not only that, but they must also have been an enterprising people to set out from a warm climate at the beginning of the last glacial period and migrate headlong into the frigid weather of Europe. Was this dynamic period of adaptation to the inclement climate reason enough to justify the modicum of technological and cultural progress in general made during these 65,000 long years? There probably was another reason, which Lee suggested to justify such a cultural lapse. Although the Neanderthal culture had a well-developed practice of sharing and maintaining a home base, localization into permanent "villages" did not occur. The life was nomadic, and as such there was no accumulation of wealth "even though the means for it—free time and raw materials"[13] were at hand. They probably had developed an "exchange" system with other communities and lived in a social organization that Marx would describe as "primitive commumism." These hunter-gatherers are generally described as *conservative* peoples not disposed to upset the status quo. This was apparently due to their efficiency in providing for their *perceived* needs and that these needs were being sufficiently met, i.e., their physical needs and their psychosocial needs were being satisfied as far as they perceived the situation. The satisfaction of their physical needs appears easier to perceive, being felt by hunger, weakness, and other physical distress. But their *psychosocial* needs generated by their having become humanized, and the satisfaction of those needs by the social order of primitive communism that they created out of the circumstances at hand was a satisfactory existence for them as perceived by them. That this period lasted as long as it did suggests that there was no sense of alienation involved. Production was shared by all; the producer was not alienated from the product nor from himself, since the product was a reification—an objectification of his and the community's efforts. Certainly the bonding and sharing trait was satisfied, since this was in the nature of the foraging economy. If we can trust Radin's description of primitive society and Lee's retrospective technique for ascribing certain basic principles of behavior to ancient society, then the freedom-of-choice trait, the unifying-orientation-of-behavior trait, the striving to satisfy one's appetites, inclinations, and native abilities trait, the self-image–self-esteem trait, the time-binding trait, the challenge-and-competence-to-control-one's-situation trait, and the creativity trait were satisfied insofar as the Neanderthals perceived themselves as not being denied the fulfilment of these human needs as they perceived these needs.

Rather than the severe nature of the climate retarding their technological development (since Neanderthals emerged and thrived during the last Ice Age), it was a stimulant, as we shall see in analyzing the remaining 25,000 years of this last glaciation. It was not the climate that made the Neanderthals so conservative. They were conservative because they had no great urge to change their social order, since foraging provided them with ample sustenance to afford them *more* leisure time than the modern worker has.[14] This leisure time finally generated into a burst of artistic energy by *Homo sapiens sapiens* during the final 25,000 year of the Ice Age.

HOMO SAPIENS SAPIENS

Hawkes describes this period from her scholarly vantage point:

During the second part of the last glaciation (which itself was marked by considerable climatic fluctuations) these hunters created the magnificent painting and sculpture of the French and Spanish caves. . . . Not only were these the first men of the highest mental capacities, able to express their new imaginative powers in art, in the dance and no doubt in oral literature and the use of musical sound (bone pipes), but they were also dynamic. Culture change was immensely accelerated and diversified, with many groups developing their own specialized forms. Undoubtedly the various cave dwellers of Western Europe from the Aurignacians to the Magdelenians had the supreme achievements both in art and ingenious tool-making, but there was also great dynamism in the Gravettians who seem to have created their culture in southern Russia and eastern and central Europe, but who extended as far east as Siberia. Theirs are some of the earliest known substantial man-made dwellings, they were successful mammoth hunters and their famous "mother goddess" figurines probably represent an advanced religious cult.

Energy and adaptability also made this age between about 35,000 and 10,000 B.C. one of the great periods of human expansion. In Europe, hunters were able to push northward into Scandinavia as the ice sheets retreated. Meanwhile the earliest settlement of the Americas was taking place—by 20,000 B.C. if not before, immigrants being able to cross by the land bridge that then linked Siberia with Alaska. The settlement of Australia, which had probably begun by 20,000 B.C., was more remarkable still. . . . About 10,000 years ago the rapid onset of warmer climatic conditions was having a drastic effect on the human environment throughout much of the northern hemisphere. In Europe north of the Alps and Pyrenees, country which in glacial conditions had been open steppe and tundra became forested, and the huge game herds on which the advanced Palaeolithic hunters had lived dwindled away or, like the reindeer, retreated northward. In north Africa, including the Sahara and some parts of southwest Asia, on the other hand, what had been grassland became dessicated. This period after the last glaciation . . . the various hunting peoples were adjusting to new conditions. . . . It was hardly possible for them to take the next big step in human history, partly owing to the forest environment, more because western Europe lacked the wild grasses and the wild sheep and goats most suitable for domestication. Ideal conditions for the development of mixed farming and the large settlements and more complex societies that went with it existed among Mesolithic peoples in the Near and Middle East.[15]

The sense of challenge, competence to control one's situation, and creativity had become inured traits of *Homo* behavior. Hawkes described these behavioral traits in these ancient folks well:

The sudden emergence of full human *creativity* [italics added] among the Advanced Hunters . . . at the end of the Old Stone Age is surely one of the most astonishing chapters in all our history. The Neanderthalers had taken a tentative step, but the Cromagnons made a graceful leap forward. . . . [They] began to think in terms of solving problems. With this new sense of *challenge* [italics added], they invented within a relatively short time the spear-thrower and thong-softener, composite hafting of flint, a variety of specialized barbed spears and harpoons, the eyed needle, a fat-burning lamp, and probably the bow and arrow. . . . The Advanced Hunting Age of Europe came to a glorious *end* in this earliest outburst of artistic creation. There was to be no other to approach it before the Old Kingdom art of Egypt some *seven thousand years later* [italics added].[16]

During the middle of the Magdelenian period in Europe, microliths and grinders for wild cereals were in use in the Near East including the Zagros range. This was 13,000 B.C., when Natufians were still in their late hunting culture. These people "chose to live where the ancestors of wheat and barley grew wild, and their equipment of reaping knives, querns, pestles, and mortars proves that they harvested the grain in quantity. It is also possible that they added to their meat supply by herding gazelles. Population grew with food supply, and so did a more settled way of life. The old tradition of realistic animal art and personal finery *lingered* [italics added] on among them."[17]

The period that Hawkes described was one in which the abundance of wild game plus the appearance of modern man brought a new quality for creative action into human evolution. This new quality had to do with the development of the imagination, the cognitive processes, as a tool to advance *Homo*'s creativity. Wild game being so plentiful, this creativity was not needed to expand the tools for food and other material things for subsistence. In the latter sphere, only *moderate* advances were made, such as devising techniques for more efficient hunting practices and developing the methods for building living abodes. But they let their imagination and refined sensibilities expand *prolifically* in painting, sculpturing, and dancing. Also, their ritual practices imply the existence of epics of past experience and legendary heroics and the verbal composition of the philosophy of living such as observances of religious cults and more explicit codification of the rules for societal conduct as Radin described in *Primitive Man as Philosopher*.

After the climate changed, the abundance of food for ample sustenance dwindled, to be replaced with dense forests. A new world came into existence. The good life, with its *leisure time* for expressing the fertilely developed imagination and humanized sensibilities in the arts, was gone. With the dwindling supply of wildlife, the logical substitute would be animal domestication. With the development of the more complex society and, as the population increased, gathering had to be converted into a more abundant generation of supply and methods of *exchange* also became more sophisticated. The answer to this was farming and a more formal method of exchange of products.

BEGINNING OF PSYCHOSOCIAL DISCORD
WITH SOCIAL ORDERS

Two million years of the Pleistocene was coming to an end. The Palaeolithic foragers with their stone tools and intellectual uniqueness, particularly during the Cro-magnon period of the last 100,000 years, were taxed, tested, and challenged by termination of the last glaciation. A new challenge and a new urge to creativity were coming into being. The need for revolutionary methods of solving problems was in the air, and solutions were rapid in coming, considering the length of time that it took for the Palaeolithic to come into existence and finally pass away. *Homo* has always responded to exigent situations, and this period was a marvelous demonstration of this resiliency. Childe so vividly described the situation whereby: "the revolutionaries were not the most advanced savages of the Old Stone Age—the Magdelenians were all too successfully specialized for exploiting [for initiating changes in the ecology for accommodating to] the pleistocene environment—but humbler groups who had created less specialized and less brilliant cultures farther south" were the ones whose new challenge to creativity demonstrated "how enormously neolithic equipment was richer than that of any palaeolithic or mesolithic savagery. The new technology which they created based on farming and herding required more sedentary type of existence and eventually the establishment and growth of villages."[18]

As the technology advanced, the villages became self-sufficient and, in a sense, specialized by concentrating on growing a particular type of food plant and the herding of a particular domesticated animal stock. Sharing continued in modified ways—modified by the new cultural developments. Traits of human nature take on the complexion of the culture of a people. *Exchange*, a basic practice that distinguishes human society from that of other primates, took on qualities inherent in the relations of this new type of village life. Production increased and surpluses accumulated. Surplus became a new phenomenon in the economic life of *Homo*. Surplus and exchange gave stimulating variety to the lives of these people.

As population grew, suitable land for cultivation and stock raising became scarce. Competition for land space added a new dimension to socioeconomic practice—conflict for space and raiding and predation for food became chronic. The two basic defects that evolved from the Neolithic mode of production were therefore:

1. Competition (uncontrolled, eliciting more primatelike responses) for land suitable for farming and herding, which led to conflict and the breaking up of the clan and kinship organization of society.
2. Self-sufficiency of each village, which did not provide protection against natural disasters such as blights, hailstorms, tempests, droughts, fires, floods, and frosts, which might spell famine and even annihilation.[19]

From the insecurity in survival created by the contradictions emerging in the Neolithic mode of production evolved the need for the coming into prominence of chiefdoms to organize the means of security for those who would accept such protection. Sharing, work practices, and exchange began taking on the incipiency of the dynamics of class society.

The traits of human nature that developed during the democratic social order of primitive communism were naturally in harmony with the prevailing social relations of that social order, but began to strain under the socioeconomic stresses of the Neolithic mode of production.

The bonding and sharing trait began to disjoin. The freedom-of-choice trait became more constricted and prone to more socially inimical choices. The unifying-orientation-of-behavior trait suffered from dislocation in social relations and surrendered to chiefdom authority, including the incipient class oriented religious authority. The striving trait became exaggerated and deflected by desires created by the imbalances in the new social order. the self-image–self-esteem trait was polarized toward the self-aggrandizement with personal power or self-negation due to depersonalization—alienation. The prospection trait became a sense of hope for some and a hopeless alienation for others. The trait of challenge and competence to control one's situation was exaggerated to competitive conflict, initiating a new quality of aggression. Creativity under these conditions initiated social relations whereby those with power organized others to produce for them. The traits of human nature have been out of harmony with the succession of social orders ever since those pristine days when freedom of choice was enhanced for the favored minority. The fruits of creativity have been augmented by intensified competition and have been directed as well toward social benefit as for use as instruments of control over people by the "power elite" since the latter years of the Neolithic revolution. The price of protection has been subjection. This is still a formula prevalent the world over. Capitalism, the fruition of the Industrial Revolution, became the social order, par excellence, for the creation of capital as the wealth of nations. Because of its bivalent nature, i.e., the tendency toward industrial and financial monopoly and government control, on the one hand, and democratic distribution of the fruits of production and of the reins of government, on the other hand, it is possible for the tendency to be pressured in either direction. Happily, the direction toward real democratic government is most likely. Under a democratic social order, the likelihood of the ecosystem harmonizing with the traits of human nature is great. As soon as the Soviet-type dictatorships around the world and those trying to imitate that genre of socialism erroneously called Marxist governments, metamorphose into democratic forms of socialism, concordance with the traits of human nature will begin to eventuate.

MARX, WORK, AND LEISURE TIME

In our consumer type of social atmosphere, our leisure time is more and more coming under the influence of a play ethos colored with sexual abandon and abuse of the various physiological processes.

Where is this leading and how is this affecting the traits of human nature? Argyle stated that: "In simpler societies, work is done in a way that gives satisfaction to those who do it, and there is no clear division between work and leisure."[20] This picture of societal adequacy is what Marx meant when he said in discussing the productively developed communist society: "For real wealth is the developed productive force of all individuals. It is no longer the labour time but the disposable time [what we call leisure time] which is the measure of wealth."[21] Is it possible that in very highly productive societies of the future, the interrelationships between the forces of production and the forces of production relations will be such that no clear division will be obtained between work and leisure? In such an atmosphere, what becomes of the play ethos? Is the concept of *Homo ludens* a serious matter? Are challenge and creativity muffled? Is there a tie-in between play time and physiological processes abuse?

It follows as the night follows the day that being "effective" cannot be accomplished without exertion. Exertion resulting in motion is an expenditure of energy, and this is the mechanical definition of work. Without work there is nothing human. Work is the conversion of one's living essence into an external entity, be it a material object, an expressed mental elaboration, or an interacting social relation. Work is a manifestation of self. It is so fundamental that the history of social systems is essentially based on the history of the interrelations between the energies (forces) man uses to work (to produce), i.e., the work relations between men in the process of producing, and the means (the various types of mechanical applications of energies) used to produce. Marx as an economist, stated that "*commodities* and hence exchange values . . . are *objectified labour*."[22] As a political economist, he described the interrelations of forces of production and production relations: "In the social production which men carry on, they enter into definite relations that are indispensable and independent of their will; these relations of production correspond to a definite stage of development of their material powers of production. The sum total of these relations of production constitutes the economic structure of society—the real foundation, on which rise legal and political superstructures and to which correspond definite forms of social consciousness."[23]

Fromm was thoroughly grounded in Marx's philosophy and was also a social psychologist grounded in political economy. He used every opportunity to associate creativity in its practical aspects expressed as work in terms of its alienation: "Work, man's exchange with nature, is such a fundamental part of human existence that only when it ceases to be alienated can leisure time become productive. This, however, is not only a question of changing the nature of work, but of a total social and political change in the direction of subordinating the economy to the real needs of man."[24] Although this is a Marxian statement and transmits Marx's concepts with clarity, Marx conceived the meaning of alienation in a more complex form than expressed by Fromm. According to Marx, labor, in a capitalist system, is not only alienated from the product and, at the same time, appropriated by the capitalist, but is also alienated from the act of production (self-alienation) and man is, at the same time, alienated from mankind (from his species, *Homo sapiens sapiens*). This, Marx claims, is so because labor, under capitalism, produces only the means to satisfy the needs for physical existence, i.e., man makes of his essence (his life activity) only a means to satisfy needs, instead of the work itself being an essential creative need for man, for satisfying his human nature.

Fromm considers that the alienation of man's labor disappears under a socialist system. Marx described the alienation of work, or as he called it, labor: "In surplus capital all the elements are the product of alien labour—the alien surplus labour which has been changed into capital. . . . But if capital thus appears as the product of labour, the product of labour also appears as capital—no more as a simple product, nor as exchangeable goods, but as capital; objectified labour assumes mastery, has command over living labour. It appears just as much the product of labour that its product appears as alien property, an independent mode of existence opposed to living labour, and equally autonomous value; that the product of labour, objectified labour, has acquired its own soul from living labour and has established itself opposite living labour as an alien force."[25]

Marx's line of reasoning led him into discussion of alienation as a contortion of human nature, which, indeed, it is:

An immediate consequence of the fact that man is estranged from the product of his labour, from his *life-activity*, from his *species-being* [humanity or *Homo sapiens*] is the estrangement of man from man [italics added]. . . . In fact, the proposition that man's *species nature* [human nature] is estranged from him means that one man is estranged from the others, as each of them is from man's essential nature [human nature].

The estrangement of man and in fact every relationship in which man stands to himself is first realized and expressed in the relationship in which a man stands to other men.

Hence within the relationship of estranged labour each man views the other in accordance with the standard and the relationship in which he finds himself as a worker.[26]

Marx's perception is acute that "work," which is an aspect of the effective competence to control one's situation trait of human nature, is indeed part of human nature. Marx's great contribution to political economy, in which "work" is one of the fundamentals and an analysis of which became the Bible of revolutionaries, apparently became exaggerated to many Marxist theorists, with work being the only essence of human nature. Thus among the enthusiastic left-wingers, many recognized theorists treat lightly or not at all such other fundamentals of human nature as relate to ethics and moral codes, freedom of choice, and the bonding force of the family. They probably never "really" studied Friederich Engels's *Origin of the Family*.

Marx described alienation as a force operating in a process of a capitalist society in relation to the origin and production of surplus value. Since the dialectics of every process call for the interpenetrative movement of two opposite unalienable forces, Marx posits the force of appropriation (expropriation from the workers becomes appropriation by the capitalist) in opposition to and as the complement of alienation. In a social setting, then, every alienation is, in a countervailing sense, an appropriation. This is a basic social phenomenon. It could not exist except in the *social* world of mankind, and this is true for any and every type of society, including socialism and communism.

A reason for the pejorative implications of the term "alienation" is because Marx used the term in a restricted historical context—in the origin and production of capital from surplus value produced under capitalism. The workers thereby became alienated from their objectified essence—from the product of their labor. In this context, emphasis was placed on the inhuman expropriation of the surplus value from the pauperized workers, rather than its being appropriated in the process of capital formation for increasingly augmenting the wealth of the community (even though the wealth be privately owned). If Marx developed the process universally as applying beyond the capitalist system, the dialectics would have changed the social sensibilities applied to the process of alienation-appropriation so that the concept of exploitation would gradually have resolved into social benefaction and would proceed to lose its antisocial implications. This is happening in the Western democracies where the impetus for the development of social services is rapidly diminishing the morally sensitive edge of exploitation. When restricted to nineteenth-century capitalism, then, Marx's treatment of surplus value, exploitation, alienation, and expropriation gives to these terms a sense of permanent malignancy, not judgment in the spirit of Marx's usual dialectic vibrancy of the dynamics of the changing relational meaning of concepts where the law of negation applies.

Another reason for the pejorative implication of the term "alienation" is Marx's sometime equivalent use of the terms "capital and capitalist"[27] and "capital and capitalism"[28] when he described the dialectics of capital formation as a permanently revolutionary process. He probably did not dream of the possibility of capitalism under democratic government utilizing surplus value under the influence of democratic ideology and increasingly establishing social services to the point of being designated welfare state (although Marx seemed to have a soft spot toward the United States). Thus the alienation inherent in surplus value becomes less and less in disharmony with the traits of human nature and so becomes the appropriation of the surplus value by capitalists, since much of it becomes taxes or assessments for social services. But because Marx believed that capitalism under democracy set a permanent boundary for itself, i.e., the boundary of the social order of capitalism with the increasing intensity of its class antagonisms, the universality toward which capital formation is perpetually driving must lead to capitalism's own destruction. In the latter description, the terms "capital" and "capitalism" could very well be taken as interchangeable, thereby negating the dialectics of the process. Thus Lenin and the subsequent Soviet interpretation of "capital" limited its existence to the duration of capitalism because they posit that surplus value, exploitation, alienation, and appropriation would disappear under socialism.[29]

Fromm repeats the same misinterpretation by believing that alienation disappears under socialism as cited above. Marx does not say specifically that capital disappears with capitalism, although the implication appears to be there. When socialism or communism or any modification of capitalism takes the place of raw (Adam Smith's) capitalism, neither alienation nor appropriation disappears. What disappears is the pejorative appearance and implications of these forces. So long as society continues to progress to the point where people work according to their abilities and get according to their needs, there will always be a necessity for the maintenance and development of work places and the machinery and equipment to produce and for the maintenance of a healthful and pleasant environment and the abodes where people live, work, play, and spend their leisure time. And since production of things whets the appetites of people, it will always have to be maintained and developed to provide such social needs. Where will the capital come from to provide such social requirements? It will have to come from the surplus value produced by the worker and appropriated or expropriated by society. The fact that the society may refuse to apply the word *alienation* to the interrelationship between the worker and the products produced as surplus value or may refuse to apply the the term "appropriation" or "expropriation" to the act of government when it collects surplus value as taxes in order to administer the multitude of social services that people under socialism consider as their needs, does not change the nature of these essential social processes, even though the tilt of such "exploitation" may have changed radically toward more human practice. Such change is actually taking place at present under democratic practice in the same sense as it is taking place under what is being practiced as socialism in the Eastern countries, except that democratic practice has the potential for being in greater harmony with the traits of human nature than socialism under a dictatorship.

The simplicity of the work concept in primitive society contrasts sharply with the complicating factors generated as cultural advancement proceeds. Yet certain aspects of work as a creative process are as valid today as they were of yore, because man must work to create to fulfill his human need and because what he produces is a crystallization of his being. He appreciates those things he produces and those activities by which he lives, except when the creativity trait is distorted by the demoralization caused by class alienation. No trait stands by itself, just as no human can stand alone and remain human.[30] Work whets the creative appetites by tending more and more to add to the possible fulfillment of desires relating to the human condition and to continually re-orient man's relations toward greater schemes of mutual aid. Challenge and psychosocial response to this fulfilment may create conditions not only salutary to man's existence but also destructive of his social well-being.

MAN: THE ACTIVE AGENT IN NATURE

The position taken in this study is that if the traits of human nature were known with specificity and if the effects of the various aspects of social dynamics on the specific traits of human nature were known, then we could make an effort to alter the interrelational structure of our social milieu so that the resulting social dynamics would be in harmony with the traits of our human nature. In this way, those disorientations of behavior that are caused by the hostile ecosystem could be prevented or at least greatly reduced. This, together with the efforts we are expending on alleviating the economic distress in our society, should result in the kind of society that man has dreamed of from time immemorial—a society in which the ecosystem is in harmony with human nature and from which the stress of poverty has been eliminated. Montagu aptly stated that: "Human nature—not animal nature—is to be the basis and guide of Human Engineering."[31]

When the elements of human nature are unbalanced by a discordant ecosystem, particularly where economic distress is the patent factor, the basis for mass revolutionary fervor and desperation is created accompanied by a variety of behavior disorientations, which eventually elicit delinquent and criminal acts, neuroses, psychoneuroses, and psychoses and, consequent to such stress, will produce psychosomatic diseases. By disturbing social stability—dynamic equilibrium—these stresses may throw the human ecology into disorder enough to allow past and present dread communicable diseases, starvation, and violence to thrive and to cause death and disability. The disturbances of social stability is a basic phase of the developmental process. Beyond certain threshold levels of disturbances, changes are accompanied by social violence and destruction and, in the physiological sphere, by pathological changes in some people due to stresses having accumulated beyond their physiological threshold.

Man is moved to action by inner cognitive initiative and external stimuli, which in turn enrich the inner initiative, or conditions may prevail to depress it. The combined expression of inner initiative and external stimuli may be manifested by physical or mental activity or a combination of both. The result of this activity is and has been the creation of human culture. Fromm discusses this aspect of man's existence as follows: "Man is the only animal who does not feel at home in nature . . . the only animal for whom his own existence is a problem that he has to solve and from which he cannot escape. He cannot go back to the prehuman state of harmony with nature, and he does not know where he will arrive if he goes forward. Man's existential contradiction results in a state of constant disequilibrium."[32] Then quoting W. S. Laughlin, Fromm says: " 'Hunting has placed a premium upon inventiveness, upon problem solving, and has imposed a real penalty for failure to solve the problem. Therefore it has contributed as much to advancing the human species as to holding it together within the confines of a single variable species.' "[33]

Dubos, in a similar vein, observed that: "Many tribes of hunter-gatherers devoted prodigious efforts to the creation of paintings in the depths of caves where they did not live. Prehistoric mankind created the stupendous megalithic statues of Northwestern Europe as well as the colossal enigmatic statues of Easter Island. The urge to create monuments having chiefly a symbolic value has continued throughout history."[34] He then continues with the modern scene: "Modern science and technology therefore constitute expressions of the genius of this era which have a collective value. But it is doubtful that these expressions will equal those of the past in imaginative richness or in influence. When evaluating them, it must be remembered that for a hundred millenia human beings devoted a large percentage of their resources and inventiveness to creations which did not contribute to their material needs, but which still enrich life today.[35]

Dubos concluded: "Most human beings desire to participate in the adventures and spectacles of collective life, but they also want to make a unique creation of their own life. All share the biological endowment of the human species; all retain some psychological aspects of the Paleolithic hunter, of the Neolithic farmer, and of the urban dweller who has experienced the splendor and miseries of civilizations."[36]

Maslow, who has studied human nature in depth, is convinced that: "This kind of primary creativeness is very probably a heritage of every human being. It is a common and universal kind of thing."[37] He further queries: "The question is, who is interested in creativity? And my answer is that practically everybody is."[38]

Matson agrees with Fromm and Dobzhansky that "no longer is man the offspring of Nature, the creature of natural selection. Science has provided him with the technology to become his own maker."[39]

Creativity is indeed a struggle in the analysis of May, and a joy in the perceptions of Dubos. May's description is that "creativity is a yearning for immortality. We human beings know that we must die. We have, strangely enough, a word for death. We know that each of us must develop the courage to confront death. Yet we also must rebel and struggle against it. Creativity comes from this struggle—out of the rebellion the creative act is born ."[40] He adds: "The creative process is the expression of this passion for form. It is the struggle against disintegration, the struggle to bring into existence new kinds of being that give harmony and integration."[41]

Dubos declared that "there exists a form of *joie de vivre* which expresses the very pleasure of being alive—a purely organic satisfaction which animals share with the human species. But there is another form of happiness, which seems peculiar to human beings. It originates from their deep awareness that their personal life is the realization of their dreams and their collective life a creative enterprise which gives concrete forms to the dreams of humankind."[42]

Dubos even came down to earth and declared cooking an act of creation, as it is: "Cooking is often a repetitive chore, but it has its creative aspects and it can transcend drudgery through uniting the family at mealtime."[43]

The fact is that most human activities associated with productive or innovative results, material and mental, are creative. The industrial worker, the actor, the teacher, the housekeeper, the artist, the discussion group, are actively and purposefully engaged in generating material and immaterial products through external and internal motivation. May has various ways of expressing this, such as: "Creativity can be seen only in the act";[44] "Creativity . . . is the encounter of the intensely conscious human being with his or her world."[45] "Creativity arises out of the tensions between spontaneity and limitations"[46] and "Limits are not only unavoidable in human life, they are also valuable. . . *Creativity itself requires limits* for the creative act arises out of the struggle of human beings with and against that which limits them."[47] May concluded: "Nietzsche, in his important book *The Birth of Tragedy*, cites the Dionysian principle of surging vitality and the Apollonian principle of form and rational order as the two dialectical principles that operate in creativity. This dichotomy is assumed by many students and writers."[48]

The dual effect of creativity in enlarging the external world and at the same time enriching the inner self by the experience is expressed by Arieti as follows: "Creative work thus may be seen to have a dual role: at the same time as it enlarges the universe by adding or uncovering new dimensions, it also enriches and expands man, who will be able to experience these new dimensions inwardly."[49] Creativity is a *human* growth factor, as Arieti states: "Although creativity is by no means the only way in which the human being can grow, it is one of the most important."[50]

Arieti's faulty judgment about the deterrent nature of paleologic thinking he expresses as follows: "We must conclude that although the appearance of symbolic thinking was an evolutionary improvement that led to what is specifically human in man, it was a dangerous improvement, because at first it emerged in the form of paleologic thinking."[51] Paleologic logic was indeed an improvement over no logic at all. It was a logic that helped create human nature—a cognitive process that realized the importance of the psychosocial bonding-sharing force in the struggle to survive and the need for the creation of an ethics to control and direct a system of inhibitions and expressions for humanizing the primate in *Homo*. There was no more danger in the evolution of man by being exposed to Paleologic cognition than to formal or dialectic logic. Man's greatest danger has always been the possible misdirection of the biphasic or contradictory nature of his traits of human nature, allowing the primate impulses to dominate the human conduct. Marshall Sahlins's the *Origin of Society* lends confirmation to the remarkable advances made by man during his Paleological evolutionary period.

Montagu expressed man's creativeness in a very generic manner: "Instead of having his responses genetically fixed as in other animal species, man is a species that invents its own responses, and it is out of this unique ability to invent, to improvize his responses that his cultures are born."[52]

Maslow wrote a book on human nature without defining the term, without listing the word in the index, and without discussing much in terms of it. But creativity and self-actualization appear to be an essence of it. The following quotes are his descriptions:

> My feeling is that the concept of creativeness and the concept of the healthy, self-actualizing, fully human person seem to be coming closer and closer together, and may perhaps turn out to be the same thing.[53]
>
> It seems to me terribly impressive, as I read the creativeness literature, that the relationship with psychiatric health or psychological health is so crucial, so profound, so terribly important, and so obvious, and yet it is not used as a foundation on which to build.[54]
>
> Self-actualizing people are, without one single exception, involved in a cause outside their own skin, in something outside of themselves. They are devoted, working at something, something which is very precious to them—some calling or vocation in the old sense, the priestly sense.[55]

Being moved to action by internal and external stimuli is described by Sarbin: "A basic postulate in the model [of role finding] is that human beings constantly strive to locate themselves in their environment. In order to make efficient choices from among behavior alternatives, a person must locate himself with regard to the world occurrence. . . . Constantly faced with the necessity of locating himself, a person's misplacement of self in the role system may lead to embarrassing, perilous, or even fatal consequences."[56] Being moved to action therefore cannot be separated from man's nature of making a choice as to the direction in which to move to secure his position—to locate himself, which is further influenced by his effective competence to control his situation in the process of accepting the challenge and eventually whether he has become demoralized and moves purposelessly or embarks on a creative role.

Being moved to action is given the name of courage by May. To him "courage . . . is the foundation that underlies and gives reality to all other virtues and personal values. . . . In human beings courage is necessary to make *being* and *becoming* possible. An assertion of the self, a commitment, is essential if the self is to have any reality. This is the distinction between human beings and the rest of nature."[57] Of course, courage can be directed toward creative action or to primatelike appetite gratification. The philosophy of life, or, in simple terms, one's mental disposition from experience in growing up, will guide the direction that motivation or courage to act will take.

Notes

1. Alfred Korzybski, *Manhood of Humanity* (New York: E. P. Dutton and Co., 1921), pp. 143, 148, 174–175.

2. Walton S. Neff, *Work and Human Behavior* (Atherton Press, 1968), p. 75.

3. Ibid., pp. 75–76.

4. Ibid., p. 78.

5. Ibid., pp. 259–60.

6. Ibid., p. 84.

7. Karl Marx, *The Grundrisse*, edited by David McLellan (New York: Harper Torchbook, 1971), p. 126.

8. Karl Marx, *The Grundrisse*, translated by Martin Nicolaus (New York: Random House, 1973), p. 504.

9. J. Hawkes, *Atlas of Ancient Archaeology* (New York: McGraw-Hill Co., 1974), pp. 9–10.

10. Ibid.

11. Robert J. Wenke, *Patterns in Prehistory* (New York: Oxford University Press, 1980), p. 176.

12.Hawkes, *loco supra citato*, p. 9.

13. Richard B. Lee, *!Kung San: Men, Women and Children in a Foraging Society* (New York: Cambridge University Press, 1979), p. 456.

14. Ibid., p. 440.

15. Hawkes, *loco supra citato*, pp. 9–10.

16. J. Hawkes, *The Atlas of Early Man* (New York: St. Martin's Press, 1976), pp. 21–22.

17. Ibid., p. 23.

18. Gordon Childe, *What Happened in History* (New York: Pelican Books, 1943), pp. 43–45.

19. Ibid., pp. 60–61.

20. Michael Argyle, *The Social Psychology of Work* (New York: Taplinger Publishing Co., 1972), pp. 251–52.

21. Karl Marx, *The Grundrisse* (New York: Harper Torchbooks, 1971), p. 145.

22. Karl Marx, *The Grundrisse* (New York: Vintage Books, 1973), p. 272.

23. Karl Marx, *A Contribution to the Critique of Political Economy* (Chicago, Illinois: Charles H. Kerr, and Co., 1904), p. 11.

24. Erich Fromm, *The Anatomy of Human Destructiveness* (New York: Fawcett, 1978), p. 244.

25. Karl Marx, *The Grundrisse, loco supra citato*, pp. 99–100.

26. Karl Marx, *Economic and Philosophical Manuscripts of 1844*, pp. 114–115. Cited also in John Torrence, *Estrangement, Alienation, and Exploitation: A Sociological Approach to Historical Materialism* (New York: Columbia University Press, 1977), p. 89.

27. Karl Marx, *Capital: Capitalistic Production,* vol. 1, (Chicago, Illinois: Charles H. Kerr and Co., 1926), pp. 648–49.

28. Karl Marx, *The Grundrisse*, edited and translated by David McLellan (New York: Harper Torchbooks, 1971), pp. 94–5.

29. A. Leontiev, *Political Economy: A Condensed Course* (New York: International Publishing Co., 1975), p. 93.

30. Ben Freedman, *Health Is Indivisible: Program Priorities* (Tel Aviv: The International Technical Cooperation Center, 1975), pp. 62–75.

31. Ashley Montagu, *Anthropology and Human Nature* (Boston Massachusetts: Porter Sargent Publishers, 1957), p. 51.

32. Fromm, *op. cit.* p. 225.

33. Ibid., p. 133.

34. René Dubos, *Beast or Angel* (New York: Scribner, 1974), pp. 107–108.

35. Ibid., p. 113.

36. Ibid., p. 100.

37. A. H. Maslow, *The Farther Reaches of Human Nature* (New York: Penguin, 1976), p. 83.

38. Ibid., p. 96.

39. Matson, *The Idea of Man*, pp. 84–5.

40. Rollo May, *The Courage to Create* (New York: W. W. Norton and Co., 1975), p. 31.

41. Ibid., pp. 139–40.

42. Dubos, *op. cit.*, p. 207.

43. Ibid., p. 150.

44. May, *op. cit.*, p. 43.

45. Ibid., p. 54.

46. Ibid., p. 115.

47. Ibid., p. 113.

48. Ibid., p. 47.

49. Silvano Arieti, *Creativity*, p. 5.

50. Ibid., p. 413.

51. Ibid., p. 73.

52. A. Montagu, *Anthropology and Human Nature* (Boston, Massachusetts: Porter Sargent, 1951), p. 139.

53. Maslow, *op. cit.*, p. 57.

54. Ibid., p. 73.

55. Ibid., p. 43.

56. T. R. Sarbin, "The Culture of Poverty, Social Identity, and Cognitive Outcomes," Vernon L. Allen, ed., *Psychological Factors in Poverty* (Markham Publishing Co., 1970), p. 36.

57. *Op cit.*, p. 13.

14

The Relation of Emotions to Traits of Human Nature

DEFINITIONS

This study is concerned with the traits of human nature about which everyone talks, but concerning which very few people really have a clear picture of the specific behavioral dynamics involved. Emotions are also basic qualities of human behavior, and they are in the routine observation of people behaving, completely integrated with the traits of human nature. It almost appears as a truism that scarcely a trait can be manifested without its intermeshing with an emotional expression. For example, the essence of the trait of "bonding-sharing" is love. Is it possible to express love without demonstrating emotion?

There is indeed a need for the science of human behavior to analyze and to distinguish comprehensively the differences in the nature of these two fundamental qualities of human behavior. Because the main body of this study concerns itself only with the problem of human nature, I am using Carroll E. Izard's very fine and comprehensive work, *Human Emotions*, to develop the comparative relations.

Izard defines emotion

as a complex process with neurophysiological, neuromuscular, and phenomenological aspects. At the neurophysiological level emotion is defined primarily in terms of patterns of electrochemical activity in the nervous system, particularly in the cortex, the hypothalamus, the basal ganglia, the limbic system, and the facial and trigeminal nerves. . . . At the neuromuscular level, emotion is primarily facial activity and facial patterning, and secondarily it is bodily (postural, visceral-glandular, and sometimes vocal) response. At the phenomenological level [subjective], emotion is essentially motivating experience and/or experience which has immediate meaning and significance for the person. The experiencing of emotion can constitute a process in consciousness completely independent of cognition.[1]

From Izard's definition, emotions are basically affective-cognitive experiences and, for the most part, on the conscious level are activated by internal and external stimuli involving physical responses of the neurophysiological and neuromuscular systems. Emotions, therefore, are psychophysical phenomena. In contrast, the traits of human nature are axiomatic patterns of behavioral responses of the genus *Homo* to the human condition. (See charts 1 and 2 in the chapter "The Nature of Human Nature.") Emotions are not just the domain of man, but are characteristic of all mammals. Human nature is only the province of *Homo*, with possible *anlage* of some traits being present in other primates. The traits of human nature are the patterns of behavior that distinguish human behavior from all other types of animal behavior. The human condition is the complex of factors originating in the struggle of the genus *Homo* to survive and to better its condition of living, given its special anatomical features, the potential of its physiological features relating to sexuality and to the nature of the reproductive process requiring intensified parenting, as well as its mental capacity for symbolizing. This special human condition directed primitive *Homo* to embark on a particular organization of society that determined cognitively new social relations and modified others from its primate past. These social relations required cognitive efforts to formulate the rules for new directions of human behavior. The human potential of this new direction of behavior was put to test when emerging *Homo* was challenged as to whether he could respond in a completely new course of behavior—human behavior—by *inhibition* of undesirable primate-stamped social behavior. But in order to contend with this new course of behavior, the affective-cognitive structure, the *conscience* had to be evolved and the incipient higher level mammalian behavioral problem, *jealousy*, had to be controlled.

The various traits of human nature are durable for reasons other than emotions and drives. The latter are psychophysical-affective responses involving such permanent phenomena as neurophysiological and neuromuscular dynamics. The traits of human nature are psychosocial behavioral responses to the new social interrelations that *Homo* had contrived in order to accommodate favorably to the new conditions. These social responses have a permanency co-terminal with the permanency of those basic factors composing the human condition. Even though the traits of human nature are universal in all human societies, different cultures give their distinctive stamp on each trait without changing its basic nature. For example, all societies have moral-ethical norms of behavior, but the resultant moral-ethical behavioral response in each society has the distinctive stamp of that culture.

We need further to distinguish the difference in the nature of these two elements of human behavior. The traits of human nature are primarily *social* phenomena molded in the form of the human condition by the natural mental and physical endowments of the genus *Homo*. Emotions are expressed primarily as individual physical phenomena. The traits are effectively and consistently manifested in communities of people, exhibiting less uniformity as well as variations in degrees of effectiveness in the individuals of a community. Emotions are the consistent attributes of all average individuals, and are individually expressed in accordance with individual circumstances. Emotions are expressed with uniformity by communities of people under special circumstances, such as wars and hurricanes. Traits of human nature when expressed are practically always accompanied by emotions. Emotions are not so axiomatically associated with expressed traits of human nature.

THE FAMILY

What present day social sophists appear to be unaware of is that the elemental behavior traits that characterize human beings have been in the process of development since those primeval times when the human family began to become a discrete unit in the management of *Homo's* societal mode of operation. One needs to analyze the nature of the family in enough detail so that an adequate understanding of how intimately every phase of the development of the family is bound up with the dynamics of the traits of human nature. We need not belabor the point that we are confronted now with a very disturbing social crisis in family life. This will be discussed in subsequent chapters. However, historically observed, a tremendous contraction of the size of the family has unrelentingly been occurring since primeval times. At present, this contraction cannot proceed further without the dissolution of the the basic family unit, the nuclear family, and exacerbation of the already critical problem of socialization of children, a problem concerning both emotions and traits of human nature.

The family came into being from the social need to control the disorder and violence created by unrestricted sexuality, which was disrupting the dynamics of productiveness of the economic life of the community and the care of children. Man's growing utilization of his cognitive powers led him to perceive that not only survival but also betterment of his condition of living was becoming a glimmer in his perception of the future: the incipient time-binding trait. The magnet of kinship relations was a heritage from his primate state. *Sensitivity* was becoming an increasingly more developed quality as the sense of the self-image–self-esteem trait became more distinct. The social organization of the primitive horde, except for its characteristic of *sharing*, was scarcely more accommodating to *Homo's* social organizational needs than his primate troop heritage. It was becoming clear that more order was becoming necessary if the improvement of social life was to be achieved. This introduced the awareness of some discipline in behavior—some *inhibitions* in the primate heritage of behavior—some control over the undisciplined sense of *jealousy*. Thus the human sense of *conscience* began to dawn. To start with, too much inhibition of the primate impulses to act would not be practical. To be expected, then, was for the control of sexuality to begin with the least individualized and least taxing impact on the existing primitive horde's social interrelations. These were necessarily endogamous[2] and on the strong side of kinship. This was the separation of the social group into generations between which sexual practice was first prohibited.

Thus began the first great revolution in human social history: the formulation of rules of individual behavior for controlling human sexuality. The impact of human emotions and application of human intelligence in determining human nature are here demonstrated by the dramatic augmentation of the already incipient trait for the need of a "unifying behavioral orientation." This trait was already in the incipient stage of development, being forged in the crucible of the forces of the *bonding and sharing* trait of human nature, which made the special characteristics of the primitive human horde possible.

The primitive human horde possessed the particular potentialities needed for the emergence of the primitive social organization eventually to become the human family. How this took place is still a moot question. Two things are sure when we examine the trend of family development in historical times: (1) There was observed a developmental change from the endogamous family to the exogamous family; and (2) the size of the family unit got increasingly smaller. As Lowie admits, "probably the most ambitious scheme of social evolution is that propounded in Lewis H. Morgan's *Ancient Society* (1876) with reference to family life and marriage."[3] This compliment is also accompanied by criticism. But this does not detract from the basic sweep of logic and detailed assemblage of vast amounts of data that still point to Morgan's work as the classic foundation for the study of the origin of the family.

Whether there ever was a Consanguine Family as posited by Morgan[4] and reaffirmed by Briffault (1927),[5] and strongly sustained against opponents of the theory by Thomson (1949),[6] this primordium of the family is asserted to have been composed of marriage groups arranged by generations. All grandparents were mutually husbands and wives, the same for their children and for their grandchildren. Engels observed that: "While the first step of organization consisted in excluding parents and children from mutual sexual intercourse, the second was the erection of a barrier between brother and sister."[7] The latter family organization was called by Morgan the Punaluan Family,[8] in which a series of natural or more remote brothers lived in mutual marriage with a number of women not their natural sisters. The constriction of the family continued as a social process. The next stage, according to Morgan, was the Pairing Family (also called by Morgan the Syndyasmian Family). It was founded upon marriage between single pairs, but without exclusive cohabitation. This marriage continued at the pleasure of the parties. Such an arrangement was too unstable to form the basis for solid social organization. But from it developed the practically universal unit of primitive social organization, the *gens*, based upon the bond of *kin*, in which intermarriage was prohibited. This was done to secure the benefit of marriage with unrelated persons.[9] Matrilineal descent in social organization gave way to patriliny at the juncture of the upper Paleolithic and the beginning of the Neolithic periods. The Patriarchal Family was founded upon marriage with several wives, followed, in general, by the seclusion of the wives.[10] The downfall of maternal law was stimulated by the development of the domestication of animals and, later, the invention of the use of slave labor. This brought into existence Monogamy, the first form of the family not founded on natural, but rather on economic conditions, resulting from the victory of private ownership over primitive and natural collectivism.[11] However, the highest state of Monogamy, as now practiced, is based on the love relations between the sexes.

EMOTIONS AS MOTIVATORS OF BEHAVIOR

The essential factors that drove forward the development of the family as an elemental human force in the social history of humankind were the same that gave shape to the nature of human nature—its traits. These traits of human nature are ceaselessly energized, pro-

voked, and expedited by the emotions, drives, affect-cognitive interactions, and affective-cognitive structures [discussed by Izard].

It needs to be emphasized that shaping of the traits of human
nature was not only the consequence of the reproductive physiology,
the human anatomy, and the symbolizing ability of man in relation
to his ecology, but also of the drives, emotions, affect-cognition interactions, and affective-cognitive structures.[12] The traits of human nature are the basic patterns of behavior that give character, recognizability,
stability, and a sense of permanence to the essential nature of human
society regardless of the differences in their cultures. The drives,
emotions, affect-cognitive interactions, and affective-cognitive structures are the motivators, the facilitators, the reinforcers, the exciters,
the energizers, and the invigorators of the positive and negative aspects
of the traits of human nature, depending on the structure function of
the social order and the individual peculiarities. If the ecology of the
social order becomes incompatible with the positive aspects of the traits
of human nature, this *loss* generates the negative influences of the
drives, emotions, affect-cognitive interactions, and affective-cognitive
structures to destabilize the physiological homeostasis and psychological equilibrium among the people. Depending on their tolerance
thresholds, the results may be psychosomatic or behavioral disorientations or both.

In this study, the traits of human nature are elaborated in detail
and their relation to the two most prominent types of social orders,
democracies and dictatorships, are brought into focus. However, the
traits of human nature manifest themselves as biphasic, the human
phase and the phylogenetic primate phase. When a trait of human
nature is expressed in the behavior of people, this expression is impossible without the affective and cognitive nature of people being
involved. For example, Polish workers, in expressing their trait of
human nature, the *freedom to choose*, chose to strike against long lines,
high prices, and lack of food at the end of the lines. In exasperation,
they expressed the freedom to choose, even though this type of freedom
was not supposed to be theirs by the nature of their present social
order. In expressing their freedom to choose, a tremendous impact of
emotions of distress, anger, fear, and contempt were generated. The
final action, to strike, was the result of the building up of these emotions to a point great enough in the people to gush over the threshold
of resistence to act. The government did not feel confident enough to
quell the strike with the finalty that would result in a bloodbath. This
set into motion most of the other traits of human nature, particularly
those relating to *challenge, striving to satisfy inclinations, prospecting*

on the future, justifying moral and ethical acts, and *engaging creative planning* for establishing a free trade union, which they dubbed Solidarity. The traits of human nature of the police and military authorities were also stimulated to respond to the situation, and a battery of emotions were triggered, but tempered with cognitive warnings, such as contempt, fear, and anger, moderated by cognitive calculations lest reprisals lead to uncontrolled bloodletting. the negative phase of the freedom-to-choose trait is exhorted in that the response to restrict the freedom to choose for the people is initiated by a course of action designed to smother the strike. In the case of the police and military, the *self-image–self-esteem* and the *challenge to prevail* traits were also brought into action.

OUTLINE OF EMOTION THEORY

In this study, the affective-cognitive factors will not be elucidated in the discussion of the traits of human nature, since the concentration is on the latter. However, the reader should be aware that it is practically impossible to express any trait of human nature without concomitantly involving affective factors. One of the very comprehensively presented theories of affective-cognitive behavior is the Differential Emotions theory of Carroll E. Izard elaborated in his book, *Human Emotions.* To give a concise outline of this theory is best done by paraphrasing his narrative.[13] Although this theory is concerned with personality, it at no time alludes to the nature of human nature. This could be due to the fact that traits are more socially oriented phenomena than personal while emotions are more personally oriented than social.

Personality, Izard states, is a complex organization of six subsystems: the homeostatic, drive, emotional, perceptual, cognitive, and motor systems. Each system has a degree of autonomy or independence, but all are completely interrelated. the homeostatic and drive systems are of primary importance in biological maintenance, reproduction, and regulation of body function. The homeostatic system is really a network of interrelated systems that operate automatically and unconsciously. Chief among these are endrocrine and cardiovascular systems, which are of importance to personality mainly through frequent interactions with the emotions system. Homeostatic mechanisms are considered auxiliary to the emotion system, but the hormones, neurohumors, enzymes, and other regulators of metabolism are important in regulating and sustaining emotion once it has been activated.

The drive system is based on tissue changes and deficits that create signals and provide information about bodily needs. The most common drives are hunger, thirst, sex, comfort (pain avoidance), fatigue, and sleepiness. Drives are obviously important when survival is at stake. These drives inevitably recruit and interact with emotions, and it is the subsequent drive-emotion interactions that often make sex and pain important for personality and behavior.

The four systems most important in personality, social interaction, and higher-order human functioning are the emotional, perceptual, cognitive, and motor systems. These four systems jointly form the basis for uniquely human behavior. Effective behavior derives from the harmonious interaction of these four systems. Ineffective behavior and maladjustment result when systemic interactions break down or become faulty.

The above abstraction from Izard pertains to subsystems in the makeup of the individual *human* being manifested as a unique *personality*. These components have a quality of specificity for the individual, while the components of human nature, the traits, have a quality of specificity for the *human race*. These are reflected within individuals in greater or lesser degree, depending on the personality. The traits of human nature give specific character to the whole human society and give distinct personal characteristics to individuals in varying proportion to their individual experiences in the process of their socialization, such as being gregarious, being egotistical, being selfish, being disposed to accept challenges, being innovative, et cetera.

Concerning Differential Emotions Theory, Izard posits that the six subsystems of personality generate four major types of motivation: the drives, emotions, affect-cognition interactions, and affective-cognitive structures. The drives resulting from tissue deficit or tissue change are usually cyclic in nature. Emotions are experiential-motivational phenomena that have adaptive functions independent of tissue needs. An affective-cognitive interaction is a motivational state resulting from the interaction between an affect or pattern of affects and cognitive processes. Such interactions are innumerable and vary with the particular person-environment transaction. Affective-cognitive structures are psychological organizations of affect and cognition—traitlike phenomena that result from repeated interactions between a particular affect or pattern of affects and a particular set or configuration of cognitions. A complex affective-cognitive structure or an interrelated set of them may constitute an affective-cognitive orientation, a more global personality trait, a trait complex, or a disposition, such as introversion. Any one of the four major types of motivation may dominate the individual and become for a time the primary determinant of behavior.

The emotions can give rise to a great diversity and complexity of motivational-experiential conditions. Such complexity is required to establish a framework for understanding both the personalities and the social interactions of human beings.

Izard lists ten fundamental emotions:

1. Interest-excitement	6. Anger-rage
2. Enjoyment-joy	7. Shame-humiliation
3. Surprise-startle	8. Fear-terror
4. Distress-anguish	9. Guilt-remorse
5. Disgust-revulsion	10. Contempt-scorn

He identifies five affective-cognitive structures or orientations:

1. Introversion-extroversion
2. Skepticism
3. Egotism
4. Vigor
5. Calmness-tranquillity

He identifies four categories of affect interactions, under which innumerable specific interactions are classified:

1. Emotion in relation to another emotion
2. Emotion in relation to drive
3. Emotion in relation to affective-cognitive structures
4. Emotion-cognitive interaction

That emotions play a critical role in the etiology of mental disturbance is a scientifically accepted principle. However, that it be the ultimate etiological cause or an accessory stimulus is still a moot point. Some hold that emotions are automatic and involuntary. Others hold that they are, for the most part, stimulated by the cognitive process, consciously or semiconsciously. According to Izard: "The principle of interaction systems* holds that the emotion system interacts with and

---

*The four systems most important in personality, social interaction, and higher-order human functioning, according to Izard, are the emotional, the perceptual, the cognitive and the motor systems.

influences the functions of the homeostatic drive, perceptual, cognitive, and actions systems. Harmonious interaction of subsystems facilitates health development and effective functioning."[14] Disharmony causes unhealthy development and problematic functioning. Izard further asserts that: "Experiments have shown that at least some people can self-generate emotion by means of affective imagery and expressive movements."[15] The newer school of psychopathology has elaborated extensively on this last observation of Izard; as Grieger and Grieger point out:

> Amidst this flux, perhaps no other phenomenon has had a greater impact on the field of psychopathology during the last two decades than the emergence of cognitive and cognitive-behavior psycho-therapy. . . . Basic to this movement is a large and growing body of literature on the cognitive basis of emotional and behavioral disorders. This theory is rich and varied, yet consistent in the view that people's psychological problems derive largely from conscious or partially conscious misconceptions and/or irrational ideas, beliefs, attitudes, or philosophies, not from the press of putative underlying personality structures in conflict. Put into the now-famous ABC theory or RET, the cognitive camp states that it is not the events we experience (at A) that determine how we react (at C), but rather our thoughts or ideas (at B) that do.[16]

The above theory of psychopathology and the behavioral process is in accord with the thesis of this book that human nature is a psychosocial-behavioral process and that cognition as understood by Izard and the Griegers is the controlling factor in the *human* aspect of behavior.

NOTES

1. Carroll E. Izard, *Human Emotions* (New York: Plenum Press, 1977), pp. 48–49.

2. George Thomson, *Studies in Ancient Greek Society: The Prehistoric Aegean* (New York: International Publishers, 1948), p. 44.

3. Robert H. Lowie, *Social Organization* (New York: Rinehart and Co. 1948), p. 33.

4. Morgan, *loco supra citato*, pp. 393–427.

5. R. Briffault, *The Mothers: A Study of the Origins of Sentiments and Institutions* (1927), pp. 614–781.

6. Thomson, *loco supra citato*, p. 70.

7. Friedrich Engels, *The Origin of the Family* (Chicago, Illinois: Charles H. Kerr and Co. 1902), p. 46.

8. Morgan, *loco supra citato*, pp. 433–54.

9. Morgan, *loco supra citato*, p. 389.

10. Ibid., p. 394.

11. Engels, *loco supra citato*, pp. 68–70.

12. Izard, *loco supra citato*, p. 44.

13. Izard, *loco supra citato*, pp. 44–47.

14. Izard, *loco supra citato*, p. 128.

15. Ibid., p. 129.

16. Russell Grieger and Ingrid Zachary Grieger, eds., *Cognition and Emotional Disturbance* (New York: Human Sciences Press, 1982), pp. 11–12.

15

Some Epidemiological Considerations about the Dynamics of Human Nature

IS HUMAN NATURE A RESEARCHABLE ENTITY?

People manifest a certain nature in their behavior because they are human beings. They manifest themselves as humane and vicious, lovable and hateful, aggressive and meek, bestial and angelic, sane and insane, destructive and creative, and so forth, like the contrarieties of Aristotle.[1] If we consider each pair of contrarieties like the positive and negative composite of a behavioral molecule, do these molecules have an organized structure as characterizes the structure of the physical world? And like the physiological domain of man concerning which biomedicine gives proof of molecular structure and function, does the human domain, i.e., the psychosocial behavioral manifestations, also have an organized dynamics? Is there a definite organizational pattern of man's basic behavioral spontaneity of reactivity to life's vicissitudes due to his potentials and the absolutely necessary social interrelations that must be maintained in order to survive and to better his lot as a sociocultural entity? Is this organizational pattern of behavior composed of behavioral traits reflecting the fundamental nature of man? Can these traits be individually identified, described, measured, and in some way even studied epidemiologically as behavior pattern that responds in a particular way to the structure and function of the ecosystem when the latter is in concordance or in discord with the individual traits of this human nature?

It is the thesis of this work that there are fundamental traits of human nature resulting from the specific patterns of behavior that *Homo* must resort to for physical survival and from specific patterns of interrelations that he has to adopt to secure continuity and betterment of social life. As an example of a trait is the morality-ethics trait, which is found in every conceivable cultural entity ever examined.

Montagu,[2] Fromm,[3] Cooley,[4] Korzybski,[5] Mead,[6] and Etzioni[7] have given strong arguments that human nature has structural dynamics. They even have described specific individual traits of human nature. They initiated the process of researching and analyzing the nature of human nature in order to do for psychosocial substance (man's cognitive processes resulting in behavior) what the physicists have been able to do for physical substance. To what extent were they aware of the ultimate potential and consequence of this process? Were they intent on developing a science capable of determining what needs to be done with the sociocultural structures and sociofunctional relations (i.e., *all* the significant social interrelational functions in the dynamics of the society) of a societal system in order to adjust this ecosystem to harmonize with the traits of human nature? Etzioni appears to display such intention. This is the crux of the problem of developing a sociology, psychology, and sociocultural anthropology that can help man to attain his greatest human potential and to maintain his psychosocial harmony with this potential so the process of untrammelled humanization becomes a reality of the future.

The lack of understanding the nature of human nature had led the International Congress of Mental Health in 1948 to formulate in the Text of the International Preparatory Commission Statement the following relativistic statement, as advocated by the anthropologist Herskovits, about human behavior: "It is therefore necessary to make clear that the concept of the plasticity of human beings is paralleled by, and interdependent with, a similar conception of plasticity of social institutions. The study of these institutions by sociologists has led along a path similar to that pursued by psychologists and psychiatrists. Just as the latter have shown that it is incorrect to assume the unchangeability of human behavior, so the former, starting from an entirely different point of departure, have shown that it is equally incorrect to say that patterns of human behavior can only find expression in certain unvarying forms."[8] The fundamental works of Cooley, Korzybski, and Mead were either forgotten or neglected or the trend toward relativism was so strong that the formulation of the above statement was inevitable even for such a prestigious body.

319

HUMAN NATURE AND ANIMAL NATURE

Human nature is different from animal nature. Animals have only animal nature. Humans have both a modified animal and a human nature. Thus man's animal nature is not the same as animal's animal nature. Such sameness is impossible, since animal nature and human nature in man are so indivisible that his animal nature of necessity has qualities unattainable in animals. In general use, the term "human nature" includes man's human as well as his primate behavior. Only for certain discriminatory purposes are they conceived separately.

Thus man, being a primate, inherited primate propensities, but as he was human, these propensities are manifested with modified human variance. For example, *competition*, which is another expression of *aggression*, is a primate characteristic, but in the human it has acquired a human quality tempered by man's cognitive processes to respond to challenges with a rationally developed competence. But this new trait cannot completely separate itself from the animal urge to compete with brute tenacity. Thus the human trait expresses itself with some degree of competition, but which when given rein can stimulate to extreme competitiveness. When the degree of competition is allowed to augment to a point of complete dominance over the human aspect of the trait, the reversion to primate behavior takes over. The results are winners and losers, which could adversely effect the whole community or society. The unrestricted exercise of this trait to boundaries beyond that of *human* behavior has allowed a whole social system, capitalism, to create social classes of the poor and the paupers and classes of the opulent, but also has allowed it to unleash powerful productive forces making possible an affluent society for all the people. An epidemiology of such social forces needs to be developed.

Being human means that human behavior has a unique quality of its own—a *humanity that predominates over animality*. Yet man has *both* dispositions to behave—his human behavior and his modified primate behavior. It is this battle—and a battle it is indeed—between these two opposite behavioral propensities that gives human behavior and, therefore, human nature their biphasic or dialectic nature. The human aspect, historically, predominates, due to man's cognitive processes being able to evaluate what is the most effective behavior for accommodating as humans to the essential conditions of existence. This concept of the nature of man's behavior is well expressed by Sahlins: "Yet the remarkable aspect of culture's usurpation of the evolutionary task from biology was that in so doing it was forced to oppose man's primate nature on many fronts and to subdue it. It is an extraordinary fact that primate urges often become not the secure foundation of human social life, but a source of weakness in it."[9] Although Sahlins refers to "culture" rather than "socio-culture," the statement applies perfectly.

CYBERNETIC EQUILIBRIUM

Thus man's psychosocial nature is expressed as the combined dynamic tensions between the human and primate forces in all the traits of humans as they respond to the particular ecosystem. In a sense, this resembles the dynamic equilibrium of the physiological processes elaborated by Claude Bernard and described by Dubos:

> More than a century ago, the French physiologist Claude Bernard asserted that . . . the constancy of the *milieu interieur* presupposes a perfection of the organism such that the external variations are at each instant compensated and brought into balance. . . . Not until the first decades of the 20th century, however, did insights into physiology and biochemistry enable us to identify some of the mechanisms that the body employs to correct departures from the ideal state and to maintain itself in a state of dynamic equilibrium. Walter B. Cannon, the Harvard physiologist . . . showed by physiological experimentation . . . the multifarious physiological and metabolic reactions that continuously adjust the internal composition of the body within safe limits. The limits are precisely defined for each organism. . . . The theoretical physicist Norbert Wiener, one of Cannon's contemporaries [described this process in these words]: "The apparent equilibrium of life is active equilibrium in which each deviation from the norm brings a reaction in the opposite direction, which is of the nature of what we call 'negative feedback.'" This cybernetic statement of homeostasis is of course quite consonant with Claude Bernard's view of stability of the *milieu interieur*. . . . Homeostatic mechanisms are the outcome of evolutionary adaptations, but because they emerged in response to the environmental challenges of the Paleolithic period some 750,000 years ago, they are better suited to the conditions of the past than to those of the present.[10]

Just as the *milieu interieur* was brought into balance with the *milieu exterieur* in the deep past, so did the complex of psychosocial responses that fitted *Homo* to a human existence come into being in the dim past and crystallize into a stable pattern of humanized behavior—the human nature. In that dim past, survival depended on ability to gather food, to provide shelter, to protect the group against a hostile environment, to raise children during their altricial period and until they became socialized, to develop tools and techniques to do all these things better, and to control the primate sex behavior in order to prevent the social dislocations that disturbed the pursuit of a rational process of humanized living. *Homo sapiens*, and probably *Homo erectus* to some extent, would have passed into paleolithic history tens of thousands of years ago if that race were unable to adapt its behavior to the above cited conditions of survival. But *Homo* had the brains and physical features to make the grade. If one examines which of the above conditions for survival (see also charts 1,2, and 3, in chapter 2) do not apply today for the human race, the answer must be loud and clear that *they all apply*. And that is the reason that the traits of human nature have remained so stable during man's history. Etzioni expresses this conclusion as follows: "What is becoming increasingly apparent is that to solve social problems by changing people is more expensive and usually less productive than approaches that accept people as they are and seek to mend not them but the circumstances around them."[11] Of course, the variations of cultures color the traits with their special overtones, but *basically* the traits are still the same. And like physiological processes, the ecosystem can disturb them while at the same time they can maintain a homeostatic condition up to their thresholds of tolerence, then pathology sets in or revolt against external conditions. Each individual has his own level of tolerance, and if the disturbance created by the ecosystem becomes too great, behavioral epidemics occur and sociopolitical turmoil may supervene. This is true when an ecosystem is in discordance with the traits of human nature, as when the *milieu exterieur* is in discordance with the physiological *milieu interieur*. Pertinent here for epidemiological study of behavior are the Manias described in Hecker's *Epidemics of the Middle Ages*, translated by B. G. Babington (1859).

WHAT IS HUMANNESS?

Historically, it is not accidental that primitive man looked upon human behavior that did not disrupt community life as normal. When this behavior was not in accordance with the local norms, the person was looked upon as possessed by an evil spirit. Biblical man looked upon behavior as guided by God or the Devil. This belief persists down to recent times. The psychosocial uniqueness of man has a biological basis—a highly developed brain and special physical features. This basis is purely potential. It does not determine the complex specific patterns of man's behavior any more than the foundation of a building determines its artistic or technical quality or the nature of the superstructure. The last paragraph of Sahlins's article on the origin of society is pertinent to this subject and is eloquently expressed. It is quoted by Nance in his interesting discussion of the Stone Age people the Tasaday: "In selective adaptation to the perils of the Stone Age, human society overcame or subordinated such primate propensities as selfishness, indiscriminate sexuality, dominance and brute competition. It substituted kinship and cooperation for conflict, placed solidarity over sex, morality over might. In its earliest days, it accomplished the greatest reform in history, the overthrow of human primate nature, and thereby secured the evolutionary future of the species."[12] In examining the above thesis, let us take as an example the sex nature of animals and man.[13] True enough, some humans behave like animals sexwise in a lot of ways and not just in sex matters. Not only is the estrous cycle different, but the qualities of the human family, which is sex-centered to a high degree, cannot be compared to the animal family when one considers the psychosocial aspects involved, i.e., the influence of cognition on behavior. Some sociobiologists shift the genetic behavior of animals to that of man. Wilson counsels the anthropologists that they need a discipline of anthropological genetics in order to understand the "human biogram" or what he designates as "human nature" in his later studies. He asks the question: "To what extent [does the human biogram] represent an adaptation to modern cultural life and to what extent is it a phylogenetic vestige?"[14] But he answers the question himself: "There is a need for a discipline of anthropological genetics. In the interval before we acquire it, it should be possible to characterize the human biogram by two indirect methods. First, models can be constructed from the most elementary rules of human behavior. . . . The rules can be legitimately compared with the ethograms of other primate species. . . . The other indirect approach to anthropological genetics is through phylogenetic analysis."[15] It is clear that to Wilson the "human biogram," which appears synonymous with the term "human nature" (which he does not even mention once in his opus magnum, *Sociobiology*) has a thorough genetic meaning. In his later work, *On Human Nature*, the latter term also has a thorough genetic meaning where he defines the term as "the full set of innate behavioral predispositions that characterize the human species."[16] Human nature to Wilson is as thoroughly genetic as animal nature. This point of view eliminates the humanness from the human being, for how can freedom to choose, a trait of human nature, be expressed in such a mechanistic framework? Wilson, however, affirms a certain sense of free will only because the nervous system is so complicated that it becomes indeterministic to the scientist's methods of delving into such a situation.[17] This is the way nineteenth-century mechanistic materialism eliminated the existence of the subjective substance known as the mind without invoking absolute denial of it.

THE NATURE OF HUMAN NATURE

Both phylogenetic and psychosocial factors are involved *intrinsically* in the nature of human nature, although cultural factors are *extrinsically* involved. For example, although man belongs in the phylum Chordata, member of his class, Mammalia, except for the very primitive Monotremes, are viviparous. But the singularly long and helpless infancy and childhood of the genus *Homo*, plus *Homo*'s highly developed neopallium, thumb-fingers opposition hand, unique voice-box structure, and bipedalism, compose the phylogenetic basis for the emergence of man's human nature, i.e., the complex of traits generated by his highly distinctive cognitive process in comprehending and devising ways to survive and develop. Thus the phylogenetic basis is not the direct genetic activator, for example, of man's moral-ethical trait of human nature. This force or *need* results from the circumstances in which man finds himself because he can imagine, understand, and plan, because he can evaluate and freely choose, because the survival of his offspring requires certain intimate acts of care, because his survival depends on his ability to trust his kin and kith, and because of a number of other essential sociofunctional interrelationships. The moral-ethical force does not manifest itself in the same configuration in every culture, yet every culture has an ethical-moral system that is affected by the cultural matrix of that particular culture. The culture, therefore, like genetics does *not* generate the moral-ethical trait. The culture merely gives the trait specific overtones, and the genetic potential makes the trait possible.

Human nature is man's pristine adaptation to a world in which survival and cultural development depend on his unique mental and physical powers to accommodate the frailties of the individual to the strength of group action and control. It is for this reason that *human nature is a potential behavioral characteristic of the individual human but the actual behavioral nature of the human group.* Various individuals express various traits of human nature to a greater or lesser degree, but for the group, *human nature is a constant and essential response to its conditions of living.* Thus human nature is predominantly and basically a social-psychological phenomenon of behavior of individuals in response to the very nature of the conditions of their social survival and struggles to better their conditions of existence. The focus of psychosocial, epidemiological studies should be thus directed. Glasser puts this in a very interesting way, actually going back to the Australopithecine period. Whether *Homo* had come into existence 3½ million years ago is still questionable, but the point made is valid:

> I call the earliest human society the *primitive survival society.* It lasted three-and-a-half million years. During that long period, man's primary goal in life was survival in a rigorous, often hostile, environment. He was able to survive because he cooperated intelligently with other members of the species in defending against predatory animals, in killing other creatures for food, in rearing the helpless human young, and in helping his fellows in myriad ways to overcome individual weaknesses. When men failed to cooperate with one another they suffered, and sometimes they died. During those several million years, the need for intelligent cooperation became built into the human nervous system by the normal evolutionary process of natural selection.[18]

This does not mean that specific genes are the bearers of the cooperative trait. It means that the whole human potential developed more and more to satisfy the need for cooperation.

EPIDEMIOLOGICAL OBSERVATIONS
FOR SOCIAL ENGINEERING

Human nature is where individual psychology blends into social psychology and sociology. It is the connecting link of these aspects of behavioral science. That is why it is best described as a psychosocial phenomenon. It is the area where social reformers and politicians should look to find solutions for social problems. It is the area to examine in order to find whether the social dynamics of the social system accommodate to the positive human aspects of the traits of human nature. A very basic aspect of human behavior that stems from the biophysiological and is a potent influence on psychosocial behavior is sexuality. The problem of violence in our society has prompted the Center for Disease Control to embark on epidemiological studies of violent deaths among young people. According to the reporting by the media, it appears that a substantial number of those deaths are sex-related. This brings us to the anthropological speculation of hominids' first social revolution as described by Sahlins:

> Sex is more than a force of attraction between adult males and females; it also operates among the young and between individuals of the same sex. Promiscuity is not an accurate term for it; it is indiscriminate. And while we might deem some of the forms perversions, to a monkey or an ape they are all just sociable. Sex is not an unmitigated social blessing for primates. Competition over partners . . . can lead to vicious, even fatal strife. It was this side of primate sexuality that forced early culture to curb and repress it. . . . This liberation of human society from direct biological control was its great evolutionary strength. Culture saved man in his earliest days. . . . The decisive battle between early culture and human nature must have been waged on the field of primate sexuality.[19]

This first hominid social revolution, which was stimulated by the need to control intragroup violence inherent in primate sexuality, took place as many as a million years ago. The last several decades has witnessed a tendency to lift these age-old inhibitions and to return to the "indiscriminate" sex practice of the primates. Therefore, if the original thesis of Sahlins about primate sex violence is correct, the statistics for the past several decades should show an increasing trend of sex violence and other criminal violence as sex-related. Other problems of sexuality are explored in the chapter "Democracy without Limits: Chaos."

Another area to examine is the complexity of modern political economy, which so confuses the observer with a myriad of extraneous factors that the true nature of *exchange* becomes difficult to observe. One must never forget that the forces of labor and capital, of strikes and lockouts, of trade deficits and balances, and of strong and weak dollars all stem from the *human* need to exchange—basically, the exchange of labor for the means to exist, although in the maelstrom of the socioeconomic superstructure, it seems to lose its moorings to its basic human origin.

The exchange process emerged into the ken of *Homo* as a humanizing step in the development of his bonding-sharing trait—sharing, at first, with the immediate family, which was held together by the phylogenetically humanized bond. As the hunting-gathering technology advanced and netted enough to share with other groups, a system of exchange came into being, later called the barter system. Exchange thus is an offshoot of human nature. This primordial system of exchange became the basis from which the dynamics of political economy evolved. This dynamic deals with the exchange of products (objectified labor) and labor time within a system of socioeconomic order that determines the distribution mechanism of the essentials and amenities for living.

This area of study, therefore, becomes the future instrument of political economy for accommodating a true people's economy to a really democratic political system, whereby the highest potential of social existence can be achieved. Basic psychosocial epidemiology must involve this factor. All the great reformers from Moses to Marx had some more or less amorphous sort of sensibilities of such a social state of existence as the nidus of their ideal. Some, like Moses and Christ, contributed the framework of moral-ethical norms of behavior; others, like Marx, gave an exposition of social forces that influence the field of political economy for creating the physical conditions for the thriving of human nature. Adam Smith liberated "exchange" from its primordial bonding-sharing nexus with such comsummation that was impossible under any other system. This liberation drove forward with unrelenting acceleration the development of the productive forces toward a theoretical infinity, unconcerned with the trail it leaves behind.

Human behavior and, therefore, human nature, to reiterate, have a genetic (phylogenetically developed) potential to respond to stimuli in certain patterns, be these stimuli internally or externally initiated. Human behavior also has a phenotypic potential, which is molded by the sociocultural experience of mankind. How much of human nature is genotypic and how much is phenotypic cannot be determined, since they are both indissolubly integrated and since man's behavior abstracted from society is experimentally impossible to attain. This, of course, does not mean that within the scientific technology for abstracting intimately occurring phenomena for studying degrees of knowledge about the nature of each force (the genotypic and phenotypic), relative quantification of each may not be attained. As an example of the nature of this problem, consider the following discussion by Newell-Smith of a citation from Piaget on justice: "What seems obvious is not always true, and Piaget found that in children 'the sense of justice' . . . is largely independent of these (parental) influences and requires nothing more for its development than the mutual respect and solidarity which holds among children themselves. It is often in spite of the adult and not because of him that the notions of just and unjust find their way into the youthful mind."[20] It is possible that this sense of the just is the result of childhood experience emerging from the early interplay of the bonding-sharing relations with the parents.

This illustrates the point that children are born with the brain potential to evaluate the immediate circumstances about them and adjust their position to such circumstances in order to prevent the violation of their well-being. They begin developing this ability in their relation to their parents from the moment they are born. In relation to other children, this potential impels them to arrive at an intergroup relationship that expresses itself as though it were an *independently* derived code of justice. Piaget's interpretation of this phenomenon as a sense of justice largely independent of parental influences is not really accurate, since what is inborn is the remarkable mind, the cognitive processes, which can recognize the self and what best agrees with this self. The citation is used to illustrate that a sense of judging values in relation to oneself and to others comes into being as the result of the interaction of life's circumstances. The remarkably resourceful mind in recognizing what is in concordance with the self is a trait of the nature of human beings.

An understanding of the traits of man's nature is basic to understanding the dynamics of man's behavior. Such an understanding is the essential knowledge required in order to fathom the process of how

$$\left.\begin{array}{l}\text{The complex of } \textit{specific} \\ \textit{traits} \text{ composing the} \\ \text{nature of human beings}\end{array}\right\} = \text{Human Nature} + \left\{\begin{array}{l}\text{concordant human} \\ \text{ecosystem} \longrightarrow \text{minimum} \\ \\ \text{discordant human} \\ \text{ecosystem} \longrightarrow \text{increased}\end{array}\right.$$

$\longrightarrow$ fear, frustration $\longrightarrow$ decreased anxiety $\longrightarrow$ well-oriented behavior

$\longrightarrow$ fear, frustration and aberrant cognition $\longrightarrow$ increased anxiety $\longrightarrow$ disoriented behavior

and what makes for the disorientation of people in a particular eco-system. If we have such knowledge, then we have arrived at the *initial position to start building a program* for correcting and eventually pre-venting the process that leads to anxiety, demoralization, and diso-rientation in a community of people. The chart summarizes this po-sition.

HOMEOSTATIC STRESS: THE ESSENCE OF LIFE

We come now to a very basic consideration of the relation of the ecosystem to the human nature: Is it possible to create an ecosystem that is in such concordance with the positive aspects of the traits of human nature and the inhibitions have so neutralized the negative aspects that complete harmony exists continually, endlessly? Luckily, such a state is impossible for a community of people. Why? Because if it were possible, it would be a catastrophic force for the deterioration, degeneration, and disappearance of the community. *Stress and adapt-ability within the threshold of maintaining mental and physical ho-meostasis are the essence of life.* An unused (unstressed) muscle or joint produces degeneration in the muscle and ankylosis in the joint. Un-stressed mental processes deteriorate the mind and disorient behavior. Contrariwise, stress and adaptability keep mind and body successfully alive. This is stated very well by Selye in the foreword to his distin-guished book on this subject: "Adaptability is probably the most dis-tinctive characteristic of life."[21] In his popular exposition on stress, he asserts that: "Stress is essentially the rate of all the wear and tear caused by life. . . . Although we cannot avoid stress as long as we live, we can learn a great deal about how to keep its damaging side-effects to a minimum. . . . Many common diseases are largely due to errors in our adaptive responses to stress. . . . In this sense many nervous and emotional disturbances, high blood pressure, gastric and duodenal ulcers, certain types of rheumatic, allergic, cardiovascular, and renal diseases appear to be essentially *diseases of adaptation.*"[22] These are really diseases of *mal-adaptation.* "Stress," Selye continues, "is not even necessarily bad for you; it is also the spice of life, for any emotion, any activity causes stress. But, of course, your system must be prepared to take it. The same stress which makes one person sick can be invig-orating experience for another. Life is largely a process of adaptation to the circumstances in which we exist." Stress produces damage, phys-ically and mentally, when it becomes greater or *lesser* than the body's threshold limits for maintaining dynamic equilibrium of the homeostatic processes. Adaptability, therefore, is possible only within limits, thereafter only if the ecosystem be changed.

As Selye[23] and Leighton[24] point out, interference with basic body responses may give way to error in our adaptive response to the stress generated, resulting in mental disorder. In a roundtable meeting sponsored by the Milbank Memorial Fund in 1959 to explore the epidemiology of mental disorders, much of the knowledge available about the causes and dynamics of mental disorders was discussed. Some of the conclusions are very interesting in that they support the thesis of this study, but in a way indicating that present-day understanding of the nature of human nature is one of the great obstacles in behavior research. For example, Dunham, a respected epidemiologist in the field of behavior, concluded that "persons who are firmly rooted and integrated in the culture of a community have a minimum probability of developing a functional mental disorder as compared to those who are not so well integrated [and the] areas of social disorganization produced disorganized persons and consequently more crime, delinquency, sickness, mental disorders, and suicide." Realizing the backwardness of the position of social scientists in the psychosocial field, he concluded that: "The task which the social scientists face here is to be able to show that certain stresses from a given position in the social structure make such an ingression into a given human experience that his mental content and behavior emerge in such bizarre forms that he cannot be fitted into the social structure at any point."[25] Dunham's solution is to find a spot in the structure where such disoriented people will fit instead of changing the causative condition in the structure which he already impugned.

THE NEED FOR STRUCTURE IN BEHAVIORAL SCIENCE

Dr. Leighton, of *My Name Is Legion* fame, chaired the above session and concluded that in all the foregoing discussion there "is the need for an explicit statement of the psychological frame of reference in thinking about *cause* [italics added]. . . . It might be wise to have clear concepts as to the framework of ideas as is the case in other forms of epidemiology with regard to infection, nutritional deficiencies, etc."[26] Dr. Leighton implied that if you deal with infection, to be effective you must have an understanding of microbiology and immunology and the pathways by which microbes get around, and if you deal with behavior, you should know the structure of human behavior, the nature of human nature, and the dynamics of its relationship to the specific item in the social structure in which people manifest their behavior. What Dr. Leighton had probably been thinking about was the contribution he had made to this subject in his two volumes of *My Name Is Legion.*

HUMAN NATURE AND THE ECOSYSTEM

Dr. Murphy's discussion of the subject was also productive of pertinent information: "What we have found is that in one type of social change situation, and only one, there is fairly unanimous agreement that those undergoing rapid change show more mental pathology than others from the same background undergoing less change.... Accordingly, I think we can say that the sum of the evidence is strongly in favor of the *associated factors* [italics added] theory, and strongly against the theory of social change as a general mental health hazard."[27] Thus Murphy correctly observed that it is not so much the social change that adversely effects behavior, but other associated factors to which he attributed etiological potency, such as "stability of family functioning," "social expectations," and "social assessment." These factors unwittingly refer to specific traits of human nature. For example, stability of family functioning is the soil in which the traits that envelop rootedness, bonding, trust, cooperation, love, ethics, and morality are rooted. In Murphy's words: "An unusually consistent finding is the fact that there is more likely to be an excess of mental breakdown in youth and in old age than in the years of adult maturity.... [C]hildhood appears to be unusually immune to pathological sequelae to broad social change ... provided only that they remain within their family and that the family, in its functioning, does not change.... Disturbances in children in wartime Britain were nearly always associated with the breaking up of the family."[28]

The following observation is an extension of what is involved in the above citations on family stability: "An interesting, general explanation can be hypothesized through the assumption that social change only has the possibility of creating mental disturbance when it occurs within what the individual perceives to be his 'own' or 'true' society."[29] What the individual perceives is really a feeling of whether the situation is in harmony with his nature and, unwittingly, with his human nature.

The time-binding trait of human nature expressed in the psychosocial motive called hope is alluded to in the concept of "social expectation": "One important social factor which I think can be deduced from the studies . . . is that of social expectations. . . . Social expectations are important here not only—and and not mainly—with respect to age roles, however; they probably are a significant factor in quite a number of other situations."[30]

The concept of "social assessment" refers to several traits of human nature, primarily to the need to appreciate one's self-image, but also to the normative trait, the need to perform competently, and, to some extent the time-binding trait is involved. Concerning this concept, Murphy states: "Closely allied to the factor of social expectation is that of social assessment. . . . Probably this mechanism of identification with society's assessment of one's group accounts for much of the marked difference in mental hospitalization rates which the East Indian demonstrates in different countries."[31]

Murphy realizes that when dealing with behavior, he is working with a set of values that are quite different from the quantitative, morphological data of biological phenomena. Behavior must have a unique structure and functional dynamics of its own, as is the case in the dynamics of the traits of human nature. Thus he asserts: "It must be admitted at this point that all the social factors which have been mentioned are ones which are not easily amenable to identification, comparison, or measurement by traditional epidemiological technique, and to move from the assessment of age as a factor to the assessment of values as a factor calls for a great technological jump. . . In the writer's opinion it is through similar attempts that this side of the epidemiology of mental disorders will have to advance."[32] He does not mention the important technology, the historical.

THE PSYCHOPHYSIOLOGICAL THRESHOLD

Murphy cites Hinkle and Wolff to affirm the latter's thesis as follows: " 'The great majority of the clusters of illness episodes that occurred in the lives of every group occurred at times when they perceived their life situations to be unsatisfying, threatening, overdemanding and productive of conflict, and they could make no satisfactory adaptation to these situations.' An important inference from this is that where a change in life situation occurred and a satisfactory mode of adaptation was discovered, no particular excess of illness developed. (It must be an inference at present, for in none of the published papers in the projects findings is this specifically demonstrated to be true)."[33] The reason why this latter inference will remain an inference and not be demonstrated to be true is because finding "a satisfactory mode of adaptation" is *not the critical issue*. When a situation is unsatisfactory and threatening and is causing clusters of illness episodes, it means that for a *certain* number of people, the impact of the situation over a certain lapse of time has broken down the *threshold* of their psychophysiological homeostasis. These people *can no longer adapt* to the situation except by some form of behavioral deviation. For example, some will probably develop schizophrenia. As Murphy points out, "one interpretation of schizophrenia is that it constitutes a pathological solution to a life problem."[34] He further states: "Schizophrenia tends to be increased in association with social change where there is an additional expectation to adapt to the change and no clear guide as to how to do so."[35] There is a tendency for psychiatrists, psychologists, and other psychosocial scientists to recommend adaptation solutions to people who develop mental illness. It is true that a small number of people can learn to further adapt to their vitiating situation. *Most people cannot change their psychophysiological threshold of homeostasis*. What they need is a change in the vitiating ecosystem in which they find themselves, i.e., a change of their ecosystem to put it in harmony with their traits of human nature. If psychiatric therapy were able to change the threshold of psychophysiological homeostasis, the extensive survey of the literature by Eysenck[36] certainly indicates the contrary.

The nature of human nature is an excellent example of how and why stress and tension are the normal state of the human being. The very fact that each trait of human nature is a biphasic tensional process between opposing forces, that every waking hour is a conscious struggle of the conscience to act human instead of as a modified primate, that no matter how favorable the ecosystem is for the expression of the human aspect of behavioral traits, the stress will still prevail, although ordinarily below the threshold in most cases for creating behavioral disorientation. The state of schizophrenia is a main escape route in many cases from the stress and tension that exceed one's threshold. Since mental and emotional stress cannot be excluded from living experience, our problem is to avoid the type and the amount of stress that produces the degree of anxiety disposed to generate behavioral disorientation.

ANXIETY

What is anxiety? Branch states concerning this term: "Anxiety has been defined in various ways: as, for instance 'a specific unpleasurable state of tension which indicates the presence of some danger to the organism', or as 'the apprehensive tension or uneasiness which stems from anticipation of imminent danger, in which the source is largely unknown or unrecognized'. However it may be described, the unpleasantness of anxiety is invariably stressed. . . . Anxiety not only warns the individual that 'something is wrong' but generally goads him into seeking out the source of danger so that it can be eliminated. In moderate degree, anxiety can be termed a constructive force, serving to increase alertness and effort."[37] From this point of view, anxiety could be an effective force in reinforcing the "challenge" aspect of the "social-role performance" trait of human nature, in which challenge is dominant in the positive aspect of this trait. The importance of anxiety is stated by May: "Every alert citizen in our society realizes, on the basis of his own experience as well as his observations of his fellow-men, that anxiety is a pervasive and profound phenomenon in the middle of the twentieth century. . . . Hence to endeavor to 'prove' the pervasiveness of anxiety in our day is as unnecessary as the proverbial carrying of coals to Newcastle."[38]

PRIMARY PREVENTION OF BEHAVIORAL DISORIENTATION

The problem we have, therefore, as social scientists, health scientists, social planners, political scientists, politicians, statesmen, and informed citizens is to generate the knowledge to enable humankind to choose intelligently what needs to be done to the ecosystem to render it as harmonious as possible to the human behavioral needs rather than support the expression of the primate impulses that still are part of man's nature, and which can vitiate the ecosystem against the traits of human nature. Let us, at least, devote an equal share of our energies to support the positive aspects of human nature as we are expending on safeguarding the physical features of our ecosystem. This does not mean that the primate impulses are altogether destructive of life. It means that primate traits of primate nature are good for primate society. It means that, as humans, we must choose to live in a human society and not a primate society, and to do so most effectively, the ecosystem must be tilted toward encouraging the expression of the human rather than the primate impulses in the population. However, during crises such as wars, the primate traits may serve us amply. How must the ecosystem be modified to succeed in effecting such accommodations?

Unless we conceive the process of the development of human behavior in the above pattern, there can be no logical methodology for primary prevention of behavioral disorientations in a community of people, such as juvenile delinquency. The questions, then, are to begin with:

Can we determine the specific traits of human nature? If so, then,

Can we determine the specific types of sociocultural patterns of interrelationships among people that are concordant with the traits of human nature? If so, then,

Can we mold those sociocultural interrelations into program patterns that, when applied to society, will be concordant with the traits of human nature? What are the techniques, the methodologies, to accomplish this?

THE USSR: THE LABORATORY TO TEST BEHAVIORAL THEORY AND SOCIOFUNCTIONAL RELATIONS

The laboratory to test the validity of the thesis of the concordant or discordant relations between the traits of human nature and the ecosystem is the place where the ecosystem has been changed and then observe the results on the behavior of the people in comparison to its history and to other social orders. The Soviet Union is such a laboratory, and it will be compared here to the American experience. Let me cite a perceptive observation by the father of modern socialist theory—a quotation that illustrates the functioning of several traits of human nature and brings to mind basic elements of political, economic, and psychological fundamentals: "Man makes his own history, but he does not make it out of the whole cloth; he does not make it out of conditions chosen by himself, but out of such as he finds close at hand. The tradition of all past generations weighs like an Alp upon the brain of the living. At the very time when men appear engaged in revolutionizing things and themselves in bringing about what never was before, at such very epochs of revolutionary crisis do they anxiously conjure up into their service the spirits of the past. . . . "[39]
This profound statement by Karl Marx has not been understood to its depths by the greatest practitioners of his philosophy. It appears that these practitioners have latched onto the first part of the statement about man making his own history in order for them to justify their revolutionary efforts, but have thoroughly misunderstood, disregarded, or misapplied the latter part of the statement about tradition and

conjuring up the past into their service. For them, the revolution is actually and primarily made for bread to fill the stomach and for more property to secure the future filling of the stomach. This certainly is all to the good. The changes in the interrelations between the means of production and production relations were supposed to do the rest of the task in changing people themselves into more human "human beings." The stomachs are indeed being filled, but that the people have been transmuted into a higher state of humanity by having changed the relation between the means of production and the production relations is a real disappointment. Why this disappointment? The disappointment arises from the fact that supplying more food and property (land and means of production) to the people does change their physical status of health and their states of fear, anger, and anxieties about some, particularly economic, aspects of their condition of existence, but does not necessarily change to the good all the sociofunctional relations (i.e., *all* basic social interrelational functions in the dynamics of the society) in the new social order so as to accommodate to all the traits of human nature. That the process of social production, i.e., the interaction of the productive means and the production relations in the pursuit of creating the material means for carrying on community life, is *one* of the *two basic social processes* is indisputable. But the other one, the process of the behavioral dynamics, is just as basic in generating the changes in sociofunctional relations in order to be in concordance with the traits of human nature. Both of these processes form a single population process, which forms the ecosystem of the social order. The sociofunctional relations, of course, include production relations,[40] but also all the other basic social interrelations, including those generated by legislation, litigation, adjudication, etiquette, customs, bureaucracy, and, very basically, by the moral-ethical code, much of which has up to the present been taught by religion. Basic sociofunctional relations are incorporated in and controlled by law, i.e., social control by government in order to prevent chaos—even such chaos resulting from oppressive government.

Having control of the means of production and production relations does put the people in a position to change the ecosystem to accommodate it to all the traits of human nature. But changing the interrelations between the production relations and the means of production does not guarantee that the interrelations between the human ecology and the traits of human nature will be changed enough to effect a state of concordance between them, thus preventing the disorientation of human behavior. Sixty years after the Russian revolution, dissidence among the people has not disappeared, traditional anti-Semitism has been brought into the service of the government through the back door, behavioral disorientations are still a heavy part of the social milieu, and alcoholism has reached a critical level.[41] Almost three decades after the Chinese revolution, their cultural revolution to change the behavior of people was a disaster. At least the Chinese political leaders realized that something went awry with that aspect of their revolution. It would be a happy circumstance if they realized what really went wrong—that instead of trying to change the human nature of the people, they should have tried to adjust their ecosystem to their human nature. The leadership of the USSR are making the same mistake.

Dictatorship and Human Nature

Considering that the nature of man is an intimate, indissoluable interpenetration of his general genotypic and specific phenotypic characteristics that include the relative freedom to make his own history and the specific elemental ecological influences that impinge upon him, Marx's statement that "man makes his own history" is more profound than the practitioners of Marxism generally acknowledge. Not only can social revolution change the social system by changing the relations between the forces of the means of production and the forces of production relations, but those who have gained control of the social forces could, if they understood the need and had the perspicacity, mold the social milieu to become consonant with the specific traits of human nature. The ecosystem should not only be changed enough to be tractable in supplying the physical needs of the body and the educational needs to nourish whatever technology the new society needs to continue to develop the productive process, but should also minister to the psychosocial needs of the people. Human behavior is a plastic essence of man, but not altogether formlessly plastic as a sculptor's clay. The human-nature aspect of human behavior has specific durable form regardless of culture. Each culture, however, engraves its imprint on the human nature of its people. From this point of view, *man can not only make his political-economic history,* but he must also pilot the establishment of salutary social relations to secure his *psychosocial* history. The leadership of the USSR have expected that the political-economic changes would take care of that. China believed otherwise and launched its disastrous, misconceived Cultural Revolution, which violently offended the traits of human nature by doing in the wrong way what needed to be done. The USSR's continuing problems in relation to workers' productiveness, alcoholism, and human rights problems that relate to the violation of "the traditions of all past generations [which] weigh like an Alp upon the brain of the living," is testimony to its leadership's insensibility to the psychosocial needs of the Soviet people. Among those "traditions" are, indeed, the psychosocial needs of the traits of human nature. Tradition has a psychosocial essence and a cognitive process patterned by the traits of human nature and the existing culture. This becomes the psychosocial heritage that weighs like an Alp upon the brain of the living.

Marxian theorists and practitioners become blinded by constantly repeating to themselves the crusade-cry that by changing the social order into a socialist dictatorship so that *material* security would pervade the ecosystem, the behavior of the people would change in time to fit the new economic-political system. Such optimism negated the need for a science of sociology in a socialist country, since the psychosocial needs are assured by the new social order. It was, therefore, not until around 1956 that the Soviet political leaders were painfully awakened to the validity and need of a science of sociology and psychosociology or social psychology.

Examples of the dictatorship methodology for shaping the personalities of people to the pattern of the dictatorship and how these methods are futile because they are in discord with the traits of human nature are given by Mikhail Tsypkin in the *Bulletin of the Atomic Scientists* in discussing the Soviet program of military conscription: "Thus, like the great majority of Soviet citizens, servicemen have no access to non-technical Western publications. To prevent enlisted men from listening to foreign radio broadcasts they have to surrender their radios to their non-commissioned officers, who return them on Sundays and holidays. The prohibition against listening to foreign radio broadcasts is such that even radio operators are afraid to receive anything but Soviet broadcasts. No precaution is considered excessive."[42] The restrictions practiced to prevent the public from becoming acquainted with the ideas of the outside world was, up to Brezhnev's regime, also practiced by ideological interference in the theoretical elaborations and interpretations of scientists. However, under Brezhnev, philosophical restrictions on scientists were relaxed, but was more than matched "by a tightening of political controls over the extra-scientific activities of scientists."[43] These restrictions, now in practice well over a half-century, have not essentially changed the reactions of the Soviet people when compared to reactions of Western people placed under similar restrictions. The Soviet system, which was supposed to mold a nation of new personalities, as China's Cultural Revolution was supposed to do, has not changed the human nature of the Soviet people from what that nature was under the czar. The dictatorship of the czar was different, but in its very essence was the same. There have been cultural modifications of these responses, to be sure, but the trait, for example, of freedom to choose still elicits mental, emotional, and physical counteractive responses to the the restrictions of dictatorship, even though the people have been inculcated with the idea that this is their dictatorship.[44,45,46,47] There is indeed a need to distinguish between the Marxian theoreticians and political practitioners, on the one hand, and Soviet scientists, on the other. The Soviet social scientists, like the physical scientists, operate by what is considered, universally, the scientific methodology, except when interfered with by the political theoreticians and practitioners as was done in the past, particularly under the regimes of Stalin and Khrushchev. The following statement is from a letter to the president of the Academy of Sciences of the USSR by a group of Soviet dissident scientists in October 1976: "In the past, in their most extreme . . . manifestations, infringements on the rights of scientists have repeatedly developed into a direct struggle with science. For a long period in the Soviet Union, the theory of relativity and quantum mechanics was regarded with suspicion; cybernetics was opposed; and genetics and contemporary biology were violently persecuted."[48] The political buffeting of science by dictatorial agents is illustrated by the following observations: "Chinese enthusiasm for plate tectonic theory may have a political component, however; Soviet geology has been a bastion of resistance to plate tectonic concepts, and Chinese scientists are known to have no wish to emulate their Soviet rivals."[49] The political use of psychiatry is another illustration: "The World Psychiatric Association took action in the last week of August 1977 in which the Soviet Union was condemned for alleged abuse of psychiatry for political purposes. The resolution was bitterly fought by the Soviet members."[50]

Except for such subject matter as "eradication of class distinction," "bringing physical and mental workers together," and "equalization of the economic and cultural conditions of urban and rural districts,"[51] the subject matter of researchers is practically the same as for sociologists in the capitalist world. Even the above exceptions are not strange subjects for social scientists in the United States and the rest of the Western world. In the Western world, however, the study of human nature is much more implied and even denoted as subject matter for study than in the socialist world. The reason is quite clear. The Soviet social scientists regard sociology as the study of how to best attain a communist society as that society is conceived by their leaders. Such a humane aim is generally similar to that of sociologists in capitalist countries, except that the idea of "communist society" is substituted for by the idea of "capitalist democracy." It appears that the Soviet social scientists' studies are aimed at developing ways to fit the Soviet people into the particular Soviet economic and political version of a Marxian socialist system, instead of how to create a society in which the psychosocial relations as well as the production relations are in harmony with the traits of human nature under a democratic form of socialism. The aim of the Soviet social scientists is no less the aim of American social scientists, except that the latter relate to the social order called capitalist democracy. The impression is also given that when the real state of communism based on the Marxian ideal is attained, there will be no further need for sociology, since such a state of existence, being a living theory, will negate the need for more theory. Such a state of existence can, however, never be attained, since it is inconceivable that culture will take on a state of suspended animation under communism and therefore no accommodation to change will ever be necessary again. Man's nature will not automatically accommodate to the social interrelations of a dictatorship maintained over such a long period of time. Man has a remarkable ability to adapt to unsuitable conditions, but always at the expense of the mental health of those individuals whose psychosocial homeostasis could not stand the strain. The *contingent* sociocultural patterns of behavior of accommodation to the Soviet system will slowly change into patterns to fit the new state of affairs. But the *essential* traits of human nature could not accommodate to the social strictures that have been created by dictatorship and have no more affinity to socialism than Nazism has to to Karl Marx's Marxism.

Human nature cannot be *molded*, but only accommodated temporarily, to any system of socialism, communism, national socialism, capitalism, or any other system. This is so unless the particular system has built-in mechanisms for accommodating to the traits of human nature. These mechanisms must be able to prevent "my" party, "my" group, "my" theory of government, or "my" thirst for self-aggrandizement (power) from prevailing against the majority will. The latter "mys" are, of course, manifestations of the negative (primate) forces of human nature prevailing over the positive (human) forces. Each government system is operated by a particular political organization, and each such organization has to be led by people who have biphasic traits of human nature and therefore have tendencies to want to remain in power. In order for these organizations to stay in power, social strictures will have to be created that will be in discord with the traits of human nature. It may not be the economic system that will be the problem, but the political organization (the state) that it fosters in order to keep the elite of its vanguard in power that is always the problem for attaining an ideal state of human existence. This is not different with the Soviet "power elite."[52] People give up power reluctantly. Dictatorships (states) of the people have the tendency to become dictatorships *over* the people, as Rosa Luxemburg, the admirable revolutionary, alluded to before her untimely death during the revolution in Germany in 1919.[53] This brings up the seemingly eternal question: How long must the Leninist dictatorship, such as exists in the Soviet Union, last in order to begin the Marxist process of the "state withering away" to a system of democratic socialism or communism? After two-thirds of a century, the dictatorship is stronger, more audacious as a dictatorship, and just as violent against dissenters as when the dictatorship began. Is it the "party" that is clinging to power or an elite group within the party that abhors democracy—for only from an atmosphere of democratic government is it possible for a "state" to wither away, but never from the milieu of dictatorship.

Etzioni, a very competent sociologist, reluctantly agrees that "social scientists like myself have begun to re-examine our core assumption that man can be taught almost anything and quite readily. We are now confronting the uncomfortable possibility that human beings are not easily changed after all. . . . Here the two assumptions about the pliability and perfectibility of human nature come into sharp focus."[54] The use of psychiatric therapy to force conformance to a particular political creed will be unsuccessful for all the foregoing reasons. And, for the same reasons, psychiatrists are unsuccessful in treating behavioral disorientations.

What is the best type of political organization that will allow for the "withering away" of power-seeking factions (who act out the negative aspects of several traits of human nature in many instances)? The answer will be found when the people insist that political organization be based on knowledge of the dynamics of the human and primate aspects of the traits of human nature, when this knowledge is applied in establishing specific norms of behavior for their leaders, and when these norms are implemented with zeal.

POLITICS, GOVERNMENT, AND FACTION DYNAMICS

At this point, it would be well to quote Lovejoy, who, in discussing human nature in relation to politicians, stated: "*How*, by means of what political device, could you bring creatures whose wills were always moved by irrational and depraved passions to behave in ways which would not be inconsistent with the 'common good'? There were several proposed solutions to the problem; the one which here concerns us and which was to play an extremely influential part in eighteenth-century political thinking was the method of counterpoise."[55] This, as Lovejoy points out, is the method recommended by Alexander Pope in his famous poem *Essay on Man*. This method, Pope expounds, is composed of two presuppositions—one that "men's actions are always prompted by their passions, not by their reason"; the other that "though these conflicting passions cannot be got rid of, they can be so combined and made to counteract one another that the total result will be social peace and order."[56] " . . . The chief framers of the Constitution of the United States . . . accepted the same two presuppositions and sought to apply them, for the first time in modern history. . . . That theory was unmistakably set forth in what has come to be the most famous of the *Federalist* papers (No.10), written by James Madison, the member of the Convention who, I suppose, now generally admitted to deserve, if any one member can be said to deserve, the title of 'Father of the Constitution'. . . . In Madison's words: 'The great menace to government on the popular model is the spirit of faction' (faction meaning a number of citizens united and actuated adversely against the rights of other citizens)."[57] "There are two conceivable 'methods of curing the mischiefs of factions: the one, by removing its causes, the other, by controlling its effects'. The first method, however, is wholly inconsistent with popular government; you could abolish factions only by totally abolishing the 'liberty' of individual citizens. . . . 'The *latent causes of factions are sown in the nature of man*. [italics added] . . . As long as the reason of man continues fallible, and he is at liberty to exercise it, different opinions will be formed. . . . As long as the connection subsists between his reason and his self-love, his opinions and his passions will have a reciprocal influence upon each other.' "[58] Thus the framers of the Constitution chose the method of counterpoise, sometimes referred to as the check and countercheck method. The separation of government into the executive, legislation, and judicial branches represents the U.S. method of counterpoise to control the effects of faction. The dictatorships were the methods chosen by most of the socialist countries to control the cause of faction. As we unravel the nature of the traits of human nature in detail, it will become evident that the way of the American Constitutional Convention of 1787 was the method resulting in lesser discord with the traits of human nature, even though in the process of economic development it may have caused greater *physical* suffering of the population. The pity, of course, is that obstacles developed in the American political-economic scene that obstructed the exploitation—the taking advantage—of the counterpoise method in creating a much more salutary atmosphere for the traits of human nature than has been rendered to date. Ideally, the counterpoise system is supposed to prevent the assumption of power to concentrate too predominantly in any *faction* of society. The two main reasons that it has not worked too well in the United States are that we have allowed: (1) industrial monopolies to develop and to control government action, (2) money (as distinguished from capital) in the hands of a faction to wield power not necessarily for the "common good." (Monopoly dynamics is discussed in other chapters.) Let me illustrate the difference between money, capital, and wealth. *Wealth* is the most general term, which subsumes the content of the other two terms, i.e., it is the abundance of valuable material possession or resources. *Capital* is that part of wealth described as the accumulated goods that are devoted to the production of other goods. It is as Marx described it the most creative instrument of *material* social development. Basically, of course, it is an accumulation of crystallized social labor. *Money* is a measure of value of wealth used as a medium of exchange or payment.

The money cult in the United States has been depreciating the traditional work ethos, which has built the greatest material culture in world history. In this milieu, a "get-something-for-nothing gusto" is being generated in an ever increasing portion of the population. This description does not refer to the profit modality of the economic system as long as it remains within the socially recognized limits of what is perceived as traditionally valid and just. One does not need to possess a too fertile fantasy-provoking mentality to imagine how the following social devices are products of the money-cult-get-something-for-nothing-work-depreciating ethos (which vicariously is being translated into the consumer's cult):

1. The increasing dependence of people on the government to *donate* for *free* more and more of their basic requirements and amenities without contributing to the production of any wealth. This has no relation to the aid for legitimate dependency.
2. The increasing expectancy and condonation that politicians are corrupt and politics is a mechanism of self-aggrandizement.
3. The use by special interests or factions of bribery devices including corrupt methods of lobbying.
4. The trend of increasing financial manipulations in order to obtain enough money to run for an elective office in government.

5. The increasing ineffectiveness and indifference in controlling the devious financial practices of monopolies, conglomerates, and cartels and the use of tax shelters.
6. The circuitous judicial practices in the process of sentencing (including endless periods of litigation) and pardoning of known unrehabilitated and unrehabilitatable criminals.
7. The acceptance by government of the rip-off system as normal economic practice in the commodity exchange process.
8. Allowing the income practices of capital and labor to contend without restraint, thus leading to pricing American goods out of competition on the world market.

There are many more flagrant examples. The money-cult system in the United States can eventually lead to the decline of American democracy, unless the genius of the American people will devise and implement a system of Madisonian countervalences to prevent money from operating as a disrupting and corrupting cult in our ecosystem against the creation of conditions harmonious to the traits of human nature. The latter does not relate to the legitimate uses of capital.

Any true epidemiological understanding of health and disease and of risk factors threatening the social well-being, but in particular the psychosocial well-being, of a community must rest on such basics as the nature of the social order's political economy, the relation of the latter's dynamics to the traits of human nature, pinpointing the particular factors that are in discord with the traits, and researching the mechanisms for change, if that be necessary. Structure and dynamics of all the socioeconomic interrelations in an ecosystem must be studied and understood in detail for effective epidemiological work on the psychosocial phenomena of an ecosystem.

The psychosocial thesis expounded above for an epidemiology in behavior science comes at a time when medical scientists in this area admit their almost complete perplexity, but do seem to imply an acceptance of an approach as here presented:

> Insofar as the causes of mental disorder lie buried at the roots of our society, the development of preventive psychiatry must attend, not only on scientific advance, but upon a complex process of political, economic and socio-cultural change. It must be said that observation of current political and social trends leave few grounds for easy optimism.

From this standpoint, the long-term future of epidemiological research in psychiatry can be seen to rest less with technological progress than with the growth of a philosophy of medicine which views the sickness of individuals in relation to the health of communities and regards disease prevention as perhaps the single most important field for the application of scientific methods to humanitarian ends.[59]

NOTES

1. Aristotle, *The Works of Aristotle Translated into English* (Oxford Press, 1930) Physica, Book 1. 6, 189a.

2. M. F. Ashley Montagu, *Anthropology and Human Nature* (Boston, Massachusetts: Porter Sargent Publ., 1957).

3. Erich Fromm, *The Sane Society* (New York: Rinehart and Co., Inc., 1955).

4. Charles H. Cooley, *Human Nature and the Social Order* (New York: Charles Scribner and Son, 1902).

5. Alfred Korzybski, *Manhood of Humanity* (New York: E. P. Dutton and Co., 1921).

6. George H. Mead, *Mind, Self, and Society* (Chicago, Illinois: University of Chicago Press, 1934).

7. Amitai Etzioni, *The Active Society* (London: Collier-Macmillan Ltd., 1968).

8. *International Congress on Mental Health, 1948,* volume 4: *Proceedings of the International Conference on Mental Hygiene, International Preparatory Commission Statement* (New York: Columbia University Press, 1948), p. 290

9. M.D. Sahlins, "The Origin of Society," *Scientific American* (September 1960), pp. 76–87.

10. Rene Dubos, "Health and Creative Adaptation," *Human Nature* (January 1978), pp. 74–82.

11. Amitai Etzioni, "Human Beings Are Not Easy to Change After All," *Saturday Review* (June 3, 1972), pp. 45–47.

12. John Nance, *The Gentle Tasaday* (New York: Harcourt Brace Jovanovich, 1975), p. 134.

13. Peter Farb, *Humankind* (New York: Houghton Mifflin Co., 1978), p. 33.

14. E. O. Wilson, *Sociobiology* (Cambridge, Massachusetts: Harvard University Press, 1975), pp. 548, 550–551.

15. Ibid., pp. 550–551.

16. E. O. Wilson, On Human Nature (Cambridge, Massachusetts: Harvard University Press, 1978), pp. 217–218.

17. Ibid., p. 7.

18. William Glasser, "The Civilized Identity Society," *Saturday Review* (February 19, 1972), pp. 26–31.

19. Marshall Sahlins, "The Origin of Society," *Scientific American*, vol. 203, no. 3, (September 1960), pp. 88–96.

20. Jean Piaget, *The Essentials of Piaget*, edited by H. E. Gruber and J. J. Vonèche (New York: Basic Books, 1977) pp. 186–93.

21. Hans Selye, *Stress* (Chicago, Illinois: ACTA Foundation, 1950), foreword.

22. Hans Selye, *The Stress of Life* (New York: McGraw-Hill Book Co., 1956), pp. vii–viii.

23. Ibid.

24. Alexander H. Leighton, *My Name Is Legion*, vol. 1 (New York: Basic Books, 1959), p. 136.

25. *Milbank Memorial Fund, 1961, Social Structure and Mental Disorders: Competing Hypotheses of Explanation*, H. Warren Dunham, pp. 245–46, 259.

26. Ibid., p. 278.

27. Ibid., H. B. M. Murphy, *Social Change and Mental Health*, pp. 309–10.

28. Ibid., pp. 310–11.

29. Ibid., p. 312.

30. Ibid., p. 316.

31. Ibid., p. 317.

32. Ibid., pp. 319–20.

33. Ibid., p. 320.

34. Ibid., p. 318.

35. Ibid., p. 323.

36. Hans J. Eysenck, "The Effects of Psychotherapy," *International Journal of Psychiatry*, vol. 1, no. 1 (January 1965), pp. 99–142.

37. C. H. Hardin Branch, *Aspects of Anxiety* (New York: J. B. Lippincott Co., 1968), p. 9.

38. Rollo May, *The Meaning of Anxiety* (New York: Ronald Press, 1950), p. 3.

39. Karl Marx, *The Eighteenth Brumaire of Louis Bonaparte* (Chicago, Illinois: Charles H. Kerr and Co., 1913), p. 9.

40. Klaus-Friedrich Kock, "A General Theory of Law, a Book Review of Donald Black's *The Behavior of Law*," vol. 197 (July 8, 1977), pp. 149–50.

41. Boris M. Segal, "Psychiatry and Psychology in the U.S.S.R.," in Samuel A. Corson, ed. *Drinking Patterns and Alcoholism in Soviet and American Societies* (New York: Plenum Press, 1976), pp. 183–201.

42. Mikhail Tsypkin, "The Conscript," *Bulletin of the Atomic Scientists*, vol. 39, no. 5 (May 1983), pp. 28–32.

43. Loren R. Graham, "Science in the Brezhnev Era," *Bulletin of the Atomic Scientists*, vol. 38, no. 2 (February 1982), pp. 23–28.

44. Marshall L. Goldman, "The Economy and the Consumer," *Bulletin of the Atomic Scientists*, vol. 38, no. 4 (April 1982), pp. 24–27.

45. David E. Powell, "Social Trends and Social Problems," *Bulletin of the Atomic Scientists*, vol. 38, no. 9 (November 1982), pp. 19–25.

46. "Soviet Succession and Policy Choices, *Bulletin of the Atomic Scientists*, vol. 38, no. 9 (November 1982), pp. 49–54.

47. D. Gale Johnson, "Agriculture—Management and Performance," *Bulletin of the Atomic Scientists*, vol. 39, no. 2 (February 1983), pp. 16–22.

48. *FAS [Federation of American Scientists] Public Interest Report*, November 1976, p. 11.

49. Deborah Shapley, "Chinese Earthquakes: The Maoist Approach to Seismology," *Science*, vol. 193, no. 4254 (August 20, 1976), pp. 656–657.

50. *Washington Report on Medicine and Health*, September 1977.

51. G. Osipov and M. Yovchuk, "Some Principles of Theory, Problems, and Methods of Research in Sociology in the USSR: A Soviet View," in Alex Simirenko, (ed.), *Soviet Sociology* (New York: Quadrangle Books, 1966), pp. 298–305.

52. Mark R. Beissinger, "The Power Elite," *The Bulletin of the Atomic Scientists*, vol. 38, no. 8 (October 1982), pp. 24–31.

53. David Mitchell, *1919: Red Mirage* (New York: The Macmillan Co., 1970), p. 180.

54. Amitai Etzioni, "Human Beings Are Not Very Easy to Change after All," *Saturday Review*, (June 3, 1972), pp. 45–47.

55. Arthur O. Lovejoy, *Reflections on Human Nature* (Baltimore, Maryland: Johns Hopkins Press, 1961), p. 41.

56. Ibid., pp. 42–43.

57. Alexander Hamilton *et.al.*, *The Federalist Papers* (New York: New American Library, 1961), pp. 77–84.

58. Lovejoy, *supra cite*, pp. 47–48.

59. Brian Cooper and H. G. Morgan, *Epidemiological Psychiatry* (Springfield, Illinois: Charles C. Thomas, 1973), p. 172.

16

Democracy without Limits: Chaos

AMERICAN DEMOCRACY AND HUMAN NATURE

The strengths of democracy are well established. However, the one great weakness of democracy is its tendency to allow its politically most popular behavior trait, that of "freedom to choose," to express itself to the limits of uninhibited, self-indulgent permissiveness, appearing as chaotic social behavior. Democracy is that system of people interrelations in organized community life that has the potential for supporting the free expressison of all the traits of human nature. The essence of this system began emerging during the dawning experience of *Homo*, as he probed for the best methods of survival as a primate possessed of mental and physical capacities that rendered him increasingly sensitive to human vicissitudes of living. Basic to his humanization process, which began molding the traits of human nature, was the need to suppress—to inhibit—certain primate traits to reduce brute violence and to magnify his primate bonding trait with the humanizing potential to *share*. Man's first mode of production, foraging, was simple enough to accommodate itself to an uncomplicated, democratic human existence in which the traits of human nature developed specific, enduring forms. With technological advancement, the agricultural (including pastoral) mode of production came into being with the economic and political latency for antidemocratic sociofunctional interrelationships in community life emerging in the form of war and the enslavement of the vanquished. Such slavery-based societies are exemplified by ancient Egypt, Greece, and Rome. What we commendatorily call Grecian democracy was a vestige from precivilization democracy, but restricted to a class of "free citizens" who depended on war and enslavement of the vanquished for production. From then on, democracy was limited to the small dominant class of society through the period of feudalism to the American Revolution and Civil War. Thenceforward, democratic practice began spreading with increasing acceleration to larger and larger sections of the world population.

Cranston asserts that: "A right . . . is something that can and, from a moral point of view, *should* be respected here and now. If it is violated, justice is abused. . . . Since human rights are not acquired by any of these means [i.e., by gift, inheritance, or work], but, so to speak, inhere in the human person, other arguments are needed to justify their existence. There is a lot to be said for the traditional view that natural rights are conferred by natural law, for in asserting the existence of human rights, one is saying that there is something about man's nature that entitles him to a respect that is different from that owed to animals or angels."[1] That there is something in "man's nature that entitles him" to human rights is the essence of this study. That something *is* human nature, i.e., the *traits of human nature,* the psychosocial phenomena that make *Homo* human. Cranston gives the right to be free (a trait of human nature) as an example of his thesis: "Nature again enters our earliest conception of a right to freedom. When Epictetus speaks of his freedom, he describes it in this way: 'I go wherever I wish; I come from whence I choose'. The Greek word he uses for freedom is *eleutheria,* and we find that the etymology of the word derives from 'to go where one wills'. . . . One of the classical arguments in favor of human rights was that a free country is safer than despotism. History gives us good grounds for continuing to think that this is true."[2] Cranston comes to the right conclusions because they are historically obvious. But they are not based on the scientific psychosocial fundamentals of being human. Therefore they lack the validity of a scientific presentation relating the human ecosystem to the traits of human nature.

To what extent does a democratic form of capitalist society create an ecosystem that is in concordance with the humanly oriented phases of the traits of human nature, and to what extent does it not? Any kind of democracy, from capitalist to socialist, will violate the traits of human nature less than any type of political dictatorship. The fact that "primitive communism," as the first *democractic* social order, lasted for so many tens of thousands of years is a cogent logical premise for such an assumption. Yet capitalist democracies that are questionably distended to the right may be scarcely any better than restrained dictatorships, while those to the left may resemble bedlam. Dictatorships like the present Soviet type provide basic material needs and education for the people and, because of the tight police control on the behavior of the people, may maintain social tranquility in the face of discordance between the ecosystem and the traits of human nature. But, as in

Poland today, the critical threshold of psychosocial accommodation can be reached in spite of police constraints, resulting in sociopolitical disturbance. It must also be realized that the influence of satisfying the basic material needs of a people is always favorable to various degrees in supporting the positive human aspects of the traits of human nature.

In the United States, where democracy is not equal for everyone yet because the power of wealth divides the population into classes, the concept of democracy is allowed to express itself within certain limits that do not threaten the power structure. However, there prevails a trend of interpreting democracy more and more as a limitless freedom—freedom that the power elite uses as a facade of real freedom for the economically discontented classes while the real freedom is its own. But those limits are sometimes strained to a breaking point, such as occurred in the violence and riots of Detroit, Watts, and Miami consequent to the depressed socioeconomic existence of the classes who vented their sense of freedom with the uninhibited brutish phase of the traits of human nature. The chaos created by the oil cartel manipulation resulted in extended lines of automobiles, each individual contending for a few gallons of gasoline. This elicited the negative phase reactions of the traits of human nature in all sections of the population when the limit of their cognitive power to inhibit rash behavior to that monopoly ploy was exceeded. How long can the fabulous force of "capital"[3] in the framework of democracy keep expanding the science, technology, and production of a country without the strength of its forward movement declining? At what point is the limit reached that Marx predicted when a change, violent or rational, becomes inevitable? The limits are set when the contradictions become intolerable for the majority of the people. But in a democratic governmental framework, social changes can very well be accomplisheed evolutionarily by ballot if the countervalence of the industrial-financial complex be not ultimately too powerful in negating the power of the ballot. This is a critical problem today in the United States. In the United States, the traits that are most likely to be violated for large sections of the population have to do with "challenge to succeed and competence to do so," "striving to satisfy one's appetites, inclinations, and aptitudes," and the "freedom to choose one's course of action." It is true that in the American democracy the obstacles to accommodating these traits are not insuperable, as in a dictatorship or absolute monarchy. The fact is that superficially the obstacles appear superable for an outsider looking in, but for a large section of the actors themselves the road to success is in a different world. The accumulating frustrations from social and economic obstacles encountered in the process of responding to life's challenges and attaining the competence to pursue one's chosen role with a reasonable perspective of success is enough to demoralize most people and to infuriate some to dehumanizing behavior. Once embarked on the road of accepting the challenge, the problem becomes centered around whether the pressures from the strains of the high levels of competition required for success are excessive and beyond the threshold of endurance for most people. The competition is not only a matter of matching talents, but is also economic and contentious in nature. Getting the chance to compete under the rules (or chaos) of present-day mores inspires the use of shenanigans or worse in gaining advantage and always requires hard-to-obtain financial support. The violation of the above cited traits constrains the feelings of satisfaction the competitors experience in their social relations by not having been able to establish a recognized place for themselves in their community as they see their own self-images. However, all traits are affected to some extent, since they all interpenetrate in their influence on one another.

Our country has reached a point where neither the politicians, statesmen, industrialists, professional government consultants, nor labor leaders really seem to know how to handle the flood of multiple economic and social contradictions that are plaguing our society and are continually getting worse. As a consequence, a sense of helplessness abounds among our people, and the traits of human nature are experiencing significant strains—strains the enemies of capitalist democracy are very successfully exploiting. We cannot sing our praise when a substantial portion of our people are in or near the poverty level, when unemployment is always a problem except in times of war, when our misconception of democratic permissiveness has relaxed ethical and moral values and created cognitive and behavioral chaos with the trait of "freedom to choose," when our elected officials are continually being convicted for fraud, when strong monopolies like those of oil and finance flagrantly practice rip-off economics with impunity, when the criminal seems to get better treatment by the law than the victim, and when we have replaced our work ethos with the attitude of getting a buck with the least effort or for nothing. These and other disturbing conditions of living have created critical disharmonies with the traits of human nature so that the "challenge" trait has become intensifed up to a state of vicious competition or frustrated to a state of inertia; the creativity trait of large sections of people is harnessed and depressed by the mishandling of the labor problems of vulnerable sections of the population, particularly, the youth and the poor; the "hope" trait for too large a section of youth has been dimmed or destroyed as the result of unmotivated involvement in poorly understood and difficult to justify warfare and monopoly infested degradation of the American economy; the commitment to a spiritually elevating frame of behavioral orientation trait keeps continually being battered by political-economic-social events of corruption; "competence" for meeting challenges dealing with the increasing numbers of school dropouts and of graduates from our schools, which ill prepare them for joining the labor force, coupled with chronic unemployment of the incompetent and even the competent; the security of the "rootedness" trait is being eroded by the many factors that are disrupting family life, such as marriages without commitment, children being born out of wedlock, community-unsupported working mothers, extreme freedom from discipline allowed children and youth, alcoholism, and drug abuse. For those in the poverty and low-income groups, all traits of human nature are vitiated in more or less degree, fortunately, representing only a relatively moderate portion of the population.

As a recapitulation, let us list the traits adversely affected and needing reaffirmed support in the United States particularly among the poor, due to the ecosystem's discordance to them:

1. the need to reaffirm our bonding and sharing trait to family and community in order to reinforce a more significant sense of prospective mutuality and relative stability in social relations;
2. the need to find one's place in one's ecosystem by being able to respond to challenge with effective competence unhindered by socioeconomic obstacles;
3. the need to feel free to evaluate situations and freely choose, *within reasonable limits,* one's course of action;
4. the need to be able to appreciate one's self-image and favorably identify with it;
5. the need to experience a sense of commitment to a unifying frame of behavioral orientation which gives direction to one's life so that the intellectual and spiritual wants be enhanced, since *man as human does not live by bread alone*;
6. the need for the opportunity of expending certain portions of one's life's experience in pursuing one's own native course of creativity;
7. the need of man to project his expectations to coming events with hope;
8. the need to be able, within the limits of acceptable social norms,

to keep striving in the direction that satisfies one's appetites, inclinations, and native abilities without unnecessary obstacles interfering.

It is not difficult to imagine, in consideration of the traits of human nature, how a social system such as primitive communism helped to support the emerging traits of human nature in that ancient society and how slavery and feudalism were bound to violate those traits. Nor is it difficult, on the same basis, to understand how primitive communism endured for so many tens of thousands of years, and how slavery and feudalism endured for relatively shorter periods of time.[4,5] Both slavery and feudalism persisted for such short periods because they had become too expensive in *human* expenditure and were impeding socioeconomic practice in developing the amenities for living that all the creativity of past experience of *Homo* had ignited in the desires of people. The more they produce, the more their desires are kindled. Feudalism was displaced by capitalism, the most democratic forms of which brought the modern world of science and technology to its present level.

Civilization's alienation of certain aspects of man's humanness from himself did not disappear with the disappearance of slavery and serfdom. With all its evils, however, capitalism's virtues were a boon to mankind. Particularly did it open up the human ecosystem to an incredible development of "capital" and to the freer exercise of practically all the traits of human nature, but not without also giving latitude for *freer exercise of the primate aspects of the traits of human nature* to move and develop in new directions. In regard to capital, Childe made the following provocative observation: "Finally [at the end of the Neolithic period], war helped to a great discovery—that men as well as animals can be domesticated. Instead of killing a defeated enemy, he might be enslaved; in return for his life he could be made to work. This discovery has been compared in importance to that of taming animals. In any case, by early historic times slavery was a foundation of ancient industry and a potent instrument in the accumulation of capital."[6] No less was the dissolution of slavery and serfdom a great revolution by freeing labor to work for wages in the great modern civilizing process of production with the fantastic ability to develop and accumulate capital.[7] Although this capitalist process of production has taken its toll in human life and misery for large sections of the population, it has forced the development of knowledge and technology and the creation of social circumstances for man to bring into focus a "utopia" for himself and his progeny, as Marx so aptly pointed out. Our ecosystem under capitalism has developed a compensatory scheme of philanthropy, a welfare system of partial economic security, a highly sensitive mass response to the inhumanities to man. But we have also developed a blind spot to the ravages committed by an unrelenting extremity in economic and sociocultural competition and the need for controlling such competition so that the challenge trait of human nature be not depressed, diverted, strangled, or ravaged and so prevented from acting competently in the process of achieving. This blind spot still allows close to 20 percent of the population to exist in poverty and near poverty levels. We spend billions of dollars a year to operate social welfare programs to alleviate this situation, but the efforts are ineffective, since they are not directed at the causes of the problems, and too much of the funds become dissipated in the scramble for money—a simulation of the uncontrolled competitive exercise in the process of making a living. The programs are ineffective because of our blind spot to relentless competition. As a consequence, there is a resistance to the granting of guarantees for making work available and compensated by a living income for those who desire to give a good day's work, but have not been entrapped in the vigorous competitive struggle as entrepreneurs. It is *not* the competition that is obstructive, but its relentless nature whereby *it is allowed to control people rather than people controlling it*. The challenge to action is a basic need of the human. If it lead to competition, then, very well. But let man control the consequences by setting normative limits to the process—limits on this side of throat-cutting and monopoly, which negate challenge and competition. No less does man have an essential need for a sense of security, but not to the extent that we create a completely protective, soporific womb out of our ecosystem, which is as destructive to creativity and the other traits of human nature as relentless competition is to that section of society that falls by the wayside in the competitive process. Security is itself *not* a trait of human nature. It is a complex of feelings that result from harmony of the ecosystem with the traits of human nature, particularly the trait that gives a sense of rootedness—the bonding and sharing trait.

The trait relating to the "need to appreciate one's self-image" is being pushed to the limit at the expense of the trait relating to the "need for rootedness in significant love-relatedness and social relations of mutuality." This, with the distorted performance in relation to the trait of "challenge" is creating havoc in the ultracompetitive atmosphere in school, on the job, in the arts, in entertainment, in sports, at the university, in politics, in labor unions, in the ministry, and in all others areas of the ecosystem. But, at the same time, the uncritical protective womb of the dole system type of welfare practiced in the United States is dissipating responsibility and pride in performance by much of the productive and service sections of the population. Dole system welfare is alienating the people from their human nature, or, expressed in a positive sense, the dole system is appropriating the human aspect of the human nature, leaving man with a negative nature. There is much misdirection in creativity and production of cultural phenomena. Psychosocial orientation to the world around us and commitment to essentials have been misguided or lost with the development of mass demoralization and behavioral disorientation expressed as antiinstitutionalism, antisociety, antiself, antieducation, and antiscience. The trait of human nature manifested in "freedom to choose" is perverted by pushing freedom to choose into randomness of choice like the "Brownian movement" of molecules in a liquid. People act as though each has an unrestricted prerogative of freedom to choose to satisfy every personal whim without the responsibility of adhering to any socially oriented guidelines. This is breaking down the boundaries of the democratic aura traditionally present in American life. In the apparent eagerness of everyone to express one's unalienable rights to democratic freedom to choose, democracy is itself being directed headlong into a maelstrom of scrambling self-seekers—a state of chaos, a process of diminishing the nature of being human. However, the American heritage of a democratic ecosystem is too strong to be destroyed. Freedom to choose will have to be humanized to get back on the human track. With all the corruption in politics, we did respond with enough popular pressure on congressional politicians to extirpate the cancer of Watergate, although not the causes of it. We have created organizations like Common Cause, Public Citizen, Inc., numerous environmental protection societies, the Federation of American Scientists, and various other save-our-society organizations which are denigrated by the military-industrial complex against which President Eisenhower warned us. Even the misdirected hippie movement had at its roots a desire to disown the follies of the fathers and to create a haven of their own.

Our democratic heritage is being exploited, with antisocial results. We must accept the thesis that the extremes of any movement will change the essential nature of its mean or moderate position, i.e., if quantity be added or subtracted enough to reach a critical threshold, the quality will then change. Democracy is not a system in which every individual or group has unrestricted freedom of movement. Democratic freedom must not be equated with the freedom of movement of molecules. Every trait of human nature would be violated if this were to take place. In fact, there would no longer be a society. Human beings have desires, but also the ability to choose how and when to satisfy those desires in order not to disrupt the community of persons with whom they associate who also have desires. The response to challenge and to ego development should be within the limits of a normative psychosocial frame of behavioral orientation. Cultural creations should not be directed to antisocial uses. The democratic rights of the individual in the United States today are being applied with such abandon that people, including the criminal element, can obtain public records of individuals, thereby creating a situation whereby the sensitive individuals who have not committed crimes are laid open potentially to blackmail and other forms of duress. There must be a better way to protect privacy and to deal with concealed documents.

The democratic rights of individuals to sue have created a very lucrative process of legal fraud and imposture that is not only corrupting sections of the legal profession, but also creating a new method for racketeers to make a lucrative living. It is also dislocating the price structure in health services and insurance costs. The democratic rights of children and adolescents are being misdirected by allowing them to make decisions for situations for which they do not have the experience and maturity to make. This is leading to a breakdown in child and adolescent behavioral relations with basic social institutions such as the family. Children have rights, but depreciating the family is not the way to protect them. There are certain immature couples whose right to family status should be abrogated. The democratic rights of the mass media have become so extended without the corresponding responsibility for content that it presents to the public. It has thereby become a potent catalyst of public orientation in directions of the media's own choosing, instead of in the direction which the community would choose if it were objectively informed. The news media insidiously *make* the news. The cult of publicity seeking that stems from the news media's practices of amplifying trivia has dangerously deflected the behavior of susceptible people and encouraged criminal and terroristic acts.

The first article of the Bill of Rights is certainly a landmark in democracy, but so are articles 4 and 9. In the first article, the freedom of speech and of the press are unconditionally protected. But article 4 unconditionally protects the right of the people to be secure in their persons against unreasonable searches, and article 9 gives people certain rights not enumerated in the Constitution. However, when one considers what searches are made by investigative reporters on individuals with the aid of the statutory support of access to practically all government records, there appears to exist contradictions between article 1 and article 4. And when article 9 is placed in apposition to articles 1 and 4, more contradictions become apparent. These contradictions disappear, however, immediately when the absoluteness of each article is interpreted as being dependent on each of the other articles, i.e., a democratic right is relative to other democratic rights. An absolute right becomes a *relative* absolute, as it should be. That is why they (the rights) are subject to the interpretation of the Supreme Court. The absolute absoluteness of the freedom of the press is as dangerous as the absolute absoluteness of the power of the president in relation to the Congress and the Supreme Court. Such rights must perforce be relatively absolute.

SEXUAL PERVERSION

What democratic rights are doing for other types of disoriented people they are also doing for homosexuals. They are all socially faulted deviations of time-tested, socially forged behavior. Deviation from what? Let us examine this question. The socialization process of man necessitated that he adopt certain patterns of behavior in order to facilitate social order. This required that the primate way of life be replaced by a primitive human society. In such a society, the cognitive process opened new vast vistas. The burgeoning traits of human nature became molded by the new conditions of existence, responding to the developing rationality for the need of behavioral changes to accommodate to a human existence in a bonding-sharing, non-violent social organization. Basic to such a change was the adoption of a system of inhibitory behavior to suppress the inherited primate nature of direct response to biological urges. As Sahlins expressed it: "This liberation of human society from direct biological control was its great evolutionary strength. . . . It is an extraordinary fact that primate urges often become not the secure foundation of human social life, but a source of weakness in it."[8] Throughout the history of humankind, the sexual urge has had a powerful influence on man's behavior. Throughout this whole period, systems of inhibitions have guarded human society from reverting to the destructive influence of primate sexuality. As Sahlins further stated concerning primate sexuality: "Sex is more than a force of attraction between adult males and females; it also operates among the young and between individuals of the same sex. Promiscuity is not an accurate term for it; it is indiscriminate. And while we might deem some of the forms perversions, to a monkey or an ape they are all just sociable. . . . Among subhuman primates sex had organized society; the customs of hunters and gatherers testify eloquently that now society was to organize sex."

How do we describe a reversion back to primate sexuality? This cannot be described in the exact terms of actual primate sexuality, since man is no longer a subhuman primate. Primate sexuality involves indiscriminate relations operating under male domination and violently uncontrolled competition, urged on by instinctive dissension and brute force. But the human has cognitive processes and a train of rationality so he can plan to pursue his biological urges in the most devious ways. He has guns and knives and poisons and other mechanical apparatus to redress his jealousies and angers against whoever stimulates his emotional madnesses. Thus the human who abandons the behavioral precepts of his humanized conduct is much more dangerous than the subhuman brute.

At this point, it is interesting to compare the activities of homosexuals to that of primates insofar as "indiscriminate" sexuality is concerned. Meredith summarizes from the statistics of the Centers for Disease Control:

> In a 1982 study of 50 AIDS victims, for example, the Centers for Disease Control found that the median number of lifetime sexual partners for these men was 1,100, with a few of the men reporting as many as 20,000. The median number of different partners for a homosexual control group without the disease (a matched sample of 120 men) was 550. These figures are consistent with the result of a 1978 survey of 685 gay men living in San Francisco. Psychologist Alan P. Bell and sociologist Martin S. Weinberg of the Kinsey Institute for Sex Research found that 15 percent of these men reported having between 500 and 1,000 partners; more than 25 percent had above 1,000. . . . Psychoanalyst Charles W. Socarides, a long-time advocate of the disease model of homosexuality, says that promiscuity among gay men is a manifestation of oedipal fixation. . . . ."The more fragile the structure of the homosexual ego, and the earlier fixed he is, the more he needs the fix of a homosexual act to allay anxiety and the more *indiscriminant* [italics added] he becomes."[9]

Thus we find that homosexuality reverts to primate indiscrimate sexual activity, where sex takes over and organizes homosexual society, from which is spawned more and more psychosocial pathology and even physical pathology in such epidemics of diseases as AIDS, Kaposi's sarcoma, and all types and complications of various veneral diseases.

Primate sexuality among brutes could never be so dangerous and disastrous.

Present-day excessive permissiveness in sexuality is reaching disturbing levels, and the pervasive possession of firearms is leading to dangerous acceleration of sex violence, killings, and maiming, not to mention the deleterious effect on children as the female-headed families with children rapidly increase. The statistics of sex killings are included in the data of the survey of the Centers for Disease Control study on violent deaths among persons eighteen to twenty-four years of age.[10] And, as pointed out by Raspberry, the female-headed black families with children increased from 8 percent in 1950 to 20 percent in 1960 to 47 percent in 1983,* while the increase of white female-headed families with children increased respectively from 3 percent to 6 percent to 15 percent in those years.[11]

Sahlin's observations that "the decisive battle between early culture and human nature must have been waged on the field of primate sexuality"[12] is perceptive indeed. The traits of *human* nature that evolved to facilitate human socialization could not tolerate the unsocial *primate* pattern of uncontrolled biological sexuality. What was valid for primate socialization was impossible in cognition-endowed man for human socialization. Although normative sexual violence has now and then been romanticized in the literature as in the time of knighthood, unbridled sex violence has since time immemorial been considered antisocial, immoral, and even criminal in human social mores. Patterns of sexual behavior have therefore been of the profoundest concern to human society since the time it emerged from primate society. The actual history of man's sexual behavior is therefore quite opposed to the light-headed and contradictory manner of Stoller, who labels homosexuals as perverts and then proceeds to describe homosexuality as "people whose crime is their sexual style" or to say "homosexuality is not a diagnosis . . . only a sexual preference. . . . There is homosexual behavior . . . but there is no such thing as homosexuality."[13] For a psychiatrist to confound such a basic problem of behavior with a barrage of ostentatious frippery is not unusual in these days of rapidly changing fads. The present swing to the extreme side of sexual freedom as a reaction against Puritanical and Victorian moral rigidity, accom-

*Data from Bill Moyers's television show of January 25, 1986 indicates that nearly 60 percent of all black children are born out of wedlock, that half of all black teenage girls become pregnant, that blacks are about 11 percent of the population but compose about 50 percent of imprisoned felons, and that among blacks aged fifteen to twenty-four the principal cause of death is murder by other blacks.

panied by the flourishing of pornography, children disadvantaged by being born out of wedlock to adolescents, the glorification of the swingers, the florid descriptions of the demise of monogamy, the terroristic increase in rape, the seduction of children, and the shrill cries for the civil rights of all these types of perverters are manifestations of the chaos resulting from unrestricted, unqualified practices, perverting the human historical significance of democratic rights—the rights of human beings to resist reverting to uncontrolled primate behavior.

HETERO- AND HOMOSEXUALITY

Because morality is manmade is no reason for a light-headed approach to its functioning. Man did not create morality out of the "whole cloth." He did so out of the relentless conditions existing around him—a world where raw natural forces completely had the upper hand. Against these forces, man interposed a perceptive psychic disposition, a bipedal stance, facile hands, creative symbolization, behavioral plasticity, language communication, and a pattern of biological urges. Out of these emerged a pattern of behavior to facilitate humanization by socialization of *Homo,* lest he perish in a sea of chaos. The result was the continuing evolution of *Homo*'s nature, of which one trait was the moral and ethical patterns of conduct that have given mankind tens of thousands of years of tolerable order in society. In these codes of conduct, sexuality has always been a potent force and heterosexuality has *always* been the accepted norm. However, homosexuality appears to have been present during the entire period of written history, sometimes more tolerated and sometimes less tolerated or proscribed, but at no time allowed to thrive as a *social movement* striving to become a political force as is occurring in the United States today. Taylor discussed the historical aspects of this problem in detail and concluded: "This sketch has left much ground uncovered, chiefly because the data are too scant. . . . As it is my thesis that attitudes toward homosexuality can change within a few generations, isolated observations do not provide a basis for generalizations. . . . All we can say is that there is probably no culture from which homosexuality has not been reported. Historical analysis also indicates that the incidence of homosexuality is unlikely to be changed radically by individual therapy, however widely it may be applied. Homosexuality, like divorce rate and other phenomena, is no more than a symptom of an underlying state of *psychosocial distress* [italics added]. The cure of the state on a broad scale can be effected only by altering the relevant social conditions."[14]

Those who would cite incidence of homosexuality in past social history to support the homosexuality as a *social movement,* presenting itself as a normal, prosocial aspect of culture can find little data. Wilbur[15] cites the concluding chapter of a study of male homosexuality published in 1962 by the Research Committee of the Society of Medical Psychoanalysis as stating:

> The capacity to adapt to homosexuality is in a sense, a tribute to man's bio-social resources in the face of thwarted heterosexual goal achievement. Sexual gratification is not renounced; instead, fears and inhibitions associated with heterosexuality are circumvented and sexual responsivity with pleasure and excitement to a member of the same sex develops as a *pathological* [italics added] alternative. This conclusion supports Rado's[16] suggestion that male homosexual adaptation is a result of "hidden but incapacitating fears of the opposite sex." Furthermore, the authors of the research study wrote: "we assume that *heterosexuality is a biological norm* and that unless interfered with all individuals are heterosexual. Homosexuals do not bypass heterosexual developmental phases and all remain potentially heterosexual."[17]

The branding of homosexuality as a "tribute to man's bio-social resources" by the Research Committeee of the Society of Medical Psychoanalysis is a clear indication how unhistorical recent psychiatry has become in relation to human sexuality. Rather than homosexuality being a tribute to man's biosocial resources, it is a reversion away from human sociality to primate behavior, in which sex relations with the same sex is a demonstration of primate sociality.

All the traits of human nature are affected by the social practices in sexuality. *In primate society, sex is the social organizer, while in human society, sex is organized by the society.* Are we drifting back to primate sociality, where dominance of sexuality preempts social decisions? In sexuality, the recent trend in behavior appears to be to release the traditional restrictions engendered by the "orientation" trait, which has for aeons controlled, within the limits of societal needs, the trait of self-disciplined "freedom to choose." This freedom-to-choose trait, now released from controls, has stimulated paths of sexual behavior to a degree that one wonders whether all stops have been abandoned in the striving to satisfy the sexual appetites and inclinations and whether the sex-fantasy–surfeited "self-image–self-esteem" trait can be sexually satisfied any longer. The drive for immediate satiety of these urges has relegated "prospection" in these matters to abeyance and has elicited an increasing sex-related violence. Challenges in resolving sex matters are no longer tempered with historical rationality, and "creative" energies are increasingly occupied in devising ways to generate "kicks" in sex-abandon using drugs for support. Thus all of the traits of human nature have been stressed and strained out of proportion in accommodating to the situation of forsaken inhibitions that are chronicled in human development as maintainers of societal order.

Now that the homosexual social movement is taking on characteristics of a *political movement,* the legitimacy of gathering adherents gains validity. Since homosexuality has its roots in childhood, this would be the most likely age group to seduce, by highlighting the "kicks" involved. Thus adherents could be added by what might be termed "seduction" of the inexperienced and the *déjà-vu sophisticated* youth. The potentially normal are thereby induced into perverted practices by impressing them that such behavior is the exciting lifestyle of the future. The adoption of the term "gay" to replace the socially pejorative term "homosexual," which emerged from the present movement for sexual freedom based on the pleasure principle and the Ludenic (play) theory of sexuality, has undoubtedly given homosexuality a flavor of normalcy according to a significant section of the population, particularly among the younger age group. This leads to the problem of whether to allow this delusion of the behaviorally disoriented to pose as normal and whether their practice of deceptively seducing the youth be allowed, thus supporting this fraud against socially accepted biological normality. The other side of the problem is the consideration that must be given to a group of people who have been incapacitated from acting normally. Certainly, they should have their civil rights, like the rest of the citizenry, including the right to medical help, but not the right to cripple others by propagating homosexuality.

Homosexuality is a mental perversion to satisfy a biological urge. It is no different from the other perversions of biological urges, all of which are unquestionably considered and treated as illnesses. For example, suppose the biological urge of hunger were satisfied by a mental perversion of eating too much, such as in the condition known as bulimia. Then the "craze" to eat and to induce regurgitation as was practiced at the Roman bacchanalia became a new modern social "lifestyle" among the sophisticated, who are already "life-styling" from perversions of the psychobiological processes with psycholeptic drugs. But suppose that the hunger urge were repressed instead by the diet passion and a rationale developed for inducing social movements of persons placating one another in their anorexia nervosa plights. To this comparison, the homosexuals will certainly respond that the bulimia, anorexia nervosa, and drug addiction cases are "really" physically sick and some are dying. Then one need only remind the homosexuals that the human race could *only* survive and develop in heterosexual practice and that an *antisurvival* disease, like Acquired Immuno-Deficient Syndrome, is testimony that homosexuality is not only fruitless behavior, i.e., barren to life, but also leads opportunistically to destruction of the basic biological defenses. For AIDS, there is no treatment, not even for relief. Most of the afflicted will die of its ravages. Luckily, the production of scientists will eventually find a method to control the destructive force of the offending retrovirus HTLV-III.

Allowing such abnormal practice to establish itself as a socio-political movement is like letting loose a plague on the community. We do not yet know what other opportunistic diseases, physical or mental, may be generated by encouraging the intensification of primate behavior to become established in human society as an accepted life-style. As repeated over and over again because of its importance, certain primate behavioral traits that are normal for nonhuman primates when practiced by humans in human society can become catastrophic, because the human has the mind and imagination to wreak havoc on the social suroundings by such practices. Sex play among the pongidae of the same sex is a way of socializing. Among mature hominids it becomes disastrously perversive, which the pongidae brain could never conceive to do. The free-wheeling of the homosexual movement could not have happened had our preoccupation with extending civil rights not led us to a near state of moral and ethical chaos. As United States Supreme Court justice William Rehnquist recently put it: "Approving civil rights for every one who claims it would be a *recipe for anarchy.*"[18] This does not apply to *a* homosexual. But it does to a homosexual *movement.* All this has not happened without cause. It has happened because our ecosystem is not in harmony with the socially acceptable phases of our traits of human nature.

Society has the right to control, in a broad sense, the conduct of its people. That is why we have moral, ethical, and legal systems in all societies. But in setting up controls, the inhibitions required to effect the controls should not violate the basic physiological and behavioral needs of the people. To wit, people need food. If there are no jobs available for some people to earn a living and no legitimate way to get food, then begging and stealing are the unsatisfactory choices left to the hungry. But if they choose to steal rather than beg, because the latter would depreciate their self-image more than stealing, then the society that makes stealing a crime has violated the basic needs of the people. The example is simplistic, but it illustrates how an essential social control can be negated, turned into its opposite, when applied under contradictory circumstances.

Just as basic a biological need as food is sexuality. The normal biological consummation of this need is based on the heterosexuality of the human. In fact, heterosexuality is the means of fruition practically in all forms of life. Desire is a mainspring of human action. Sexual desire is fundamental to animal life. Blind pursuit of the gratification of sexual desire would render *human* society impossible to maintain due to the violently uncontrolled primate competition, instinctive dissension, and brute force generated. Mankind solved this problem by humanizing the response to sexual desire very early in the evolution of *Homo.* This was done by invoking an intellectually devised code of inhibitory conduct to guide his response. The present code of behavior in relation to heterosexuality, taboo of incest, and the importance of the family is as old as the beginning of the humanization of man. It is true that in different cultures and in different times of history variations existed, but they did not negate the essences of those three fundamentals of social life. Whenever the dynamics of social development begins to press for changes in these fundamentals, it is the obligation of society to delve profoundly into the causes and the rationale of such pressures for change and to decide whether the causes and the rationale are valid and warrant changes in our social conduct. The time has come for man to become the forthright master of the future of his life-style and the structure and substructure of his social system.

In a recent comprehensive compilation of the results of studies on "homosexualities" published by the Institute For Sex Research, Bell and Weinberg concluded that "numerous investigations have failed to show any consistent or clear-cut difference between homosexuals and heterosexuals in terms of their psychological adjustment." However, among the studies that did find "more pathology among homosexual than heterosexual samples" were those by E. W. Bruce (1942), W. T. Doige (1956), F. E Kenyon (1968), M. T. Saghir and E. Robins (1973), M. S. Weinberg and C. J. Williams (1974), F. L. Myrick (1974), and R. L. Freidberg (1975). "Other studies have been unable to distinguish homosexual and heterosexual individuals on the basis of their psychological adjustment."[19] They are: J. Chang and J. Block (1960), M. J. Freedman (1967), H. P. David and W. Rabinowitz (1952), J. N. DeLuca (1967), E. Hooker (1967), D. M. Wayne, *et al.* (1947), T. R. Clark (1975), and M. T. Saghir and E. Robins (1975).

It must be repeated over and over again that a people have a right to enshrine into its moral and ethical norms such rules of behavior that it believes to be most suitable to itself. Such norms do not necessarily have a scientific basis any more than art does, although it may. *It is important,* nevertheless, *that the norms do not violate the traits of human nature.* If one were to examine the comments made by various categories of homosexuals concerning various notable circumstances in their lives, as listed by Bell and Weinberg in their study on homosexuality, one would be impressed that these people are troubled by many problems, many of which are similar to those of a cross section of the population, but with differences. It seemed that the most impressive factor is that they are "conditioned" people whose *circumstances and personal sensitivities influenced* them toward homosexuality more impressively than others so exposed. Among the various age groups studied, that of the twenty-five years and younger group composed 24 percent of the white males, 43 percent of the black males, 26 percent of the white females, and 27 percent of the black females.[20] Therefore, quite a large proportion of homosexuals were youngsters. An amazing 43 percent of the black males were under twenty-five years of age, an indication that something in black male socialization was influencing them as children to homosexuality. From the above mentioned listing of comments by the homosexuals, what is very impressive is that a large proportion of these comments fell into the three categories: disturbed, timid people; immature people; and those who plainly indicated that they were conditioned into homosexuality. When considering the various circumstances in the lives of young children that could condition the highly sensitive among them into homosexual feelings, and considering further the sparseness and weakness of sex education and guidance available to American children, and particularly these days with the spectacular, dissolute, and vulgar manner that sex and homosexuality are presented in the mass media, what can one expect? Prudery is not defended, but there is serious human depreciation in cheapening so essential a function as sexuality.

Homosexuality does not appear to depress nor to activate the talents of people. This is demonstrated by the creativity of such homosexuals as Erasmus, Tchaikovsky, Herman Melville, John Maynard Keynes, Leonardo da Vinci, Lord Byron, Somerset Maugham, Walt Whitman, Serge Diaghilov, Marcel Proust, Frederick the Great, and Lawrence of Arabia.

The problem of gender identity is relevantly related to that of homosexuality insofar as both are problems of sexuality in which the affective aspects of consciousness are involved in the learning process during the most impressionable years in the lives of children. Thus a strong indication concerning early childhood conditioning as the cause of homosexuality is found in a recent issue of *Science* in which its entire contents is devoted to sexual dimorphism. Ehrhardt, *et al.*, after reviewing the experimental literature on prenatal sex hormone effects on gender-related behavior, cite Money, *et al.*, who "suggested that gender identity is formed in early postnatal years and that gender identification typically depends on a person's sex of rearing even when this is in contrast to some of the biological factors of sex. . . . Once gender identity has been established it cannot be reversed easily." And further in the study: "Thus, the available data on genetic male inter-sexes suggest that sexual orientation mainly follows the sex of rearing and identity, and therefore, is based on social learning rather than on hormones. . . ."[21]

In 1976, Patrick C. Lee, chairman of the early childhood education program at Columbia University, edited a volume on sex differences in which twenty-five contributors from the fields of psychiatry, anthropology, sociology, psychology, and bioethology, from Freud to Malinowski to Parsons to Tinbergen, contributed. The following is an extraction of statements that are pertinent to the thesis of this chapter.

Lee commented: "For the anthropologist, male-female dimorphism is a psychobiological constant to which every known human society has made accommodations. . . . Taken collectively, these accommodations are known as 'sex-role' and they include whatever behaviors, attitudes, values, and expectations a given society regards as appropriate for either males or females, but not for both. The basic questions anthropologists raise about sex-role are these: How variable versus universal are sex roles across human cultures? What means are used to teach and persuade members of a culture to assume the sex role which corresponds to their biological sex? In what way is sex role adaptive and in what way is it maladaptive?"[22] Lee continues: "But it would be a mistake to conclude that human sex role is an infinitely malleable phenomenon or that there are no universal tendencies. In fact, there are some universal practices, although they appear to be negative rather than positive. For example, there is no known society in which women are unequivocally the dominant sex, although there are some in which they share dominance with men. More specifically, in most societies men have clear control of political and military apparatus, and there are no known societies in which women have such control. . . . It does appear, then, that there is cross-cultural *consensus*, if not unanimity, on some aspects of sex role."[23] Lee further observes: "Although the nuclear family is universal, it is an autonomous unit in only 25 percent of human societies. In the majority of societies, its economy, loyalty, and membership are incorporated into larger extended familial networks."[24]

The anthropologist Linton observed: "In all societies, certain things are selected as reference points for the ascription of status. . . . The simplest and most universally used of these reference points is sex. . . . Family relationships, the simplest and most obvious being that of the child to its mother, are also used in all societies as reference points for the establishment of a whole series of statuses."[25] Lee further observed:

By ascribing one role to females . . . and another to males, there is an automatic economy of socialization energy. By ascribing these roles from birth, society ensures that the child will have the primary and sustained exposure to role expections prerequisite to the easy acceptance of one's adult role. If these roles prescribe functions and temperamental dispositions which correspond to the basic physiology of sex, then they would appear to have further adaptive value. Thus . . . there are near-universal tendencies for males to be dominant, achievement-oriented, and self-reliant, while women tend to be nurturant and domestically oriented in their functions. These functional and temperamental characteristics conveniently fit the physiological facts of female childbearing and nursing and of male size and degree of muscularity. Finally, these are economic and kinship factors which tend to dictate the degree of sex-role differentiation found in a given society."[26]

Continuing, Linton states that

the double standard [male dominance and his tendency to accumulate and hold females as opposed to female monogamy] is probably as old as the primate order. In man . . . the combination of continuous sexual activity and male dominance makes for the continuity of sexual partnerships. Practically all societies have tacitly recognized the existence of these tendencies and capitalized them to a greater or less degree in their formal organization. . . . In a very large number of societies marriage has become a means of assuring male assistance to the woman and her children. . . . Man's continuity of sexual interests is reflected in a jealousy which gives conflict over women an unusually high emotional content. . . . All societies inhibit the male's tendency to collect females to some degree, setting limits to the competition for them and, through marriage, assuring the male of the possession of those which he has already gathered. Any society which failed to do this would be constantly disrupted by fights.[27]

From the news media, it is easy to get the distinct impression that violent acts and deaths among our youth, fifteen to twenty-four years of age, have been increasing. This has also been reported in federal statistics[28] for the last several decades—a period in which the customary inhibitions in sexual behavior and related matters have practically been abandoned and where chaotic confusion abounds. In examining the news reports, sex-related violence appears as a potent cause, although statistical data are difficult to come by. Concerning the matter of systems of sexual norms in human society, Linton writes: "The direct expression of any one of the tendencies arising from continuous sexual activity and male dominance can be inhibited, and all of them are inhibited by one social system or another. At the same time, such inhibition requires the development of a series of compensating patterns, even if these do nothing more than provide the individual with intensive inhibitory training. . . . Culture plays such an important part in both the inhibition and encouragement of jealousy that it may very well be asked whether jealousy is one of the innate qualities of human beings."[29]

Concerning the importance of the division of function between male and female, Parsons views: "This complementarity of function reduces competition between parents and enables them to present a united sex-differentiated front to the children. Thus, the children are encouraged to assume functional roles which correspond to the roles of their same sex parents."[30] He discussed the whole problem of the sex role in preventing family and social disruption:

On the basis of these considerations, we suggest that from the family point of view the primary function of the repression of eroticism is to prevent the assumption of either parental role by the child or its encouragement by the parent. In the mechanisms involved on the social system level two points stand out. The first is the very general fact about groups . . . namely that the stability of a small group is highly dependent, both on the differentiation of instrumental [male] and expressive [female] leadership roles and on a coalition of the instrumental and expressive leaders. From this point of view, denial of the child's impulses to assume either of the parental roles vis-à-vis the other (equally of the parents' complementary impulses) is a protection of the integration of the family as a system against a *disruption* [italics added] tendency. Secondly, the erotic relation between the marriage partners is a primary symbolic focus of their solidarity. It both symbolizes the differentiation of their roles in the family system and their integration with each other. The child's earlier erotic attachment to the mother can be defined as non-competitive with her attachment to the father, but beyond a certain point, particularly where the child's role becomes sufficiently active, this non-competitiveness tends to break down. It is a well-known principle of differentiation of social structures that competitive pressures can be eased by qualitive differentiation of roles.[31]

The above thesis by Parsons, when retrospected to the time that primitive *Homo* first began to organize as a society, was engagingly described by Sahlins as the first great social revolution of mankind—the sex revolution: "The decisive battle between early culture and human nature must have been waged on the field of primate sexuality."[32] How does this relate to the problem of homosexuality? This is pertinent to the latter problem because it is in the process of socialization of children that sex identity is established. Whiting, who has done much in the field of psychological anthropology, asserts that: "It is our thesis that the aim of socialization in any society is to produce an adult whose attributed, subjective, and optative identities are isomorphic: 'I see myself as others see me, and I am what I want to be.' " Whiting assumes that sleeping arrangements provide the best index for gauging the identification process in infancy:

Arrangements in infancy lead to *primary identification,* whereas those in childhood lead to *secondary identification. . . .* In most societies the world over, an infant sleeps during the nursing period in his mother's bed, or a crib or cradle right next to it, and within easy reach. Of over 100 societies on which we have data on sleeping arrangements, the American middle-class is unqiue in putting the baby to sleep in a room of his own. For our purpose, the big difference lies in whether or not the father also sleeps with the mother. . . . According to our theory, these two arrangements should be profoundly different in their effect on the infant's first or primary identification. . . . Thus, the male infant in societies with exclusive mother-child sleeping arrangements should have a primary cross-sex optative identity, whereas the boy reared in societies in which the father sleeps with the mother should have a primary adult optative identity.[33]

Whiting further observed: "The draft at the beginning of World War II made possible several studies comparing middle class children from father-absent homes with those from father-present households. These studies indicated that boys from father-absent households behaved like girls both in fantasy behavior and in overt behavior, especially with respect to producing very little aggression. . . . The boys whose fathers had been absent but were then returned continued to be effeminate in overt behavior, but there was a marked change in their fantasy behavior. These . . . are the conditions we have indicated should produce conflict over sexual identification."[34]

The psychologists Terman and Miles have the following to say about the male-female dichotomy:

> The masculine-feminine contrast is probably as deeply grounded, whether by nature or by nurture, as any other which human temperament presents. Certainly it is more specifically rooted in a structural dichotomy than the cycloid-schizoid or extrovertive-introvertive contrasts. Whether it is less or more grounded in general physiological and biochemical factors than these remains to be seen. . . . The fact remains that the M-F dichotomy, in various patterns, has existed throughout history and is still firmly established in our mores. . . . The nature-nurture problem occupies a central position in any theory of sex temperament. . . . At present, no one knows whether the M-F deviant is primarily a problem for the neurologist, biochemist, and endocrinologist or for the parent and educator. The question cannot be answered without thoroughgoing search for the constitutional correlates of M-F deviation. . . . Accordingly, although the evidence in favor of a considerable nurture influence is in our opinion very weighty, it is by no means crucial.[35]

In Tyler's study of the psychology of human differences, she confirmed the childhood influence on the adult personality: "There is overwhelming evidence that in the large majority of cases, the type of interests that characterize an individual in his late adolescence will go with him through life. Even considerably earlier than this, in the first years of high school, it has been shown that interest scores are fairly stable."[36]

Bandura and Walters, who represent the "social-learning" school of sex-role development, assert that:

> Failure to develop sex-appropriate behavior has received considerable attention in clinical psychology and psychiatry and has

customarily been interpreted as a manifestation of underlying psychodynamic processes, especially latent homosexuality. To present these processes as internal causal factors does little to clarify the genesis of sex-inappropriate behavior. On the other hand, to identify the influence of external social-learning variables, such as the distribution of rewarding power within the family, on the formation of deviant sex-role behavior both assists in the understanding of the development of deviant sexuality and directs attention to the manner in which culturally approved patterns may be formed. . . . Thus, within one family even same-sex siblings may exhibit quite different patterns of behavior, owing to their having selected for imitation different elements of their father's and mother's response repertories.[37]

Kohlberg and Zigler, using the "cognitive-developmental" approach, describe the sex-role problem as follows:

The fact that sex-role concepts have physical dimensions suggests that the formation of a sex-role identity is in large part the comprehension and acceptance of a physical reality rather than a process primarily determined by sexual fantasies, social reinforcement, or identification with models. The child's basic sex-role identity is largely the result of a self-categorization as a male or female *made early in development* [italics added]. While dependent on social labeling, this categorization is basically a cognitive reality judgment rather than a product of social rewards, parental identifications, or sexual fantasies. . . . The motivational forces implied in such reality judgments are general . . . motives . . . which orient the child both toward a structured reality and toward the *maintenance of self-esteem* [italics added].[38]

HOMOSEXUALITY AND
THE AMERICAN PSYCHIATRIC ASSOCIATION

It is necessary to comment on the most recent classification devices developed and used by the American Psychiatric Association (APA) in advocating diagnostic methodology for mental disorders. Muscari has this to say about the APA's issue of its diagnostic manual titled *DSM-III (Diagnostic and Statistical Manual of Mental Disorders* (1980) in his most comprehensive philosophic discussion of the subject:

> [I]n the hope of redirecting future inquiry this paper will argue:
> (1) that the recent trend towards multivariate statistical methods
> of psychiatric classification—what has been regarded by DSM-III
> collaborators as "a major investment of the profession" (Spitzer,
> et al., 1980, p. 162)[39]—might appear to be clinically beneficial,
> but in point of fact it is riddled by unsound theoretical conclusions
> which leave the field without a deeply reaching base for under-
> standing and treating mental disorder, and (2), that, *a fortiori*,
> "mental disorder" is best conceived as not a cluster of properties
> and events, nor a metaphorical reaction to a breakdown in social
> interrelations, but a deeply laid condition characterized by the
> absence of an imaginally integrated system. Such an account, to
> be sure, hinges upon a successful explanation of imagery.[40]

In Muscari's definition of mental disorder, the subjects present an "absence of an imaginally integrated system," i.e., the imagery of "the recesses of the inner person . . . becomes a journey without maps."[41] Homosexuality, he states, does not fit this definition and is not a mental disorder, but rather a functional disability, i.e., "homosexuals [are] disturbed by their inability to function heterosexually. . . ." Muscari's definition of mental disorder is simpler than that of the APA in its manual *DSM-III*. He disregards the factor of social interrelations in the definition, even though it impossible to consider any reality of mental disorder in a meaningful way for professional (scientific) purposes without a developmental perspective of it unfolding. This approach can only be implemented by analyzing and synthesizing the social interrelations of the case historically. Individuals are social organisms. Their mental conditions are social phenomena expressed objectively in behavior and subjectively in the cognitive dynamics of their imaginations and emotions. We are not here considering mental disorders resulting intrinsically from traceable physiological pathology.

The definition of mental disorder by the APA is: "In DSM-III, a mental disorder is conceptualized as a clinically significant behavioral or psychological syndrome or pattern that occurs in an individual and that is typically associated with either a painful symptom (distress) or impairment in one or more important areas of functioning (disability). In addition, there is an inference that there is a behavioral, psychologic or biologic dysfunction and that the disturbance is not only in the relationship between the individual and society. When the disturbance is limited to a conflict between an individual and society, this may represent social deviance, which may or may not be commendable, but is not by itself a mental disorder."[42]

Concerning whether homosexuality is a mental disorder, Spitzer stated:

> On the one hand, the gay activists and their supporters argue that homosexuality represents no impairment in an "important area of functioning" since *sexual* functioning is unimpaired. They refuse to accept *hetero*sexual functioning as the norm. . . . The DSM-III position (and the 1973 decision) can be viewed as acknowledging that at the present time mental health professionals are unable to agree on whether it is *hetero*sexual or *sexual* functioning that should be regarded as an "important area of functioning," so that inability to function in that area justifies the designation of mental disorder. Therefore, in DSM-III only those homosexuals distressed by their inability to function heterosexually are classified as having a mental disorder (Ego-dystonic Homosexuality). In other words, in this controversial condition it is the *patient* who judges whether or not the absence of his or her heterosexual functioning represents impairment in an important area of functioning.[43]

A functional disturbance is certainly not a life-style that functionally undisturbed people would adopt except when nonconditioned children are recruited and conditioned to malfunction sexually. There are, of course, some immature adults who are as susceptible as children. The period of distress during which sexual malfunction is developing and the accompanying critical cognitive and emotional processes that drive individuals to homosexual action may last a shorter or longer time. After the crisis is over and the pattern of sex satisfaction has become established, the distress symptoms may subside in most cases and the behavior of these subjects socially may not be distinguishable from the rest of the population. The malfunction has become to the mentally marred a routine pattern of living. Calling this a life-style is like calling the pattern of life adopted by hemiplegics a normal state of living. In the bold and dramatic experiment of Rosenhan in relation to diagnostic validity as practiced today in psychiatry, he asserted: "But one thing is certain: any diagnostic process that lends itself so readily to massive errors of this sort (errors in distinguishing between sane and insane individuals) cannot be a very reliable one. . . . It is clear that we cannot distinguish the sane from the insane in psychiatric hospitals."[44]

Marmor discussed the problem of defining homosexuality and finally concluded that "for a homosexual adaptation to occur, in our time and culture, these factors must combine to (1) create an *impaired* [italics added] gender-identity, (2) create fear of intimate contact with members of the opposite sex, and (3) provide opportunities for sexual release with members of the same sex."[45] This is in agreement with the above discussion of the dysfunctional nature of homosexuality. Marmor further stated that the eighteen contributors to the book which he edited on sexual inversion were of a similar mind about homosexuality: "The clinicians represented in this volume present convincing evidence that homosexuality is a potentially reversible condition. There is little doubt that much of the recent success in the treatment of homosexuals stems from the growing recognition among psychoanalysts that homosexuality is a disorder of adaptation."[46] Among the clinicians cited is Dr. Stoller, who stated that, considering that the nature of this dysfunction is the inability to function heterosexually, these people are "turned away," i.e., perverted from the intrinsic biosocial heterogeneous process. Stoller is convinced that historically and today homosexuals were and are perverts.[47] He titled his book *Perversion*.

There is a need to discuss further the qualified term for homosexuality as used by the American Psychiatric Association in its latest manual, *DSM-III*—ego-dystonic homosexuality. But this term does not include the "nondistressed" homosexuals. What does ego-dystonic mean, and why is it used? In 1972, due to the clamor raised by the sympathizers, hidden or patent, with homosexuals, the general membership of APA was asked to vote on the question whether to eliminate homosexuality from the classification manual *DSM-II*. The result was that the category "Sexual Orientation Disorder" replaced the category "Homosexuality" in 1973. This still did not satisfy some. Thus the final solution was to designate this category as "Ego-dystonic Homosexuality," to be used only for those homosexuals who admitted that they are distressed. The 1960 edition of the *Psychiatric Dictionary* defined ego-dystonic as "anything that is unacceptable to the ego." This then is the compromise—the arbitrary concession—to the homosexual sociopolitical *movement* in the United States. What a scientific solution!

THE HUMAN OUTLOOK

Considering the nature of this problem, is it valid to use the term "pervert" or "perversion," or "invert or inversion," to describe homosexual or homosexuality? The fact is that there is absolutely no indication or suggestive evidence that homosexuality is genetic or physiological. There is, however, very much evidence that these people are or were at one time in their lives and continue to be potential heterosexuals. That being the case, how did they become homosexual? We certainly do need to direct our future research into longitudinal studies of the lives of the adolescent and young adult homosexuals in relation to the circumstances of their childhood to try to discover at what age and under what circumstances conditioning to homosexuality is most likely and what type of sex guidance must be developed for youngsters in the age groups where influence may lead them to homosexuality. Why cancel out such influences? Are homosexuals not good people? Is their status to be avoided? The American Psychiatric Association says that they are not mentally ill. Is perversion an illness?

Heterosexuality is preferable because nature made us that way. We have not learned to change that fact, even though we have learned the mechanism of gene splitting. So far, no one has offered any good reason why man should revert to the status of most bacteria, in which patent heterosexuality does not exist, with very rare exceptions. Biologically, heterosexuality is the fundamental for survival as a race. But *Homo sapiens* is an ingenious species. It has devised a number of unique ways of living, called cultures. Some are less unique, so they are dubbed subcultures. Within these systems of living there are various modes of expressing thought and behavior, various manners of expression that are characteristic of an individual, period, school, or even nation, and various ways of acting or performing that have been designated as life-styles. Life-styles or patterns of behavior may not be deleterious to the physical health. Others may or may not be deleterious to mental health. Still others may be or may not be deleterious to both. Smoking and overeating may be injurious to physical health, but being much overweight may also be injurious to mental health in our culture. The life-style—the battery of behavioral patterns—of children of broken homes may become what we call juvenile delinquency. Some of these children, when they become adults, move into the life-style of the criminal,[48] most of whom are unrehabilitatable.[49] The life-style of homosexuality, if that designation be valid in this case, is at a different level of social concern than any of the other life-styles. The others are either at the superficial level, such as hair or dress styles, or at the physiological level of nutrition or toxicology, like the effects of smoking, but homosexuality is at the biological and physiological levels—at the level of the survival functions of the species where the fertile mind of humankind has, since the sexuality revolution at the dawn of the emergence of *Homo*, woven the most sublime legends, the most binding moral-ethical codes, and the most personal and private privileges. But more than this, it is the biosocial area in which the human family has developed, and out of which the psychosocial traits of human nature are generated. This is the area concerning which the compromising gesture (certainly from social pressures of homosexuals) of the American Psychiatric Association reduces the biosocial behavior of homosexuality to the level of the physiological or more superficial areas of behavior. For a "scientific" body to do this with the weak apology that this life-style is not a mental illness, even though it "happens to be out of favor with current cultural conventions," is completely inexcusable.

The facts must not be misassociated and thereby confused. The overwhelming majority of people practice heterosexuality, which is *normal* biosocial behavior. If the American Psychiatric Association defers to label homosexuality a life-style of behavior, then this life-style must stand by itself at the most fundamental level—the biological and, in the human context, at the bisocial level. If the apparent homosexuality of animals is invoked as a support for human homosexuality, then how can the blind sexual impulses of male animals, which may now and then accidentally mount other males, be likened to the human male and female conditioning process toward his or her own sex? A ridiculous comparison! Homosexuality conditioning begins in childhood or adolescence. What looks like freedom of choice to be homosexual is actually an insidious process of conditioning that later appears as freedom of choice. Here the basic trait of human nature, the need to have freedom to choose, is vitiated. The homosexual chooses homosexuality only after his or her biological nature has been *perverted* by conditioning to choose this perversion of behavior, usually while he or she is not mature enough to make such choices rationally. Society is not and has not done anything in the past to prevent such perverted conditioning. Social practice in the past concerning this problem was contemptuous condemnation. Homosexuals should not be condemned, nor penalized, nor harassed, nor deprived of their civil rights nor their human rights within the context of what the community decides is normal biosocial living. Since homosexuality is not normal biosocial living, the community has the right to do everything within its understanding to prevent children and adolescents from becoming conditioned to homosexuality. Therefore, homosexuals should have only one restriction—not to do anything, public or private, that might pervert impressionable youth away from heterosexuality. All other civil rights and human rights must be theirs. The present-day clamor for visibility that homosexuals have organized to redress the injustices against them and to gain their civil and human rights must be discouraged, while, at the same time, guaranteeing to them their human and civil rights. But they must also cease their irrational behavioral responses of clamoring for recognition as practitioners of a highly desirable life-style, lest the publicity and propaganda effects of this clamor continue to be transmitted to our youth. The perpetuating effects of homosexuality as a sociopolitical movement based on freedom of choice must be halted, so also the perpetuation of the injustice against homosexuals. The American Psychiatric Association should join the scientific community and never again allow sociopolitical pressure to influence its professional rendering of decisions. We need, rather, to allay the disorder that is building up in our country in the tension between the meaning of human rights and the practice of democracy—a tension that is subverting the traits of human nature.

The American Psychiatric Association, instead of having declared that homosexuality is a valid life-style like any other life-style, should have recommended to the distressed community of homosexuals to use their organizational thrust to help alleviate their psychobiologically disoriented behavior. Alcoholics made such a salutary move by organizing Alcoholics Anonymous. Why does the American Psychiatric Association not recommend that homosexuals muster their efforts to attain a socially acceptable self-image–self-esteem and a biophysiologically desirable status by creating a Homosexuals Anonymous? Such a technique for lightening the burden of homosexuals would be less likely to support the spread of such opportunistic diseases as Acquired Immuno-Deficient Syndrome (AIDS), Pneumocystis Carinii Pneumonia (PCP), Kaposi's Sarcoma (KS), candidiasis, cryptcoccosis, toxoplasmosis, cytomegalovirus infections, and mycobacterium avium-intracellulare infections.

CONSENSUAL ADULTERY

The other vexing problem that is also disruptive of the fundamental biosocial structure of society, particularly the family, its effect on the behavior of the children, and the vitiation of the traits of human nature, is related to the pleasure-seeking perverters of the family, the advocates of consensual adultery.

One of the most aggravating problems plaguing the advocates of *consensual* adultery is jealousy, although they claim that jealousy is less a problem in consensual adultery than in *conventional* adultery.[50] They even claim that jealousy is not an emotionally involved behavior but merely a type of behavior,[51] resulting from "loss of another person" or "loss of status."

Freud considered jealousy a character trait,[52] but one associated with "intensity of feeling."[53] He asserted that jealousy is a *normal* affective state: "Jealousy is one of those affective states like grief, that may be described as normal."[54] He also asserted that this normal or competitive stage of jealousy is "compounded by grief . . . and a greater or lesser amount of self-criticism.[55] Alfred Adler agreed with Freud on the above points about jealousy.[56] Malinowski found jealousy in the primitive Trobianders,[57] and Lloyd opined that "all our emotions are finally one emotion—self-love—and our jealousy roots in selfishness."[58] The modern advocates of consensual adultery "found that jealousy behavior is a significantly smaller problem among enduring groups [those groups of multilateral marriage whose relations lasted longest]. . . . Thus, it appears that groups did learn with time to cope with jealousy. . . . Jealousy was also a function of age: all respondents under age of thirty-one listed jealousy as a problem."[59]

Among the latest studies on jealousy, Virginia Adams reviews the studies on jealous love done during the last decade. Commenting on those who believe that they have learned to transcend the age-old problem of sexual jealousy, Adams remarked: "If so, their achievement is remarkable, for sexual jealousy was the undoing of numerous failed Utopias in the past and is assumed by many to be an all but universal emotion."[60] The significant indicator observation, however, is the relation of jealousy to self-esteem, a trait of human nature, as Adams pointed out: "Most psychologists also believe that jealousy entails a threat to self-esteem as well as to a valued relationship." One of the traits of human nature is the need to appreciate one's self-image as generated by the awareness of the self as an object scrutinized and judged by the social world that interrelates with that individual. On the basis of this fact, it is the responsibility of the community to reject any type of social interrelations that are out of tune with any trait of human nature or that evoke emotional responses that are in discord with any such trait. There is an argument that, by training, individuals can learn to transcend or even to eliminate the jealousy response and if we would organize a movement to transcend monogamy,[61] sexual jealousy would disappear. These beliefs are not born out in fact. Ralph Linton, in describing sexual relations on the Marquesas Islands, observed that

both men and women enjoy an unusual degree of sexual freedom both before and after marriage. Both sexes begin to have intercourse at a very early age and are almost completely promiscuous until marriage, which is rather late. There is then little opportunity for an early conditioning to the idea of exclusive sexual possession of any individual by another. Moreover, group marriage is, or rather was, the normal form, so that even after marriage there were few exclusive partnerships. . . . Any manifestation of sexual jealousy still exposes the individual to ridicule, and the natives rarely show any signs of it when sober [when inhibitions are under control]. However, when they are drunk such jealousy *promptly* (italics added) manifests itself and leads to numerous fights among both the men and the women.[62]

This expression of primate impulses certainly cannot be attributed to the capitalistic social system of outmoded monogamy, as the Smiths judge this problem.[63]

The advocates of consensual adultery seem to be unaware that sexual jealousy is tied up with a biphasic trait of human nature. The Smiths preach for their consensual colleagues that

Sexual liberation in the form of realistic individual autonomy in a viable dyadic relationship is at least as relevant and necessary for personal and interpersonal fulfilment in marriage as liberation from socio-economic dependency and procreative (and anti-nonprocreative) institutions which serve the continuancy of traditional family structure. . . . For most couples, the most difficult part of achieving such a relationship [an open, free marriage] is liberation from sexual possessiveness and all that it feeds and thrives on in the self and the environment. This is the damnable consequence of a process of repressive primary sexual socialization which, in fostering the cultural ideology of monogamy and perpetuating the procreative sex ethic as the indispensible dual standards of sexual relationships and sexual expression, eventuates in feelings of sexual jealousy and renders many persons emotionally lame and even physiologically impotent in the adult years. Their sexuality is stifled, truncated, and subject to a myriad of minor handicaps and self-negating blind spots. This, then, is the cultural and psychological point of departure for an overwhelming number of marital relationships and the partial cause of failure for a substantial portion.[64]

FALSE LOGIC IN CONSENSUAL ADULTERY

The above citation is the crux of the rationale of the consensual adultery movement. All those arguments are supposed to have been derived from "scientific study." But there are so many half-truths, specious logic, and unproven "facts." Let us list the more obvious of these faulty facts.

First, as already mentioned, the statement disregards the fact that sexual jealousy is thoroughly involved with the traits of human nature and if provoked too often leads to violent discord with the traits.

Second, the claim that the cultural ideology is the cause of sexual jealousy is admission that the opposite—consensual adultery or promiscuity—will eliminate sexual jealousy. Not only do the nonmonogamous sexual relations on the Marquesas Islands, as described by Linton, and the primitive sex relations on the Trobiand Islands, as described by Malinowski, refute completely the idea that monogamy is causing all the horrible sexual jealousy problems attributed to it, but many other studies of primitive societies, by reputable anthropologists such as Sahlins, affirm that sexual jealousy is as old as the history of the genus *Homo* and something similar was even a potent problem among the higher primates below man. As Sahlins pointed out, the first great revolution in the progress of *Homo* was in creating norms to control the destructiveness of sexual jealousy. This took place hundreds of thousands of years before monogamy was even thought of.

Third, sexual liberation means different things to different groups. To some, it means equal sexual rights and equivalent responsibilities for both sexes. For others, it means unisex—no difference in the behavior responses to conditions of living by either sex. To the advocates of consensual adultery, it means freedom for married couples to express their erotic inclinations toward others fortuitously and without involvement and yet to maintain their married relations as long as they can last. What is in the background of the latter relations creates the need to formalize the relationship between the sexes that will satisfy the eventuality of the recent sexual freedom movement. In order to do this, it became necessary for the advocates of open marriage to overcome the formidable sexual jealousy factor by depreciating its intrinsic nature with superficial arguments and by depreciating monogamy as a ritual of sexual possessiveness and the etiological factor of sexual jealousy. In the present spirit of "human" equality between the sexes, the sexual possessiveness is no longer one-sided. A mutual love commitment has an inevitable aspect of mutual possessiveness that is a wonderful love aura. It is this sense of mutual possessiveness that can only persist and develop in an orientation whereby people are conscious of the need to win and to strengthen each other's love bond as a continuous process. As Masters and Johnson so elequently presented the case[65] this all must begin with commitment, which the advocates of open marriage discuss[66] with a sociopsychological shallowness characteristic of their other presentations.

Fourth, the recently accelerated sexual freedom movement is a spinoff of the extreme liberalization of behavior and civil policy and involves adversely at least several traits of human nature. The relaxation of the norms of behavior involves the need of a mentally unifying frame of orientation trait, which has been generating some chaotic behavior in our midst. The trait expressing the need to feel free to evaluate situations and to freely choose, within the context of social justice of others, between alternative options has been so freed of inhibitions as to seem like chaotic choice making. The trait manifested by striving in the direction that satisfies appetites, inclinations, and talents is operating in such loose fashion of acceptability that almost any mode of behavior in satisfying erotic fantasy has become acceptable. This uninhibited freedom of behavior of open-marriage orientation is, in a sense, directed toward sex-selfishness and indiscriminate sexuality, which borders on a return to primate sexuality that was so destructive of societal development that it had to be abandoned by early *Homo* in order to achieve enough harmony to start humanizing society.

Fifth, the advocates of "beyond monogamy" appear to be very weak in their concern for the fate of children. They indicate that they really do not know what to do with the children.

DO CHILDREN COUNT?

The problem of children, always basic to society, has become critical in present-day society. Motherhood as a full-time vocation has emerged only since the middle of the nineteenth century.[67] This began to take place when the child began to lose its place as a contributor to the rural household economy. His training, therefore, by productive participation began disappearing as more and more families migrated from rural to urban areas. His closely supervised behavior as a participant in the family productive operations began being replaced by the full-time mother. Thus the modern family unit was in the process of coming into being.

All the native talents involved in mothering (parenting) were given opportunity to develop.[68] The legendary mother of song and story came into being. But the acceleration of social change kept up its momentum. Industrialization was creating metropolitan giants of urbanization. Amenities for living kept continuing to increase. Costs of such standards kept continuing to increase so that more and more full-time mothers had to get involved in contributing to the family income by working at part-time and full-time jobs. The family unit had to make more and more adjustments, particularly in relation to children. With as much as half of full-time mothering having disappeared, with no training unit, such as the rural household economy, available for child rearing and training, what next?

Rossi stated the problem well: "All women work, and they always have—sometimes as providers of goods and services on the land and in the household, sometimes for wages in the marketplace. The questions now are where women work during pregnancy, how adequate the support system is that provides assistance to mothers of very young children, and what the best conditions are for the healthy development of the preschool child."[69]

Our concern, of course, is just as great for the elementary and secondary school age child. Rossi further made the critical observations, such that never seems to occurred to the sex-pleasure–seeking irresponsible philosophers of the open-marriage doctrine: "Unfortunately, the rationale for child-care programs in the past has been the needs of the economy or the needs of the mother, not the needs of the children. . . . As a consequence, little has yet been done to disturb the idea that under the best of all circumstances, the best place for young children is in the home under the mother's care" or, rather than in an impoverished home, at least part of the day in a "growth center as a kind of third parent that could contribute creatively to the child's development in ways the best home could not provide."[70] Could multifamily households in which the sexual and parenting lines of the nuclear families remain intact, but which include overlapping and shared living space, possibly serve the same purpose as growth centers? Would the traits of human nature be served in this case, for example, the "bonding of the mother and the newborn," the generation of an "orderly scheme of behavior norms" for the child, "the development of a positive self-image and self-esteem," the guidance of the "striving impulse" in directions consonant with self and society, et cetera?

In relation to the family and child rearing, Rossi gave the following cautions to those who would exercise their fancies with schemes of sexual relations and child rearing as substitutes for the evolutionary structures of child-parent relations:

> The application of a biosocial perspective to current explorations of marriage and parenthood puts serious questions to the *cultural determinism* [italics added] to which the social sciences have long adhered. The sexual and parenting scripts underlying much contemporary literature on the family is one-sided in its stress on the male-female relationship and its virtual ignoring of the birth and rearing of children. An egalitarian ideology in fact involves profound difficulties when applied to child-rearing. Communally reared children, far from being liberated, are often neglected, joyless creatures. . . . By far the wiser course to such a future [a balanced life] is to plan and build from the most fundamental root of society in human parenting and not from the shaky superstructure created by men in that fraction of time in which industrial societies have existed.[71]

NOTES

1. Maurice Cranston, "Are There Any Human Rights?" *Daedalus: Journal of the American Academy of Arts and Science* (Fall 1983), pp. 1–17.

2. Ibid.

3. Karl Marx, *The Grundrisse,* edited and translated by David McLellan (New York: Harper Torchbook, 1971), pp. 94–95.

4. William L. Werterman, *The Slave System of Greek and Roman Antiquity* (Philadelphia, Pennsylvania: The American Philosophical Society, 1955).

5. V. Gordon Childe, *Social Evolution* (Henry Schuman, 1951).

6. V. Gordon Childe, *Man Makes Himself* (C. A. Watts and Co., 1948), p. 134.

7. Karl Marx, *loco supra citato,* pp. 94–95.

8. Marshall D. Sahlins, "The Origin of Society," *Scientific American,* vol. 203, no. 3 (September 1960), pp. 88–96.

9. Nikki Meredith, "The Gay Dilemma," *Psychology Today* (January 1984), pp. 56–62.

10. *Morbidity and Mortality Weekly Report,* Public Health Service, vol. 32, No. 35 (September 9, 1983).

11. William Raspberry, "Focus on the Black Family," *Times-Picayune/The States Item,* February 3, 1984.

12. Marshall D. Sahlins, "The Origin of Society," *Scientific American,* vol. 203 (September 1960), pp. 76–87.

13. Robert J. Stoller, *Perversion* (New York: Pantheon Books, 1975), p. 199.

14. Gordon Rattray Taylor, "Historical and Mythological Aspects of Homosexual Behavior," in *Sexual Inversion: The Multiple Roots of Homosexuality,"* Judd Marmor, ed. (New York: Basic Books, 1965), p. 162.

15. Cornelia B. Wilbur, "Clinical Aspects of Female Homosexuality," in Judd Marmor, ed., *Sexual Inversion: The Multiple Roots of Homosexuality* (New York: Basic Books, 1969), p. 268.

16. I. Bieber, H. J. Dain, P. R. Dince, C. B. Wilbur, T. B. Bieber, M. G. Drellich, H. G. Grand, R. H. Grundlach, M. W. Kremer, A. R. Rifkin, *Homosexuality* (New York: Basic Books, 1962) p. 303.

17. S. Rado, "An Adaptational View of Sexual Behavior," in P. Hoch and J. Zubin eds., *Psychological Development in Health and Disease* (New York: Grune and Stratton, 1949) pp. 186–213.

19. A. P. Bell and M. S. Weinberg, *Homosexualities: A Study of Diversity among Men and Women* (New York: Simon and Schuster, 1978), pp. 196–197.

20. Ibid., p. 277, table 2.2.

21. "Effects of Prenatal Sex Hormones on Gender-Related Behavior," A. A. Ehrhardt and H. F. L. Meyer-Bahlburg, *Science,* vol. 211, no. 4488 (March 20, 1981), pp. 1312–28.

22. P. C. Lee, "Anthropology and Sex Differences," in Patrick C. Lee and Robert S. Stewart, eds., *Sex Differences* (New York: Urizen Books, 1976), p. 153.

23. Ibid., p. 154.

24. Ibid., p. 155.

25. Ralph Linton, "Selections from The Study of Man," in Patrick C. Lee and Robert S. Stewart, eds., *Sex Differences* (New York: Urizen Books, 1976), p. 172.

26. Lee, *loco supra citato,* p. 157.

27. Linton, *loco supra citato,* pp. 182–83.

28. *Morbidity and Mortality Weekly Reports,* Public Health Service vol. 32, no. 35 (September 9, 1983), pp. 453–57.

29. Linton, *loco supra citato,* p. 183

30. Talcott Parsons, "Family Structure and the Socialization of the Child," in Lee and Stewart, eds., *Sex Differences.* p. 203.

31. Ibid., p. 209.

32. Sahlins, *loco supra citato.*

33. Roger V. Burton and John W. M. Whiting, "The Absent Father and Cross-Sex Identity," in Lee and Stewart, eds., *Sex Differences,* pp. 235–36.

34. Ibid., p. 242.

35. Lewis Terman and Catherine Cox Miles, "Sex and Personality: Studies in Masculinity and Femininity," in Lee and Stewart, eds., *Sex Differences,* pp. 386, 389, 392.

36. "Sex Difference in Personality Characteristics," in Lee and Stewart, eds., *Sex Differences* p. 401.

37. Albert Bandura and Richard H. Walters, "Theories of Identification and Exposure to Multiple Models" in Lee and Stewart, eds., *Sex Differences,* pp. 430–31.

38. Lawrence Kohlberg and Edward Zigler, "Physiological Development, Cognitive Development, and Socialization Antecedents of Children's Sex-Role Attitudes," in Lee and Stewart, eds., *Sex Differences,* p. 439.

39. Paul G. Muscari, "The Structure of Mental Disorder," *Philosophy of Science,* vol. 48, no. 4. (December 1981), pp. 553–72.

40. Robert L. Spitzer, *et al.,* "DSM-III: The Major Achievement and an Overview," *American Journal of Psychiatry,* vol. 137 (1980) pp. 151–64.

41. Muscari, *loco supra citato.*

42. Spitzer, *loco supra citato.*

43. Ibid.

44. D. L. Rosenhan, "On Being Sane in Insane Places," *Science,* vol. 179, no. 4070 (January 19, 1973), pp. 250–57.

45. Judd Marmor, ed., *Sexual Inversion* (New York: Basic Books, Inc. 1965), p. 5.

46. Ibid., p. 21.

47. Robert J. Stoller, *Perversion* (New York: Pantheon Books, 1975), pp. 3–11.

48. Frank Schmalleger, "World of the Career Criminal," *Human Nature* (March 1979), pp. 50–56.

49. Constance Holden, "The Criminal Mind: A New Look at an Ancient Puzzle," *Science,* vol. 199 (February 3, 1978), pp. 511–14.

50. James R. Smith and Lynn G. Smith, "Co-Marital Sex and the Sexual Freedom Movement," in James R. Smith and Lynn G. Smith, eds., *Beyond Monogamy* (Baltimore, Maryland: Johns Hopkins University Press, 1974), p. 207.

51. L. L. Constantine and J. M. Constantine, "Sexual Aspects of Multilateral Relations," in James R. Smith and Lynn G. Smith, eds., *Beyond Monogamy* (Baltimore, Maryland, Johns Hopkins Press, 1974), p. 281.

52. Sigmund Freud, *Collected Papers* (Honolulu: Hogarth Press, 1953), vol. 5 p. 192.

53. Ibid., vol. 4, p. 194

54. Ibid., vol. 2, p. 232

55. Ibid.

56. Alfred Adler, *Understanding Human Nature* (Garden City, New York: Garden City Publishing, 1927), p. 221.

57. Bronislaw Malinowski, *Sex and Repression in Savage Society* (Harcourt, Brace and Co., 1927).

58. J. William Lloyd, "Sex Jealousy and Civilization," in V. F. Calverton and S. D. Schmalhausen, eds., *Sex in Civilization* (Macaulay Co., 1929), p. 233.

59. Constantine/Constantine, *loco supra citato*, p. 281.

60. Virginia Adams, "Getting at the Heart of Jealous Love," *Psychology Today*, vol. 13, no. 12 (May 1980) pp. 38–47, 102–106.

61. Smith/Smith, *loco supra citato*, pp. 2–3.

62. R. Linton, *The Study of Man* (Appleton, Century, Crofts, 1936), p. 137.

63. Smith/Smith, *Beyond Monogamy*, p. 33.

64. Ibid., pp. 2–3.

65. W. H. Masters and V. E. Johnson, *The Pleasure Bond* (New York: Bantam Books, 1975) pp. 267–285.

66. Smith/Smith, *loco supra citato*, J.W. Ramey, "Emerging Patterns of Innovative Behavior in Marriage," pp. 103–37.

67. Tamara K. Hareven, "Family Time and Historical Time," *Daedalus* (Spring, 1977), pp. 57–70.

68. Alice S. Rossi, "A Biosocial Perspective on Parenting," *Daedalus* (Spring 1977), pp. 1–31.

69. Ibid.

70. Ibid.

71. Ibid.

17

Human Nature and Governmental Life-Style: Marxian Implications

THE DREAM

Seldom does an emergent theory in social science strike the sensitivity of an ordered mind so acutely as to clarify the many contradictions and philosophic dilemmas in the politicosocial practices of nations. Seldom does such a theory bring to light the reasons for the discordant impact of nations' social systems on the behavior patterns of their people, i.e., the reasons why their social systems traumatize the nature of their people's human nature. The social theories of the visionary utopians like Plato, Thomas More, Tommasco Campanella, Francis Bacon, Robert Owen, Claude Henri Saint-Simon, Charles Fourier, and Jean Jacques Rousseau were unique contributions to the endless quest and yearning of people through the ages for a world where, without unnecessary mundane obstacles, the body is nourished, the spirit inspired, and the creative impulses encouraged. But they lacked the historical insight to realize that such a world was not yet possible. They were not aware of the basic social forces brought into play by the civilized world whose interplay impelled the process of social development. They were not cognizant that knowledge, i.e., science and technology, had not yet reached the stage necessary to realize their dream, that the prerequisite for freedom to participate in all social relations for everyone was bound up inseparably with society's mastery of the physical sciences and their productivity, and that a social system, in order to satisfy the needs of its people, must not only assure their material needs, but must also operate in concordance with the traits of human nature. Culture has now developed to a point of no return to a social system like primitive communism, which had satisfied *Homo* for hundreds of thousands of years. Under present conditions, the satisfaction of the traits of human nature by a social system would require a production capacity and capital accumulation no nation has yet reached.

The Origin of the Dream

There is a relationship between human nature and socioeconomic systems that mankind had developed during its history up to the present time. These systems were foraging, agriculture and herding, agricultural surplus, metallurgy, urbanization and slave-serf labor, mercantilism and emergence of the bourgeoisie, and Machine Age industrial production and emergence of the industrial working class. Each system is either in accord or in discord with some or all of the traits of human nature. At the very beginning of human prehistory, when *Homo* was groping for a type of social interrelationship that would change the primate bonding force to the human force of behavior, i.e., bonding and sharing, the traits of human nature were mostly potential and inchoate. Primate sexual behavior kept disrupting and plaguing the social relations among the bands of primitive man. The problem of the increasing lengthening of the altricial period of childhood had to be dealt with. The dynamics of foraging and sharing needed to be developed. The social relations technique for keeping behavior controlled within the needed limits for maintaining an ongoing operational family and band had to be formulated. These were the problems that drove *Homo* to become psychosocially humanized. His cognitive processes were gathering momentum. None of these problems has disappeared from humankind's ken to this very day—nor ever will in the foreseeable future. The traits of human nature therefore have an essense of permanence, although each culture adds its specific aspects in the expression of each trait. Each socioeconomic system of society brings into being its special sociofunctional interrelations that impinge on each trait of human nature. None of the socioeconomic systems has acted in concord with all the traits of human nature, with the possible exception of the foraging system or what Marx called "primitive communism." But, as Lee pointed out, even this stage of existence had its built-in struggles—the struggles of *Homo* exerting itself to maintain its human behavior against the ever-present urge of primate behavior, forcing itself to dominate, to wit:

Having declared that the foraging mode of production is a form of primitive communism, it would be a mistake to idealize the foraging peoples as noble savages who have solved all the basic problems of living. Like individuals in any society, the foragers have to struggle with their own internal contradictions, and living up to the demands of this strongly collective existence presents some particularly challenging problems. *Sharing,* for example, *is not automatic*; it has to be learned and reinforced by culture. Every human infant is born equipped with both the capacity to share and the capacity to be selfish. This observation is confirmed by studies of early childhood (Garvey). Learning to receive an offered toy, to hand it back, and to extend the hand to receive it again is one of the earliest complex behaviors exhibited by young infants in Western society (Waterhouse and Waterhouse).[1]

The predominant system today is what Marx dubbed as capitalism after the main feature of its productive process, capital, the United States being its staunchest supporter in today's world. But its antithesis is the Soviet Union's Leninist adaptation of Marx's philosophy, Soviet socialism. These are the two main magnetic poles of political economy today.

The human rights theories of the American colonists shaped significantly the political and economic orientation of the modern world toward what we call democracy. We became the epitome of the laissez faire economy Marx panegyrized as the greatest force for the eventual development of socialism in our time: "Thus capital first creates bourgeois society and the universal appropriation of nature and of social relationships themselves by the members of society. Hence the great civilizing influence of capital, its production of a stage of society compared with which all earlier stages appear to be merely *local progress* and idolatry of nature. Nature becomes for the first time simply an object for mankind, purely a matter of utility; it ceases to be recognized as a power in its own right; and the theoretical knowledge of its independent laws appears only as a strategem designed to subdue it to human requirements, whether as the object of consumption or as the means of production"[2] This American economic giant, capital, became the envy of the world as its ability to produce and create wealth became legendary. In the wake of this triumph were created powerful industrial monopolies and the means to fragment them, trade unions, unique scientific communities, racism and the means to abolish it, large sections of impoverished people and governmental apparatus to ameliorate poverty, and powerful special interest lobbies like those of the oil, bank, and insurance company monopolies, but not enough will to control them, although laws were passed to do so. Capital also created a democracy that allows for the organization of public movements for the election of people's candidates as a counterforce to powerful special interests and for social security programs that have mitigated the conditions of the elderly and the poor, although with regrettable ineptness. This capitalist vanguard nation, with its good and bad, has created for its people the highest *material* level of living among the nations of the world.

THE NIGHTMARE

Laissez-faire began as a principle of political economy that stimulated freedom of action in the process of producing wealth—a freedom that created all types of social inequalities in the scramble for wealth while, at the same time, fomenting movements for political freedom: democracy. It is a foregone conclusion that uncontrolled freedom of action will eventually change into its opposite. Actually, this practice of laissez-faire, even though confounded with an imposing facade of regulatory impedimenta has allowed such economic freedom to generate the present-day mighty monopolies, and has nurtured this sense of freedom also to infiltrate as a self-serving ethos into every facet of the social life of the country. This has occurred to an extent that the community norms that used to control conduct have now been negated so that individuals have arrogated to themselves the right of choosing their own norms of behavior, thus driving toward community chaos. Accordingly, the overconcern with criminals' civil rights by manipulation of trial procedure technicalities, as compared to their victims' rights, has given the criminal a checkrein over the freedom of action of their victims (the public). The greater freedom for decision making given by the courts to those incapable of making mature or wholesome decisions, such as children and the mentally disoriented, is denying the responsibility of the family. The way the government remains silent or pretends to regard as normal business conduct the flagrant economic blackmail and "rip-off" practices abounding everywhere is turning freedom into confusion and denial of freedom. Allowing those for whose education society is responsible to dictate the curricula and methods of education is turning over to the uneducated the authority to educate. Favoring the use and abuse of the legal system in suing and countersuing for causes incidental, accidental, or planned frivolity but expressly as an exploitative method for making money, or, by pursuing a course of prolonging and complicating trial procedure, giving legitimacy to a process of increasing costs and wasting time in order to obfuscate results, is negating the instrument of justice to serve its opposite, injustice. And wantonly and unnecessarily destroying the environment in order to create commodities and more profits is transmuting the salutary commonalty into a forbidding dispossession.

Examples of the "democratic" disorder created by the unprincipled application of laissez-faire in the name of American freedom or the American way of life can be multiplied amply. It is indeed ironic when one considers how restrictive and constrictive life can become living under a purely unrestrictive laissez-faire system. The greatest and most fancy-free freedom for all is a sure way of creating chaos in which little freedom for anyone prevails except for those who know how to use such chaos to maintain their own preeminence and power or to take the route of open theft and violence as an appropriate way for a livelihood. Even where chaos has not supervened, an atmosphere of swindle as an accepted mode of conduct may exist. Take, for instance, the tradition that has developed in expecting elected officials to be crooked, rich persons or firms to have "made it by hook or crook," or take, for instance, the dread that envelops many families during a period of economic depression, which is an inherent phenomenon in such a system, or the fear of being mugged and robbed, particularly when older ladies step out of their homes, or the terror of being raped that grips younger and older women when not in protected company, or the anxiety that pervades many a community because of the prevalence of burglary associated with violence. What a life-style for living! What is wrong with a system that tolerates such an atmosphere? What kind of democracy is this? Or is our capitalist democracy losing its way, as predicted by Marx and Lenin?

The social and economic theories of the scientific utopians like Karl Marx, Friederich Engels, Max Weber, Sidney and Beatrice Webb, and Vladimir Lenin were unique contributions to the modus operandi of the political process for attaining the governmental power to realize the social aims of their theories. The Marxian political-economic theories with Leninist variation have been the most successful in attaining power and in influencing world movement. Therefore, let us examine the comparative relationship between the Marxian and capitalistic principles and whether their application results in concordance or antagonism with the traits of human nature. The practitioners of Marxian theory certainly are not of one mind. Such theoriests as Edward Bernstein, Karl Kautsky, Otto Bauer, and G. V. Plekhanov were considered variants from the orthodox. Rosa Luxemburg, an early and longtime friend of Lenin and a dynamic activist, disagreed with Lenin's one-party dictatorship, but not with the temporary dictatorship of the proletariat. Angelica Balabanoff, also a close and respected friend of Lenin, was in continual disagreement with his undemocratic tactics. Other variations in the interpretation and application of Marxian theory as dogmatized by the Russian theorists are the Chinese, which in turn are different from that of the Yugoslavs, which are different from that of the Rumanians and Hungarians, and which were different from that of the Czechoslovaks before 1968. Are all these differences so great as to cause the kind of enmity that exists between the Soviets and the Chinese, or between the Yugoslavs and the Soviets, or between the Albanians and the Soviets, or that existed between the Czechoslovaks before 1968 and the Soviets?

WHITHER THE U.S.A.?

We accept the thesis that the direction of the socialist movement is aimed toward humanistic practice. What harm, in the historical perspective, does some variance in interpretation make, even though one theoretical scheme may lead more quickly to attaining the objective than another? Which country appears to be making most ominous maneuvers against those who do not hold to its orthodoxy? It seems that the Soviet Union stands first and China is a close second. From all indications, the positions taken by these two countries are mostly the result of vying for leadership among the socialist-oriented countries. From a historical point of view, this competition has already led to senseless violence on the part of the Soviet Union and to the stirring up of violent rhetoric by China against the Soviet Union. If this competition for attaining the position of leader and practitioner of the only version of correct Marxian principles were vital in protecting the socialist countries against capitalistic incursions and counterrevolutionary cabal, one could understand the positions taken. But such circumstances have practically ceased as a real threat. The United States, the only possible threat, does not even have enough of its "old-time" imperialistic spirit to react with dignity toward the economic war the OPEC countries have openly declared against the U.S.'s lifeline—energy. It does not even earn the Chinese rubric for pretentious power—paper tiger. The rest of the capitalist world has responded to this threat against their jugular vein with craven opportunism. These are the countries that threaten the USSR! Even Reaganism is only a disposition to *react* to provocation rather than an initiative to act against existential forebodings.

Neither the capitalist countries nor the socialist countries have approached the problem of developing a modus operandi in their social systems to accommodate to the behavioral needs of their people—to the traits of human nature. The interest of both have been: (1) to satisfy the material needs of their people, (2) to do this while holding onto the power to govern those people, and (3) to gain favor and controlling influence over other nations in order to maintain leadership in political and economic competition. These comparisons are words of blasphemy to the socialist leadership. To them, this so-called competition is in reality maneuvering to further deteriorate the capitalistic economies and to bring to fulmination the contradictions in the capitalist social system. This is what the socialist politicians would like the people to believe. But anyone with any sophistication and knowledge of what is going on is as dismayed with the socialist camp of leaders as with the capitalist camp of leaders and how they are reacting to various national and international crises without concern for accommodating the eco-system to the human-nature needs of the people.

The leaders of the socialist nations must have developed enough acumen to realize that the mass movements of peoples all over the globe are now caught up in a relentless process that is directed unal-terably toward effecting greater humanization of governmental proc-esses and that these movements have generated a momentum too accelerated to be stopped by any combination of capitalist forces. Nor is there any sign that such a combination of forces would be mustered into action if the mass movements within each country were allowed to mature on their own energies. For what other purpose, then, could the socialist leaders be activating their countries' military machines so impetuously, if not for the same old imperialistic motives of which they had in the past, with ample justification, accused the capitalist nations? What is actually happening is that many more people are and will continue to be killed and maimed by prematurely forcing the creation of "socialist dictatorships" in underdeveloped countries than by encouraging them first to develop their "capital" bases competitively as Marx had historically propounded in his *Grundrisse*: "Capital's ceaseless striving toward the general form of wealth drives labour beyond the limits of its natural paltriness (Naturbedürftigkeit) and thus creates the material elements for the development of the rich individuality which is as all-sided in its production as in its consump-tion, and whose labour also therefore appears no longer as labour, but as full development of activity itself, in which natural necessity in its direct form has disappeared; because a historically created need has taken the place of the natural one. This is why *capital is productive;* i.e., *an essential relation for the development of the social forces.*"[3] This would be the quickest way to humanize the world without the bloodshed resulting from unnecessarily and prematurely *forcing* the establishment of "socialist dictatorships" in underdeveloped countries. Such dictatorships are, in reality, not socialist but the direct opposite, and if they claim to be dictatorships of the proletariat or of the people, they are, in reality, dictatorships *over* the proletariat or the people and, tragically, farcical at that. The foregoing quotation from Marx would indeed be the quickest and least blood-letting course for humanizing the world, and is not such humanization the ulterior goal of all the utopian and scientific socialist theories, even the theories of *democratic* capitalism as nourished by Ben Franklin, Thomas Jefferson, and Abraham Lincoln.

It is plainly impossible to distinguish anymore between the atrocities and stupidities fomented by the nations in either camp. *Not one* country that calls itself socialist is making an intelligent effort to become the *showcase* of humaneness and humanity—to become a paragon for other nations to emulate. Certainly, no capitalist country is such a paragon. But there is an irony in this long historical struggle of people toward greater humaneness of government—an irony that challenges the fate of a capitalist democracy like the United States. If humanization of man's condition becomes the *all-consuming motive* of government, and this is beginning to happen in the United States, to be achieved by creation of conditions in the ecosystem that would be in harmony with the positive phases of the traits of human nature, then, could a capitalist country as well as a socialist country become such a paragon?

Today, the political struggles in the world, as seen by the left, are between the humanistic concepts and theories of socialism and the villainous practices of capitalism. Such a simplistic understanding of the world is, to a significant extent, valid but not without significant qualification. Marx himself explained this really complex struggle as the dialectic movement of *capital*, toward inevitable socialism, which is fascinating indeed:

> But to the degree that large industry develops, the creation of real wealth comes to depend less on labour time and on the amount of labour employed than on the power of the agencies [such as machines] set in motion during labour time, whose powerful effectiveness is itself in turn out of all proportion to the direct labour time spent on their production, but depends rather on the general state of science and on the progress of technology, or the application of this science to production. . . . No longer does the worker

insert a modified natural thing [his direct work] as middle link between the object and himself; rather, he inserts the process of nature, transformed into an industrial process, as a means between himself and inorganic nature, mastering it. He steps to the side of the production process instead of being its chief actor. In this transformation, it is neither the direct human labour he himself performs, nor the time during which he works, but rather the appropriation of his own general productive power, his understanding of nature and his mastery over it by virtue of his presence as a social body—it is, in a word, the development of the social individual which appears as the great foundation-stone of production and of wealth. *The theft of alien labour time, on which the present wealth* [during Marx's time] *is based,* appears a miserable foundation in face of this new one [high level of scientific production], created by large-scale industry itself. As soon as labour in the direct form has ceased to be the great well-spring of wealth, labour time ceases and must cease to be its measure, and hence exchange value must cease to be the measure of use value. The *surplus labour of the mass* has ceased to be the condition for the development of general wealth, just as the *non-labour of the few,* for the development of the general powers of the human head. With that, production based on exchange value breaks down, and the direct, material production process is stripped of the form of penury and antithesis. The free development of individualities, and hence not the reduction of necessary labour time so as to posit surplus labour, but rather the general reduction of the necessary labour of society to a minimum, which then corresponds to the artistic, scientific, etc., development of the individuals in the time set free, and with the means created, for all of them. *Capital itself is the moving contradiction, in that it presses to reduce labour time to a minimum, while it posits labour time, on the other side, as sole measure and source of wealth. Hence it diminishes labour time in the necessary form so as to increase it in the superflous form; hence posits the superflous in growing measure as a condition—question of life or death—for the necessary.* [italics added] On the one side, then, it calls to life all the powers of science and of nature, as of social combination and of social intercourse, in order to make the creation of wealth independent (relatively) of the labour time employed on it. On the other side, it wants to use labour time as the measuring rod for the giant social forces thereby created, and to confine them within the limits required to maintain the already created value as value. Forces of production and social relations—two different sides of the development of the social individual—appear to capital as mere means and are merely means for it to produce on its limited foundation. In fact, however, they are the material conditions to blow this foundation sky-high.[4]

This explains the Marxian view of how capital creates the conditions for socialism and blows the foundation of capitalism sky-high.

The lengthy foregoing citation from Marx's famous critique on the theory, principles, and philosophy of political economy is the gist of his historical perspective in relation to the dialectics of capital. In the United States and the rest of the Western world, the essence of this dialectic movement of capital is remarkably well illustrated. Science and technology have certainly initiated changes in our time which demonstrate that "as soon as labour in the direct form [the worker applying his energy directly on the thing being produced] has ceased to be the great well-spring of wealth, labour time ceases and must cease to be the measure of use value." This is explained by Marx's penetrating dialectics in analyzing the meaning of the terms "use value" and "exchange value" as they relate to the worker himself and to the dynamics of capital. To the worker who needs to sell his labor in order to get money, his labor possesses only *use value* insofar as he can use it as *exchange value* for acquiring wages. While it is only *exchange value* for capital insofar as the objectified labor (that which labor produces) has *use value* for the buyer in the exchange process. Thus, in the free market, the labor time expended on production of material has always been the measure of *use value* that capital used in exchanging the products in the marketplace. But when the free market is faulted by monopoly, this relation is abolished and disorder, disorganization, and licentiousness supervene. Thus monopoly abolishes the relations between labor time, use value, and exchange value that are basic to the *productive* functioning of capital, but with disastrous results for the people. Instead of *capital* itself creating conditions for its own metamorphosis from master of society to society's mastery over it by the very plenitude of its production, thus leading to socialism or some semblance of this relation of capital to the social organization, private monopoly (capital's power play) incites to capitalism's destruction. Monopoly thereby tries to accomplish, as a private instrument, what democratic society itself would have the power and inclination to do after its productive forces are able to produce every thing amply for all its people. As a socio-politico-economic concept, monopoly per se is not necessarily a destructive process. It depends on how and who uses it. Government monopoly of the essential agents of social needs, such as energy, banks, insurance agencies, public education, and public hygiene, including the economic implementation factors basic for community well-being, are the areas where government monopoly is socially beneficial. Thus monopoly abolishes the relation between use-value and exchange-value, because it operates as a government, with all its prerogatives. When the monopoly is by private enterprise, it operates as a private government within a public government and not in the interest of all the people. Only when the relation between the forces of production and the social relations (which include production relations) are altered in favor of all the people will the definitions of use-value and exchange-value take on a new meaning and their relations to one another will evolve into a new level of humanistic practice, since labortime then "must cease to be the measure of use-value."

The present drive toward more and more monopoly is being strengthened by the movement to form conglomerates. This is one of the most chimerical schemes for the devious manipulation of rip-off profits for negating the capital formation use of capital, since the scheme wastes rather than produces capital. The movement is directed toward the rapid siphoning off of profits and gaining tax exemptions for the immediate increase of dividends for stock holders. This movement reinforces the ability of monopoly to increase its destructive rip-off intrigues in a process of vitiating the capital formation power of capital and accelerating the dissolution of capitalism.

The 1982 winner of the Nobel Prize for economics, George J. Stigler, is credited with giving "birth to an economic analysis of political processes based on the pursuit of self-interest by both elected officials and politically potent economic constituencies."[5] Professor Stigler has a long history of researches along the theme of the antisocial practices of big business, to wit, his popular article on the case against big business in the May 1952 issue of *Fortune*. The economic literature for the past century has become more and more charged with studies on this subject, some discoursing in polemic generalities and others fluent with excellent compilation of pertinent data of a particular industry, such as John M. Blair's "The Control of Oil." But Professor Stigler's comprehensive and incisive research leading to well-founded principles in political economy and his straightforward interpretation of data are refreshing indeed. Economics professor Demsetz of the University of

California, who wrote the article in *Science* describing Stigler's Nobel honor, asserted that:

> Increasingly these (Stigler's studies) showed not that the effect of regulation was nil, but that it was *perverse* [italics added]. Where commissions were created to protect consumers, they functioned by protecting the industries they regulated from competition—to the disadvantage of the consumers. . . . This work (*The Behavior of Industrial Prices by Stigler and Kendahl,* National Bureau of Economic Research, New York, 1968) helped give birth to an economic analysis of political processes based on the pursuit of self-interest by both elected officials and politically potent economic constituencies. The powerful reasoning and mounting evidence yielded by this view of the functioning of democracy has completely undermined naive political theories based on the presumption that democratically elected governments seek primarily the interests of the broadly based electorate. This new application of economic models of self-interested behavior has increased substantially our ability to understand political behavior. . . . Stigler's work, along with that of J. M. Buchanan and G. Tullock, has given rise to a fascinating and burgeoning economic theory and accompanying empirical study of democracy.[6]

What Professor Demsetz did not say is that the principles derived by Professor Stigler in relation to economics and big business are really a confirmation of what Marx developed in his major opus, *Capital,* in great detail concerning antisocial capitalist's business practices in relation to the welfare of the community. It was not capital that Marx derided, but those who used it for pursuit of pure self-interest. Consequently, those individuals and their practices need to be controlled, lest they destroy the vigorous productive capacity of capital. At the present time, the greatest destroyers of capital are the boards of directors of the large oil companies and their allies who control OPEC. To illustrate: The cost of gasoline before 1973 was based on the cost of production plus the constrained profit that a competitive market extracted. Only by eliminating the competitive aspect was it possible to extract more than the market constrained profit. This was accomplished by limiting exploration for oil in the United States and allowing, over the years, the production within our country to lag more and more. The scarcity thereby resulting in home-produced oil created the pressure for the United States to import more and more of the oil produced by the multinational oil companies in the Middle East and

North Africa. Our country was thus maneuvered into the most vulnerable position for being exploited by the oil companies monopoly in collaboration with the cartel of the oil-producing countries. Within a few years, the price of a barrel of crude oil increased ten times. The extraction of the profit on the competitive market was transformed anon into an extortion of booty by a pirating monopoly. The craven weakness of the response of the government to this obvious illegal monopolistic maneuver stirred bold repercussions in the rest of the economy. Suddenly a predicted freeze in a small coffee-growing area sent the price of coffee sky-high. A drought in a small peanut-growing area increased suddenly the price of peanut butter by over 150 percent. Rumors about the coming shortage of sugar (which never came to be) tripled and quadrupled the price. Similar hyperbolizing of contrived rumors inflated the prices of bread, meat and other basic needs for routine living. This was followed by the skyrocketing of costs of housing, clothes, medical care, ad infinitum. The labor-management accepted relationship between "labor-time" and "use-value" as worked out in our mechanized processes of production were thrown completely out of kilter. Labor-time ceased to have meaning in relation to use-value, but not because there was no longer any need to maintain this relation, due to our attainment of an almost utopian level of potential in production and the "general reduction of the necessary labour of society to a minimum," as Marx predicated, but, on the contrary, because labour-time ceased to be the measure of use-value as the result of the power of the illicit monopoly of the oil companies in conspiration with the cartel of the feudal dictatorships, mainly of the Middle East and North Africa. The conspirators were strong enough politically to blackmail the entire world with the greatest example of extortion ever perpetrated in world history. It was this event that initiated the catastrophe of corrupting the relation between labour-time and, ultimately, *wages* and use-value. The extortion was so debilitating to the lesser developed countries as to threaten to throw eighty-seven of them into bankrupcy. By the end of 1981, their debt was $418 billion. They were unable even to meet the payment of the interest on this debt, a situation "that could "shake the world's banking monopoly."[7,8] Capitalism, by destroying its foundation, the free market, in a very essential area of world economy was able to invalidate thereby the basic relation between labour-time, use-value and exchange-value. Instead of the cessation of the relations between these basic values being due to the production having reached the level for everyone to have what everyone needed and thereby leaving ample time for self-development of all individuals, the cessation of relations was forced by falsely creating an economy of scarcity and this with the covert condonation of the government, ingloriously swayed by the oil and banking interests. But just as destructive of capital were the nonproductive uses made of the hundreds of billions of dollars accruing to the oil profiteers, as explained elsewhere.

Is the United States going to follow in the course Marx depicted in his prediction of the relentless movement of capital to its final destruction of capitalism, where the monopolists are leading the world, or will this democratic system be ingenious enough to be master of its fate in the drive of capital pushing beyond "the reproduction of the traditional way of life"? Will it be able to accommodate to the changing conditions created by the development of capital and continue to evolve while preserving the best of its system and shedding its impedimenta?

The rationale of Marx's prediction about the movement of capital is that it moves by accretion by exploiting labor, the exploitation being manifested by "the theft of alien labour time on which the present wealth" appears as a "miserable foundation in the face of new" and high level of scientific industrial production. "The surplus labour of the mass has ceased to be the condition for the development of general wealth, just as the non-labour of the few [capitalists] for the development of the general powers of the human head." When highly developed machines take over production, Marx noted, a certain amount of workers' time spent in production becomes superflous. Universal education and democratic sociocultural heritage have conditioned our people to act out the pressures for expression of their traits of human nature, at times even behaving in extremes by expressing the primate aspects of their nature. Education sharpens the cognitive processes for apprehending the forces of which Marx elaborated in his thesis on alienation. Democracy further accelerates this apprehension and even tempers the cognitive processes in expressing the actions mobilized by the people to redress their grievances. The tempering process might, by ingenious social engineering, even modify the production process whereby the traits of human nature are disencumbered and the fruits of production become objects for the people, i.e., alienation of the workers is dissolved.

Since, in Marx's day, there were no special nations among the capitalist countries where the longevity of "capital accretion" could have been predicted with some probability to be indefinitely prolonged, the United States, like any other capitalist country, was expected to eventually have its day of reckoning with the forces of self-destruction followed by socialism. What socialist theoretician has ever reckoned with the possibility that a capitalist country could ever modify the "inexorable" movement of its capital in relation to its productive forces in such a way that all the material needs of its people could reasonably be met, and, at the same time, to accede to a commitment to accommodate the dynamics of its social relations to the traits of human nature? Let us examine this anomaly.

Marx did not denegrate capitalist society malevalently in his philosophic contemplations where his sense of objectivity was unquestionable. He stated that capital created capitalist society, its productive forces, and its exploitive social relations: "Hence the great civilising influence of capital, its production of a stage of society compared with which all earlier stages appear to be merely *local progress* and idolatry of nature . . . capital has pushed beyond national boundaries and prejudices."[9] How does the United States stand today in relation to the possibility of veering into favorably modifying its "capital" movement to accommodate to the changing world of economic and social justice?

It has already been pointed out how chaotic social movement has become in United States. Reich describes in detail the impact of the American chaos.[10] Let us consider the main factors that have created this chaos:

1. The social trauma caused by the fulminating contradictions predicted by Marx that capital would engender eventually irreconcilable antagonisms between the tremendous ability to produce and the constrictions prevailing in the relation of the workers to the owners of capital, i.e., the relation of the workers to the products of social labor.

2. The completely unrestrained (pure laissez-faire) spirit and conscience of American democracy epitomized in the freedom of the individuals to make socially irresponsible choices (the primate aspect of a trait of human nature). This irresponsible freedom is being encouraged and reinforced by legal means such as extreme interpretations of civil rights and human rights laws. This abandon is being supported by court decisions, by educational means, as illustrated in the lack of reasonable restraints and discrimination in distinguishing between the human and primate aspects of teaching content in schools and in evaluating the behavior of students, by welfare practices such as social security programs that motivate either morale building or demoralization, and by organized labor's right to strike and bargain even when injury and death in the community are involved. Laissez-faire in the behavior of the individual is condoned as balance for the invisible privileges of monopoly in political economy.

3. The failure to create a rational system of social relations, agreed upon by the overwhelming majority of the people, based upon their material needs and conforming harmoniously to the traits of human nature.

Is there any wonder that chaos has taken over, but not the kind of chaos that makes for a revolutionary situation as described by Lenin[11] and in the hearings before the Committee on Foreign Relations of the United States Senate.[12] The chaos is of a benign type when considered in relation to civil disturbance, but malignant enough for those who are still unemployed, or whose income is still in the poverty level, or who are the victims of criminal violence, or who have suffered from fraud, rackets, or "rip-off" experiences like the emotion-laden waiting in gasoline station lines, or the epidemic increase in alcoholism and drug abuse, or who are bored or angered with the pattern of their existence.

Why is the United States not threatened with a large left wing party, except for some misplaced radicalism in the schools,[13] that is part of the political system of every Western capitalist democracy?

The answer is not explainable in the light of Marx's theory that capital created capitalism and will be capitalism's undoing. Capital in the United States has been so successful that, up to recently, it produced an inordinate percentage of the world production in relation to the size of its population, i.e., one-third of world production (1974). At this rate of production, the Marxian would expect that the socioeconomic contradictions in the United States should be nearing the stage of ripeness for a radical change in economic policy and practice. The doctrinaire Marxian would be expecting revolutionary change in this social system. That a change is taking place can even be seen by the blind. What will be the nature of the change? Will it be a revolution to socialism by a tame process as took place in the 1950s and 1960s in what is called the Black revolution? Will it be more violent or more extensive in time? Or is it possible that in the American Corporate State, as Reich describes the United States, an "immensely powerful machine, ordered, legalistic, rational, yet utterly out of human control, wholly and perfectly indifferent to any human values"[14] can, in a struggle to save itself, become rational to human needs? If "the great historical feature of capital is that it produces . . . surplus labor,"[15] surplus value, and increasing wealth, can a substantial amount of this surplus objectified labor be diverted for the wages and well-being of the producers to completely eliminate poverty and yet retain enough to be plowed back in producing more surplus value? Can the individual corporations that compose the Frankenstein Corporate State and that can, theoretically, according to law, more and more become subject to the will of large numbers of small stockholders—stockholders who could eventually be the workers and families of the corporation—be converted into a benevolent organization concerned with the human values of its workers? Can Marx's "surplus value" (wealth accumulated from profit, which implies that it is founded on poverty)[16] be transmuted to "social disposable time or non-working time" (measure of wealth in a society that has eliminated exploitation of the worker)[17] and eventually develop into a system that will be consonant with the traits of human nature? Can this happen without destroying the elements of challenge and modulated competitiveness by containing the latter, i.e., by keeping it from running wild and eliminating itself by development of cartels? Can the "Public State" of Galbraith[18] be accommodated to the needs not only of the material wants of life, but also to the psychosocial wants, the traits of human nature? If not, how can they be modified to so accommodate? If not, what other politicoeconomic system can be so accommodated?

The expectations that the modification or outright change in the American socioeconomic system will continue at an evolutionary course is credible, based on the fact that the vast majority of the American population have lived and continue to live under material conditions tolerable to human endurance, and although the rich become richer in comparison to the vast majority, the material lot of the latter continues to get better. Even Marx somewhere in his voluminous writings opined that social change in the United States may not be accomplished by violent revolution. Certainly, this appeared to be a valid prediction based on the exceptional development of capital generated by a fabulous application of science and technology by an exceptionally industrious, enterprising people in material creations. If, as is expected, change in the American socioeconomic system will be by evolution, it is not extravagant to expect that "capital" will continue to play a vital role in development of American social change.

Bankruptcy of Government Economic Stress Policies

It is most important that we concern ourselves with Marxian theory, for the reason that it is the most potent socioeconomic theory contending in the world today—much more potent as contender than traditional American economics, which does not seem to be working so well, or at least, its intelligent application by the American leadership is getting increasingly disjointed. Traditional American economic theory is losing its respectful place in the eyes of the American public since it has been demonstrated in the last decade that the government is unable to deal with the critical inflation, unemployment, energy, and crime problems. The inflated strength of the dollar on the international exchange is mostly a problem of high interest rates charged in response to the inordinate federal deficit and to the reckless loans made to Third World countries with bank-gorged Arab petrodollars, which the predatory increased price of oil made impossible for those countries to repay. Neither traditional economics nor Keynesian nor Friedman money supply theory works any more. Even the Scandinavian countries have given up on their use of Keynesian economics.[19] Such variant economists as Galbraith and Tyler are not even listened to, regardless of whether they are right or wrong. Reich's methodology for social change is entirely too hazy for application. His book, *The Greening of America,* made quite a stir only because the American people are longing for a change that its leadership is unable to deliver.

The economists whom the government uses and has used as advisors in the economic affairs of the country have not been able to render demonstrably sound advice in the past or at present on how to deal with capitalism's stubborn cycle of prosperity-depression-unemployment since this cycle began in 1790. Their palliatives have been less than moderate in effectiveness in contrast to the auspicious pronunciamentoes of many of them.

The essence of humankind's economy, the practice of exchange, springs from its most basic trait of human nature, that of bonding-sharing. Exchange was a human practice before *Homo* began to produce things for survival, i.e., before farming and stock raising. Because the ecosystem of the ancient hominid hordes varied in natural productiveness of items for survival, their nature to share expanded to the practice of exchanging the excess of one ecosystem for the excess of another ecosystem. The rewards of exchange generated the cognitive processes resulting eventually in human production, circulation, and money as the economic basis of exchange. The story is a long and fascinating one, but not for presentation here.

It is a fact that economic depression or recession occurs concomitantly with a decrease in consumer buying power, followed by a decrease in stock replenishment, followed by a decrease in production, followed by an increase in unemployment. Then, before monopoly was powerful enough to prevent deflation, the latter was a sure adjunct of depression. All this happened because society, in the guise of government, *failed to act at the critical point* to prevent this *manmade cycle* from setting in. The critical point, of course, is somewhere in the prosperity phase of the cycle. What needs to be done is to prevent those forces that tend to negate prosperity from setting in, since they already become active during prosperity. Why has this not been done before? Because those who controlled the forces of production and the economic interrelationships obtaining in the production process had neither the mental disposition, nor the emotional urge, nor the intellectual perspicacity, nor the dedicated skill to contend with one of the fundamental characteristics of capitalism, the prosperity-depression-unemployment cycle.

If the critical point for introducing a modulatory intercession is during the phase of prosperity, is it in the area of circulation that then redounds on the process of production or in the process of production that, in turn, reflects on the process of circulation, or both? If it be in circulation, a phase of exchange, then basically it relates to the amount of money available to the producer to *buy* the raw or semiprocessed materials and labor and machines for production and for the people to buy the commodities for consumption. If it be in production, then basically it relates to the quantity and quality of the raw or semiprocessed materials, of labor and machines, of the commodities produced, and getting the latter to the market. But also to be taken into account must be the *time* it takes to produce what is needed without overproducing.

Circulation of money and commodities cannot happen without *people*. To control or modulate circulation by narrowly limited monetary policies such as restricting or amplifying the amount of money in circulation or by varying interest rates on borrowing money, or by narrowly limited fiscal policies relating to revenue collection has never worked well and certainly has not stopped recession and unemployment from threatening the lives of the people. These are scarcely palliative measures and are initiated with less concern for the people than for special interests. Controlling production by limiting or increasing the amount of commodities produced in order to maintain prices instead of primary concern for employment and livable wages again fails to take into consideration the people.

Any policies for the control or elimination of the economic cycle of prosperity-depression-unemployment that does not *primarily* take into consideration the people must inevitably be unsatisfactory in a democracy under capitalism, because it will destroy the competitive system of production and possibly democracy itself. If the American political economy is so inflexible that it cannot devise a method for interposing at a critical point in the process of production-circulation to arrest or negate the pernicious cycle of unmodulated capitalism without destroying the challenge trait of human nature and without penalizing the economic life of the people, then it does not deserve to be saved.

The highly respected traditional economist George P. Shultz is indeed pessimistic about the economy of the United States in his book *Economic Policy Beyond the Headlines*.[20] This longtime advisor on economic policy to the United States government opined: "Nearly everyone—economists, pundits, politicians, even policymakers themselves—would like to think it possible to achieve high employment with stable prices and to adjust the economy continuously to maintain that objective. *The primary tools available are fiscal policy and monetary policy* [italics added]. We shall be concerned here almost exclusively with fiscal policy because that is where our own experience has been concentrated." Is there any wonder that the government approach to the basic "production relations" problem plaguing this country, i.e., the relation of labor to capital, and the relation of both to government, and the tremendous influence of monopolies, unemployment produced by government monetary and fiscal policy (supply side economics), and contention between labor and capital on government economic policy and practice, including the foreign policy and influence of the State Department policy such as on the oil monopoly,* is as unproductive as the desert sands for the well-being of the people. How is it possible for narrowly perceived fiscal and monetary policies and practice without wide perspective on people's problems *to solve the following contradictions* in the U.S. economy unless there be *effective disciplinary* control over the critical points of "production relations" so that people can work and be compensated enough to buy what is produced according, at least, to an average standard of living made possible by the country's productive ability while, at the same time, adequate profit is made for increasing the country's wealth.

1. In the past, increases in unemployment occurred, for the most part, as the reaction to overproduction. At present, increased unemployment also occurs with underproduction.
2. In the past, increase in unemployment was accompanied by deflation of prices. At present, increased unemployment is accompanied by inflation of prices (monopoly control of prices made possible by creating a scarcity market).

*See the report to Congress by the Comptroller General of the U.S. January 3, 1978, *More Attention Should Be Paid to Making The U.S. Less Vulnerable to Foreign Oil Price and Supply Decisions.*

3. In the past, the law of supply and demand prevailed (as long as the term "demand" was not identified with real social need), i.e., the greater the supply, the more the demand is satisfied and followed by the lowering of price. This law is now turned on its head by monopoly: the *control* of supply prevents satisfaction of demand and forces the acceptance of increase in prices. Reduced production in large production units in itself increases cost of production because fixed capital remains fixed regardless how much is produced. This increased cost is a trifle compared to the extortion prices that monopoly usually demands.

4. In the past, prices were determined by competition in the free market. At present, monopoly determines price at the whim of its will, i.e., the rip-off system is applied in accordance to what the people will bear.

Corollaries:
   a. Profits can increase while production (supply) stagnates or decreases.
   b. Instead of producing to satisfy the market demand, production is restricted to increase prices.

5. Wages and prices in the past decreased with economic recession and increased somewhat with prosperity. At present, both continue to increase regardless of prosperity or recession. Labor unions and management are in a continual struggle in the upward movement of wages, which increase is immediately passed on to the consumer by increased prices, the worker mostly coming out on the short end, but, nevertheless, as a responsible instrument in the process of pricing American goods out of the world market.

These contradictions make it clear that neither the traditional nor the Keynesian nor the more recent monetarist nor any combination of them will work without better accommodation of the forces of *production relations* to the needs of the people. That the old methods do not work is well stated by Professor Woolley: "Periods of crisis present opportunities to alter, to redirect, and to redefine the role the state plays in the economy and the way in which economic policy is made. To judge from many current commentaries, we are now in such a crisis: old understandings of how the economy and politics work no longer seem adequate; expectations are unmet; forecasts fail. The crisis is felt not only in the realm of economic thought, but in political thought and in political life. The crisis is further revealed in the fact that serious consideration is given to the possibility of reversing the previously expanding role of government in the economy."[21] Contrary to the present conservation trend in spending and its relation to the well-being of the economy, Professor Cameron asserts with assuredness that although "a few nations have experienced such dramatic increase in government spending that the generation of capital has been impeded . . . most [such nations] have not, and in these nations the public economy has expanded without hindering capital formation and, in all likelihood, will continue to expand in the foreseeable future."[22] But the expanding of the economy cannot take place in the matrix of the new maneuver of severing the humanism from the process of exchange. Exchange is no longer a process of human sharing, but a spin-off of the human brain, using the primate heritage to convert the exchange process to a system of extortion. Although classical free enterprise has continued to change in the medium of scientific, technological, and social change, the humanistic nature inherent in the practice of exchange in democratic society has elevated the level of living of the entire society, regardless of the social class up to recent times. In recent decades, with the coming of age of monopoly and cartelism, this humanistic nature in exchange is gradually disappearing and exchange itself is changing into a dehumanized system of extortion and inflation.

Although the monopolistic price gouging of the oil cartel (OPEC and the multinational oil companies) initiated the precipitous worldwide inflation trend in 1973, sight must not be lost of the international socio-polito-economic significance of the gradual inflationary trend that began during the interval between the end of the Great Depression and the end of World War II. These two trends are illustrated by the changes in the worth of the dollar. During the thirty-two years between 1940 and 1973, the worth of the dollar decreased by 66 percent, while the decrease during the much shorter twelve-year interval between 1972 and 1983 was practically equivalent: 63 percent. This was an inflation rate of three times as fast as for the previous thirty-two years. For the four decades before 1940, the inflation rates were too small to be of consequence. The period beginning with World War II was associated with great social unrest and political changes. The League of Nations, which was established in 1920, had a membership of thirty-five nations at its peak in 1935. The United Nations was established in 1945, with a membership of 51 nations, which increased by 1983 to 157 nations. The postwar explosion of independent countries was the result of the restiveness of ethnic entities, declaring their human rights based on the belatedly recognized theme of Woodrow Wilson of self-determination. This restiveness was undoubtedly the result of the growing awareness of colonial peoples of their economic exploitation and of their rearing against the ethnical restraints placed on them by the political will of the Western industrialized nations. To impassion this revolutionary animation and aggressive leadership the socialist nations of Eastern Europe and later of Asia lent their deft efforts. The growing appreciation of people in the underdeveloped countries of the amenities for living decently made them easy converts to political action, and the spread of social and political movements based on human rights was further advanced through the declarations and encouragement of the United Nations. The usual high birth rates and the recently falling death rates were another significant factor in straining the economic plight of these nations.

This worldwide push of the awakened economically underdeveloped nations gradually began increasing the demand on the world market of commodities and sources of finances. These nations' economies improved and their opportunities were increased to borrow the petrodollars deposited in the Western banks by the OPEC members. Thus there occurred an increased demand for and drain of the commodities on the world market. Prices therefore tended to increase, due to pressures of supply and demand. But, almost at the same time, the oil cartel's precipitous increase in the cost of oil initiated the worldwide economic depression and an increase in interest rates that, in turn, retarded capital formation in the economically underdeveloped countries making it impossible for them to even pay the interest on their loans, much less being able to reduce the principals on their national debts.

Over the long run, cost of production continued to increase as the wages in the industrialized advanced countries continued to increase, and standards and levels of living continued to get better for the people as a whole. The technology for producing continued to grow. But the possibility of "real" overproduction, as distinguished from monopoly controlled production, would be small if the developing and underdeveloped counties were to continue to develop economically. This would have been the case if the oil cartel had not been allowed to plunder the industrialized countries and to pillage and plague the economies of the developing and underdeveloped countries. Even such catastrophes cannot last too long, considering the mood of the world. Considering this mood, the Third World will continue to develop economically and the income of workers will continue to increase. Such a process will continue to cause an acceptable inflation rate until the world economies produce adequately for comfortable subsistence and a measure of the amenities accruing to the world's population.

The Essentiality of Production Relations

The facts are that the vicarious maneuvers of the propounders of the simplistic political economic schemes treat the economy like a machine, rather than a human organization expressing one of its vital humanizing characteristics generated by its basic bonding-sharing trait: exchange. This exchange is a system of sociofunctional interactions whereby a mutual process of giving and taking occurs. When it relates to material (capital) and services (labor), it manifests itself as "production relations."

The basic relations encompassed in the meaning of the term "production relations" are:

1. the relations of the owners of the means of production (excluding labor) to the production process;
2. the relations of the workers to the production process;
3. the relations of item 1 to item 2 to the production process, which includes:

    a. the compensation of the worker, his productivity, the length of the working day, and the status of his family;
    b. the participation of the workers in the policy-making and management process;
    c. the share-holding interest of the workers in the enterprise;
    d. the employment-unemployment problems relating to the enterprise's operations;
    e. The relation of capital-labor matters generated by the internationalization of the American economy;
    f. the capital-labor relations generated by the immigration of labor into the American labor market;
    g. government operations related to the production process; and
    h. the dislocation of the relations between workers and owners of the means of production by the fouling of the process of exchange.

The failure to modulate at critical points the relations of the owners to the production process allows expansion of ownership to the point of national and international monopoly. If the products controlled by monopoly are socially essential enough, the owners become private powers capable of controlling government while, at the same time, eradicating free enterprise in relation to those essential items of production. This has already happened to the production of energy—a monopoly of oil companies, reinforced by partnership with OPEC. Monopolies can control and, in the case of oil, do control the amount of production and the prices.[23,24] They use their profits to help elect government officials and to "subtly" bribe them to perform in their favor. As previously cited, this was well elucidated by Nobel laureate Stigler. Monopoly can control the quality of products and dampen the vigor of capital formation by eliminating competition, and building conglomerates, thus taking capital out of production—the eventuality being the deterioration of the economy. The influence in government bureaucracy, particularly in the State Department of American-based international monopolies, would be an excellent topic for a Ph.D. dissertation.

In spite of the power of money in our culture, we are a democracy and labor has forged its place in the power structure of our society. The operational wealth of labor organizations is not a trifle in the political arena of government. Labor laws, for the most part, favor labor union organization. Labor has the undiluted right to negotiate contracts with capital. Regardless whether there be depression, recession, or prosperity, this right continues to operate. In many areas of production of products or services, labor has been successful in negotiating wages and salaries that have elevated its members' level of living to a very comfortably high standard. However, in relation to unemployment, its power is dead. Capital has certainly not lost anything by this state of affairs. It has continued to add these increases in the level of living of workers to the price of products and of services. Such uncontrolled maneuvering by capital and labor must have a threshold beyond which the society is vitally effected. Such has been happening for the past several decades. The American shipping industry has practically dried up since the cost of labor has outpriced itself on the competitive world market. This has been happening to the automobile industry so that it has been in a state of financial crisis for the past several years. The quality and price and cost of operation have outdone the American-produced cars. The manufacture of electronic items such as televisions and appliances and such other items as textiles is suffering the same fate. Eventually, such an uncontrolled situation must lead to chronic unemployment, recession, or depression, with short intervals of weak normalcy.

A more viable interrelationship between capital and labor must eventually be worked out for the good of both, since the monetary and fiscal policy of government has been fruitless in solving such "production relations" problems that cause the dislocations in our economy: unemployment, inflation, and stagnation of economic growth. The latter, therefore, are symptoms of economic dislocations, not causes. Most of the American economists are oriented toward trying to remedy dislocations of the economy by treating symptoms. In medical science, we know the weakness of this approach, although we treat symptoms when we do not know what causes them. Thus the Keynesians would increase government spending to fight depression and withdraw such spending in times of prosperity. The monetarists would center their major concern on fighting inflation, but mainly with varying prime interest rates and control of the money supply. The supply theorists concern themselves with deficit spending by government and liberalizing taxation for business and the wealthier class in order to increase investment for stimulating production, hoping thereby to decrease inflation, unemployment, and deficit spending and increase the growth of the economy.

All the foregoing types of economists use limited monetary or fiscal or both means in treating dislocations caused by disrupted socioeconomic relational problems such as unemployment, labor-capital confrontation with prices and wages spiraling, and the economic despotism of monopoly. The economic cycles of prosperity, depression, unemployment, and economic recovery have been going on since 1790, and luckily, the recovery phase of the cycle always turns up, regardless of the fiscal and monetary gimmicks used since 1933. The gimmicks have never stopped the cycles, because their causes are not limited to monetary or fiscal but to socioeconomic problems, i.e., production relations. The existing production relations, particularly between capital and labor, are sacred to both because they represent the essence of the heritage of the seventeenth century laissez-faire freedom of the entrepreneur to do as he pleased and the freedom of the worker to sell his labor to the highest bidder—even though such freedoms exist no more. It is always hoped by these contenders that the strong will get and do almost what they will for their self-aggrandizement—labor by organizing, if possible, all workers into unions and capital by controlling more and more of the production machinery. However, interrelational forces must be controlled at points where they disrupt the socioeconomic equilibrium, for example, by outpricing the products and the services from competition on the world market. They can be controlled without destroying the best that capitalist society has given to mankind. These are an ecosystem that creates challenges and stimulates the development of competence that untrammels the trait of freedom to choose, that frees the trait to be creative, that releases the trait to strive to satisfy ones inclinations and talents, that makes possible the blossoming of the trait of self-image–self-esteem, and that activates the trait that gives hope to life's aims.

Galbraith agrees that monetary policy is a passive instrument and that primary economic policy deals with management of interrelationships in the production process, such as:

1. Controls of wages and prices should be applied only to those large industries (which he identifies as involved in the planning system) that participate in collective bargaining.
2. Wage increases should be confined to average productivity gains in the large industries.
3. The power of big industry needs to be minimized in its ability to determine compensation and in maintaining the great income differentials.
4. The need to develop a control system for prices and wages whereby those industries and workers in the lower level category of productivity gain and the lower prices and wages category catch up to the average.
5. Effective controls by government must be instituted, because big business is so powerful in its control of the market system.[25]

Thus both fiscal and monetary policies have pragmatic value if used wisely in consonance with production relations, for example, to maintain a balance between wages and prices, between productivity and price-wage equity, between production and employment, and to sustain worker participation in enterprise management and profit sharing. But fiscal and monetary policies will not work to the satisfaction of all the people unless government regulations based on legislative statutes steer the economic forces, particularly the production relations. This is so because big business, with support from government bureaucracy, is the force that serves as the planner of the economy in the interest of big business instead of for the public well-being. This is the nature of capitalist democracy *if unrestrained.* If an efficient capital formation system is to be maintained under democratic government, the administration of economic justice must be legislatively spelled out. Galbraith's solution to the problem of planning is to replace a "technostructure" planning system for the present planning system composed of big business supported by the government bureaucracy. Even under this system, the watch over monopoly will have to be observed vigorously. not that monopoly under partnership with democratic government and operated for the commonweal could not be beneficial, but that monopoly in the wrong hands leads to corruption and self-serving manipulations and is destructive of democracy and is discordant to the traits of human nature.

The Weakness of Fiscal and Monetary Nostrums

Let us see in more detail how valid the methods used for treating socioeconomic symptoms of dislocation are. The modern conservative monetarists believe that:

1. Stagflation (recession and inflation at the same time) is caused by increased government deficit spending, which in turn increases money supply beyond what is economically beneficial, thereby dampening the rate of economic growth while decreasing the value of the dollar and increasing prices.
2. The increased government spending is accompanied by increased unemployment, which is caused by depression of economic growth.
3. The ways to treat the above situations are to:

   a. increase interest rates to decrease borrowing and money supply;
   b. decrease government spending in order to decrease government borrowing and thereby decrease inflation; and
   c. reduce the taxation in places, which would stimulate capital formation through increased investments by business and the wealthier section of the population. This would: (1) increase long-term economic growth in order to (2) reduce unemployment and also (3) reduce government spending.

The weakness of the interrelations on which the conservative economists base their attack on inflation, unemployment, and government deficit spending is very well revealed by Cameron in his study of the relationships among nineteen advanced capitalist nations between increases in spending and lower rates of economic growth, higher unemployment, increases in deficits, and inflation. He asks: "Is there . . . a fundamental tension or incompatibility between capitalism and a highly developed fiscal role for the state? Is the capitalist form of economic organization therefore likely to impose limits on the extent and continued increase of government spending?"*[26]

Cameron found that "all nations experienced, simultaneously a dampening of the rate of economic growth. In the early 1960s, the average rate of growth in real GDP (gross domestic product) in the 19 nations was 5.7 percent per year. By the late 1970s the average had dropped to 2.7 percent and in several nations—Sweden, Denmark, Belgium, and Britain—the volume of GDP increased by less than 2 percent a year." He asked whether these decreases were related to increased government spending relative to the GDP. Statistically he found these to correlate. But he found that in spite of the correlation, "the magnitude of the decrease is quite insignificant: An increase in total spending of one percentage point of GDP between the early 1960s and late 1970s lowered the growth rate in the late 1970s only five one-hundredths of one percent. Thus a very dramatic increase in spending in the range of 20 percentage points of GDP—a magnitude of increase that occurred in a few nations such as Sweden, the Netherlands, and Denmark—would have *reduced the rate of economic growth by only one percent*" (italics added).[27] Thus the real correlation was weak indeed! But the economists usually chosen by the American government as consultants belabor this point into maximum sensitivity as a measure.

Another interesting observation made by Cameron is that the "American government has throughout the period, especially in the 1970s, been much less in deficit than most nations, including many whose economic performance became the subject of envy and emulation" and that "the United States is the only nation in which the size of the budget deficit as a proportion of GDP has decreased over the two decades."

How valid is the claim that increased government spending increases the rate of unemployment? Cameron's study shows that there is a weak correlation between the two, but that this is largely due to "the very weak relation between increased spending and lower economic growth, the harmful effects on employment [being] almost invisible." And further: "An increase in total spending equivalent to one percent of GDP increased unemployment by 0.04 percent. In other words, the mediated effect of increased expenditure on unemployment is virtually zero."

Cameron cites studies on the effect of public spending on employment by the nature of the political party running the government:

"Various studies have noted that government by leftist parties [as in Denmark and Sweden], compared to government by nonleftist parties, is associated with a lower rate of unemployment. . . . This direct partisan effect on unemployment clearly exceeds any indirect effect on unemployment associated with the impact of increased government spending—also a product of leftist-dominated government—on economic growth."

To what extent does deficit spending by government cause inflation? Addressing this question, the Cameron study found that: "When one systematically compares, across nations, the magnitude and increase over time in the budget deficit of all governments with a measure of inflation, defined as the acceleration in the rate of change in prices over time, one finds no indication that deficits contribute to inflation. . . ." Contrary to the inherent logic of the Phillips curve and to findings of Hibbs, control of government by leftist parties is not associated with higher rates of inflation. In fact, the reverse is true. The nations in which leftist parties have governed most frequently experienced smaller increases in the rate of change in consumer prices over the long term than did the nations that were most frequently governed by centrist and rightist parties." The main reason for this is *because the leftist governments have more influence with workers' organizations in maintaining a favorable wage restraint in relation to what the economy will bear* (italics added) without causing imbalance: "The variation among nations in the increase in average rate of change in real earnings [of manufacturing workers] is a very powerful predictor of inflation. . . . Thus an increase of one percent in the average rate of change in real earnings is associated with an increase in inflation in excess of one percent. . . . Rather than being incompatible with and harmful to capitalism, a large and expanding welfare state may be beneficial and helpful to a capitalist economy" since it "assists in limiting labor's share of national income, thereby increasing corporate profits and the funds available for capital investment." Cameron should also have advised that unless the debilitating effects of unrestrained private enterprise monopoly on capitalism is prevented, such a relation of labor to capital would become unfeasible.

Capital formation for the purpose of capital accumulation and investment is the most fundamental requisite of capitalist economies. Cameron formulates the conservative economists' arguments concerning this basic thesis as follows: "It is not the effects of spending on growth or those of growth on unemployment or those of deficits on inflation that matter *most* [italics added] and that may necessitate limitations on government spending [but] the necessity to curb the flow of funds to the public sector—through either tax revenues or payments for deficit-generated securities—that would otherwise be invested in capital goods." That capital formation is basic to a capitalist economy is undisputable: "Among the 19 nations during the 1960s and 1970s, one observes a consistently strong relationship between the rate of capital investment . . . and the rate of economic growth, unemployment, and inflation." Cameron further found that "among the 19 nations, Britain and the United States experienced the lowest rates of capital formation throughout the two decades." This was due to the governments' espousal of what Cameron calls a "liberal international order," which tolerates and encourages massive exports of capital rather than domestic investments and the inability or unwillingness to direct a "large share of the economic product into investments." Cameron does not discuss the other abuses that are perpetrated by monopoly capital, such as conspiring with OPEC to raid the wealth of nations, the use of these enormous profits in buying up other large industries, thereby eliminating these profits from use in capital formation and at the same time decreasing government revenues by manipulating tax exemptions inherent in such maneuvers, and to sell tax deductions credits to other cocontrivers when they have overextracted such tax avoidance schemes for their own use.

Nowhere in the world is production so highly developed that unrestricted socialism could be practiced effectively. Therefore, some form of capitalist production is still desirable even for the most productive capitalist countries. But in order to maintain vigorous capitalist production, is there a limit of government spending beyond which capital formation is hindered? Cameron asserts that: "The experience of these nations [Germany, Italy, Switzerland, Sweden, and the Netherlands] suggests that public economy has approached, in size relative to the entire economy, the limits . . . imposed by the fundamental requisites of a capitalist economy. In Sweden and the Netherlands, in particular, one finds evidence that the expansion of government spending to the range of 60 percent of the GDP has hindered and contributed to the decrease of investment." The United States government spending, as a percentage of the GDP, has been 33.3 during the same period, about half of the above estimated limit. Such limits are important indicators that the level of production of these countries has not reached the level necessary for real socialist practice.

Who Controls the U.S. Economy?

There is plenty of evidence that the American economy is controlled by highly effective private monopoly, particularly composed of oil companies, banks, and insurance companies. This situation has become most critical since the end of the Second World War. Never before has monopoly been powerful enough to control both production and prices during recessions and periods of prosperity. The world oil resources are plentiful and the market could be easily glutted, yet prices keep going up and the chain reaction on the rest of the economy is disastrous for the poor and middle-income families. If anyone doubts how concentrated the wealth and power of the American economy has become in the talons of a few organizations, they should examine the latest (1980) *CDE Stock Ownership Directory: Energy,* which was reviewed by Robert Sherrill in the *Nation* of October 25, 1980 and which was inserted into the November 19, 1980 *Congressional Record* by Congressman John Conyers.[28] Sherrill wrote: "It is a marvelously rich lode of information about 142 largest U.S. energy companies." For example: "Citicorp is among the top five stockholders of Atlantic Richfield, Conoco, Phillips, Standard of Indiana, Standard of Ohio, and Getty Oil. (Dropping into the second tier of five, it is No. 6 at Exxon, No. 8 at Texaco, No. 8 at Marathon, No. 8 at Union Oil.) Chase Manhattan is among the top five at Exxon, Standard of California, Conoco, Standard of Indiana, Sun Oil and Mobil. (It is No. 10 at Atlantic Richfield.) Similar interlocking interests are given for Bankers Trust of New York, Manufacturers Hanover, J. P. Morgan, and the Chemical Bank of New York. . . . Prudential Life Insurance Company is the second largest stockholder in Marathon Oil, the third largest in Union Oil of California, the fourth in Shell and Gulf, the fifth largest in Standard of Indiana, the seventh largest in Mobil and Atlantic Richfield, fifteenth largest in Exxon," et cetera. Sen. Lee Metcalf's subcommittee's investigators' study showed that "three of the largest energy companies had indirect interlocks with most of their major *competitors* [italics added]. . . . The nation's largest energy company, Exxon, indirectly interlocked with its leading competitors as follows: Atlantic Richfield (four times); Mobil (six times); Shell (once); Standard of California (six times); Standard of Indiana (twice); Texaco (twice). . . . The intense concentration is seen not only in the stock ownership but also in the sharing of lawyers." If any doubt that free enterprise is past history in the United States, except for smaller businesses where the banks do not reach them through loans, let them study further the 1968 report of Rep. Wright Patman's staff, Senators Metcalf and Muskie's 1974 subcommittee report, and the Senate Interior Committee's report of 1976.

The philosophy of competition between nations is such that when political-economic policies of the contenders for favorable positions for extracting unreasonable advantages from competitors reach certain limits, the policies pass over into warlike aggressiveness or outright war when circumstances are opportune. When the Arab oil countries declared an oil embargo against the United States in 1973, this was actually a declaration of economic and political war by the monopoly of the Arab oil complex, composed of the multinational oil companies and the American private money-changing institutions, against the American people. Previous profits were not great enough. The Arab component of the complex wanted to wrest political advantage against Israel by blackmailing its best friend, the American people. The intensification of the economic plundering, therefore, was, by mutual cognition of the Arab oil countries' leaders, the multinational oil companies' boards, and banks' boards, the most powerful monopoly force in the entire world. But since these financial and economic interests were so powerful in their influence on the leadership of the United States government, the latter meekly did practically nothing about the blackmail, although later during an unguarded moment, President Carter declared the oil companies to be the greatest enemy of the American people. What could one expect a politicized president to do when caught in such a power play? After all, there was actually no interruption of "political commerce" between the United States government and the monopoly of the Arab oil complex. Therefore, there was no reason for business as usual not to continue. The interruptive action was *only* against the American people. They have taken it in the past, and the monopoly-government perpetrators are confident and hope the American people will continue to take it in the future. As the most eminent student of war, Karl von Clausewitz, put it: "We see, therefore, that War is not merely a political act, but also a real political instrument, a *continuation* [italics added] of political commerce, a carrying out of the same by other means."[29] Thus government, in collusion with the Arab oil complex, continued its "political commerce" as if nothing had happened, while the political war was intensified against the people, not against their exploiters. Political-economic monopoly reinforced by government collusion rather than partnership for the public well-being is the most pernicious force eating away at the structural stability of capitalist democracy.

One of the basic problems we have to deal with is the nature of human nature, about which many claim to know a good deal, but few really appreciate its essentiality and specificity. What the fiscal and monetary policies are supposed to do is to control human behavior. And, indeed, such policies can influence human behavior to act in a manner traditional for a capitalist society when none except the moneyed class of the socioeconomic groups was strong enough to deflect the resultant mass movement of the random actions of the myriad competitors in the traditional "free" market economy. But when any of the other socioeconomic groups do become strong enough to manipulate the free market, behavior begins to change, because the negative nature of the capitalist system begins to change in favor of the majority. We are now in that changing, transitional, chaotic, leaderless period. The aphorism "power corrupts" is such a common observation of human behavior that it is almost a superficiality. It is, however, a primate trait that the leader of a simian troop demonstrates until deposed by a more powerful competitor, who takes over leadership by physically defeating in combat the old leader. The human, of course, has the advantage of rationality and therefore by his cognitive powers can be much more devious and dangerous in gaining power and maintaining it. In many instances, the power is held by outright terrorism, as in the more brutal forms of dictatorship. This is a negative or primate aspect of human nature. Human nature is expressed in the average behavior of people. It is manifested as a complex of particular traits of behavior. Each trait has a dialectic nature, i.e., is expressed as a tension between opposite directions or inclinations to behave. All of the eight traits distinguished here operate in an interpenetrating manner when manifesting themselves. The primate aspects may gain dominance and corrupt the behavior of man. In considering the quality of behavior described as "power corrupts," the negative aspects of the eight traits come into play. The trait of challenge, generated in man's urge to perform well in striving to satisfy the self-image–self-esteem trait, may get involved in a power struggle where challenge may generate impelling competition when conditioned by a frame of orientation nurtured in an ecosystem such as favors unrestricted laissez-faire. "Power corupts" is therefore a "normal" manifestation of human nature where the negative phase of the diphasic nature of the challenge trait is not controlled by the cognitive powers that generate inhibitions. President Nixon and Chairman Stalin are good examples where the primate orientation of this behavioral trait predominates. Albert Einstein and Albert Schweitzer are good examples where the trait is humanly oriented. Whether people usually respond humanly or primatelike will depend on the pattern of the ecosystem in which they were reared and whether that ecosystem and its social relations are consonant or in conflict with the positive traits of human nature, particularly, those traits relating to the need to be devoted or engaged to a unifying frame of mental and behavioral orientation and the need to feel free to evaluate situations and to choose freely one's course of action. Devotion or commitment can be deflected to a course of ruthless pursuit for making money at any cost or attaining power or status for personal aggrandizement or to a course of devotion to community development and attaining recognition for contributing to community social well-being. For people living in the United States, the general frame of orientation that guides them is freedom to choose one's role in life's pursuit, the most predominant role being getting property for status or power-attaining roles. A more recent ego-oriented role is toward uninhibited sexual expression. The freedom roles have become so unrestricted that inhibition, a basic characteristic of being human, is losing social favor and ethics and morality in such pursuits have sunk to the point where hidden corruption in business practice and other ways of making a living and even outright stealing and burgulary by confirmed criminals are given similar silk-glove treatment by the legal system in the name of a growing humanity of the spirit, while the family and child socialization is increasingly suffering disruption. Since such primatelike, self-aggrandizing behavior is found so frequently among the wealthy who have power, among the politically powerful, and even among artists, scientists, and other professionals, is there any wonder that the aphorism "power corrupts" is universally accepted as a truism of human nature? Yet this negative manifestation need not come into being if the ecosystem of a country were oriented toward a philosophy of life—a unifying frame of orientation—whereby the humanly oriented side of the traits of human nature were truly reinforced so that there was equilibrium between the social and the egoistic predilections in everyday behavior, which is transmitted to the children as a way of life. In social life, power must be vested in some people called politicians and bureaucrats so that certain needed social functions in governing be tended to. Individual responsibility of such people must be balanced with social orientation.

LENINISM AND HUMAN NATURE

As previously observed, the Marxian side of the present-day sociopolitical movements needs to be discussed freely, because at least half of the people of the world are living under governments professing to adhere to Marxian philosophy, which is really a Leninist version of Marxism. The Marxist-Leninist movement has been most successful in attaining political power yet, although capitalism has met the basic problem of rapidly increasing the capital of the nations practicing it, it has met neither the material needs of *all* the people of such countries nor their psychosocial needs. But neither have the nations professing to practice Marxist-Leninist theory. Due to the mass communications media not usually being government controlled in the highly developed capitalist countries, their socioeconomic failures in relation to the poor section of the population have become more universally known than the various types of failures in the socialist dictatorships, and, for the same reason, the propaganda of the latter has been more effective. Also the practitioners of the Marxist-Leninist philosophy have either forgotten or misinterpreted Marx's deliberations on the theme of *alienation,* which consider in depth the psychosocial aspects of man's behavior—his (Marx's) contributions to a basis for the science of sociology and psychology. The misuse of power by the practitioners of Marxist-Leninist political economy, particularly by imposing strictures on behavior through the prolonged maintenance of the dictatorship of the proletariat beyond what is necessary for stability, has created conditions that are discordant with the traits of human nature. It appears that the dictatorship *of* the proletariat has, by this prolongation, been negated and transformed into a dictatorship *over* the proletariat, resulting in the alienation of the power of the people by a government masquerading as of the people. A very striking example of this is the spreading strike of the Polish workers and farmers, which began at the Lenin shipyard in Gdansk, and which in several weeks engulfed about ten million industrial workers and farmers. The proletariat had come to feel that the government's union just did not really represent them, which union, based on Lenin theory that since the government dictatorship is of the people, by the people, and for the people, must be their (the proletariat's) union. A similar feeling is and has been the perceptivity of the American workers. But there is a difference. The American worker knows that his government, representing various classes, could not operate a union representing his interest alone, which a union is supposed to do. The Polish worker is supposed to know and feel that there are no classes in Poland but one, the working class. Yet he does not perceive it to be so. He perceives that there also exist two classes in Poland—the working class and the government class.

The practitioners of Marxist-Leninist theory have developed a philosophy of government that they conceive as a scientific methodology to change the social system to a configuration that would eliminate the various alienations caused by capitalist social organization. This they believe can be achieved by eliminating classes, by changing the socioeconomic conditions that generate classes, and by guaranteeing everyone a job and an opportunity for an education. Certainly, such conditions will support a degree of harmony with the traits of human nature, but dictatorship supervenes to nullify substantially these salutary effects. The plasticity of the human is his behavioral distinction. It gives him the ability to tolerate discordant ecosystems for even long periods when he foresees hopeful termination of the discordant factors. The workers therefore can tolerate dictatorships so long as they have hope that these dictatorships will disappear. But a long dictatorship of the proletariat builds power corruption in those who wield power, i.e., it generates the desire for those in power to continue in power not for the good of the proletariat, but for the sake of egotistic power. What these practitioners do not seem to understand is that the sociology of Marx is based on solving the socioeconomic problems, the powerful causes of alienation, but that satisfying the material needs does not satisfy all of what Marx called *man's species being*[30] (which is equivalent to human nature), but does open the vistas to create social conditions that accord with all the traits of human nature. Those practitioners' constricted view of Marxian philosophy is confirmed by the fact that the Soviet Union did not recognize the validity of a science of sociology for the first four or five decades of its existence.

THE BIPHASIC NATURE OF HUMAN NATURE

Does the accommodation of the whole world ecosystem to the traits of human nature mean the eventual tranquillity of *Homo* by complete domestication of all individuals into patterns of conformity and by muffling of their national and cultural differences? Such an eventuality would be a catastrophic outcome of the social effort to completely humanize a species that has a biological history and therefore a phylogenetic heritage. To superhumanize *Homo* would mean to erase his primate nature, as if all his primate nature were bad. This, of course, is not so. The biphasic nature of *Homo* is what makes him human. His primate nature alone would dehumanize him. The human aspect of his nature alone would most probably enervate him. For example, being self-centered is, for the most part, primate behavior. The broadening of *Homo*'s sociofunctional relations for societal growth and solidarity is, for the most part, human behavior. But the human aspect would lose its potency if the self-centered drive for self-development were not there to give the human aspect the force to act socially with vigor. Together, the dynamic equilibrium of the two forces gives *Homo* his distinct nature. Exaggeration of the primate potential results in unhuman-antisocial behavior. Exaggeration of the human potential will tend to reduce the dynamism of behavior. In a sense, Heer, in his introduction to *Great Documents of the World,* succinctly expressed the above concept: "Man is an ultimately untamable creature." This does not refer to man's ultimate animality but precisely to the opposite, to his ultimate humanness. Humankind without its conflicting psycho-social nature is no longer human. That is the reason that man needs government, a code of ethical-moral norms, a democratic social organization, and a built-in sociopolitical mechanism for continually studying and shaping the ecosystem to conform to the needs of the traits of human nature.

Being human creates a richness in the world of people that generates varieties of cultures and subcultures, each developing untrammelled. Such localized creativeness must be strongly encouraged. But each culture must also be aware that the only area to which cultures must adhere is that their sociofunctional practices not violate the needs of the traits of human nature, which are basically psychosocial, not cultural, in origin. Concerning the conflicting nature of human nature, Heer further observes: "Being human means living with the conflicts that each self, each society, each nation, each period bears within it."[31] Here he refers to one of man's traits of his human nature, expressed as "boundless desire and freedom to choose." What is boundless includes a myriad of contradictions, and the inherent drive to be free to choose creates dilemmas and conflicts. The untamability of man means his native motivations, which express themselves as his traits of human nature, each of which is inherently biphasic in a sense like Aristotle's contrarieties but more like Hegel's Principle of Contradiction).[32] To tame man not to express his human nature would be a state of ultimate domestication, of routinizing every response to internal and external stimuli, of quenching his morale, of denying him his humanness, like a dictatorship or a limitless chaotic democracy could very well accomplish, given enough time.

THE FIRST AND SECOND REVOLUTIONS OF HUMAN BEHAVIOR

Sahlin's acute perception of human society's first great revolution in behavior, i.e., control of indiscriminate sexuality, illustrates the changeover from primate to biphasic human behavior: "The decisive battle between early culture and human nature must have been waged on the field of primate sexuality. . . . Competition over partners . . . can lead to vicious, even fatal strife. It was this side of primate sexuality that forced early culture to curb and repress it. The emerging human primate, in a life-and-death economic struggle with nature, could not afford the luxury of a social struggle."[33] With an intellect capable of developing a culture and controlling behavior, "it became possible to regulate sex by moral rules; to subordinate it to higher collective ends."[34] Thus the trait of human nature expressed as "boundless desire and freedom to choose" gave birth to a moral code to guide man's choice as man himself saw fit to choose. Thus arose the human behavioral quality of *self-restraint* or inhibition—a quality of behavior that helps significantly to humanize society, by guiding man's behavior according to intellectually arrived at conclusions and planning that serve the interest of society as well as the individual.

There is a need to comment about Sahlins's use of the term "human nature." If the sexuality revolution were the first instance when man modified his primate behavior, then the phrase "the decisive battle between early culture and human nature" assumes that there was human nature before that "battle." It may very well be that there was, but the human nature was purely *potential*; otherwise the sexuality battle could not have been the first. Considering the fact that the traits of human nature came into being as the result physical changes, particularly that of the brain, which had evolved to distinguish *Homo* from *Australopithecus* in behavior to the conditions of life, the new behavioral potential could very well have begun to manifest itself long before the sexuality revolution which itself could have lasted over a span of tens of thousands of years. From that point of view, Sahlins's use of the term "human nature" could be considered valid, although its state of development certainly was rudimentary and scarcely being formed. The concept of "first revolution" need not necessarily mean that this revolution initiated the forming of the first trait of human nature, the need for a unified frame of orientation of conduct. It is just as possible that the need of molding into the "bonding" trait the act of "sharing" was even more primordial, since the need to control sex impulse in order to prevent disruption in societal function implied that the bonding and sharing trait already existed and could even have been transmitted to man in an embryonic form from *Australopithecus* and therefore came so gradually as not to be considered a revolution. Will these fine points ever be solved? Nevertheless, Sahlins's perception of that period is very commendable.

Man has learned of the impossibility of satisfying his boundless desires—impossible because of their contradictory nature and because his survival depends on satisfing the needs of the group, which needs are not always compatible with self-satisfaction. He has learned to do this by creating moral and ethical norms as guides for individual conduct for group survival. These norms do not obstruct the individual's freedom to choose, since such norms relate only to the types of behavior that are critical for societal survival and dynamic equilibrium of the group. Restrictions in this area are normally accepted and desirable inhibitions. This leaves a myriad circumstances where the individual can express his freedom to choose.

This brings us to a second great revolution in human behavior that must one day come to pass—a revolution in our social organization so that the conditions of living will be kept so organized as to be continually in concordance with the traits of human nature. To date, no such system has ever existed in historical times. It could not have existed except incidently since the individual traits of human nature had not been specifically defined, recognized, and accepted as a unified system that civil society must reckon with as an essential responsibility of government. This is what the present study is all about. Once these traits have been recognized as the valid aspects of human nature, the revolution will be initiated when the majority of the people accept the thesis that the conditions under which we live must be adjusted to conform to the dynamic expression of these traits. It is one thing for the intellectual recognition of the validity of the traits of human nature, but quite another to have the knowledge of how to adjust the social dynamics to be in consonance with them. A great deal of research and wisdom will be needed to devise the methodology and social engineering to accommodate the social system to these traits.

Democratic systems as prevail in the Western world and are exemplified by the United States have the potential for being accommodated to the nature of human beings. Attitudes and institutions will need modification. The attitude that politics is naturally self-seeking and therefore self-aggrandizement of politicians is expected and tolerated *must* be changed. Will the American dream of a true Jefferson-Madison-Lincoln-Dewey democracy come to pass without dampening its ingenious ability at capital formation and meshed to a system compatible with the traits of human nature? Will the American dream become the real showcase of human living to the world?

Social systems based on Marxian theory as developed by Lenin, which prevail in Central and Eastern Europe and in Asia, started out as dictatorships. They came into existence three to six decades ago. They still are dictatorships. Instead of striving to set examples of how good socialist systems could satisfy the needs of the material and social and spiritual aspirations of people, they have continued to waste stupendous quantities of their resources building their military might long after a real need for it has disappeared. They have embarked on the repulsive imperialist game for world domination based on the obsolete excuse of capitalism's unyielding intent on destruction of socialist countries, ignoring the tremendous influence they might have if they could demonstrate that their system can generate capital formation quotas at such a rate as Marx and Engels predicted would be necessary to develop real "scientific" socialism. However, as long as dictatorship remains the essential nature of the Soviet social order, it will not be able to implement the social dynamics to accommodate to the needs of the whole spectrum of human nature, particularly not to the trait that generates the drive responding to "challenge and competence" for initiating innovations.[35] Dictatorship of the Soviet pattern is limited mostly to accommodate to the material and partially to the literacy needs of the people.

NOTES

1. Richard B. Lee, *!Kung San: Men, Women and Children in a Foraging Society* (New York: Cambridge University Press, 1979), p. 460.

2. Karl Marx, *The Grundrisse*, edited and translated by David McLellan (New York: Harper Torchbooks, 1971), p. 94.

3. Karl Marx, *Grundrisse*, translated by Martin Nicolaus, (New York: Vintage Books, 1973), p. 325.

4. Ibid., pp. 704–06.

5. Harold Demsetz, "The 1982 Nobel Prize in Economics," *Science,* vol. 218, no. 4573 (November 12, 1982), pp. 655–57.

6. Ibid.

7. "Bankers Fear Default by Oil-Poor Countries," *Times Picayune* July 12, 1981.

8. W. R. Johnson and E. J. Wilson III, "The Oil Crises and African Economics," *Daedalus* (Spring 1982), pp. 211–41.

9. Marx, *op. cit.,* p. 94.

10. Charles A. Reich, *The Greening of America* (New York: Bantam Books, Inc., 1971).

11. V. I. Lenin, *State and Revolution* (New York: International Publishers, 1932).

12. *The Nature of Revolution* (Washington D.C.: U.S. Government Printing Office, 1968).

13. Herbert Marcuse, *Counter-revolution and Revolt* (Boston, Massachusetts: Beacon Press, 1972), p. 129.

14. Reich, *supra cite,* p. 92.

15. Marx, *op. cit.,* p. 85.

16. Ibid., p. 145, and Karl Marx in *Das Capital,* vol. 3 (Chicago, Illinois: Charles H. Kerr, 1909), p. 49.

17. Ibid., p. 145.

18. John K. Galbraith, *Economics and the Public Purpose* (New York: Houghton Mifflin Co., 1973), pp. 265–85.

19. Erling Olsen, "The Dilemma of the Social-Democratic Labor Partries," *Daedalus* (Spring 1984), pp. 169–94.

20. George P. Shultz and Kenneth W. Dam, *Economic Policy beyond the Headlines* (New York: W.W. Norton and Co., 1977), p. 20.

21. John T. Woolley, "Monetarists and the Politcs of Monetary Policy," *Annals of the American Academy of Political and Social Science,* vol. 459 (January 1982), pp. 142–60.

22. David R. Cameron, "On the Limits of the Public Economy," *Annals of the American Academy of Political and Social Science,* vol. 459 (January 1982), pp. 46–62.

23. W. R. Johnson and E. J. Wilson III, "The Oil Crises and African Economies," *Daedalus* (Spring 1982), pp. 211–41.

24. J. M. Blair, *The Control of Oil* (New York: Pantheon Books, 1976), p. 281.

25. Galbraith, *op. cit.,* pp. 313–16.

26. David R. Cameron, "On the Limits of the Public Economy," *Annals of the American Academy of Political and Social Science,* vol. 459 (January 1982), pp. 46–62.

27. Ibid.

28. "Who Owns the Oil Companies?," *Congressional Record,* November 19, 1980, pp. E 5018–E 5019.

29. Col. Joseph I. Greene, *Living Thoughts of Clausewitz* (New York: Longmans, Green and Co., 1943), p. 169.

30. Karl Marx, *The Economic and Philosophic Manuscripts of 1844* (New York: International Publishers, 1964), pp. 114, 147.

31. Frederick Heer, ed., *Great Documents of the World* (New York: McGraw-Hill Book Company, 1977), p. 6.

32. Wm. Wallace, *The Logic of Hegel* (New York: Oxford University Press, 1931), p. 221.

33. Marshall D. Sahlins, "The Origin of Society," *Scientific American,* vol. 203 (September 1960) pp. 76–87.

34. Ibid.

35. Loren R. Graham, "Science in the Brezhnev Era," *Bulletin of the Atomic Scientists,* vol. 38, no. 2 (February, 1982), pp. 23–28.

18

The Essence and Essentiality of Capital

CAPITAL: GOOD AND EVIL

In the history of political economy, the most important factor that plays the leading role in nationhood development is the dynamic performer of *capital*. Without this royal executor of miracles, the steam engine would probably still be a hazy dream. But certainly, the aeon-long dream of utopia would still be a vagary in a poetic epic instead of the reality of present strivings of people around the world. And no less is such striving at the highest level of the people's ambition in the United States and the Western world than in the Soviet Union and the Third World. "The modern history of *capital* dates from the creation in the 16th century of a world-embracing commerce and a world-embracing market"[1] as Marx described it. This social force—this capital—has indeed been a miracle worker toward the utopian dream. In spite of the fact that Marx railed against capitalist exploitation of workers, as he did so vividly in his major work, *Das Capital*, which was an application of his principles and theories to the living world, for example: "Capital is dead labour that, vampire-like, only lives by sucking living labour, and lives the more, the more it sucks."[2] In part 7 and part 8 of that work, he described in very great detail the manner in which *new* capital accumulation originally took place in the sixteenth and seventeenth centuries, and he concluded in chapter 32 with: "Capital comes dripping from head to foot from every pore, with blood and dirt."[3] This indictment of capitalism, in line with the prophetic and foreboding tone of the *Communist Manifesto,* written two decades before *Das Capital* was published, has quite a different temper than his major work. Marx clarified his principles and theories as a logically measured philosophy of society, *Grundrisse* (principles),[4] written around the time when Marx was organizing his material for the first volume of *Das Capital*. This was the time Marx's digestion of information from his

427

studies of the iniquities of capitalism had become immersed in the stream of history so that the civilizing influence of capital emerged as a tremendous creative force. In this work, another side of Marx was revealed, the dispassionate, reflective, philosophic exerciser of complicated concepts into understandable analysis without simplistic judgments. This is the side that the revolutionarily involved politicians deliberately evade, since the adjectives of passion, of violence, of exhortation, and of inflammation on which political movements thrive are muted and mostly absent. Instead of the vitriolic polemicist, the following judgments illustrate the logical sweep of Marx the philosophic historian:

> Thus capital first creates bourgeois society and the universal appropriation of nature and of social relationships themselves by the members of society. Hence the great civilizing influence of capital, its production of a stage of society compared with which all earlier stages appear to be merely *local progress* and idolatry of nature. Nature becomes for the first time simply an object for mankind, purely a matter of utility; it ceases to be recognized as a power in its own right; and the theoretical knowledge of its independent laws appears only as a stratagem designed to subdue it to human requirements, whether as the object of consumption or as the means of production. Pursuing this tendency, capital has pushed beyond national boundaries and prejudices, beyond the deification of nature and the inherited, self-sufficient satisfaction of existing needs confined within well-defined bounds, and the reproduction of the traditional way of life. It is destructive of all this, and permanently revolutionary, tearing down all obstacles that impede the development of productive forces, the expansion of needs, the diversity of production, and the exploitation and exchange of natural and intellectual forces. . . . The universality toward which it is perpetually driving finds limitations in its own nature, which at a certain stage of its development will make it appear as itself the greatest barrier to this tendency, leading to its (capitalist production's) own self-destruction.[5]

In this paragraph, Marx displays an historical insight that is seldom matched when examining a forecast written a century and a quarter before. We have seen what "capital" has been able to accomplish worldwide since Marx forecast the above, especially have we seen it happen in the United States, Marx's favorite capitalist country. We have seen it happen in the Soviet Union during the past half-century, although in a modified way, since socialist countries, no less than capitalist countries, must operate on a capital intensive economy if they wish to make progress. Only real communism is supposed to be able to change capital to a less than primary status in social operations, maybe, depending on whether the politicians applying Marx's theory really know how better than the present ones.

In Marx's perception of the "self-destruction" drive of capitalism, he was attempting to describe the dialectic process by which the forces of the means of production and production relations reached a level of development whereby the productive forces had grown to such proportions that its potential to humanize living conditions of all the people had been reached while at the same time the production relations had not changed enough to bring into reality their tremendous potentiality for the betterment of the living conditions of all the people. This contradiction between what *is* and what potentially *could be* would create forceful changes in production relations, i.e., between the workers and the caretakers of the accumulated capital whereby the workers would appropriate the capital in the form of the means of production—make these public property, thereby abolishing them as a means of exploitation of the workers. This is the meaning of Marx's pithy summarization that "The universality toward which it is perpetually driving [i.e., the infinite ability of capital to expand in order to provide for man's infinitely expanding desires] finds limitations in its own nature [i.e., it creates overproduction and thereby limits production because workers' income limits their ability to buy what has been produced], which at a certain stage of its development will make it appear as itself the greatest barrier to this tendency [i.e., the tolerance threshold of all the traits of human nature is reached at a certain level of limitations on living conditions], leading to its own self-destruction" [i.e., capitalism is transformed into socialism.] We will discuss below whether the latter action really changes "capitalism's capital," into something else, i.e., whether surplus value created by capital as public property no longer retains its exploitative (in the dehumanizing sense of the pre–social security epoch) nature. In the foregoing process, "capital", which was being developed by exploiting the workers would go through a change in *quality* and would therefore require a *new* definition in order that the "surplus value (surplus labor)" which becomes capital be declared as derived by nonexploitative means.

DIALECTICS OF EXPLOITATION

What Marx could not have foreseen was that the quality of capital was changing even before the tolerance threshold of the traits of human nature of the workers was being reached necessitating their appropriation of capital. *The dialectics of the process of capital formation, rather than destroying itself, is instead, in the process of negating the very nature of exploitation.* No doubt, the specter of the socialist revolution staring the capitalist countries in the face, beginning with the Russian revolution, plus the very nature of the dynamics of capital formation in developing the technostructure[6] of corporate monopoly is changing the nature and the definition of exploitation in relation to capital. But let it not be forgotten also that this change in definition of the meaning of exploitation in relation to capital was, to a significant degree, also stimulated by the humanizing changes in the dynamics of workers' relations in the democratic ecosystem in the United States and the other Western democracies. Marx's appreciation of the socio-economic force of the United States was well expressed in his correspondence during the Civil War and after, when he predicted and hoped that the "Yankees" would win, and in the first preface to *Capital,* where he wrote in 1867: "As in the eighteenth century the American War of Independence sounded the tocsin for the European middle class, so in the nineteenth century the American Civil War sounded it for the European working class."[7] Marx appreciated the dynamic nature of capitalism in American democracy in furthering without revolution the interests of the workers.

As indicated above, there is an intimate relation between the term "exploitation" and Marx's concept of the nature of "capital." Marx was the greatest student of this subject, and, as previously observed, his political-economic and social theories are what the Western world today has most to contend with. This is not only true insofar as the 'socialist' countries are concerned, but also insofar as all the underdeveloped countries are concerned and even the countries of Western Europe such as Italy and France. This is his definition paraphrased but without the pejorative "exploitation" implication: *Capital*[8] is all the wealth that is created by stored-up wage-labour; it is the surplus labour time appropriated by the owners of the means of production by which value and surplus value are produced, the owners appropriating the greatest possible amount of surplus labour. This is the process of valorization by which capital reproduces and increases its value and becomes money, i.e., exchange value.[9] The important idea to remember about capital is that it "does not mean anything without wage-labour, value, money, price, etc."[10] "Capital is the all-dominating economic power of bourgeois society. It must form the starting point as well as the end."[11] "Capital is, therefore, not a personal, it is a social power."[12]

In order to emphasize the point that capital is a capitalist society phenomenon, that it is evil because it represents the exploitation of the proletariat's labor, the communist political economist Leontiev gave Lenin's definition for capital as a carrier of social relations particularly concerned with special production relations, i.e., the relation of the wage-earner to the exploiter of his labour: Capital is "a special historically definite social production relation."[13] What we have here is an attempt by Leontiev to restrict the description of the term "capital" to the pejorative aspect of its nature without implying even that it had a remarkable progressive aspect in its nature as Marx described its historical importance. Let it not be forgotten that the word *exploitation* has both a positive and negative meaning: utilization or working of a natural resource; an unjust or improper use of another person for one's own profit or advantage (Webster).

The problem posed here is the need for a critical discussion of the meaning of "exploitation" from a historical point of view in relation to political economy. We are all acquainted with its meaning in England at the beginning of the Industrial Revolution, when, to give an emotion-laden example depicted by Winslow: "Under the insanitary conditions which surrounded those wretched children, both in the factory and in the barracks (where they slept by relays in filthy beds which were never allowed to cool), it is small wonder that epidemic disease raged as in a hotbed of contagion."[14] Is this exploitation a reversion, a retrogression to savagery or barbarism? According to Marxist interpretation, the answer is a decided No! Friederich Engels, in describing, in *The Condition of the Working Class in England,* the "process of driving the workers from hearth and home as it took place in the eighteenth century in England," responds to Proudhon's description of this as retrogression in the following historical perspective: "But could it enter my head to regard this, which was in the circumstances an absolutely necessary historical process of development, as a retrogression 'below the savages'? Impossible! The English proletariat of 1872 is on an infinitely higher level than the rural weaver of 1772 with his 'hearth and home.' "[15] Is exploitation good or evil? From a historical point of view, it is neither in the cold perspective of the historian perched on the peak of Mount Olympus or Mount Ida scanning the historical horizon. To the social scientist, it is both good and evil, the evil pertaining to the present situation and the good to the eventual progress. To the exploited worker, it is plainly and categorically evil. To Marx and Engels, the humanitarians, there was a need to organize the exploited in order to change the system of exploitation. To Marx and Engels, scientists of the historical process, the inhumane effects of the exploitation is "an absolutely necessary historical process of development." Thus the dialectics of human, of societal, progress is well demonstrated in the intellectual dynamics of the two greatest dialecticians. Marx and Engels demonstrated the same dialectic approach in relation to the economic instrument called "capital" as they did to "exploitation"—two inseparable instrumentalities on which human progress categorically depends. There will *always* be a need for production as long as society exists. Therefore there will always be a need for the means of production and the human relations that pertain to these means of production by those who use them. But without a continuously available stock of accumulated goods devoted to the process of production, there can be no production. At what point is this stock of accumulated goods and means of production usually called capital, not capital, and at what point in the relation between the producers (workers) and this capital, inherent in the forces of production relations, not exploitation? Is exploitation the only source of *surplus value*? Here is how Marx described surplus value: "What happens to be surplus value on the part of capital appears on the worker's side to be, precisely, surplus labour far beyond his requirements, that is to say, far beyond his immediate needs for the maintenance of his livelihood. The great historical feature of capital is that it produces this surplus labour, which is superfluous labour from the standpoint of ordinary use value and mere subsistence . . . This is why capital is productive; *it is an essential relationship for the development of the productive forces of society* (italics added). . . . Capital, as capital . . . exists only through either direct forced labour and slavery, or intermediary forced labour, this is, wage-earning labour."[16]

It is clear then that, according to Marxian theory, capital is created by surplus value, which is surplus labor and which is derived by exploitation of the worker directly by slavery or forced labor or indirectly by forced wage-earning labor. *But even the wage-earning process has a dialectic nature that was still not apparent in Marx's day.* The aspect that was apparent to Marx at that time was expressed by him in the *Communist Manifesto*: the "class of labourers . . . live only so long as they find work, and who find work only so long as their labour increases capital."[17] The modern aspect of the wage-earning process was always inherent but in Marx's time not apparent in the concept of wage-labor. It relates to the modern capitalist democracies and some of the present-day socialist states where wage-labor more and more takes on the appearance of being relatively free to negotiate its working conditions with the owners of the means of production. In the capitalist democracies this relative freedom is supported by:

1) the strength of organized labor;
2) unemployment insurance provided by law and by some affluent unions;
3) welfare support by various governmental programs;
4) prevalence of hospital and medical insurance and government-provided hospital and medical facilities;
5) the growing strength of labor in the political field;
6) the growing financial strength of labor union funds invested in American business;
7) more and more investment of workers in the stocks of various private enterprises;
8) the increasing number of enterprises that have programs for worker involvement in profit sharing systems; and
9) many other types of social services provided by official and voluntary agencies.

SOCIALISM, DEMOCRACY, AND FOLLY

It appears that workers in the Western democracies have greater freedom in work relations than exists in the socialist countries, where dictatorships of a single party prevails. The recent strike of workers in Poland for a "free" labor union has brought this appearance to the surface as reality. Although the influence of exemplification of trade unions in the capitalist democracies may have been involved in a minimal way with stimulating the Polish workers to dissidence, this can not be blamed for the bursting forth of this explosion of workers' and farmers' energy with the force of 10 million souls as was revealed recently.

From what is going on in the capitalist democracies, the clear-cut determination that accumulated surplus value or capital is generated by an undiluted practice of naked exploitation associated with the most pejorative meaning of exploitation no longer holds for most workers in most capitalist democracies. The democratic forces in capitalist democracy have changed profoundly since the days of Lenin and certainly since the time of Marx and Engels.

Since the time of Marx, many countries have become socialist and some have professed to be socialist, especially among the less economically developed nations, most of the latter really being feudal dictatorships or just plain personal or military dictatorships. Therefore, we now have had many years of experience since 1917 to observe and judge whether that aspect of the definition of capital that applies to its essentiality as a capitalist exploitative phenomenon still has validity. Bitter experience taught Marx that disciplined education on valid revolutionary theory took time,[18] that the transition from capitalism to communism would take a certain duration, that the withering away of the state would take time, and part of that would be taken up by passing through the socialist phase, or what Lenin called the proletarian state or semistate or dictorship.[19] The socialist states of Eastern Europe were all at a rather low stage of capitalist production when their revolutions occurred, but that of the Soviet Union was the lowest among them. They are now trying to develop their social productive forces in order to reach the level whereby their *states* (a *state*, in Marxian terms, meaning a coercive force) will be able to wither away. Their economies are based on state control of the means of production and labor being compensated by a wage scheme. Every one of these states is still very short of the capital it needs for its productive forces to grow and develop to the point where the state could be allowed to wither away. Among the underdeveloped nations, some are at a very low level of capitalist production, but none of the Black African states until recently could have been considered to have a capitalist system, except for some colonial exploitation that was being carried on. Some of these call themselves the unaligned states of the Third World. Most of these countries are dictatorships and as such are holding back their own development by their dictatorship type of organization, which is *preventing* the formation of capital.[20] They are being misguided by the Eastern European socialist states and China by fumbling with the incredible task of mimicking "socialist" dictatorships in order to develop their productive forces. Rapid capital formation and growth are most efficiently accomplished by the laissez-faire competitive system. Socialism is an anachronistic concept under a primitive stage of economic development. Both Marx and Engels would have denounced this trend of encouraging such countries to simulate socialism as reactionary authoritarianism. The most important need of every one of these states is capital, and the most important reality among these states is that they do not know how to use or generate capital, and dictatorships are the most inappropriate way to do this. A shining example of this is the People's Republic of the Congo (Brazzaville). This state is neither a real state nor a socialist system. If it were not such a serious problem, this episode might be called the "comedy of the Congo."

The colonial experience of the Black African countries gave to the natives very little skill or knowledge in the field of entrepreneurship for generating capital.[21] The multinational enterprises extracted much of the natural resources and left these governments a generous gift of weakness except where oil is produced. And there, they and their OPEC partners contribute only the immoral practices of plunder and black-mail. What these countries need is a good dose of what Marx would have recommended for them—the revolutionary influence of capital, not doles from the "rich" countries or dictatorships and economic dogma from so-called people's political sages. The push for capital investments and employment of local people to learn business technology and modern craft technique, the freedom to generate challenge and to precipitate economic competition are the immediate needs. Under these circumstances, the generosity of the rich countries will bear fruit. Applying socialist economic theory to generate capital in economically underdeveloped countries is the greatest misapplication of Marxian economic theory—example: the economic debacle in Cuba. As Marx pointed out, capitalist production will find its own time for socialism.

At this point, let us take note of an important dialectic principle, the bifurcation of unity. Thus it is not the transitional "capital" that destroys itself as Marxian theory has been formulated, but blind capitalism's drive for profit that allows multinationals to control the destiny of free enterprise and thus to destroy the system that capital created and that created capital. It appears that a process of bifurcation is taking place in the meaning and dynamics of "capital," that associated with naked exploitation and that associated with increasing democratic wage labor practice in the use of capital.

As explained above, under capitalism a certain amount of the value of workers' production, of their labor, is funneled off by the owner of the means of production for further use in the production of more commodities. Marxian economics does recognize a certain aspect of ownership per se of the means of production as a valid reason for being compensated for the use of those means, since the cost of those means and their depreciation are reckoned in calculating the cost of production. It is the surplus beyond the wages and other costs that comes into question. This accumulating and perpetually increasing surplus value is the capital used to continue the process of more and more production. Under socialism, the very same process takes place except for the fact that the surplus value is no longer privately owned, but state owned. At this point, we run into the problem of whether every government that declares itself socialist is indeed a government of the people and therefore whether the surplus value that redounds to the state really belongs to the people. Let us take an example.

Mali, a former French colony, declared itself a single-party socialist state in 1964 and was set "irreversibly" on the path of socialism, mainly of the Maoist variety. Large numbers of Chinese communist experts were brought in to help organize state enterprises and farm collectivization according to socialist economic theory. Pres. Modito Keita acquired into his person all state power. The people were increasingly terrorized by the president's private militia, which also became a threat to the regular army. In 1968, a bloodless coup by army officers set up a new government under Lt. Moussa Traoré. Farm collectivization was abolished and state enterprises were converted into mixed economy enterprises, private business was encouraged, and incentives were adopted to encourage private foreign investment. As a result, farm production was markedly increased and the availability of goods was substantially augmented. Ties with the Soviet Union and China have been maintained, and the country still considers itself socialist. Is this a government of the people? There is as much evidence and as many reasons for a negative as for a positive answer. Is the capital being developed in this country really capital or capital by some other name in order to eschew the implication of exploitation? The lesson is plain enough. Marx was right about the power of capital. If an underdeveloped country is to be set on the road to economic progress, the competitive bourgeois system of practice is the method of choice. Dictatorship may be another way, but at the exhorbitant cost of life and the vitiation of the traits of human nature to a greater degree than the competitive system of laissez-faire. Stalin's farm collectivization program is another example of the misapplication of Marx's economic theory, as it is related by Nikita Khrushchev:

> Our difficulties in providing food were a direct result of Stalin's victory over his opponents in the campaign to collectivize agriculture. Stalin forced collectivization on our farmers by police methods. His policy was an utter perversion of the principles Lenin had bequeathed to us when he died. When Lenin said that only through cooperation could we develop our agriculture, he had something very different in mind from the Stalinist means employed during collectivization. . . . Even though he called himself a Leninist, Stalin perverted Lenin's principles by imposing collectivization without proper preparation. . . . As a result of Stalin's form of collectivization, we experienced severe shortages in Moscow. Other parts of the country suffered terrible famine. . . . Peasants couldn't bring anything to the peasant markets because private trade was outlawed. We were back to rationing—just like

the period after the Civil War, before the institution of the New Economic Policy. (Lenin instituted the NEP in 1921 to encourage private enterprises as a device to restore morale and productivity, especially in agriculture.) . . . Hundreds of thousands of lives were lost—maybe even millions. I can't give an exact figure because no one was keeping count. All we knew was that people were dying in enormous numbers. . . . Certain theoreticians and even literary figures [took] a Stalinist position . . . that collectivization represented a historically inevitable period of transition from capitalist production . . . to a socialist economy; they say that this process inevitably required sacrifice—and that the loss of lives was justified as long as it was on the altar of socialist progress. What nonsense! What a foolish rationalization of murder and the perversion of Leninist policy.[22]

This is what can happen in the name of a people's government. This is what Rosa Luxemburg was so afraid could happen to the dictatorship of the proletariat when it becomes a dictatorship of the party and finally gets into the hands of a clique of the party.[23]

Morgenthau, in her review of the changing circumstances in the developing African states and the effect of multinationals coming into those states to extract the natural resources, declares that these enterprises usually do very little good for the general welfare of the population. In order for these enterprises to have a favorable effect on the whole population, she recommends that there should be "better distribution of income, more diverse and larger sources of revenue, stronger and more effective institutions connecting leaders and the rest of the population, more avenues of social mobility."[24] What these recommendations actually mean is that the way for assuring that production of wealth by a multinational will favorably influence that country is for it to be democratically organized and have a capitalist economic way of practice. This, of course, is impossible with the world cartels like the combination of oil companies and OPEC (Organization of Oil Exporting Countries). Their method of practice is a complete contradiction to the free enterprise principles of capitalism. The key in the recommendations that predicate the need for a capitalist type economy for these states is: "more diverse and larger sources of revenue." For an economically underdeveloped country to generate more diverse and larger sources of revenue, it needs an economy that is operating in many areas of the country's needs with a large section of its people competing in the generation and control of the capital. Where else could more revenues from diverse sources come from?

THE SYSTEM PAR EXCELLENCE FOR CAPITAL FORMATION

It has become evident from the scramble by the strong nations for political and economic influence, one way or another, over the developing states that the Soviet Union and the Chinese Republic have completely foresaken the principles of Marx and Engels about the course of developmental stages required for a country to pass through in finally attaining a mature level of socialism. Of course, some countries could go through various stages in shorter or longer periods, depending on circumstances. By catapulting an underdeveloped country into socialism without passing through the stage of effective capital formation and accumulation is a real crime against the people of that country—an uncalled for type of ruthless exploitation of those people. The Soviets and Chinese are actually retarding the growth of those countries toward socialism by preventing them from passing through the free enterprise stage and, in the meantime, are creating ecosystems based on dictatorships that are more discordant to their traits of human nature than any free enterprise or mature socialist system could provide.

Engels, in the introductory chapter to his book explaining the meaning of the first volume of Marx's *Capital*, written in 1868, stated: "Just as sharply as Marx stresses the bad sides of capitalist production, does he clearly prove that this social form was necessary to develop the productive forces of society to a level which will make possible an equal development, worthy of human beings, for *all* members of society. All earlier forms of society were too poor for this. Capitalist production for the first time creates the wealth and the productive forces necessary for this. . . ."[25]

The reason why capital creates wealth by the development of the social productive forces is very aptly described by Marx: ". . . Capital, with its restless striving after the general form of wealth, drives labour out beyond the limits of its natural needs . . . the place of natural needs . . . [being] taken by needs that are historically produced. This is why capital is productive: it is an essential relationship for the development of the productive forces of society."[26] What Marx alluded to is that capital, by its extreme competitive nature, creates the conditions that challenge and exhort the people to strive for more wealth because increased production creates new cultural desires, new products to be desired, that only more wealth will satisfy. This happens more facilely under a democratic form of government than under dictatorship.

LENIN'S AVERSION TO DEMOCRACY

The psychological advantages of democracy over dictatorship are obvious. Personal political power pushes to propagate, sustain, and perpetuate itself. Select group power pushes to unify itself in one. The wielding of concentrated power tends to limit the freedom of those subject to that power and thus violates the traits of human nature of those involved including those who wield the power. Lenin would not have agreed with the latter remarks on democracy and dictatorship. He opined in his usually strong polemical pronouncements: "But it never enters the head of any of the opportunists who shamelessly distort Marx that when Engels speaks . . . of the state 'withering away' or 'becoming dormant,' he speaks of democracy. But is 'unintelligible' only to one who has not reflected on the fact that democracy is also a state, and that, consequently, democracy will also disappear when the state disappears."[27] Lenin quoted a good deal from Engels's *Origin of the Family* in his *State and Revolution*. He was too careful a scholar to make mistakes often. But in his latter statement and in his following quote from Engels, he stretched Engels's meaning to the limit: "For Marx and me—Engels writes [January 3, 1894]—it was therefore quite impossible to choose an elastic term [as Social-Democrat] to characterize our special point of view. Today things are different, and the word *Social Democrat* may perhaps pass muster *(mag passieren)*, however unsuitable *(unpassend)* it still is for a party whose economic programme is not merely Socialist in general, but directly Communist, and whose ultimate political aim is to overcome the state, and therefore democracy as well."[28] Here Engels is not rejecting the essential concept of democracy, which he ennobled in *The Origin of the Family* and which is the same as depicted by John Dewey,[29] neither concept engendering a political organization—a state. Engels was rather rejecting the use of the word *democracy* or *democrat* in the names of the European socialist parties that were called "social-democratic." He vigorously disagreed for years with the "bourgeois" tendencies and deviations of the social-democratic parties. Democracy as used by them referred to a type of state apparatus rather than a concept of interrelations inspired and supported by government. It was the use of the word *democracy* and not the concept democracy Engels rejected in the above quotation cited by Lenin. The latter, to press his point, failed to recall Engels's very clear statement on democracy in the concluding paragraph of *Origin of the Family*, which refuted his (Lenin's) foregoing statement attributed to Engels. Engels asserted: "Democracy in government, brotherhood in society, equality in rights and privileges, and universal education foreshadow the next higher plane of society to which experience, intelligence, and knowledge are steadily tending."[30]

The admirable revolutionary during the first World War, Rosa Luxemburg, good friend of Lenin from his earlier political years, was a believer in the dictatorship of the workers as a whole *class* and therefore always disagreed with Lenin. She wrote: "The proletariat, when it seizes power . . . should and must at once undertake socialist measures in the most energetic, unyielding, and unhesitant fashion, in other words, exercise a dictatorship, but a dictatorship of the *class,* not the party or of a clique—dictatorship of the class, that means in the broadest public form on the basis of the most active, unlimited participation of the mass of people, of unlimited democracy . . . to create a social democracy to replace bourgeois democracy—not to *eliminate democracy altogether"* (italics added).[31] Her disagreement with Lenin was based on her belief that it violated the principles of Marx's teachings.

The United States is a capitalist democracy, with all its socioeconomic troubles. The socialist countries of Eastern Europe are single political party dictatorships with all their socioeconomic troubles. The latter are neither democracies nor wholly socialist states. They are very clearly dictatorships to the point of acting extremely ruthless, the justification being that it was a defense against capitalist imperialism. Angelica Balabanoff, the first secretary of the Communist International, longtime friend of Lenin, who worked with the latter in the early years after the Russian Revolution in setting up the communist party control, wrote about Lenin's divergence from Marxism: "Bolshevism as doctrine and as *antithesis* [italics added] to socialism was entirely Lenin's creation . . . *He even acted contrary to Marx's theory that a social revolution presupposes a certain level of technical and industrial development and a corresponding political maturity of the working classes.* (italics added) This condition did not obtain in Russia. . . . Lenin's views on dictatorship were substantiated by the regime he introduced in Russia," Balabanoff wrote and then quoted Lenin's dictum: "Dictatorship is a word charged with blood and ruthlesness, it spells implacable fight between two classes, two worlds, two epochs on a worldwide scale," and further, "this end [socialism] cannot be achieved overnight; the transition from capitalism to socialism requires considerable time." Although nowhere in Marx's writings is there any place for resort to terrorism or even sympathy with such a practice, Balabanoff, who knew Lenin's thinking intimately, quoted him incisively on this subject: "We never declared ourselves contrary to terrorism, nor could we ever do so. It is a weapon which, under certain circumstances, is not only useful, but even indispensable. We are far from denying the usefulness of single acts of terrorism, but we feel impelled to warn against an infatuation with terrorism, against its exclusive use in battle. . . ."[32] Lenin did draw a line on the use of terrorism, however tenuous that line may be in the minds of those who are impelled to stretch it to the limit, as Stalin did. In relation to the murder of the Austrian prime minister in 1916, Balabanoff quoted from a letter by Lenin: "As to our view of that murder, we remain of the opinion, confirmed by decades of experience, that political murder is not a *rational* means. Acts of individual terrorism are useful only in connection with revolutionary mass movements."[33]

Terrorism is the expression of violent primate impulses nourished by the most treacherous complex of influences: the cognitive processes of *Homo*. To think and to plan terrorist acts are a reversion of the human to the farthest reaches of the abysmal. In 1920, Leon Trotsky wrote a book titled *Terrorism and Communism* as a polemic against a brochure by the same name written the previous year by the influential German socialist leader Karl Kautsky, who was severely critical of the conduct of the Bolsheviks in the 1917 Russian Revolution. In this work, Trotsky, in line with Lenin's severe polemics against Kautsky, gave Bolshevism's rationale on the subject of terrorism. He described terrorism as it pervaded the major social revolutions since the Reformation (not mentioning the American Revolution). Trotsky, like Lenin, was an accomplished historian of revolutionary situations, and indeed, they were realists. They may not have appreciated the phylogenetic nature of *Homo,* but they did appreciate the violent nature of humankind in periods of stress. They experienced, personally, the violence, the anxiety, and the fear of persecution and also the inflamed urgency and anger to destroy the persecutors. They probably did not rationalize about the biphasic nature of man's human nature, but they knew how, under chronic unbearable stress, it expressed itself—as Trotsky put it: "But terror can be very efficient against a reactionary class which does not want to leave the scene of operation. *Intimidation* is a powerful weapon of policy, both internationally and internally. War, like revolution, is founded upon intimidation. A victorious war, generally speaking, destroys only an insignificant part of the conquered army, intimidating the remainder and breaking their will. The revolution works in the same way. It kills individuals and intimidates thousands."[34] The human problem, therefore, is how to deal with this aspect of human nature: how to prevent the ecosystem from contradicting and thereby conflicting with the traits of human nature; how to handle the chronic welling up of anger against the current circumstances of living; how to abolish the exploitation of people in the process of trying to make a living; how to bring the circumstances of living into harmony with the traits of human nature; how to prevent a political entity from maintaining itself in power over and against the majority will.

COMPARATIVE DATA: U.S. AND USSR

All countries of the world operate their economies with capital, which in socialist countries is no less capital than the capital of the capitalist countries. The name socialist state, the magic term that has motivated political aspirants among the underdeveloped countries, such as Tanzania, Mali, Guinea, the Congo, and Mozambique, is a decided misnomer, and this is no less true for such somewhat developed states as Syria, Iraq, Egypt, and South Yemen, where party, clique, or personal dictatorships prevail.

As previously discussed, the political pressure exerted toward the establishment of "socialist" dictorships in underdeveloped countries is one of the great political crimes of our time, since such practice delays the advancement of the process of capital formation—that which these countries need most of all. It does this by suppressing various traits of human nature in the vise of dictatorship, particularly the "challenge and competence" and "freedom to choose" traits. Without the morale to drive these traits into a striving course of action, capital formation is markedly retarded.

The Western democracies developed their wealth under the system of laissez-faire economy. Free enterprise today is not what it was when analyzed by Adam Smith. Unqualified free enterprise as described by the latter is impossible today. Technology has so increased volume of production, speed of communications, and facility for record keeping, computation, and management that enterprises are impelled toward growing larger without limit. At the same time, democratic influences have forced governments of these democracies to introduce increasingly more humanized programs and practices to negate the exploitation of labor by capital. Such elaborately expensive programs in health and social services have had and are having decided beneficial effects on the productive forces of their countries. The fantastic growth of technologies has not slighted the allocation of funds for the development and production of military hardware, nor their purchase by even the poorest of the Third World countries, nor by the socialist states. The inordinate expenditure of funds for the military has revealed several lessons:

1. The capitalist countries are no longer the only fomentors of military adventures. The responsibilities for such international misconduct is well distributed among countries with various socioeconomic philosophies and with various stages of socioeconomic development, each with its own "peace-loving" self-righteous propaganda. Nor has the United Nations been a deterrent force in this area, and to some extent, it has actually been an active fomentor of trouble.

2. No country in the world has an adequate productive capacity to sustain progressively improving social services for all its people and also a military program to nourish an attitude of military swagger, and, at the same time, to successfully support a real socialist functioning government, operating on the basis of present-day amemities. This was well illustrated by Pres. Lyndon Johnson's misdirection when he claimed that the United States could afford to finance a Great Society program and a Vietnam War. This misadventure initiated the increased escalation of the national debt, which process was uncontrollably intensified by the OPEC oil company monopoly's contrived price swindle since 1973.

3. One of the greatest deterrents to capital formation and capital investment for growth of production and maintenance of full employment is the capital wasted for "defense" purposes. This is particularly devastating under dictatorships, which must maintain oppressive force against its people as well as, in many cases, external adventurism.

We cannot ignore such expenditures, since they are confounding the process of capital formation all over the world. The problem is basically a mutually generated confrontation between the Soviet Union and the United States, although, historically, it was initiated by the Western powers after World War I. Today the United States finds itself in a very uncomfortable moral position by being the greatest armament producer and seller and, at the same, mouthing the most vocal protests against violators of human rights. For the United States and the Soviet Union, the continuing augmentation of their nuclear stockpiles even though each already has enough to destroy civilization three times over, is as vicious a behavior as any ever demonstrated by the species *Homo sapiens*. The immorality of this practice is not only in relation to the potential destruction of humanity, but what it deprives in the meanwhile in social services for the people by depressing capital formation.

Thus it should be clear from the above that when we speak of modern free enterprise, we must be aware of the tremendous influence government itself exerts on the free enterprise system, which has the flavor of an emerging socialist or dictatorial force. This is partially a facade because it is big business with significant support of government bureaucracy and obligated elected legislators who control the system, even though the electorate is gaining more and more clout in directing the course of government. The dilemma in which the government finds itself is that the pressures by the people to spread democracy in production relations is contradicted by the strength of the monopoly powers, particularly that of the oil cartel, financial institutions, and insurance companies. In spite of antitrust laws, monopoly is not being adequately controlled. The efforts to neutralize the practice of the exploitation of the worker by modality changes in production relations can be far more effective than some of the expensive government programs. By changes in *production relations* is meant changes of worker relation to corporations, to government operations related to production processes, to participation in planning in the production process, to organization, operation, and management of the production process, and to wages and profit sharing.

Let us make some comparisons of basic areas between the government operations in the United States and the Soviet Union:

1. Government operating funds are derived mainly from:
    U.S.—Income taxes, Social Security trust fund, excise taxes, estate and gift taxes, custom duties, state enterprises
    USSR—Sales, rent, exports, taxation, custom duties, postal, telephone and other services, natural resources, interest from loans to state enterprises, state enterprises
2. Source of funds for the people's living expenses are derived:
    U.S.—overwhelmingly from wages and salaries
    USSR—overwhelmingly from wages and salaries
3. Government operative branches:
    U.S.—Significant degree of distinction between the legislative, administrative (executive), and judicial functions
    USSR—No sharp distinctions

4. Choosing of Candidates:
   U.S. candidates are chosen by:
       The various existing political parties
       Free elections
   USSR candidates are chosen by:
       The single party
       Listing a single name for each position
5. Election of Government Officials:
   U.S. legislators are elected:
       From a multiple-candidate ballot
       By universal suffrage
   USSR legislators are elected:
       From single-candidate ballots
       By universal suffrage
6. Making of Laws:
   U.S. Laws are made by legislative bodies *directly* elected to the House and the Senate.
   USSR Laws are made by legislators *indirectly* elected to the Supreme Soviet by six steps or levels removed from the electorate, but the laws originate by dictation from the party.
7. Execution of Laws:
   U.S. laws are executed by the president, who is elected *directly* by popular vote, and the president's bureaucracy, the Cabinet and departments approved by the Senate.
   USSR laws are executed by the All-Union Council of Ministers, elected by the Supreme Soviet, which is elected from single-candidate ballots chosen by the party whose powers are exercised by its presidium chosen by the party.

The foregoing comparisons of government organizational and administrative dynamics are clear enough in eliciting the difference between capitalist democratic government and socialist Soviet dictatorship. Even though a Soviet corporation has many aspects of organization and administration that resemble the large American corporation, there are, nevertheless, very basic qualitative differences due to their settings in capitalist democracy, on the one hand, and Soviet type socialism, on the other. The settings are the nature of the government to which each one is responsible, as listed in the above outline of comparisons. Thus the president, senators, and the representatives in the United States are elected directly by universally franchised electorate and do represent the people, who freely choose to vote. But do the USSR central government officers represent the people when they are six steps removed from the voting people and the entire six-step process is guided by a single-party apparatus whose candidates are dictated by the party? This can be countered by the facts that the U.S. system of choosing candidates is so expensive as to be beyond the means of most people, that the critical sources of campaign funds come from special interests that obligate those elected to support special interest biases.

This kind of quibbling gets us nowhere. Facts are not changed by such quibbling. But there is no doubt that plenty of people in the Eastern European socialist countries do not feel that their own will and judgment are represented in their government's operations, just as many people in the United States feel the same way. The difference is that the latter are individually not muzzled from expressing their grievances if done without inciting to riot, and even then they are not always muzzled. Dictatorship cannot hide itself from the people. The latter feel it because it violates too many of the traits of human nature, particularly the traits pertaining to the freedom to choose, the need to respond to challenge, the impulse to strive to satisfy one's appetites, inclinations, and talents, and the urge to respond to one's creative feeling. Violations of the traits of human nature cause behavioral disorientations among those people whose thresholds of flexibility to adaptation are overriden. Thus, in the Soviet Union, the stress disorder of alcoholism is epidemic, as it is in the United States, but for different stress-producing factors, the one from too little freedom to choose, the other from too much freedom and permissiveness in an exaggerated adversary atmosphere.

There is general agreement that the Western capitalist countries are democracies, the United States being the paragon among them. Even Lenin called them democracies, but with disparaging implications rather than the approbatory use of Marx and Engels in their historical perspective. Yet, in the showdown, the American monopolies, hiding their political weight behind fascinatingly beguiling facades, have such critical influence in the shaping of significant policies in the federal government that real democracy is thereby compromised. The extent of this undemocratic influence, for example, as described by Tyler, concerning the multinational oil companies, is so great that even the blackmail perpetrated against the people of the United States and the world by them in collusion with the oil-rich Arab countries is tolerated by our government as normal routine business practice.[35] The real democracy alluded to by Engels as a higher plane of society is still lacking in the Western democracies as, indeed, it is lacking even more in the socialist countries of Eastern Europe, as patently demonstrated in Poland today.

From the comparison of the United States and the Soviet Union government operations, it is clear that the Soviet economy is operated by the use of "capital," just like in the rest of the world, even though ideological restraints may create a Soviet aversion to using the term "capital." This reluctance is illustrated in the case when the Soviet economist Liberman recommended a method of stimulating more incentive in production by paying bonuses to enterprises based on profitability.[36] The term "profitability," was circumvented although the fact was "profit," the result of *surplus value*. Here is the way Schwartz translated an article by an eminent Soviet economist in *Pravda* summarizing the positive aspects of the first full post-Stalin decade: "About 60 per cent of the industrial production of the entire period of the Soviet State's existence was produced in these ten years; *capital* [italics added] investments during that time accounted for more than two-thirds of the total invested during the 46 years. . . ."[37] Whether the original article used the word *capital* or whether it was so used in the translation is not known by this author, but that the word meant capital is certain.

IMPERIALISM

Will the United States be so weak, so lacking in ingenuity, in determining its future as to let Lenin's predictions about the self-destruction of such countries as ours come true for this country? He dubbed the United States the chief imperialist country in the world. His definition of imperialism includes the following five characteristics:

> 1. The concentration of production and capital developed to such a stage that it creates monopolies which play a decisive role in economic life;
>
> 2. The merging of bank capital with industrial capital, and the creation, on the basis of this "finance capital," of a financial oligarchy;
>
> 3. The export of capital, which has become extremely important, as distinguished from the export of commodities;

4. The formation of international capitalist monopolies which share the world among themselves:

5. The territorial division of the whole world among capitalist powers is completed.

Imperialism is capitalism in that stage of development in which the domination of monopolies and finance capital has established itself.[38]

The above description is today quite inadequate in relation to finance capital. The greatest and most effective finance capital cartel today is, in a sense, the oil producing Third World nations—industrially underdeveloped countries. The OPEC countries, particularly Saudi Arabia, have been allowed to blackmail the entire world and have created havoc with the world economy. This they could not have done without the heavy hand of the multinational oil monopolies, which have no allegiance to nation or people, but only to the power structure of their profit-making machine, which has decisive influence over governments.

THE AMERICAN EVOLUTIONARY REVOLUTION

Where there is life, there are problems. The great depression of the thirties accentuated and brought under microscopic examination the chronic socioeconomic problems of the United States. The Social Security Act of 1935, the Agricultural Adjustment Act of 1933, and government intervention in the national economy during depression by adoption of the Keynesian practice initiated a new epoch in American history—an epoch that justifies the description of an evolutionary revolution that reached critical levels around 1965, with the crisis continuing to sharpen up to the present time. The blame for the crisis has been pointed in the direction of too much social service, and therefore too much government spending. The reason for this, although a spurious indictment, is because so many sociopolitical events associated with social service converged and became more acute about 1965. The civil rights radicals, disillusioned with liberalism and "participatory democracy," became more revolutionary, particularly the blacks. The students, not a poverty group, activated their rebellion against conventional norms of society, including the rejection with scorn of scientific education. Government and industry began reducing productivity in research and technology. The sales of American technological products such as automobiles and machinery began to be replaced by Japanese and West German products. Productivity per man, which used to be the highest in the world, began to decline and has continued to do so. United States's first place in electronics began to erode, and it has continued to lose status internationally. United States production of oil began a rapid decline as a result of reduced exploration efforts. The oil monopoly was preparing the country for the gasoline rip-off act. In a few years American self-sufficiency was reduced to almost 50 percent importation of oil. Crime, juvenile delinquency, alcoholism, drug abuse and addiction, and illegitimate births to teenagers began to rise dramatically, and so did our involvement in the Vietnam War, with a surging increase in casualties.

But so were other events crowding the mass communications media for public attention. President Johnson won a resounding victory in 1964, with the winning slogan "to keep us out of war," which he immediately violated, claiming that the waste of production on war could be easily absorbed by our wondrous economy at the same time that he launched his Great Society program with special vigor. The nature of the Second American Revolution was aptly described in his State of the Union message on January 4, 1965: "We are in the midst of the greatest upward surge of economic well-being in the history of any nation. But we are only at the beginning of the road to the Great Society. Ahead is a summit where freedom from want of the body can help fulfill the needs of the spirit. The Great Society asks not how much, but how good; not how to create wealth, but how to use it; not only how fast we are going, but where we are headed." He outlined a list of glittering goals to be attained.

A flood of social service and environmental quality control legislation began pouring out of Congress, such as Medicare, Medicaid, civil rights, Head Start, EPSDT (Early Periodic Screening, Diagnosis, and Treatment for medically indigent children), the Food Stamp Program, WIC (Women, Infant, and Children) nutrition program, the belated Equal Opportunity and Full Employment Act of 1976, and various environmental acts. Johnson's description of the Great Society program and what came out of Congress in the form of laws was a reflection of the sanguinary battle that was taking place between the old and the new perceptual dynamics in that august body. The compromises that produced those legislative acts not only were hopelessly inadequate to solve the problems toward which they were directed, but they created as many problems as they solved. In the meantime, the casualties in Vietnam kept getting greater, the end of the "police action" was nowhere in sight, the cost of the war and the cost of implementing the social legislation began to create greater deficit spending by the federal government than was anticipated. Even though the war ended in 1973, the budget deficit kept growing.

What was becoming clear was that the United States economy was not as strong as portrayed by the patriotic prating of politicians and that OPEC's price-pirating adventure beginning in 1973 stimulated a hefty increase in the annual budget deficits,[39] which had already been augmented by the wastefulness of capital during the Vietnam War. From 1963 to 1970, the deficits hovered between $3 and $5 billion, except for 1967 and 1968, when it rose to $8.7 and $25.2 billion respectively. This picture was only slightly higher than for the preceding decade. But for the last three years of the Vietnam War, the deficits really began to grow. For 1971, 1972, and 1973, it was respectively $23.0, $23.2, and $14.8 billion. What a waste of capital to extract it from the world economy and to render it nonproductive, for the most part, by using it for war or, as OPEC and the oil company monopoly has been using it to buy political and economic power and to wield it for destabilizing governments and increasing the purchase and production of armaments. The greatest sufferers from the vulpine machinations of the oil cartel are the developing countries where the trade imbalance, as shown in table 2, is reflected in the World Bank figures that show that the Third World debt in 1981 was $517 billion and it was headed for $600 billion for 1982.[40]

The destabilization of the world economy is being blamed on everything except the real culprit, the oil cartel. The acceptance of the power-profit jag of the latter as the sacred expression of free trade, although it has become the greatest force ever created for destroying free trade and productive capital, is an illustration of the influence of monopoly on the elequent articulations of the powers that be in government.

The effect of the oil cartel on the American economy was spectacular, considering its (the American economy's) legendary strength. The United States budget deficit in 1975 climbed to $45.1 billion. Then from 1976 to 1980 the deficits were respectively $66.4, $45.0, $48.8, $27.7, and $40.0 billion. The 1982 deficit was estimated at $196.0 billion, but here other complicating factors of mismanagement also came into being. Production continued to stagnate; unemployment continued to rise, reaching to just about 11 percent by the end of 1982. For an opulent country like the United States, a deficit in the balance of trade between imports and exports is not a very detrimental problem, except as a symptom of economic dislocation. But for the developing countries, the problem can be catastrophic. Table 1 shows how this problem developed in the United States before and after 1973. Whereas, generally, the balance was favorable before that critical year, thence except for 1975, the balance continued to be unfavorable through 1979, due mostly to the cost of importing oil and gas. The depression had spread worldwide. Bankruptcies continued at an alarming rate. The alliance of Dark Age feudalism with monopolistic finance capitalism inaugurated a new level of monopoly development—the blood-sucking stage whereby a life-sustaining commodity (energy) was being used to drain the life of nations.

What will be the mechanism by which the objectives of the Great Society can be attained without hindering the tremendous productive power of the American "free" enterprise system when it is linked to a guiding star of social responsibility? Those who say that this linkage is not possible are relegating the future of the United States to the cauldron of Lenin's and, for that matter, Khrushchev's "self-destruction" prediction. The election of 1980 showed that the majority people want the free enterprise system *and* the social and environmental services toward which we have been aiming since the passage of the Social Security Act. What the people do not want are the ineffective legislative methods devised to solve our problems and to operate the programs, the waste, and the impotent fragmented administration of them, the demoralizing effect of the dole system, the lack of concern for quality workmanship, the antiscientific education atmosphere among the youth, the lack of ethical judgment engulfing conduct in all areas of living, the latter being sparked to a large extent by the ethos of getting something for nothing or the scorn directed toward conventional norms. What is not generally realized is that this depreciated side of the American scene is the consequence of the accumulated repercussions of the influence of the conscienceless monopolies selling their conscienceless attitude through the mass media into every niche of American society and to their supporters in the halls of Congress. Not that monopolies are inherently bad, but that they are bad when operated as conscienceless technostructures concerned only with profit and power and the spread of their nonsocial influence, such as the rip-off system of economics, throughout the social structure.

The contradictions that are generated by the above seminal antagonisms are:

1. *The liability of benefits:* The benefits of the dole system for the unemployed are so administered as to discourage the demoralized from wanting to work and to demoralize those who would want to work.

Table 1.
Exports and Imports of Merchandise, 1960 to 1979, U.S., in Billions of dollars

	1960	1965	1970	1972	1973	1974	1975	1976	1977	1978	1979
Exports	20.6	27.5	43.2	49.8	71.3	98.5	107.6	115.0	121.2	143.7	181.8
Imports	14.7	21.4	40.0	55.6	69.5	101.0	96.9	120.7	147.7	172.0	206.3

Statistical Abstracts of the United States, 1980.

TABLE 2.
Exports and Imports, Developing Countries, Excluding Oil-exporting Countries, 1970 to 1979, in Billions of dollars

	1970	1971	1972	1973	1974	1975	1976	1977	1978	1979
Exports	44.4	46.5	55.6	80.5	116.0	113.1	133.0	156.7	178.0	226.4
Imports	58.6	66.0	72.1	98.6	158.2	168.7	174.2	198.6	232.4	287.9

Statistical Abstracts of the United States, 1980.

TABLE 3.
Exports and Imports for Oil-exporting Countries,
1970 to 1979, in Billions of dollars

	1970	1971	1972	1973	1974	1975	1976	1977	1978	1979
Exports	17.3	22.0	24.8	39.0	119.3	109.8	133.0	146.0	141.8	207.5
Imports	9.6	11.1	13.8	20.1	32.1	51.3	62.2	83.9	94.9	100.3

Statistical Abstracts of the United States, 1980

TABLE 4.
Federal Budget Surpluses or Deficits
from Receipts and Outlays: 1940 to 1980

1940	1945	1950	1955	1960	1961	1962	1963	1964	1965	1966
-3.1	-47.5	-3.1	-3.0	.3	-3.4	-7.1	-4.8	-5.9	-1.6	-3.8

1967	1968	1969	1970	1971	1972	1973	1974	1975	1976	1977
-8.7	-25.2	3.2	-2.8	-23.0	-23.4	-14.8	-4.7	-45.1	-66.4	-45.0

1978	1979	1980
-48.8	-27.7	-39.8

Statistical Abstracts of the United States, 1980

2. Free enterprise unguided by social concern and effective government control will negate itself by becoming monopolized. *Unrestricted free enterprise negates free enterprise and freedom.*

3. The concern with quantity of work only for higher profits and power and for higher wages sacrifices quality of product and morale of those workers instilled with pride in their creative arts. *Concern for only quantity of an activity may compromise the quality of its result,* such as when the *bottom line* becomes the beginning and the end of the perceptions of executive boards of production enterprises.

4. The extreme consequence of uncontrolled competition for profit and power breeds a psychosocial behavior of seeking more for less and leads corporations to form monopolies whereby control of production makes feasible the control of prices without regard to demand. Such is the breeding soil for corruption and crime, particularly in government. The morale of the people caught in the mesh of such contradictions is tortured into a state of demoralization. *Uncontrolled human effort easily changes to rationalized primate behavior,* a legacy of the Australopithicines.

5. Under a truly free enterprise system, the way to control inflation would be to increase production, but where monopoly prevails, this does not work, because the monopoly controls the amount of production placed on the market and the price thereof. Therefore, under a free enterprise system, where the government does not provide interposing planned practices, increasing production to overproduction reduces prices and leads to reduced production to the point of inducing recession, which will increase unemployment and will reduce profits and revenue collections by limiting the amount of money workers have to spend on product. Under monopoly, which controls the amount produced and the prices of the products, prices can be kept inflated even in depressison. Thus during the present spell of inflation and recession, the oil glut temporarily reduced prices at the pump while OPEC got busy reducing production. Almost immediately prices for the consumer increased again. Another way relates to the 1981 orange crop in Florida, which was partly destroyed by a frost, while the crop in California was most abundant. The orange monopoly made sure, with the support of the Department of Agriculture, that enough oranges were fed to cattle and buried underground to keep the abundant supply off the market. This kept the price as high as those people with ample incomes were willing to pay. *Private monopoly profits produces public privation.*

The above contradictions and more are playing havoc with the ecosystem's relation to the traits of human nature, as demonstrated by the present epidemics of alcoholism; drug abuse and addiction; crime, including white collar crime; juvenile delinquency; and corruption of politicians. The trend for community concern in solving social problems, nevertheless, has been accelerating since the Great Depression. In spite of inadequate legislation created by compromise with the forces for unrestricted profit and the power seekers, the American Second Revolution continues to grind its way to eventual solution. The solution would have to include universal opportunity and civil rights, guaranteed full employment, and a living wage for all who wish to work, with no benefits for the able-bodied who refuse to work, and a system of personal health care and education available to everyone according to need. The solution should also include a mechanism in government to study the ecosystem's harmony or disharmony with the traits of human nature and to implement adjustments in social dynamics needing changes. We must create and preserve a pattern of human interrelations in which those positive aspects of the traits of human nature will thrive that endow the people with the free, creative, compassionate, and rational spirit that, even when available to a restricted fortunate section of the population, has made America great.

It should be clear to the American people that the nation is coping contentiously and with some success with the contradictions tearing at its foundations. The Soviet Union, no less, is plagued with its contradictions, which cannot be solved under dictatorship.

CAPITALIST AND SOCIALIST PRODUCTION

To this very day, two of the most critical socio-economic problems of the Soviet Government are:

1. Generating enough capital to do what needs to be done to fulfill the various five-year plans; and
2. Stimulating incentive among the workers to generate the capital needed by increasing productivity.

One reason for the Soviet government having to contend with these two problems is because their socialist revolution took place in one of the most *backward capitalist* countries. The problem, therefore, of generating capital was almost like starting from scratch, particularly after the destruction that took place during the years of fighting for power and then, again, by the Second World War. But another important reason, besides the tremendous waste in producing mountains of armaments, is that the generation of capital is taking place under circumstances where the universal stimulus of capital striving to create more and more surplus value is everywhere dampened by governmental restrictions on individual initiative. It must be remembered that a real communist ideological life-style is impossible where the forces of production have not reached the level where they produce enough for everyone's needs at the highest standard of living. One of the few countries in the world where production is *only beginning* to reach that level is the United States. The Soviets have trouble stimulating their people to produce at the highest individual level, because the generation of capital by the method adopted in the East European countries up to recently was much less stimulating to capital formation than in a freewheeling laissez-faire system. Even Stalin's highly publicized "Stakhanov" movement for stimulating farm production helped very little. That is why socialism works best in a country that has reached the highest level of production under capitalism and where the emergence of private monopoly has been controlled effectively enough not to allow it to destroy the morale of enterprising people, as it is beginning to do in the United States, with destructive effect on the economy.

There is a need to consider the problem of the similarities between the methods of capital formation in the United States and other Western developed capitalist countries and the Soviet Union and its socialist partners in Eastern Europe. One thing is certain and that is that the industrial corporations operate in both areas. In the Eastern bloc of socialist countries, the corporations are state controlled, with certain liberalized variations, as in Yugoslavia and Hungary. In the Western capitalist countries, the corporations are privately organized and controlled, but the larger the corporation, the more is it *jointly* controlled by private and state apparatuses. In fact, the Marxian theorists have for many decades theorized that the larger and more monopolistic capitalist corporations became, the easier could they be transformed into socialist corporations. The growing closeness of state and private collaboration and control of monopolies was discussed by Bukharin in 1915: "It is a fact, however, that economic evolution . . . must and does lead to a situation where the bourgeoisie as a whole is more tolerant regarding monopolistic interference of the state power. The basic reason for this is the ever growing closeness between state power and the leading spheres of finance capital. State and private monopoly enterprises merge into one entity within the framework of the state capitalist trust. The interests of the state and the interests of finance capital coincide more and more. On the other hand, a maximum of centralization and a maximum of state power are required by the fierce competitive struggle on the world market."[41] This process was proceeding so sufficiently during the years of the First World War that some eager social theorists were predicting the development of state socialism out of this obvious state capitalism.[42] This study, to which Lenin wrote the introduction in 1915, preceded Lenin's famous *Imperialism, the Highest Stage of Capitalism* by two years.

The close collaboration of the State Department with private monopoly is well illustrated by the incursion of American oil companies into Arabian oil. The California Standard Oil Company was created by the split-up of the Standard Oil Trust in 1911. "British fumbling and the energetic intervention of the State Department transformed the California company into one of the partners in the world oil company cartel. It began on the Island of Bahrain, lying off the Arabian coast but claimed by Iran. In 1925 a British group obtained a concession from the ruler which in turn was transferred to an American group two years later. In 1928 Standard of California appeared as the owner of the concession to the consternation of the [British] Colonial Office which could only regard this as a form of poaching on Imperial preserves, for the Sheikh's foreign relations were shepherded from London. At this point, the State Department stepped in, and the Colonial Office was obliged by 1930 to concede Standard's position in Bahrain."[43]

In the United States, the longtime build-up of State Department career personnel has supported the monopolies and, on the international level, has always played prominent, though unpublicized, roles in aiding the schemes of these monopolies in increasing their power and profits. In the mid-twenties, the State Department fought valiantly to forcibly introduce the emerging American oil monopoly into the Persian Gulf area against the British pressure to the contrary. In the 1950s, it was advantageous for the State Department to support the British oil monopoly against Iranian prime minister Mossadeq's threat to nationalize Iran's oil industry and oust the British. This eventuated with the ouster of the latter and the consolidation of the shah's power. When the oil monopoly and its OPEC partners decided that the opportunity was ripe to rip off the world with its oil blackmail, making Israel the scapegoat, (not for the first time),[44] they did this during the crisis of the Yom Kippur War. The State Department's collusion with the Arab section of OPEC's anti-Israel declaration of conditions for normalizing the oil supply was demonstrated in all of its dealings with the problem of the Arab refugees. Further demonstration of the State Department collusion with the oil monopoly is the graceful way in which it rejected the recommendations of the General Accounting Office's Report[45] on how to counter the predation perpetrated against the American people by the OPEC oil company monopoly. So strongly established do the oil companies feel that they thumb their noses at the Department of Energy when the latter asks for data on their operations.[46] No significant action is ever taken against the oil monopoly, even when it is openly blamed by Sheikh Yamani for price gouging, and the sheikh should know: "The ones who want that [price increases] are first and foremost, the oil companies. Obviously, when the price rises, their profits increase. And unless the system changes, unless, for instance, Saudi Arabia takes over 100 percent control of Aramco, as I hope will happen in the future, the companies will keep on demanding increases."[47]

All these embarrassing situations led President Carter, in a moment of truth and riled by the frustrations of handling the economy, to let down his guard and declare the oil lobby as the greatest threat to our economic life, and then to proceed to treat the oil price rapacity as legitimate and proper business practice. Some will claim that, in accordance with the above description, things have not changed in our country since monopoly capitalism came into being. Such a sweeping conclusion is certainly not warranted considering what has been going on in the American political-economic scene. Regardless of whether one agrees with Reich's[48] analysis of the American condition and its promise, nevertheless, the conditions and the alienations created by the "corporate state" do exist. His description of Consciousness III of the New Generation is an attempt to elucidate the fact that exciting changes have been occurring in the thinking and attitudes of American people. These changes, he avers, *will* alter the political structure without violence and will bring the social world into harmony with the nature of the human being. His recommendations on how this will happen lack definiteness and a basic understanding of the principles of political economy. But this does not negate his premise that the movement for change toward the better life for all our people is on its way and that the American people will not accommodate Lenin with his prediction of the dire fate of American imperialism.

What Reich and the impetuous polemicists for change lack in understanding the principles of political economy, Galbraith and his school of economists make up. Galbraith's discussion of the dynamics and anatomy of the corporation in modern industrial nations is penetrating indeed. He chides the conservative businessman with the observation that: "Among the least enchanting words in the business lexicon are planning, government control, state underwriting, and socialism. To consider the likelihood of these in the future would be to bring home the appalling extent to which they are already a fact."[49] He lays down several principles, which appear to be obvious, that "modern large-scale production with heavy requirements of capital and sophisticated technology" demand elaborate organization and planning;[50] also that "large-scale industrialism requires . . . that the market and the consumer sovereignty be extensively superseded,"[51] that "large-scale organization also requires autonomy," and that "the same imperative operates in the socialist economy."[52] He also posits: "Nothing in our time is more interesting than that the erstwhile capitalist corporation and the erstwhile Communist form, under the imperatives of organization, come together as oligarchies of their own members. Ideology is not the relevant force. . . . It is autonomy that allows the firm authority over its planning. . . . Thus, convergence between the two ostensibly different planning systems occurs at all fundamental points."[53]

Galbraith quotes from Richman's *Management Development and Education in the Soviet Union*: " 'The Soviet industrial enterprise is some hybrid of an American Corporation and an American factory. It operates as an autonomous financial entity with its own bank account(s). It also operates on a profit-and-loss basis, although the earning of profit is not a requisite for survival. In essence and law, the Soviet enterprise is the key unit for the administration of state property and productive resources.' "[54]

The need for the technostructure of a corporation to be autonomous in planning is the core of the problem of large-scale production not only in a capitalist economy (where planning is *not for* the people), but in the socialist economy (where planning is supposed to be *for* the people) as reflected in Galbraith's observation: "The technical complexity, planning and associated scale of operations that took power from the capitalist entrepreneur and lodged it with the technostructure removed it also from the reach of social controls."[55] What is the mechanism by which the need for autonomy in planning is modified so that the planning does aim at the social goals of the society without reducing the effectiveness of planning by the technostructure?

THE MEANING OF EXPLOITATION

Throughout history, social revolutions were generated and sparked by exploitation. Formally and theoretically, the working people in the Soviet Union hold all *state* power through the soviets, but in reality if the meaning of the concept "exploitation" were broadly applied to all phases of human interrelations involved in capital accumulation, such as working for the state (which is, according to Marxism, a coercive force) so it could augment its capital for increasing production, then such exploitation still exists in the Soviet Union. The question is: At what share of the surplus value given to the worker for the value of the work he contributes is the term "exploitation" no longer valid? Is the "freedom of choice" in doing that work the factor in determining the meaning of exploitation? Is the nature of the social system itself, regardless of other factors, the determining factor of what is exploitation? When three persons do the same kind of work and receive the same level of compensation to allow them each to live at the same comparably adequate level of physical, mental, emotional, and social comfort, but one works in the Soviet Union, another for the United States government, and the third for an American private corporation, are any of them being exploited? In a technologically developed world, capital formation is as basic an activity as living itself. One without the other is improbable, unless we return to living in the nontechnological world. Capital formation, therefore, in the socialist world is as essential as it is in the capitalist world. But an activity such as capital formation is impossible without the production of "surplus value." Is surplus value produced in a Soviet type of "socialism" not produced by exploitation, while that in a capitalist democracy is produced by exploitation? From a human point of view, the important considerations are:

1. Under what conditions are the surplus value produced considering the need to protect the physical health and the traits of human nature?
2. What portion of the value produced is given to the needs of the worker, what proportion to the maintenance of the production plant, what proportion to the maintenance of the owner of the plant (be the owner an individual, a private corporation, or a governmental corporation), and what proportion for developing increased production?

Marx's definition of *surplus value* is: "The worker begins by adding so many new forms to the value of the raw material and the instrument, through the utilization of the instrument as an instrument and the transformation of raw material, as would equal the working time that is contained in his own wages. Anything more that he adds is surplus working time, surplus value."[56] He continues: "What appears to be surplus value on the part of capital appears on the worker's side to be, precisely, surplus labour far beyond his requirements, that is to say, far beyond his immediate needs for maintenance of his livelihood. The great historical feature of capital is that it produces this surplus value, which is superfluous labour from the standpoint of ordinary use value and mere subsistence. . . . This is why capital is productive; it is an essential relationship for the *development of the productive forces* [italics added] of society."[57] In the United States, surplus value is recirculated to the worker by way of:

1. Social Security system
2. Unemployment compensation
3. Various types of health insurance and direct health services
4. Various types of social services
5. Free education systems
6. Free trade union bargaining with employers
7. Retirement systems
8. Minimum wage laws

Under such conditions, is the American worker an exploited victim? This certainly could not be true for the largest majority of the workers. Nor does this mean that a substantial sector of the population is not having income problems and difficulty in finding employment. In the sector of low income families, unemployment, and training for job competence, the United States has serious unresolved but "easily" solvable problems which could be solved by passing a law guaranteeing a job for those who want to work, a living wage for those who do work, and training for those desiring it.

In the Eastern European socialist countries it is claimed that exploitation does not exist. Yet the relation of worker to employer and the technostructure of the firm to the government apparatus is practically the same as in capitalist countries. Workers do feel exploited to some degree, as do American workers. Otherwise how does one explain the demand of about 10 million workers and farmers in Poland for better wages and free choice of unions independent of the government? The American worker strikes when he feels that he is not getting his fair share. He does not have to strike for the freedom to do so, since he already has it. In the industrialized countries, therefore, exploitation of the workers does not have the same meaning that it had when Marx was analyzing the political economy of nineteenth-century capitalism. The big change took place between the First and Second World Wars. The question remains: At what level of production and workers compensation do we have an exploitative threshold above which the surplus value or capital is no longer regarded as the product of exploited workers? Must a specific type of social system prevail in order to make this determination?

Does the meaning of *exploitation* depend on who takes possession of the surplus value? In the Soviet Union, it is taken by the government for its operations, but the government is supposed to belong to the people. In the United States, the surplus value from government production goes to the government, which is also supposed to belong to the people. However, in the United States, a great part of production enterprises are operated by private business. But even here a major part of the surplus value is paid as taxes to the government, which in turn pays for most of the Social Security and other social service programs that benefit the workers. So who is better off in a material way, the majority of the Soviet workers or the majority of United States workers? Who among these are the most exploited? Who among these live in an ecosystem more in concordance with the traits of human nature?

The Marxian definition of *capital* as being fundamentally a historically based social production relation places the Soviet "social wealth" as much in the sphere of "capital" as American capital approaches the sphere of "social wealth." How much difference the term "governmental" as meaning the "people" or "social" there exists in comparing the Soviet Union with the United States is a good question for a scholarly thesis. Both are *states* and from that viewpoint are coercive. Just imagine what more advantage would accrue to the American worker if the posture of the United States government operations in relation to monopolies was to take a decided direction in harnessing the development of monopoly without eliminating the challenge factors of free enterprise and so help capital maintain its great productive capabilities. Under such circumstances, the United States productive machine could make economic paradise of this country long before the Soviet Union could come close to doing the same for its people. The Soviet Union could never achieve this (including the psychosocial harmony) under a dictatorship.

Violent social revolution is not to be expected in the United States. Some economic changes are bound to occur, lest the United States economy degenerate out of control, and the latter is also not to be expected. The changes that will occur, in order not to be violent, must not destroy the productive power of capital. The productive nature of capital, while being kept alive, will also have to be regulated against unethical and vicious, inhuman competitive operations. The dynamics of the regulations will have to be such as will divest from the process of production whatever alienating factors that may come into existence in relation to the workers. The American genius is certainly not daunted at the challenge that this presents!

THE RIP-OFF SYSTEM THAT UPSET THE WORLD ECONOMY

A new type of exploitation has come into existence, exploitation by monopoly of a life artery of the social organism. There was a time when the world would respond with philanthropic masses of food when famines occurred anywhere in the world. No food, no life. It was as simple as that. No other item has been shared with the same sanctity throughout the history of *Homo* as food. Exploitation of this essential in the face of famine has never been an indictment in human practice. However, we are now living in a different world, where, although in certain areas of the world people are in the throes of starvation and there is scarcely enough of food *energy* available to them to supply the living organisms nor the transportation energy to distribute the food from afar to these starving. The *direct* sharing of food with the starving is even in this day a moral practice, the violation of which humankind would not tolerate. But the *indirect* withholding of food from the starving by constricting the availability of energy is an entirely new form of exploiting the human race. It is a practice made possible by monopoly of the energy that the machines of world production requires to produce food, i.e., oil. For the less developed countries of the world, this problem is acute. No oil (energy)—no food, no life.

The whole world economy has been fundamentally dislocated because a fundamental process in human society has been disrupted: the process of *exchange*. One of the essential characteristics of human society that distinguishes it from other primate "societies" if troops can be called societies, is the exchange of things which one group has or produces and the other needs or wants. The first item that entered the exchange process, historically, was food. In the whole history of humankind, those interrelations between people where food is concerned have always been ethically and morally formulated in sacred and generous rules of exchange. The first written record to be found is in the tithe system in the Bible, an ethological principle of giving to the poor in exchange for social good. This was so because people cannot maintain a social existence without food. No food—no society, no life. It was as simple as that. It would be very difficult to find an instance where food had been monopolized and used as a political weapon of one people against another. In a less formalized way, human interrelations where shelter is concerned is similarly wrapped in the ethics and morality of mankind.

Thus, in *our* world, the *direct energy* driving the human being, food, is generally dependent on a supply of *indirect energy* in the form of petroleum. Energy in this form has therefore, like food, become one of the very essentials for life. The exchange process must not be disrupted that *directly* or *indirectly*, supplies the food of mankind. Therefore, OPEC, the petroleum cartel, in collusion with the oil company oligopoly disrupted the basic dynamics of the human production and exchange processes in which food exchange is carried on for the nations of the world. Thus where hundreds of millions of people are adversely effected in their daily struggle to live, OPEC and the oil companies are criminal instrumentalities, ethically and morally.

What is sad and revulsive about this situation is that the United Nations appears to be oblivious to the political immorality involved and that the Western nations, after reacting unbeguilingly in 1973 to OPEC's and the oil company oligopoly's evil act against humanity, subsequently embraced this turpitude with craven obsequiousness. And those nations whose land yielded petroleum, though not belonging to OPEC, soon allowed their oil companies to imitate this criminal act.

For a country like the United States, whose land is favored with long-term petroleum reserves, the solution to the problem is to nationalize the oil industry. Then the government could set the price of oil, which would be measured by its relation to the cost of production, as with other items of production. Then, also, an intensive research and development program would be organized for other sources of energy. Another solution is for the government to organize a partnership with private enterprise, not necessarily with any of those belonging to the American oil monopoly, and regulate the price of oil to accommodate the needs of the American Economy. This would not interfere with the operation of free enterprise. It would, rather, stimulate free enterprise by preventing the cost of production in general from being artificially inflated, thus depressing sales, increasing unemployment, increasing bankruptcies, increasing risk in making loans and thereby increasing interest rates, and maintaining high prices in the face of depression.

Never, never, should human society allow criminal control of a life-dependent commodity! As Johnson and Wilson opined about a remark by Kissinger in his address to the United Nations in September 1974: "Implicit in speeches of leaders like Kissinger was the threat that Robert W. Tucker stated explicitly—armed intervention against the Arabs, specifically in the coastal area from Kuwait to Qatar" [Oil: The Issue of American Intervention," *Commentary*, vol. 59, no. 1 [January 25, 1975, p. 21].[58] Economic war as expressed by the Arab oil embargo of 1973 against supporters of Israel is the mutual counterpart of military action as counseled by Clausewitz.

OIL USED AS A POLITICAL INSTRUMENT

As asseverated by Kissinger and others who should know and confirmed in the record of the Senate Committee on Energy and Natural Resources: "Oil has become a political instrument in the hands of the oil producing nations."[59] The Middle East Arab nations have used oil as a weapon over the heads of the Third World nations to command their votes in the United Nations and as an embargo threat over the industrialized nations in an effort to use them for the destruction of Israel.[60] This is all done with the general support of the State Department, the arrant industrialized nations, and the United Nations.

Blair, the former chief economist of the Senate Subcommittee on Antitrust and Monopoly, stated:

> On October 6, 1973, Egypt and Syria invaded Israel, setting off the "Yom Kippur" war. Two days later, a previously scheduled meeting was convened in Vienna between officials of the major oil companies and representatives of the Organization of Petroleum Exporting Countries. The subject for discussion was a revision in the price of oil. . . . OPEC on October 16 announced an immediate increase of approximately 70 percent—from $3.00 to $5.11. . . . To support the higher prices, OPEC's Arab members . . . announced on October 17, 1973, that they would cut production below the September level a minimum of 5 percent in October and by a further 5 percent each subsequent month "until Israeli withdrawal is completed from the whole Arab territories occupied in June 1967 and the legal rights of the Palestinian people are restored"! Because of their conspicious friendship with the Israelis, the United States and the Netherlands were to be cut off completely. . . . In the United States, already suffering from a domestic shortage artificially created earlier in the year, the reaction approached pure panic.[61]

Those who know the petroleum industry are well aware that the Israel ploy by the Arab oil producers is a subterfuge to hide their traditional cupidity and violent habits and the modern technique to satisfy their power-hunger, which they learned well from their teachers in the oil company monopoly or, better, as Blair calls it: oligopoly.[62] Abdullah Taraki, the inventor of OPEC and former Saudi oil minister, sharply defined the greedy prodigality of the Arab leadership with the terse assertion: "They are just consuming money."[63] And, indeed, they are accumulating so much and wasting tens of millions on inciting conflict and many times that on disrupting the world economy.

A LESSON IN FREE ENTERPRISE

Even Lenin did not foresee that the world could be held hostage by monopoly, which the hostages could so easily destroy if they wished. The unholy alliance between OPEC and the oil companies was a stroke of genius by the frustrated oil companies, mostly American, which were conniving for years to shape circumstances for completing the stranglehold of their monopoly. They thereby could defy the basic principle of the free economy—the "law" of supply and demand*—so they could manipulate the price of oil. The oil companies problem was that up to 1970, this monopoly was *not* completely organized. There were smaller oil companies, which kept successfully competing against them and thereby holding down the price of oil. These oil companies were all making plenty of profit, the cost of production of a barrel of oil being so low that the selling price of about $1.50 was still a welcome bonanza profit on oil produced by the oil companies as concessionaires in foreign countries, based on a fifty-fifty profit division arrangement with the foreign governments.[64]

The independent smaller oil companies were always a thorn in the side of the major companies. In the early 1930s, with the discovery of new fields, "the United States . . . led the world in low-cost production, exporting more than it imported."[65] Foreign oil field discoveries soon reduced the price of imported oil below that of the United States–produced oil. By 1957, control on imported oil was instituted. The 1958 recession decreased the market for oil so the United States imposed an import quota in 1959 so that independents who were involved in foreign production became a most harassing element by forcing majors to compete.

How did the independents become such competitors with the majors? King Idris of Libya developed a deliberate policy of giving oil concessions to the newcomers to the world of international oil in order to prevent the powerful multinational oil monopoly from getting a foothold in his country. He wanted the young companies that had no concessions elsewhere, so they would stand or fall by their success in Libya. These independents became competitors on the world market

*Marx claimed that supply and demand explained nothing but the oscillation of prices (*Capital* [Chicago, Illinois: Charles H. Kerr and Co., 1926], p. 589).

by 1960: "It was in this setting that the independents (Occidental, Continental, Marathon, Amerada, Bunker Hunt) began to put their product on the world market. Under strong pressure by the Libyan government to produce, and with no established 'market position,' price cutting was their only viable option. . . . As a consequence, Mideast prices declined throughout the 1960s . . . reaching a low of $1.30 in 1967."[66]

Exxon was so provoked by the competition of the independents that in responding to the chief economist of the Senate Subcommittee on Antitrust and Monopoly, concerning the deterioration of the price of oil during the 1965–68 period he said that the "deterioration [is] a result of competition."[67] The chief economist retorted: "As a result of competition. Competition has been intense, particularly in Europe, where you have a considerable number of independent refiners."

The *Times Picayune* stated: "As early as 1960, Exxon in its internal annual Forecast recognized the *threat* [italics added] of an expanding Libyan output to Mideast production".[68] The situation kept getting more threatening for Exxon Mideast production due to Libyan competition. "But it was not until 1968 that the panic button was pushed"[69] in Exxon's Forecast. The oil companies monopoly was afraid that the Libyan independents' competition would so reduce the price that the governments of their four established concessions, in Iraq, Iran, Kuwait, and Sauda Arabia, would abrogate the oil companies' concessions due to reduced revenue.[70]

The evisceration of the Libyan independents was an absolute necessity for Exxon and the majors to plug the cracks in their monopoly in order to control production and prices and thereby destroy the basic thesis of capitalism's free-trade world market. This was accomplished by the majors utilizing Colonel Qadaffi's megalomaniac illusions of world power. He needed money to finance his illusions. This he accomplished by nationalizing oil production of the independents and assuming majority (51 percent) ownership for the Libyan government in oil production by the end of 1973.[71] This went "a long way toward achieving Colonel Qadaffi's objective of gaining 'full control over the sources of oil wealth'; it (Libya) had taken over or severely curtailed the operation of those companies whose shipments of Libyan oil had most seriously *demoralized* [italics added] world markets,"[72] i.e., had kept the price of oil at a reasonable relation to the cost of production. It was Colonel Qadaffi who initiated the rip-off jag in world oil prices. It worked because the Western powers accepted it for business-as-usual after manifesting an initial shock. Blair comments: "In addition to the usual symbiotic relation between the companies and the [oil-producing] countries (a higher price inuring to the benefit of both), the relationship in Libya was symbiotic in still other respects. . . . They were interested in increasing their unit per barrel income in order to be able to cut back on their production. . . . The curtailments on the independents . . . meant the attainment of greater revenues with lower output [and] the end of the Libyan danger to the world price structure. . . . [This] was the necessary prerequisite to the staggering price increases of late 1973 and early 1974."[73] Blair further comments: "The price increases of 1973–74 had as their necessary prelude the unnoted evisceration of a few independent oil companies operating in one of the world's most sparsely populated and little-known countries."[74]

The conduct of the oil companies and the socially malignant dictators illustrates how power corrupts because it releases conduct from all the inhibitions that compose the human side of human nature. How malign people can become is shown when they express only, but with *Homo*'s mental capacity, the primate impulses of their human nature while living in a human setting, and how far such people can go to dislocate a "capital formation" social system and generate the forces for its destruction when society places no restrictions on such conduct. The United States government, aided by the State Department and against the basic interest of our country and the world economy, allowed the multinational oil companies' monopoly in collaboration with a coterie of pirating dictators to fleece the public and American business as has never been imagined before. The plunder of the robber barons of the nineteenth century was tolerable in comparison. They never took the world hostage by controlling the essentials of life. The House Energy and Commerce Investigations Subcommittee, chaired by Rep. John Dingell of Michigan, reported that "virtually all the growth of the U.S. economy is flowing into oil company treasuries . . . at the expense of the rest of the country," noting that "96 percent of the total net income increase" in profits ($19.2 billion) accrued to 82 oil and gas companies out of the 1,000 companies listed by *Fortune* magazine, while only 4 percent accrued to the rest of the 918 companies. "The shift in the profits . . . is important . . . because it deprives U.S. industry of the capital it needs to build and expand plants. . . . The shift into energy exploitation has reduced the U.S. to the status of a lesser developed country [being now] a net exporter of food and raw materials, such as lumber and coal and . . . a net importer of value-added products such as machine tools." The report cited "substantial evidence of illegal and questionable practices by the [oil] industry."[75]

THE PROCESS OF POLITICAL PILLAGE

Let us examine how the oil cartel's morally and ethically corrupt price fixing of oil in collusion with the oil companies monopoly was the initiating spark that exploded into the worldwide economic depression. Even the greatest "capital" generating economy that ever existed was battered into submission by this new instrument of world exploitation. This instrument is no longer exploitation of workers alone, the exploitation of other industries by competitors, or the exploitation of raw material (oil) producing countries. It is *total* exploitation of all the people of all the *other* industries, of all the non-oil producing countries in the world and some nations like the United States, which is oil-producing. All this with the connivance of the United States government. Supply and demand forces are no longer complementary opposites that controlled prices in a capitalist free economy where the value of a commodity was tied to the potential availability of raw material plus cost of production, which included a reasonable profit. The latter items determined the *supply,* and the funds available to the people needing the commodity determined the *demand.* But the oil controlling complex *controlled* the amount of the raw material available, the amount of refined oil, the price of both the crude oil and the gasoline, and the distribution. The result: with potential supply amply available in the United States at least for the next three or four decades, the cost of producing a barrel of crude oil in 1965, when competition was still not completely throttled and OPEC had not yet begot the gall to implement its hidden cabal was $0.10 and posted or selling price per barrel was $1.80. In 1973, the cost of production was still the same, but the posted price was raised to $3.01. In 1974, the cost of production was still the same, but the posted price was raised to $11.65.[76] At the present time, with a liberal estimated 600 percent increase in cost of production projected to $0.60, the price ranges from $34.00 to $41.00 per barrel. The entire world economy has been thrown out of kilter, the rip-off system having spread its evil into every nook of the economic world, the underdeveloped countries suffering the most because the high cost of energy is holding down their ability to generate capital. Billions of people are thereby being held back from developing a human ecosystem compatible with living as human beings. The two most responsible nations whose impact is the strongest in causing this human catastrophe are Saudi Arabia and Libya, whose combined population is less than 11 million, of which but a handful are receiving the benefits of this tremendous wealth.

The *Times Picayune* states: "The International Monetary Fund estimates that by the end of this year [1981], 87 poor countries that do not produce oil will be $418 billion in debt,"[77] although they were only about $100 billion in debt to the Western world banks in 1973 before OPEC sprang the rip-off system. A later estimate is that these countries will have accumulated a debt approaching $600 billion by the end of 1982.[78]

In 1972, Saudi Arabia's revenue from oil was $3.1 billion. By 1979, this had increased to $65 billion. At the same time, United States imports of petroleum and petroleum products increased from $7.1 billion in 1973 to $56.0 billion in 1979, and the United States trade balance changed from a highly favorable status to one of deficit by many billions of dollars. If such an economic reversion could happen to the greatest producing country in the world, it is not difficult to picture what happened to the rest of the Western world and to the unfortunate non–oil producing countries of the Third World. Saudi investments, internationally, rose from $3 billion in 1972 to $132 billion in 1979, of which $70 billion was invested in the United States. One can imagine the flood of petrodollars that are invested in the Western world now (in 1986), considering the booty that the rest of the OPEC nations are also investing. A very large proportion of those investments are in the banks of the United States and the other countries of the Western world, particularly West Germany, Britain, and Switzerland. Thus the banks were inundated with petrodollars that needed to be put to "work." This is when another impetus to the world economic crisis was added.

When OPEC raised the price of petroleum in 1973, the greatest sufferers were the Third World countries. The increased cost of energy dislocated their struggling economies. As Johnson and Wilson described this situation:

> The flood of high import prices that swept over African economies in the 1970s severely imbalanced their international payments, knocked African development plans out of their traditional moorings, and nearly drowned the new states in a sea of debts. The flood broke dramatically on the African consciousness with the OPEC price increases of 1973–74. . . . Secretary of State Henry Kissinger's famous "Age of Interdependence" speech to the United Nations, in September 1974, exemplifies that attitude of OPEC's critics: the high cost of oil is not the result of economic factors. . . . Rather, it is caused by deliberate decisions to restrict production and maintain an artificial price level. . . . [A result is] to magnify

the despair of the least developed who are uniquely vulnerable to exorbitant prices and who have no recourse but to pay. What has gone up by political decision can be reduced by political decision.[79]

The critical need was created for more loans by the Third World countries. These borrowing countries assumed that prices in their economies would also increase and the loans paid off thereby. Therefore they took advantage of the lending stampede. Petrodollars flowed like water. This resulted in a Third World financial debt, as previously cited. Thus extortionist prices of oil produced a sudden flush of cash in the coffers of the OPEC countries, which turned to the international banks to recycle these petrodollars. Banks competed with each other to lend out the excess of ill-gained pelf to the countries whose economies have been dislocated by the inflated prices of imports, most of which countries are now unable to pay the annual interest on the loans, much less reduce the size of the principals themselves.

Compounding their problem, many of these countries gambled and borrowed on short-term expecting interest rates to come down soon. This did not happen and caught them holding notes that they could not pay. Interest rates did not come down mainly because the United States government's monetary and fiscal policies were directed toward trying to reduce the rate of inflation at the risk of depression and unemployment. This policy affected the countries of the Western world also by draining off investment funds. Thus in the process of trying to control inflation by controlling money supply and keeping interest rates high, production was depressed, unemployment increased, and contrary to past depressions, prices kept increasing and deepening the depression and the unemployment—all this, essentially, to keep recycling the noxious flood of petrodollars. Further complicating the situation was the augmentation of the risk factor in accommodating the debtor countries with more loans, i.e., the risk of throwing good money after bad money. The "cure" being urged on the debtor countries, instead of loans at lower rates, was to "brace up" in an austerity program. But such a cure becomes increasingly hazardous, as it could lead to riots and political upheaval. The monetary problems of the Third World are not less troublesome in the Western world so far as the industrial and commercial enterprises and the workers are concerned, where bankruptcies and unemployment keep climbing.

What a waste of capital! What a waste of human beings! What a waste of opportunity! What a compliance to Lenin's wishes and predictions about greedy capitalists destroying the system that created their wealth! To wit: "We have seen that the economic quintessence of imperialism is monopoly capitalism. This fact determines its place in history, for monopoly that grew up on the basis of free competition, and precisely out of free competition, is the transition from the capitalist system to a higher social-economic order."[80] This forecast was written between 1914 and 1917. The oil companies seem to be committed to proving its validity.

NOTES

1. Karl Marx, *Das Capital* (Chicago, Illinois: Charles H. Kerr and Company, 1926), p. 163.

2. Ibid., p. 257.

3. Ibid., p. 834.

4. Karl Marx, *Grundrisse,* translated by M. Nicolaus (New York: Vintage Books: 1973), p. 60.

5. Karl Marx, *The Grundrisse,* edited and translated by David McLellan (New York: Harper Torchbooks, 1971), pp. 94–95.

6. John K. Galbraith, *The Industrial State* (New York: Mentor, 1979).

7. Friederich Engels, *Capital,* (New York: International Publishers, 1937), p. 13.

8. Marx, *Das Capital, loco supra citato,* book 1, p. 257.

9. Marx *The Grundrisse, loco supra citato,* p. 80.

10. Ibid., p. 34

11. Ibid., p. 41.

12. Karl Marx and Friederich Engels, *Manifesto of the Communist Party, Selected Works,* Vol. 1 (New York: International Publishers), p. 220.

13. A Leontiev, *Political Economy: A Condensed Course* (New York: International Publishers, 1975), p. 93.

14. C. A. Winslow, *The Evolution and Significance of the Modern Public Health Campaign* (New Haven, Connecticut: Yale University Press, 1923), p. 18.

15. Friederich Engels, *The Housing Question* (Lawrence and Wishart Ltd., 1942), p. 24.

16. Marx, *The Grundrisse, loco supra citato,* pp. 85–86.

17. Karl Marx, *Selected Works,* Vol. 1: *Manifesto of the Communist Party* (International Publishers), p. 212.

18. Karl Marx, *Grundrisse,* translated by M. Nicolaus (New York: Vintage Books, 1973), pp. 8–9.

19. V. I. Lenin, *State and Revolution* (New York: International Publishers, 1932), p. 17.

20. U. Lele, "Rural Africa: Modernization, Equity, and Long-Term Development, *Science,* vol. 211, no. 4482 (February 6, 1981), pp. 547–53.

21. Ruth Schachter Morgenthau, "The Developing States of Africa," *Annals of the American Academy of Political and Social Science,* vol. 432 (July 1977), pp. 80–95.

22. Nikita Khrushchev, *Khrushchev Remembers: The Last Testament,* translated and edited by Strobe Talbot (Boston, Massachusetts: Little, Brown and Co., 1974), pp. 107–09.

23. Rosa Luxemburg, *The Russian Revolution: Leninism or Marxism?* (Ann Arbor, Michigan: University of Michigan Press, 1961), p. 76.

24. Morgenthau, *loco supra citato,* p. 91

25. Friederich Engels, *Engels on Capital* (New York: International Publishers, 1937), p. 20.

26. Marx, *The Grundrisse, loco supra citato*, pp. 85–86.

27. V. I. Lenin, *State and Revolution* (New York: International Publishers, 1932), p. 17.

28. Lenin, *loco supra citato*, p. 67.

29. John Dewey, "Democracy," in Louis M. Hacker, ed., *The Shaping of American Tradition* (New York: Columbia University Press, 1947),

30. Friederich Engels, *The Origin of the Family* (Chicago, Illinois: Charles H. Kerr, 1902), p. 217.

31. Rosa Luxemburg, *The Russian Revolution: Leninism or Marxism?* (Ann Arbor, Michigan: University of Michigan Press, 1961), pp. 76–77.

32. Angelica Balabanoff, *Impressions of Lenin* (Ann Arbor, Michigan: University of Michigan, Press, 1968), pp. 137–41.

33. Ibid., p. 139.

34. Leon Trotsky, *Terrorism and Communism* (Ann Arbor, Michigan: University of Michigan Press, 1972), p. 58.

35. Gus Tyler, *Scarcity* (New York: Quadrangle/The New York Times Book Co., 1976), pp. 152–76.

36. J. N. Westwood, *Endurance and Endeavor Russian History, 1817–1971* (New York: Oxford University Press, 1973), p. 390.

37. Harry Schwartz, *The Soviet Economy Since Stalin* (New York: J. P. Lippincott Co.), from an article by Academician Arzumanyan, *Pravda*, February 24, 1964.

38. V. I. Lenin, *Imperialism, the Highest Stage of Capitalism* (New York: International Publishers, 1939), p. 89.

39. Prof. B. R. Bergmann, "Who's to Blame for the Economy?" *New York Times*, 10/17/82

40. W. J. Holstein, "Debt Strains International Financial System," *Times Picayune*, October 10, 1982.

41. Nicolai Bukharin, *Imperialism and World Economy* (New York: International Publishers, 1929), p. 155.

42. Ibid., pp. 154–60.

43. Harvey O'Connor, "World Crisis in Oil," *Monthly Review Press* (1962), p. 17.

44. W. B. Ziff, *The Rape of Palestine* (New York: Longmans, Green and Co., 1938), pp. 539, 563.

45. "More Attention Should Be Paid To Making The U.S. Less Vulnerable To Foreign Oil Price And Supply Decisions," January 3, 1978.

46. John M. Blair, *The Control of Oil* (New York: Pantheon Books, 1976), p. 114.

47. Ibid., p. 281.

48. Charles A. Reich, *The Greening of American* (New York: Bantam Books, 1971).

49. John K. Galbraith, *The New Industrial State* (New York: Mentor, 1978), p. 352.

50. Ibid., p. 352.

51. Ibid., pp. 352–53.

52. Ibid., p. 353.

53. Ibid., p. 353.

54. Ibid., p. 97.

55. Ibid., p. 96.

56. Marx, *The Grundrisse, loco supra citato*, p. 88.

57. Ibid., pp. 85–86.

58. "The 'Oil Crises' and African Economies: Oil Wave on a Tidal Flood of Industrial Price Inflation," *Daedalus* (Spring 1982), pp. 211–41.

59. "The Geopolitics of Oil," *Science*, vol. 210 (December 19, 1980), pp. 1324–27, Report of the Senate Committee on Energy and Natural Resources, November 1980.

60. W. R. Johnson and E. J. Wilson, "The Oil Crises and African Economics," *Daedalus*, (Spring 1982), p. 211–41.

61. John M. Blair, *The Control of Oil* (New York: Pantheon Books, 1976), pp. 261–64.

62. Ibid., p. 119.

63. *Times Picayune*, December 22, 1980.

64. *Loco supra citato,* p. 270.

65. Ibid., pp. 169–70.

66. Ibid., p. 213.

67. Ibid., p. 214.

68. Ibid., p. 215.

69. Ibid., p. 216.

70. Ibid., p. 218.

71. Ibid., pp. 227–29, 233–34.

72. Ibid., pp. 229–30.

73. Ibid., pp. 233–34.

74. Ibid., p. 234.

75. *Times Picayune,* November 19, 1981.

76. Blair, *loco supra citato,* p. 269.

77. *The Times Picayune,* July 12, 1981.

78. William J. Holstein, "Debt Strains the International Financial System," *The Times Picayune,* October 10, 1982.

79. W. R. Johnson and E. J. Wilson III, "The 'Oil Crises' and African Economies: Oil Wave on a Tidal Flood of Industrial Price Inflation," *Daedalus* (Spring 1982), pp. 211–41.

80. V. I. Lenin, *Imperialism, the Highest Stage of Capitalism* (New York: International Publishers, 1939), p. 123.

19

Human Engineering and Political Action

CAPITAL AND SOCIALISM

Since the development of civilization, the political activists, as far as we know, have always dominated in the leadership of historical movement. Since the American Revolution, the great leaders of capitalist enterprising and politics more and more became centered in the United States. After the Second World War, Harold Laski opined: "World history is more likely to be shaped by American history for the next half-century than by any other element in its making."[1] To date, this prediction has been correct. But the political, economic, and sociocultural atmosphere of the world has been changing so quickly during this period, to the point that half the world population is now dominated by a political-economic philosophy that *promises the ideals* of the American dream but in a much shorter period than the American way would achieve it. I refer to the Leninist application of the Marxian philosophy and its derived methodology for achieving it by a revision of the Marxian concept of the dictatorship of the proletariat. Mattick put it this way:

> Lenin's Marxism did not express the practical necessities of the modern international, anti-capitalist class struggle, but was determined by conditions specific to Russia. Russia required not so much the emancipation as the creation of an industrial proletariat, and not so much the end of capital accumulation as its acceleration. The Bolsheviks overthrew Czarism and the Russian bourgeosie in the name of Marx and by revolutionary means only to become themselves a dictatorial force over the workers and the peasants. And this in order to lead them, eventually, by way of intensified suppression and exploitation into socialism. Lenin's Marxian "orthodoxy" existed only in ideological form, as the false consciousness of a non-socialist practice.[2]

475

MARXISM AND LENINISM IN PRACTICE

It is clear that the Marxian revolutions in Russia and Eastern Europe and China based on Lenin's revision of Marxian theory and his development of the "dictatorship force" to achieve, "eventually," socialism "by way of intensified suppression and exploitation" have had a tremendous influence for socioeconomic change all over the world. Therefore, in considering the *effect* of the Leninist form of dictatorship and the capitalist achievements in capital formation and rising "physical" standards and levels of living on the traits of human nature and subsequent orientation and disorientation of the behavior of the exposed populations, an acquaintance with the teachings of Marx and Engels can not be avoided. What most people do not realize is that Marx was not an eccentric, wild-eyed, oddball zealot, although he did have a beard, and that Engels was owner and operator of a cotton mill in Manchester, England. Marx was a devoted family man, highly educated, scholastically and intellectually a genius, married to a highly intelligent Westphalian lady of aristocratic birth, whose admirable loyalty to Marx and their children during a life of economic hardships is legendary. Marx was a cosmopolitan whose interest in the development of the American democracy was extensively manifested by his sense of favorable expectations and hope in the voluminous letters he wrote to his friends about the American Civil War[3] and the ten years he served as European correspondent for the *New York Daily Tribune,* whose editor, Charles A. Dana, a disciple of the utopian socialist Fourier, had a great deal of respect for Marx's opinion and political analytic contributions.

The appearance of Marxian philosophy was not a sudden emergence on the sociopolitical scene that captivated the imagination of the downtrodden masses. It was a world outlook consuming about sixty years of intellectually active and sociopolitically contentious lives of Marx and Engels.

This was a period of political effervescence in Europe, and like the vapor of a boiling caldron, social and political theories emanated and swirled through the atmosphere. Marx and Engels were in the middle of the storm. They were proud of their philosophic heritage. As Engels wrote: "We German Socialists are proud of the fact that we are derived not only from Saint-Simon, Fourier and Owen, but also from Kant, Fichte and Hegel."[4]

Many ideas Marx recommended as revolutionary acts are today traditional provisions in United States governmental practice. For example, among the measures Marx recommended in *The Communist*

Manifesto in 1848 to be implemented in order to transform capitalist society to socialism are: "A heavy progressive or graduated income tax" and "free education for all children in public schools. Abolition of children's factory labour in the present form. . . ."[5] In the United States, the tax measure become law in 1912. Public education by 1860 had become a progressive and irreversible fact. While the Child Labor Law was passed and declared unconstitutional in 1918, every state has since then adopted child labor laws.

An interesting area that needs exploration is, what is meant by the concept of "socializing the means of production"? The Soviet politicians and academicians teach that the only way to do this is as Lenin recommended and carried out. The only problem with this advice is that the Soviet Union preached it with forked tongue. For example, *Soviet Manual on the Fundamentals of Marxism-Leninism* states: "The Communist Parties are fighting not only for a united working-class front; they are striving to unite broader sections of the people. Working class unity should be the basis for the unity of a broad democratic movement."[6] The entire text of almost 900 pages expounds on the virtues of democracy. Just study the following statement and compare it to what Stalin did in relation to the Russian peasantry: "The *socialist method* of reorganizing agriculture is by voluntary cooperation of the peasants. It was clearly foreseen by the founders of Marxism. "When we are in possession of state power," Engels wrote (in *Selected Works of Marx and Engels*), "we shall not even think of forcibly expropriating the small peasants (regardless of whether with or without compensation), as we shall have to do in the case of big landowners. Our task relative to the small peasant consists, in the first place, in effecting a transition of his private enterprise and private possession to co-operative ones, not forcibly but by dint of example, and the proffer of social assistance for the purpose."[7] What Stalin and his party did to the Russian peasants was graphically described by Khrushchev.[8] Stalin's method of socializing production was certainly not in accordance with the counsel of Engels. Actually, the details of methodology of socializing production after political power has been seized are nowhere to be found in the writings of Marx or Engels. Mattick explored this problem and concluded: "When dealing with the question of the socialist organization of the economy, Lenin's proposals were . . . almost exclusively of a pragmatic type, and no attempt was made to relate them to Marxian theory. Of all the socialists who have written about socialism, Lenin said rightly, none had dealt concretely with the issues involved."[9] The methods of socializing production in the present-day socialist countries, both Soviet and Maoist oriented, have only one element in common with Marxism, the dictatorship of the proletariat, but even this principle has been stretched and twisted, for the most part, to satisfy the modus operandi adopted by groups and cliques to stay in power. Lip service is given to the concept of democracy, but practically never is it practiced when party dogma is expounded. How long the dictatorships will last in each country seems to be related to how long each group can stay in power. The "withering away of the state," as Marx and Engels understood it and as Rosa Luxemburg's studies of the latter interpreted the concept, is quite different from the comfortable theory perceived by Lenin whereby the time element for the dictatorship is an indefinitely flexible factor. The fact is that instead of withering away, the *socialist state* becomes more dictatorial.

Certainly, the socialist countries have not yet developed a higher level of humanization of society than exists in the Western democracies. But Marxism predicted that socialism would be a higher state of humane society. Engels wrote in 1844:

[Adam] Smith was right to eulogize trade as humane. There is nothing absolutely immoral in the world. Trade, too, has an aspect wherein it pays homage to morality and humanity. But what homage! The law of the strong hand, the open highway robbery of the Middle Ages, became humanized when it passed over into trade; and trade became humanized when, in its first stage characterized by the prohibition to export money, it passed over into the mercantile system. Now the mercantile system itself was humanized. Naturally, it is in the interest of the trader to be on good terms with the one from whom he buys cheap as well as with the other whom he sells dear. A nation therefore acts very imprudently if it fosters feelings of animosity in its suppliers and customers. The more friendly, the more profitable. Such is the humanity of trade. And this hypocritical way of misusing morality for immoral purposes is the pride of the free-trade system.[10]

It is this hypocritical and immoral type of humanity that socialism is supposed to eliminate from interrelations. It was, indeed, the aim of Marxian thinking to eliminate from social behavior this type of immoral motive feigning behind the screen of the trait of human nature "to share by *exchange*." It is no less the hope of capitalist democracies to achieve this aim. The fact is that "consciousness" of the human is everywhere forcing greater and greater humaneness in conscience and in behavior. Can pure humaneness become prevalent everywhere without vitiating the human nature trait of "challenge," which may generate extreme destructive competition? These are problems that relate to the nature of governing.

There is a need at this point to remark concisely on the subject of the nature of the "state." To Marx and Engels, the state was essentially a *coercive* political instrument used by the dominant social class to maintain its dominance. The impact of the biphasic nature of humankind's behavior had not yet related itself to social structure in Marxian theory. Therefore, coercion was the essential nature of class society and would be abolished under communism. The fact, however, is that the nature of human nature is such that under the sphere of small, sparse populations, as existed prior to the emergence of civilization, primate behavior was controlled by the pressure of rejection of the violator by one's family and associates. This is practically impossible to achieve in an atmosphere of crowding as exists today in the world. Since bivalent behavior is a permanent nature of human behavior, a community instrument for control is certainly necessary to maintain order. This is a coercive force that all forms of society will require.

DICTATORSHIP DEPRESSES CAPITAL FORMATION AND VIOLATES HUMAN NATURE

It is becoming more and more clear that the one-world concept is a reality today. Not one world as a unity of nations and peoples, but one world as a multiplicity of ethnic and national units intimately interrelated by mass communications, both in transport and in informational media. The most economically underdeveloped countries know what the most advanced are doing and vice versa. The concept of "quality of life," which the politicians in the advanced countries bandy about, has impressed the leadership of the underdeveloped countries. Everywhere people are aware that the "good life with quality" is a feasible aim—a long-term aim. Some of the leadership in the underdeveloped countries want this so intensely that they bluster their desires for immediate satisfaction in the halls of world conferences, with threats directed at the most advanced countries if they do not get something for nothing. These dangerous demands for the immediate realization of the unrealizable are unfortunately instigated and supported by the more advanced socialist countries who are pursuing this anti-Marxian self-aggrandizing political strategem of world revolution against free enterprise instead of concentrating on developing real socialism at home to serve as a paragon for the rest of the world. Encouraging "socialist" dictatorships in those economically backward countries is creating havoc in the world and delaying the development of the means for rapid capital formation in these countries. The latter is a tragic mistake since the poor countries are not going to generate capital in the most effective way under this so-called socialist dictatorship. As Marx pointed out over a hundred years ago: "Free competition expresses the real development of capital. . . . The domination of capital is the prerequisite of free competition."[11] Dictatorships are the antithesis of the freedom needed to develop the forces for rapid generation of capital. Such ecosystems are more discordant with the traits of human nature than democratic capitalism. Under dictatorships, the formation and accumulation of capital is depressed.

The socialist theoreticians are continually misjudging the length of time that it takes for the dictatorship of the proletariat to eventuate into real socialism. Lenin, in 1920, in addressing the Soviet Young Communist League, counseled: "And so, the generation of those who are now fifteen years, and will be living in a communist society in *ten* or *twenty* [italics added] years' time, should tackle all its educational tasks in such a way that every day . . . the young people shall engage in the practical solution of some problem of labour in common. . . ."[12] Sixty years later, the Soviet Union is still a long way off from being a real socialist society, let alone a communist society, precisely because of its lag in capital formation and because it is still a dictatorship, which is antithetical to socialism and communism.

Because of the one-world nature of the means of communication and because capital formation and accumulation have such a long way to go, particularly among the lesser developed peoples who compose about two-thirds of the world's population, therefore, to raise the world economic level to socialist standards, the *competition for material things* will remain a strong factor in people's behavior. So long as competition for material things remains an important behavioral characteristic in any sizable area of the world, we will have difficulties of displacing it from the psychosocial sphere of "challenge" even in the most advanced countries, where socialism otherwise would reduce the need for such competition as an aspect of the trait "challenge."

It is necessary as a first priority of a social scientist, to be able to focus historically and urgently on the very first priority of effective social theory, i.e., to deal with man's physical survival. This is what made Marxism such a powerful sociopolitical theory. At the burial of Karl Marx in 1883, his lifelong collaborator, Friederich Engels, in his farewell address summed up the historical and human values of Marx's life effort: "As Darwin discovered the law of evolution in organic nature, so Marx discovered the law of evolution in human history: the simple fact, previously hidden under ideological growths, that human beings must first of all eat, drink, shelter, and clothe themselves before they can turn their attention to politics, science, art, and religion."[13] Unfortunately, most Marxian practitioners have advanced no farther in their *practice* than controlling the means of production of their countries, almost completely disregarding Marx's pioneering researches in the broadening of the horizon of economic science to include its impact on the whole psychosocial dynamics of the population involved, reaching to the essence of *Homo*'s humanness, to his human nature. This he did by predicating *human interrelations* as a most basic factor in social development.

Firstly, he declared production *relations* as the complementary force to the forces of production in the socioeconomic process of production, and

Secondly, he declared that production relations as practiced under the raw capitalism of his time created a state of *alienation* in the producers, the workers, the creators whereby the objectification of their labor became independent objects (anonymous commodities) as something alien to them and that these commodities even became something hostile and opposed to them in the form of power in the hands of capitalists. (The capitalists also became alienated from the humanistic social process.) In this way, the alienation of the workers affected their whole (physical and mental) way of life and their "species nature," i.e., Marx's term for their human nature.

Those practitioners of Marxian philosophy who do interest themselves in alienation usually do not pursue the matter any further than its bare relation to the economic exploitation of workers. They probably never searched their souls as to what Marx meant by the term "species nature." That the species of man is *Homo sapiens,* and that *Homo* implies being *human,* and that "species nature" means "human nature" does not seem to occur to these practitioners. Therefore, not being concerned with the nature of man but only with his belly, dictatorship as a form of social order was one convenient way to attain "socialism," regardless of its effects on the traits of human nature. As observed over and over again, dictatorship is a flagrant violator of these traits when its duration lasts beyond the endurance threshold of a large enough plurality of the people so subjected. This problem was thoroughly exposed by Lenin's friend Rosa Luxemburg, [14] who completely disagreed with Lenin's theory that dictatorship should be directed by the Central Committee of the party rather than by the working class. She feared lest the Central Committee, in order to remain in power, would prolong the dictatorship by the emergence of a select clique of power-hungry politicians. Power hunger is the negative aspect of several traits of human nature.

Power hunger is the negative aspect of several traits of human nature, particularly those of challenge and competence and self-image–self-esteem. Challenge is the response of self-consciousness to an encounter, physical or mental, that stimulates the cognitive processes to act in the most capable manner to attain a goal. Such response, in the humanized context, leads to creativity and the satisfaction of the self in having accomplished. This is the human as distinguished from the animal instinctive response to a confrontation. Children love to play because in such activity they have the opportunity to feel the pleasure of controlling situations.[15] As psychologist Kipnis describes this behavioral phenomenon: "No one wants to be powerless. Psychologist Rollo May observed that people who are unwilling or unable to use power condemn themselves to lives of frustration. . . . Yet, while the absence of power often creates problems, so may its presence. Writers and social philosophers have noted since the time of Sophocles that the control of power produces strong psychological changes. Power holders start to exploit those they control; they become puffed up with their own importance; their moral values become self-serving. Power thus changes people's view of themselves and of others."[16] Good intentions by the leaders of social movements easily slide into unintended power-play maneuvers to keep the movement in line with their perception of what should be, and then those good intentions metamorphose into psychic hunger for power to control the situation. The situation becomes an endless chain of situations. There is no return again to the good intentions. This was surely not what Marx and Engels intended in their recommendation that: "As, therefore, the 'state' is only a transitory institution which is used in the struggle, in the revolution, in order to *hold down one's adversaries by force* [italics added], it is pure nonsense to talk of a 'free people's state'; so long as the proletariat still *uses* the state, it does not use it in the interests of freedom but in order to hold down its adversaries, and as soon as it becomes possible to speak of freedom, the state as such ceases to exist."[17] This quotation is the most critical that separates Luxemburg's interpretation of Marxism from that of Lenin's.[18] And it certainly appears that Luxemburg is more correct in her interpretation. In the quote above, Engels specifically states that the state becomes "a transitory institution" after the people have taken control of it, and since state power is used "to hold down [*niederzuhalten*] one's adversaries by force" and is not used "in the interests of freedom," then whom is this transitional state going to *hold down* by force if not the *internal bourgeois* adversaries who are entertaining plans for counter-revolution? The 'state' here is reckoned to be the 'dictatorship' of the party. But, as Luxemburg theorizes, such counter-force should not last over prolonged periods if democratic *freedom* is to be implemented for all the working class as soon as counter-revolution is eliminated. When, therefore, is the Presidium of the Soviet Union (which replaced the politburo) or the Central Committee of the Communist Party going to decide how many decades or generations must pass before dictatorship of the proletariat is ended and there is no more reason for the state to hold down adversaries against the people? Who are the adversaries *in* the Soviet Union? Are they the same as in Poland—the workers? *External* adversaries are not held down; they are fought and defeated and possibly eliminated. Therefore, the state is maintained to control—*to hold down*—*internal* adversaries. Are the Soviet people the adversaries of the Soviet state? The state is a force against people—a contradiction to the "interests of freedom." How long will the government in the Soviet Union consider that it must *hold down* its internal enemies? Does democracy change a "state" into a "government"?

AMERICAN DEMOCRACY

Any political party in the United States that has for its aim the revolutionary overthrow of the government is completely out of touch with the sociopolitical atmosphere and forces in our country. The United States is destined to keep evolving into a democratic state to which the frozen rubrics such as socialism, communism, capitalism or other isms will not apply. This will be true for an extended period of time. That does not mean smooth sailing without a struggle. Violence is a historical heritage of the American people, but there is also a yearning for a deep and abiding freedom for peaceful pursuit of self and community development within a democratic framework. The fact that man's nature is biphasic is reason to believe that the state will not "wither away" as Engels predicted the state would under communism. Jefferson's concern with man's factional behavior in his Federalist Paper No. 10 is a profound recognition of this nature of human nature—of the people of the United States.

Lenin considered democracy a political form of bourgeois government. He therefore railed against it. Yet the USSR's *Manual on Fundamentals of Marxism-Leninism* supports the term as compatible with socialism-communism. Marx, in criticizng the Gotha Program, which was drafted for unifying the two socialist parties (the Social-Democratic

Workers Party and the General Association of Germen Workers) in Germany at the Gotha Congress in 1875, was so disgusted with the weakness of the theoretical aspects of the program that he spit fire in critique of the Gotha Program in criticizing article 3, which contained the phrase "democratic control of the toiling people." His criticism was of the *misuse* of the adjective *democratic* and not of the noun *democracy.* Ten years earlier, on January 7, 1865, the International Workingmen's Association had sent a letter, of which Marx had been prominent in drafting, to President Lincoln on his reelection for his second term. In this letter, the United States as a democratic republic was cited for the eminently progressive role it had played in the sociopolitical development of the modern world: "[W]here hardly a century ago the idea of one great democratic republic had first sprung up, whence the first Declaration of the Rights of Man was issued, and the first impulse given to the European revolution of the eighteenth century. . . . The workingmen of Europe feel sure that, as the American War of Independence initiated a new era of ascendency for the middle class, so the American Anti-slavery War will do for the working class."[19] This does not ring like the raucous denigration of democracy that comes from the Leninists.

Engels, in 1894, disgusted with "the Proudhonists in France and the Lassalleans in Germany who called themselves Social-Democrats and whose theoretical soundness both Marx and Engels denounced, for the first time depreciated the term "democracy,"[20] which as recently as 1884 he had used with the highest esteem.[21] However, it must be noted that Engels was here referring to an unacceptable type of political organization being supported by the Social *Democratic* parties and not as a broad concept referring to a way of life in a free society. Rosa Luxemburg, a devoted scholar of Marx and Engels, uses the term *democracy* to describe basic interrelational aspects of socialism and communism, finding the terms broadly complementary rather than politically contradictory.[22] Dewey's following definition of democracy is compatible with Marx's, Engels's, and Luxemburg's understanding of the term and quite at odds with Lenin's:

> Democracy is much broader than a special political form, a method of conducting government, of making laws and carrying on governmental administration by means of popular suffrage and elected officers. It is that, of course. But it is something broader and deeper than that. The political and governmental phase of democracy is a means, the best means so far found, for realizing ends that lie in the wide domain of *human relationships* and the

development of *human personality* [italics added]. It is, as we often say, though perhaps without appreciating all that is involved in the saying, a way of life, social and individual. The keynote of democracy as a way of life may be expressed, it seems to me, as the necessity for the participation of every mature human being in formation of the values that regulate the living of men together: which is necessary from the standpoint of both the general social welfare and the full development of human beings as individuals. . . . The foundation of democracy is faith in the capacities of *human nature* (italics added).[23]

Marx's understanding of democratic practice in relation to human nature is quite similar. He mostly discusses this subject under "alienation" without mentioning the word *democracy*.[24,25,26,27] But the conditions that he described where alienation would disappear certainly would be in harmony with the traits of human nature, and therefore *real* democracy would prevail. However, Marx's discussion of democracy specifically as a concept is done with philosophic mastery, as one would expect from his genius in his *Contribution to the Critique on Hegel's Philosophy of Law*. There is significant similarity between the concept of democracy as conceived by Marx and that of John Dewey. To Dewey, democracy is a philosophy of community life expressed in the interrelations of people. Therefore, this concept goes beyond the structure and dynamics of the state, although the structure and dynamics of the state must conform to the philosophy of the *interrelations* between people of the community in order to be able to live that philosophy. To Marx, the meaning is, at the same time, both that of a philosophy of human interrelations in community living and as the structure and dynamics of the state. This double meaning is expressed by Marx: "Democracy is the genus Constitution. Monarchy is one species, and a poor one at that. Democracy is content and form. Monarchy is *supposed* to be only a form, but it falsifies the content."[28] Here it is clear that content means the philosophy of living interrelations, while the form is the political structure. This is further elucidated by Marx: "In monarchy, the whole, the people, is subsumed under one of its particular modes of being, the political constitution. In democracy the *constitution itself* appears only as *one* determination, that is, the self-determination of the people. In monarchy we have the people of the constitution; in democracy the constitution of the people. Democracy is the solved *riddle* of all constitutions. Here, not merely *implicitly* and in essence but *existing* in reality, the constitution is constantly brought back to its actual basis, the *actual human being*, the *actual people*, and established as the people's *own* work . . . Hegel starts from the state and makes man the subjectified state; democracy starts from man and makes the state objectified man."[29]

SOCIAL STRUCTURE AND THE TRAITS OF HUMAN NATURE

In systematizing the concepts of the social dynamics that would be required in hammering out and sustaining a human ecology that would be in harmony with the traits of human nature, we are overwhelmed by the great social and cultural effort that would be needed to effect the sociopolitical changes to attain such harmony. The fact that these objectives appear to be visionary rather than practical, as were those of the social philosophers of the eighteenth and nineteenth centuries in relation to democratic republican government, must not deter our drive in the direction of attaining them. There are ample historical lessons to illustrate the eventual practicality of visionary objectives. In the present state of rapid social change, the attainment of such objectives is more possible and more feasible than at any previous period of social development, since *change* is the theme of the times. Unfortunately, we have no examples anywhere in the world to give us guidance in our present task. But we do have more and more people with such a dream in their mind's eye and the spirit to reach for its realization. As the eminent American public health teacher and philosopher Rosenau dreamed: When young men have vision, the dreams of old men come true.

When one examines the traits that compose the complex of human nature, it becomes clear that the facilities and mode of operation of hospitals and clinics are not the means for dealing with behavior problems resulting from disorientations of the traits of human nature since the causes are the incompatibilities with the nature of the social order. These traits are psychosocial phenomena, and dealing with them becomes a task in prevention and therefore for social engineering, i.e., the social-medical-political-economic maneuvering and the guiding of people in their sociocultural interrelations. Culture and social relations in life-style must be kept concordant with the traits of human nature. This recommendation does not assume the organization of a dictatorship in order to direct people how to behave. The exact opposite is necessary. In discussing the traits of man's sense of "judging values and freedom to choose between them," it was made clear that freedom to choose was not license to create chaos, but that it involved the responsibility to consider the social good as well as that of the individual desire. Dobzhansky declared that: "Perhaps freedom is even the most important of all the specifically human attributes.... Ethics emanate from freedom and are unthinkable without freedom. Ethics are, consequently, a human responsibility. We cannot rely on genes or on natural selection to guarantee that man will always choose the right direction of his evolution."[30] Thus man must be *responsible* for the choices he makes as a free agent who has chosen to behave in accordance with a *socially positive* frame of orientation. If he were not, there would be no society. As Dobzhansky declared: "Man was formed for society."[31] Man now has the potential to make the society of his choice—a society that is in harmony with all of the traits of human nature. Humankind, however, cannot, under present circumstances, make a choice that will satisfy all individuals. We have not reached that point yet. People's values do not always correspond to the human aspects of the biphasic traits of human nature. For example, the present value of excessive self-indulgence is out of tune with the human aspect of the trait of self-image–self-esteem by its very excessiveness. Such excessiveness in a society of real material scarcity would lead to no society at all. The result would be a return to contention to satisfy self-centered appetites—a primate trait. The value between people of different social classes may be different, although their aims, collectively, may be the same due to their human nature. Yet demogogic influences may temporarily divert them in the direction of their primate behavioral potentials, such as occurred with the influence of Hitler on the bulk of the German people.

In a sense, the present-day atmosphere in the political arena of the United States finds every politician giving lip-service to the needs of the lower and middle income classes, since they make up the majority of the voters. In this democratic field of contention, the will of the majority will one day soon win out. At the same time, this democratic heritage is beginning to be pushed to an extremity, giving rise to an atmosphere of irresponsible permissiveness that is moving toward bedlam. The perfunctory liberal and left-wing soothsayers interpret this as the degeneration of capitalist America. I have nothing against the liberals or left-wingers, if only they would stop following the doctrinaire sophists and start thinking for themselves. To some extent their foreboding has validity. But they miss the real point of this seeming chaotic development, which is actually the emergence of a social conscious groping for a better way of living. The people in the United States are pushing toward a two-goal type of democracy in which *economic freedom* is based on a firm ethical free enterprise system in a social justice process of making a living and an *individual freedom* ethic based on a system of social interrelations that satisfy the traits of human nature. What must not be lost sight of is that the gradual disappearance of economic injustice is a process in which coming-to-be and passing-away[32] take place at the same time—the coming-to-be of economic and individual freedom and the passing-away of what Marx called *exploitation* of the individuals and classes—an exploitation that causes alienation in the whole range of sociocultural interrelations. This process begins by capitalists' appropriation of workers' labor and estranging them from the products they produce and ends by alienating the whole community of people from their human nature and estranging man from man in the process of living. This process has been taking place in the United States since the American Revolution, but the explosion of American "capital," as Marx envisioned it,[33] brought incredible benefit to the vast majority of the people precisely because it took place in a very free capitalist democracy. The impetus of this contradictory process has been gathering speed all these years, but the acceleration has been greatest in the past half-century. Let not the statistics mongers overwhelm our sympathies with figures that show the increasing difference in incomes of economic classes and thereby divert our attention from the real meaning of the present trend, which shows also the increasing number of social welfare programs for the needy, such as:

<table>
<tr><td>Old Age and Survivors Insurance</td><td>Public Housing</td></tr>
<tr><td>Civil Service and Retirement</td><td>Disability Insurance</td></tr>
<tr><td>Unemployment Insurance</td><td>Veterans Benefits</td></tr>
<tr><td>Food Stamps</td><td>Railroad Insurance</td></tr>
<tr><td>Supplementary Medical Insurance</td><td>Child Nutrition, including WIC program</td></tr>
<tr><td>Medicare</td><td>Hosptital Insurance</td></tr>
<tr><td>Medicaid</td><td>Other programs, including military</td></tr>
</table>

An important phenomenon that is masking the real progress being made in the United States in satisfying the basic physical needs of the poor is associated with the deliberate violation of the traits of "freedom-to-choose" and "Unifying Orientation of Behavior," although other traits are involved. The inordinate permissiveness being sanctioned by society and law concerning irresponsible sexual behavior, particularly among teenagers and resulting in hundreds of thousands of children with babies flooding the welfare rolls, and the millions of babies born to other single women who swell the welfare ranks are the main reasons why the statistics of the poor are increasing rather than decreasing. This is not due to government retrenchment against the poor, but to liberalism not being aware that thresholds in freedom-to-act must be part of the norms of behavior. The sophisticated intelligentsia such as the American Civil Liberties Union is not as sophisticated as it pretends to be. It needs to understand the role that human nature has played in the history of the development of society. Our present *transitional* stage, with its excesses, could be controlled to become a phase in the swing of the pendulum toward the better life.

The important sociopolitical factor that we must preserve is our democratic essence. Just what could happen in a country with the American productive power and a sociopolitical history that even Marx could extol? Can our social system support a program that will guarantee to every person who wanted to work a job, for which he will receive a living income in accordance with the nature of his work? Can we inaugurate a system wherein enterprises are sternly subject to a code of ethics that modulated the production and circulation processes that would make it close to impossible for private forces to wield antisocial influence over government? Can we develop a system of challenge under the above circumstances where the competitive process could be cleansed of the primate-like aggressiveness resulting in economic piracy as practiced by the multinational oil companies? If these things could be accomplished within a democratic framework, recognizing the contradictory nature of egalitarianism,[34] this country would become the paragon of the world. In such an atmosphere, we could have the freedom to study the specific traits of human nature, research the types of ecosystem processes that would foster such sociofunctional relations among people in which the positive aspects of the specific traits of human nature would predominate. As information becomes available about such matters, we would work for their implementation by community education through all the sociopolitical avenues of our democratic society. Such a society must operate by the principle that there should exist concordance between the rights and well-being of individuals, which will satisfy the positive phase of each trait, on the one hand and the sociocultural relations devised by society for sustaining those rights and well-being of individuals, on the other hand, so that behavior based on ethics formulated to harmonize with a society supportive of social organization in concordance with the traits of human nature is a higher state. Indeed, the highest state of democratic expression of individual human and social rights. Such a society could never be a static organization, since social progress will require a continual effort of adjustment for maintaining dynamic societal equilibrium.

ECOSYSTEM COMPATIBILITY WITH HUMAN NATURE: THE ESSENCE OF LABOR VALUE

It is not necessary to belabor the fact that the ecosystem, which includes the socioeconomic system, conditions its population to respond to life's events in various complexes of behavior. It is well established that community life starts with labor, i.e., making a living, and the socioeconomic interrelations that this involves, and that a society based on free-wage labor has the tendency, more or less, to generate alienation in the wage-laboring population. The laboring process must, therefore, and without subterfuge, be divested of the quality of inducing alienation by bringing the working condition of the wage workers into concordance with the traits of human nature. How do we bring the living conditions of the wage workers into concordance with the traits of human nature without destroying capital? The nature of capital will determine this. The critical problem is, can a system of creating capital be devised whose accumulating capital does not wrest control of the system from those who create it?

"Capital" in the modern world is a contradiction, just as it was in the time of Marx, the contradiction being, first that it was and is the generator of the "good life," and secondly, that it was and is the master of those who produce it and those who appropriate it. The human concern with the inherent nature of capital is because of the need to *control* it for comprehensive *human* use. In the days of Marx, the complete freedom of the operation of the second phase of the contradiction allowed for the most rapid accumulation of capital, but with much exploitation of the worker, while, at the same time, raising all levels and standards of living. Thus capital controlled the worker, but also the capitalist, by pushing him to appropriate more and more capital. In more modern times, technological development infused capital with logarithmic growth, driving its benefaction abroad to the whole population of the nation so disposed. In the past, therefore, capital was the taskmaster of those who produced it and the blind power-bound obsessionist of those who appropriated it. Modern democratic society has gradually been changing that by implementing control over the first phase and helping capital accumulation to be diverted more amply to the benefit of the producers. Exploitation began, thereby, to change its face and to lose its grip, particularly in the Western democracies. It is still the blind aggressive manipulator of profit in the Third World. Exploitation in the democratic world is being perceived generally as a repugnant practice even among a substantial portion of industrial and commercial leaders.

This study makes so great ado about *value* as the measure of labor invested in a commodity or service because it is the basis for most of the ideological contention in the world today, and it has been so since time immemorial, although not in these recognizable terms. But the significance of this concept has been relegated to past history or not even mentioned as a plausible subject in modern economics. Its significance does not appear to be comprehended by the propagators of modern economic theory. However, with a little perspective, it becomes evident that every social order is and was essentially a mechanism for the production, distribution, and exchange of labor value. A humanistic social philosophy would be fruitless without relating human value to labor value to social value. Marx's concept of exploitation, which is the foundation of his humanism, is based on the Franklin definition of *value*, and so his three volumes of *Capital* are a thesis on labor value and exploitation.

The basic criterion that distinguishes the structure and content of the capitalist from the socialist philosophy of social science is how the *exchange process* of human behavior, which emanates from *Homo*'s bonding-sharing trait of human nature, is evaluated. This most fundamental trait that has phylogenetic roots in the bonding trait of the mammaliam class is humanized by the cognitive processes of man not only to *share* but to extend that process to *exchange*. At first, the exchange act was not related to specific object value, as to the need as humans to share: "We have more of this which you need; you have more of that which we need. Let us trade." As the trading process extended beyond the clan or tribe to less familiar groups, there developed a sense of equating the value of the things exchanged, resulting in the barter system. This value measure was probably intuitively arrived at. But then the process developed mediums of exchange such as money. But as our own Ben Franklin pointed out: "For many ages, those parts of the world which are engaged in commerce have fixed upon gold and silver as the chief and most proper materials for this medium [of exchange]. . . . But as silver itself [as well as gold] is of no certain permanent value, being worth more or less according to its scarcity or plenty, therefore it seems requisite to fix upon something else, more proper to be made a *measure of value,* and this I take to be *labor.*"[35] As a man of clear vision who saw complicated phenomena in their simplest, basic form, he clearly identified labor as the essence of commodity value. Value, after all, is a human quality. There could be no value without human involvement, At first, values were shared humanistically. There could be no exchange without human involvement. There could be no ubiquitously developed behavioral quality of sharing among any other living organism except the human species. A commodity is merely an item invested with human labor and offered for exchange for another item of comparable labor.

The resolution of the meaning of value as hidden in the complexities of the modern production process and exchange market is similar to the situation as was presented to the world by Copernicus, but in an inverse manner. Copernicus simplified the understanding of the movement of the planets from a ptolemaic system of confusing multiellipsoidal rotations around the earth to simplified rotations centered around the sun. Value of a commodity when observed as the resultant of the maze of all the present-day socioeconomic factors as apparent to modern economists renders the concept practically meaningless except as an empirical measure of the "ratios at which different goods are exchanged for each other,"[36] which simulates exchange-value. Thus *value* as a meaningful concept in economic theory becomes lost in the multifaceted medium of exchange value. Only when value is conceived as man-centered rather than ecosystem-centered does the concept become simplified and meaningful and useful as an instrument in political economy and in sociology. This, of course, is anathema to an economic class interested and involved only in the "bottom line." The maelstrom in which this concept is battered about is well expressed by Nobelist Stigler: "The most pervasive problem of economic life is of course that of value, and this is why the routine and undramatic problem of value has elicited the supreme effort of the greatest theorists."[37] Actually, very many economics textbooks do not mention value as a basic economic concept. This has become a forgotten area.

We must build our theory of human enterprise on human beings' activities, lest it lose its human meaning and orientation altogether, like some of the abstruse mathematical formulations of economic theory that the eminent economist Leontief declaims, as already noted, because they identify little in the human world of economics. What is the value of human labor (mental or physical or both), i.e., the value of that part of human life that is objectified in a commodity or service? From a human point of view, it is valuable to the point of being unmeasurable. Therefore, regardless of the price of a commodity or service, the only relation of any significance between the commodity and its value has been the type of skill involved in the production process or the rendering of the service, and even then this comparative relation is measureless in finite quantities, but only as preference for the occasion. When the one commodity and its use value are compared to the skill and time for the production of another commodity, a more defined value relation emerges from the comparison, considering the relative survival and living needs of the producers.

With the tendency to consider Franklin's definition of value outmoded, and with the development of the electronic and robotic machines, the meaning of value has apparently been so extenuated that its rarefied meaning no longer conveys an apprehensible concept of value. So it seems. *Value* is a philosophic term. It has moral and ethical implications. The value of life cannot be measured in nonhuman terms. It cannot be quantified any more than motherhood can be quantified. Excluding the moral and philosophic qualities from value would be equivalent to excluding humanism from the process of living. The existing contradiction between value as the object of creation and the *ability* to produce value must be understood. In the history of political economy there exists an inverse significance between value as the object of man's creativity and the increasing ability of society to produce the objects of value. What must further be understood is that the contradiction between value per se and the objects of value does not invalidate the concept of value, since the former is the essence of creativity and the latter the creation itself. Value, as already observed, is a philosophically measureless concept whereas the product as objectified labor value is measurable. The reason is that when that *object of value becomes a commodity* in the market, its *philosophic value as the essence of human creativity disappears* to become a *marketable use-value* with a relatively specific *exchange-value.*

Man's abililty to produce value at an increasingly rapid rate does not invalidate the Franklin concept of value. This is so because the technology exists not independently by itself. It is the creation of human labor. This is what Marx meant when he asseverated: "The total labor-power of society, which is embodied in the sum total of the values of all commodities produced by that society, counts here as one homogeneous mass of human labor-power, composed though it be of innumerable individual units."[38]

Marx's definition of capital stemmed historically from the dissolution of feudalism, freeing a large class of serfs to become wage-laborers who sold their labor-time to the possessors of money and the means of production in return for a subsistence wage to keep body and soul together. Capital, therefore, is composed of "constant capital or value of the means of production, and variable capital or labour-power, the sum total of wages . . . Growth of capital involves growth of its variable constituent or the part invested in labour-power."[39] The variable capital is the value of the labor expended by the worker in producing the commodity. This labor value is distributed in the wages paid the worker for his subsistence and in the product created by the worker. This latter objectified labor is what was expended by the worker beyond what he received as wages for creating the object. It is what Marx called the surplus labor or the surplus value generated by the worker and appropriated by the owner of the means of production and what Adam Smith called "the labor of inspection and direction" and the "share" of the "owner of the stock."[40]

The *excess labor* appropriated by the owners of the means of production is the essence of what Marx defines as *exploitation,* and it is the frozen *nonhistorical* definition used today by the Soviet political economists for the meaning of capital. Thus the definition of *exploitation* depends on one's definition of *value* of a commodity. Like Marx, Smith agreed with Franklin's definition of value, without giving him credit for it. According to Smith, "Labour alone, therefore, never varying in its own value, is alone the ultimate and real standard by which the value of all commodities can at all times and places be estimated and compared. It is their real price; money is their nominal price only."[41] After declaring such a definition, Smith proffers many reasons why, on the open market, real value disappears into a variable exchange value, thus helping to make contemplation of the concept of surplus value unseemly. In this fundamental is where Marx and Smith part company. For Marx, the real value of a commodity is not subject to legerdemain variation, since such measurable value can be nothing other than of human creation. The exchange-value contains that part that replaces value of the means of production used up in producing the commodity and the wages paid the worker, the rest of the exchange-value being the balance of the value of the labor used in making the commodity that is appropriated by the owner of the stock as his share. Therefore the profit becomes surplus-value, i.e., labor that the owners of the means of production extracted from the worker for no compensation. This process Marx profaned as exploitation.

Marx's theory of value and surplus value was and continues to be a revolutionary body of knowledge for humanizing the conditions of living of the broad masses of people in economically lesser developed capitalist countries. In Marx's day, most people worked to keep body and soul together. The subsistence level was at a minimum. The death rate for the large section of the population was between 25 and 30 deaths per 1,000 people—three times greater than today. Social services were limited to the paltry aid of the poor laws and the poor houses and debtor prisons. The social conscience of the affluent was a mockery of virtue.

Ben Franklin's definition of value must have been an exciting discovery for a sophisticated mind that penetrated the misery of the masses with a social conscience that called for action. This was Marx, the Hegelian philosopher who was in the process of turning Hegel upside down. Franklin's formula for value of a commodity was logical, had scientific validity, and was unencumbered with philosophic proclivity except for being thoroughly centered in the human being. It therefore could be adopted by any particular philosophic turn of mind. It was adopted by Adam Smith's capitalist turn of mind without reservation and was later welcomed by Marx's revolutionary turn of mind, when he built a formidable structure of political economy upon it. Whereas Smith made little ado about value, Marx embodied the workers' labor in it and threw his theory into the faces of the political economists of the newly developing capitalist social order with his devastating theory of surplus value, which pushed capitalism toward humanistic change while it was accelerating its ability to generate and accumulate capital.

Had Marx's theory been applied to Western Europe during the dissolution of feudalism, without mercantilism or capitalism having had an opportunity to take hold, what would have resulted to world progress in commodity production and capital accumulation is a speculation based on historical perspection. However, my surmise is that the generation of capital (if it would have been called by that name) would have been *greatly* retarded, and probably this would also have been true of science as well. Based on historical theory, this retardation would have occurred because profits or surplus value could not very well have been applied vigorously to such an economy. Both Marx and Engels, from their writings on the dialectic interpretation of history, would have agreed with this appraisal.

Surplus-value, as already noted, was Marx's humanistic concept, based on a moral principle on which his revolutionary theory rested. This principle, like all moral principles, revolves around what is right or wrong in human behavior as this behavior relates to the essence of being human. If, it argues, the value of a commodity is measured by the human labor expended in producing it, then the nature of the value in exchange-value must also be based on the Franklin formula. If, however, the exchange-value has the characteristic of containing a portion that is appropriated as profit by the owner of the stock after the exchange is negotiated, then this profit must be the equivalent in value of the surplus labor expended by the worker in producing the commodity. Marx claimed that human labor expended in producing a commodity is in essence a crystallization of human life and therefore must not be treated as a commodity to be bought and sold as property. This is an extended version of slavery—that instead of owning the slave outright as property, only his labor is property owned by the master. And this morally is wrong, just as is slavery. Marx called this exploitation of the human being.

Adam Smith was more the amoral savant in his objectivity toward science rather than, like Marx, the moral humanist in relation to science. Smith correctly ascribed the profit motive to man's human nature—actually to two traits of human nature, that is, the bonding-sharing trait, which eventuated into the exchange process, and the self-image–self-esteem trait, which developed to the extreme phase of self-love,[42] as manifested in the accumulators of capital—the merchants and manufacturers. Smith put it as follows: ". . . [I]t is the power of exchanging that gives occasion to the division of labour. . . The division of labour arises from a propensity in human nature to exchange."[43]. But "without the assistance and cooperation of many thousands"[44] of labor subdivisions "the very meanest person in a civilized country could not be provided." Among these subdivisions of labor, the critical ones are the workers and the owners of the means of production. Smith asserted labor to be the "real measure of the exchangable value of all commodities."[45] Then he asserted that "[T]he whole produce of labour does not always belong to the labourer. He must in most cases *share* [italics added] it with the owner of the stock which employs him."[46] The owner of the stock therefore buys labour as he buys commodities, but he does not buy them at their exchange-value worth. He buys them at a wage low enough to make his desired profit. What Smith called the "share . . . [of] the owner of the stock" is exactly what Marx called surplus-value. Smith did not call labor a commodity, but certainly treated it as a commodity. The buying of labor he designated as *natural law*. Adam Smith's theories supported the free expression of the traits of human nature, particularly that of "challenge and competence" which stimulated inventive and proficiency pursuits to succeed, that of "freedom-to-choose," which unboggled the minds to sense inspirational independence, and that of "striving to satisfy one's appetites, inclinations, and talents," which generated a torrent of individual pursuits to satisfy wants in all directions. For a much larger portion of the population than the feudal nobility, freer expression of the remaining traits of human nature became possible. However, the unlimited expression of the "challenge" trait spilled over into *extreme* expression of *competition* in economic matters, which became the trademark of capitalism and the miraculous development of *capital*. As more capital accumulated, the greater became the antagonisms between those who controlled capital and those who were hired to *produce* it. But, nevertheless, the greater the antagonism, the more benefits spilled over to the masses of producers (the workers), and the more dissatisfied the *producers* became because *democracy* induced in them a stream of creative cognitions that inspired *hope* that they could also share more and more of this capital that they produced. Along came Karl Marx and Friederich Engels to show how workers morally deserved to share in this capital and how they could attain that hope.

The psychosocial basis of Adam Smith's theory rested on a premise inspired by the traits cited above, which expressed extreme aspects of those traits. This premise was *self-interest*. Such a premise by itself could not have been acceptable as having complete human worth unless Smith further theorized that out of the maelstrom of laissez-faire emerged the *social benefaction*. In this cauldron of economic competition, all the traits of human nature were conditioned by the new cultural developments. Capitalism in a democratic framework opened the pent-up traits of human nature from their feudal constrictions. The more one had control of capital, the more freedom one had to express one's human nature as far as material independence could free them toward either the positive or negative aspects of the traits, depending upon how the social conditions effected the traits. The higher the wages became for the "producers," the more the oppressive weight on man's human nature lightened. The theory of Marxism magnified the "producers" hope for lifting the oppressive weight from his ability to express the urges of the traits of his human nature. Whereas Smith attributed the extremities of free expression tò *natural law,* Marx profoundly steeped himself in the philosophic deliberations of the nature of man in his exposition of the complex process of alienation and estrangement.

In a modern Western capitalist democracy, the theory of surplus-value loses its sting, since the workers benefit from taxes collected by government, and from the benefits won by the labor unions from owners of industry, to an extent large enough to enervate the validity of surplus-value. Also, considering the highly developed organization of administrative and sales technology necessary to operate big industry, these activities plus taxes must also share in the surplus value (capital) repository. Thus surplus-value was a workable theory for developing class consciousness among the workers to struggle for better living conditions. But this was true only for the eighteenth, nineteenth, and the first several decades of the twentieth centuries in the Western democracies. It still holds for other economically depressed areas of the world.

The variable applicability of the theory of surplus value depending on historical situations is not the case for the applicability of the definition of *value* itself as Franklin stated it. In human society, value is created by human energy. This is a relative absolute for human society—relative only so far as human society remains viable and absolute as long as human society exists. A diamond is worthless without human society and without being processed by the energy of human beings. In a capitalist democracy like the United States, where freedom of choice is now being practiced in the extreme, social scientists and social conscious elements in the population profess orientations from communist to capitalist, from liberal to conservative, from one extreme to the opposite extreme, while hosts of middle-of-the-roaders exist. One of the extreme points of view needs discussion here since it accepts the extreme position of the human nature trait that deals with freedom of choice and uses it to apologize for the extremist behavior of OPEC and the oil companies monopoly. This is done by the vitiation of the meaning of *value*.

There are highly regarded academicians who justify the rapaciousness of cartelism. Professor Scott of the Harvard Business School absolves the OPEC countries from the inordinate prices of oil and blames the crisis on the American life-style. This is tantamount to saying that the world economic depression of the 1970s following the Arab oil embargo was due to the American people. This is political-economic theory with a vengence. He makes such an evaluation on the basis that this commodity's *use-value* is in extreme demand, i.e., has an inordinately high use-value. Professor Scott seems to be living in the academician's dreamworld. Why, according to his theory, are potable water and nourishing food not in the same category? And why are the prices of these commodities not more than ten times higher than they were ten years ago? The eminent economist Leontief, in a letter to the journal *Science,* exploded in exasperation at the economic academician's "irrelevant theoretical conclusions. . . [N]o one taking part in the elaborate and solemn procession of contemporary U.S. academic economics seems to know it [that the 'King is naked'] and those who do, don't dare speak up."[47] Does the professor not have enough practical economic acumen to realize that any life-sustaining commodity has a high use-value? The real use-value of a life-sustaining commodity becomes manifest when it is scarce. If a cartel were able to control the production and distribution of food and water, as is being done with oil, the result would be the same.

The experience of the world has been that when an item becomes scarce, some way is always found to replace it. The amount of natural oil is limited. But, from estimates, there is enough for at least twenty years, not considering that a great part of the world has not yet been explored for this item. From what is known in science today, there is no doubt that another source of energy will be available when natural oil resources are exhausted. There is no scarcity now. Scarcity can be created by those (the oil cartel) who produce it. When food became unavailable due to drought, as in the case in Africa today or as was the case in China in the past, the countries that had food responded with human concern. However, if they were brigands as OPEC and the oil companies are, they surely would not respond.

Scott's interpretation is the most abject apology for the new rip-off system that could be devised. Such a high use-value should place this commodity in the category of needing government control, since its market scarcity at present would disrupt social life. The gist of Scott's apology is stated by him as follows: "At the heart of the United States misconception is an inability to see oil in any other terms but the consumer's. It is cheap to produce—only $1 or $2 per barrel in the Middle East—so the price should be low (at marginal cost, according to our economics texts). But that premise ignores the high *value oil has in use* [italics added], ranging beyond $100 per barrel in petro-chemicals and as fuel in automobiles."[48] An economy cannot exist without consumers and producers. The producer produces for the consumer, and this could not possibly be otherwise. Beginning with Adam Smith,[49] every theory of economics has dealt with use-value, but acceptable theory has not misused the term as Scott has. A free market abhors production control by private agents for controlling prices. Neither Marxist, Soviet, nor capitalist economic theory allows for the wild interpretation of use-value as described by Scott. This description of the function of use-value in economics is equivalent to an academic technique of sanctioning brigandism.

Price is the money-name of labor realized in a commodity that fluctuates with supply and demand and with use-value, if that were to fluctuate also. Supply and demand, therefore, do not determine the value of the commodity, but only actuates the fluctuation of the price above or below a certain mean. That certain mean is the money-name of the labor realized in the commodity. The use-value per se has no quantitative objective *measurable* value in itself, but is usually *identical* to the exchange-value converted to price in an *uncontrolled* market, based on the fluctuations affecting it by the supply and demand for the commodity. A measure for use-value separate from exchange-value is completely arbitrary. The only place where such an unpredictable value system exists is in relation to rare art or antique items like a Rembrandt portrait or a Gutenberg Bible. Such items are usually not considered commodities. A commodity is an item with a reasonably predictable exchange-value, based on the cost of production, and created for exchange in the market. Only a devious mechanism where man loses control of this basic human activity and that destroys the predictable meaning of exchange-value and introduces the legitimacy of the rip-off system in the economy would equate the method of evaluating the Michelangelo statue of David with a barrel of oil, such as by justifying the exchange-value of a $2 barrel of oil to be $100 or $1,000. Scott, by misrepresenting the classical and modern accepted meaning of *use-value,* exculpates the criminal intent of monopoly operators, and the market becomes so chaotic that it differs little from the economy of piracy.

Professor Scott was not as wise in giving his advice to the oil princes as "one dose" Machiavelli was in advising Lorenzo the Magnificent, son of Piero Di Medici, in the least painful way to *take* in order to assuage the loser: "Whence it is to be noted, that in taking a state, the conqueror must arrange to commit all his cruelties at once, so as not to have to recur to them every day, and so as to be able, by not making fresh changes, to reassure people and win them over by benefitting them."[50]

To preclude such Machiavellian practices from becoming the legitimate process of modern exchange, which unfortunately the monopolies and cartels are foisting with increasing frequency upon the public, and to counteract the "deindustrialization" process whereby labor-intensive production is being shifted from advanced industrial nations to less-developed and nearly developed nations and thereby increasing the ranks of the permanent unemployed and reducing the level-of-living of the workers in the advanced industrial nations, an industrial restructuring must be undertaken.[51]

Restructuring

Production, accumulation, and mobility of capital are the inseparable tripartite essence of the free enterprise profit-making system, while the well-being of the workers and the communities in which they live is the ultimate aim of a democratically organized humane societal system. Can these two systems be integrated into a stabilized social order? This is one of the paramount problems of the Western democracies. Upon its solution hinges the future existence of democratic Western countries.

Management decisions of private enterprises are driven by a supreme commitment to the pursuit of lowest costs and highest short-term profits (the bottom line) on investments, long-term considerations being secondary or in limbo. This is due to the nature of the investment process and is influenced mightily by the operation of the stock market. The multinational corporations tied up in monopolies and cartels are the ultimate organizational manifestation of this process. Is this process the only way to prevent dictatorship of the right or the left? The multinational corporations think so, even though they come very close to operating and do operate as dictatorships of the right.

Does the United States government have the disposition to make public investments for the nation's good? In their support of such investments, Blakely and Shapira state: "America has a long and rich history of deep and far-reaching public interventions that have fundamentally changed the nation's economic and social course: The Louisiana Purchase is one example; the development of the West, the promotion of the railroads, and the formulation of the land-grant universities are others."[52] To this should be added the Tennessee Valley Authority and the whole network of the nation's highways and dams and coastal waterways. The American life-style of supporting the human nature traits of challenge and competence, freedom to choose, and cumulative creative action, can be given even greater opportunity for developing our country by government intervention in dispelling the economic chaos and restraining monopoly and conglomerate formation from spreading through the economy and by introducing certain types of controls that will give the economic forces their needed predictability to act for the good of the nation.

The restructuring should include the development and implementation of a new national framework of economic stratagems to replace the Keynesian, monetary, and supply-side formulations favored by various economists and parties, which obviously do not work in our present situation. Industrial restructuring will require policies for increasing social control over economic change and for investment stratagems. These are:

1. Elimination of the loopholes in the tax structure that provide incentives to close plants, which increases the mobility of capital by moving plants overseas for cheap labor, and which encourage the practise of wasteful conglomerate acquisitions whereby capital is used to buy money instead of investing in production of new capital.

2. Establish national policies for government to review all corporate
maneuvers that have the potential for producing results deleterious
for the workers, for their communities, and for the national well-being.
3. Establishing national policies for involving workers and their communities to participate in and bargain over decisions for corporate
investment germane to the local situation.
4. The major corporations should provide ongoing information to their
work-force on corporation strategies concerning production, investment plans, overseas operations, major shutdowns and the like. To be
useful, such reporting should be of a similar nature as impact studies
required in environmental operations. Such statements would give the
workers and the communities the ability to decide whether to keep the
plant open or explore the feasibility of the community or the workers
taking over the ownership.
5. A National Planning and Industrial Investment Agency should be
established.[53] The planning system's aim should be directed toward:

    a. inquiring into and devising ways of measuring the needs and
the means of satisfying the needs of the essential community
resources which the government has the responsibility to operate,

    b. exploring the effective impact of the operations of private en-
terprising on the community and devise the methodology of
preventing such operations from impinging unfavorably upon
the community without disturbing legitimate private enterprise, and

    c. Stimulating research and development in areas needing sup-
port for community well-being, such as the development of new
sources of energy.

The National Investment System would:

    a. invest in large national firms and basic sectors, and

    b. establish state-level industrial development agencies to make
investments in medium-sized regional enterprises.

In this way, social control over key elements of the economy would
be strengthened. To further strengthen the economy, investment in
public goods production could be instituted, including public services,
transportation, energy, housing, health, and various aspects of development.
6. Developing the means for inducing corporations to incorporate the

long-term community development view in their planning process and for taking the responsibility for accountability to the community for their operations.

7. Monopolies and cartels must be controlled to prevent the irresponsible disruptive manipulation of production whose purpose is usually to create scarcity and arbitrary price-fixing unrelated to the cost of production or to the natural availability of the raw material. The strangle-hold on competitive activities is thereby released. Energy, an essential factor in the lifeblood of community survival and which practically controlled by the oil companies, banks, and insurance companies, must be released from their stifling grip.

8. Developing a system for increasing the stockholdings of those who work in a particular industry or commercial firm in accordance with longevity on the job so that such employees accumulate enough worth during the years to live decently in their older years of retirement. This would help reduce the Social Security load, resolve the alienation of workers, and reduce the confrontational relations between capital and labor and eventually eliminate it without restraining the challenge and competence trait of human nature.

9. A creative and self-perpetuating mechanism needs to be established dedicated to the principles of:

    a. fostering community projects in those areas of lower economic development and poorer health status;

    b. helping enterprising individuals or groups with sound business-venture plans to obtain the necessary training, capital, and consultation on how to get started; and

    c. aiding in the retooling and reorganizing of ongoing enterprises, which needs to keep abreast with the latest technology in order to compete in producing efficiently and with quality (a type of Reconstruction Finance Corporation for the small neophyte venturer).

The plan could be accomplished by establishing a revolving fund for stimulating and encouraging the productive forces of the local economy. This fund would be replenished by the repayment of loans as projects begin to become self-sustaining.

The revolving fund should be controlled by a relatively independent body established by law. This body should be composed of persons well versed in business administration and practice, agriculture and farm management, practical politics and government, banking and finance, public health and education.

The organization, in order to be creatively helpful, should study and be knowledgeable concerning:

a. the ecological potential and feasibility for raising various flora and fauna from various parts of the world in particular localities of the area without impairing the ecology,

b. the possibilities of profitably exploiting the land and water resources without impairing the ecology,

c. developing methods of inducing the needy population into profitable pursuits in agriculture, commerce, or industry; and

d. the latest technologies for application to the local pursuits in order to keep competitive.

10. Increasingly more industrial and governmental funds should be invested in control of environmental pollution, housing, health, education, and recreation. Where industry cannot employ people, government must do so for the purpose of rehabilitating the urban and rural environment which has become excessively deteriorated.

11. Dedicate adequate funds for a vigorous research program. Research in the psychosocial sciences to establish the most workable methodology and dynamics for orienting the direction of social organization to the best patterns of social interrelations for creating an ecosystem that will be in harmony with the traits of human nature. Also to maintain surveillance of research activities in general, to prevent regression in knowledge development.

12. Let us never forget the creative urge in humankind, which, if given an opportunity to develop, brings a great deal of satisfaction into the lives of those who develop their skills to engage in such pursuits as that of the artist and the artisan. Just like the formation, reproduction, and accumulation of capital to satisfy the material needs of all the people and to give rise to more and more disposable time (recreational time) for the individual, so must encouragement be given for the development of crafts, the rediscovery of crafts that have been lost, the development of new crafts, and the pursuits of the arts. The time may even come when the distinction between the artisan's and the artist's creations may blend. Mechanized production must never depress or negate the individual creativeness of people.

13. Health and education services have a very high priority and must be planned so that every young educable adult is of optimum health and trained in a skill for making a living. There must be no barrier for an individual who has committed himself to a higher education. Vocational schools should be of the highest quality and utilized to the highest degree.

14. During the period before the government has learned to prevent economic crises with unemployment and part-time employed reaching into the millions of souls, and inflation still plaguing the economy and persistently reducing the value of fixed incomes of the aging population, the government must not hesitate to institute:

    a. a program of job security;
    b. price control on commodities, rent, and services;
    c. wage controls on a selective bases, depending on how far behind the inflation cycle some categories of wages have lagged;
    d. nationalization of the whole field of energy production and distribution, particularly petroleum and gas;
    e. development of arrangements with private oil and gas prospectors for profitable exploration activities, and development of a modus operandi for cooperative government-private enterprise in exploration and production of oil and gas and other sources of energy; and
    f. maintaining interest rates at a reasonable 4 to 6 percent for enterprises concerned with commodity production, including agriculture, construction, and essential services, such as health and education. This may be considered discriminatory legislation, but with such great changes taking place in our society, practices of this nature will have to become possible lest the government take over the responsibility completely.

SOCIAL ENGINEERING

Mass education in socio-economic-political needs based on the aim of initiating *social movement* is the first step for a campaign for social engineering and political action. The term "social engineering" is not a concept invented by modern social theorists. Korzybski in 1921 introduced the term "human engineering," which implied the same meaning as "social engineering": "There is no doubt that the engineering of human society is a difficult and complicated problem of tremendous ethical responsibility, for it involves the welfare of mankind throughout an unending succession of generations. The science of Human Engineering can not be built upon false conceptions of human nature."[54] The latter observation that "Human Engineering can not be built upon false conceptions of human nature" is a profound observation indeed. Since human or social engineering must be based on anthropological, psychological, and sociological theory, how can such theory have any validity lest it clearly expounds the dynamics of man's nature. The only significantly great sociological theories developed since the Industrial Revolution were those discussed above of Adam Smith and Karl Marx. Both were great from the point of view of having basic impact upon social development over the entire world. But both were great also because they led to untrammelling the yoke of the oppressive social practices that for many centuries had inhibited the traits of human nature from free expression.

Social engineering is basically a discipline for adjusting and maintaining social relations in equilibrium with the traits of human nature. Both Smith and Marx perceived that the social relations involved in "exchange" were associated with the dynamics of human nature—to the bonding-sharing nature inherent in social behavior. Exchange is not a natural law, as claimed by Smith, but a psychosocial behavioral manifestation issuing from bonding-sharing trait and therefore being a biphasic human-primate complex as human nature itself is. Its being an expression of human nature was pointed out recently by anthropologist Lee.[55] Being biphasic, it manifests itself as a moral-ethical problem, as treated by Marx, contending between being human or aggressively primate, this depending to a large extent on the nature of the ecosystem.

Marx, therefore, was the first modern exponent of human engineering in the moral-ethical scientific sense of Korzybski. Marx was very concerned in development of a social structure that was not only conducive to physical health, but was also in harmony with the traits of human nature, as he understood the practical side of the psychosocial needs of human beings, according to the available knowledge at that time.

When Ben Franklin enunciated his theory of value,[56] the Industrial Revolution was just around the corner, but the forces for its moving forward were already driving for recognition. At this period, the various side currents that might influence the status of value one way or another had not yet come into existence. Therefore, Franklin's clarity in comprehending the concept of value was not side-tracked and blurred, as are the visions of present-day economists by the growing amount of new factors and accompanying trivia composing the maelstrom of the present-day "market." To him, it was clear that no other factor was as basic in determining the value of the life-sustaining commodities and the more ordinary amenities resulting from science and technology than the labor required to produce the commodities.

Human engineering is a sociological movement for arranging the social forces so they will initiate the development and maintenance of social institutions and mores that will support the essential patterns of human behavior—the traits of human nature—and that are determined by the psychosocial response of man to his biosocial conditions of living. This study leads to the conclusion that the ultimate aim of society should be the practice of human engineering to orient the development of society toward a social order that will be in concordance with the traits of human nature, and, as Korzybski declared, this cannot be ventured upon with "false conceptions of human nature."[57] The eight traits of human nature expounded in this study are completely intertwined with one another. Any social condition that is discordant in its effect on any trait will have its disturbing effect on the other traits. Every social system's structure, organization, and operation, in order to support the most essential *human* conditions for living, must:

1. Guarantee to people a just way of satisfying their physical survival and physiological needs, and their pursuit for betterment of the material conditions of living.
2. Engage in molding the social institutions to support such sociofunctional interrelations that will be in harmony with the psychosocial needs of the people, i.e., to nurture the positive aspects of the traits of human nature.

We have some of the knowledge to do many of the primary tasks of human engineering to accomplish the above. There are, however, many facets of the task that must be researched in order to achieve a dynamic pattern of societal functioning as elaborated in the work of Etzioni[58] and Brown and Harris.[59] What we must guard against in the process of changing is dispensing with the good in the life that we already have for scientifically unsupported inspirational or demagogic patterns of paradise, the contemplation of which animates the spirit, fires the mind, but, for those who nurture a rational approach to social change, "puzzles the will, and makes us rather bear those ills we have, than fly to others that we 'know not of,' " as Hamlet so aptly put it.

Rational social change is as much an art as a science. The direction in which we move forward, the mores and institutions that we leave behind and those we carry forward, and the new replacements that we institute *should be rationally and scientifically* dictated as far as possible. The methodology used in making changes is mostly involved with the *art* of dealing with people. In historical times, most social changes were not dictated by the populace but by those who had the power to dictate, and even then, the direction taken was not always the choice of the dictators, because they did not understand the nature of the prevailing socio-economo-political and psychosocial forces. But now, for the first time in history, there is an opportunity for humanity to make its own history in the direction that aggrandizes the whole of humankind, materially and mentally. Since the nature of *Homo* is both primate and human, and since human society, from the very beginning, has always been specifically organized to maintain and to preserve the human phase as dominant over the primate phase, the direction that will most aggrandize the whole of humankind will be where the social interrelations generated will be in the highest possible harmony with the traits of human nature.

NOTES

1. Harold Laski, *The American Democracy* (New York: Viking Press, 1948), p. 761.

2. Paul Mattick, *Marx and Keynes* (Boston, Massachusetts: Porter Sargent Publisher, 1969), p. 307.

3. Karl Marx and Friederich Engels, *The Civil War in the United States* (New York: International Publishers, 1937).

4. Karl Marx, *Selected Works*, vol. 1 (New York: International Publishers), p. 137.

5. Ibid., p. 228.

6. *Fundamentals of Marxism-Leninism* (Moscow: Foreign Language Publishing House), p. 463

7. Ibid., p. 679.

8. Nikita S. Khrushchev, *Khrushchev Remembers: The Last Testament* (Boston, Massachusetts: Little, Brown and Co., 1974).

9. Paul Mattick, *Marx and Keynes* (Boston, Massachusetts: Porter Sargent Publisher, 1969), p. 307.

10. Karl Marx, *The Economic and Philosophic Manuscripts of 1844* (New York: International Publishers, 1964), pp. 202–03.

11. Karl Marx, *The Grundrisse* (New York: Harper and Row, 1971), pp. 129–30.

12. V. I. Lenin, *On Proletarian Culture* (Moscow: Novosti Press Agency Publishing House, 1969), p. 34.

13. Franz Mehring, *Karl Marx* (Ann Arbor, Michigan: University of Michigan Press, 1979), p. 531.

14. Rosa Luxemburg, *The Russian Revolution and Leninism or Marxism?* (Ann Arbor, Michigan: University of Michigan Press, 1961), pp. 76–85.

15. S. K. Kuczaj II, *Crib Speech and Language Play* (New York: Springer-Verlage, 1983).

16. David Kipnis, "The View from the Top," *Psychology Today* (December 1984), pp. 30–36.

17. Karl Marx, *Critique of the Gotha Program* (New York: International Publishers, 1938, Appendix I, from the Correspondence of Marx and Engels Concerning the Gotha Programme, Friederich Engels to August Bebel, 1875), p. 31.

18. V. I. Lenin, *State and Revolution* (New York: International Publishers, 1932), p. 71.

19. Karl Marx and Friederich Engels, *The Civil War in the United States* (New York: International Publishers, 1937), pp. 280–281.

20. Marx, *Critique of the Gotha Programme, loco supra citato*, p. 67.

21. Friederich Engels, *Origin of the Family, Private Property, and the State* (Chicago, Illinois: Charles H. Kerr and Co.), p. 217.

22. Luxemburg, *loco supra citato*, pp. 22–24.

23. Louis M. Hacker, *The Shaping of American Tradition* (New York: Columbia University Press, 1947), pp. 1161–62.

24. Marx, *The Grundrisse, loco supra citato,* pp. 70–73,77, 96–102.

25. John Torrance, *Estrangement, Alienation, and Exploitation* (New York: Columbia University Press, 1977).

26. Marx, *The Economic and Philosophic Manuscripts of 1844, loco supra citato,* pp. 120–64.

27. Henry Lefebvre, *The Sociology of Marx* (New York: Random House, 1968), pp. 138–83.

28. Karl Marx, *Collected Works,* Vol. 3, *Contribution to the Critique of Hegel's Philosophy of Law, 1843–44* (New York: International Publishers, 1976), p. 29.

29. *Ibid.*

30. T. Dobzhansky, *The Biological Basis of Human Freedom* (New York: Columbia University Press, 1956), p. 134.

31. Ibid., p. 124.

32. Aristotle, *The Works of Aristotle, translated into English,* vol. 2.

33. Marx, *The Grundrisse, loco supra citato,* pp. 94–95.

34. Douglas Rae, "The Egalitarian State," *Daedalus* (Fall 1979), pp. 37–54.

35. Benjamin Franklin, *The Works of Franklin,* edited by Jared Sparks, vol. 2, *Essays on Political Economy* (Charles Tappan, Publisher, 1844), p. 265.

36. Raymond T. Bye, *Principles of Economics* (F. S. Crofts and Co., 1936), p. 282ff.

37. George J. Stigler, *Essays in the History of Economics* (Chicago, Illinois: University of Chicago Press, 1965), p. 22.

38. Karl Marx, *Capital,* vol. 1 *Capitalist Production* (Chicago, Illinois: Charles H. Kerr and Co.), p. 46.

39. Karl Marx, *Capital,* vol. 1: *Capitalist Production* (Chicago, Illinois: Charles H. Kerr, 1926), p. 671.

40. Adam Smith, *The Wealth of Nations* (New York: Modern Library, 1937), pp. 48–49.

41. Ibid., p. 33.

42. Ibid., p. 14.

43. Ibid., p. 17, 13.

44. Ibid., p. 12.

45. Ibid., p. 30.

46. Ibid., p. 49.

47. Wassily Leontief, "Academic Economics," *Science,* vol. 217 (July 9, 1982), pp. 217–18.

48. B. R. Scott, "OPEC, the American Scapegoat," *Harvard Business Review,* vol. 59, no. 1.

49. Smith, *op. cit.,* p. 28.

50. Niccolo Machiavelli, *The Prince* (New York: New American Library, 1937), p. 61.

51. Edward J. Blakely and Philip Shapira, "Industrial Restructuring: Public Policy for Investment in Advanced Industrial Scoiety," *Annals of the American Academy of Political and Social Science,* vol. 475 (September 1984), pp. 96–109.

52. Ibid.

53. Ibid.

54. Alfred Korzybski, *Manhood of Humanity: The Science and Art of Human Engineering* (New York: E. P. Dutton and Co., 1921), p. 69.

55. Richard B. Lee, *!Kung San: Men, Women and Children in a Foraging Society* (New York: Cambridge University Press, 1979), p. 490.

56. Benjamin Franklin *The Works of Franklin,* vol. 2, edited by Jared Sparks (Charles Tappan, Publisher, 1844), p. 265.

57. Kirkpatrick Says, "U.N. Worsens Conflict," *Times Picayune,* February 2, 16, 1982.

58. Korzybski, *loco supra citato,* p. 69.

58. Amitai Etzioni, *The Active Society* (New York: The Free Press, 1968).

59. George W. Brown and Tirril Harris, *Social Origins of Depression* (New York: The Free Press, 1978).

INDEX

Abrahms, Eliot, 162, 183, 259
Acheuleal, 288
Adams, Virginia, 248, 377
Adaptation, 99, 104, 107, 135, 152, 160,
    163, 205, 226
Adler, Alfred, 206, 207, 377
Adultery, 155, 247
Affective-cognitive, 312, 313, 314
Africa, 280, 288, 289, 291, 470, 499
Aggregation, 128, 129, 130, 131
Aggression, 3, 24, 25, 55, 77, 118, 119, 124,
    125, 131, 157, 210, 217, 280, 286,
    320, 489, 491
Agricultural Adjustment Act, 448
Agriculture, 65, 224, 227, 386, 505
AIDS, 209, 376, 357, 362
Alcock, John, 95
Alcoholism, 33, 39, 41, 42, 101, 104, 106,
    337, 351, 376, 449, 455
Alcoholics Anonymous, 376
Alien labor, 287
Allee, W.C., 131
Allport, G.W., 212, 243
Alverdes, F., 131
Alienation, 3, 98, 99, 100, 101, 177–181,
    287, 298–300, 352, 398, 403, 420,
    421, 458, 481, 488, 490, 497
Altricial infant, 51, 56, 61
Altruism, 24, 123, 137, 158, 159, 164, 165,
    169, 205
America, 291
American Civil War, 347, 476, 484
American democracy, 483, 486
American experience, 335, 342, 349, 389,
    401, 408
American Psychiatric Association, 253,
    370, 373–376
American Revolution, 347, 441, 475, 484,
    488
Animal nature, 320, 323, 375
Anlage, 308
Anorexia nervosa, 5, 208, 362

Anthropology, 3, 5, 7, 8, 9, 13, 14, 21, 22,
    39, 44, 48, 60, 61, 63, 73–75, 80, 84,
    89–91, 101, 102, 112, 113, 115, 116,
    120, 124, 135, 141, 150, 155, 162,
    163, 180, 190, 224, 319, 323, 505
Antisemitism, 336
Antony, Marc, 246
Anxiety, 101, 148, 163, 180, 212, 245, 266,
    271, 286, 328, 333, 334, 336
Apes, 24–26, 75–78, 132, 134, 141, 170, 221
Appollonian principle, 303
Aquinas, Thomas, 28
Arabs, 402, 416, 446, 457, 464, 465, 498
Aramco, 458
Archeologists, 132, 164, 221, 224, 225
Ardrey, Robert, 187
Argyle, Michael, 296
Arieti, Silvano, 303
Aristotle, 21, 27, 28, 318
Art, 290, 293, 323
Asia, 407
Assimilation, 25
Attachment, 169
Avogadro, Amedeo, 14
Aurelius, Marcus, 218
Aurignacian culture, 291
Australopithecus, 50, 71, 209, 221, 222,
    279, 423, 454
Australia, 291
Awareness, 79, 279
Axelrod, R., 129

Babington, B.G., 322
Bacchanalia, 361
Bacon, Francis, 385
Bachofen, J.J., 162
Bahrain, 457
Bailey, F.R., 58
Balabanoff, Angelico, 389, 440
Baldwin, James Mark, 204, 205
Bandura, A., 369
Bankruptcies, 451

Barash, David P., 85, 95
Barley, 292
Barron, F., 212
Barter system, 491
Base camp, 278
Battered children, 101
Batto, Bernard F., 199
Bauer, Otto, 389
Beck, A.T., 163
Behavior, 12, 13, 23, 24, 25
Behavioral anatomy, 26
Behavioral disorientation, 12, 13, 102, 103, 107, 119, 121, 126, 154, 166, 167, 170, 183, 189, 192, 207, 218, 245, 246, 259, 301, 328, 329, 333, 446
Behavioral theory, 335
Behaviorism, 136
Belgium, 413
Bell, Alan P., 357, 363, 364
Benedict, Ruth, 116
Bernard, B., 94
Bernard, Claude, 321
Bernstein, Edward, 389
Bible, 463, 500
Bidney, David, 7, 13, 22
Biogram, 81, 82, 128, 133, 135, 137, 144, 323
Biological sexuality, 358
Biological nature, 302, 323, 356, 357
Biological needs, 286, 358, 359
Biomedical knowledge, 26, 318
Biosocial structure of society, 274, 376
Bioto, Arrigo, 160
Bipedality, 50, 53, 59, 62, 79, 130, 132, 268, 324, 359
Biphasic behavior process, 4, 12, 27, 28, 30, 37, 47, 58, 69, 72, 90, 93, 94, 95, 97, 113, 119, 142, 151, 192, 211, 217, 229, 235, 259, 273, 304, 312, 338, 418, 421, 422, 479, 483, 487, 506
Black African States, 434, 435
Blair, John M., 229, 395, 465, 467, 468
Blakely, Edward J., 501
Block, J., 363
Boaz, Franz, 21, 113, 115
Bohr, Niels, 7
Bonding-sharing trait, 13, 37, 50, 52, 54, 58, 60, 74, 88, 90, 95, 107, 123, 128, 129, 130, 133, 135, 136, 137, 141, 144, 145, 147, 148, 149, 154, 155, 156, 157, 158, 159, 162, 163, 165, 166, 169, 170, 171, 295, 303, 307, 310, 327, 328, 331, 347, 351, 352, 386, 408, 423, 506
Boredom, 287

Borneo, 76
Bouglé, C., 67
Bowlby, J., 138, 150
Boyle, Robert, 14
Brain, 9, 23, 24, 27, 28, 51, 56, 59, 61, 79, 80, 90, 104, 125, 129, 130, 132, 134, 136, 137, 141, 142, 170, 182, 205, 210, 216, 217, 221, 222, 279, 322, 323, 328, 406
Brezhnev, Leonid, 1, 338
Bribery, 343
Briffault, R., 311
Britain, 413, 457, 470
British museum, 175
Brown, George W., 507
Brownian moement, 354
Bruce, E.W., 363
Brutus, 246
Buchanan, J.M., 396
Buddha, 218
Bukharin, Nicolai, 456
Bulimia, 5, 208, 362
Byron, Lord George G., 364

Caesar, 246
California, 454
California Standard Oil Company, 457
Cameron, David R., 406, 412, 413, 414, 415
Campanello, Tommasco, 385
Candidiasis, 376
Cannon, Walter B., 321
Capital, 3, 14, 143, 232, 287, 299, 300, 343, 344, 352, 391, 395, 396, 398–401, 404, 406, 408, 409, 410, 427, 429–432, 434, 447, 450, 455, 461, 462, 488, 490, 493, 501
Capital accumulation, 43, 228, 232, 352, 392, 398, 414, 429, 459, 480, 490, 491, 494, 495, 504
Capitalism, 2, 142, 143, 152, 162, 167, 168, 177, 179, 234, 277, 295, 297–299, 339, 348, 352, 353, 387, 392, 396, 400, 403, 414, 418, 419, 425, 428, 429, 434, 437, 440, 445, 448, 455, 458, 483, 495, 497
Capitalist countries, 229, 232, 233, 420
Capitalist production, 287, 390, 401
Capitalist society, 431, 440, 443, 460, 465, 480
Carrying devices, 66
Cartels, 228, 229, 344, 349, 401, 406, 450, 457, 469, 498, 499, 503
Carter, James E., 417, 458
Cave dwellers, 291, 302
Centers for Disease Control, 357, 358

Challenge, 3, 36, 37, 38, 56, 57, 60, 71, 74,
    107, 170, 178, 180, 192, 217, 223,
    224, 228, 268–282, 289, 290, 292,
    300, 305, 312, 313, 334, 349, 350,
    353, 355, 401, 403, 418, 435, 442,
    446, 462, 478, 480, 481, 496, 510,
    503
Chang, J., 363
Chaos, 35, 39, 40, 41, 72, 121, 151, 162,
    176, 194, 195, 198, 199, 202, 209,
    213, 214, 349, 380, 399, 422
Charles, Jacques, A.C., 14
Chauvin, Nicholas, 232
Chess, Stella, 96, 106, 107
Child abuse, 24, 25
Childe, V. Gordon, 293, 352
Chile, 33
Children, 101, 328, 331, 351, 355, 358, 359,
    361, 364, 365, 367, 368, 369, 370,
    374–376, 380, 381, 431, 449, 477,
    482, 488
Chimpanzee, 25, 66, 77, 78, 132, 133, 135,
    148
China, 3, 38, 337–339, 434, 436, 438, 499
Chinese theorists, 390
Chordata, 78, 324
Christ, 327
Circadian system, 26
Circulation, 403, 489
Civilized Identity Society, 248–250, 253
Civilized Survival Society, 248
Civil Liberties Union, 489
Civil rights, 348, 361, 362, 376, 388, 399,
    448, 455
Clan, 92, 141, 154, 156, 159, 165
Clark, T.R., 363
Class, 154, 189, 190
Clausewitz, Karl von, 417, 464
Clinard, Marshall B., 247
Code of behavior, 36, 37, 53, 55, 58, 60, 70,
    72, 74, 98, 107, 115, 119, 124, 143,
    144, 151, 164, 183, 186, 187, 193–195,
    199, 202–204, 206, 208, 213, 214,
    217, 227, 324, 327, 422
Cognition, 9, 11, 12, 14, 23, 26, 29–33, 40,
    47, 48, 50, 55–57, 64, 69, 70, 73, 75,
    79, 80, 84, 85, 87, 89, 90, 102,
    112–114, 120, 121, 125, 126, 134,
    138, 142, 148, 149, 163, 167, 170,
    173, 175, 176, 179, 182, 187, 188,
    192–195, 198, 201, 213–218, 220,
    259, 272, 281, 284, 301, 303, 304,
    308, 310, 312–316, 324, 338, 357,
    358, 398, 418, 432, 491, 497
Cohen, Avner, 20

Collectivism, 311
Collectivization, 436
Combe Grenal Valley, 289
Commitment, 25, 36, 115, 147, 160, 162,
    165, 166, 193, 198, 206, 212, 231,
    232
Common Cause, 354
Communism, 429, 434, 440, 456, 477, 479,
    483
Communist Manifesto, 427, 432, 476, 477
Communist society, 296, 298, 339, 340,
    352, 439, 459
Competence, 36, 37, 51, 56, 107, 166, 168,
    192, 223, 224, 228, 251, 264, 266,
    268–282, 290, 292, 350, 351, 353,
    461, 481, 501, 503
Competition, 3, 16, 24, 52, 57, 62, 77, 80,
    95, 122, 133, 138, 143, 151–153, 217,
    225, 228, 230, 233–235, 268, 274–277,
    280, 320, 323, 326, 344, 350, 352,
    357, 363, 367, 368, 390, 391, 396,
    397, 405, 409, 411, 418, 422, 423,
    435, 436, 438, 454, 462, 467, 480,
    489, 497
Concentration of economic power, 228, 230
Conflict, 281, 294, 332, 422
Conglomerates, 344, 501
Congo, 434, 442
Congressional Library, 175
Consanguine family, 311
Conscience, 1, 24, 25, 36, 48, 56, 58, 72, 79,
    97, 114, 115, 136, 141, 157, 158, 169,
    170, 173, 176, 177, 180, 181, 182,
    195, 198, 199, 201, 204, 209, 213,
    216, 230, 241, 250, 308, 310, 495
Consciousness, 1, 20, 21, 23, 28, 56, 60, 63,
    79, 93, 124, 156, 157, 173, 201, 308,
    458, 475, 478, 497
Consensual adultery, 376, 378, 379
Constitution of United States, 342, 355
Consumer cult, 343
Contradictions, 4, 27, 58, 69, 70, 113, 119,
    122, 151, 174, 185, 186, 207, 234,
    349, 350, 355, 356, 391, 393, 399,
    400, 404, 405, 422, 429, 444, 490,
    493
Contrarieties, 27, 318
Cooley, Charles H., 12, 47, 49, 85, 94, 95,
    97, 105, 186–188, 205, 319
Cooperation, 25, 75, 80, 92, 94, 129, 130,
    143, 147, 152, 159, 250, 276–278,
    280, 281, 323, 331
Copernicus, 492
Cortex, 307
Cournand, André, 214

Count, Earl W., 75, 137, 138–140, 144
Courtship, 24
Cranston, Maurice, 348
Creativity, 36–38, 42, 44, 50, 51, 57, 59,
    65, 68, 71, 72, 78, 83, 107, 124, 125,
    142, 164, 168, 169, 170, 173, 175,
    176, 178, 192, 193, 199, 200, 201,
    217, 224, 225, 227, 228, 230, 271,
    272, 281, 284–305, 351, 352, 354,
    355, 364, 422, 446, 454, 493, 497,
    501, 504
Crime, 39, 41, 42, 101, 189, 190, 208, 209,
    231, 301, 335, 350, 358, 388, 449,
    454, 464
Croce, Benedetto, 188
Cro-Magnon, 206, 224, 265, 292, 293
Cryptococcosis, 376
Cultural determinism, 161, 166, 169
Cultural revolution, 338
Culture, 5, 21, 22, 32, 51–54, 56, 57, 59,
    60, 62, 63, 71, 75, 80, 83, 85, 89, 90,
    97, 102, 116, 120, 122, 124, 125, 132,
    133, 141, 142, 143, 150, 152, 153,
    157, 160, 165, 173, 174, 183, 210,
    216, 221, 222, 223, 224, 227, 281,
    284, 286, 301, 309, 324, 326, 335,
    337, 338, 340, 355, 358, 359, 365,
    374, 378, 379, 382, 409, 423
Culture gens, 87–89
Cybernetics, 321, 339
Cytomegalovirus infections, 376
Czechoslovakian theorists, 390

Dalton, John, 14
Dana, Charles A., 476
Darling, F.F., 131
Darwin, Charles, 87, 115, 162, 274, 480
Darwinian, 81, 135
Das Capital, 427, 438, 491
David, H.P., 363
Dawkins, Richards, 87
Delinquency, 101, 301, 335
DeLuca, J.N., 363
Declaration of Independence, 261
Deflation, 404
Democracy, 2, 15, 16, 34, 35–39, 41, 44, 54,
    121, 177, 195, 214, 228, 232–235,
    287, 295, 299, 312, 326, 327, 340,
    344, 347, 349, 352, 354, 355, 356,
    388, 389, 396, 398, 399, 400, 403,
    406, 411, 412, 417, 422, 424, 430,
    432, 433, 437, 439, 440, 445, 446,
    477, 480, 483, 484, 485, 489, 490,
    491, 497, 498, 500, 501

Demoralization, 38, 42, 43, 207, 209, 259,
    300, 305, 328, 354, 399, 451
Demsetz, Harold, 395, 396
Denmark, 413, 414
Depersonalization, 253, 295, 406, 429
Depression, 148, 162, 163, 183, 259, 286
Descartes, René, 20, 28
Desire, 55, 67, 69, 173, 175–177, 181–186,
    189, 216, 218, 220, 223, 230, 231,
    349, 422, 423, 487
Detroit, 349
Deuteronomy, 33
Developmental process 26
Dewey, John, 34, 43, 47–49, 94, 113, 424,
    439, 484, 485
Diaghilov, Serge, 364
Dialectics, 298, 299, 303, 304, 394, 430,
    432, 435, 495
Dictatorship, 2, 15, 33, 37, 38, 41, 42, 45,
    54, 126, 177, 195, 271, 280, 295, 300,
    312, 337–340, 347, 489, 391, 392,
    418, 420–422, 424, 434, 436, 437,
    440, 442–446, 455, 462, 476, 480–483,
    498, 501
DiGiusseppe, Raymond, 163
Di Medici, Piero, 500
Dingell, John, 468
Dionysian principle, 303
Discipline, 230
Disequilibrium, 13, 14, 106, 107, 214
Disorganization, 330
Disposable time, 296, 401
Distractability, 25, 77
Division of labor, 278
Dobzhansky, Theodosius, 87, 97, 183, 184,
    302, 487
Doige, W.T., 363
Dole system, 354
Domestication, 224, 250, 292, 294, 352, 422
Dominance, 77, 121, 139, 152, 169–171,
    217, 220, 323, 357, 366, 367
Donne, John, 258
Drug abuse, 5, 41, 42, 104, 208, 228, 361,
    449, 455
Dubos, René, 72, 81, 95, 183 184, 203, 244,
    245, 247, 261, 277, 301–303, 321
Dunham, H. Warren, 330
Dynamic equilibrium, 13, 14

Eastern Europe, 447
Ecology, 104
Economic depression, 43, 113, 389, 402,
    406, 407, 409, 410, 412, 454, 455,
    498

Economic organization, 31, 66, 132, 148, 188, 221, 233, 343
Economics, 3, 13, 14, 15, 42, 112, 113, 143, 147, 148, 155, 165, 178, 179, 180, 189, 201, 229, 233, 234, 235, 296, 351, 402, 436, 492
Economic struggle, 152, 229, 351, 381, 440, 469
Economy world, 229
Educability, 27, 50, 51, 79, 80, 122, 153, 203
Education, 38, 43, 55, 57, 59, 61, 155, 212
Egalitarianism, 160, 162, 168, 183, 205, 489
Egocentrism, 25
Ego development, 247, 276, 355
Egypt, 292, 347, 442, 455
Ehrhardt, A.A., 365
Einstein, Albert, 418
Eisenburg, Leon, 48
Eisenhower, Dwight D., 354
Ellis, A., 163, 218, 245
Ellis, Havelock, 113
Emergence of society, 281, 284, 324, 352, 359, 423
Emotions, 32, 85, 96, 102, 114, 117, 120, 122, 137, 148, 163, 166, 167, 169, 178, 179, 181, 182, 198, 202, 208, 218, 307–316, 357, 377, 403
Energy, 403, 463, 503, 505
Engels, Frederick, 14, 19, 27, 63, 113, 154, 162, 163, 205, 298, 311, 389, 431, 432, 438, 439, 446, 476–480, 482–484, 495, 497
England, 288, 431, 476
Environment, 16, 73, 93, 94, 107, 120, 125, 130, 131, 136, 142, 163, 166, 173, 184, 186, 189, 220, 222, 223, 226, 231, 286, 289, 293, 304, 322, 325, 354, 389, 449, 451, 502
Enaterprise, free, 229, 385–425, 427, 472, 475, 478, 479, 500
Epictetus, 218, 348
Epidemiology, 1, 2, 4, 12, 33, 42, 44, 106, 318, 320, 322, 455
Epigamic characteristics, 51, 53, 54, 55, 62
Epigenetic rules, 86, 87, 88, 89
Equilibrium, 14, 113, 175, 321, 330, 411, 419, 421, 424
Erasmus, D., 364
Erikson, Erik H., 95, 165, 188, 212, 247, 263, 265, 266, 273, 274
Estrangement, 178, 179, 297, 298, 388
Estrus, 76, 151, 223

Ethics, 16, 250, 273, 281, 298, 313, 319, 324, 327, 331, 336, 359, 362, 364, 375, 378, 419, 422, 506
Ethologists, 25, 29, 39, 41, 61, 77, 114, 163, 186, 187, 246
Ethos, 252
Etzioni, Amitai, 47, 85, 99–101, 178, 319, 322, 341, 507
Europe, 289, 291, 292, 302, 407, 430, 434, 446, 456, 461, 467, 476
Exchange, 9, 14, 15, 17, 53, 54, 63, 64, 66, 90, 129, 130, 132, 133, 136, 142, 143, 147–149, 156, 170, 179, 222, 226, 294, 326, 327, 393, 402, 406, 408, 463, 464, 478, 481, 491, 492, 496, 506
Exchange value, 179, 290, 393, 397, 402, 430, 494–496, 499, 500
Exogamy, 115, 116
Expectations, 227, 331, 343, 351, 401, 406
Exploitations, 9, 54, 155, 206, 232, 299, 300, 350, 388, 398, 401, 407, 417, 427, 430–433, 442, 459–463, 469, 488, 490, 491, 494, 495
Exports, 452
Expropriation, 298, 300
Exxon, 467
Eysenck, Hans J., 333

Factions, 342, 343
Faith, 35, 36, 39, 198
Familialism, 139, 140, 143
Familialize, 143, 144, 169
Family, 92, 101, 106, 107, 121, 126, 138, 140, 141, 151, 152, 158–161, 165, 166, 169, 175, 178, 194, 205, 212, 220, 234, 235, 249, 251, 298, 309, 310, 323, 327, 331, 351, 365–369, 380, 381, 419, 439
Farb, Peter, 75, 77
Federalist Papers, 342
Federal papers, 121, 235, 483
Federation of American Scientists, 354
Feudal, 347, 352, 434, 451, 493, 495, 496
Fichte, I.H., 476
Fire making, 73
Firth, Raymond, 80
Fiscal policy, 404, 410, 412, 471
Fletcher, R., 122
Florida, 454
Foragers, 261, 270, 271
Foraging economy, 222, 223, 224, 225, 242, 268, 290, 347, 386, 387
Fourier, Charles, 385, 476

515

France, 484
Frank, Lawrence K., 80, 81
Franklin, Ben, 14, 392, 491, 493, 498, 506
Fraser, J.T., 259
Frederick the Great, 364
Freedman, M.J., 363
Freedom-to-choose trait, 35, 37, 38, 44, 45,
  50, 58, 60, 70, 74, 97, 101, 153, 166,
  168, 170, 173–195, 208, 214, 230,
  250, 258, 290, 295, 312, 313, 347,
  349, 350, 354, 360, 380, 419, 422,
  423, 424, 442, 446, 460, 488, 496,
  501
Freidberg, L., 363
Freud, Sigmund, 1, 4, 23, 27, 107, 113–125,
  131, 157, 216, 365, 377
Fromm, Erich, 7, 47, 72, 74, 75, 85, 95–97,
  113, 156, 180, 182, 184–186, 198,
  206, 212, 243–245, 278, 279, 299,
  301, 302, 319
Frustration, 100, 101, 124, 148, 178, 266,
  329, 482

Gabor, Dennis, 251, 261, 272, 273
Galbraith, John K., 401, 402, 411, 412,
  458, 459
Gallup, G.C., 77
Gdansk, 420
Gender identity, 373
Gene-culture-coevolution theory, 86, 183
General Accounting Office report, 457
Genetic, 130, 131, 135
Genetic assemblages, 88
Genicide, 231
Gens, 141, 154, 165, 311
German nation, 192
Germany, 341, 415, 441, 449, 470, 476, 484
Glaciation, 289
Glasser, W., 248, 325
GNP, 238, 413, 415
Goals, 275, 482
Goethe, Johann, W. von, 113
Goldberger, Joseph, 42
Goldstein, M.S., 212, 243
Goodall, J.V.L., 132
Goodness-of-fit, 107
Gordon, Milton M., 85, 95
Gotha Program, 483
Governmental lifestyle, 385
Gravettians, 203, 291
Great Depression, 233
Greece, 347
Greed, 58
Grieger, Russel & Ingrid Z., 148, 316
Grundrisse, 427
Guinae, 442

Haeckel, E., 74
Hallowell, A. Irving, 7
Hamburg, David A., 104
Hamilton, W.H., 129
Hands, 324, 359
Harris, Marvin, 82, 102, 116
Harris, Tiril, 507
Hate, 25
Hawkes, Jacquetta, 203, 287, 288, 289, 292
Hecker, J.F.C., 322
Heer, Frederick, 421, 422
Hegel, George Wilhelm F., 19, 113, 177,
  180, 422, 476, 485, 486, 495
Helsinki Agreement, 177
Helvetius, Claude A., 47
Heredity, 136, 354
Herkovits, Melville, 93, 101
Herrick, C. Judson, 67, 68
Heterosexuality, 360, 363, 372
Hibbs, Douglas A., 414
Hierarchical arrangement in science, 18,
  19, 20, 21
Hiller, E.T., 88
Hinkle, L.E., 332
Historical method, 6
Hitler, Adolph, 123, 192, 231
Hobbes, Thomas, 47
Home base, 66, 147, 150, 222, 223, 226, 278
Homeostatic system, 104, 122, 207, 208,
  313, 316, 321, 322, 328, 330
Homo, 1, 3, 4, 5, 13, 14, 16, 22–25, 27, 29,
  32, 40, 41, 45, 49, 54–56, 60, 61,
  63–65, 69–71, 73, 75, 79, 88–90, 113,
  116, 118–121, 123–125, 133, 137,
  138, 141, 142, 148–150, 159, 170,
  171, 174, 175, 182, 191, 201, 202,
  209, 211, 217, 220, 221, 241, 258–260,
  270, 274, 281, 292, 293, 304, 308,
  309, 319, 322, 347, 368, 374, 379,
  386, 421, 441, 463, 468, 491, 508
Homo contendens, 275
Homo erectus, 5, 71, 113, 220–222, 288,
  322
Homo habilis, 113, 221, 288
Homo ludens, 296, 361, 376, 381
Homo sapiens, 71, 72, 73, 120, 153, 204,
  221, 244, 265, 279, 289, 322, 374,
  444
Homo sapiens neanderthalensis, 5, 71, 222,
  265
Homo sapiens sapiens, 4, 26, 79, 84, 174,
  222, 224, 289–281, 297
Homosexuality, 5, 101, 194, 213, 357–365,
  368, 370–376
Homosexual political movement, 361, 363,
  373, 376

516

Homosexual social movement, 359, 360, 362, 373, 376
Homo's evolution, 287, 292
Homo Steinheim, 288
Homo Swanscombe, 222, 288
Hooker, E., 363
Hope, 36–39, 55, 60, 71, 170, 203, 206, 216, 217, 235, 260, 263–266, 350, 411, 497
Horney, Karen, 271
Human biogram, 323
Human engineering, 262, 301, 325, 398, 424, 475–508
Human intelligence, 250
Humanization, 27, 32, 57, 69, 71, 72, 85, 94, 123, 133, 147, 154, 155, 169, 170, 174, 182, 214, 260, 261, 319, 322, 347, 359, 363, 386, 391, 392, 408, 423, 429
Human nature, 1, 8, 25, 27, 32, 34, 43, 45, 47, 48, 50, 70, 72, 81, 82, 83, 84, 86, 87, 90, 101, 113, 119, 125, 126, 133, 134, 135, 141, 147, 148, 153, 159, 174, 182, 183, 185, 186, 187, 192, 202, 204, 205, 206, 207, 210, 211, 224, 230, 244, 245, 248, 250, 251, 256, 274, 279, 280, 282, 287, 297, 298, 301, 302, 308, 311, 314, 318, 319, 320, 322, 323, 325, 327, 331, 334, 337, 347, 349, 350, 376, 377, 385, 418, 420, 421, 425, 441, 481, 496, 505, 506
Humanness, 282, 322, 422
Human relations, 9, 13, 14, 16, 69, 70, 79, 88
Human rights, 348, 361, 407, 443, 489
Hume, David, 47
Hungarian theorists, 390
Hungary, 33, 456
Hunger, 68, 93, 94
Hunters, 278, 279, 289, 291, 292, 293, 301, 357
Hunting-gathering, 327
Hypothalamus, 307

Iago, 27, 168
Ideology, 2, 31, 105, 160, 166, 190, 376–379, 447, 456, 481
Ilfeld, F., 162
Imagination, 284, 324
Imitation, 25, 79, 205
Imperialism, 447, 457, 471
imports, 452, 471
Incest, 115, 116, 143, 151, 152, 194, 213
Income, 236
India, 191

Indiscriminate sexuality, 356, 357, 380, 422
Individual freedom ethic, 487, 488
Individualism, 220, 280
Industrialization, 166, 253, 254, 381, 407, 461
Industrial revolution, 295, 431, 506
Inequality, 190
Inflation, 229, 234, 402, 404, 406, 408, 410, 412, 414, 415, 454, 464, 471, 505
Inhibition, 17, 24, 25, 27, 35, 36, 48, 49, 68–72, 90, 118, 121, 133, 143, 149, 151, 153, 168, 170, 175, 176, 182, 189, 193, 207, 209, 211, 227, 230, 250, 303, 308, 310, 361, 363, 367, 380, 419, 423, 506
Instinct, 3, 29, 47, 54, 70, 74, 82, 96, 113, 114, 118–125, 131, 135, 150, 176, 216, 217, 220, 270
Instinctual renunciation, 126
Institute for Sex Research, 363
Institutional, 92, 98, 115, 152–154, 160
Intelligence, 250
International Monetary Fund, 470
Interrelationship, 14, 21, 34–37, 41, 42, 45, 50, 54–57, 80, 115, 118, 121, 126, 128, 130, 131, 136, 138, 169, 187, 214, 224, 225, 232, 319, 335, 336, 377, 411, 439, 455, 459, 478, 481, 487, 488, 489, 504
Iraq, 33, 467
Iran, 467
Iroquois confederation, 175
Irrationality, 77, 121, 148, 163, 194
Israel, 457, 464, 465
Italy, 415
Iteroparity, 52

Jacob, Francois, 18, 19
Jahoda, Maria, 212, 242, 243, 247
Japanese, 449
Jealousy, 154, 166, 167, 168, 220, 225, 247, 308, 310, 357, 367, 377, 378
Jefferson, Thomas, 392, 424, 483
Jensen, A.R., 96
Johnson, Lyndon, 443, 449
Johnson, V.E., 162, 380
Johnson, W.R., 464, 470
Juvenile delinquency, 335, 449

Kagan, Jerome, 166, 205, 251
Kant, Emmanual, 476
Kaposi's sarcoma (KS), 376
Kardiner, Abram, 120
Kautsky, Karl, 389, 441
Keita, Modito, 436

Kenyon, S.E., 363
Keynes, John Maynard, 364, 402, 405, 410, 448, 501
Khrushchev, Nikita, 436, 451, 477
King Idris, 466
Kinsey Institute for Sex Research, 357
Kinship, 24, 25, 63, 75, 131, 137, 141, 144, 151, 152, 159, 198, 294, 310, 311, 323, 324, 366
Kipnis, David, 482
Kissinger, Henry, 464, 465, 470
Klaus, M.H., 156
Klein, G.S. 94
Kluckhohn, Clyde, 80
Knaus, William, 259
Kohlberg, Lawrence, 370
Korzybski, Alfred, 12, 47, 49, 85, 204, 256, 258, 260, 262, 263, 265, 266, 269, 319, 505, 506, 507
Kosa, John, 263
Kroeber, A.L., 7, 75, 116, 150
Kuczai, Stan A., 173
!Kung San people, 31, 63, 65, 67, 75, 132, 133, 148, 182, 225, 226, 242, 270
Kuwait, 464, 467

Labor, 14, 143, 154, 160, 165, 169 177, 223, 227, 297, 393, 399, 404, 405, 408, 410, 430, 433, 488, 490, 491, 492, 494, 495, 500, 501, 506
Labor time, 292, 394, 395, 397
Laissez-faire, 386, 387, 389, 399, 410, 434, 436, 442, 456
Lancaster, Jane E., 130
Language, 79, 130, 142, 170, 173, 199, 359
Laryngopharyngeal sound-producing organ, 50, 53, 59
Laski, Harold, 475
LasSalle, Ferdinand, 484
Laughlin, William S., 278, 301
Lawrence of Arabia, 364
League of Nations, 175, 406
Learning, 25, 75
Lee, Patrick C., 365
Lee, Richard B., 9, 31, 57, 63, 65–67, 75, 132, 133, 148, 182, 183, 225–227, 261, 270, 290, 365, 366, 386, 506
Leighton, D.C., 123, 217–220, 269, 330, 331
Leisure time, 66, 227, 293
Lenin, V.I., 299, 341, 387, 389, 400, 419, 420, 431, 433, 434, 436, 439, 440, 441, 446, 447, 451, 457, 458, 466, 475, 477, 478, 480, 481, 483, 484
Leonardo de Vinci, 277, 364
Leontief, Wassily, 15

Leontiev, A., 431, 494, 498
Levi-Strauss, Claude, 63
Levine, Maurice, 84, 193, 194, 210, 273
Lewin, K., 264
Lewis, J.M., 95, 247
Libya, 466–469
Lifestyle, 104, 281, 361, 362, 363, 374, 376, 385, 456, 498, 401
Lincoln, Abraham, 392, 424, 484
Linder, Marc, 2
Linton, Ralph, 120, 366, 367, 377
Litigation, 344
Lloyd, J. William, 377
Loeb, Jacques, 113
Loevinger, Jane, 95, 157, 176, 204, 206, 247
Louisiana Purchase, 501
Lorenz, Konrad, 25, 81, 95, 186, 187
Love, 25, 54, 71, 80, 95, 99, 101, 123, 147, 150, 155, 157–159, 163, 164, 165, 169, 185, 203, 219, 220, 232, 266, 331, 353, 380
Lovejoy, Arthur O., 47–49, 341, 342
Lovejoy, C. Owen, 61, 63, 67
Lumsden, C.J., 86–89
Luxemburg, Rosa, 341, 389, 437, 440, 478, 481–484

Machiavelli, Nicolo, 500
MacKinnon, John, 24
Madison, James, 47, 235, 342, 344, 424
Magdelinian culture, 291, 292, 293
Malaysia, 76, 77
Mali, 436, 442
Maliciousness, 24
Malinowski, Bronislaw, 365, 377, 379
Mammalia, 136, 138, 140, 141, 145, 149, 160, 276, 324
Manhattan Project, 175
Manipulation, 25
Marcus, Herbert, 400
Marketplace, 393, 499, 506
Markham, Edwin, 147, 148
Mark Twain, 82
Marmor, Judd, 372, 373
Marquesas Islands, 377, 379
Marshack, Alexander, 265
Marshall, Lorna, 183, 242
Marxism, Karl Marx, 1, 3, 8, 14, 19, 23, 27, 31, 32, 57, 63–66, 86, 98, 99, 101, 113, 115, 143, 162, 177–179, 182, 185, 202, 205, 225, 232, 249, 282, 287, 290, 295, 296–299, 327, 355, 337–339, 340, 343, 349, 352, 385, 386, 387, 389, 390, 391, 392, 393, 394, 396, 397, 398, 399, 400, 401,

419, 420, 421, 424, 425, 427, 429, 430, 431, 432, 433, 434, 435, 436, 437, 438, 439, 440, 446, 456, 460, 461, 462, 466, 475, 476, 477, 478, 479, 480, 481, 482, 483, 484, 485, 488, 489, 490, 491, 493, 494, 495, 496, 497, 499, 506
Maslow, A.H., 82, 83, 84, 187, 212, 243, 247, 263, 281, 302, 304
Massacre at Rosewood, Florida, 192
Mass communications media, 194, 195, 208, 214, 231
Masters, W.H., 162, 380
Materialism, 324
Matrilineal descent, 311
Matson, Lloyd W., 84, 86, 187, 188, 282, 302
Mattick, Paul, 477
Maugham, Sumerset, 364
May, Rollo, 95, 193, 209, 302, 334, 482
Mayman, M., 212
Mayr, Ernst, 22, 89, 278, 279
McCarthy, Joseph, 192
McDougall, W., 247
McLennan, J.F., 162
Mead, George H., 13, 47, 49, 85, 91, 93, 94, 95, 205, 244, 319
Mead, Margaret, 116, 276
Melville, Herman, 364
Memory, 260, 266
Mental attributes, 278
Mental disorders, 163, 174, 189, 253, 330, 331, 333
Mentality, 79, 468
Mental wellbeing, 31, 32, 33, 181, 374
Merchantilism, 386
Meredith, Nikki, 357
Mesolithic people, 292, 294
Mesopotamia, 288
Meta-human, 70
Meta-primate behavior, 6
Metallurgy, 386
Miami, 349
Michelangelo, 500
Middle East, 280, 292, 499
Miles, Catherine C., 369
Miller, A.M., 58
Milton, John, 262
Money, J., 365
Money cult, 343, 353, 418, 419
Monetary policy, 404, 410–412, 471
Moist, 436, 477
Monogamy, 62, 68, 155, 159, 161, 162, 166, 167, 194, 213, 311, 359, 377–379, 380
Monopology, 228, 229, 230, 234, 235, 343, 344, 350, 351, 387, 388, 394, 395, 397, 398, 399, 404–406, 409–412, 414–417, 446, 448, 449, 451, 454, 456–458, 462, 465–467, 472, 501, 503
Monotony, 271
Monotremes, 324
Montagu, Ashley, 47, 73, 80, 85, 95, 96, 163, 164, 186, 204, 260, 277, 280, 281, 301, 304, 319
Montaigne, Michel de, 96, 245
Morale, 38, 39, 43, 207, 231, 437, 442, 454
Morality, 48, 49, 67, 72, 102, 115, 120, 121, 143, 152, 153, 173, 179, 182–184, 186, 188, 193–195, 201, 204, 205, 208, 211–214, 234, 235, 273, 281, 298–313, 319, 324, 327, 331, 336, 350, 358, 359, 362, 364, 375, 419, 422, 423, 497, 506
More, Thomas, 385
Morgan, Lewis H., 60, 61, 63, 162, 310, 311
Morganthau, Ruth S., 437
Morris, D., 187
Moses, 327
Mossadeq, 457
Mothers, 252, 351, 368, 380, 381, 493
Motivation, 173, 176, 191, 202, 207, 223, 227, 263, 287, 311, 314, 315
Mousterian culture, 289
Mozambique, 442
Muller, Steve, 212, 213
Multinational oil companies, 229, 390, 396, 407, 409, 415, 435, 436, 446, 448, 450, 458, 464, 466, 467, 469, 501
Mumford, Lewis, 188
Murphy, H.B.M., 331, 332, 333
Muscari, Paul G., 370
Mycobacterium avium intracellular infection, 376
Myrick, F.L., 363

Napoleonic Code, 144
National Planning and Industrial Investment Agency, 502
Natufians, 292
Nature of human nature, 3, 13, 21, 30, 31, 40 47–107, 112, 136, 188, 210, 308, 324, 330, 337, 349, 376, 385, 418, 425, 441, 481, 496, 505, 506, 507
Nazism, 340
Neanderthal, 164, 184, 203, 206, 242, 244, 258, 265, 279, 288–290
Neff, Walton S., 285–286, 287
Neolithic, 221, 224, 294, 295, 302
Neopallium, 324

Netherlands, 413, 415, 465
Neuromuscular, 307, 308
Neurophysiology, 18, 20, 21, 24, 28, 29, 40,
    82, 90, 91, 134, 307, 308
Neurosis, 101, 112, 114–117, 189
New Economic Policy (NEP), 437
Newell-Smith, P.H., 327
News media, 355
New York *Tribune*, 476
Nietzsche, F.W., 157, 303
Nirvana, 218
Nixon, Richard, 418
Nuclear family, 62, 159, 121, 309, 365

Objectified labor, 287, 296
Objective, 9, 23, 24, 28, 399
Odum, Eugene P., 19, 20
Oedipus complex, 114, 118, 124
Old Stone Age, 292, 293
Olduvai Gorge, 222, 223, 288
Olympics, 228
OPEC, 229, 390, 396, 407, 409, 415, 435,
    437, 443, 448, 450, 454, 457, 463,
    465, 466, 469, 470, 471, 498, 499
Opler, Marvin K., 96
Opportunistic diseases, 362, 376
Orangutan, 76
Order primate, 137
Ornstein, E., 94
Othello, 168
Overproduction, 404, 407, 429
Owen, Robert, 385, 476

Painting, 293, 302
Pair bonding, 62, 68
Pairing family, 311
Paleolithic, 224, 293, 294, 302–304, 311,
    321
Paleolithic hunters, 291
Palestine, 288
Palestinians, 465
Paranthropus, 221
Pareek, Udai, 191, 192
Parental, 24, 49, 52, 56, 61, 68, 78, 89, 91,
    107, 138, 139–141, 150, 151, 157,
    160, 162, 170, 231, 379–381
Parsons, T., 365, 367, 368
Pasteur, Louis, 12
Patriarchal family, 311
Pavlov, I.P., 40
Pellagra, 42, 43, 44
Permissiveness, 39, 41, 121, 153, 166, 194,
    208, 213, 150, 347, 350, 358, 488
Personal freedom, 41

Perversion, sexual, 356, 361, 362, 373, 375,
    376
Petrodollars, 402, 407, 470, 471
Pfeiffer, J.E., 84, 186, 281
Phillips, A.W., 414
Phillips curve, 414
Philosopher, 6, 7, 22, 47, 63, 92, 162, 177,
    202, 218, 482, 484, 495
Philosophic, 29, 47, 67, 87, 94, 101, 113,
    162, 177, 205, 385, 399, 428, 493,
    497
Philosophy, 36–38, 71, 82, 113, 115, 143,
    166, 168, 183, 198, 204, 207, 209,
    212, 214, 231, 232, 305, 316, 335,
    345, 387, 393, 394, 419, 421, 443,
    475, 476, 485, 491
Phylogenetic, 6, 13, 54, 69, 70, 81, 90, 114,
    123, 128, 130, 136, 137, 139, 141,
    145, 164, 170, 176, 274, 280, 312,
    323, 324, 491
Phylogenetic behavior traits, 5, 13, 54, 69,
    81, 119, 123, 128, 327
Phylum Vertebra, 136, 138, 139, 145
Physical science, 4, 12, 13, 385
Physiological process abuse, 296
Piaget, Jean, 78, 138, 327, 328
Plasticity, 245, 319, 337, 359, 421
Plato, 28, 385
Play, 24, 25, 173
Pleasure principle, 176, 361, 376, 381
Pleistocene, 73, 75, 220, 221, 261, 287, 293
Plekhanov, G.V., 389
Pliocene, 73, 75
Pneumocystis Carinii pneumonia (PCP),
    376
Poland, 312, 349, 420, 433, 447, 483
Political economy, 9, 13, 32, 44, 123, 179,
    180, 225, 276, 296, 337, 344, 385,
    388, 394, 408, 420, 427, 430, 458,
    461, 475, 498, 505, 507
Political theory, 3
Pongidae, 362
Poor, 351, 387, 388, 400, 401, 488, 489
Poorness-of-fit, 107
Pope Alexander, 262, 342
Population development, 30, 32, 106, 113,
    135, 212
Pornography, 212, 213, 214, 359
Poverty, 189, 190, 191, 263
Power to control, 174, 178
Power of science, 393
Predation, 77
Predictability, 15, 16, 17, 18, 40, 44, 75,
    115, 194, 198, 207, 398, 406, 414,
    451, 457, 500, 501

Primary prevention, 27, 104, 105, 119, 121,
    126, 328, 334, 486
Primate, 17, 24, 25, 27, 35, 37, 40 41, 44,
    57, 59, 65, 66, 69, 75, 121, 133, 141,
    149, 174, 200, 221, 259, 304, 320
Primate behavior, 75, 77, 83, 90, 113, 114,
    119, 125, 142, 167, 168, 170, 171,
    174, 183, 192, 217, 220, 280, 334,
    356, 362, 398, 399, 421, 422, 486,
    506, 507
Primate instincts, 27, 40, 119, 125, 142,
    202, 352, 359, 378, 386, 489
Primate sexuality, 357, 358
Primate troop, 143, 220, 334, 418, 463
Primeval behavior, 173
Primeval horde, 27, 141, 310
Primitive communism, 63, 221, 227, 270,
    290, 294, 348, 385, 386
Primitive identity society, 248
Primitive man, 53, 69, 75, 76, 147, 167,
    174, 182, 201, 203, 206, 209, 220,
    222, 242, 249, 260, 261, 291, 356
Primitive philosophy, 293
Primitive society, 201, 220, 248, 251, 270,
    276, 290, 309, 326, 358, 360
Primitive survival society, 248, 250
Primordial, 27, 40
Private property, 119, 154, 167
Production, 15, 290, 294, 398, 403, 404,
    405, 409, 432, 436, 443, 444, 447,
    450, 454, 455, 459, 460, 489, 492,
    493, 503, 505
Production relations, 15, 42, 43, 98, 103,
    296, 336, 395, 400, 404, 408, 410,
    411, 429, 431, 444
Productive forces, 63, 67, 97, 103, 132, 133,
    152, 154, 165, 179, 222, 232, 233,
    294, 296, 327, 336, 347, 393, 395,
    398, 403, 407, 430, 432–434, 477,
    493, 494, 496, 503
Productive nature of capital, 387, 391
Profits, 237
Promiscuity, 326
Prospection, 56, 58, 256–267, 312, 360
Prostitution, 155
Protection, 25, 75, 150, 158, 159, 170, 295
Protohuman, 226
Protoexchange, 148
Proudhon, Pierre Joseph, 431, 484
Proust, Marcel, 364
Psychic stress, 272
Psychiatrists, 319
Psychoanalysis, 114, 115, 116, 117, 123,
    126
Psychology, 23, 39, 40, 44, 74, 77, 78, 84,

    85, 89, 91, 94, 101, 102, 112, 114,
    116, 117, 118, 120, 133, 150, 161,
    162, 166, 176, 180, 188, 201, 204,
    205, 206, 218, 219, 325, 330, 420,
    482, 505
Psychoneurosis, 41, 189, 217, 218
Psychophysiological homeostasis, 333
Psychosocial homeostasis, 340
Psychosocial
    behavior, 29, 58, 60, 61, 69, 72, 83,
        84, 88, 89, 93, 102, 105, 114,
        126, 133, 134, 145, 157, 169,
        175, 179, 191, 198, 210, 216,
        269, 272, 318, 319, 320, 322,
        326, 357, 361, 481, 506, 507
    discord, 293, 322, 357, 361, 179, 507
    distress, 359
    nature, 15, 23, 59, 82, 85, 88, 90,
        105, 106, 113, 116, 119, 120,
        121, 123, 124, 134, 139, 142,
        147, 148, 150, 153, 165, 174,
        176, 180, 182, 192, 193, 206,
        211, 213, 227, 235, 278, 322,
        323, 340, 422, 497
    needs, 290, 419, 500, 507
    science, 4, 13, 14, 17, 18, 21, 47, 48,
        142, 149, 156, 167, 180, 253
    stimuli, 250, 269
    traits, 5, 8, 14, 22, 93, 190, 219
Psychosomatic diseases, 12, 272, 312
Public citizen, 354
Punaluan family, 311
Puritanical, 358

Qaddafi, Muammar el, 33, 467
Quatar, 464

Rabinowitz, W., 363
Radin, P., 164, 182, 201, 208, 220, 242, 260,
    281, 290, 293
Rado, S., 360
Rae, Douglass, 168
Randomness, 14, 15
Rape, 24, 101, 252, 359
Raspberry, William, 358
Rational, 81, 122, 148, 153, 187, 192, 200,
    206, 230, 418, 437, 454, 507
Recession, 234, 402, 409, 410, 412, 416, 454
Reconstruction Finance Corporation, 503
Redfield, Robert, 8, 13, 80, 86
Reductionist, 19
Rehnquist, William, 362
Reich, Charles A., 399, 402, 458
Relations, 14, 21, 34–37, 41, 68, 70–72, 79,
    80, 92, 93

Relativism, 5, 7, 21, 93, 102, 188, 210, 219, 356
Religion, 114–116, 118, 121, 201–203, 206, 212, 220, 224, 481
Rembrandt, 500
Repetition, 25, 26
Repetitive process, 26
Repetitiveness, 271, 303
Res cogitans, 20
Research, 504
Res extensa, 20
Responsibility, 35, 37, 55, 81, 87, 115, 130, 149, 162, 169, 174, 184, 194, 198, 231
Retirement, 503
Revenue collections, 239
Revolutionary, 66, 70, 105, 118, 133, 141, 155, 168, 201, 224, 228, 250, 281, 293, 299, 301, 310, 326, 335, 336, 337, 338, 352, 379, 400, 401, 407, 422–424, 429, 430, 434, 439–441, 449, 455, 459, 462, 476, 482, 494, 495
Revolving fund, 503
Richman, Barry M., 459
Ricoeur, P., 157
Rights, 35, 41
Riots, 349
Rip-off system, 344, 388, 400, 405, 463, 469, 500
Risk taking, 66, 104, 156, 226, 270, 272
Robins, E., 363
Robinson, James H., 260
Rogers, Carl, 243
Roheim, Gesa, 116
Roland, Romain, 113
Role, 36, 71, 84, 100, 158, 160, 168, 189, 201, 203, 207
Romania, 33
Romanian theorists, 390
Rome, 347, 361
Rootedness, 244, 331, 351, 353, 491
Rosenau, Milton, 486
Rosenhan, D.L., 372
Rossi, Alice S., 139, 140, 159, 161, 168, 251, 381
Rothchild, J., 161
Rowan, Carl T., 252
Rousseau, Jean Jacques, 47, 385
Ruben, Harvey L., 274, 275
Russell, Bertrand, 113, 218
Russia, 273, 291, 430, 440, 441, 475, 477
Russian theorists, 390

Saghir, M.T., 363
Sahara, 291

Sahlins, Marshall, 24, 63, 66, 74, 118, 141–143, 151–154, 201, 304, 323, 326, 356, 358, 368, 379, 422, 423
Saint-Simon, Claude Henry, 385, 476
Samuelson, Paul A., 2
Santayana, George, 113, 273
Sarbin, T.S., 189, 304
Saudi Arabia, 448, 458, 467, 469, 470
Schizophrenia, 181, 333, 359
Scientific methodology, 40, 339
Schmalleger, Frank, 209
Schneirla, T.C., 176, 272
Schopenhauer, A., 48
Schwartz, Harvey, 447
Schweitzer, Albert, 418
Scott, B.R., 498, 499, 500
Security, 75, 164, 180, 226, 227, 251, 281, 338, 352, 353, 399, 461, 462, 503, 505
Self, 20, 21, 48, 56, 57, 94, 96, 157, 165, 166, 167, 180, 194, 200, 201, 202, 204, 205, 208, 209, 212, 224, 225, 243
Self-actualization, 83, 243, 304
Self-awareness, 86, 247, 250
Self-evaluation, 264, 265
Self-image–self-esteem trait, 35, 37, 38, 45, 56–58, 60, 71, 74, 83, 99, 107, 144, 167, 180, 192, 201, 205, 208, 217, 229, 231, 235, 241, 242–254, 258, 268, 271, 290, 295, 313, 332, 350, 351, 353, 360, 377, 411, 418, 487
Self-interest, 396, 410, 412, 419, 421, 424, 479, 497
Selfishness, 77
Self-love, 142
Selye, Hans, 329, 330
Serfdom, 277, 386
Sex violence, 358, 361
Sexual behavior, 24, 41, 49, 52, 55, 62, 68, 70, 71, 75, 78, 84, 91, 93, 94, 112, 113, 114, 118, 122, 133, 136, 137, 138, 139, 140, 143, 144, 150, 151, 152, 155, 160, 161, 162, 165, 166, 167, 168, 169, 201, 206, 208, 216, 217, 219, 220, 227, 250, 308, 310, 311, 323, 356, 357, 360, 361, 363, 364, 365, 366, 367, 368, 370, 377, 380, 381, 488
Shakespeare, 168, 241, 246
Shanidar cave, 168, 241, 246
Shapiro, Philip, 501
Sharing, 25, 63, 90, 132, 221, 223, 289, 290, 294, 310, 347, 387, 463, 491, 496
Shaw, G. Bernard, 113
Schultz, George P., 404

Simpson, G.H., 183, 194
Single mothers, 489
Slavery, 277, 347, 352, 381, 432, 495
Slum dwellers, 247
Smith, Adam, 3, 8, 14, 47, 142, 299, 322,
    442, 478, 494–497, 499, 506
Smith, Jane R., 161, 166, 167, 378
Smith, Lynn G., 161, 166, 167, 378
Smith, M. Brewster, 94, 264
Smithsonian Institute, 175
Snow, C.P., 273
Socarides, Charles W., 357
Sociability, 95, 96, 143
Social, 5, 13, 21, 22, 88, 89, 90, 129, 130,
    131, 142
Social development, 32, 165
Social engineering, 505, 506
Social organization, 75, 79, 91, 92, 99,
    100–102, 105, 115, 116, 118, 122,
    134, 176, 186, 187, 188, 189, 191,
    192, 222, 223, 234, 261, 276, 291,
    293, 295, 296, 309, 310, 311, 319,
    325, 385, 220, 490, 506, 597
Social production, 31, 276
Social relations, 5, 13, 21, 23, 25, 68, 69,
    83, 88, 89, 92–96, 115, 118, 142, 143,
    147, 148, 150, 151, 158, 159, 179,
    183, 198, 199–205, 210, 219, 284,
    400
Social-role performance, 334
Social scientists, 339
Social structure, 486
Socialism, 2, 229, 232, 233, 295, 298, 299,
    338, 340, 348, 387, 393, 394, 400,
    415, 429, 433, 434, 436, 438, 439,
    444, 445, 455, 457, 477, 481
Socialist countries, 33, 38, 232, 425, 460
Socialist economic theory, 435
Socialist economy, 437
Socialist movement, 390
Socialist nations, 407, 429, 430, 434, 442,
    446, 447, 461
Socialist party, 38, 119
Socialist philosophy, 32, 177, 480
Socialist world, 339
Sociality, 136, 137
Socialization, 24, 25, 27, 90, 94, 96, 100,
    121, 136, 137, 153, 154, 160, 166,
    170, 175, 189, 191, 195, 204, 209,
    230, 231, 268, 272, 314, 356, 358,
    359, 366, 418
Social Security Act, 448, 451
Social service, 234, 235
Society, 18, 30, 31, 98, 99, 129, 131, 141,
    149, 154, 174, 177, 199, 214, 220,
    440
Sociobiologists, 20, 24, 25, 29, 39, 77, 81,

82, 85, 89, 95, 96, 158, 159, 164, 211,
    275, 323
Sociobiology, 86, 87, 89, 114, 133, 323
Socioeconomic system, 386
Sociofunctional relations, 13, 17, 30–33,
    38, 42, 44, 67, 72, 90, 319, 324, 335,
    336, 347, 386, 421, 422, 489
Sociological theory, 2, 3, 4, 8, 13, 21, 39,
    80, 88, 89, 94, 177, 180, 287, 385,
    430
Sociology, 91, 94, 95, 101, 102, 141, 161,
    177, 178, 180, 205, 287, 319, 338,
    339, 420, 421, 492, 505
Solecki, Ralph S., 203
Song of the Sea, 199
Sophocles, 482
South Yemen, 442
Soviet Union, 3, 33, 39, 41, 42, 167, 177,
    180, 229, 232, 299, 335, 337–341,
    348, 387, 390, 391, 421, 429, 434,
    436, 438, 442–447, 455, 456, 459,
    460, 462, 477, 480, 483, 499
Speciation, 22
Species being, 178, 297, 421
Species nature, 178, 297, 481
Speech, 130, 132
Sperry, Rogers. 9, 23, 28, 29, 40
Spicer, E.H., 150
Spinoza, Baruch, 218
Spitzer, Robert L., 372
Spivak, G., 163
Stagflation, 234, 412
Stalin, Joseph, 180, 229, 339, 418, 436,
    437, 441, 447, 477
Standard Oil Trust, 457
State Department (U.S.), 404, 409, 457,
    465, 468, 469
Steiner, G.A., 94
Stent, G.S., 20, 22, 23
Stigler, George J., 395, 396, 409, 492
Stockholders, 401, 408
Stoller, Robert J., 358, 373
Stone Age, 151, 153, 164, 323
Stotland, Ezra, 264
Straus, Edwin W.M., 20
Stress, 328, 329, 330, 333, 334, 441, 446
Striving trait, 3, 36, 38, 55, 60, 71, 99, 107,
    123, 124, 126, 169, 176, 204, 207,
    216, 218, 220, 222, 223, 227, 228,
    230–235, 269, 271, 312, 352, 359,
    360, 380, 411, 418, 427, 442, 446,
    496
Subjective, 4, 9, 17, 23, 24, 28, 29, 31, 40,
    87, 90, 112, 206, 307
Suicide, 252, 330
Sumatra, 76, 77
Supply and demand, 230, 405, 466, 499

Suppression, 271
Supreme Court of the United States, 356, 362
Surplus labor, 393, 400, 429, 430, 432, 496
Surplus production, 66, 227, 393
Surplus value, 179, 232, 233, 235, 287, 298, 299, 300, 400, 401, 429, 430, 432, 447, 456, 460, 461, 492, 495, 498
Sweden, 413, 414, 415
Swingers, 359
Switzerland, 415, 470
Symbolization, 90, 114, 130, 132, 134, 136, 141, 142, 149, 170, 199, 224, 265, 266, 268, 289, 308, 312, 359
Syndyasmian family, 311
Syria, 442, 465

Tanzania, 442
Taraki, Abdullah, 465
Tasaday, 74, 323
Taylor, Gordon R., 359
Tchaikovski, Peter, 1, 364
Technology, 278, 282, 293, 294, 302, 323, 337, 352, 392, 393, 407, 442, 448, 449, 504, 506
Technostructure, 412, 430, 451, 459
Teleology, 4, 14, 15, 17, 35, 39, 55, 57, 115, 124, 176, 177, 195, 198, 207, 212
Tenant farmers, 43
Ten Commandments, 115
Tennessee Valley Authority, 501
Terman, Lewis, 369
Terrace, H.S., 78
Territoriality, 24, 222
Terror, 37, 440, 441
Theories of human nature, 4
Thomas, Alexander, 96, 106, 107
Thomson, George, 311
Threshold, 246, 301, 312, 322, 333, 349, 430
Thumb-finger opposition, 59, 132
Time-binding, 37, 39, 71, 77, 107, 189, 194, 212, 250, 256–267, 270, 284, 285, 290, 310, 331, 332
Tinbergen, N., 365
Tool-making, 25, 65, 66, 73, 75, 77, 130, 221–223, 288, 289
Torrence, John, 178
Totemism, 115, 116, 118, 206
Toxoplasmosis, 376
Tradition, 338, 348, 360, 389, 401, 418, 428, 465
Traits of human nature, 2, 3, 4, 7, 9, 13, 16, 17, 21, 22, 23, 26, 27, 29, 30, 32, 33, 34, 35, 36, 38, 39, 42, 44, 54, 57, 58, 61, 63, 67, 69, 71, 74, 77, 80, 85, 86, 88, 91, 93, 94, 95, 97, 98, 99, 100, 101, 105, 107, 115, 119, 122, 125, 126, 129, 133, 135, 138, 142, 148, 161, 163, 165, 166, 168, 169, 174, 180, 181, 188, 189, 190, 192, 193, 195, 200, 206, 211, 212, 213, 216, 223, 227, 232, 234, 256, 259, 262, 264, 269, 270, 272, 273, 277, 278, 284, 294, 295, 300, 307, 308, 309, 311, 312, 313, 322, 324, 328, 329, 332, 333, 335, 338, 340, 341, 342, 344, 347, 348, 352, 353, 358, 360, 364, 375, 379, 380, 385, 386, 389, 391, 392, 398, 399, 400, 419, 420, 422, 423, 424, 429, 436, 438, 439, 446, 455, 460, 462, 476, 478, 481, 482, 486, 487, 489, 490, 491, 495, 496, 497, 498, 501, 504, 505, 507, 508
Traoré, Moussa, 436
Tribal society, 92, 280
Trickery, 24
Trobianders, 377, 379
Trotsky, Leon, 441
Tsypkin, Mikhail, 338
Tucker, Robert W., 464
Tullock, G., 396
Tyler, Gus, 402
Tyler, Leona E., 369

Uncontrolled conduct, 77
Uncontrolled power corrupts, 229
Underdeveloped countries, 391, 392, 402, 407, 408, 434, 437, 442, 443, 448, 450, 465, 469, 470, 471, 479, 491
Unemployment, 271, 351, 402, 403, 408, 410, 412, 414, 415, 450, 454, 461, 471, 505
Uniformitarianism, 6, 9, 65, 182, 225
Unifying orientation of behavior trait, 290, 295, 310, 351, 354, 355, 360, 380, 418, 419, 423, 488
Unisex, 140, 160, 169
United Nations, 165, 175, 407, 464, 465, 470
United States, 232, 233, 234, 299, 342, 343, 344, 349, 354, 359, 373, 387, 390, 399, 400, 401, 402, 404, 409, 413, 415, 416, 419, 420, 424, 429, 440, 442, 443, 444, 445, 446, 447, 448, 449, 450, 451, 455, 456, 457, 458, 461, 462, 464, 465, 466, 468, 469, 470, 471, 483, 484, 487, 488, 498, 499, 501
United States Public Health Service, 218
Urbanization, 166, 253, 254, 381, 386

Use value, 393, 394, 395, 397, 493, 498, 499
Utopia, 352, 377, 385, 389, 392, 397

Vaihinger, H., 207
Valentine, Charles A., 190
Value, 9, 412, 491–494, 498, 506
Values about living, 67, 68, 69, 71, 101, 102, 107, 124, 148, 168, 179, 190, 191, 218
Variable capital, 493, 494
Verdi, Giuseppe, 168
Vertebrates, 136, 137, 138, 145
Victorian, 358
Vietnam War, 443, 449, 450
Violence, 252, 309, 358, 366, 367, 378, 389, 390, 392, 423, 437, 462
Voice-box, 324

Wages, 287, 405, 409, 411, 444, 454, 460, 490, 496
Wallis, Wilson D., 80
Walters, R.H., 369
Watergate, 354
Watsonian, 245
Watts, 349
Wayne, D.M., 363
Wealth, 343, 393, 462, 469, 472
Webb, Beatrice, 389
Webb, Sidney, 389
Weber, Max, 389
Webster, Noah, 285
Weinberg, Martin S., 357, 363, 364
Wenke, Robert J., 220, 221, 222, 288
Westmarck, E.A., 162
Western world, 339, 446, 464, 470

Wheat, 292
Whiting, John M.W., 368, 369
Whitman, Walt, 364
Wiener, Norbert, 321
Wilbur, Cornelia B., 360
Williams, C.J., 363
Williams, Leonard, 60, 143
Wilson, E.J., 464, 470
Wilson, E.O., 20, 25, 81, 82, 86–89, 96, 128, 131–136, 323, 324
Wilson, Woodrow, 407
Winnebago Indians, 164, 209
Winslow, C.E.A., 431
Withering away of the state, 341, 434, 483
Wolf, S.B., 161
Wolff, H.G., 332
Wooley, John T., 405
Work, 65, 66, 132, 252, 272, 274, 280, 281, 284–287, 295, 297, 298, 489
Workers, 177, 178, 298, 312, 399, 408, 414, 420, 429, 432, 454, 455, 460–462, 484, 488, 495, 497, 500, 502
World Psychiatric Association, 339
World War, 406, 416, 440, 443, 455, 457
Wright, Henry T., 132, 133

Yamani, Ahmed Zaki, 458
Yerushalmi, Josef Hayim, 202
Yom Kippur War, 457, 465
Young, J.Z., 96
Yugoslavia, 33, 456
Yugoslavian theorists, 389

Zagros range, 292
Zigler, E., 370